The
Nation's Health

The Nation's Health

A Courses by Newspaper Reader

Edited by

Philip R. Lee
Nancy Brown
Ida VSW Red

Health Policy Program
School of Medicine

University of California
San Francisco

Courses by Newspaper is a project of
University Extension, University of California, San Diego

Funded by
The National Endowment for the Humanities

Boyd & Fraser Publishing Company
San Francisco

Courses by Newspaper
The Nation's Health

Academic Coordinator

Philip R. Lee, M.D., Professor of Social Medicine and Director, Health Policy
Program, School of Medicine, University of California, San Francisco

Project Director

George A. Colburn, University of California, San Diego

Editorial Director

Jane L. Scheiber, University of California, San Diego

Research Associates

Nancy Brown, M.A., Research Associate, Health Policy Program,
School of Medicine, University of California, San Francisco

Ida VSW Red, M.A., M.S.L.S., Resource Director, Aging Health Policy Center,
University of California, San Francisco

National Board

David P. Gardner, Chair; President, University of Utah
Carl N. Degler, Professor of History, Stanford University
Robert C. Elliott, Professor of Literature, University of California, San Diego
Georgie Anne Geyer, Columnist, Los Angeles Times Syndicate
Richard Leonard, Editor, *Milwaukee Journal*
Thomas O'Connell, President, Bellevue (Washington) Community College
Paul D. Saltman, Professor of Biology, University of California, San Diego
Gerald Warren, Editor, *San Diego Union*

Faculty Committee, University of California, San Diego

Paul D. Saltman, Chair; Professor of Biology
Stanley A. Chodorow, Professor of History
Doris A. Howell, Professor of Community Medicine
Edward Reynolds, Associate Professor of History
Jacqueline P. Wiseman, Professor of Sociology

Philip R. Lee, Nancy Brown, and Ida VSW Red, editors
THE NATION'S HEALTH
A Courses by Newspaper Reader

Published by Boyd & Fraser Publishing Company
3627 Sacramento Street, San Francisco, CA 94118

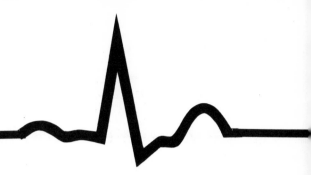

Contents

Part III: Problems in Paradise

Part IV: The Search for Solutions: Frontiers of Knowledge

Acknowledgments

CHAPTER 1

René Dubos, "Health and Creative Adaptation." Abridged from *Human Nature,* January 1978. Copyright © 1977 by Human Nature, Inc. Reprinted by permission of the publisher.

John S. Chapman, "Health and Medicine," *Architecture Environment Health,* June 1974. Reprinted with permission of Heldref Publications, 4000 Albemarle Street, N.W., Washington, D.C. 20016.

Arthur Kleinman, "The Failure of Western Medicine." Adapted from *Human Nature,* November 1978. Copyright © 1978 by Human Nature, Inc. Reprinted by permission of the publisher.

Robert J. Haggerty, "The Boundaries of Health Care." Reprinted from *The Pharos* of Alpha Omega Alpha, July 1972, Volume 35, Number 3, pp. 106–111, with the permission of the Editor. Copyright © 1972 by The Pharos of Alpha Omega Alpha.

Howard Brody and David S. Sobel, "A Systems View of Health and Disease," from *Ways of Health,* edited by David S. Sobel, copyright © 1979 by David S. Sobel. Reprinted by permission of Harcourt Brace Jovanovich, Inc.

CHAPTER 2

Brian MacMahon and Joyce E. Berlin, "Health of the United States Population." Reprinted from *The Horizons of Health,* edited by Henry Wechsler, Joel Gurin, and George F. Cahill, Jr., Cambridge, Mass.: Harvard University Press, Copyright © 1977 by the President and Fellows of Harvard College.

Thomas McKeown, "Determinants of Health." Abridged from *Human Nature,* April 1978. Copyright © 1978 by Human Nature, Inc. Reprinted by permission of the publisher.

Walsh McDermott, "Medicine: The Public Good and One's Own," from *Perspectives in Biology and Medicine,* Volume 21, Number 2, Winter 1978. Copyright © by the University of Chicago. Reprinted with permission of the University of Chicago Press. All rights reserved.

Lewis Thomas, "Notes of a Biology Watcher: On Magic in Medicine." Reprinted by permission from the *New England Journal of Medicine,* Volume 229, pages 461–463, August 31, 1978. Copyright © 1978 by The Massachusetts Medical Society.

CHAPTER 3

Ivan Illich, "Medical Nemesis." *The Lancet,* Volume 7863 (May 11, 1974), pages 918–921. Copyright © 1974. Reprinted by permission of the publisher.

Irving Kenneth Zola, "Healthism and Disabling Medicalization." Reprinted from *Disabling Professions.* Boston: Marion Boyars, Inc., 1977, $4.95, paperback. Copyright © 1977 by Irving Zola. By permission of the publisher.

Renée C. Fox, "The Medicalization and Demedicalization of American Society." Reprinted from *Doing Better and Feeling Worse: Health in the United States,* edited by John H. Knowles, M.D., with the permission of W. W. Norton, Inc. Copyright © 1977 by the American Academy of Arts and Sciences.

Rose Elizabeth Bird, "A Hard Look: Cancer and Mortality." Remarks by Rose Elizabeth Bird, Chief Justice of California, at the First Annual Community Forum on Breast Cancer, Los Angeles, California, May 3, 1980. Reprinted by permission of the Chief Justice.

CHAPTER 4

Robert B. Greifinger and Victor W. Sidel, "American Medicine," *Environment,* Volume 18, Number 4, May 1976. Copyright © 1976 by Scientists Institute for Public Information. Reprinted with permission of Heldref Publications, 4000 Albemarle Street, N.W., Washington, D.C. 20016.

Barbara Ehrenreich, "The Health Care Industry: A Theory of Industrial Medicine," *Social Policy,* November/December 1975. Copyright © 1975 by Social Policy Corporation. Reprinted with permission of the publisher.

Ronald L. Numbers, "The Third Party: Health Insurance in America," in Judith Walzer Leavitt and Ronald L. Numbers, editors, *Sickness and Health in America: Readings in the History of*

Medicine and Public Health (Madison: The University of Wisconsin Press; © 1978 by the Regents of the University of Wisconsin), pages 139–149. Reprinted with permission of the publisher.

CHAPTER 5

Paul R. Torrens, "Overview of Health Services in the United States," in Stephen J. Williams and Paul R. Torrens, editors, *Introduction to Health Services.* Copyright © 1980 by John Wiley & Sons, Inc., Publishers. Reprinted with permission of the publisher. This material is an adaptation of material previously presented in *The American Health Care System: Issues and Problems* by Paul R. Torrens, published by C. V. Mosby Company.

William H. Glazier, "The Task of Medicine," *Scientific American,* Volume 28, Number 4, April 1973, pages 13–17. Copyright © April, 1973, by Scientific American, Inc. All rights reserved. Reprinted with permission.

Eric J. Cassell, "Our Sickness Care System," *The Wall Street Journal,* March 3, 1980, page 16. Reprinted by permission of *The Wall Street Journal,* Copyright © Dow Jones & Company, Inc., 1980. All rights reserved.

"America's Health Care System: A Comprehensive Portrait," adapted from "A New Survey on Access to Medical Care," Special Report Number One/1978. Copyright 1978 by the Robert Wood Johnson Foundation. Reprinted with permission of the publisher.

Allan Parachini, "All-Night Vigil at Emergency Hospital," *Los Angeles Times,* April 29, 1980. Copyright © 1980, Los Angeles Times. Reprinted by permission.

CHAPTER 6

Emmet Rixford, "Levi Cooper Lane, M.D." Originally published in *California and Western Medicine,* Volume 38, 1933, pages 37–39. Copyright © 1933 by the California Medical Association. Reprinted by permission from *The Western Journal of Medicine.*

Christine E. Bishop, "Health Employment and the Nation's Health," *Current History,* Volume 72, May/June 1977. Copyright © 1977 by Current History. Reprinted by permission of the publisher.

C. Glenn Pickard, Jr., "Midlevel Practitioners: Nurse Practitioners and Physicians' Assistants," in John Noble, editor, *Primary Care and the Practice of Medicine,* copyright © 1976 by Little, Brown and Company. Reprinted with permission of the publisher.

Nicholas Lemann, "Let the Nurses Do It." Reprinted with permission from *The Washington Monthly.* Copyright 1979 by The Washington Monthly Co., 1611 Connecticut Ave., N.W., Washington, D.C. 20009.

Rosemary Stevens, "Health Manpower," in *Regionalization and Health Policy,* edited by Eli Ginzburg. U.S. Department of Health, Education, and Welfare, Public Health Service, 1977. Reprinted with permission of the publisher, Health Resources Administration.

CHAPTER 7

Philip R. Lee and Albert R. Jonsen, "The Right to Health Care," *American Review of Respiratory Disease,* June 1974. Copyright © 1974 by the American Review of Respiratory Disease. Reprinted with permission of the publisher.

Daniel Callahan, "Health and Society: Some Ethical Imperatives." Published in *Daedalus* 106:1, Winter 1977. Copyright © 1977 by the American Academy of Arts and Sciences. Reprinted by permission.

Dan E. Beauchamp, "Public Health as Social Justice." Reprinted, with permission of the Blue Cross Association, from *Inquiry,* Volume 13, Number 1 (March 1976), pages 3–14. Copyright © 1976 by the Blue Cross Association. All rights reserved.

Brian Abel-Smith, "Minimum Adequate Levels of Personal Health Care." *Milbank Memorial Fund Quarterly/Health and Society,* Volume 56, Number 1, Winter 1978. Copyright © 1978 by Milbank Memorial Fund. Reprinted with permission of the publisher.

CHAPTER 8

"Health Costs: What Limit?" Reprinted by permission from *Time,* The Weekly Newsmagazine; Copyright Time, Inc., 1979.

Philip R. Lee, "Technology and the Cost of Medical Care—The Physician's Responsibility." Reprinted from *Stanford M.D.* (Fall 1979/Winter 1980). Copyright © by the Stanford Medical Alumni Association.

David Mechanic, "Rationing Medical Care," published in *The Center Magazine*, Volume 11, Number 5, September/October 1978, pages 22–31. Copyright © 1978 by David Mechanic. Reprinted with permission of the author and the publisher.

CHAPTER 9

Harold S. Luft, "Poverty and Health: Discussion of the Issues." Reprinted with permission from *Poverty and Health: Economic Causes and Consequences of Health Problems.* Copyright 1978, Ballinger Publishing Company.

David Mechanic, "Inequality, Health Status, and the Delivery of Health Services in the United States." From *Public Expectations and Health Care.* Copyright © 1972 by John Wiley and Sons, Inc. Reprinted by permission of John Wiley & Sons, Inc.

Karen Davis, "The Impact of Inflation and Unemployment on Health Care of Low-Income Families," excerpted from *Health: A Victim or Cause of Inflation,* edited by Michael Zubkoff, Copyright © by Milbank Memorial Fund. Reprinted with permission of the publisher.

Raymond Wheeler, "Health and Human Resources." Reprinted from the Southern Regional Councils' *New South* (Fall 1971), pages 3–4, by permission from the publisher. Copyright © 1971 by the Southern Regional Council.

CHAPTER 10

Milton Silverman and Philip R. Lee, "The Revolution in Drugs." Reprinted from *Pills, Profits, and Politics.* Copyright © 1974 by The Regents of the University of California. Reprinted by permission of the University of California Press.

Robert L. Kane, "Iatrogenesis: Just What the Doctor Ordered," *Journal of Community Health,* Volume 4, Number 3 (Spring, 1980), pages 149–158. Reprinted by permission from Human Sciences Press, 72 Fifth Avenue, New York, New York 10011. Copyright © 1980 by Human Sciences Press.

Donald Kennedy, "Creative Tension; FDA and Medicine." Reprinted by permission from *The New England Journal of Medicine,* Volume 298, pages 846–850, April 13, 1978. Copyright © 1978 by the Massachusetts Medical Society.

Milton Silverman and Philip R. Lee, "Future Strategy: Prescriptions for Action." Reprinted from *Pills, Profits, and Politics.* Copyright © 1974 by The Regents of the University of California. Reprinted by permission of the University of California Press.

CHAPTER 11

Lewis Thomas, "Natural Science" from *The Lives of a Cell: Notes of a Biology Watcher* by Lewis Thomas. Copyright © 1973 by the Massachusetts Medical Society. Originally appeared in *The New England Journal of Medicine.* Reprinted by permission of Viking Penguin, Inc.

Renée C. Fox, "The Sociology of Modern Medical Research," from Charles Leslie, ed., *Asian Medical Systems: A Comparative Study* (Berkeley: University of California Press), pages 102–114. Copyright © 1976 by The Regents of the University of California. Reprinted by permission.

Henry Wechsler, Joel Gurin, and George F. Cahill, Jr., "Biomedical Research: An Overview." Excerpted by permission of the publishers from *The Horizons of Health,* edited by Henry Wechsler, Joel Gurin, and George F. Cahill, Jr., Cambridge, Mass.: Harvard University Press, Copyright © 1977 by the President and Fellows of Harvard College.

Matt Clark with Sharon Begley and Mary Hager, "The Miracles of Spliced Genes." From *Newsweek,* March 17, 1980. Copyright 1980 by Newsweek, Inc. All Rights Reserved. Reprinted by permission.

Robert Sinsheimer, "Caution May Be an Essential Scientific Virtue." Reprinted from *Moral Choices in Contemporary Society,* edited by Philip Rieff and Isaac Finkle. Copyright © 1977 by The Regents of the University of California. By permission.

CHAPTER 12

H. Jack Geiger, "Health Policy, Social Policy, and the Health of the Aging: Prelude to a Decade of Disaster." Reprinted from *Generations,* Volume 4, Number 1, May 1980, page 11. *Journal of the Western Gerontological Society.* Copyright © 1980 by the Western Gerontological Society. By permission of the publisher.

Carroll L. Estes, "The Social Construction of Reality: A Framework for Inquiry," from C. L. Estes, *The Aging Enterprise.* San Francisco: Jossey-Bass, 1979. Copyright © 1979 by Jossey-Bass, Inc., Publishers. Reprinted by permission.

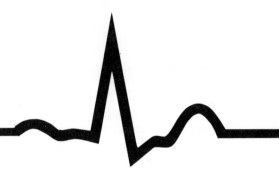

Preface

The *Nation's Health* is the fourteenth in a series of books developed for Courses by Newspaper (CbN). A national program, originated and administered by University Extension, University of California, San Diego, and funded primarily by the National Endowment for the Humanities, Courses by Newspaper develops materials for college-level courses that are presented to the general public through the nationwide cooperation of newspapers and colleges and universities.

The program features a fifteen-part series of articles written by some of the nation's leading experts, who address an audience of millions through the pages of approximately 450 participating newspapers. Interested readers can pursue the subjects further in this book of readings and in a study guide. In addition, approximately 300 colleges and universities offer college credit for a course based on these materials, and many community organizations sponsor public forums and discussion groups on the CbN themes.

This volume supplements the fifteen newspaper articles written especially for the fourteenth Course by Newspaper, "The Nation's Health." The weekly series was developed for newspapers throughout the nation, with a starting date of January 1981.

We would like to thank the hundreds of newspaper editors and publishers who have contributed valuable space to bring the newspaper series to their readers, and the faculties and administrations of the many colleges and universities participating in the program, who have cooperated to make credit available on a nationwide basis.

We would also like to acknowledge those who contributed to the development of this course. The authors of the newspaper articles—Lester Breslow, Irene Butter, Daniel Callahan, René Dubos, Carroll Estes, Paul J. Feldstein, H. Jack Geiger, Edward F. X. Hughes, Donald Kennedy, Lowell Levin, Joann E. Rodgers, Paul D. Saltman, Stephen M. Shortell, and Rosemary Stevens—contributed valuable suggestions for this anthology and the bibliographies that appear at the end of the volume. In addition, the National Board and the CbN

Faculty Committee made important contributions to the conception of the course. Also deserving thanks is Jude Thomas May of the University of Oklahoma Health Sciences Center, whose provocative paper on humanistic aspects of health care played a major role in the formative stage of the course.

Deserving special mention at the University of California, San Diego, is Paul D. Saltman, professor of biology, who has chaired the Faculty Committee and guided the project since its inception, in addition to serving as the first academic coordinator in 1973. Special thanks also go to George Colburn, Project Director of Courses by Newspaper, and the other members of the CbN staff—Yvonne Hancher, Stephanie Giel, Elliot Wager, Linda Wood, Beverly Barry, Sally Cirito, Sharon Fluck, and Gwen Bargsten—who have played crucial roles in developing and administering the program.

A number of people have provided invaluable assistance in the production of this book. David Sobel, a Fellow of the Health Policy Program at the University of California, San Francisco (UCSF), and Policy Chief of Preventive Medicine, Kaiser-Permanente Medical Center, San Jose, deserves special mention. Dr. Sobel read hundreds of articles in order to assist in the final selections for the Reader, and he oversaw the completion of Part I, which presents an overview of the relationship between medicine and health. He was present at the original planning meetings for the course, and his input contributed considerably to the quality of the final product.

We also want to thank Lauren LeRoy, Senior Research Associate of the Health Policy Program, for her willingness to spend long hours critiquing articles for the Reader and for her advice to the editors. Members of the Health Policy Program administrative staff have cooperated on every stage of this project. Special appreciation goes to Eunice Chee, who oversaw the clerical work, and to Les Gates, Dennis Seely, Cathy Kulka, Tedi Dunn, and Pat Franks, who gave generously of their time and talents. This staff effort was made possible, in part, through the support of the Robert Wood Johnson Foundation of Princeton, New Jersey, and the National Center for Health Services Research, Department of Health and Human Services, to the Health Policy Program.

In addition, we wish to thank Carroll Estes, director of the Aging Health Policy Center, School of Nursing, University of California, San Francisco, for generous contributions, including released time for the major efforts by the Center's resource director, Ida Red.

Mark Tuschman, a freelance photographer, took most of the illuminating photographs that appear in this volume. He kindly worked with the editors to develop the themes of this book in real-life images.

In connection with the photographs, we would like to thank the following people and institutions for their generosity in allowing us to photograph their facilities and patients: Mrs. Susan Jergesen and others at the Visiting Nurse Association of San Francisco, an organization that keeps the spirit of personal health care alive by visiting people of limited mobility and treating them medically in their homes; Dr. David Smith and his staff of the Haight Ashbury Clinic in San Francisco, an organization that treats individuals outside the mainstream of American society; Michael Lerner and his staff at Commonweal in Bolinas, California, one of the few facilities in the country that are supplementing medical care by treating children for behavior problems with social and environmental improvements; Pat Wizeman of UCSF Hospital Administration, who helped arrange sessions in the hospitals and clinics; and Dace Mitchell in Ambulatory Care Clinic, UCSF, who allowed us to photograph patient treatment, as did Doris Weyl, nurse practitioner in obstetrics and gynecology. Thanks also are due to Dr. Willard Fee at the Stanford University Hospital and to the Alza pharmaceutical company.

Finally, we wish to express our gratitude to our funding agency, the National Endowment for the Humanities. The Endowment, a federal agency created in 1965 to support education, research, and public activities in the humanities, has generously supported this nationwide program since its inception.

Although Courses by Newspaper is a project of the University of California, San Diego, and is supported by the National Endowment for the Humanities, the views expressed in course materials are those of the authors only and do not necessarily reflect those of the funding agency or of the University of California.

Jane L. Scheiber
Editorial Director, Courses by Newspaper

Nancy Brown
Research Associate

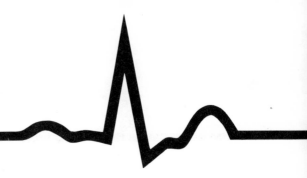

Prologue

I in this volume, we have attempted to provide a clear view of the factors affecting the health of Americans, including the role of medicine. Although the subject of health is important to everyone, the determinants of our health are, in fact, poorly understood. Medical care and biomedical research have dominated health care until relatively recently, when social, economic, and environmental factors, as well as life style, have been acknowledged as major forces that determine health and well-being. Modern industrial society has produced new diseases and new approaches to health care. All aspects of the health care system have undergone a vast revolution in the twentieth century. From the simple doctor of eighty years ago, a gigantic maze of practitioners, facilities, agencies, institutions, schools, industries, and research complexes has developed in the United States.

We intend this Reader to reflect our optimism about the future, particularly about the continuing improvements in health and in the American health care system. The picture, however, is not all bright. There are chapters that reflect bleak aspects of the system. Some avenues medicine is traveling could lead to failure, but promising alternatives are available to individuals and society. Undoubtedly, much of what is in this book will provoke dissent from myriad camps, not because the text represents a narrow point of view, but precisely because it reflects an entire spectrum of views. There are no simple solutions to the problems explored in this text. There are heated controversies as well as neglected ideas, and we have attempted to present some of the most articulate advocates covering the entire range. We have tried to be provocative as well as prudent.

Despite the extraordinary complexity of the issues, one clear message rings through: Americans over the decades have abdicated a large portion of responsibility for their health to physicians, drugs, hospitals, and modern technology. Individuals and health professionals in our society have pursued an imbalanced approach to well-being, and this is rapidly heading toward a dead end. We have distorted the relationship between medicine and health.

Health is not just a matter for science and medicine; it also involves social, economic, philosophical, and ethical issues—issues that cut to the core of American values and institutions.

In this book, we have critically examined the contributions of modern medicine. Rather than merely emphasizing its many contributions in the care of the sick and in improving the health of the population, we have looked at the web of issues, policies, controversies, problems, and solutions that surround the health care system. While acknowledging the inevitability of death and disease, we would like to explore a means to greater health and longevity for everyone. We hope that this volume will contribute to a realization of that aim.

I The Role of Medicine: An Overview

What is health? How do we measure it? What are the major determinants of our health? What is the role of medical care in promoting health? What role do we play in determining our health? What are the consequences of the increasing influence of medicine in our lives?

These are some of the major questions addressed in this first section of *The Nation's Health*. While the questions are easy to pose, they are not that easy to answer. Consequently, we encounter many sharp differences of opinion and points of view on these issues.

There is general agreement that we are healthier today as a nation than ever before in history. It is also clear that we are investing an increasing proportion of our national resources in medical care and that medicine has become a dominant social institution. Yet there is a striking paradox: we are at the same time concerned about our health and more critical of our medical care system.

Chapter 1 presents a broad overview of health and medicine, and of the relationship between them. Chapter 2 focuses on our health status—the difficulties involved in measuring it and the factors that determine it. The role of medicine as a social institution and as a cultural phenomenon is assessed in Chapter 3, which discusses the medicalization of American society.

1 Medicine and Health

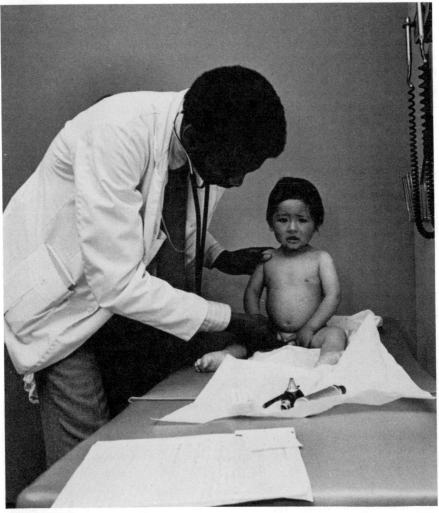

MARK TUSCHMAN

T here has been a major shift in our health problems over the last one hundred years. In the past, infectious diseases and nutritional deficiencies predominated. These diseases yielded to a combination of improved environments and, to a lesser degree, more effective medical treatments. Today the major health problems are accidental death, homicides, suicides, heart disease, cancer, and strokes; they appear to result, at least in part, from the ways we choose to live and the environments we create. Management of these problems, therefore, requires a different strategy. We cannot rely on the cures of modern medicine or collective public health measures. Today, health requires, perhaps more than ever, a stronger commitment of personal responsibility and conscious decisions. Even so, physicians still have a role to play. When cures cannot be effected, medical care can still facilitate rehabilitation, offer reassurance, and help us to function as well as possible in the face of serious disease.

In "Health and Creative Adaptation," René Dubos, the famed microbiologist and environmentalist, describes health as the reflection of a person's success in adapting to environmental challenges. The adaptability of the human organism, though remarkable, does have its limits. Rapidly accelerating social and technological change presents novel challenges which at times exceed our adaptive capacities. The chronic and degenerative diseases as well as accidents and violence have been called the "diseases of civilization" because they reflect some of the costs of industrialization, urbanization, and rapid social change. Against these diseases the narrow analytic approach of contemporary scientific medicine has been relatively ineffective, largely because health increasingly depends on the choice of healthy ways of living.

Perhaps we have confused medicine and health. The assumption that the way to improve health is by increasing medical care is challenged by Dr. John S. Chapman of the University of Texas in "Health and Medicine." He maintains that medicine has focused almost exclusively on disease. Therefore, it is little wonder that we know so little about health and how to promote it other than by preventing specific diseases.

Arthur Kleinman, who is both a physician and an anthropologist, further explores the limitations posed by Western medicine's exclusive focus on the biological dimensions of sickness, namely disease. What about the human experience of illness, the meaning of disease for the patient, family, and

4

friends? In "The Failure of Western Medicine," Kleinman argues that to be more effective, medicine must not only attempt to cure the biological dysfunction of disease but should also address the illness experience as well—the personal and social consequences of being sick.

In a similar vein, Dr. Robert J. Haggerty urges medicine to extend its boundaries and influence. In "The Boundaries of Health Care," he echoes the theme that "illness care" can produce only marginal gains in health relative to measures aimed at social and environmental factors. He contends that by working in the "boundary areas" of lifestyle, housing, pollution, life stresses, and political institutions, medicine is likely to contribute far more to health than would further concentration on curative, personal medical care. Several contributors in Chapter 3, as we shall see, express serious concern about this expanded role of medicine.

If the boundaries of health care are to be extended, as Haggerty suggests, how can we organize and think about the complex, interrelated biological, environmental, and behavioral determinants of health? Physicians Howard Brody and David S. Sobel introduce "A Systems View of Health and Disease." They characterize health as the ability of a system (for example, a cell, organism, family, or society) to adapt to a wide variety of environmental challenges (for example, physical, chemical, infectious, psychological, or social). Disease is the pattern of disruption which can spread through the cellular, organic, personal, group, or societal system levels. Therefore, treatment or preventive interventions should be aimed at multiple levels of the system. This view of health and disease can provide a common vocabulary and framework to facilitate communication and teamwork across professional and disciplinary boundaries.

René Dubos

Health and Creative Adaptation

"Although human beings can never adapt biologically to the diseases of civilization, creative adaptation allows us to shape our lives and our responses to disease." In this introductory article, biologist René Dubos defines health as the ability to adapt to environmental challenges, and healing as restoring to an individual the freedom to make choices. Human health goes beyond the purely biological health of animals because it involves value judgments by which we select our modes of life.

Anyone who has ever undergone a routine medical checkup knows that body functions are commonly described by cryptic abbreviations like EKG and technical terms like serum triglyceride. Health is expressed in numbers such as 120/80 and 98.6, which are interpreted as being inside or outside the range of normal. All too often, however, the measurements extracted from a test tube of blood or a sample of urine are normal while the patient continues to insist that something is wrong. The explanation of the discrepancy is that these measurements indicate only biological fitness, which is appropriate to animals in the wild but insufficient to describe the health of human beings.

For human beings, health transcends biological fitness. It is primarily a measure of each person's ability to do what he wants to do and become what he wants to become. Good health implies an individual's success in functioning within his particular set of values, and as such it is extremely relative. The bookish scholar in a library has a concept of health that is different from that of the financier who worries about coronary occlusion and peptic ulcer during a business lunch.

Animals in their natural habitats appear healthy and free of disease for the simple reason that any animal seriously handicapped by genetic abnormalities, old age, or disease is likely to be abandoned by the other members of its group and to fall victim to starvation or predators. The health of wild animals depends on their ability to adapt biologically to their environment, an ability based on anatomical and physiological mechanisms developed during evolu-

6

tion and encoded in their genes. In the human species, also, the state of health reflects a person's success in adapting to environmental challenges, but the interplay between human beings and their environment involves many factors not encountered in animal life.

Animals rarely leave the environment in which they evolved, an environment for which they are biologically suited. In contrast, human beings have settled over practically all the earth even though they essentially retain the genetic legacy acquired in the region of their biological origin, probably the warm grasslands of East Africa. Human beings are biologically semitropical animals, yet they now live in all climatic zones. In order to colonize the earth, they have been compelled to fashion habitats that enable them to function and multiply in environments where they are biological misfits. . . . Wherever it exists, human life has modified nature profoundly, often with unpredictable consequences for biological health and the quality of the environment.

Human beings also long for new experiences. . . . For the sake of adventure, they commonly expose themselves to situations to which they are biologically or socially ill-adapted.

Because of the pressures generated by new ways of life, most social and technological changes have, throughout history, been marked by an increase in the prevalence of disease. Epidemics of plague during the Renaissance were the result of an increase in intercontinental travel. The migration of people from rural areas into crowded, urban tenements during the first phase of the Industrial Revolution certainly played a role in the rampant spread of tuberculosis and other infectious diseases. In our own time, prosperity and modern technologies account at least in part for the increase in the so-called diseases of civilization, such as heart disease, stroke, and probably cancer.

The effects of the environment on health are further complicated by the human propensity to turn events into symbols and to react to the symbols as if they were physical challenges. Thus an individual's responses to a particular environment reflect not only its physical and chemical characteristics but also the experiences that the individual associates with that environment. Memories and emotions can metamorphose the most trivial as well as the most sublime events and can cause unexpected physiological reactions.

Similarly, anticipation, whether conscious or unconscious, can profoundly affect an individual's response to a stimulus. The sight of a food associated with the memory of a disgusting event may cause nausea. A sudden drop in the stock market or the end of a love affair can exacerbate a latent peptic ulcer or reawaken a tuberculous infection. The hope or fear of a situation that has not yet occurred may cause irregular heartbeats. The symbol of any real or imagined experience commonly becomes as effective as the experience itself in evoking physiological responses that govern health or disease.

Health in human societies, thus, has far more complex determinants than has the health of animals in the wild. However, the sociocultural view of human health also has a biological basis in the fact that *Homo sapiens* is the least specialized of animal species. Unlike animals, whose physical capabilities are rather narrowly defined, human beings can walk, run, creep, climb, and swim. They can live at sea level, at an altitude of 15,000 feet in the Peruvian Andes, or at 1,000 feet below sea level near the Dead Sea. Some people prefer the sun and others prefer the shade. All can derive nourishment—if they wish—from a completely carnivorous or herbivorous diet, or from a combination of both. Ever since the Stone Age, human beings have developed cultural mechanisms that enhance still further the adaptability provided by their low level of anatomical and physiological specialization. . . .

*   *   *

The most polluted, traumatic, and crowded cities of the world have great appeal for people of all races and ages. Some of the most rapid increases in population occur under living conditions biologically so detestable that they seem incompatible with life. Humankind seems capable of adjusting to environmental pollution, inadequate diets, intense crowding, as well as to monotonous, ugly, and stressful surroundings.

These adjustments, however, are bought at a high price. The smoke and fumes in the air around us; the filth in our streams, lakes, and oceans; the mountains of wastes that spoil landscapes and cityscapes; the noise, glaring lights, and other unnatural stimuli that shatter our nerves—all these environmental insults contribute to the pattern of diseases peculiar to modern civilization. Authorities once believed that disorders of the cardiovascular system, various forms of cancer, and chronic and degenerative diseases in general are more prevalent simply because more people are surviving long enough to fall victim to such disorders. But the truth is that the increase in chronic and degenerative diseases is due in large part to the environmental and behavioral changes associated with industrialization and urbanization.

Unfortunately, humankind can never overcome the diseases of civilization by becoming biologically adapted to pollution or other environmental insults, because many changes in the human organism that appear adaptive on first sight are destructive in the long run. Air pollution, for example, elicits from the lung an overproduction of mucus that at first protects delicate lung tissues from pollutants. Eventually, however, the protective response gives way to chronic pulmonary disease. Continued exposure to loud noises gradually reduces one's perception of them but impairment of the hearing apparatus also limits the ability to hear musical tones and the finer qualities of the human voice. Life in extremely crowded environments generates psychological attitudes that block out excessive environmental stimuli, but these attitudes can impoverish human relationships. Such mutilations of the physical and mental being should not be regarded as adaptation but rather as undesirable mechanisms of tolerance.

Deeper biological reasons than these prevent humankind from genetically adapting to the diseases of civilization. The most important reason is that insults from the modern environment generally do not dramatically impair health during the first decades of life. Since susceptibility to environmentally induced disease does not interfere with reproductive ability, natural selection cannot work against it. If a certain air pollutant causes cancer, for example, the chances are great that people sensitive to the carcinogens will have children before the disease becomes incapacitating. As a consequence, the children will be as susceptible to the cancer-producing agent as their parents were.

Even if we could adapt to automobile fumes, the noise of jackhammers, or the traumatic experience of rush hour in the subway, adaptation through genetic changes proceeds slowly and many, many generations would be required for the changes to be significant for society as a whole.

In practice, then, the only biological adjustment we can make to the deleterious environmental factors is not true adaptation but a form of tolerance achieved at the cost of impaired functioning. We must learn to design environments suited to human health, and where we fail we must deal with environmental insults either by developing ways of life that protect us from them or by treating the diseases they cause.

More than a century ago, the French physiologist Claude Bernard asserted that, in higher animals as well as in human beings, survival and health depend upon the ability of the organism to maintain its internal environment in an approximately constant state, despite exposure to endless and often large variations in the external environment. The composition of our body fluids, for example, remains remarkably constant regardless of the kind of food we eat. Recognizing a fundamental truth long before it could be scientifically demonstrated, Bernard boldly claimed in a famous phrase that "the constancy of the *milieu intérieur* [internal environment] is the essential condition for free and independent life."

In his most explicit statement of this concept, Bernard wrote: "The constancy of the *milieu intérieur* presupposes a perfection of the organism such that the external variations are at each instant compensated and brought into balance.... All the vital mechanisms, however varied they might be, always have one purpose, that of maintaining the integrity of the conditions for life within the internal environment."

... Not until the first decades of the 20th century did insights into physiology and biochemistry enable us to identify some of the mechanisms that the body employs to correct departures from the ideal state and to maintain itself in a state of dynamic equilibrium. Walter B. Cannon, the Harvard physiologist who adapted x-rays to the study of the digestive system, introduced the word *homeostasis* to denote this equilibrium.

As Cannon showed by physiological experimentation, the phrase "homeostatic processes" describes the multifarious physiological and metabolic reactions that continuously adjust the internal composition of the body within safe limits. The limits are precisely defined for each organism. The cybernetic nature of this adjustment was recognized by the theoretical physicist Norbert Wiener, one of Cannon's contemporaries. In Wiener's words, "The apparent equilibrium of life is an active equilibrium in which each deviation from the norm brings on a reaction in the opposite direction, which is of the nature of what we call negative feedback." This cybernetic statement of homeostasis is of course quite consonant with Claude Bernard's views of the stability of the *milieu intérieur*.

Cannon was so impressed by the perfection of the mechanisms involved in the maintenance of homeostasis that he barely mentioned illness in his book. He seemed to imply that homeostatic negative feedback always manages to return the organism to normal and thus assures the maintenance of health. But in reality, perfect homeostatic reactions are probably the exception rather than the rule. . . .

In many situations, homeostatic mechanisms have indirect and delayed consequences that are responsible for chronic disorders. The production of scar tissue, or fibrosis, is a homeostatic response that heals wounds and helps to check the spread of infection, but fibrosis destroys the liver in alcoholic cirrhosis, freezes the joints in rheumatoid arthritis, and stifles breathing in a diseased lung. Dangers are also inherent in behavioral homeostasis when reactions such as anger and excitement give way to obsessions, maniacal episodes, and other forms of pathological behavior in response to incidents that may be minor.

The ultimate value of homeostatic reactions cannot be judged, therefore, until all of the consequences of such changes have been recognized. All too often the wisdom of the body is a short-sighted wisdom. . . .

Purely homeostatic processes are largely unconscious. Similarly, a large percentage of responses to environmental forces are determined by instincts that operate outside consciousness and free will. Instincts come ready-made, so to speak, and enable the organism to deal decisively and often successfully with life situations similar to those experienced by the species during its evolutionary past.

But precisely because instincts are so pointed and mechanical, they are of little use in new circumstances. We have no instinct to warn us of the dangers inherent in odorless chemical fumes, invisible radiation beams, or subliminal forms of brainwashing. Instincts do not enable us to deal successfully with the unforeseeable complexities of human life.

Whereas instincts stand for biological security in a static world, awareness, knowledge, and motivation account for the adventurous liberty and creativity of the human spirit. . . . To the extent that the brain can make choices, it can direct adaptive responses. Since the evolved wisdom of the body is blind and often faulty, we must substitute for it a wisdom based on knowledge of present conditions and on anticipation of future consequences.

In the final analysis, we can make choices concerning our behavior and surroundings, choices that will prevent or minimize undesirable changes in the *milieu intérieur*. Manipulation of the external environment inevitably affects mental characteristics and the constituents of some body tissues, as well as the quality of social relationships. Thought processes also play an important role in shaping the internal environment since they can profoundly alter hormonal secretions and consequently physiological mechanisms. . . .

The concept of health as a creative adaptive process that requires choices and conscious participation by the whole organism seems at odds with the dominant trends of modern scientific medicine. Like other aspects of Western science, modern medicine emphasizes the analytical approach to knowledge, an attitude reflected in the diagnosis and treatment of a specific disease. Most other forms of medicine, by contrast, deal with the patient as part of the total environment. This fundamental difference in attitude is evident in a comparison of Western and traditional Chinese medicine.

Ever since the 17th century, medical science has been shaped largely by Cartesian analytical philosophy. Its ideal is to subdivide every anatomic structure, physiological function, and biochemical process into smaller and smaller subunits so that each can be studied in greater and greater detail. The most sophisticated and successful application of this analytical approach is the reduction of medical problems to phenomena of molecular biology.

*   *   *

In contrast, traditional Chinese medicine seems to be more concerned with the interplay between the components of biological systems than with the description of these individual components. It studies, for example, the way the liver relates to other parts of the body rather than the anatomical or physiological characteristics of the liver as an isolated organ. It also pays much attention to the relationships between the living organism and its environment—the place, the seasons, the weather, the time of day, the social milieu. To a large extent, all systems of medicine except those based on modern Western science derive from an emphasize an integration of the body, the mind, and the environment.

There is no doubt, of course, that the Western analytical approach has yielded phenomenal achievements in preventive and therapeutic medicine during the past half century. But it is also true that some of the greatest triumphs of Western medicine emerged not from reductionist analysis but from an integrated view of disease and of man's relation to his total environment. . . .

Many people assume that the successful medical and public health practices of the past were just lucky accidents. In reality, they were based on a method of reasoning that was scientific but that differed from ours in content. In most cases, they involved an implicit awareness that living organisms respond to environmental challenges by active processes that have adaptive value. . . .

An approach to medicine that is based on concepts of organismic and social adaptation is certainly compatible with scientific developments. In fact, such an attitude leads to the conclusion that the scientific medicine of our time is not scientific enough because it neglects, and at times completely ignores, the multifarious environmental and emotional factors that affect the human organism in health and in disease, and to which the organism can consciously respond in an adaptive, creative way. . . .

All forms of organic and mental disease inevitably interfere with the ability of patients to live as they would like: to take the social roles that appeal to them and to reach the goals they formulate for themselves. Such an interference amounts to a loss of freedom. Patients go to a healer—any member of the health profession—in the hope of recovering this lost freedom. Even when there is no treatment known to cure the disease, the healer can often help the patient to function in a fairly normal way, either by the use of drugs and other forms of medical technology, or by advice based on knowledge of human nature.

Recovery from disease may follow two different courses. The organism may return to the exact condition in which it was before the illness, or it may undergo lasting changes that go beyond mere reversal of damage and result in a new adaptive state. The first type of healing, which is rare, corresponds to the classical homeostatic *reactions* of the body; the second constitutes the creative adaptive *responses* of the whole organism.

I have used the word *reaction* for homeostatic healing processes and *response* for creative healing processes. The difference in wording conveys my belief that homeostatic reactions are determined to a large extent by unconscious physiological and biochemical mechanisms of the body, whereas creative responses tend to be goal-oriented and to involve the conscious participation of the organism as a whole.

To heal does not necessarily imply to cure. It can simply mean helping people to achieve a way of life compatible with their individual aspirations—to restore their freedom to make choices—even in the presence of continuing disease.

MARK TUSCHMAN

Children at Commonweal, a residential community in Bolinas, California, take part in a unique living experiment. Here, young people with learning and behavior problems are provided with a wholesome diet and supportive environment as enhancements to medical treatment.

John S. Chapman

Health and Medicine

The contemporary tendency to associate health with the practice of medicine is a mistake, according to Dr. John S. Chapman of the University of Texas. In the following article he argues that medicine has always concerned itself with disease. Chapman proposes that health be studied and promoted by new professionals and institutions altogether separate from physicians and medical schools, the experts in disease.

The institution with which I am associated has recently undergone re-baptism. What was formerly a medical school with some attached and relatively minor instruction of other technical and professional personnel has become a "Health Science Center." The new term has the advantage of bombast, solecism, and imprecision, all qualities in high esteem along Madison Avenue.

In fact, the institution remains predominantly a medical school and, as such, is about as scientific as a good school can get. And, like all medical schools, this one has little or nothing to do with health. One accepts "center" to avoid quibbling.

However, what is important is an institutionalization of the metonymy,* "health = medicine" or "medicine = health." These concepts are more truly antonymous, as the discussion will demonstrate. Much more importantly, misuse of language produces misapprehension, unfulfilled expectations, and consequential revolt. In short, the misapprehension consists of the notion that if there is enough medicine or enough medical care, the population will be healthy.

In truth, however, the purpose of medicine has never been to produce health, but rather to recognize the signs of disease and institute suitable procedures to set the disorder right again. The conceptual structure underlying the entire discipline is pathology—the disorder of structure and function. Students enter medical schools with the expectation that they will learn how to repair the disordered human to the point that he may resume function, or at least remain alive. It should be obvious that this preselection of per-

Ed. note: A figure of speech in which an idea is evoked by naming an associated idea.

sonnel, followed by four years of concentrated study of processes of disease and confirmed by training in hospitals, does not and cannot be expected to produce an expert in health.

Not much more promising is the student who elects to enter Public Health and Preventive Medicine. His preselection for interest in the morbid (the old term for "pathological") and the four years of disease-oriented medical school have set deeply in him reference points from which he can escape only in the most unusual circumstances. Operations in the field of public health still function to control or prevent specific illness or injury. The inclusion of Preventive Medicine adds not much, except a more generalized concept: the basic element still consists of prevention of some or many specific ill effects as they may arise from occupation, environment, or habit. The statement remains accurate whether the mechanism of prevention be exercise, diet, or regular checkups.

These distinctions acquire importance from the present "crisis" in medical care. (To what degree the crisis may be an artifact of statistical manipulation or of political ambition is beside the point.) The people of the United States, including a good many experts in many areas, *believe* there is a crisis and for that reason have undertaken to respond. Their reasoning apparently takes the following form. The people of the United States are not healthy. Medicine produces health. Therefore, there is not enough medicine. The response has assumed the form of proliferation of medical schools, the development of nurse-practitioner and medical aide programs, clamor for all kinds of mechanized procedures, including computer diagnosis, and various new systems of delivery of medical care.

All of these remedies and responses refer to "health," but they all apply essentially to medical service. Furthermore, under the rubric of "health crisis" these various actual and proposed solutions in reality deal with distribution of medical service, costs of hospitalization and medical care, transportation, staffing of hospitals, and quite a lot of other considerations that may have more to do with convenience and preference than either with the quality of medical care or with health. If the aim is health, as proclaimed, people will strive in vain as long as they try to achieve that goal by proliferation of medical personnel or facilities. For all of these instrumentalities produce health only incidentally, one may say, negatively, through control or correction of disorder.

Medicine has indeed very little knowledge of or techniques for production of health as a positive activity. Even there hardly exists a vocabulary, other than in the humanities, to deal with ideas of health. So little have these concepts received attention since the Renaissance that one has to turn to the Greeks and even to primitive peoples to find definitions. Among them one encounters the idea of internal harmony—and the modern promptly adds, whatever that is. Most of our other ideas of health are similarly expressive but undefinable.

We can speak easily of a healthy child, by which we mean a child who is lively and energetic, but then we have to add, not often sick. The negative is measurable, but the positive adjectives are not. In like fashion, we speak of a "well-preserved" old person, and imply an individual who, in spite of years, retains an active mind and a fund of physical energy. These are all qualitative expressions, quite as familiar to the humanist as to a scientist. But they are observable in crude measure and they are aspects of a biological form. Therefore, theoretically, it should be possible to determine mechanisms underlying and to quantitate these attributes.

The suggestion naturally follows that conceptualization may be directed from the normal to the morbid quite as readily as from diseases to normality. In this reorientation, health becomes the goal and illness an incident. In a reversal of emphasis of this kind, it should promptly occur to one that the preparation of the student or practitioner or scientist of health should not be in medical schools, but in a quite different type of training in which pathology has no part.

Except for the fears of disease and of death that have afflicted thinking man from his beginning, the evolution of some kind of expert in health might have been anticipated. It is a curious phenomenon that while in human biology we have remained preoccupied with morbid processes, we have simultaneously produced animal husbandrymen and agronomists. The function of both professionals is to produce environmental and nutritional milieus that protect their species against disease, and in a far more compassionate fashion than one can find in human affairs to produce disease-resistant strains.

The argument leads inevitably to the proposition that a rational society might turn its attention to the production of a profession devoted to the understanding and furtherance of health as a positive goal. The scientific base of the profession should be human anatomy, biochemistry, genetics, physiology, and cellular biology. The practitioners' function would be the production of health to the extent that knowledge at any moment and that change in human attitude permit. On the basis of present knowledge of health, the profession might well face scorn: we know little more than the Greeks or our grandmothers, but this does not imply that we must remain forever ignorant.

The reorientation of goals does not mean that medicine would undergo a rapid atrophy. There will be always sufficient departures from health to require a large profession of human repairmen. The reorientation will demand a redirection of cultural attitudes and practices, a change that may take place more slowly than professional development. Yet the prospect for cultural change is less discouraging than one may think. There is some evidence that the countercurrent exists, although in curious and irrational eddies.

Where and what are these precursors? They are the food-faddists, the health nuts, the exercise enthusiasts, and the body-builders. Our derogation indicates how far they are from the mainstream of culture. But the fact that they exist demonstrates a tribal or cultural Gestalt that by performance of the "right" and avoidance of the "wrong" rituals one may render himself resistant to the ills which assail mankind. That a major part of this activity is in the hands of biological illiterates is of minor importance. Medicine was little more than pompous quackery till the 19th century. What it all signifies is that if a reasonable amount of intelligence, study, and investigation should go into the meaning and nature of health rather than into morbid incidents of maiming or lethal potential, we might find a far more rational solution to our difficulties than in a multiplication of trouble-shooters.

There are two reasons that such a direction of study and guidance may never develop. First, humans in groups tend to behave irrationally. Second, the responsibility for health rests on self-discipline, and the human individual almost without exception will trade a deferred benefit for present gratification.

All our lives long, every day and every hour, we are engaged in the process of accommodating our changed and unchanged selves to changed and unchanged surroundings; living, in fact, is nothing else than a process of accommodation.

—Samuel Butler

Arthur Kleinman

The Failure of Western Medicine

In the following selection, psychiatrist Arthur Kleinman deplores the tendency for Western physicians to concentrate on disease rather than on the patient as a whole individual. He argues that widespread dissatisfaction with modern medical treatment may be caused by the fact that most doctors concern themselves only with the diagnosis and treatment of disease, while patients experience illness as a multifaceted disruption of their lives. By adding some of the social and behavioral approaches of alternative healers to their biological methods, Western physicians could offer patients more humanistic, satisfying medical care.

Increasing numbers of patients are turning from professional health care to alternative forms of treatment—from orthopedic surgeons to chiropractors, from ophthalmologists to optometrists, from physicians to native healers. This lack of confidence in Western medicine springs, I believe, from the physician's disregard for the patient apart from his or her disease. This was not always so.

Several decades ago, before their ability to control disease began to increase dramatically, Western physicians were interested in treating both disease *and* illness—the way the patient perceives and experiences his disorder, in the context of family and society. Today, however, most physicians limit their care to the cure of disease—the biological disorder. If, for instance, a person has cancer, the physician uses surgery, radiation, and chemotherapy to treat the malignant tumor. But the modern physician's training leaves him unequipped to treat the illness: how the cancer is experienced by the patient, what meaning it holds for him, his family, friends, and fellow workers.

In one interview I witnessed, an anxious twenty-year-old patient with kidney disease asked his doctor, "When will I be able to return to school?" The physician replied, "We'll see. I'm sorry I have to go now. I can't answer any more questions. Why don't you speak to the nurse?" When I asked the doctor why he failed to answer the patient's questions on this and five other occasions, he said, "The patient's questions don't matter. Nothing is gained from talking to him, except getting him to take the medicine properly and to follow the right diet. It is much more important to study the laboratory findings. They show what is really going on inside his kidneys."

In this frank expression of the "veterinary" tendency in modern medicine, the physician failed to recognize that the experience of a biological disorder is distinct from the disorder itself. Sickness begins with a person's awareness of a change in his bodily feelings that is labeled either by the sufferer or his family as being "ill." The person does not experience the presence of bacteria or organ malfunction; he senses pain, disorientation, and distress. Others do not see the patient's disease. They respond to his behavior, to his illness. But instead of treating the patient's experiences, the modern physician restricts himself to attacking the bacteria or restoring the organ's function; there is no regular relationship between the disease and the illness. Patients with the same disease—a heart ailment, for instance—may experience different illnesses: one person may be debilitated and another not. The web of personal significance surrounding each illness represents some special combination of threat, loss, and gain. In addition, illness may, and often does, occur without disease. Fifty percent of patients' visits to doctors are for complaints without any clear biological basis.

Because the illness exists apart from the disease, but each is affected by the other, physicians may diagnose a disease properly but fail to cure it. Patients who do not understand the treatment or who disagree with the physician's explanation often fail to follow the prescribed treatment. In one case, a professor insisted that he did not have coronary artery disease and resisted treatment, believing that to admit the disease would make him an invalid. It was not until a psychiatrist intervened that the cardiologist discussed the disease frankly with the patient and described the limited changes in his way of life that the treatment would entail.

This lack of concern with illness has contributed to the increasing tendency of patients to disregard doctors' instructions, the dissatisfaction with the quality of medical care, the explosive growth in malpractice suits, and to the trend in many industrial countries toward self-care. As a result, many scholars are re-evaluating the effectiveness of Western medicine; others are recording native-healing practices in various countries and comparing them with the methods of Western physicians.

Unlike physicians, native healers focus on the patient's illness. They concentrate on the social and cultural aspects of treatment, dealing with sickness as a human problem that affects family functions and tears at the web of meaning that integrates day to day life, not as just an isolated event in the life of the patient. Native healers primarily use symbolic, religious, and ritualistic treatments. Their definition of illness as a social and cultural experience is a crucial part of the healing process. . . .

Western physicians could broaden their own skills and knowledge, allowing them to treat both disease and illness. I am recommending not that Western physicians learn to go into trances or ask patients to burn spirit money, but that they learn to treat sickness in the context of the patient's psychology and culture. Physicians need, for example, to question patients about what they think caused their problems; how they think their illnesses should be treated; what threats, losses, and gains their sickness represents; and what conflicts they perceive between their values and the doctor's professional values.

Doctors need to be as precise in defining the life problems created by an illness as in investigating its biological basis. They should be as competent in prescribing behavioral and social management strategies for treating the illness as in prescribing technological interventions for the disease. This takes time, effort, and training. But only when physicians again treat the patient's illness, as well as his disease, and treat it with a systematic approach based on the findings of clinical social science, not with a folksy parody of shamans or old-time general practitioners, will the persistent dissatisfaction with modern medicine begin to fade. Following the example of the native healer, though not his specific methods, may be the best way to introduce humanistic medicine into the developed world.

Health signifies that one's life force is intact, and that one is sufficiently in harmony with the social, physical, and supernatural environment to enjoy what is positively valued in life, and to ward off misfortunes and evils.

—Bantu African Medical Thought

Robert J. Haggerty

The Boundaries of Health Care

By addressing the questions of what factors affect health and where health services properly end and other human services begin, pediatrician Robert J. Haggerty proposes new directions for the development of medicine. Beyond biomedical research, curative medicine, public health, and social medicine, are health boundaries that offer new challenges to medical professionals. Research on the environmental, behavioral, educational, social, and political factors that affect health will require the cooperation of biological and social scientists.

N ational priorities have now been set for health services in our country: they are to increase access, to moderate cost, and to maintain or increase quality. Most of the current efforts are directed to the first two of these goals—getting existing types of services to those who do not now receive them and reorganizing and financing care to improve efficiency and contain costs. Solutions to these first two goals are in sight although considerable struggles still lie ahead before they are achieved.

While the public and the professions are most concerned with these two issues today, I suspect that the next crisis will center around the issue of quality—and by quality I mean effectiveness of the whole process of health services and what factors produce health. I will review a few studies that bear on this and then discuss what role medicine can play in the production of health as opposed to merely providing health services. This will lead me on into several areas not now a part of traditional medical care. This future oriented area, I think, is appropriately titled "The Boundaries of Health Care."

I. Health Services and Their Effect on Health

First, I would like to review... the effectiveness of health services in changing health. Health itself is difficult to measure, but there can be little argument that it is somehow the reciprocal or absence of mortality, morbidity, disability and distress....

In the absence of our ability to show much reduction in death, disease and only occasionally in disability as a result of medical care, most of us have turned to measure other factors that we felt might be more responsive to care—costs, utilization of services such as hospitals, office visits and compliance with preventive or curative regimens. Here the evidence that different types of medical care have different effects is much better.

... There is not much evidence that illness care (which is what most medical care consists of) reduces mortality or morbidity very much. When well organized, it can reduce utilization of expensive facilities such as hospitals and emergency rooms and can reduce other costs such as laboratory and pharmacy without any measurable difference in health status. In other words, the effect of illness care after a point produces only marginal gains in health.

I need to make perfectly clear that I am well aware that we do have some data on the effectiveness of specific aspects of curative medicine—penicillin for pneumonia, antimicrobial treatment of meningitis, drug therapy for essential hypertension and a few other conditions that have been shown by controlled clinical trials to be positively affected by modern therapy. And I certainly do not wish to belittle the very important effects of our role as relievers of pain and distress. Individuals and society need someone who provides hope by not giving up when the outcome is death. They need the comfort that there is access to such people as physicians even for conditions that will be self-limiting. Medicine satisfies a deep human need for someone else to provide help. I need also to make clear that I, as a clinician who has spent my entire professional life caring for children and their families, like to practice medicine. I am not disillusioned, bitter or tired of practice. But I also believe that we need to be humble about what we clinicians accomplish and raise our sights a bit to see if there may not be other things that we or someone in society could do to improve health much more than we are doing today. . . .

David Mechanic, who expresses so many things so well, said that "medicine has three principal tasks: (1) to understand how particular symptoms, syndromes or disease entities arise, either in individuals or among groups of individuals; (2) to recognize and cure these or shorten their course or minimize any residual impairment; and (3) to promote living conditions in human populations which eliminate hazards to health and thus prevent disease." The first of these tasks has generally been the province of biomedical research, the second of curative medicine and the last of public health and social medicine. The time is now at hand to join these three and to move into what I like to call the boundaries of health care.

The problem is simply stated. Where do health services end and other human services begin? Or, what factors affect health? The answers are far from clear. Let me first discuss the evidence.

II. Social and Environmental Factors' Effect on Health

On a superficial level it is easy for everyone to accept that the way we live, our diet, our pace of life, our housing, our political and social structure, all contribute to health—perhaps sharing only with our genes predominance as the factor most responsible for our state of health. In comparison, what we as doctors do for people is rather insignificant. Let me spend just a few moments documenting this bold statement since it is said with a good deal more conviction than the facts often allow.

A. *Lead poisoning* is an easy example with which to start. Most lead poisoning in children results from ingestion of paint from housing with high lead content paint. The outcome of therapy, once symptomatic poisoning occurs, is bad—mortality and especially late intellectual morbidity are high. We can now diagnose body lead burdens above normal before symptoms appear and have fairly good chelating agents to accelerate its elimination, although we still do not know the long term consequences of asymptomatic lead burdens. But the poisoned child usually must remain in his same environment where he will continue to ingest lead. To date no cure for his desire to eat paint has been found to be successful. We must remove him from the lead. Even if we move him, however, another family with a small child is likely to move into the same house and become poisoned. Getting landlords and even parents to remove the paint from the housing has been disappointing—it is costly, time consuming and, with absentee landlords and poorly prosecuted housing codes, often impossible to accomplish. What is medicine's role? Should it stop at treatment of the symptomatic child? At surveillance programs to detect and then treat the asymptomatic child? At getting social workers to move the child to a new home? At enforcing housing codes that may require the physician's attendance in court if he pushes hard enough? At promotion of building new, safe housing for his community? At political action? At building the new housing himself? Clearly, each of us stops somewhere along this spectrum, usually before building the new housing himself. But until new housing has been built to replace all the old, or complete renovation of the old achieved, there will not be a solution to lead poisoning, any more than there was a solution to the problem of rickets until vitamin D was put in all milk.

B. *Environment:* A second example of the effect of physical environment on health is the ... work of H. Sultz and W. Winkelstein. ... They showed that on days when there was high air pollution, there were also many more asthmatic children having acute attacks and coming to physicians. What role should we as clinicians play in air pollution control when it directly affects the health of our patients?

One of the most strikingly successful stories of such a role in altering environment by a physician is that of L. Colebrook, a surgeon in Britain, who became incensed that little girls were frequently severely burned by standing close to open hearth fireplaces and catching their clothes on fire. He collected data, presented it and got legislation passed requiring that every fireplace have a grate six inches in front of the fire. Such burns were significantly reduced as a result. As a clinician he contributed more to health by this move than by all his surgical skills.

C. *Way of Life:* Let me now take a third example from adult medicine. L. Breslow and his colleagues in California have been engaged for some years in the Human Population Laboratory conducting a longitudinal study of the health status of a random sample of people and correlating this with various aspects of life style. He found that five factors in the way people live—the amount of sleep (less than six hours/night vs. 7–8), diet (erratic or regular), alcohol consumption (less or more than five drinks per day), regular exercise and tobacco use—were significantly associated with health. Good health practices were associated with good health, and the relation was cumulative—the more of these factors that were "good" the better the health. In fact, people of 55–64 who had had these "good" habits had the health, as determined by their functioning, of 25–34 year olds who had these "bad" habits. To the epidemiologists there are, of course, many missing links. Most important to the clinician is the question, can such "bad" habits, if present, be changed and how; and if changed, will that alter a person's health? For the purpose of this discussion the issues I would like to have you think about include, "Is it medicine's job to educate people on how to sleep, eat, drink, exercise and smoke?" Is this within or beyond the boundary? The implications are that if we could change men's function this much by altering life habits, we would accomplish more than through all of our therapeutic medicine.

D. *Schools and Health:* The next example I would like to mention is the role of medicine in schools. Traditional school health programs of "laying on of hands," inspections, referrals without follow-up have been shown to be a waste of time. But at the same time one quarter of the referrals of children to our pediatric clinic are now sent for "school learning problems." We find very few traditional medical problems among such children. But the suffering of the child and family with such problems is still just as real, and the management requires that we alter the child's environment—the school and the home. We have been quite unsuccessful, even after doing rather complete work-ups in the clinic, if we only make recommendations or treat with drugs.

When we have moved out of our offices into the schools, we have achieved greater success. We need to join with teachers to help them understand how children grow and develop, with psychologists to understand how they learn, and sociologists to learn how the organization of the school affects learning. While the data to support the effectiveness of such new programs are not all in, we as doctors either have to decide that we do not have anything to offer such parents and children or we have to join forces with other professions to seek solutions to the problems by crossing the boundaries of traditional health services.

The schools also offer remarkable settings for health education to achieve more healthy patterns of living that may then affect health. The boundary between medicine and education is not difficult to accept, but few of us have crossed it.

III. Population vs. Individual Health Care

Most of these examples could be thought of as in the range of traditional public health—that is population medicine—and the clinician would be quite correct to say that the boundary problem is largely one between population medicine, where responsibility for such things as housing, group health in schools and community-wide health education is the province of the public health physician, while the provision of curative medicine of individual patients is his domain.

One of our own studies illustrates that the problem of boundaries exists even for the clinician dealing with individuals. For some time we have been interested in the clinical observation that family-life stress seemed to be positively related to illness and also to the timing of seeking health care related to such stress. We have studied two types of family stress—long term or chronic, such as poverty, divorce, poor housing, unemployment, and short term, such as quarrels in the family, deaths in near relatives, loss of jobs, moves and interpersonal problems outside the family.... Long term or chronic stress is very strongly associated with illness—in fact it accounts for as much as 20 per cent of all illness in families with children. Likewise short term stress has a strong association with illness, but little over-all relation to when people seek health care. There are interesting and important differences in the relation of stress (controlling for the amount of illness) and where care is sought. Telephone, emergency room, and OPD contacts are two to three times more likely if there is family stress, while office visits show no difference.

There is a considerable body of other data in this field of stress and illness. L. E. Hinkle's documentation of the greater occurrence of illness in workers in a telephone company at times of stress, and a study by R. H. Rahe, J. D.

McKean, and R. J. Arthur of navy men's greater illness at times of life changes (moves, deaths of close relatives, job changes) give credence to our view that life stress is an important cause of physical illness.

The important point is again the boundary problem. If this type of family-life stress and life change is a major factor in causing illness and in determining when and where people seek care, what should be the physician's role in helping families to avoid or learn to cope in more healthy ways with stress? What is the physiologic pathway by which such stress works its havoc? What could social changes, such as income maintenance, or various educational efforts, such as operant conditioning (to teach families how to manage life crises without the stress that leads to illness), do to improve health? What should be the doctor's role in these boundary problems? Should we become engaged in these areas? I think it is clear that, as a society, we must find ways to manage boundary problems if we are to improve health. As physicians we do have another reason for involvement.

G. Caplan many years ago proposed the crisis intervention theory. In brief, he postulates that at these times of crisis, people are more amenable to changing ways of life that are unhealthy than at more stable times. If this is so, and we obviously need data to prove or disprove it, then crisis-related illness and crisis-related use of health services bring the clinician into the middle of social medicine.

By working in these boundary areas it seems likely that we will contribute more to health than we will by sticking purely to our curative, traditional medical care. . . .

*   *   *

Perhaps the major thing medicine has to contribute is the ability to meld biology and social sciences—drawing people from both discipines to work on the complex problems of social and family life and how they affect health. We and society may then end up by developing new helping groups or professions that actually deal with or deliver the care at these boundaries. . . .

The boundaries of medical care offer exciting challenges to the future oriented biosocial physician. By successful blending of social and biologic research we may finally, as physicians, contribute to improved health and not merely to the production of health services.

Howard Brody and David S. Sobel

A Systems View of Health and Disease

If, as Dubos, Chapman, Kleinman, and Haggerty propose, the study of health and disease requires consideration of information from a broad spectrum of nonmedical fields, how can new information be organized and utilized? Howard Brody, a resident in family practice, and David S. Sobel, of the Health Policy Program at the University of California, San Francisco, suggest taking a systems view of the hierarchy of living spheres in order to integrate information from different disciplines. They argue that both total patient care and effective health planning require intervention at various levels by a multidisciplinary team taking a systems view and coordinating efforts to understand health and illness.

Western scientific medicine, long used to an information explosion within its own territory, is now confronted with a barrage of information from other disciplines and medical systems. Within the Western scientific tradition, disciplines such as psychology, sociology, and ecology are turning up new factors that influence human health and disease but that fall outside medical boundaries as traditionally defined. Also from outside the Western tradition there is increased interest in ancient, non-Western and alternative approaches to healing.

Western medicine has to decide whether and how to incorporate this new information. The analytic and reductionist tendencies that have served scientific medicine so well up to now suggest two possible strategies—either to reject this new information as perhaps interesting but not relevant; or to accept it in a condescending way, meanwhile being confident that it will soon be replaced by "hard" knowledge once the "real" physical-chemical underlying processes are understood. Both strategies amount to turning one's back on important, different ways of knowing more about human health.

Information becomes knowledge only when it is fitted within a wider framework, so that the relationship between the new information and existing knowledge becomes more useful and clearer. The framework that we have found most helpful for this purpose we call a systems view of health and

27

Figure 1. A Hierarchy of Living Systems

disease. The systems view shows how the scientific-medical, the scientific-nonmedical, and the non-Western ways of knowing the world all complement one another, each providing pieces of a puzzle that would otherwise remain incomplete.... Our most modest goal is to provide a structured way of shifting one's viewpoint, so that the same phenomenon can be looked at from a number of different perspectives, and the resulting data can be assembled in an orderly manner instead of remaining fragmented. Although the systems approach has been used widely in many areas, including health care management, there have been few attempts to apply it as a framework for understanding health and disease.

To begin, the terms "system," "hierarchy," "information," and "environment" need to be clarified, for we will be using them in a somewhat technical way. A system is an organized set of components that is conveniently regarded as a whole consisting of interdependent parts. It is characteristic of a system that if one part or subcomponent is replaced by a different but similar part, the system functions as before; if the organization among the parts is changed, however, the system's function is altered even though the parts remain the same. Any system (for example, the liver) can be viewed as a whole composed of parts (for example, cells) or as a component of a higher level system (for example, the body), depending upon what is most convenient for the purpose of inquiry.

When systems are ranked in order of increasing complexity we have a

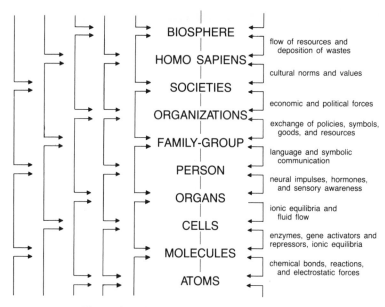

Figure 2. Information Flow in the Hierarchy

hierarchy—that is, atoms are subcomponents of molecules, which are sub-components of cells, which are subcomponents of tissues, which are subcomponents of organs, and so on. Biologists are accustomed to thinking in terms of such a systems hierarchy that begins with atoms and molecules and moves up in complexity through organelles, cells, tissues, organs, organ systems, and finally to the individual organism. It is useful, however, to continue the hierarchy beyond the individual level, with persons viewed as subcomponents of still-higher-level systems such as families, communities, and nations.

This hierarchical pattern can be illustrated by a variety of graphic conventions, including concentric circles, nesting boxes, or a linear array. Figure 1 demonstrates one simplified way of depicting the levels of a hierarchy of living systems. . . .

The patterns of information flow determine the orderly organization among the subcomponents permitting the system to function as more than a random collection of parts. The flow of information commonly takes the form of feedback loops, in which component A influences component B and the new state of B then "feeds back" to influence A. There are two basic types of feedback regulation. The first, known as negative feedback, acts to reduce any deviations and return the system to equilibrium. For example, in the human organism each organ depends upon a certain level of blood flow to carry out its particular activities. When the heart begins to pump too slowly or too quickly, a complex series of neural and hormonal feedback mechanisms is activated to return the heart to homeostatic normal limits. Thus, each subsystem has the freedom to function within certain limits, but once it crosses these limits the negative feedback mechanisms act to return it to its proper role in the functioning of the larger whole. The second type of feedback mechanism is called positive feedback because it tends to amplify, rather than dampen, deviation within the system. Most growth and maturation processes are regulated in this manner.

The general patterns of information flow appear to exist at all hierarchical levels, but the actual nature of the information will be different at each level. Atoms maintain equilibrium configuration within a molecule by means of electrostatic attractions and repulsions; family members relate to each other largely through language and symbols; and organizations regulate individual behavior by enforcing rules and social norms (See Figure 2). Information flows not only within a given level or between adjacent levels but also between widely spaced levels, as, for example, when a nation communicates directly with an individual via income tax laws or requirements for immunization.

Living systems are continuously exchanging matter, energy, and information with their environments and must periodically adapt their internal processes to accommodate change in the environment. . . .

Health and Disease Defined

The description of a hierarchy of living systems suggests characteristic features of a concept of "health," which can be summarized as the *ability of a system (for example, cell, organism, family, society) to respond adaptively to a wide variety of environmental challenges (for example, physical, chemical, infectious, psychological, social).*

This view of health suggests several advantages over more traditional definitions. Health is seen as a positive process, not as the mere absence of the signs and symptoms of disease. Furthermore, this definition is not restricted to biological fitness or somatic well-being; rather, it demands a consideration of the broader environmental, sociocultural, and behavioral determinants of health. Also the level of health is dynamically changing; encounters with environmental challenges result in either a lower level of health, a restoration of customary equilibrium, or a growth-enhancing response. This latter response involves more than a passive reaction or homeostatic adjustment. It refers to a creative adaptation that leaves the organism or system at a higher level of functioning than before the challenge. Immunizations, major life-style changes following illness, and the development of an international peace-keeping force are examples of such adaptations.

Our definition of health clearly does not exclude the central role played by value judgments in evaluating health. In particular, health must be viewed as only one among many possible human values. For example, health is not necessarily equivalent to happiness, and individuals will often sacrifice their health to pursue other goals. Furthermore, what is judged as healthy or unhealthy varies from person to person and, even more dramatically, from culture to culture because of highly individual requirements and relative social norms.

Given this systems view of health, "disease" can be seen as *a failure to respond adaptively to environmental challenges resulting in a disruption of the overall equilibrium of the system*. The disruption may be due to feedback constraints that have become too rigid to permit compensatory responses of the component parts. More commonly, however, the disruption results from perturbing forces in the environment to which the usual feedback mechanisms cannot accommodate. Perturbations may take the form of an excessive stress (for example, germs or toxins) or a lack of necessary stimuli (for example, food or love). These perturbations may impinge upon one hierarchical level—radiation, for example, primarily affects the molecular level—or they may impact across many levels, as in the trauma of an automobile collision.

As a rule, however, a disease does not stop at one level since all the levels are interconnected by the information circuits. Therefore, unless the homeostatic mechanisms at contiguous levels can restore a level of normal function and "buffer" the disruption, it will tend to spread up and down the hierarchy. For example, in diabetes, genetic and environmental factors interact to produce an initial disruption at a biochemical level that can lead to pathological changes in cellular function and a disruption of organ systems (for example, kidney and eye). Such changes are likely to disrupt the individual's behavior and may strain the family as well as produce a potential resource drain on the community. A disruption can also travel downward through the hierarchy, as when economic or natural disasters produce societal disruptions creating upheavals in community and family function and, in turn, precipitating a variety of psychosomatic or sociosomatic symptoms among individuals.

Therefore, from a systems view diseases are not regarded as discrete entities localized in one organ or tissue but as *patterns of disruptions* manifested at various levels of the system at various times. Patterns may differ in regard to where the disruption arises, which hierarchical levels are most affected, the type of environmental force that initiated the disturbance, and so on, allowing us to classify diseases by the traditional diagnostic categories.

The systems view, however, predicts certain features of disease that traditional classifications do not make explicit. For instance, the systems approach accommodates very well a multiple-causation understanding of disease. The development, expression, and course of disease is seen to depend as much on the stability and adaptive capacity of the host system as on the nature of specific perturbing forces impinging on the hierarchy. In fact, the actual signs and symptoms of disease not infrequently represent the failing efforts of the system to restore order (for example, autoimmune diseases). The systems view also eliminates the sharp distinction between mind and body which has plagued medical thought. If disruptions are seen to move up and down the hierarchical levels, then we might expect that psychosocial disruptions can cause tissue or biochemical manifestations and vice versa.

Implications for Health Care

When a system is disrupted, it may attempt to restore equilibrium by activating special reserve information circuits and subsystems. For example, during an infection white blood cells may be mobilized to remedy the disruption or, at least, to keep it from spreading. If some components die, they can often be replaced by the activation of growth processes. Sometimes, however, the inherent self-regulatory mechanisms alone are not sufficient and some form of therapy is required. In traditional Chinese medicine two distinct and complementary therapeutic strategies have been described: the *iliao* approach, involving active therapeutic intervention, and the *yang sheng* approach, aimed at strengthening the natural powers of resistance of the organism.

In modern systems terminology the former consists essentially of a disruption from the environment designed to oppose a specific disease-disruption, as when antibiotics are used to treat bacterial infections. The difference between a therapeutic disruption and a disease-producing disruption lies in the value judgments placed on the predicted outcomes of each. However, in practice, the distinction is often blurred because of the so-called side effects, or iatrogenic diseases, produced by therapeutic interventions. Until recently, medical thought has regarded the ill effects of therapy as freak occurrences, or the losing end of a calculated risk, rather than as expected outcomes due to the intrinsic nature of therapeutic measures and the interconnectedness of living systems. On the whole, however, the active therapeutic interventions that characterize modern medicine, whether surgical or chemical, have appeared so dramatic and successful that complementary health strategies have tended to be overlooked.

Ancient systems of healing are replete with examples of another therapeutic approach that attempts to support the inherent healing powers of the body. In systems terms this can be viewed as attempts to improve the information flow in the system in order to accommodate disruptions and facilitate the restoration of equilibrium. For example, such techniques as yogic therapy, meditation, and biofeedback training operate at psychophysiological levels to improve (or, in the case of biofeedback, to add) feedback circuits in order to enhance the self-regulatory capabilities of the organism. Similarly, immunization and the more recent developments in immunotherapy for the treatment of cancer represent methods of stimulating the body's inherent capacities to manage and prevent disease. In the absence of specific disease, this approach can be extended to general health promotion. Improving the feedback and communication among family members, for example, can stabilize the hierarchy at that level, rendering the system more capable of handling challenges and resisting disruption. The same rationale may be applied to other health-promotive measures such as improved nutrition, exercise, and relaxation techniques.

In general, Western scientific medicine has focused on the lower levels of the hierarchy—the biological causes of disease and physical and chemical interventions. This approach has been remarkably successful for diseases in which the primary disruptions are largely confined to the biological levels. But, even here the strict biomedical approach is limited. By failing to attend to the person and sociocultural levels, where disease is shaped into the human experience of illness, contemporary medicine undermines its own effectiveness. The attempt to treat disease as a purely physicochemical dysfunction also ignores that many ailments presented as somatic complaints are due primarily to disruptions at the person, family, or societal levels. But, as Abraham Maslow has observed, "If the only tool you have is a hammer, you tend to treat everything as if it were a nail."

The treatment of human sickness can never be reduced to a completely technical and impersonal matter. Disease most often involves multiple levels, disrupting the person and social group, and therefore requires multiple interventions directed at different levels. Many of the traditional healing systems of other cultures recognize the importance of the sociocultural dimensions of disease. Although these systems often ignore the biology of sickness, we can still learn a great deal from their management of the illness experience as a personal and social phenomenon. Also, a recent approach to the treatment of cancer patients illustrates how standard biological therapies (radiotherapy, chemotherapy, and surgery) can be combined with adjunctive support at the person level (various meditation and relaxation exercises) as well as the family level (group work and counseling).

Intervention at multiple levels, however, must be systematically integrated as part of total patient care, not added on as an afterthought or left to chance. This will require a team effort, for no single individual can be expert in the various modes of interventions at each hierarchical level. At the same time, if the members of the team all share a common language, a common framework, and an understanding of one another's specializations, then a real coordination of effort becomes possible. The systems model can potentially provide an integrating framework to inform the actions of the individual members of such a team.

The systems approach also emphasizes that prevention and cure are not the only objectives of health-related interventions. When a disease-disruption cannot be prevented or removed, it can often be confined to allow a maximum degree of normal functioning. An individual with organ-level dysfunction can often be supported so as to lessen person-level and family-level disruption. One can therefore speak of "a healthy way to live a disease" and the importance of helping patients develop confidence that they can to some degree control their illness.

The systems view also avoids the problem of confusing the level of intervention with the level of disease. While diseases may represent patterns of disruption affecting many hierarchical levels, a therapy aimed at just one level may be highly efficacious because it can affect other levels via the interconnected patterns of information flow. Thus, chemotherapy for depression is often strikingly effective even though depressive disorders are characterized by complex mixtures of genetic, biochemical, behavioral, and social factors. Therefore, to conclude from a clinical trial of a drug that depression is only a biochemical disease would be to ignore the true complexity of the illness. This confusion might also lead to the systematic neglect of other possible preventive or health-promotive strategies that could be directed at higher system levels.

In trying to prevent many of the complex health problems that confront us today, the biomedical approach needs to be broadened and complemented by interventions aimed at higher levels of the hierarchy. The physician has been likened to a man rescuing drowning people from a river, too busy to investigate why all these people were falling in upstream. The systems view encourages us to look upstream, to consider the behavioral, social, political, and environmental, as well as the biological, determinants of health and ill health.

Clearly there is no way that the doctor, or even an interdisciplinary health care team as presently constituted, can address the problems of preserving health across all these levels. For instance, we look to politicians to handle disruptions that occur at the society-nation level; are politicians then to become members of the health care team? On the other hand, we cannot deny that the various hierarchical levels are interconnected and that events at the social level have major implications for the health or sickness of all individuals.

These arguments lead to the conclusion that it cannot be the task exclusively of the medical profession to preserve health, but that the efforts and domain of the medical profession need to be placed in perspective and integrated as part of a more holistic approach to health.

Implications for Health Planning and Policy

The systems view suggests a more rational approach to planning health interventions and evaluating their outcomes. Ideally, in considering a particular health problem, planners would examine the problem as it relates to each hierarchical level. For example, nutrition presents many different, yet interrelated, concerns at each level. At the molecular and cellular levels we might be concerned with the intricate metabolic roles of nutrients. At the person level, the question of individual food selection and eating habits arises. At the institutional level, issues concerning agribusiness, food production, processing, and distribution emerge. At the level of societies, we must consider cultural beliefs about food and nutrition. And at the biospheric level, ecological considerations about climate, soil, and the limits of the earth in terms of food production become critical concerns. Of course, all the hierarchical levels interact in a systems model: nutrient requirements change with various stressors or drugs, eating habits are influenced by commercial food advertising, climatic and political changes modify food production, and so on.

The systems model provides an orderly and systematic way of inquiring into these interactions between levels and avoids the risk of viewing each level in isolation. For example, if the individual is not viewed in terms of the social, political, and economic context that constrains and conditions individual behavior, we run the risk of developing a policy that "blames the victim" for poor health.

With this broader picture in mind, the planner can then look for possible interventions at each level and assess the likely consequences, good and bad, of alternative strategies. The interventions promising the greatest efficacy at lowest cost and with the lowest level of unwanted side effects would be adopted. Thus, in dealing with lung cancer, appropriate studies might determine, for instance, that a societal policy of buying out tobacco growers and converting the land to other crops might be more effective in the long run than increased efforts in chemotherapy, surgery, radiotherapy, or public health education. The evaluation of alternative strategies is particularly important since increasing health care costs and the allocation of scarce resources have become critical issues.

The systems approach can also be used to evaluate interventions in terms of their short-run and long-run consequences at different hierarchical levels. For example, in testing new drugs, food additives, and pollutants, physiological side effects such as cancer production are often considered, while potential toxicities at a behavioral level are ignored. Similarly, in massive technological interventions like the building of a dam, the promised economic benefits may blind us to the disastrous public health problems that may result. Public policy interventions, therefore, often produce unintentional side effects at a different level than the original intervention and after a considerable time lag. Of course, these unintentional consequences may be positive as well as negative, as when automobile fatalities were reduced following the lowering of the speed limits to save energy.

Thus, the systems perspective, which reminds us of the interconnectedness of the hierarchical levels, not only clearly warns of the probability of short-range and long-range side effects but also provides a checklist of where they might occur. It also reminds us that modest attempts to aid the natural restorative actions of the system generally cause less trouble than heroic interventions. Therefore, longer-range, higher-level changes in the system that make it more adaptable and better able to cope with stresses are preferable to one-shot interventions after disease has occurred. For instance, while antibiotics have been regarded as one of the greatest medical advances of this century, their effect on infant mortality in Western countries has been only a fraction of the effects of general improvement in nutrition, chlorination of water, and pasteurization of milk.

Implications for the Health Sciences

At each hierarchical level, new functions and properties emerge due to the interaction among the component parts. These properties are "lost" when the system is analyzed at a lower level of organization and the components examined in isolation. This is what is meant by the phrase "the whole is more than the sum of the parts." The "more" arises from the relationship of the components. For example, the human capacities for symbolic communication, decision-making, and goal-setting cannot be fully explained in terms of molecules, cells, or organs. Therefore, from a systems view, it makes no sense to say that the processes of the mind are nothing but biochemical and biophysical occurrences in the brain. It makes very good sense, however, to attempt to investigate which biochemical and biopysical processes are *correlated with* higher-level mental functions. The systems approach is, therefore, not opposed to analysis—breaking complex systems down into component parts—as long as the limits of analysis for understanding whole-system behavior are appreciated.

Unfortunately, much of contemporary scientific research is characterized by marked disciplinary rigidity and isolation. This situation is particularly tragic in the study of human health and disease since these subjects clearly demand an understanding that transcends disciplinary boundaries. The current scientific disciplines of biophysics, biochemistry, cellular biology, physiology, psychology, sociology, anthropology, and political science roughly correspond to each of the levels of the hierarchy. The systems approach attempts to bridge and unify, not replace, these levels of study. However, since each discipline requires specialized methods of inquiry and a scientific notation appropriate for its level, it makes no sense to say that the social sciences are less scientific than the biological sciences. The difference between the so-called hard natural sciences and soft social sciences can be attributed largely to the different levels of the hierarchy that each deals with.

Many complex problems, particularly in the health field, involve multiple levels and, therefore, demand multidisciplinary investigation. For example, in examining the efficacy of traditional healing practices, a complete research strategy would include not only pharmacological analyses of the herbs used by native healers but also an assessment of the sociocultural context within which the healers live and practice.

Research aimed at the hierarchical levels of the person, family, community, or ecosystem are not meant to replace basic biomedical research. Rather, studies in these areas are likely to stimulate biomedical research as attempts are made to correlate behavior at higher hierarchical levels with changes at the physiological and biochemical levels.

The systems approach can provide a framework and language to facilitate communication across disciplines. It illustrates how the various disciplines can complement one another in addressing complex, multilevel problems such as ecological, sociopolitical, psychosomatic, and ethical questions. Issues concerning human health, because they span the entire hierarchy, can also stimulate information flow between the disciplines and promote a unification of the human and physical sciences. Again, the systems view, while not necessarily providing the answers to the complex problems of human health and disease, can at least provide a useful way of asking the appropriate questions.

Health is not a condition of matter, but of Mind; nor can the material senses bear reliable testimony on the subject of health.
                                                    —*Mary Baker Eddy*

2 Health Status and Its Determinants

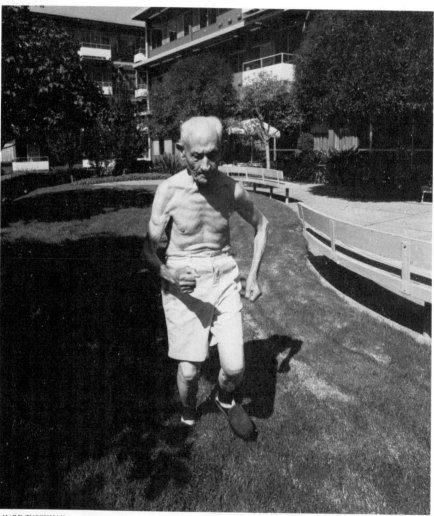

Since the eighteenth century, there has been a dramatic improvement in the health and life-span of Americans. This largely reflects a decline in the infectious diseases that once claimed the lives of many children. For the first time in history parents can now be confident that their children are likely to survive into adulthood. In the 1950s and early 1960s, little further progress was made in improving the health of the population in spite of massive increases in expenditures on medical care. However, from the late 1960s to the present, there has once again been a dramatic decline in infant deaths and deaths from coronary heart disease.

What accounts for this most recent improvement in health? Many observers argue that healthier ways of living—particularly changes in health habits such as smoking, eating, drinking, and exercise—are the major determinants of health, maintaining that we have overrated the impact of medical care on health.

The difficulty of measuring health status in the first place, let alone assessing its determinants, is discussed by Brian MacMahon and Joyce Berlin, of the Harvard School of Public Health, in "Health of the United States Population." In this introduction to the vocabulary and methods of health measurement, they acknowledge that nearly all of the measures are actually of *ill health* (mortality, morbidity, prevalence of disease, etc.) and not *good health*. Also, since health status is complex and has many dimensions, a combination of different measures, each sensitive to different characteristics, is necessary.

Using primarily data on death rates (mortality), British physician Thomas McKeown, in "Determinants of Health," discusses the reasons for the dramatic decline in the death rate which has taken place since the eighteenth century. He notes that the vast proportion of this improvement in health took place before the introduction of specific medical interventions, such as antibiotics. Therefore, McKeown argues, improved nutrition and a safer, cleaner environment were more significant determinants of health than medical care. He also believes that for future improvement in health we should look more towards changing our ways of living and personal health habits than to continued reliance on modern medicine.

Dr. Walsh McDermott, in "Medicine: The Public Good and One's Own," directly counters McKeown, offering a defense of the impact of personal medical care on health. He maintains that statistics like death rate greatly underestimate many of the valuable contributions of medical care, especially the supportive, reassuring, and caring functions of medicine. Even when a disease cannot be cured, years of productive life for the patient can be added by appropriate application of the science and art of medicine. The system in which physicians treat patients on a one-to-one basis may also have played a significant role in the recent declines in coronary heart disease and infant mortality. McDermott is not ready to jump on the bandwagon with those who claim that health can be improved only by fundamental changes in personal health habits and in the social, economic, or physical environments.

A similar reservation about the evidence linking personal lifestyle habits and health is made by Lewis Thomas in "On Magic in Medicine." He strongly believes in scientific medicine's promise to identify the specific biological mechanisms of disease (see his other selection in Chapter 15). Thomas, a pathologist, compares the recent enthusiasm for healthy lifestyles to some of the ancient magical beliefs about the causes of ill health.

Brian MacMahon and Joyce E. Berlin

Health of the United States Population

The health status of the population can be described and measured in a variety of ways. Brian MacMahon and Joyce Berlin, both of the Harvard School of Public Health, describe the common methods used to determine and compare death rates, life expectancy, and patterns of disease occurrence for acute and chronic conditions. Since the causes of illness and death have changed significantly in recent years, epidemiology—the science of measuring health in populations—is necessary to planning future health care strategies.

W hat does it mean to talk about the health of a population? To measure or even define something as elusive as good health is extremely difficult and what is actually measured is usually ill health. Specifically, the numbers of people suffering different types of death and illness can be counted. If the same measures are used over a period of time and in different populations, changes in the degree and kind of ill health can be assessed and populations can be compared.

The science of measuring health in populations is epidemiology. In the past the word epidemic (and the science of epidemics) was used only in the context of infectious diseases, but the term literally describes excessive disease prevalence, regardless of the type of disease. For example, the United States is currently suffering epidemics of heart disease and cancer that are as truly epidemic as were the great plagues of infectious diseases of the past.

Several kinds of rates are used to describe the frequency of disease in a population, and it is important to keep their different implications in mind. For example, when enquiring about the health of an individual, we often ask "How are you?" or "How have you been?" In the social context the two questions may be used interchangeably, but interpreted rigorously they have different implications. The first question asks about the individual's health at this particular point in time; the second, about health-related events that the individual may have experienced over some recent time period.

A similar distinction must be made when describing the frequency of disease in a population. Prevalence rates describe what pattern of disease one would find if one were able to examine the entire population at a single point in time—how many people would be found to be ill, to what degree, and with what diseases. Incidence rates, in contrast, describe the frequency of health-related events (onset of illness or death) that occurred in the population over a fixed period of time, commonly a year. Estimates of the frequency of death have the basic characteristics of incidence rates, since they are counts of events during a fixed period of time (incidence of death), but these are usually referred to as mortality rates to specify that they refer to rates of death from, rather than occurrence of, a particular disease.

Why is it important to distinguish between these types of rate? The answer is that no single rate can paint an adequate picture of the significance of any disease in a population. A disease with a very high incidence but short duration, like the common cold, will appear as a minor cause of disease prevalence at any one point in time (unless the data happen to be collected during a severe epidemic). On the other hand, a disease which can occur only once to an individual (and of which incidence rates will therefore be low) but which has long-lasting consequences—such as multiple sclerosis—will make a major contribution to disease prevalence. Consumption of medical and social resources is generally a function of disease prevalence rather than incidence, while the emotional, economic, and social trauma associated with acute illness (and death) relate more directly to disease incidence and mortality. One's purpose and values therefore determine which types of rate one chooses to consider most relevant in a particular context.

Mortality

Death is unequaled as an objective and readily ascertainable index of health status or lack thereof. For this reason, as much as for its intrinsic significance, the frequency of death has long been studied around the world. A common way of summarizing the effect of different levels of mortality is in terms of expectation of life. This is the average duration of life that a population would experience if the observed age-specific death rates were to continue throughout the population's life span.

The annual death rate in the United States is now about 7 per 1,000 population, less than half the rate at the beginning of the century. In 1900 the average expectation of life in the United States was about 48 years for men and 51 years for women. Now the value for men is about 68 years, and for women, 75 years. Death rates for males stabilized between 1955 and 1970; the rates for females are still declining, but at a slower rate than in previous decades.

This historical increase in average life expectancy is due primarily to the decline in mortality rates in infancy and childhood. Death rates are relatively high during the first year of life, particularly during the first 28 days, and then decrease until around age 15. After that there is a steady increase; the rates approximately double with each decade of age. While infants still have a higher death rate than young adults, newborns now have a vastly better chance of survival than they did at the turn of the century. The present infant mortality rate—about 18 deaths under one year of age per 1,000 liveborn infants—is less than one fifth of what it was 60 years ago. During this time, the life expectation for an infant has increased by approximately 22 years. In contrast, the life expectancy for a person of 40 has increased by only six years.

Despite these improvements, death rates in the United States—particularly among males—do not compare favorably with those in many other developed countries. In 1960, for females, New Zealand, the Netherlands, Norway, and Sweden had lower age-adjusted mortality rates than the United States; Canada, New Zealand, and six European countries had lower mortality rates for males.

There have been tremendous changes in the causes of death during this century. In 1900 the leading causes of death were influenza and pneumonia, with tuberculosis a close second. By 1970 influenza and pneumonia had dropped to fifth place and tuberculosis had so diminished that it was no longer among the leading causes of death. In general, over the century, mortality rates due to infectious disease have declined dramatically. At the same time, deaths due to chronic degenerative diseases—ischemic heart disease (caused by inadequate blood flow to heart muscle), malignant neoplasms (cancer), cerebrovascular disease—have increased. Table 1 lists the ten leading causes of death in the United States. Together, these causes account for 80 percent of all deaths in this country. Heart disease and cancer lead the list; these two disorders now account for more than half of all American deaths. At least 75 percent of all deaths are now attributable to noninfectious diseases.

Table 1. Percentage of deaths attributed to the ten leading causes, United States, 1970

Ischemic heart disease	34.7
Malignant neoplasm	17.2
Cerebrovascular disease	10.8
Accident	6.0
Influenza and pneumonia	3.3
Diabetes mellitus	2.0
Arteriosclerosis	1.6
Cirrhosis of the liver	1.6
Bronchitis, emphysema, and asthma	1.6
Suicide	1.2

Changes in the causes of infant mortality have been as dramatic as the overall changes in causes of death. While infectious diseases 60 years ago accounted for about 70 percent of infant deaths, they now account for only about 10 percent. The most common cause of infant death is now prematurity, and congenital malformations (which cause 15 percent of infant deaths) have become more significant than the infectious diseases.

At all ages, death rates are higher for males than for females. The excess is particularly marked in the younger years (ages 15 to 29) and in the later years (ages 55 to 69), when death rates for men are nearly double those for women. Males have had higher death rates than females in nearly all times, places, and races, but the extent of the difference is greatest in modern times in the industrialized nations. The greater mortality for males in the young adult ages is due primarily to accidents, especially automobile accidents. Many of the twentieth-century epidemics like heart disease and lung cancer also affect men more than women. The increasing frequency of early and prolonged widowhood is just one social consequence of this difference in death rates between males and females.

Mortality rates vary not only with respect to sex and age but also according to race and geographic location. Death rates for nonwhites are higher than those for whites, except at the oldest ages. The nonwhite mortality rate is lowest in the Pacific and Mountain states (where much of the nonwhite population is of Oriental or American Indian ancestry) and highest in the South Atlantic division (where the majority are black). Overall, age-adjusted mortality rates are higher by about 5 percent in metropolitan areas than in nonmetropolitan areas of the United States.

One final, important variable closely related to mortality is socioeconomic status. The highest socioeconomic groups have the lowest mortality. This relationship, although also seen in adults, is particularly marked in infancy. The lower socioeconomic groups have infant death rates almost 50 percent higher than those of higher socioeconomic groups.

Acute Illness

There are many difficulties in attempting to measure the frequency of illness, particularly illnesses of limited duration. In the United States the most useful information comes from the Health Interview Survey of the National Health Survey. In this program, representative samples of the population are asked about illnesses that have occurred during the two weeks prior to the interview. Acute conditions are defined as those that lasted less than three months, involved either medical attention or restricted activity, and do not appear on a list of conditions defined as chronic (including, for example, arthritis, heart disease, and mental illness).

In 1974, the average person surveyed suffered about two acute illnesses; these conditions caused an average of nine days of restricted activity (including four days in bed), and nearly three days lost from work for each employed person. Respiratory illnesses, especially the common cold and flu, made up the largest number of acute conditions; second to respiratory diseases were

Table 2. Number of acute conditions per 100 persons per year by sex, age, and condition group, United States, 1974

Condition	Total	Male	Female	−6	6–16	17–44	45+
Respiratory conditions	94.4	92.2	96.5	172.6	131.3	92.5	47.5
Injuries	30.4	36.0	25.2	33.9	38.1	33.8	19.9
Infective and parasitic diseases	19.5	18.1	20.9	47.4	30.3	16.0	8.0
Digestive system conditions	7.8	6.0	9.5	7.3	10.6	8.8	4.8
All other acute conditions	23.5	19.2	27.5	47.8	26.4	24.1	13.3

injuries. The incidence of acute illnesses varies according to age and sex, as seen in Table 2.

The study of acute conditions gives a very different picture of national health than do the observed mortality rates. In contrast to deaths, acute illnesses decline in frequency with age and, except for injuries, tend to be more frequent in females than in males. It is a curious paradox that women are more likely to suffer acute or chronic disease, but death rates are higher in men. . . .

Chronic Illness

The impact of chronic illness is best seen through prevalence, rather than incidence, rates. The best sources of data are the same Health Interview Survey and the Health Examination Survey, also part of the National Health Survey. In the Health Interview Survey, chronic conditions are defined as those which appear on a special list, or which lasted more than three months. In the Examination Survey, participants are actually examined by physicians; the diagnosis of disease is thus more accurate than in the Interview Survey. But the Examination Survey also has disadvantages. It uses a much smaller sample and does not permit examination of changes over time, since, to date, no age group in the population has been examined more than once. A limitation of both surveys that is particularly important in the context of chronic illness is that the samples are drawn from the noninstitutionalized population.

In spite of these drawbacks, these surveys have provided valuable estimates of the impact of chronic disease on the American population. In 1974 approximately 26 million persons (13 percent of the population)—and almost half of people aged 65 or over—reported some limitation of activity due to one or more chronic conditions (Figure 1). The leading causes of activity

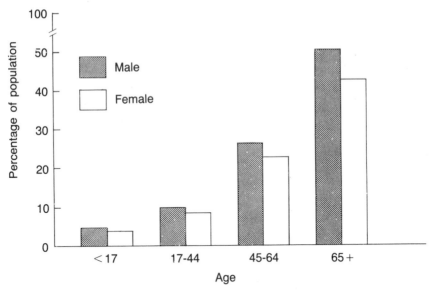

Figure 1. Percentage of population with limitation of activity due to chronic conditions by age and sex, United States, 1974. From P. W. Ries, "Current Estimates from the Health Interview Survey, United States–1974," *Vital and Health Statistics,* series 10, no. 100 (Washington, D.C.: National Center for Health Statistics, September 1975).

limitation in persons aged 17 to 64 were heart conditions, arthritis and rheumatism, impairments of the back and spine, and mental and nervous conditions. In persons aged 65 and over, the first two conditions remained the most frequent, but visual impairments and hypertension were third and fourth.

Chronic illness may impair the individual's ability to function or may call for continuous medical care to such an extent that institutionalization becomes necessary. At any given time, approximately 1 percent of the U.S. adult population is in a long-stay medical institution of some kind. For persons aged 65–74, the figure is approximately 2 percent, and for those 75 and older it is over 7 percent. Almost half of these institutionalized persons are in mental hospitals, almost half in nursing homes, and the remainder are in geriatric and chronic disease hospitals. Among residents of nursing homes more than 60 percent have some form of cardiovascular problem, over 30 percent have arthritis or rheumatism, and close to 30 percent have had a stroke. In recent years, the number of elderly people in mental hospitals has decreased substantially; but the number in nursing and personal care homes—which are assuming an increasing proportion of the care of the aged mentally ill—has increased.

The impact of a chronic disease is measured not only in terms of its effect on the individual but also in terms of its prevalence in the population. The diseases of the mouth (particularly dental caries and periodontal disease) do not make their presence felt in measures either of reported activity limitation or institutionalization; yet they are the most widespread diseases in the United States. Estimates of the extent of dental disease were made in the Health Examination Survey. The average DMF score—the number of permanent teeth that are "decayed, filled, and either missing or indicated for extraction"—was 18.7 for white adults and 12.2 for blacks. The difference between whites and blacks was largely accounted for by a higher prevalence of filled teeth among whites.

Implications

Patterns of disease and death have changed greatly in the past several decades. The infectious diseases still account for a large number of acute illnesses in the United States, particularly among the young. However, they are rapidly disappearing as causes of mortality. Ischemic heart disease, cancer, and stroke are now the major cases of death; heart disease and stroke also frequently disable those they do not kill. Among the nonfatal though disabling chronic diseases, mental illness and dental conditions are now the most prevalent.

As the most widespread and serious diseases are identified, effective ways of preventing them are also being sought. Cigarette smoking plays a major role in some prominent diseases, notably cardiovascular disease and certain cancers; if everyone stopped smoking, between 100,000 and 200,000 deaths could be prevented each year. The social use and abuse of alcohol also contributes, to an unknown extent, to the nation's burden of disease. But beyond paying attention to these two sources of illness, there is relatively little that can be done in disease prevention that is not already being done. The great majority of deaths and the great preponderance of disability are due to diseases of unknown cause for which preventive measures have not been developed and for which therapy is often ineffective. It appears, therefore, that research into causation should have a high priority in efforts to improve the health of the population.

The studies discussed [here] give some picture of the magnitude of the problems facing us and of the relative importance of the major disease categories. In determining research directions, the frequency of a disease is only one factor to be considered. Also required is an estimate of the likelihood that a particular approach to a particular disease will be successful. The originality of the approach, the competence and resources of the investigator, and many other factors all affect the chances that research will succeed. Research support should not be withheld simply because the disease involved is uncommon. But at the same time, prevalent diseases are important to study simply because they affect the greatest numbers of people. The data indicate that cardiovascular disease, cancer, stroke, mental illness, dental disorders, and prematurity and congenital malformations in infants are types of diseases that are certainly widespread enough to warrant more research into their causation.

Every society creates its own casualties.

—J. N. Morris

Thomas McKeown

Determinants of Health

Measuring health status is simpler than explaining its causes, as the determinants of health include broad environmental and behavioral factors as well as medical care. Thomas McKeown, professor emeritus of social medicine at the University of Birmingham, England, credits improved sanitation, food supply, and birth control with modern increases in health and long life. He argues that future strategies to improve health will require balanced public attention to environmental factors and to personal behavior.

Modern medicine is not nearly as effective as most people believe. It has not been effective because medical science and service are misdirected and society's investment in health is misused. At the base of this misdirection is a false assumption about human health. Physicians, biochemists, and the general public assume that the body is a machine that can be protected from disease primarily by physical and chemical intervention. This approach, rooted in 17th-century science, has led to widespread indifference to the influence of the primary determinants of human health—environment and personal behavior—and emphasizes the role of medical treatment, which is actually less important than either of the others. It has also resulted in the neglect of sick people whose ailments are not within the scope of the sort of therapy that interests the medical professions.

An appraisal of influences on health in the past suggests that the contribution of modern medicine to the increase of life expectancy has been much smaller than most people believe. Health improved, not because of steps when we are ill, but because we become ill less often. We remain well, less because of specific measures such as vaccination and immunization than because we enjoy a higher standard of nutrition, we live in a healthier environment, and we have fewer children.

For some 300 years an engineering approach has been dominant in biology and medicine and has provided the basis for the treatment of the sick. A mechanistic concept of nature developed in the 17th century led to the idea that a living organism, like a machine, might be taken apart and reassembled if its structure and function were sufficiently understood. Applied to medicine, this concept meant that understanding the body's response to disease would allow physicians to intervene in the course of disease. The consequences of the engineering approach to medicine are more conspicuous today than they were in the 17th century, largely because the resources of the physical and chemical sciences are so much greater. Medical education begins with the study of the structure and function of the body, continues with examination of disease processes, and ends with clinical instruction on selected sick people. Medical service is dominated by the image of the hospital for the acutely ill, where technological resources are concentrated. Medical research also reflects the mechanistic approach, concerning itself with problems such as the chemical basis of inheritance and the immunological response to transplanted tissues.

No one disputes the predominance of the engineering approach in medicine, but we must now ask whether it is seriously deficient as a conceptualization of the problems of human health. To answer this question, we must examine the determinants of human health. We must first discover why health improved in the past and then go on to ascertain the important influences on health today, in the light of the change in health problems that has resulted from the decline of infectious diseases.

It is no exaggeration to say that health, especially the health of infants and young children, has been transformed since the 18th century. For the first time in history, a mother knows it is likely that all her children will live to maturity. Before the 19th century, only about three out of every 10 newborn infants lived beyond the age of 25. Of the seven who died, two or three never reached their first birthday, and five or six died before they were six. Today, in developed countries fewer than one in 20 children die before they reach adulthood.

The increased life expectancy, most evident for young children, is due predominantly to a reduction of deaths from infectious diseases. Records from England and Wales (the earliest national statistics available) show that this reduction was the reason for the improvement in health before 1900 and it remains the main influence to the present day.

But when we try to account for the decline of infections, significant differences of opinion appear. The conventional view attributes the change to an increased understanding of the nature of infectious disease and to the application of that knowledge through better hygiene, immunization, and treatment. This interpretation places particular emphasis on immunization against diseases like smallpox and polio, and on the use of drugs for the treatment of other diseases, such as tuberculosis, meningitis, and pneumonia. These measures, in fact, contributed relatively little to the total reduction of mortality;

the main explanation for the dramatic fall in the number of deaths lies not in medical intervention, but elsewhere.

Deaths from the common infections were declining long before effective medical intervention was possible. By 1900, the total death rate had dropped substantially, and over 90 percent of the reduction was due to a decrease of deaths from infectious diseases. The relative importance of the major influences can be illustrated by reference to tuberculosis. Although respiratory tuberculosis was the single largest cause of death in the mid-19th century, mortality from the disease declined continuously after 1938, when it was first registered in England and Wales as a cause of death.

Robert Koch identified the tubercle bacillus in 1882, but none of the treatments used in the 19th or early 20th centuries significantly influenced the course of the disease. The many drugs that were tried were worthless; so, too, was the practice of surgically collapsing an infected lung, a treatment introduced about 1920. Streptomycin, developed in 1947, was the first effective treatment, but by this time mortality from the disease had fallen to a small fraction of its level during 1848 to 1854. Streptomycin lowered the death rate from tuberculosis in England and Wales by about 50 percent, but its contribution to the decrease in the death rate since the early 19th century was only about 3 percent.

Deaths from bronchitis, pneumonia, and influenza also began to decline before medical science provided an effective treatment for these illnesses. Although the death rate in England and Wales increased in the second half of the 19th century, it has fallen continuously since the beginning of the 20th. There is still no effective immunization against bronchitis or pneumonia, and influenza vaccines have had no effect on deaths. The first successful treatment for these respiratory diseases was a sulfa drug introduced in 1938, but mortality attributed to the lung infections was declining from the beginning of the 20th century. There is no reason to doubt that the decline would have continued without effective therapeutic measures, if at a far slower rate.

In the United States, the story was similar; Thomas Magill noted that "the rapid decline of pneumonia death rates began in New York State before the turn of the century and many years before the 'miracle drugs' were known." Obviously, drug therapy was not responsible for the total decrease in deaths that occurred since 1938, and it could have had no influence on the substantial reduction that occurred before then.

The histories of most other common infections, such as whooping cough, measles, and scarlet fever, are similar. In each of these diseases, mortality had fallen to a low level before effective immunization or therapy became available.

In some infections, medical intervention *was* valuable before sulfa drugs

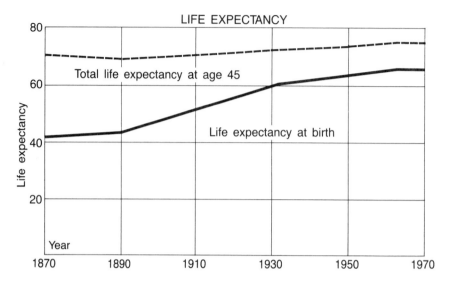

and antibiotics became available. Immunization protected people against smallpox and tetanus; antitoxin treatment limited deaths from diphtheria; appendicitis, peritonitis, and ear infections responded to surgery; Salvarsan was a long-sought "magic bullet" against syphilis; intravenous therapy saved people with severe diarrheas; and improved obstetric care prevented childbed fever.

But even if such medical measures had been responsible for the whole decline of mortality from these particular conditions after 1900 (and clearly they were not), they would account for only a small part of the decrease in deaths attributed to all infectious diseases before 1935. From that time, powerful drugs came into use and they were supplemented by improved vaccines. But mortality would have continued to fall even without the presence of these agents; and over the whole period since cause of death was first recorded, immunization and treatments have contributed much less than other influences.

The substantial fall in mortality was due in part to reduced contact with microorganisms. In developed countries an individual no longer encounters the cholera bacillus, he is rarely exposed to the typhoid organism, and his contact with the tubercle bacillus is infrequent. The death rate from these infections fell continuously from the second half of the 19th century when basic hygienic measures were introduced: purification of water; efficient sewage disposal; and improved food hygiene, particularly the pasteurization of milk, the item in the diet most likely to spread disease.

Pasteurization was probably the main reason for the decrease in deaths from gastroenteritis and for the decline in infant mortality from about 1900.

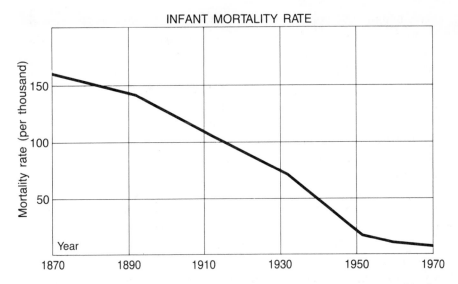

In the 20th century, these essential hygienic measures were supported by improved conditions in the home, the work place, and the general environment. Over the entire period for which records exist, better hygiene accounts for approximately a fifth of the total reduction of mortality.

But the decline of mortality caused by infections began long before the introduction of sanitary measures. It had already begun in England and Wales by 1838, and statistics from Scandinavia suggest that the death rate had been decreasing there since the first half of the 18th century.

A review of English experience makes it unlikely that reduced exposure to microorganisms contributed significantly to the falling death rate in this earlier period. In England and Wales that was the time of industrialization, characterized by rapid population growth and shifts of people from farms into towns, where living and working conditions were uncontrolled. The crowding and poor hygiene that resulted provided ideal conditions for the multiplication and spread of microorganisms, and the situation improved little before sanitary measures were introduced in the last third of the century. . . .

A further explanation for the falling death rate is that an improvement in nutrition led to an increase in resistance to infectious diseases. This is, I believe, the most credible reason for the decline of the infections, at least until the late 19th century, and also explains why deaths from airborne diseases like scarlet fever and measles have decreased even when exposure to the organisms that cause them remains almost unchanged. The evidence demonstrating the impact of improved nutrition is indirect, but it is still impressive.

Lack of food and the resulting malnutrition were largely responsible for the predominance of the infectious diseases, from the time when men first aggregated in large population groups about 10,000 years ago. In these conditions an improvement in nutrition was necessary for a substantial and prolonged decline in mortality.

Experience in developing countries today leaves no doubt that nutritional state is a critical factor in a person's response to infectious disease, particularly in young children. Malnourished people contract infections more often than those who are well fed and they suffer more when they become infected. According to a recent World Health Organization report on nutrition in developing countries, the best vaccine against common infectious diseases is an adequate diet.

In the 18th and 19th centuries, food production increased greatly throughout the Western world. The number of people in England and Wales tripled between 1700 and 1850 and they were fed on home-grown food.

In summary: The death rate from infectious diseases fell because an increase in food supplies led to better nutrition. From the second half of the 19th century this advance was strongly supported by improved hygiene and safer food and water, which reduced exposure to infection. With the exception of smallpox vaccination, which played a small part in the total decline of mortality, medical procedures such as immunization and therapy had little impact on human health until the 20th century.

One other influence needs to be considered: a change in reproductive behavior, which caused the birth rate to decline. The significance of this change can hardly be exaggerated, for without it the other advances would soon have been overtaken by the increasing population. We can attribute the modern improvement in health to food, hygiene, and medical intervention— in that order of time and importance—but we must recognize that it is to a modification of behavior that we owe the permanence of this improvement.

But it does not follow that these influences have the same relative importance today as in the past. In technologically advanced countries, the decline of infectious diseases was followed by a vast change in health problems, and even in developing countries advances in medical science and technology may have modified the effects of nutrition, sanitation, and contraception. In order to predict the factors likely to affect our health in the future, we need to examine the nature of the problems in health that exist today.

Because today's problems are mainly with noncommunicable diseases, physicians have shifted their approach. In the case of infections, interest centers on the organisms that cause them and on the conditions under which they spread. In noninfective conditions, the engineering approach established in the 17th century remains predominant and attention is focused on how a disease develops rather on why it begins. Perhaps the most important question now confronting medicine is whether the commonest health problems—heart disease, cancer, rheumatoid arthritis, cerebrovascular disease—are essentially different from health problems of the past or whether, like infections, they can be prevented by modifying the conditions that lead to them.

To answer this question, we must distinguish between genetic and chromosomal diseases determined at the moment of fertilization and all other diseases, which are attributable in greater or lesser degree to the influence of the environment. Most diseases, including the common noninfectious ones, appear to fall into the second category. Whether these diseases can be prevented is likely to be determined by the practicability of controlling the environmental influences that lead to them.

The change in the character of health problems that followed the decline of infections in developed countries has not invalidated the conclusion that most diseases, both physical and mental, are associated with influences that might be controlled. Among such influences, those which the individual determines by his own behavior (smoking, eating, exercise, and the like) are now more important for his health than those that depend mainly on society's actions (provision of essential food and protection from hazards). And both behavioral and environmental influences are more significant than medical care.

The role of individual medical care in preventing sickness and premature death is secondary to that of other influences; yet society's investment in health care is based on the premise that it is the major determinant. It is assumed that we are ill and are made well, but it is nearer the truth to say that we are well and are made ill. Few people think of themselves as having the major responsibility for their own health, and the enormous resources that advanced countries assign to the health field are used mainly to treat disease or, to a lesser extent, to prevent it by personal measures such as immunization.

The revised concept of human health cannot provide immediate solutions for the many complex problems facing society: limiting population growth and providing adequate food in developing countries, changing personal behavior and striking a new balance between technology and care in developed nations. Instead, the enlarged understanding of health and disease should be regarded as a conceptual base with implications for services, education, and research that will take years to develop.

The most immediate requirement in the health services is to give sufficient attention to behavioral influences that are now the main determinants of health. The public believes that health depends primarily on intervention by the doctor and that the essential requirement for health is the early discovery of disease. This concept should be replaced by recognition that disease often cannot be treated effectively, and that health is determined predominantly by the way of life individuals choose to follow. Among the important influences on health are the use of tobacco, the misuse of alcohol and drugs, excessive or unbalanced diets, and lack of exercise. With research, the list of significant behavioral influences will undoubtedly increase, particularly in relation to the prevention of mental illness.

Although the influences of personal behavior are the main determinants of health in developed countries, public action can still accomplish a great deal in the environmental field. Internationally, malnutrition probably remains the most important cause of ill health, and even in affluent societies sections of the population are inadequately, as distinct from unwisely, fed. The malnourished vary in proportion and composition from one country to another, but in the developed world they are mainly the younger children of large families and elderly people who live alone. In light of the importance of food for good health, governments might use supplements and subsidies to put essential foods within the reach of everyone, and provide inducements for people to select beneficial in place of harmful foods. Of course these aims cannot exclude other considerations such as international agreements and the solvency of farmers who have been encouraged to produce meat and dairy products rather than grains. Nevertheless, in future evaluations of agricultural and related economic policies, health implications deserve a primary place.

Perhaps the most sensitive area for consideration is the funding of health services. Although the contribution of medical intervention to prevention of sickness and premature death can be expected to remain small in relation to behavioral and environmental influences, surgery and drugs are widely regarded as the basis of health and the essence of medical care, and society invests the money it sets aside for health mainly in treatment for acute diseases and particularly in hospitals for the acutely ill. Does it follow from our appraisal that resources should be transferred from acute care to chronic care and to preventive measures?

Restricting the discussion to personal medical care, I believe that neglected areas, such as mental illness, mental retardation, and geriatric care, need greatly increased attention. But to suggest that this can be achieved merely by direct transfer of resources is an oversimplification. The designation "acute care" comprises a wide range of activities that differ profoundly in their effectiveness and efficiency. Some, like surgery for accidents and the treatment of acute emergencies, are among the most important services that medicine can offer and any reduction of their support would be disastrous. Others, however, like coronary care units and iron treatment of some anemias are not shown to be effective, while still others—most tonsillectomies and routine check-ups—are quite useless and should be abandoned. A critical appraisal of medical services for acute illnesses would result in more efficient use of available resources and would free some of them for preventive measures.

What health services need in general is an adjustment in the distribution of interest and resources between prevention of disease, care of the sick who require investigation and treatment, and care of the sick who do not need active intervention. Such an adjustment must pay considerable attention to the major determinants of health: to food and the environment, which will be mainly in the hands of specialists, and to personal behavior, which should be the concern of every practicing doctor.

Walsh McDermott

Medicine: The Public Good and One's Own

Challenging McKeown and other critics of medicine, Walsh McDermott classifies the work of physicians and admits that there have been no effective measures of its social outcome. He argues, however, that the personal-encounter physician system is effective and, along with the public health system and changes in personal health habits, has contributed to the nation's improving health status and longevity. He believes physicians can find a balanced way to provide for their professional needs as well as the health requirements of their patients. McDermott is emeritus professor of public health and medicine at the Cornell University Medical College in New York.

Medicine, like so many of our other institutions, is under intensive scrutiny today. Long immune from serious outside looks, medicine now has extramural critics by the score, and they join forces or dispute with those medically trained. Much of what they have to say is familiar to us all. Indeed, some of it is more than 50 years old. A fair amount of the criticism is knowledgeable and pertinent; some of it is not. In view of its familiarity, to take up this subject at all might properly call for the standard wine-in-new-bottles apology. The apology can be skipped, however, because recently a new idea has been going around. It is not really a single new idea but a whole range of ideas—whole schools of thought, if you will—that are all based on one central conclusion, namely, that that part of our health care system that is operated by individual doctors and their hospitals has very little demonstrable influence on the health status of our society.

In short, with increased medical costs has not come increasing benefits in terms of health. This situation is bound to continue—so goes the argument—because today's major health problems are so heavily related to environment and life-style. Consequently, they can be alleviated only by major social

The fourth William S. Paley Lecture on Science and Society, Cornell University Medical College, New York, October 7, 1976.

changes. From this it is concluded that further investments in the system of individual doctors caring for individual patients should be curtailed in favor of what in the trade has acquired the title "alternative strategies for health."

I do not propose to present a detailed review of these strategies because the purpose of this paper lies not with them but with the validity of major arguments used in their presentation. About all I shall say is that they mostly take the form that there is a known set of health habits which, if learned, taught, and practiced by us, would result in significantly longer and healthier lives. This is to say it is postulated that the group *as a group* would have longer and healthier lives. To what extent this would comfort the individual cannot be stated. I am trying to avoid being pejorative when I say that, except for the long-known obvious excesses, there is really no solid evidence that could identify one way of living as significantly different from another in terms of health. Indeed, such evidence would be very hard to come by for it would involve careful lifelong epidemiologic studies of people whose life habits could be periodically observed and recorded. Retrospective studies, as pointed out by the authors of a recent one, can at best be only suggestive, although certainly the careful accumulation of even suggestive evidence is to be encouraged. But as things stand, what seems to be the principal case presented for the serious consideration of major investment in these alternative health strategies comes from the proposition on which they are all founded, namely, that the personal encounter physician system has failed and will continue to fail to improve our people's health.

It is my analysis of this proposition that I plan to present today. Those who base the major part of their case on this assumption by no means agree on anything else. For the group ranges all the way from passionate spokesmen such as Ivan Illich and Rick Carlson, with their books *Medical Nemesis* and *The End of Medicine,* to the physician-historian Thomas McKeown, in his "Historical Perspective on Science and Health," to the dispassionate economist Victor Fuchs, with his book, *Who Shall Live?*, and to Aaron Wildavsky in his Michael Davis Lecture, "Can Health Be Planned?" . . .

Before interjecting myself into the debate, however, I would like to point out how this issue exemplifies the dilemma we face with each of our major policy issues today. For most issues of public policy today—and for all that are science related—we must form our judgments from hearing an argument between those whose comprehension of the question may be grossly warped because they do *not* know the subject from the inside and those whose perceptions may be grossly warped because they *do* know it from the inside. Obviously, it is as one from the inside that I speak.

*   *   *

I will start with the assertion that what the doctor does is something that is extraordinarily difficult to analyze and measure. To do so requires that we go back to first principles, so to speak. Hence I will start with definitions of health, health care, and medicine.

Health, like happiness, cannot be defined in exact measurable terms because its presence is so largely a matter of subjective judgment. About as precise as one can get is that health is a relative affair that represents the degree to which an individual can operate with effectiveness within the particular circumstances of his or her heredity and physical and cultural environment. What *can* be measured is disease, and in a particular society the pattern of disease closely reflects major features of that society. As there are only some four or five different disease patterns, it is possible to classify different societies by level of health, that is, by their possession of a particular disease pattern.

Health care is partially done by onself, but in large measure is done "by others." It comes in two forms: the public health system, which embraces the activities of a wide range of health professionals serving with various degrees of autonomy and only loosely and indirectly related to the physician; and the personal-encounter physician system, in which a considerably narrower range of health professionals work in a much more direct relationship to the physician. The personal-encounter physician is the doctor familiar to us all—the one who deals with one patient at a time on a direct doctor-to-person basis. Hence the term includes all surgeons as well. These two systems—the encounter system and the public health system—exert a biomedical influence on us all, and we are also influenced by a third force—the way of living, the lifestyle—permitted by our socioeconomic or technologic status.

Medicine itself is deeply rooted in a number of sciences, but it is also deeply rooted in the Samaritan tradition. The science and the Samaritanism are both directed toward the same goal of tempering the harshness of illness and disease. Medicine is thus not a science but a learned profession that attempts to blend affairs of the spirit and the cold objectivity of science. Everything that the physician does, therefore, is a blend of technology and Samaritanism. By the technology or the "interventionist" technology is meant those products of medical science that are useful in altering disease in a predictable fashion— medicine's science-based rationalism. By "Samaritanism" is meant that collection of acts, big and little, that lend reassurance—or at least give support— to someone troubled by disease or illness. I have tried to define this function elsewhere:

> . . . The Samaritan function has a number of aspects. In the last analysis it can
> be defined as the "diagnosis and treatment of the patient's illness as opposed to
> his disease." By the illness is meant what the patient is experiencing and by

disease, what he has. Based on compassion, Samaritanism is by no means simply an exercise in love; its proper performance also requires a mastery of science and technology. In large measure but not yet *in toto,* Samaritanism is an *indirect* but nevertheless real use of science and technology. For over the long pull the greatest effect of Samaritanism lies in reassurance—in human support. Sometimes the reassurance can be quickly and decisively delivered; sometimes it takes more time.

I think most of us would agree that a patient's primary feeling when he seeks medical care is an intense wish to find out that whatever it is that is wrong, it is not something that will cause him awful harm. Lower on the priority list is curiosity as to the precise nature of what may be wrong. This is really a matter of secondary interest. But for one human being to make the judgment about another that whatever is "wrong" is not a serious threat and make that judgment stick, requires that the judge, in this case the physician, have a legitimatizing base. Prior to fifty years ago, the legitimatizing base for such judgments and the reassurance they formed, was mostly dogma—a dogma mellowed and well-polished by experience. *Today's doctor derives his legitimatizing base, the base that permits him to dispense reassurance, from his expertise in the use of a broad spectrum of scientific and technical knowledge.*

These two functions, the technologic and the Samaritan, are separable in the world of analysis but not in the world of real life. Here they are inseparable. A doctor cannot get a passing grade by being proficient at one or the other; he must be good at both, for they are to be regarded as opposite sides of the same coin. In a nutshell, a major part of what the physician tries to do in exercising these two functions is to give someone *peace of mind.* . . .

*   *   *

What the personal encounter physician does . . . falls into four categories: technologic use, Samaritanism, physiologic supportive management, and the technology-based capability to report negatives authoritatively and hence help maintain peace of mind.

We have devised no indicators to measure the effectiveness of these four categories of professional activity on the health status of a society. The fact that this is so is something that is not understood. There is a general failure to realize that what are known as "the usual indices of health status" are indicators that have been developed through the years to measure the public health system. They are based on births and deaths and enumeration of the diseases that cause the most deaths. The births that are counted might be considered as successes; the deaths in a society, in effect, are failures. From these data, which can be refined to include such information as comparisons of infant with preschool mortality, it is possible to construct a crude outline of the disease and demographic patterns of a society. As mentioned above, there are only four or five such patterns. They are sufficiently distinctive to form a hierarchy of levels of health, and a society with fatalities from yellow fever and tetanus of the newborn would be ranked at a different level than, say, present-day Philadelphia. The ranking is based on knowledge acquired over more than a century to the effect that diseases, for example, yellow fever in Philadelphia, can be prevented by public health technology.

What the doctor *does,* however, is something quite different from counting disease fatalities. It is performing an act or series of acts, and the influence of what he does depends upon what the acts are aimed at, how well the doctor manages his technology, and how effective is the technology itself. As we know, the Samaritan component cannot now be measured. But what is not realized by medicine's extramural critics is that the physiology management component—the significant prolongation of life, say, in a person with heart disease—is also not measurable at present. Yet this is the most important aspect of managing the illness of chronic disease—a major occupation for the physician today. And we have no indicators for it. The technology-based capability to be convincing about negatives is likewise not susceptible to measurement.

As a consequence, we have no way of measuring the *successes* of the encounter physician system. The only exceptions are when, as was the case with tuberculosis, the disease was quite common in occurrence and its actual spread was prevented by the treatment of those afflicted. Neither the permanent successes obtained by surgery nor those resulting from the various specific medical therapies show up to be counted. Everything that does show up in effect shows up as a failure.

To be sure, if the encounter system had *enough* successes involving enough people with some one condition sufficiently common so that the total annual mortality from all causes underwent change, some of the system's influence should be picked up on the public health system's indicators, even though we realize that only a part of the encounter system's influence would be thus detectable. It is appropriate to underline the conditions that must be met for this to happen: (1) a highly effective technology must be suddenly introduced and widely applied; (2) the technology would have to affect a disease or diseases in large numbers of people in order that an effect on deaths could be seen in the 2,000,000 or so deaths that occur each year. This means that within a single year the new technology must actually prevent the deaths of large number of people who all have the same disease or who have different diseases but are all affected by the same technology.

A rather common cause of death must thus be significantly lowered within quite a short period of time. Obviously, such a combination of circumstances would be expected to occur only rarely, yet it has occurred at least a few times in the past four decades....

*   *   *

With full realization that the conventional indices of health are able to reflect only a small portion of the encounter system's total impact on the public's health, one can nevertheless demonstrate substantial effects from the encounter system. But it can be, and is, said that, whatever may have been the reasons for what has occurred in the past, the targets of opportunity are largely gone. What remains, it is said, are conditions closely related to social ills, including intemperance in the use of food, alcohol, and cigarettes and the misuse of drugs. Hence, the prospect of the encounter system having significant effects on today's disease pattern is most unlikely. Arguments based on predictions as to what the future might bring are hard to answer, but there is one way this one could be put to the test, namely, what in fact is actually happening to the U.S. disease pattern today. The encounter system is very much involved in the attack on this pattern. Consequently, if this disease pattern were showing no change for the better, there would be strong support for the argument that the encounter system had little capacity to affect it. Contrariwise, if the pattern *were* showing change for the better, it would show that the disease patterns could be affected by *something* going on now, whether the encounter system or something else.

Let us examine the data for the most recent 5-year period for which final data are available, that is, 1971–1975, inclusive.... The age-adjusted death rate had become stabilized in 1954 following the sharp drops due to the introduction of the antimicrobial drugs. It remained essentially stable or showed a slight fall through the 1960s. But in the first 5 years of the 1970s, the age-adjusted death rate dropped by almost 9 percent. This is six times as fast as in the preceding 5-year period. What are some of the things that have been going on that are reflected in that fall in death rate?

By far the greatest single cause of death is heart disease, which for the most part is coronary heart disease. Among the earliest diagnostic studies of this disease in living man was one made by Dr. Herrick, in Chicago, in 1912. There were relatively few cases recognized until 1921, but from then on recognition of cases increased markedly. Thus, by the early 1930s, when I was in medical school, the diagnosis was not at all unusual. The fatalities from coronary heart disease increased steadily throughout the 1930s, 1940s, and 1950s until, as mentioned before, it was by far the major part of fatal heart disease which itself was the leading cause of death.

It was quite widely thought that these fatalities from coronary heart disease were on the increase well into the seventies. In point of fact, this increasing toll of deaths reached a peak in 1963; and in the 5-year period from 1963 to 1968, deaths fell by 4 percent. This was not appreciated at the time, and it was not until 1973, or 10 years after the peak, that it was recognized that a fall had occurred. Not only did the death rate fall 4 percent in the 5-year period; it has fallen 14.5 percent more in the next 7-year period, that is, from 1968 to 1974. A fall of 14 percent may not seem large, but remember the total group involved is larger than 650,000 people. Not only is a fall occurring; there is some reason to believe that it is accelerating.

Here is a major cause of death. It is showing a substantial fall in the United States; yet nobody knew it for quite a while. Although the first publication on it was in the March 1974 *Journal of the American Medical Association,* this striking phenomenon is not noted at all in the 1975 and 1976 books mentioned at the beginning of my talk. It must be remembered that the total number of cases of coronary heart disease is still high and possibly increasing. But this is solely a consequence of increased population, and when the data are corrected to allow comparability from one point in time to another, they show this very pronounced fall.

*   *   *

The infant mortality data are equally exciting. One hears a great deal about infant mortality, and the reason is that it is a sensitive reflector of all three forces that influence our health—the socioeconomic level, the public health physician, and the encounter physician systems, of medical care. For example, the black-white differences in the U.S. infant mortality disappear above a certain modest but nonpoverty level.

Infant mortality is the number of infants who fail to survive to their first birthday out of every 1,000 infants who were born alive that year. In 1965 that number was more than 20 per 1,000 per year, and for the subgroup of the minority poor, it was more than 35. In 1970 U.S. infant mortality was just at 20 with a white rate of 17.8 and "all other" or "minority poor" rate of 30.9 (see Table 1). Five years later, in 1975, the provisional U.S. infant mortality rate was 16.1. This represents a decrease of 3.6 percent from the final rate of just the year before. Such a drop is unprecedented, but it is almost certainly real. Like the death rate from coronary heart disease, this infant mortality rate is still falling. For our white population of about 192,000,000 people, the rate was 14.4, thus beginning to approach the rates in those tiny European countries with which our record is always being compared. The infant mortality rate for the U.S. "minority," that is, nonwhite population, had fallen from 30.9 to 22.9 in a 5-year period.

Either one of these two developments (the fall in fatal coronary heart disease or infant mortality) would be startling in itself, but we are seeing both

Table 1. U.S. infant mortality

Year	Total	White	All Other
1970	20.0	27.8	30.9
1971	19.1	17.1	28.5
1975	16.1	14.4	22.9

together in a 5–10-year period. Moreover, these are not the only beneficial changes in the usual health indices that have occurred: the death rate from peptic ulcer is down, and the (age-adjusted) death rate from strokes has dropped more than 33 percent in the 15-year period, including 1975. Among middle-aged women this fall is especially marked. Cirrhosis of the liver, the seventh leading cause of death, had shown a rather rapid increase until 1973, particularly among black males; since that time it has been falling. The one major disease *not* showing a fall was cancer, which showed a slight rise — really limited to those 55 years and over.

*   *   *

To what can these spectacular results be attributed? They do not appear to have been caused by chance because the trends are consistent over time, and there are no inexplicable deviations. They certainly appear to be a consequence of one or more of the three major forces we know can affect the disease pattern. Clearly the results provide no support at all for the idea that the nature of today's disease patterns is such that things are at a standstill.

Can we attribute these striking improvements to the encounter physician system? Certainly not, for, except for historically special situations such as those cited, it is simply impossible to separate the effects of the encounter system, which are almost certainly here, from effects of the public health system or from the effects of change in health habits or socioeconomic status. To be sure, the last named seems unlikely as a major factor because, during the period in question, the economy has not generally favored increases in living standards, nor has it been harsh enough to inflict widespread spartan living. (The automobile speed limit of 55 miles per hour, rather widely obeyed in 1973, is thought to have had effects on the overall death rate but presumably had no effects on the individual disease rates cited above.) Changes in health habits, however, might be playing a role. Although adolescent cigarette smoking is up, we can now see, for the first time, that adult cigarette smoking is down. The wide promotion of unhydrogenated fats in cooking and on our bread conceivably might contribute to such a change. But not only is it not known how widely the public accepts these fats, but the scientific judgment as to their role in diseases remains uncertain. The amazing falls in infant mortality are rich food for speculation and have occurred in a setting of great efforts to attack the problems through the personal-encounter system. But when all is said and done, that is all it can be — just speculation. A major problem in attribution, particularly with socioeconomic factors, is that there might be a 10- or 20-year period between a particular change and its reflection in a change in death rates from, say, heart disease.

Indeed, the more one examines the pattern of these falls in death rates, the less it appears as if any one factor or system were involved. Instead they appear exactly as one would expect them to appear if all three of the relevant forces were involved. Expressed differently, it looks as if the public health system, some beginning changes in health habits, and the encounter physician were all having effects. But above all, the results certainly do not support the widely proclaimed cries that our infant mortality cannot be lowered despite continued poverty or that today's predominant disease pattern is so linked to multifactors, including improper health habits and the environment, that its medical management has come to a standstill.

The ultimate object of analyses such as those by Illich, Carlson, McKeown, Fuchs, Wildavsky, and others, and in this essay, is to isolate and characterize as sharply as possible a social issue so that its importance and suitability for major investment can be weighed against the available alternatives.

The issue here, as we know, is whether the encounter physician system merits continuing major investment or whether some other way, largely based on acquiring good habits of health, represents a better investment opportunity for the long run. To be sure, none of the credible critics proposes actually doing away with the encounter physician system, at least not in the short run. But it would definitely be downgraded in priority for support and investment, and in the level of mastery of the science and technology required by those who would function within it. In terms of public policy, therefore, the issue is key, for it will govern what we will be working toward and what we will have to work with. Decisions on questions of this sort inevitably have to be made on less than complete information. But our capability to evaluate the impact of service programs, such as education or transport, even programs in which application of a technology is involved, is at a very elementary stage. For the outside critic especially, it is very easy to fail to realize what a particular indicator reflects and to fail to realize when it is being used to measure something it could not possibly indicate.

In the present analysis I cannot pretend to have developed a set of indicators for the annual measurement of the encounter physician system. But using whatever relevant observations I could find, I believe certain conclusions are justified. First, the proposition that the personal encounter physician system is not sufficiently effective to warrant continued major investment is clearly not proved. Indeed, certain predictive parts of the proposition would seem to have been overtaken by recent events.

Second, there are no established indicators by which to measure the effectiveness of the personal-encounter system. Only a small part of the total impact of the system could possibly show up in the usual indices of the health of a society—indices that were devised for quite a different purpose.

Third, despite our present lack of indicators, examination of the four categories of activity representing what it is the doctor does clearly show that in the encounter system we have an instrument that exerts a great influence on our nation's health and is one of *potentially* great social value. Contrary to what is now being widely stated, therefore, there is every reason to give high marks to the *functional* effectiveness of the personal-encounter physician system as something that is meeting great needs of the individual and many of the needs of the group. . . .

Lewis Thomas

On Magic in Medicine

Since the remaining barriers to improved health status and longevity are often diseases of mysterious origin, theories of causation, avoidance, and cure are numerous and varied. In the following article, Dr. Lewis Thomas of the Sloan-Kettering Cancer Center points out that the lack of understanding of common killers, such as heart disease and cancer, leaves the field open for "magic" or folk explanations and therapies. Until research fills these gaps in scientific knowledge, those who assert that individuals must take responsibility for their own health may win advocates among both conservatives and social activists.

Medicine has always been under pressure to provide public explanations for the diseases with which it deals, and the formulation of comprehensive, unifying theories has been the most ancient and willing preoccupation of the profession. In the earliest days, hostile spirits needing exorcism were the principal pathogens, and the shaman's duty was simply the development of improved technics for incantation. Later on, especially in the Western world, the idea that the distribution of body fluids among various organs determined the course of all illnesses took hold, and we were in for centuries of bleeding, cupping, sweating and purging in efforts to intervene. Early in this century the theory of autointoxication evolved, and a large part of therapy was directed at emptying the large intestine and keeping it empty. Then, the global concept of focal infection became popular, accompanied by the linked notion of allergy to the presumed microbial pathogens, and no one knows the resulting toll of extracted teeth, tonsils, gallbladders and appendixes. The idea of psychosomatic influences on disease emerged in the 30's and, for a while, seemed to sweep the field.

Gradually, one by one, some of our worst diseases have been edited out of such systems by having their causes indisputably identified and dealt with. Tuberculosis was the paradigm. This was the most chronic and inexorably progressive of common human maladies, capable of affecting virtually every organ in the body and obviously influenced by crowding, nutrition, housing and poverty; theories involving the climate in general, and night air and insufficient sunlight in particular, gave rise to the spa as a therapeutic institution. It was not until the development of today's effective chemotherapy that it became clear to everyone that the disease had a single, dominant, central cause. If you got rid of the tubercle bacillus you were rid of the disease.

But that was some time ago, and today the idea that complicated diseases can have single causes is again out of fashion. The microbial infections that can be neatly coped with by antibiotics are regarded as lucky anomalies. The new theory is that most of today's human illnesses, the infections aside, are multifactorial in nature, caused by two great arrays of causative mechanisms: the influence of things in the enviroment; and one's personal life-style. For medicine to become effective in dealing with such diseases, it has become common belief that the environment will have to be changed, and personal ways of living will have to be transformed, and radically.

These things may turn out to be true, for all I know, but it will take a long time to get the necessary proofs. Meanwhile, the field is wide open for magic.

One great difficulty in getting straightforward answers is that so many of the diseases in question have unpredictable courses, and some of them have a substantial tendency toward spontaneous remission. In rheumatoid arthritis, for instance, when such widely disparate therapeutic measures as copper bracelets, a move to Arizona, diets low in sugar or salt or meat or whatever, or even an inspirational book, have been accepted by patients as useful, the trouble in evaluation is that approximately 35 per cent of patients with this diagnosis are bound to recover no matter what they do. But if you actually have rheumatoid arthritis and then get over it, or if you are a doctor and observe this to happen, it is hard to be persuaded that it wasn't *something* you did that was responsible. Hence, you need very large numbers of patients and lots of time, and a cool head.

Magic is back again, and in full force. Laetrile cures cancer, acupuncture is useful for deafness and low-back pain, vitamins are good for anything, and meditation, yoga, dancing, biofeedback and shouting one another down in crowded rooms over weekends are specifics for the human condition. Running, a good thing to be doing for its own sake, has acquired the medicinal value formerly attributed to rare herbs from Indonesia.

There is a recurring advertisement, placed by Blue Cross on the Op-Ed page of the *New York Times,* that urges you to take advantage of science by changing your life habits, with the suggestion that if you do so, by adopting seven easy-to-follow items of life-style, you can achieve 11 added years beyond what you'll get if you don't. Since today's average figure is around 72 for all parties in both sexes, this might mean going on until at least the age of 83. You can do this formidable thing, it is claimed, by simply eating breakfast, exercising regularly, maintaining normal weight, not smoking cigarettes, not drinking excessively, sleeping for eight hours each night and not eating between meals.

The science that produced this illumination was a careful study by California epidemiologists, based on a questionnaire given to about 7000 people 45 years of age or older. Five years after the questionnaire, a body count was made by sorting through the county death certificates, and the 371 people who had died were matched up with their answers to the questions. To be sure, there were more deaths among the heavy smokers and drinkers, as you might expect from the known incidence of lung cancer in smokers and cirrhosis and automobile accidents in drinkers. But there was also a higher mortality among those who said they didn't eat breakfast, and even higher in those who took no exercise, no exercise at all, not even going off in the family car for weekend picnics. Being up to 20 per cent overweight was not so bad, surprisingly, but being *underweight* was clearly associated with a higher death rate.

The paper describing these observations has been widely quoted, and not just by Blue Cross. References to the seven healthy life habits keep turning up in popular magazines and in the health columns of newspapers, always with that promise of 11 more years.

The findings fit nicely with what is becoming folk doctrine about disease. You become ill because of not living right. If you get cancer it is, somehow or other, your own fault. If you didn't cause it by smoking or drinking, or eating the wrong things, it came from allowing yourself to persist with the wrong kind of personality, in the wrong environment. If you have a coronary occlusion, you didn't run enough. Or you were too tense, or you *wished* too much, and didn't get a good enough sleep. Or you got fat. Your fault.

But eating breakfast? It is a kind of enchantment, pure magic.

You have to read the report carefully to discover that there is another, more banal way of explaining the findings. Leave aside the higher deaths in heavy smokers and drinkers, for there is no puzzle in either case; these are dangerous things to do. But it is hard to imagine any good reason for dying within five years from not eating a good breakfast, or any sort of breakfast.

The other explanation turns cause and effect around. Among the people in that group of 7000 who answered that they don't eat breakfast, don't go off on picnics, are underweight and can't sleep properly, there were surely some who were already ill when the questionnaire arrived. They didn't eat breakfast because they couldn't stand the sight of food. They had lost their appetites, were losing weight, didn't feel up to moving around much and had trouble sleeping. They didn't play tennis, or go off on family picnics, because they didn't *feel* good. Some of these people probably had an undetected cancer, perhaps of the pancreas, others may have had hypertension or early kidney failure, or some other organic disease that the questionnaire had no way of picking up. The study did not ascertain the causes of death in the 371, but just a few deaths from such undiscerned disorders would have made a significant statistical impact. The author of the paper was careful to note these possible interpretations, although the point was not made strongly, and the general sense you have in reading it is that you can live on and on if only you will eat breakfast and play tennis.

The popular acceptance of the notion of seven healthy life habits, as a way of staying alive, says something important about today's public attitudes, or at least the attitudes in the public mind, about disease and dying. People have always wanted causes that are simple and easy to comprehend, and about which the individual can *do* something. If you believe that you can ward off the common causes of premature death—cancer, heart disease and stroke, diseases whose pathogenesis we really do not understand—by jogging, hoping and eating and sleeping regularly, these are good things to believe even if not necessarily true. Medicine has survived other periods of unifying theory, constructed to explain all human disease, not always as benign in their effects as this one is likely to be. After all, if people can be induced to give up smoking, stop overdrinking and overeating, and take some sort of regular exercise, most of them are bound to feel the better for leading more orderly, regular lives, and many of them are surely going to look better.

Nobody can say an unfriendly word against the sheer goodness of keeping fit, but we should go carefully with the promises.

There is also a bifurcated ideologic appeal contained in the seven-life-habits doctrine, quite apart from the subliminal notion of good luck in the numbers involved (7 come 11). Both ends of the political spectrum can find congenial items. At the further right, it is attractive to hear that the individual, the good old free-standing, free-enterprising American citizen, is responsible for his own health and when things go wrong it is his own damn fault for smoking and drinking and living wrong (and he can jolly well pay for it). On the other hand, at the left, it is nice to be told that all our health problems, including dying, are caused by the failure of the community to bring up its members to live properly, and if you really want to improve the health of the people research is not the answer; you should upheave the present society and invent a better one. At either end, you can't lose.

In between, the skeptics in medicine have a hard time of it. It is much more difficult to be convincing about ignorance concerning disease mechanisms than when you are making claims for full comprehension, especially when the comprehension leads, logically or not, to some sort of action. When it comes to serious illness, the public tends, understandably, to be more skeptical about the skeptics, more willing to believe the true believers. It is medicine's oldest dilemma, not to be settled by candor or by any kind of rhetoric; what it needs is a lot of time and patience, waiting for science to come in, as it has in the past, with the solid facts.

3 The Medicalization of American Society

MARK TUSCHMAN

There is little doubt that medicine as an institution and way of thinking is assuming a greater role in American society. Divorce, alcoholism, aging, crime, and learning problems—once considered legal, social, and religious issues—are now being redefined as medical problems requiring diagnosis and treatment. What are the consequences of placing so many aspects of life in a medical context? Does the public have unrealistic expectations of the medical profession? Are mental and social well-being the proper aims for medicine?

Perhaps the most strident critic of contemporary medicine is Ivan Illich, who maintains in "Medical Nemesis" that medicine is a major threat to our health. He addresses iatrogenesis, when health problems are generated by physicians and the medical care system. He cites the clinical hazards posed by unnecessary surgery, drug side-effects, and hospital-acquired infections. Other problems are created by focusing our attention and resources on costly medical care instead of attending to the social and political conditions that foster ill health. Lastly, Illich denounces the psychological dependence or addiction to medical care that destroys the ability of people to cope autonomously with their own bodies, own suffering, and own death.

Sociologist Renée Fox, while somewhat critical of Illich's broadside of contemporary medicine, is also concerned with the increasing medicalization of American society by which sinfulness was transformed to crime, which in turn has become sickness and thereby a problem requiring medical attention. In "The Medicalization and Demedicalization of American Society," she argues that society's fundamental decisions about life, death, and humanity are being recast in medical terms. The extent of societal commitment to medicine is also evidenced in the greater allotment of resources and increasing numbers of people employed in health care. Fox, however, also notes an emerging trend toward demedicalization. The feminist revolt, the patient's rights movement, and the rise of midwifery, home births, and self-care, while appearing to deemphasize professional control, still illustrate the increasing public concern and involvement with health issues.

Irving Zola, also a sociologist, further illustrates the evolution of medicine as an institution of social control in "Healthism and Disabling Medicalization." Medicine presents itself as a morally neutral way to deal with social problems. However, Zola maintains that the moral judgments do not disappear just by relabeling problems in terms of health and illness. Further, such medicalization can blind us to the need for fundamental social changes instead of medical Band-aids.

The abstract issues of medicalization and demedicalization are brought to a personal level in California Chief Justice Rose Elizabeth Bird's account of her own encounter with breast cancer, "A Hard Look: Cancer and Mortality." Like Zola, she believes that doctors exercise too much control; we have left the responsibility for diagnosis and treatment as well as management of death to the demi-gods, the physicians. What a shock it must have been, then, when her own doctor died of cancer while she had to face a recurrence of her own cancer. She makes a personal plea for more realistic expectations of doctors and more active and responsible participation of patients in their own care (a plea that is echoed by Norman Cousins in Chapter 14). Our health is too precious to surrender completely to the control of others.

Ivan Illich

Medical Nemesis

In the following article, based on his book Medical Nemesis, *social critic Ivan Illich claims that the medical professions, both directly and indirectly, are dangerous to our health. Medicine, he argues, has so pervaded our society that it destroys health by diminishing people's ability to cope independently with their problems. Illich views this destructive role of medicine as part of a broader backlash of industrial progress.*

W ithin the last decade medical professional practice has become a major threat to health. Depression, infection, disability, dysfunction, and other specific iatrogenic diseases now cause more suffering than all accidents from traffic or industry. Beyond this, medical practice sponsors sickness by the reinforcement of a morbid society which not only industrially preserves its defectives but breeds the therapist's client in a cybernetic way. Finally, the so-called health-professions have an indirect sickening power—a structurally health-denying effect. I want to focus on this last syndrome, which I designate as medical Nemesis. By transforming pain, illness, and death from a personal challenge into a technical problem, medical practice expropriates the potential of people to deal with their human condition in an autonomous way and becomes the source of a new kind of un-health.

Much suffering has always been man-made: history is the record of enslavement and exploitation. It tells of war, and of the pillage, famine, and pestilence which come in its wake. War between commonwealths and classes has so far been the main planned agency of man-made misery. Thus, man is the only animal whose evolution has been conditioned by adaptation on two fronts. If he did not succumb to the elements, he had to cope with use and abuse by others of his kind. He replaced instincts by character and culture, to be capable of this struggle on two frontiers. A third frontier of possible doom has been recognized since Homer; but common mortals were considered immune to its threat. Nemesis, the Greek name for the awe which loomed from this third direction, was the fate of a few heroes who had fallen prey to the envy of the gods. The common man grew up and perished in a struggle with Nature and neighbor. Only the elite would challenge the thresholds set by Nature for man.

Prometheus was not Everyman, but a deviant. Driven by Pleonexia, or radical greed, he trespassed the boundaries of the human condition. In hubris or measureless presumption, he brought fire from heaven, and thereby brought Nemesis on himself. He was put into irons on a Caucasian rock. A vulture preys at his innards, and heartlessly healing gods keep him alive by regrafting his liver each night. The encounter with Nemesis made the classical hero an immortal reminder of inescapable cosmic retaliation. He becomes a subject for epic tragedy, but certainly not a model for everyday aspiration. Now Nemesis has become endemic; it is the backlash of progress. Paradoxically, it has spread as far and as wide as the franchise, schooling, mechanical acceleration, and medical care. Everyman has fallen prey to the envy of the gods. If the species is to survive it can do so only by learning to cope in this third group.

Industrial Nemesis

Most man-made misery is now the byproduct of enterprises which were originally designed to protect the common man in his struggle with the inclemency of the environment and against wanton injustices inflicted by the elite. The main source of pain, disability, and death is now an engineered—albeit non-intentional—harassment. The prevailing ailments, helplessness and injustice, are now the side-effects of strategies for progress. Nemesis is now so prevalent that it is readily mistaken for part of the human condition. The desperate disability of contemporary man to envisage an alternative to the industrial aggression on the human condition is an integral part of the curse from which he suffers. Progress has come with a vengeance which cannot be called a price. The down payment was on the label and can be stated in measurable terms. The installments accrue under forms of suffering which exceed the notion of "pain."

At some point in the expansion of our major institutions their clients begin to pay a higher price every day for their continued consumption, in spite of the evidence that they will inevitably suffer more. At this point in development the prevalent behavior of society corresponds to that traditionally recognized in addicts. Declining returns pale in comparison with marginally increasing disutilities. *Homo economicus* turns into *Homo religiosus*. His expectations become heroic. The vengeance of economic development not only outweighs the price at which this vengeance was purchased; it also outweighs the compound tort done by Nature and neighbors. Classical Nemesis was punishment for the rash abuse of a privilege. Industrialized Nemesis is retribution for dutiful participation in society.

War and hunger, pestilence and sudden death, torture and madness remain man's companions, but they are now shaped into a new *Gestalt* by the Nemesis overarching them. The greater the economic progress of any community, the greater the part played by industrial Nemesis in the pain, discrimination, and death suffered by its members. Therefore, it seems that the disciplined study of the distinctive character of Nemesis ought to be the key theme for research amongst those who are concerned with health care, healing, and consoling.

Tantalus

Medical Nemesis is but one aspect of the more general "counter-intuitive mis-adventures" characteristic of industrial society. It is the monstrous outcome of a very specific dream of reason—namely, "tantalizing" hubris. Tantalus was a famous king whom the gods invited to Olympus to share one of their meals. He purloined Ambrosia, the divine potion which gave the gods unending life. For punishment, he was made immortal in Hades and condemned to suffer unending thirst and hunger. When he bows toward the river in which he stands, the water recedes, and when he reaches for the fruit above his head the branches move out of his reach. Ethologists might say that Hygienic Nemesis has programmed him for compulsory counter-intuitive behavior. Craving for Ambrosia has now spread to the common mortal. Scientific and political optimism have combined to propagate the addiction. To sustain it, the priesthood of Tantalus has organized itself, offering unlimited medical improvement of human health. The members of this guild pass themselves off as disciples of healing Asklepios, while in fact they peddle Ambrosia. People demand of them that life be improved, prolonged, rendered compatible with machines, and capable of surviving all modes of acceleration, distortion, and stress. As a result, health has become scarce to the degree to which the common man makes health depend upon the consumption of Ambrosia.

Culture and Health

Mankind evolved only because each of its individuals came into existence protected by various visible and invisible cocoons. Each one knew the womb from which he had come, and oriented himself by the stars under which he was born. To be human and to become human, the individual of our species has to find his destiny in his unique struggle with Nature and neighbor. He is on his own in the struggle, but the weapons and the rules and the style are given to him by the culture in which he grew up. Each culture is the sum of rules with which the individual could come to terms with pain, sickness, and death—could interpret them and practice compassion amongst others faced by the same threats. Each culture set the myth, the rituals, the taboos, and the ethical standards needed to deal with the fragility of life—to explain the reason for pain, the dignity of the sick, and the role of dying or death.

Cosmopolitan medical civilization denies the need for man's acceptance of these evils. Medical civilization is planned and organized to kill pain, to eliminate sickness, and to struggle against death. These are new goals, which have never before been guidelines for social life and which are antithetic to every one of the cultures with which medical civilization meets when it is dumped on the so-called poor as part and parcel of their economic progress.

The health-denying effect of medical civilization is thus equally powerful in rich and in poor countries, even though the latter are often spared some of its more sinister sides.

The Killing of Pain

For an experience to be pain in the full sense, it must fit into a culture. Precisely because each culture provides a mode for suffering, culture is a particular form of health. The act of suffering is shaped by culture into a question which can be stated and shared.

Medical civilization replaces the culturally determined competence in suffering with a growing demand by each individual for the institutional management of his pain. A myriad of different feelings, each expressing some kind of fortitude, are homogenized into the political pressure of anesthesia consumers. Pain becomes an item on a list of complaints. As a result, a new kind of horror emerges. Conceptually it is still pain, but the impact on our emotions of this valueless, opaque, and impersonal hurt is something quite new.

In this way, pain has come to pose only a technical question for industrial man—what do I need to get in order to have my pain managed or killed? If the pain continues, the fault is not with the universe, God, my sins, or the devil, but with the medical system. Suffering is an expression of consumer demand for increased medical outputs. By becoming unnecessary, pain has become unbearable. With this attitude, it now seems rational to flee pain rather than to face it, even at the cost of addiction. It also seems reasonable to eliminate pain, even at the cost of health. It seems enlightened to deny legitimacy to all non-technical issues which pain raises, even at the cost of disarming the victims of residual pain. For a while it can be argued that the total pain anesthetized in a society is greater than the totality of pain newly generated. But at some point, rising marginal disutilities set in. The new suffering is not only unmanageable, but it has lost its referential character. It has become meaningless, questionless torture. Only the recovery of the will and ability to suffer can restore health into pain.

The Elimination of Sickness

Medical interventions have not affected total mortality-rates; at best they have shifted survival from one segment of the population to another. Dramatic changes in the nature of disease afflicting Western societies during the last 100 years are well documented. First industrialization exacerbated infection, which then subsided. Tuberculosis peaked over a 50–75-year period and declined before either the tubercle bacillus had been discovered or anti-tuberculosis programs had been initiated. It was replaced in Britain and the U.S. by major malnutrition syndromes—rickets and pellagra—which peaked and declined, to be replaced by disease of early childhood, which in turn gave way to duodenal ulcers in young men. When that declined the modern epidemics took their toll—coronary heart-disease, hypertension, cancer, arthritis, diabetes, and mental disorders. At least in the U.S., death-rates from hypertensive heart-disease seem to be declining. Despite intensive research no connection betwen these changes in disease patterns can be attributed to the professional practice of medicine.

Neither decline in any of the major epidemics of killing diseases, nor major changes in the age structure of the population, nor falling and rising absentee-ism at the workbench have been significantly related to sick care—even to immunization. Medical services deserve neither credit for longevity nor blame for the threatening population pressure.

Longevity owes much more to the railroad and to the synthesis of fertilizers and insecticides than it owes to new drugs and syringes. Professional practice is both ineffective and increasingly sought out. This technically unwarranted rise of medical prestige can only be explained as a magical ritual for the achievement of goals which are beyond technical and political reach. It can be countered only through legislation and political action which favors the de-professionalization of health care.

The overwhelming majority of modern diagnostic and therapeutic interventions which demonstrably do more good than harm have two characteristics: the material resources for them are extremely cheap, and they can be packaged and designed for self-use or application by family members. The price of technology that is significantly health-furthering or curative in Canadian medicine is so low that the resources now squandered in India on modern medicine would suffice to make it available in the entire sub-continent. On the other hand, the skills needed for the application of the most generally used diagnostic and therapeutic aids are so simple that the careful observation of instruction by people who personally care would guarantee more effective and responsible use than medical practice can provide.

The deprofessionalization of medicine does not imply and should not be read as implying negation of specialized healers, of competence, of mutual criticism, or of public control. It does imply a bias against mystification, against transnational dominance of one orthodox view, against disbarment of healers chosen by their patients but not certified by the guild. The deprofessionalization of medicine does not mean denial of public funds for curative purposes, it does mean a bias against the disbursement of any such funds under the prescription and control of guild-members, rather than under the control of the consumer. Deprofessionalization does not mean the elimination of modern medicine, nor obstacles to the invention of new ones, nor necessarily the return to ancient programs, rituals, and devices. It means that no professional shall have the power to lavish on any one of his patients a package of curative resources larger than that which any other could claim on his own. Finally, the deprofessionalization of medicine does not mean disregard for the special needs which people manifest at special moments of their lives; when they are born, break a leg, marry, give birth, become crippled, or face death. It only means that people have a right to live in an environment which is hospitable to them at such high points of experience.

The Struggle against Death

The ultimate effect of medical Nemesis is the expropriation of death. In every society the image of death is the culturally conditioned anticipation of an uncertain date. This anticipation determines a series of behavioral norms during life and the structure of certain institutions.

Wherever modern medical civilization has penetrated a traditional medical culture, a novel cultural ideal of death has been fostered. The new ideal spreads by means of technology and the professional ethos which corresponds to it.

In primitive societies death is always conceived as the intervention of an actor—an enemy, a witch, an ancestor, or a god. The Christian and the Islamic Middle Ages saw in each death the hand of God. Western death had no face until about 1420. The Western ideal of death which comes to all equally from natural causes is of quite recent origin. Only during the autumn of the Middle Ages death appears as a skeleton with power in its own right. Only during the 16th century, as an answer European peoples developed the "arte and crafte to knowe ye Will to Dye." For the next three centuries peasant and noble, priest and whore, prepared themselves throughout life to preside at their own death. Foul death, bitter death, became the end rather than the goal of living. The idea that natural death should come only in healthy old age appeared only in the 18th century as a class-specific phenomenon of the bourgeois. The demand that doctors struggle against death and keep valetudinarians healthy has nothing to do with their ability to provide such services: Ariès has shown that the costly attempts to prolong life appear at first only among bankers whose power is compounded by the years they spend at a desk.

We cannot fully understand contemporary social organization unless we see in it a multi-faceted exorcism of all forms of evil death. Our major institutions constitute a gigantic defense program waged on behalf of "humanity" against all those people who can be associated with what is currently conceived of as death-dealing social injustice. Not only medical agencies, but welfare, international relief, and development programs are enlisted in this struggle. Ideological bureaucracies of all colors join the crusade. Even war has been used to justify the defeat of those who are blamed for wanton tolerance of sickness and death. Producing "natural death" for all men is at the point of becoming an ultimate justification for social control. Under the influence of medical rituals contemporary death is again the rationale for a witch-hunt.

Conclusion

Rising irreparable damage accompanies industrial expansion in all sectors. In medicine these damages appear as iatrogenesis. Iatrogenesis can be direct, when pain, sickness, and death result from medical care; or it can be indirect, when health policies reinforce an industrial organization which generates ill-health: it can be structural when medically sponsored behavior and delusion restrict the vital autonomy of people by undermining their competence in growing up, caring, aging; or when it nullifies the personal challenge arising from their pain, disability, and anguish.

Most of the remedies proposed to reduce iatrogenesis are engineering interventions. They are therapeutically designed in their approach to the individual, the group, the institution, or the environment. These so-called remedies generated second-order iatrogenic ills by creating a new prejudice against the autonomy of the citizen.

The most profound iatrogenic effects of the medical technostructure result from its non-technical social functions. The sickening technical and non-technical consequences of the institutionalization of medicine coalesce to generate a new kind of suffering—anesthetized and solitary survival in a world-wide hospital ward.

Medical Nemesis cannot be operationally verified. Much less can it be measured. The intensity with which it is experienced depends on the independence, vitality, and relatedness of each individual. As a theoretical concept it is one component in a broad theory to explain the anomalies plaguing health-care systems in our day. It is a distinct aspect of an even more general phenomenon which I have called industrial Nemesis, the backlash of institutionally structured industrial hubris. This hubris consists of a disregard for the boundaries within which the human phenomenon remains viable. Current research is overwhelmingly oriented towards unattainable "breakthroughs." What I have called counterfoil research is the disciplined analysis of the levels at which such reverberations must inevitably damage man.

The perception of enveloping Nemesis leads to a social choice. Either the natural boundaries of human endeavor are estimated, recognized, and translated into politically determined limits, or the alternative to extinction is compulsory survival in a planned and engineered Hell.

In several nations the public is ready for a review of its health-care system. The frustrations which have become manifest from private-enterprise systems and from socialized care have come to resemble each other frighteningly. The differences between the annoyances of the Russian, French, Americans, and English have become trivial. There is a serious danger that these evaluations will be performed within the coordinates set by post-cartesian illusions. In rich and poor countries the demand for reform of national health care is dominated by demands for equitable access to the wares of the guild, professional expansion and sub-professionalization, and for more truth in the advertising of progress and lay-control of the temple of Tantalus. The public discussion of the health crisis could easily be used to channel even more power, prestige, and money to biomedical engineers and designers.

There is still time in the next few years to avoid a debate which would reinforce a frustrating system. The coming debate can be reoriented by making medical Nemesis the central issue. The explanation of Nemesis requires simultaneous assessment of both the technical and the non-technical side of medicine—and must focus on it as both industry and religion. The indictment of medicine as a form of institutional hubris exposes precisely those personal illusions which make the critic dependent on the health care.

The perception and comprehension of Nemesis has therefore the power of leading us to policies which could break the magic circle of complaints which now reinforce the dependence of the plaintiff on the health engineering and planning agencies whom he sues. Recognition of Nemesis can provide the catharsis to prepare for a non-violent revolution in our attitudes towards evil and pain. The alternative to a war against these ills is the search for the peace of the strong.

Health designates a process of adaptation. It is not the result of instinct, but of autonomous and live reaction to an experienced reality. It designates the ability to adapt to changing environments, to growing up and to aging, to healing when damaged, to suffering and to the peaceful expectation of death. Health embraces the future as well, and therefore includes anguish and the inner resource to live with it.

Man's consciously lived fragility, individuality, and relatedness make the experience of pain, of sickness, and of death an integral part of his life. The ability to cope with this trio in autonomy is fundamental to his health. To the degree to which he becomes dependent on the management of his intimacy he renounces his autonomy and his health *must* decline. The true miracle of modern medicine is diabolical. It consists of making not only individuals but whole populations survive on inhumanly low levels of personal health. That health should decline with increasing health-service delivery is unforeseen only by the health manager, precisely because his strategies are the result of his blindness to the inalienability of health.

The level of public health corresponds to the degree to which the means and responsibility for coping with illness are distributed amongst the total population. This ability to cope can be enhanced but never replaced by medical intervention in the lives of people or the hygienic characteristics of the environment. That society which can reduce professional intervention to the minimum will provide the best conditions for health. The greater the potential for autonomous adaptation to self and to others and to the environment, the less management of adaptation will be needed or tolerated.

The recovery of a health attitude towards sickness is neither Luddite nor Romantic nor Utopian: it is a guiding ideal which will never be fully achieved, which can be achieved with modern devices as never before in history, and which must orient politics to avoid encroaching Nemesis.

Renée C. Fox

The Medicalization and Demedicalization of American Society

Illich's attack on the modern medical establishment is critiqued in this selection by sociologist Renée C. Fox of the University of Pennsylvania. Fox comments on health and illness as symbols in modern society for biological, social, cultural, and metaphysical ideas with both positive and negative values. In reaction to this medicalization, a movement to demedicalize political and social thinking is evident, for example, in the current shift of emphasis from institutionalized medical care of illness to self-maintenance of health.

The statement that American society has become "medicalized" is increasingly heard these days. During the past decade or so, the allegation has been made by social scientists, jurists, politicians, social critics, medical scientists, and physicians. In many instances, it has been accompanied by the claim that society is now "overmedicalized," and that some degree of "demedicalization" would be desirable. There are those who not only espouse "demedicalizing the society," but who also predict that, in fact, it will progressively come to pass.

One of the most extreme statements of this kind is Ivan Illich's monograph, *Medical Nemesis,* which opens with the assertion that "the medical establishment has become a threat to health," and goes on to develop the many damaging ways in which the author considers modern medicine to be responsible for "social" as well as "clinical" and "structural" iatrogenesis....

There are numerous grounds on which Illich's thesis can be criticized. He minimizes the advances in the prevention, diagnosis, and treatment of disease that have been made since the advent of the bacteriological era in medicine, and he attributes totally to non-medical agencies all progress in health that has ensued. He implies that modern Western, urban, industrialized, capitalist societies, of which the United States is the prototype, are more preoccupied with pain, sickness, and death, and less able to come to terms with these integral parts of a human life, than other types of society. Although his volume appears to be well documented, a disturbing discrepancy exists between the data presented in many of the works that Illich cites in his copious footnotes and the interpretive liberties that he takes with them. Perhaps most insidious of all is the sophistry that Illich uses in presenting a traditional, orthodox, Christian-Catholic point of view in the guise of a vulgar Marxist argument. For he repeatedly claims that "when dependence on the professional management of pain, sickness and death grows beyond a certain point, the healing power in sickness, patience in suffering, and fortitude in the face of death must decline." In Illich's view, this state is not only morally dubious, but also spiritually dangerous. Because it entails the "hubris" of what he deems arrogant and excessive medical intervention, it invites "nemesis": the retribution of the gods.

But whatever its shortcomings, Illich's essay is a kind of lightning rod, picking up and conducting the twin themes of medicalization and demedicalization which have become prominent in the United States and a number of other modern Western societies. These themes will concern us here. We shall begin by identifying the constellation of factors involved in what has been termed "medicalization," offer an interpretation of these phenomena, and consider and evaluate certain signs of demedicalization. Finally, some speculative predictions about the probable evolution of the medicalization-demedicalization process in American society will be offered.

*   *   *

One indication of the scope that the "health-illness-medicine complex" has acquired in American society is the diffuse definition of health that has increasingly come to be advocated: "a state of complete physical, mental, and social well-being," to borrow the World Health Organization's phrase. This conception of health extends beyond biological and psychological phenomena relevant to the functioning, equilibrium, and fulfillment of individuals, to include social and cultural conditions of communal as well as personal import. Such an inclusive perspective on health is reflected in the range of difficulties that persons now bring to physicians for their consideration and help. As Leon Kass picturesquely phrased it:

> All kinds of problems now roll to the doctor's door, from sagging anatomies to suicides, from unwanted childlessness to unwanted pregnancy, from marital difficulties to learning difficulties, from genetic counseling to drug addiction, from laziness to crime. . . .

A new term has even been coined by medical practitioners to refer to those clients who seems to have some legitimate need of their therapeutic services, but who technically cannot be considered to be ill. With discernible ambivalence, such persons are often called "the worried well."

Accompanying the increasingly comprehensive idea of what constitutes health and what is appropriate for medical professionals to deal with is the growing conviction that health and health care are rights rather than privileges, signs of grace, or lucky, chance happenings. In turn, these developments are connected with higher expectations on the part of the public about what medicine ideally ought to be able to accomplish and to prevent. To some extent, for example, the rise in the number of malpractice suits in the United States seems not only to be a reaction to the errors and abuses that physicians can commit, but also a reflection of the degree to which the profession is being held personally responsible for the scientific and technical uncertainties and limitations of their discipline. The vision of an iatrogenesis-free furthering of health, which social critics such as Illich hold forth, is also an indicator of such rising expectations.

One significant form that the process of medicalization has taken is the increase in the numbers and kinds of attitudes and behaviors that have come to be defined as illnesses and treatment of which is regarded as belonging within the jurisdiction of medicine and its practitioners. In an earlier, more religiously oriented era of a modern Western society like our own, some of these same kinds of attitudes and behaviors were considered sinful rather than sick, and they fell under the aegis of religious authorities for a different kind of diagnosis, treatment, and control. In a more secular, but less scientifically and medically oriented, stage of the society than the current one, certain of these ways of thinking, feeling, and behaving were viewed and dealt with as criminal. Although sin, crime, and sickness are not related in a simple, invariant way, there has been a general tendency in the society to move from sin to crime to sickness in categorizing a number of aberrant or deviant states to the degree that the concept of the "medicalization of deviance" has taken root in social-science writings. The sin-to-crime-to-sickness evolution has been most apparent with respect to the conditions that are now considered to be mental illnesses, or associated with serious psychological and/or social disturbances. These include, for example, states of hallucination and delusion that once would have been interpreted as signs of possession by the Devil, certain forms of physical violence, such as the type of child abuse that results in what is termed the "battered child syndrome," the set of behaviors in children which are alternatively called hyperactivity, hyperkinesis, or minimal brain dysfunction, and so-called addictive disorders, such as alcoholism, drug addiction, compulsive overeating, and compulsive gambling.

This "continuing process of divestment" away from sin and crime as categories for abnormality, dysfunction, and deviance and toward illness as the explanatory concept has entailed what Peter Sedgwick calls "the progressive annexation of not-illness into illness." "The future belongs to illness," he proclaims, predicting that "we ... are going to get more and more diseases, since our expectations of health are going to become more expansive and sophisticated." If we include into what is considered to be sickness or, at least, non-health in the United States, disorders manifested by subjective symptoms which are not brought to the medical profession for diagnosis and treatment, but which do not differ significantly from those that are, then almost everyone in the society can be regarded as in some way "sick."

> At least two ... studies have noted that as much as 90 percent of their apparently healthy sample had some physical aberration or clinical disorder.... It seems that the more intensive the investigation, the higher the prevalence of clinically serious but previously undiagnosed and untreated disorders. Such data as these give an unexpected statistical picture of illness. Instead of it being a relatively infrequent or abnormal phenomenon, the empirical reality may be that illness, defined as the presence of clinically serious symptoms, is the statistical *norm*.

Such a global conception of illness acutely raises the question of the extent to which illness is an objective reality, a subjective state, or a societal construct that exists chiefly in the minds of its social "beholders," a question that will be considered in greater detail below.

*   *   *

The great "power" that the American medical profession, particularly the physician, is assumed to possess and jealously and effectively to guard is another component of the society's medicalization. In the many allusions to this medical "power" that are currently made, the organized "autonomy" and "dominance" of the profession are frequently cited, and, in some of the more critical statements about the physician, these attributes are described as constituting a virtual "monopoly" or "expropriation" of health and illness. The "mystique" that surrounds the medical profession is part of what is felt to be its power: a mystique that is not only spontaneously conferred on its practitioners by the public, but, as some observers contend, is also cultivated by physicians themselves through their claim that they command knowledge and skills that are too esoteric to be freely and fully shared with lay persons.

However, it is to the biotechnological capacities of modern medicine that its greatest power is usually attributed: both its huge battery of established drugs and procedures and its new and continually increasing medical and surgical techniques. Among the actual or incipient developments that are most frequently mentioned are the implantation of cadaveric, live, or mechanical organs, genetic and other microcellular forms of "engineering," and *in vitro* fertilization, as well as various chemical, surgical, and psychophysiological methods of thought and behavior control. The potentials of medicine not only to prevent and to heal, but also to subjugate, modify, and harm are implicated in such references.

The high and rapidly growing cost of medical and health care is still another measure of increased medicalization. In 1975, Americans spent $547 per person for health care and related activities such as medical education and research. This represented 8.3 per cent of the GNP. In 1950, 4.6 per cent and in 1970, 7.2 per cent of the GNP was spent. From 1963 to the present, health expenditures have risen at a rate exceeding 10 per cent annually while the rest of the economy as reflected in the GNP has been growing at a rate between 6 and 7 per cent.

In addition to allocating an ever increasing proportion of society's economic resources for health care, greater amounts of political and legal energy are also being invested in health, illness, and medical concerns. The pros and cons of national health insurance, which continue to be vigorously debated in various arenas, are as much political, ideological, and legal issues, as they are economic ones. The volume of legislation relevant to health care has grown impressively. In 1974, for example, more than 1,300 health-care bills were introduced in the Congress, and more than 900 such bills in the state legislature in New York alone. The health subcommittees of the Senate and the House of Representatives are particularly active, and they have become prestigious as well. Furthermore, partly as a consequence of various congressional investigations and hearings, the federal government is now significantly involved in bioethical questions (especially those bearing on human experimentation) in addition to their more traditional interests in medical economic and health-care-delivery problems.

During the past few years, a number of medico-legal decisions have been made that are of far-reaching cultural importance, affecting the society's fundamental conceptions of life, death, the body, individuality, and humanity. These include: the Supreme Court's decisions in favor of the legal right of women to decide upon and undergo abortion; the Court's ruling against the involuntary, purely custodial confinement of untreated, mentally ill persons; the Uniform Anatomical Gift Act, adopted in fifty-one jurisdictions, which permits persons to donate all or parts of their bodies to be used for medical purposes after their death; death statutes passed in various states which add the new, "irreversible coma" criterion of "brain death" to the traditional criteria for pronouncing death, based on the cessation of respiratory and cardiac function; and, in the case of Karen Ann Quinlan, the New Jersey Supreme Court's extension of "the individual's right of privacy" to encompass a patient's decision to decline or terminate life-saving treatment, under certain circumstances.

One other, quite different, way in which medical phenomena have acquired central importance in the legal system is through the dramatic escalation of malpractice suits against physicians. An estimated 20,000 or more malpractice claims are brought against doctors each year, and the number seems to be rising steadily. In New York, for example, the number of suits filed against physicians rose from 564 in 1970 to 1,200 in 1974; in the past decade, the average award for a malpractice claim grew from $6,000 to $23,400, with far more very large awards being made than in the past.

Increasing preoccupation with bioethical issues seems also to be a concomitant of the medicalization process. Basic societal questions concerning values, beliefs, and meaning are being debated principally in terms of the dilemmas and dangers associated with biomedical advances. Consideration of particular medical developments such as genetic engineering, life-support systems, birth technology, organ implants, and population and behavior control have opened up far-reaching ethical and existential concerns. Problems of life, death, chance, "necessity," scarcity, equity, individuality, community, the "gift relationship," and the "heroic" worldview are being widely discussed in medical, scientific, political, legal, journalistic, philosophical, and religious circles. A bioethics "subculture" with certain characteristics of a social movement has crystallized around such issues.

The unprecedented number of young people who are attempting to embark on medical careers is also contributing to the medicalization process. In this country, on the average, more than three persons apply for each medical-school place available to entering first-year students, and there is as yet no sign of a leveling off. Paradoxically, this is happening during a period when medicine and the medical profession are being subjected to increased scrutiny and criticism.

*   *   *

Complex, and by no means consistent, the process of medicalization is not an easy one to analyze. Several preliminary *caveats* seem in order. In part, they are prompted by two sorts of assumptions made by critics of medicalization in America: one is that the central and pervasive position of health, illness, and medicine in present-day American society is historically and culturally unique, and the other, that it is primarily a result of the self-interested maneuvers of the medical profession. Neither of these assumptions is true without qualification.

To begin with, in all societies, health, illness, and medicine constitute a nexus of great symbolic as well as structural importance, involving and interconnecting biological, social, psychological, and cultural systems of action. In every society, health, illness, and medicine are related to the physical and psychic integrity of individuals, their ability to establish and maintain solidary relations with others, their capacities to perform social roles, their birth, survival, and death, and to the ultimate kinds of "human condition" questions that are associated with these concerns. As such, health, illness, and medicine also involve and affect every major institution of a society, and its basic cultural grounding. The family, for example, is profoundly involved in the health and illness of its members, and, especially in non-modern societies, the kinship system is as responsible for health and illness as are specialized medical practitioners. The institutions of science, magic, and religion are the major media through which the "hows" and "whys" of health and illness, life and death are addressed in a society, and through which culturally appropriate action for dealing with them is taken. The economy is also involved in several ways: the allocation of resources that health, illness, and medicine entail; the occupational division of labor relevant to diagnosis and therapy; and the bearing of health and illness on the individual's capacity and motivation for work. The deviance and social-control aspects of illness have important implications for the polity which, in turn, is responsible for the organized enforcement of health measures that pertain to the community or public welfare. And in all societies, the influence, power, and prestige that accrue to medical practitioners implicate the magico-religious and stratification systems as well as the polity.

As the foregoing implies, there are certain respects in which health, illness, and medicine are imbued with a more diffuse and sacred kind of significance in non-modern than in modern societies. For example, in traditional and neo-traditional Central African societies, the meaning of health and illness, the diagnosis and treatment of sickness, and the wisdom, efficacy, and power of medical practitioners are not only more closely linked with the institutions of kinship, religion, and magic than in American society; they are also more closely connected with the overarching cosmic view through which the whole society defines and orients itself. One indication of the larger matrix into which health, illness, and medicine fit in such a society is that in numerous Central African languages the same words can mean medicine, magico-religious charms, and metaphysically important qualities such as strength, fecundity, and invulnerability, which are believed to be supernaturally conferred.

In the light of the multi-institutional and the cultural significance of health, illness, and medicine in all societies it is both illogical and unlikely to believe that the current process of medicalization in American society has been engineered and maintained primarily by one group, namely, the physicians. What the manifestations of medicalization that we have identified do suggest, however, is that the health-illness-medical sector has progressively acquired a more general cultural meaning in American society than it had in the past.

Within this framework, the medicalization process entails the assertion of various individual and collective rights to which members of the society feel entitled and which they express as "health," "quality of life," and "quality of death." The process also involves heightened awareness of a whole range of imperfections, injustices, dangers, and afflictions that are perceived to exist in the society, a protest against them, and a resolve to take action that is more therapeutic than punitive. Medicalization represents an exploration and affirmation of values and beliefs that not only pertain to the ultimate grounding of the society, but also to the human condition, more encompassingly and existentially conceived.

Thus, in American society, health and illness have come to symbolize many positively and negatively valued biological, physical, social, cultural, and metaphysical phenomena. Increasingly, health has become a coded way of referring to an individually, socially, or cosmically ideal state of affairs. Conversely, the concept of illness has increasingly been applied to modes of thinking, feeling, and behaving that are considered undesirably variant or deviant, as well as to more forms of suffering and disability. In turn, this medicalization of deviance and suffering has had a network of consequences.

Talcott Parsons's well-known formulation of the "sick role" provides important insights into what these effects have been. According to him, the sick role consists of two interrelated sets of exemptions and obligations. A person who is defined as ill is exonerated from certain kinds of responsibility for his illness. He is not held morally accountable for the fact that he is sick (it is not considered to be his "fault"), and he is not expected to make himself better by "good motivation" or high resolve without the help of others. In addition, he is viewed as someone whose capacity to function normally is impaired, and who is therefore relieved of some of his usual familial, occupational, and civic activities and responsibilities. In exchange for these exemptions which are conditionally granted, the sick individual is expected to define the state of being ill as aberrant and undesirable, and to do everything possible to facilitate his recovery from it. In the case of illness of any moment, the responsibility to try to get well also entails the obligation to seek professionally competent help. In a modern Western society, such as the United States, this obligation involves a willingness to confer with a medically trained person, usually a physician, and to undergo the modes of diagnosis and treatment that are recommended, including the ministrations of other medical professionals and hospitalization. Upon entering this relationship with institutionalized medicine and its professional practitioners, an individual with a health problem becomes a patient. By cooperating and collaborating with the medical professionals caring for him, the patient is expected to work toward recovery, or, at least, toward the more effective management of his illness.

The fact that the exemptions and obligations of sickness have been extended to people with a widening arc of attitudes, experiences, and behaviors in American society means primarily that what is regarded as "conditionally legitimate deviance" has increased. Although illness is defined as deviance from the desirable and the normal, it is not viewed as reprehensible in the way that either sin or crime is. The sick person is neither blamed nor punished as those considered sinful or criminal are. So long as he does not abandon himself to illness or eagerly embrace it, but works actively on his own and with medical professionals to improve his condition, he is considered to be responding appropriately, even admirably, to an unfortunate occurrence. Under these conditions, illness is accepted as legitimate deviance. But this also implies that medical professionals have acquired an increasingly important social-control function in the society. They are the principal agents responsible for certifying, diagnosing, treating, and preventing illness. Because a greater proportion of deviance in American society is now seen as illness, the medical profession plays a vastly more important role than it once did in defining and regulating deviance and in trying to forestall and remedy it.

The economic, political, and legal indicators of a progressive medicalization cited above also have complex origins and implications. For example, the fact that activities connected with health, illness, and medicine represent a rising percentage of the gross national product in the United States is a consequence of the fee-for-service system under which American health-care delivery is organized; the central importance of the modern hospital in medical care; the mounting personnel, equipment, and maintenance costs that the operation of the hospital entails, and the development of new medical and surgical procedures and of new drugs, most of which are as expensive as they are efficacious. Some of this increase in costs results from the desire for profits that medical professionals, hospital administrators, and members of the pharmaceutical industry share to varying degrees. But how much is difficult to ascertain, though radical ideological criticisms and defensive conservative statements on the point are both rife at present.

In addition to such political and economic factors, the heightened commitment to health as a right and the medicalization of deviance have also contributed to the growth of health expenditures. Because health is both more coveted and more inclusively defined, and because a greater amount of medical therapeutic activity is applied to deviance-defined-as-illness, increasing economic resources are being invested in the health-illness-medicine sector of the society.

The political and legal prominence of questions of health care and medicine in American society at the present time reflects in part a widespread national discontent with the way medical care is organized, financed, and delivered, and with some of the attitudes and behaviors of physicians. The inequities that exist in access to care, and in its technical and interpersonal excellence, are among the primary foci of political and legal activities. Another major area of current political and legal action concerns the internal and external regulation of the medical profession better to insure that it uses its knowledge and skill in a socially as well as medically responsible way. Various new measures, which represent a mixture of controls from within the medical profession and from outside it, have been set into motion. For example, in 1972, the Professional Standards Review Organization was established through the passage of amendments to the Social Security Act which were designed to provide quality assessment and assurance, utilization review, and cost control, primarily for Medicare and Medicaid patients. Over the course of the years 1966 through 1971, a series of government regulations were passed which mandate peer review for all biomedical research involving human subjects, supported by the Department of Health, Education, and Welfare (and its subunits, the National Institutes of Health and the Public Health Service), as well as by the Food and Drug Administration. In 1975, the American College of Surgeons and the American Surgical Association set forth a plan for systematically decreasing the number of newly graduated doctors entering surgical training. In part, this plan represented an organized, intraprofessional attempt to deal with what appears to be an oversupply of surgeons in the United States, and thereby to reduce the possibility that federal health manpower legislation would have to be passed to remedy this maldistribution.

The fact that an extraordinary number of young people are opting for careers in health, particularly as physicians, is the final concomitant of medicalization previously mentioned. Reliable and valid data are not available to explain the mounting wave of young persons who have been attracted to medicine since the nineteen-sixties. We do not know as much as we should about how they resemble their predecessors, or differ from them. We are aware that more women, blacks, and members of other minority groups are being admitted to medical school than in the past, partly because of "affirmative action" legislation. But we do not have overall information about the characteristics of those who are accepted as compared with those who are not. Only sketchy materials are available on the impact of those changes in medical-school curricula during the past decade that were designed to make students more aware of the social and ethical dimensions of their commitment to medicine. We do not know whether their attitudes, their professional decisions, or their medical practice actually changed. More data are needed before we can interpret the short- and long-term implications of the rush of college youth toward medicine. As pre-medical and medical students themselves are first to testify, the prestige, authority, "power," autonomy, and financial rewards of medicine attract them and their peers to medicine, along with scientific interests, clinical impulses, and humanitarian concerns. But there is also evidence to suggest that even among those who readily contend that their reasons for choosing medicine are self-interested, a "new" medical-student orientation has been emerging. In fact, the very candor that medical students exhibit—and in some cases flaunt—when they insist that, regrettably, like their predecessors, their competitiveness, desire for achievement, and need for security have drawn them into medicine is part of this new orientation. Activist and meditative, as well as critical and self-critical, the "new medical student" not only wants to bring about change in the medical profession, but to do so in a way that affects other aspects of the society as well. The structural and symbolic meaning acquired by health, illness, and medicine has led such students to hope that their influence will be far-reaching as well as meliorative. How many students with this ostensibly "new" orientation will maintain it throughout their medical training and whether their entance into the profession will significantly alter the future course of medicalization in American society remains to be seen.

*   *   *

Along with progressive medicalization, a process of demedicalization seems also to be taking place in the society. To some extent the signs of demedicalization are reactions to what is felt by various individuals and groups to be a state of "*over*-medicalization." One of the most significant manifestations of this counter-trend is the mounting concern over implications that have arisen from the continuously expanding conception of "sickness" in the society. Commentators on this process would not necessarily agree with Peter Sedgwick that it will continue to "the point where everybody has become so luxuriantly ill" that perhaps sickness will no longer be "in" and a "backlash" will be set in motion; they may not envision such an engulfing state of societally defined illness. But many observers from diverse professional backgrounds have published works in which they express concern about the "coercive" aspects of the "label" illness and the treatment of illness by medical professionals in medical institutions. The admonitory perspectives on the enlarged domain of illness and medicine that these works of social science and social criticism represent appear to have gained the attention of young physicians-and nurses-in-training interested in change, and various consumer and civil-rights groups interested in health care.

This emerging view emphasizes the degree to which what is defined as health and illness, normality and abnormality, sanity and insanity varies from one society, culture, and historical period to another. Thus, it is contended, medical diagnostic categories such as "sick," "abnormal," and "insane" are not universal, objective, or necessarily reliable. Rather, they are culture-, class-, and time-bound, often ethnocentric, and as much artifacts of the preconceptions of socially biased observers as they are valid summaries of the characteristics of the observed. In this view, illness (especially mental illness) is largely a mythical construct, created and enforced by the society. The hospitals to which seriously ill persons are confined are portrayed as "total institutions": segregated, encompassing, depersonalizing organizations, "dominated" by physicians who are disinclined to convey information to patients about their conditions, or to encourage paramedical personnel to do so. These "oppressive" and "counter-therapeutic" attributes of the hospital environment are seen as emanating from the professional ideology of physicians and the kind of hierarchical relationships that they establish with patients and other medical professionals partly as a consequence of this ideology, as well as from the bureaucratic and technological features of the hospital itself. Whatever their source, the argument continues, the characteristics of the hospital and of the doctor-patient relationship increase the "powerlessness" of the sick person, "maintain his uncertainty," and systematically "mortify" and "curtail" the "self" with which he enters the sick role and arrives at the hospital door.

This critical perspective links the labeling of illness, the "imperialist" outlook, and capitalist behavior of physicians, the "stigmatizing" and "dehumanizing" experiences of patients, and the problems of the health-care system more generally to imperfections and injustices in the society as a whole. Thus, for example, the various forms of social inequality, prejudice, discrimination, and acquisitive self-interest that persist in capitalistic American society are held responsible for causing illness, as well as for contributing to the undesirable attitudes and actions of physicians and other medical professionals. Casting persons in the sick role is regarded as a powerful, latent way for the society to exact conformity and maintain the status quo. For it allows a semi-approved form of deviance to occur which siphons off potential for insurgent protest and which can be controlled through the supervision or, in some cases, the "enforced therapy" of the medical profession. Thus, however permissive and merciful it may be to expand the category of illness, these observers point out, there is always the danger that the society will become a "therapeutic state" that excessively restricts the "right to be different" and the right to dissent. They feel that this danger may already have reached serious proportions in this society through its progressive medicalization.

The criticism of medicalization and the advocacy of demedicalization have not been confined to rhetoric. Concrete steps have been taken to declassify certain conditions as illness. Most notable among these is the American Psychiatric Association's decision to remove homosexuality from its official catalogue ("Nomenclature") of mental disorders. In addition, serious efforts have been made to heighten physicians' awareness of the fact that because they share certain prejudiced, often unconscious assumptions about women, they tend to over-attribute psychological conditions to their female patients. Thus, for example, distinguished medical publications such as the *New England Journal of Medicine* have featured articles and editorials on the excessive readiness with which medical specialists and textbook authors accept the undocumented belief that dysmenorrhea, nausea of pregnancy, pain in labor, and infantile colic are all psychogenic disorders, caused or aggravated by women's emotional problems. Another related development is feminist protest against what is felt to be a too great tendency to define pregnancy as an illness, and childbirth as a "technologized" medical-surgical event, prevailed over by the obstetrician-gynecologist. These sentiments have contributed to the preference that many middle-class couples have shown for natural childbirth in recent years, and to the revival of midwifery. The last example also illustrates an allied movement, namely a growing tendency to shift some responsibility for medical care and authority over it from the physician, the medical team, and hospital to the patient, the family, and the home.

A number of attempts to "destratify" the doctor's relationships with patients and with other medical professionals and to make them more open and egalitarian have developed. "Patients' rights" are being asserted and codified, and, in some states, drafted into law. Greater emphasis is being placed, for example, on the patient's "right to treatment," right to information (relevant to diagnosis, therapy, prognosis, or to the giving of knowledgeable consent for any procedure), right to privacy and confidentiality, and right to be "allowed to die," rather than being "kept alive by artificial means or heroic measures . . . if the situation should arise in which there is no reasonable expectation of . . . recovery from physical or mental disability."

In some medical milieux (for example, community health centers and health maintenance organizations), and in critical and self-consciously progressive writings about medicine, the term "client" or "consumer" is being substituted for "patient." This change in terminology is intended to underline the importance of preventing illness while stressing the desirability of a non-supine, non-subordinate relationship for those who seek care to those who provide it. The emergence of nurse-practitioners and physician's assistants on the American scene is perhaps the most significant sign that some blurring of the physician's supremacy vis-à-vis other medical professionals may also be taking place. For some of the responsibilities for diagnosis, treatment, and patient management that were formerly prerogatives of physicians have been incorporated into these new, essentially marginal roles.

Enjoinders to patients to care for themselves rather than to rely so heavily on the services of medical professionals and institutions are more frequently heard. Much attention is being given to studies such as the one conducted by Lester Breslow and his colleagues at the University of California at Los Angeles which suggest that good health and longevity are as much related to a self-enforced regimen of sufficient sleep, regular, well-balanced meals, moderate exercise and weight, no smoking, and little or no drinking, as they are to professionally administered medical care. Groups such as those involved in the Women's Liberation Movement are advocating the social and psychic as well as the medical value of knowing, examining, and caring for one's own body. Self-therapy techniques and programs have been developed for conditions as complicated and grave as terminal renal disease and hemophilia A and B. Proponents of such regimens affirm that many aspects of managing even serious chronic illnesses can be handled safely at home by the patient and his family, who will, in turn, benefit both financially and emotionally. In addition, they claim that in many cases the biomedical results obtained seem superior to those of the traditional physician-administered, health-care-delivery system.

The underlying assumption in these instances is that, if self-care is collectivized and reinforced by mutual aid, not only will persons with a medical problem be freed from some of the exigencies of the sick role, but both personal and public health will thereby improve, all with considerable savings in cost. This point of view is based on the moral supposition that greater autonomy from the medical profession coupled with greater responsibility for self and others in the realm of health and illness is an ethically and societally superior state.

> We have the medicine we deserve. We freely choose to live the way we do. We choose to live recklessly, to abuse our bodies with what we consume, to expose ourselves to environmental insults, to rush frantically from place to place, and to sit on our spreading bottoms and watch paid professionals exercise for us. . . . Today few patients have the confidence to care for themselves. The inexorable professionalization of medicine, together with reverence for the scientific method, have invested practitioners with sacrosanct powers, and correspondingly vitiated the responsibility of the rest of us for health. . . . What is tragic is not what has happened to the revered profession, but what has happened to us as a result of professional dominance. In times of inordinate complexity and stress we have been made a profoundly dependent people. Most of us have lost the ability to care for ourselves. . . . I have tried to demonstrate three propositions. First, medical care has less impact on health than is generally assumed. Second, medical care has less impact on health than have social and environmental factors. And third, given the way in which society is evolving and the evolutionary imperatives of the medical care system, medical care in the future will have even less impact on health than it has now. . . . We have not understood what health is. . . . But in the next few decades our understanding will deepen. The pursuit of health and of well-being will then be possible,

but only if our environment is made safe for us to live in and our social order is transformed to foster health, rather than suppress joy. If not, we shall remain a sick and dependent people.... The end of medicine is not the end of health but the beginning....

The foregoing passage (excerpted from Rick Carlson's book, *The End of Medicine)* touches upon many of the demedicalization themes that have been discussed. It proclaims the desirability of demedicalizing American society, predicting that, if we do so, we can overcome the "harm" that excessive medicalization has brought in its wake and progress beyond the "limits" that it has set. Like most critics of medicalization on the American scene, Carlson inveighs against the way that medical care is currently organized and implemented, but he attaches exceptional importance to the health-illness-medicine sector of the society. In common with other commentators, he views health, illness, and medicine as inextricably associated with values and beliefs of American tradition that are both critical and desirable. It is primarily for this reason that in spite of the numerous signs that certain *structural* changes in the delivery of care will have occurred by the time we reach the year 2000. American society is not likely to undergo a significant process of *cultural* demedicalization.

Dissatisfaction with the distribution of professional medical care in the United States, its costs, and its accessibility has become sufficiently acute and generalized to make the enactment of a national health-insurance system in the foreseeable future likely. Exactly what form that system should take still evokes heated debate about free enterprise and socialism, public and private regulation, national and local government, tax rates, deductibles and co-insurance, the right to health care, the equality principle, and the principle of distributive justice. But the institutionalization of a national system that will provide more extensive and equitable health-insurance protection now seems necessary as well as inevitable even to those who do not approve of it.

There is still another change in the health-illness-medicine area of the society that seems to be forthcoming and that, like national health insurance, would alter the structure within which care is delievered. This is the movement toward effecting greater equality, collegiality, and accountability in the relationship of physicians to patients and their families, to other medical professionals, and to the lay public. Attempts to reduce the hierarchical dimension in the physician's role, as well as the increased insistence on patient's rights, self-therapy, mutual medical aid, community medical services and care by non-physician health professionals, and the growth of legislative and judicial participation in health and medicine by both federal and local government are all part of this movement. There is reason to believe that, as a consequence of pressure from both outside and inside the medical profession, the doctor will become less "dominant" and "autonomous," and will be subject to more controls.

This evolution in the direction of greater egalitarianism and regulation notwithstanding, it seems unlikely that all elements of hierarchy and autonomy will, or even can, be eliminated from the physician's role. For that to occur, the medical knowledge, skill, experience, and responsibility of patients and paramedical professionals would have to equal, if not replicate, the physician's. In addition, the social and psychic meaning of health and illness would have to become trivial in order to remove all vestiges of institutionalized charisma from the physician's role. Health, illness, and medicine have never been viewed casually in any society and, as indicated, they seem to be gaining rather than losing importance in American society.

It is significant that often the discussions and developments relevant to the destratification and control of the physician's role and to the enactment of national health insurance are accompanied by reaffirmations of traditional American values: equality, independence, self-reliance, universalism, distributive justice, solidarity, reciprocity, and individual and community responsibility. What seems to be involved here is not so much a change in values as the initiation of action intended to modify certain structural features of American medicine, so that it will more fully realize long-standing societal values.

In contrast, the new emphasis on health as a right, along with the emerging perspective on illness as medically and socially engendered, seems to entail major conceptual rather than structural shifts in the health-illness-medical matrix of the society. These shifts are indicative of a less fatalistic and individualistic attitude toward illness, increased personal and communal espousal of health, and a spreading conviction that health is as much a consequence of the good life and the good society as it is of medical care. The strongest impetus for demedicalization comes from this altered point of view. It will probably contribute to the decategorization of certain conditions as illness, greater appreciation and utilization of non-physician medical professionals, the institutionalization of more preventive medicine and personal and public health measures, and, perhaps, to the undertaking of non-medical reforms (such as full employment, improved transportation, or adequate recreation) in the name of the ultimate goal of health.

However, none of these trends implies that what we have called *cultural* demedicalization will take place. The shifts in emphasis from illness to health, from therapeutic to preventive medicine, and from the dominance and autonomy of the doctor to patient's rights and greater control of the medical profession do not alter the fact that health, illness, and medicine are central preoccupations in the society which have diffuse symbolic as well as practical meaning. All signs suggest that they will maintain the social, ethical, and existential significance they have acquired, even though by the year 2000 some structural aspects of the way that medicine and care are organized and delivered may have changed. In fact, if the issues now being considered under the rubric of bioethics are predictive of what lies ahead, we can expect that in the future, health, illness, and medicine will acquire even greater importance as one of the primary symbolic media through which American society will grapple with fundamental questions of value and belief. What social mechanisms we will develop to come to terms with these "collective conscience" issues, and exactly what role physicians, health professionals, biologists, jurists, politicians, philosophers, theologians, social scientists, and the public at large will play in their resolution remains to be seen. But it is a distinctive characteristic of an advanced modern society like our own that scientific, technical, clinical, social, ethical, and religious concerns should be joined in this way.

Irving Kenneth Zola

Healthism and Disabling Medicalization

Concern that the world is becoming a hospital and all the people in it, patients, is not new. During the past century, problems that were once considered the concern of the church or courts of law have been increasingly referred to medicine for solutions. Sociologist Irving Zola of Brandeis University traces the spread of this medicalization of society and sees the health area as the prime example of today's identity crisis: the field in which race, class, and gender differences are to be resolved.

My theme is that medicine is becoming a major institution of social control incorporating the more traditional institutions of religion and law. It is becoming the new repository of truth, the place where absolute and often final judgments are made by supposedly morally neutral and objective experts. And these judgments are no longer made in the name of virtue or legitimacy but in the name of health. Moreover this is not occurring through any increase in the political power of physicians. It is instead an insidious and often undramatic phenomenon, accomplished by "medicalizing" much of daily living, by making medicine and the labels "healthy" and "ill" *relevant* to an ever increasing part of human existence.

A Speculative History

Concern with medical influence is not new. Over a hundred years ago Goethe feared that the modern world might turn into one giant medical institution. Philip Rieff updated this concern when he noted that "the hospital is succeeding the church and the parliament as the archetypal institution of Western culture." This shift, one that is far from complete, has spanned centuries. To understand this phenomenon we must be aware of two rather important characteristics of professions: their control of their work and their tendency to generalize their expertise beyond technical matters. Everett Hughes stated these characteristics rather concisely:

> Not merely do the practitioners, by virtue of gaining admission to the charmed circle of colleagues, individually exercise the license to do things others do not,

but collectively they presume to tell society what is good and right for the individual and for society at large in some aspect of life. Indeed, they set the very terms in which people may think about this aspect of life.

How a profession gains the exclusive right and license to manage its work has been documented very well by others. For now I wish to dwell on the second aspect . . . a profession's desire to extend its limits beyond its technically and traditionally ascribed and assumed competence to wider more diffuse spheres. It is here that we enter our brief examination of religion, law and medicine.

The Christian ministry as the prototype of all professions is as good a place as any to start. Ever since Christianity achieved its European dominance in the early Middle Ages, its ministry wrestled with the conflicts between its limited and diffuse functions. The former involved the specific administration of the means of grace to individuals, while the latter involved the functions of prophecy—the direct application of the message of the gospel to the structure of the community. It is in the conveyance and elaboration of "this message" that the Christian ministry wove itself deeply into communal life. Thus, well into the Reformation one could claim that all communities were in a real sense religious ones, all leaders religiously committed, and the meaning and values of all relationships derived from a religious framework.

But during the seventeenth and eighteenth centuries the influence of religious teachings on community life faded. . . . As the Industrial Revolution drastically altered the relationship within and between communities, families and people, a new basis to explain as well as define (and perhaps to control) these relationships was sought. . . . Tracts were being written about the nature of man based on a less transcendental framework. They embodied the concept of the social contract. . . . The American and French Constitutions perhaps enthroned the tools and transformation of this thinking. They spoke of human affairs without religious reference but rather in secular terms such as justice, right, duty, franchise, liberty, contract. And as once it had been in religious teaching, so now the search for the meaning and understanding of human life was sought in the law. In America it was a sentiment well expressed in the colloquialism "there ought to be a law." And this law was a more earthly task-master. Where once we sought truth in delineating the wisdom of God, now we sought answers in deciphering the nature of man. And when we found such truth we reified it, at least in rhetoric, saying "that no man was above the law."

Religion of course did not fade away but concentrated more on matters of the inner life leaving the secular sphere to law. And flourish it did with little challenge for over a century. But two world wars including "a war to end all wars" led to the questioning of such untoward confidence. And two legal events ironically chimed its death knell—a set of trials in Nuremberg and Jerusalem where men as their defense against charges of genocide evoked without success their obedience to law and authority. In addition, in the United States at least, despite the laws, the poor still seemed poorer, the minorities still exploited, the consumer cheated, until the idea of law itself began to be questioned. The symbol of justice as blindfold was being replaced by one with its eyes slightly open and with its hand slightly extended. In America, a relatively new concept emerged, one almost "unthinkable" a couple of decades previously, the concept of a "bad law." An old tactic caught fire again—civil disobedience and with it debates arose as to the circumstances under which it was just to violate the law. Again the interpretative system of values was beginning to crumble. . . .

But again there was another group of codifiers waiting in the wings—new purveyors of both truth and authority. Medical Science was there to fill the vacuum. . . .

The Medicalizing of Society

The burgeoning influence of medicine is . . . more insidious and undramatic than the forces of religion and law. Its full exercise awaited the twentieth century. Only now is the process of "medicalization" upon us—a phenomenon which Freidson has operationalized most succinctly: "The medical profession has first claim to jurisdiction over the label of illness and *anything* to which it may be attached, irrespective of its capacity to deal with it effectively."

For illustrative purposes this "attaching" process may be categorized in four concrete ways:

1. Through the expansion of what in life is deemed relevant to the good practice of medicine.

2. Through the retention of absolute control over certain technical procedures.

3. Through the retention of near absolute access to certain "taboo" areas.

4. Through the expansion of what in medicine is deemed relevant to the good practice of life.

1. The expansion of what in life is deemed relevant to the good practice of medicine. The gradual change of medicine's commitment from a specific etiological model of disease to a multi-causal one as well as its increasing acceptance of such concepts as comprehensive medicine and psychosomatics has enormously expanded that which is or can be relevant to the understanding, treatment and even prevention of disease. Thus, it is no longer merely necessary for the patient to divulge the symptoms of his body but also the symptoms of daily living, his habits and his worries. Part of this is greatly facilitated in the "age of the computer." For what might be too embarrassing, or take too long, or be inefficient in a face-to-face encounter can now be asked and analyzed impersonally by the machine, and moreover be done before the patient ever sees the physician. With the advent of the computer, a certain guarantee of privacy is necessarily lost, for while many physicians might have probed similar issues, the only place the data was stored was in the mind of the doctor and only rarely in the medical record. The computer, on the other hand, has a retrievable, transmittable and almost inexhaustible memory.

It is not merely, however, the nature of the data needed to make more "accurate" diagnoses and treatments but the perspective which accompanies it—a perspective which pushes the physician far beyond his office and the exercise of technical skills. To rehabilitate or at least alleviate many of the ravages of chronic disease, it has become increasingly necessary to intervene to change permanently the habits of a patient's lifetime—be it of working, sleeping, playing, and eating. In Prevention, the "extension into life" goes even deeper. Since the very idea of primary prevention means getting there *before* the disease process starts, the physician must not only seek out his clientèle but once found must often convince them that they must do something *now* and perhaps at a time when the potential patient feels well or not especially troubled. The recent findings of genetics push this perspective even further. For individuals are now being confronted with making decisions, not about diseases which may occur in their own life span, but in those of their children or grandchildren.

2. Through the retention of absolute control over certain technical procedures. In particular this refers to skills which in certain jurisdictions are the very operational and legal definition of the practice of medicine—the right to do surgery and prescribe drugs. Both of these take medicine far beyond concern with ordinary organic diseases.

In surgery, this is seen in several different subspecialties. The plastic surgeon has at least participated in, if not helped perpetuate, certain aesthetic standards. What once was a practice confined to restoration has now expanded beyond the correction of certain traumatic or even congenital deformities to the creation of new physical properties from the shape of one's nose to the size of one's breast. Again and again it seems as if medicine is trying to prove Ortega y Gasset's statement that man has no nature, only a history. Thus, many of the accompaniments of formerly considered "natural processes" come under medical purview—as in aging. Now failing sight, hearing, teeth become of greater medical concern and chemical and surgical interventions to deal with wrinkles, sagging and hair loss become more common. Alterations in sexual and reproductive functioning have long been a medical concern. Yet today the frequency of hysterectomies seems not so highly correlated with the presence of organic disease, and what avenues the very possibility of sex change will open is anyone's guess. Though here too we are reminded of medicine's responsibility.

The surgical treatment of the conditions of hermaphroidism and pseudo-hermaphroidism to correct nature's mistakes, that the sexual identity and function of such persons may be established, has long been accepted as a contribution of medical science to suffering mankind.

Transplantations, despite their still relative infrequency, have had a tremendous effect on our very notions of death and dying. And at the other end of life's continuum, since abortion is still essentially a surgical procedure, it is to the physician-surgeon that society is turning (and the physician-surgeon accepting) for criteria and guidelines as to when life begins.

In the exclusive right to prescribe and thus pronounce on and regulate drugs the power of the physician is even more awesome. Forgetting for the moment our obsession with youth's "illegal" use of drugs, any observer can see, judging by sales alone, that the greatest increase in drug use of the last ten years has not been in the realm of treating any organic disease but in treating a large number of psychosocial states:

—To help us sleep or keep us awake.

—To stimulate our appetite or decrease it.

—To tone down our energy level or to increase it.

—To relieve our depression or activate our interests.

—To enhance our memory, our intelligence and our vision—spiritually or otherwise.

A former commissioner of the U.S. Food and Drug Administration went so far as to predict: "We will see new drugs, more targeted, more specific and more potent than anything we have.... And many of these would be for people we would call healthy."

3. Through the retention of near absolute access to certain "taboo" areas. These "taboo" areas refer to medicine's almost exclusive license to examine and treat, that most personal of individual possessions—the inner workings of our bodies and minds. My contention is that if anything can be shown in some way to affect the workings of the body and to a lesser extent the mind, then it can be labeled an "illness itself, or *jurisdictionally* a medical problem." The sheer statistical import of this can be seen by looking at only four such problems: aging, drug addiction, alcoholism, pregnancy. The first and last were once regarded as normal, natural processes and the middle two as human foibles and weaknesses. Now this has changed and to some extent medical specialties have emerged to meet these new needs. Numerically it expands medicine's involvement not only in a longer span of human existence but opens the possibility of its services to millions if not billions of people. In the United States, the implication of declaring alcoholism a disease (the import of a Supreme Court decision as well as laws currently under consideration in several state legislatures) would reduce arrests in many jurisdictions by ten to fifty percent and transfer such "offenders" when "discovered" directly to a medical facility. It is pregnancy, however, which produces a most illuminating illustration. For in the United States it was barely 70 years ago when virtually all births and their concomitants occurred outside the hospital as well as outside medical supervision. I do not have a precise documentary history, but with this medical claim solidified so too was medicine's claim to whole hosts of related processes: not only birth but prenatal, postnatal and pediatric care; not only conception but infertility; not only the process of reproduction but the process and problems of sexual activity itself, not only when life begins in the issue of abortion but whether it should be allowed to begin at all as in genetic counseling. The labeling of pregnancy as a disease has had still further implications in the political and social role of women and their right to control their own bodies. What has happened in this arena becomes even of greater concern when we talk about aging. For while some of us take drugs, and a few more of us drink, and half of us have the possibility of having babies, all of us age. The tone is set by Ilya Metchnikoff, a pioneer in anti-aging research:

> It is doubtless an error to consider aging a physiological phenomenon. It can be considered normal because everyone ages, but only to the extent that one might consider normal the pains of childbirth that an anesthetic might relieve; on the contrary, aging is a *chronic sickness* for which it is much more difficult to find a remedy.

Already this disease model has surfaced in the specter of heroic measures to save a life at all costs. Will it soon redefine and unwittingly make even worse what it is to be old in a society of youth?

Medicine is also increasing its involvement in another taboo area—what used to be called problems of the soul but now are located in the psyche. A recent British study reported that within a five-year period there had been a notable rise (from 25% to 41%) in the proportion of the population willing to consult the physician with a personal problem. Partly this is through the foothold that medical personnel already hold in "the taboo." For it seems as reported in many studies that access to the body opens up access to other intimate areas as well. . . .

Modern living arrangements have also contributed. For whether we look at the suburban spread or the concrete cylinders called "modern urban communities," there seems to be an absence of informal and comfortable places to gather and talk and thus a further reduction in "informal networks of help." Thus, people must of necessity turn to more formal institutions. And they do so in increasing numbers to the only one ready and waiting—medicine.

4. Through the expansion of what in medicine is deemed relevant to the good practice of life. Though in some ways the most powerful of all "the medicalizing of society" processes, the point can be simply made. Here we refer to the role of medicine directly in creating the good life or fending off the bad one.

The most far-reaching social involvement of medicine may well come in the burgeoning field of genetics and its applied arm, genetic counseling. A 1974 United States government report indicated that the list of recognized genetic disorders now includes nearly 2,000 caused by a single gene and is growing at the rate of 75–100 newly identified disorders each year. Disorders caused by multiple genes or chromosomal defects, such as Down's syndrome (mongolism) are not included, so the number of known disorders is even larger. The list also does not include conditions suspected of a genetic component nor the still largely unknown mutagenic effect of exposure to various environmental factors. From such data it is not especially surprising that a November 1974 article in the *Journal of the American Medical Association* gave the conservative estimate, based on existing studies, of chromosome defects occurring in one of every two hundred *live* births. In me this provokes the following sociological prediction: Any society that for whatever reason finds itself with a declining birth rate will inevitably be concerned with the quality of those lives that will be produced. And though this inevitably starts with a deselection process whereby we choose *not* to have children with certain genetic defects, the next step is selection to heighten certain characteristics or at least to protect the individual and the society against certain negative ones. And like it or not, the responsibility will land back in the lap of medicine and the health-related professions. . . .

The Politics of Medicalization

All this medicalization has political consequences although we do our best to deny them. There is an ever increasing use of the metaphor, health and illness, as an explanatory variable if not the explanation itself of a host of social problems. A look at the *New York Times* in a recent year yielded medical and psychiatric commentaries on such diverse phenomena as divorces, race riots, black power, juvenile delinquency, racial and religious intermarriage, the users of heroin, LSD and marijuana, college drop-outs, disrespectful children, hippies, civil rights workers, student protesters, anti-war demonstrators, medical critics, non-voters, draft resisters, and female liberationists. I do not wish to argue whether feminists and protesters have clinical maladies. My concern is what happens when a problem and its bearers become tainted with the label "illness." Any emphasis on the latter inevitably locates the source of trouble as well as the place of treatment primarily in individuals and makes the etiology of the trouble asocial and impersonal, like a virulent bacterium or a hormonal imbalance. While this may have a pragmatic basis in the handling of a specific organic ailment when a social problem is located primarily in the individual or his immediate circle, it has the additional function of blinding us to larger and discomfiting truths. As a disease it is by definition not social and at the same time the expected level of intervention is also not social. If it has to be handled anywhere or if anyone is to blame it is individuals—usually the carriers of the problem—and certainly not the rest of us, or society at large. . . .

Still another appeal of the medical model is its assumed moral neutrality. Herein, however, lies the greatest potentiality for obfuscating moral issues. Illness, in the medical perspective, assumes something painful and undesirable, and thereby something that can and should be eliminated. It is because of the latter element that great caution must be exercised in the equating of social problems or unpleasant social phenomena with illness. For a social illness, like an individual one, is by definition to be eliminated, *regardless* of the wish of the individual.

The word "regardless" is a key element. In the process of labeling a social problem an illness, there is a power imbalance of tremendous import. For illness is only to be diagnosed and treated by certain specified licensed and mandated officials—primarily doctors. In such a situation the potential patient has little right of appeal to the label-diagnosis. In fact when a patient does object to what is being done for him, the social rhetoric once again may obscure the issue, i.e., since he is sick, he does not really know what is good for him, and certainly not whether the behavior he's engaged in is "worthwhile." The treater-diagnosticians, of course, think they *do,* since there is nothing "in it" for them, the experts who made the diagnosis. The very expertise, being socially legitimated, makes this judgment seem morally neutral. It is in such reasoning that there is the greatest deception. Even granting that the illness diagnosticians and their tools may be morally neutral, something which I seriously doubt, for society to decide that any particular social problem is relevant to their province is not without moral consequences. This decision is not morally neutral precisely because in establishing its relevance as the key dimension for action, the moral issue is prevented from being squarely faced and occasionally even from being raised. By the very acceptance of a specific behavior as an illness and the definition of illness as an undesirable state the issue becomes not *whether* to deal with a particular problem but *how* and *when.* Thus, the debate over homosexuality, drugs, abortion, hyperactive children, antisocial behavior, becomes focused on the degree of sickness attached to the phenomenon in question (and its carriers) or the extent of *a* "health" risk which *is* involved. And the more principled, more perplexing, or even moral issue of *what* freedom should an individual have over his/her body, or what else, besides the individual, needs treating is shunted aside.

In Conclusion

Basically my contention is that the increasing use of illness as a lever in the understanding of social problems represents no dramatic shift from a moral view to a neutral one but merely to an alternative strategy. Thus, the shift in the handling of such social problems is primarily in those who will undertake the change (psychiatry and other medical specialties) and where the change will take place (in the individual's psyche and body). The problem being scrutinized and the person being changed is no less immoral for all the medical rhetoric. It or he is still a "problem," though the rhetoric may convince us that he and not the society is responsible, and he not the society should be changed. Even the moral imperatives remain, in the idea that if such a problem-person can be medically treated-changed, it-he *should* be.

But in addition to the basic depoliticizing effect of the labels "health and illness," there is also an exclusionary one. That the Women's Movement is making its most important inroads in the delivery of medical services is no accident. In a powerful movie called *Taking Our Bodies Back* and an extraordinary book, *Our Bodies, Ourselves,* women not only decry what power they have given up but also how biological and supposed health differences have been used to exclude them from many aspects of life. I fear that this phenomenon of "anatomy being destiny" will become even more widespread. Where once one was excluded from jobs because of race, ethnicity, gender, and age, now one will become ineligible for promotion, inappropriate for work, pushed to early retirement—all on the basis of one's physical status or health. If you do not think ours is already an exclusionary society look at the architectural barriers we have created to exclude full access and participation of our citizens from schools, restaurants, theaters, public buildings, courthouses and even private dwellings. Look at the social barriers wherein a youthful and beauty aesthetic makes us repelled by the old or people in any way deformed. Look at the communication barriers that prevent us from talking comfortably with those who are blind and deaf, gazing directly at someone who is facially disfigured, and listening for long to anyone with a speech defect.

The reasons for all this go deep. As long as the deliverers of service are markedly different in gender, economic class, and race from those to whom they offer services, as long as accessibility to medical care is a privilege rather than a right, as long as the highest income groups are health care professionals, as long as the most profit-making enterprises include the pharmaceutical and insurance industries, society is left with the uncomfortable phenomenon of a portion of its population, living, and living well, off the sufferings of others and to some extent even unwittingly having a vested interest in the continuing existence of such problems.

A web of political, economic, and even social psychological forces support this system, and only with awareness can the dismantling begin. It is for all these reasons that I am convinced that the health area is the example *par excellence* of today's identity crisis—what is or will become of the self. It is the battleground not because there are visible threats and oppressors but because they are almost invisible, not because the perspective, tools, and practitioners of medicine and the other helping professions are inherently evil, but because they are not. It is so frightening because there are elements here of the banality of evil so uncomfortably written about by Hannah Arendt. But here the danger is greater for not only is the process masked as a technical, scientific objective one but one done for our own good. In short, the road to a healthist society may well be paved with supposedly good intentions.

Rose Elizabeth Bird

A Hard Look: Cancer and Mortality

This personal account of a struggle with cancer by the Chief Justice of the California Supreme Court deals candidly with the fear and denial of death common to the threatened patient, the medical profession, and modern society at large. Overcoming a sense of hopelessness and helplessness, Bird became an active participant in her own treatment decisions. Her faith in the medical establishment was shaken when her own doctor died of cancer, and she read widely about her disease and took responsibility for improvements in diet and stress control. These remarks were delivered at the request of the doctors of Los Angeles' Brotman Memorial Hospital, which sponsored the First Annual Community Forum on Breast Cancer in May 1980.

I t is a pleasure to be with you today at this First Annual Community Forum on Breast Cancer. In inviting me to speak, Dr. Plotkin and Dr. Frileck asked that I talk about my own personal experience with cancer. That request gave me a moment of pause.

Although I have discussed the matter privately with many women who were facing the same thing, this marks the first time that I have delivered a public address on the subject. I would note that I do so as an individual—as a woman who has had cancer and a mastectomy and who also happens to be the Chief Justice of California.

As a basically private person, it is with some reticence that I undertake this "oral history." But if my remarks prove helpful to others facing this disease, then my participation will have been worthwhile. I would only ask that you hear me through. My message is essentially a positive one, though its words may at times convey the fear and pain that are part of coming to terms with having cancer.

Let me begin with some facts. My right breast was removed in 1976 using modified radical surgery techniques. It is almost impossible to put into words the shock and terror you feel when you learn you have this dreaded disease. Your emotions run the gamut from disbelief to fear to feelings of great loss.

Disbelief, because cancer is always something that happens to the next person, not to you. Fear, because everyone living in this society has been conditioned to believe that a diagnosis of cancer is equivalent to a death warrant. It is not true, but that is the popular conception. Accepting our own mortality is difficult under any circumstances. But in a society which finds euphemisms for the very word "death" and which encourages its people to pursue youth with a vengeance, it is doubly difficult. We come to the task ill-equipped, and our society does little to help prepare us.

No one in my family has ever had cancer, as far as I was able to learn. I was in my late thirties and had never in my life had a major illness of any sort. The only operation I had ever had was a tonsillectomy, which was done routinely when I was a child in the doctor's office. I simply could not and would not believe that at my age and with my health I could possibly have cancer. But it was a fact I had to face. My doctor was encouraging after my mastectomy and indicated there was little chance of reoccurrence.

I dealt with the situation by denying that possibility. I went through the operation, forced myself back to work in less than two weeks, and promptly attempted to forget all about it. I chose to deny rather than to deal with the myriad conflicting emotions that one needs to face and understand. I threw myself into my work.

Despite my efforts, it proved impossible to totally blot out what had happened. Whenever you have had a disease that may reoccur, you become very sensitized to the messages that your body sends to your mind. Whether it is a cold or a simple ache or pain, you experience the fear that this might signal a reoccurrence of some sort. And that fear brings with it the larger fear that the disease will inevitably cause your death. It is essential to face these fears and to come to terms with them for you will know no peace until you do. Fortunately, there is a very positive side to this confrontation—I learned for the first time to listen to my body and what it was saying to me. But this self-knowledge did not come quickly or easily.

After my operation I submerged myself in my work and became the picture of the traditional workaholic. I suppose I fell prey to the "macho man" complex in which I wanted to prove to myself and those around me that my illness was just a minor happenstance and did not really affect my life. However, about seven months after I became Chief Justice, I noticed a very small nodule on the muscle above where my breast was removed. It was at this juncture that I was forced to confront all the frightening possibilities that I had been unwilling to face before.

My surgeon removed the nodule in his office and told me that he would let me know the pathologist's findings. He called me a few days later during the

Los Angeles calendar of the court and told me what I had dreaded and had hoped never to hear. It was cancerous. It was a reoccurrence. He said we had to talk about what the next steps should be. He would see me that following Monday when I returned to the Bay Area.

I cannot begin to explain what a devastating blow that news was to me. However, I was in the midst of a very heavy calendar of cases and as a result had little time to ponder the situation. Besides, I did not want to worry my family or my staff so I kept the news to myself.

Upon my return that next Monday, I kept my appointment with my doctor. Unfortunately, he could not keep his with me. The nurse greeted me with tears in her eyes. She was very sorry, but my doctor would not be able to see me because he was unable to leave his home. For the first time I learned that he, too, had cancer. His was of the pancreas, and they did not expect him to live very long. He died about three weeks later, and I was never to see him again.

This shock was one that sent me reeling. How was it possible that my surgeon, who had seen me through so much, was himself a victim of cancer? How could this have happened? How could I cope; whom should I see; what should I do? If the medical establishment was unable to save my doctor, whom could they save? It was a terrifying revelation, and it made me very skeptical about whether doctors really could treat this disease and about how advanced the state of the art really was.

As a direct result of these two circumstances, I went through a type of catharsis. I began to read as much of the literature as I could. I felt I needed to know as much as the doctors did. For the first time since my mastectomy, I forced myself to face the statistics on breast cancer and the mortality rates. And for the very first time in my life, I had to seriously consider the possibility that I might have only a few years left to live.

As I observed earlier, this society does not prepare us very well for that eventuality. During most of our lives, we deny, defy, or attempt to ignore the fact of death. We place our old people in homes or hospitals beyond our line of sight so that we need not face their suffering—out of sight, out of mind, as the old saying goes. We would worship instead at the fountain of youth. We sand our skin, lift our chins, and dye our hair or replace it. We fool ourselves by creating an illusion, instead of marking proudly the milestone that each grey hair and wrinkle signify.

When you face the fact of your own mortality, you must also face the facts about what you have done with your life. In a peculiar way, death can teach you what life is all about. It is a painful lesson and a difficult journey, but I am personally grateful that I was made to travel this path at a relatively early age.

For I have learned much about myself, much about what I want out of life, and much about how precious life and people are. It is our relationships with others, especially those whom we love, that give the fullest meaning to life. I don't think I ever really knew that, emotionally or intellectually, until my second bout with cancer.

After my second operation, I set about trying to modify my behavior so that I might live a healthier, more normal life. I changed my diet to one that largely consists of fresh fruits and vegetables with little or no meat. There are some in the field who believe that stress may suppress the immune system, so I tried to deal more effectively with the stresses in my life. However, my personal experience with cancer was not at an end.

A few months after a particularly nasty and personalized political campaign in the fall of 1978, I had my second reoccurrence. As a result of my previous self-evaluation, I found myself in much better shape to handle this last blow. I suppose the greatest problem for a person suffering from a disease like cancer is the feelings of helplessness and loss of control, as well as the gnawing sense of inevitability. You hope and pray for remission, but each reoccurrence reinforces the fear that death, and a painful one at that, may be unavoidable. I believe it is important to maintain a positive frame of mind about cancer, but I would be less than honest were I to tell you that it is always possible to do so.

Thankfully, there are today many hopeful signs in the treatment of cancer. It does not mean an automatic death sentence. But it is a disease for which there is presently no complete cure. That is a reality which each person who contracts cancer must acknowledge. That fact also presents special problems for the doctors who treat cancer patients. With many other diseases, there are proven cures, tried and tested plans of treatment, courses of action that bring respite and relief. With cancer, there is only trial and error, remission and reoccurrence, expectation and frustration.

If I might be so bold, I would like to leave a few thoughts with the doctors who may be attending this Forum. Cancer is a difficult disease for the patient to deal with for some of the same reasons that it must be frustrating for the doctor. The patient must come to terms with the fear of death in a society that denies death's existence. The patient must deal with a disease that makes him or her feel helpless, since the conventional courses of treatment give the patient absolutely no role to play. All too often, the patient becomes a passive object for the interplay of surgery, radiation, and chemotherapy. The surgeon's knife, the nuclear medicine machine, and the vial of toxic chemicals become the actors in this drama, and the patient is simply written out of the script. There is perhaps no feeling more helpless than that. It's your life, but you no longer have any control over it. I think that is a principal reason why patients find cancer so very difficult to deal with.

The doctor also has a diminished role to play for he has no cure. He is no longer the traditional giver of life, the healer that he is accustomed to being. He will be challenged more often by frustrated and frightened patients. His knowledge and even his authority will be questioned, and he, too, will feel that he has lost a measure of control over his professional life.

Understandably, many doctors feel threatened by these encounters with uncertainty and react by adhering even more firmly to the conventional methods of treatment, almost as though they were articles of religious faith. This sort of intransigence on the part of many in the medical profession compounds the problem of dealing with cancer both for the patient and for the doctor. For example, many doctors refuse to consider the possibility that diet may be a factor that should be part of an overall treatment program. Or, they dismiss the idea by saying that if diet does make a difference, it was the diet you were fed as a youngster that counts. But if we know that the incidence of cancer is much higher among people living in affluent areas where the ingestion of animal protein and fat is high, what is wrong with experimenting with diet as part of a therapy program? At the very least, if patients are allowed to play some part in their treatment through regulating their diet, they feel less helpless. They become less like objects to be acted upon and more like individuals who can take responsibility along with their doctors in dealing with a disease for which neither of them has the answer.

Another area where the patient may be able to participate is the control of stress. Many degenerative diseases are considered to be stress-related since stress may play a part in suppressing our immune systems. Although it has not been scientifically shown, why not allow and encourage patients to come to terms with stress in their own environment? Why not work cooperatively with psychologists in this area? If it accomplishes nothing else, it permits patients to deal constructively with many of the emotions they experience as a result of facing a serious disease. Further, it cannot hurt anyone to review his or her life style and to try to lead a less stressful existence. Again, the patient is given an active role in what has been a very passive treatment process. Encourage your patients to try meditation, biofeedback, and other methods of coping with stress.

From my own experience, I can tell you that such things are helpful. During the two reoccurrences that I have had, I have been in the public spotlight. Anyone who has been in public life during times of societal transition can tell you that at best it amounts to cruel and unusual punishment. If you do not come to terms with the spotlight's constant focus upon you and the unrelenting criticism that comes with that public glare, it would be impossible to remain in the position.

If I had not come to terms with the possibility of my own death and my mortality, if I had not been able to accept the fact that I had cancer and to face the fears that cancer creates, I would have been devastated by many of my everyday experiences. Let me provide you with a couple of examples. About one week after my third operation was discussed in the press, one of my most vocal critics began to make public speeches about the importance of getting rid of the "cancer" at the top of the court. That, of course, was a euphemism for getting rid of me. I was surprised at the venom that such a statement revealed, but I was able to keep some perspective and even my sense of humor about it precisely because I had come to terms with my disease.

On numerous occasions, my secretary has received perhaps five phone calls a day from the press. The callers would indicate that they had been informed by some reliable source that I was seriously ill and that my death was imminent. I later learned that the systematic nature of these calls was due to the fact that the rumors were being deliberately spread to the press for political advantage. As you might imagine, it can be very disconcerting, to say the least, to be bombarded by callers asking how soon you are going to die. One might almost think that someone intended that I give the suggestion serious consideration. In fact, as recently as two weeks ago, a major California newspaper printed an article referring to rumors about my impending death and speculating on who might be my successor. If I had not already come to terms with the reality of my disease, I would not have been able to see the gallows humor in all of this. But thankfully I can observe along with Mark Twain that the reports of my death are greatly exaggerated.

If I may leave the doctors here today with one suggestion, it is this: let your patients have a role in the treatment of their disease. Don't shut them out, don't resent their questions, don't close your mind to alternatives. Remember that it is the patients' lives that are at stake here, and they should have some say about what happens. Be concerned not only about the quantity of their lives but also about the quality. Let the patients make the ultimate decisions along with you. Don't let them become pawns to be moved about at will; don't let them become helpless objects to be acted upon. Instead, let them become partners with you. Let them take some responsibility for their own lives. Their dignity as individuals and your dignity as physicians depend upon it.

For those of you who are facing this disease and for those of you who may one day face it, let me say to you what Franklin Roosevelt said at a difficult time in our nation's history: "The only thing we have to fear, is fear itself."

Have courage, face the facts, and you will find that when you have faced your fears and stood your ground there occurs a kind of liberation. It is not an easy journey. It can be quite painful and lonely. But it is a journey that must be made.

I want you to know that it is not a hopeless situation. It is neither too painful nor too fearful to face. Most importantly, it is an opportunity to find out about life. And isn't that really why each of us has been placed here?

Thank you and good luck.

Part

II The Health Care System

Part II of this book introduces us to the flesh and bones of the health care system. It is not possible to consider the broad issues raised in Part I without confronting the everyday realities in health care. Although the average patient is not able to see it, behind the physician and nurse, behind the hospital and clinic, lies a giant structure that performs an extraordinary range of services for millions of people every day.

In Chapter 4 we come to know the history of the medical system through the social and scientific forces that have shaped its character. Today, health care comprises the nation's third largest industry, and Chapter 5 focuses on the complex structure of the system itself and the various controversies that surround it. Chapter 6 explores the health care work force, which includes over seven million people and is the largest single employer of women in the country. This chapter looks back at the vanishing breed of general practitioners and measures the benefits and losses we have witnessed with the onset of specialization. Chapter 7 introduces us to the sensitive world of medical ethics—the issues that physicians, nurses, and families used to confront privately but which now are subjects for national discussion and political debate. At the core of these issues lies the question: Is medical care a right or a privilege?

4 The Shaping of Our Medical System

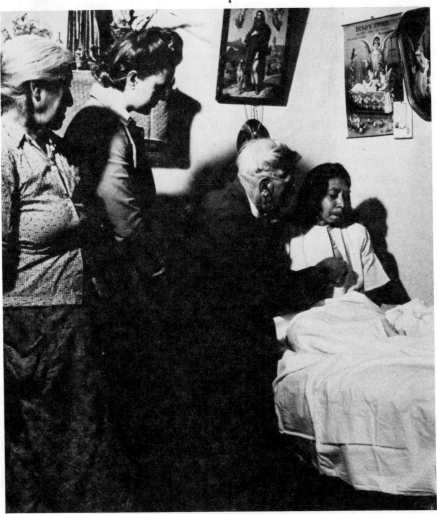

In this chapter, we shift our perspective from disease and disability, life and death, in order to look at the extraordinary social and cultural enterprise we have constructed to treat our ill, disabled, and dying citizens. As we have seen in earlier chapters, the causes for sickness and death have dramatically changed in the two hundred years since American independence; so have medical treatment, medical education, costs and methods of payment for care, the role of the government in health care, and the attitudes and values of the American people.

A look at the history of American medicine reveals the societal forces that have shaped modern medical care. We began with a system of faith and superstition subscribed to by the colonists, and we progressed to a system based on a highly developed technology, which has produced remarkable accomplishments. We can trace two major influences on the evolution of medicine: (1) the free enterprise system, with its emphasis on competition, private practice, and fee-for-service, as well as the predominance of private hospitals, drug companies, and nursing homes; and (2) the science-based, disease-oriented system of medical research and education.

The results of these forces are manifest in a complex structure involving over seven million health care workers, most of them highly specialized; 7,100 hospitals that are equipped with streamlined medical electronics systems for diagnosis and treatment; giant private health insurance companies that serve in some capacity over 80 percent of the population; and federal, state, and local governments that provide direct care for millions and finance care for the aged and the poor—to the tune of billions of dollars a year. The dramatic increase in the size and scope of health care has transformed the medical care of only fifty years ago, when physicians practiced more art than science and prospects for cure were severely limited. Increasing industrialization, urbanization, and modernization have created a host of new disease problems that have largely replaced those that responded earlier to the advances in medicine and public health. Many of these problems are as much social as they are medical, and they are deeply troubling to the entire population. The selections in Chapter 4 trace the cultural and scientific roots of these issues.

Doctors Robert B. Greifinger and Victor W. Sidel, in "American Medicine: Charity Begins at Home," shed some light on eighteenth- and nineteenth-century cultural factors that influenced the direction of modern medicine, particularly the development of active intervention to control and prevent disease. They provide an account of the growth in influence of the American Medical Association, which encouraged the emphasis on scientific medicine as well as private-enterprise medicine. The old-fashioned general practitioner who treated patients in the context of family and community was lost in an explosion of technology, and many of the ill and disabled could not afford care.

Barbara Ehrenreich, in "The Health Care Industry: A Theory of Industrial Medicine," discusses the patterns of race, class, and sex stratification in the U.S. health care system from a strong feminist point of view. The issues she raises concerning the subordination of women by modern Western medicine reflect a different social and historical perspective from the previous writers in this Reader. She also traces the origins of our current system to preindustrial society and charts its course through cultural history.

The two final articles in this chapter focus on specific issues. Medical historian Ronald L. Numbers, in "The Third Party: Health Insurance in America," details the evolution of third-party payers through the twentieth century as they waxed and waned in importance, and he keeps in balance the question of what tangible benefits we have enjoyed as a result of health insurance.

Robert B. Greifinger and Victor W. Sidel

American Medicine:
Charity Begins at Home

In an overview of the development of a medical practice peculiar to the values and social structure of the United States, Robert Greifinger and Victor Sidel, physicians at a large medical center in New York, discuss the historical forces that shaped today's health care system. Tracing the evolution of medicine in America from reliance on providential intervention or superstitious tokens to today's reliance on advanced technology and drugs, they identify the historical roots of the current separation of public from private medical practice, and of institutions caring for the ill from those promoting health.

I n discussing the forces which have shaped medical care as it is now given and received in the United States and as it reflects the historical values and present social structure of our nation, some fundamental questions must be asked. Some are common to all countries with a highly developed technology: For example, how did services for the healthy, for the purpose of protecting and promoting good health (services such as the provision of uncontaminated food and water, safe disposal of sewage, immunization against infectious disease, and education and motivation of people to lead lives which might in part prevent major killers such as degenerative diseases and accidents) become separated from services for those who are sick and injured? What are the implications of this separation in understanding our present situation, and what are its social consequences?

Other questions of concern to most industrialized societies relate to the nature of medical services developed since the Industrial Revolution and the impact of technology on the nature and distribution of these services. Since the turn of the century, people have become increasingly dependent on large, impersonal, institutional providers of medical care and have relied less on mutual aid.

Some questions are peculiar to our own country: How did it come to pass that we, alone among the world's industrialized nations, have no social insurance mechanisms to cover medical expenses for all those who are sick?

What are the consequences of this absence of insurance coverage for everyone in our society? How did it happen that we have a lower ratio of primary-care physicians to specialists than does any other nation? And what are the consequences of this emphasis on specialization—or at least on the appearance of specialization?

Before our present position and its implications for the health and the medical care of the American people can be evaluated, an outline of the history of American medical care is appropriate, intertwining the highlights of that history with the other historical forces at work in the United States.

During the seventeenth century, most of the immigrants to North America brought with them a rather static understanding of the world, one which accepted a predetermined and immutable law based on the Bible, along with the purpose of establishing a "City of God on Earth." Medical care at that time had no prospects of cure as we know it but rather a special kind of preventive approach. It was believed that a person might maintain "grace" by adhering to what Max Weber much later described as the "Protestant Ethic"; in effect, by leading a life compliant with fundamental law, replete with productive works for one's family and community, a person could have health, satisfaction, and maintenance of his covenant with God. There were, of course, many remedies for relief of pain and of some other symptoms of illness, but there were no major attempts to interfere with what was seen as God's will.

The early settlers and their several succeeding generations relied on the post-Renaissance understanding of the world as a combination of four substances—fire, air, water, and earth—and on a view of human physiology as a harmony of four humours—black bile (melancholy), green bile (what we call bile), white bile (mucus), and sanguis (blood). American native medical care was more complex, not only in its remedies but also in its methods of controlling what were seen as positive and negative forces in nature and, thereby, in the body. Both cultures, however, accepted their leaders as having spiritual powers for healing, and, in fact, there was little separation of roles in social, religious, and medical hierarchies. This similarity and the empirical observation that many native remedies seemed superior to European remedies may have been responsible for the integration of many native herbal medicines into the lives of the new Americans.

Nevertheless, a number of medical developments were imported from the Old World. As early as 1690, Cotton Mather attempted to have smallpox inoculation (immunization through the use of actual smallpox virus rather than with cowpox virus, as is done today) mandated by law in Massachusetts. This early public health measure was surrounded by tremendous controversy—again, mainly because it was seen as an interference with God's will;

it was defeated, which was probably just as well since, by modern standards, the method was unpredictable and dangerous.

Old Beliefs Questioned

By the time of the Great Awakening in the colonies, around 1740, there had been several cultural changes which allowed the development of active intervention in health matters. The view of nature was changing to a more positive one, in line with the view that "all men are created equal," have natural rights, and can realize their potential through assertion and individual achievement. People began to contract with each other for services, thereby accepting the notion that another person could aid an individual's achievement with a specialized service. Folk medicine and self-care were also extremely important. By the late eighteenth century, "patent" medicines, which could be widely publicized through the new technology of printing, were sold on a mass scale in the colonies as well as in England. Manuals for home use, including the Reverend John Wesley's *Primitive Physic,* which went through some 30 editions in England and in America, had wide public appeal.

These Old World patterns underwent major modifications when transplanted to the New World. In most of America, as indeed in much of rural England, there was no place for the guild distinctions. The few European-trained doctors who were available were often required to fulfill a wide variety of functions. Most doctors were trained by apprenticeship and practiced general forms of medicine. The small, isolated settlements on the frontier could not support fully trained doctors, and advice on health care came from itinerant peddlers of nostrums, remedies, and balsams of life. Women as well as men could play an important role as healers and had a special role in health care as midwives, since men were usually prohibited from the practice of obstetrics.

In the great seaboard cities, physicians trained in European universities began to challenge the prevalent folk medicine and the doctors who were locally trained by apprenticeship. These European doctors came in increasing numbers to develop an academic, intellectual style of medical care. A medical school on this model was started at the University of Pennsylvania in Philadelphia in 1765, and others followed in New York (1786), Boston (1782), and New Haven (1813). The great American physicians of the time became well-respected leaders, and, in fact, many were representatives in the Continental Congresses and were signers of the Declaration of Independence. Almost the only model available for medical care as the United States came into being was entrepreneurial fee-for-service medical care, and little thought was given to medical services provided by local or federal government. Neither public health nor medical care is mentioned in the Constitution, either as powers of the federal government or as powers reserved to the states or to the people. A forerunner of the U.S Public Health Service was formed in 1798, but its charter was limited solely to the care of merchant seamen in the port cities, who often had difficulty obtaining medical care from local sources.

The seventeenth century saw the introduction of medical practice in what was to become the United States; the nineteenth century brought hospitals, medical schools, and attempts at public health measures. . . . Hospitals in the United States were largely built . . . for poor incurables. People healed or died at home and, in fact, were by all accounts much safer there than in the hospital, where infections diseases ran rampant and killed many patients. Nonetheless, hospitals in Philadelphia, New York, and Boston became teaching hospitals and established the tradition of training physicians, surgeons, and nurses within the confines of an institution, outside the medical office and the home. . . . The hospital's role in curative medicine did not arise until the late nineteenth century, following the development of anesthesia, improved surgical techniques, and a better understanding of human physiology. . . .

While the hospital and the academic medical school became dominant as centers for medical education and for specialized practice in the port cities of the East Coast, farther west, the situation was different. During the early nineteenth century, there was a tremendous expansion of the land area of the United States, and with this westward expansion came movements of large groups of people from the eastern seaboard and Europe. The concept of manifest destiny was realized in a sense, along with a notion that new communities needed to be formed and that opportunities for individuals increased with communal associations. Although there was a sense that nature could be worked with for mutual gain, there was also a growing need for surgeons and, even more so, for apothecaries.

During the period before the Civil War, populism found its medical expression through the widespread practice of lay healing. Lay practitioners preferred treatment with herbs, diet, and human warmth to the more dangerous—and, at that time, not necessarily more effective—ministrations of trained doctors. Women continued to play a significant part in health care as lay practitioners. But by 1830, thirteen state governments—significantly, not the federal government—had passed medical licensing laws outlawing "irregular" practice and establishing trained doctors as the only legal healers. The battle raged in one form or another until the end of the century, when a combination of state and national medical societies, with large funding from foundations, finally drove out much "irregular" practice and with it much of the role of women in medicine.

In the developing cities of the Midwest, small medical colleges appeared, often with little or no equipment or affiliation with hospitals. Physicians were used not only for medical services but also for advice on education, sanitation, and control of infectious diseases. They came to be viewed as experts in both prevention and treatment, and, although there came to be some separation of these functions in the largest cities, most doctors did both. Almost all medical practice involved a fee or a payment in kind, such as food or clothing, for the services rendered. But many of the public preventive services were performed solely for the public good; this helped to establish a tradition of charitable medical service in the United States which was prevalent among physicians until the onset of Medicaid legislation 150 years later. As early as 1818 in Germany and 1861 in Russia, physicians were hired by governments to deliver personal medical services and were considered civil servants. Over the next century and a half, this concept spread throughout Europe, but it has never taken root in the United States.

Urban Industrial Diseases

With the Industrial Revolution of the mid-nineteenth century, great numbers of factories appeared, spawning large groups of what we now call the working poor. Mass migrations of Europeans, especially from Ireland during the early nineteenth century, filled the demand for labor in the new factories. Unable to live off their land and poorly educated, the immigrants clustered in shoddy, congested urban housing. The resulting malnutrition and crowding made these unskilled laborers prime candidates for the diseases of poverty, and infectious diseases were able to spread easily, rapidly, and widely.

Tuberculosis, rickets, and scurvy were endemic among the poor. On the other hand, epidemics of typhus, typhoid fever, yellow fever, smallpox, cholera, and syphilis affected the rich and poor alike.... These "egalitarian" diseases stimulated interest in disease control; it was recognized that prevention was possible through isolation (quarantine) and sanitation and not only through the ministrations of physicians and surgeons. Thus, the public health movement in the United States began as a reaction to the effects of poverty and has continued, in the areas of sanitation, water supply, and control of communicable diseases, quite apart from personal health services....

Another factor in the mid-nineteenth century which had an impact on the nature of both public and personal medical services was the beginning of registration of causes of death in New York and Massachusetts.... The recording and interpretation of statistics brought the alarming infant and maternal mortality rates and the deaths from diseases which were recognized as preventable to the attention of the public. But there is evidence that because of crowding, changes in sources of food, and other consequences of industrialization and urbanization, these problems actually increased during the remainder of the nineteenth century.

Disease Causes Questioned

Before the Civil War, there were great controversies about the causes of various diseases; these revolved mostly around the miasmic theory, which attributed epidemics to poisonous atmospheric or other environmental conditions, and the specific contagion theory, which postulated specific identifiable causes for each disease. In England and, later, in Germany and France, the two theories were merged, with the understanding that infectious diseases arose from a combination of environmental factors and specific contagious factors. The remarkable work of Louis Pasteur and Robert Koch in the identification of specific microbial agents capable of causing disease was interpreted in divergent ways on either side of the Atlantic. The theory prevalent in Europe stressed the interplay of many factors, while the specific agent theory prevailed in the United States. This simplistic acceptance of a single, specific cause for each disease was to prevail until well into the twentieth century in the United States and had a considerable impact on the manner in which medical care developed here.

The issue of states' rights was strong in the early nineteenth century, and state and local governments, with the specific agent theories as their major guide, began to feel a responsibility for controlling the spread of bacteria, parasites, and other microorganisms; they felt far less obligation, however, to modify the social conditions which promoted this spread of disease. The states assumed responsibility for treatment of mental disease and tuberculosis, and large public hospitals were built by the cities and the states. Public water supplies and sewage control were taken out of the realm of medical care and began to be managed by engineers. Although the boards of health which were developing in the cities during the pre–Civil War era had an interest in these issues, it was not until after the war that they were given the legal mandate to keep public water supplies clean, to monitor food for contamination, and to quarantine victims of infectious diseases. It was not until 30 years later that health standards were legally required for milk and other foodstuffs. A national board of health was started in 1875, but it was disbanded in 1882 because public health was not considered a province of the federal government.

Physicians and surgeons, who had long commanded respect and power in American society, were faced with a dilemma. Since remarkable changes in health were now available by means of environmental control, would doctors become part of the public health care establishment, or would they try to maintain their role outside government? The growing use of anesthetics such as nitrous oxide and chloroform along with a better understanding of human pathology, brought the opportunity to develop medical services which could be effectively performed on a one-to-one basis. Hospitals, already controlled by physicians, were ideal for both the teaching and the practice of medicine. As a result, the great majority of physicians and surgeons chose to remain outside government and in one-to-one practice.

As in politics, education, and industry, issues of power and control of resources became significant in the post–Civil War development of medical care. During the late nineteenth century, as many as 400 medical schools were founded in the United States; most lasted only a short time, but at least 147 medical schools were operating near the end of the century. These were privately owned institutions, and, lacking standardized graduation requirements, they produced physicians and surgeons who had inconsistent and often inadequate education.... Local medical societies were organized during the nineteenth century, and in 1847 the American Medical Association (AMA) was formed....

Rise of the AMA

The twentieth century is the era that will be identified with the explosion of science and technology in medicine and with the concomitant use of power in medical schools and research institutes.... During the first decade of the century, as the AMA was developing a strong leadership and a large following, it began to take positions on social issues.... Over a period of twenty years, the AMA had become outspoken on the subject of coordination and equitable distribution of medical services within society. Thus, at a time when power groups such as labor unions were being organized to promote the desires and rights of various segments of the populace, the AMA became the voice of the physician in American society.

At the same time, a radical change in the nature of medical education in the United States was taking place. The Carnegie Commission had authorized Abraham Flexner, a non-physician, to evaluate medical education throughout the country. In 1910, the Flexner Report disclosed many of the inadequacies in medical education and, within a few years, brought about the closing of many of the "borderline" medical schools. The public was responsive to the report's suggestions that commercialism, incompetence, and avarice should be removed from the practice of medicine and that America should create a new breed of physicians. This advice, however, also had other consequences—the concentration of medical education in the laboratory and hospital rather than in the home and the doctor's office and the concentration of control of medical education by the AMA and other professional organizations.

Science had provided a new vocabulary for the university, and the use of anesthetics had given both credibility and renewed power to practitioners of healing arts. Within a short period of time, surgery became known as a field

(To Be Tacked Inside of the Privy and NOT Torn Down.)

Sanitary Privies Are Cheaper Than Coffins

For Health's Sake let's keep this Privy CLEAN. Bad privies (and no privies at all) are our greatest cause of Disease. Clean people or families will help us keep this place clean. It should be kept as clean as the house because it spreads more diseases.

The User Must Keep It Clean Inside. Wash the Seat Occasionally

How to Keep a Safe Privy:

1. *Have the back perfectly screened against flies and animals.*
2. *Have a hinged door over the seat and keep it CLOSED when not in use.*
3. *Have a bucket beneath to catch the Excreta.*
4. *VENTILATE THE VAULT.*
5. *See that the privy is kept clean inside and out, or take the blame on yourself if some member of your family dies of Typhoid Fever.*

Some of the Diseases Spread by Filthy Privies:

Typhoid Fever, Bowel Troubles of Children, Dysenteries, Hookworms, Cholera, some Tuberculosis. The Flies that You See in the Privy Will Soon Be in the Dining Room.

Walker County Board of Health

Some of the first attempts at organized public health occurred in the early 1900s, when this handbill for privy sanitation was issued.

of curative medicine. These insights, combined with an understanding, in later decades, of specific methods of treatment such as insulin, antibiotics, cortisone, and tranquilizers, allowed the development of a power base of persons who could perform services seen as efficacious.

The emphasis on the utilization of scientific theory in medical care, especially in a society wedded to the "single agent theory" of the genesis of illness, developed into a focus on disease and symptoms rather than on therapy, prevention of disability, and caring for the "whole person." The old-fashioned family doctor had viewed patients in relation to their families and communities and had apparently been able to help people cope with problems of personal life, family, and society; the vigor with which American medicine adopted science left many of these qualities in the lurch. Science allowed the physician to deal with tissues and organs, which were much easier to comprehend than were the dynamics of human relationships, being propounded by Sigmund Freud and Carl Jung, or the complexities of disease prevention. Many physicians made efforts to integrate the various roles; however, the main thrust within society was toward academic science.

Public Medical Services

There were other changes in American society which had an impact on the nature of modern medical services. Until the turn of the century, medical care had been relatively inexpensive and accessible, even to the poor. But in the early twentieth century, medical care became more complex, expensive, and limited. At the same time, the urban poor grew in numbers as a result of immigration from Europe and migration from rural areas; the demand for health services for the poor increased. Academic medicine had a use for such people in its teaching and research activities, and in fact the poor in many cases received advanced, specialized medical care on the basis that charity cases were acceptable to physicians as a contribution to medical education.

In addition to the development of publicly supported general hospitals, local governments for the first time became involved in the delivery of specialized personal health services outside the hospital. During the first decade of the twentieth century, New York and, later, other large cities allowed their boards of health to take a special interest in maternal and child health care at the public expense. Efforts were organized around requirements for clean milk and the development of other nutritional programs for children, especially within public schools. . . . School systems around the country were increasingly required to provide medical services for children who were not otherwise receiving them, including children with remediable deficiencies such as poor vision and hearing. Thus began a new era of medical intervention in public institutions, which later developed in some instances into attempts to provide comprehensive care. . . .

What was of great importance to medical care in the social security legislation of the 1930s was the shift from local control of health and welfare issues to more centralized control. The cost of caring for children, the elderly, and, subsequently, the poor became the province of the state and federal governments. The ideas of workmen's compensation, pensions, unemployment insurance, and certain kinds of medical services came to be perceived by the people as part of their collective responsibility nationwide. A national health survey was first performed in 1935. A cooperative effort was seen as necessary for recovery from the effects of the Depression and, later, for national defense during the rapid rise of the Nazi power in Europe. The seeds were being sown for the use of health insurance and health services as part of a process of more just distribution of society's resources.

Insurance for Workers

The same period saw the rise of powerful labor unions, some of which began to demand certain forms of health insurance as part of collective bargaining with employers. In the early 1940s, the Blue Cross and Blue Shield plans were developed in each state, largely by physicians, who recognized the importance of these plans both to themselves and their patients. These forms of insurance covered many hospital and surgical costs (what we now call "catastrophic" insurance), but the costs of drugs, out-of-hospital care, and other services were excluded. Furthermore, these plans were only available to those who could pay for them—or whose employers could bear the costs. The poor continued to depend on public welfare institutions.

During World War II, major construction projects were begun in isolated areas of the western United States, where workers and their families had no access to medical services. A medical care system (which later became the Kaiser-Permanente Health Plan) was formed specifically for the care of these workers, and the costs were contracted on a yearly basis; this was the first major private prepaid group practice of medical care in the United States. The Kaiser-Permanente model has expanded and currently enrolls over three million people who pay for their medical care in advance, either individually or through their employers. (This was the model for what was named Health Maintenance Organizations during the Nixon Administration and has recently had widespread promotion, albeit little implementation.)

The introduction of hospitalization insurance and the incredible postwar explosion in medical technology led Congress to authorize federal funding of hospital construction through the Hill-Burton laws. This provided a further stimulus to make hospitals the central focus for the development of medical care. . . .

Major health legislation was not enacted, however, until the burst of social legislation which followed the assassination of Kennedy and Lyndon Johnson's assumption of the Presidency. . . . Two specific programs were enacted as amendments to the Social Security Act. One, Medicare, was an expansion of the social security system to provide coverage for the costs of health services for essentially everyone over the age of 65 and was largely federally administered. The other, Medicaid, was a form of welfare for the "medically indigent" and was designed and administered on a state-by-state basis with federal matching funds. . . .

During the 1970s, the major movement in publicly supported medical services has been toward attempting to control costs while maintaining quality. . . .

Context for Change

. . . The current status of institutions and services in the United States is largely determined by historical forces and by the current cultural, economic, political, and social context in which the institutions and services operate. Given the history of the United States and the state of its current society, it is not surprising that we have a medical care system which is highly technical, disease-oriented rather than health-oriented, largely fragmented and uncoordinated, and which uses methods of organization which often seem to be based on private gain rather than on the most effective or efficient attainment of the public good.

Since the present medical care system is a product of its own history and values, it is within this context that we must search for ways to change it. . . .

In America the passion for physical well-being . . . is general.

—Alexis de Tocqueville (1835)

Barbara Ehrenreich

The Health Care Industry: A Theory of Industrial Medicine

Just as Greifinger and Sidel found the roots of our current system of providing care in the particular history of U.S. health care, so Barbara Ehrenreich surveys medical history for the origins of the subordinate position of women in today's health work force. She analyzes the social factors that perpetuate women's subordinate roles along with the sexism and hierarchic organization in which medicine reflects the structure of U.S. society at large. An editor of Health Right *and coauthor of a book on the sexual politics of medicine, Ehrenreich originally presented this paper at the International Conference on Women in Health in Washington, D.C., in 1975.*

To say that women occupy a subordinate position within the U.S. health industry is hardly to say anything new or startling. After all, women occupy a subordinate position within U.S. industry in general. Women are clustered in low-paying service and clerical occupations and are underrepresented in top professional and managerial job categories as well as in the skilled crafts. Within any particular industry or industrial sector, one will find an occupational hierarchy grossly parallel to that in health: white males in positions of maximum authority and pay, females and nonwhite males in positions of minimum authority and pay.

But even against this background of job discrimination and segregation, the situation of women in the U.S. health industry stands out in stark relief, for two reasons. First, because the health workforce is an overwhelmingly female workforce.... Second, the women in the health workforce are, relative to the bulk of the women in the paid workforce in this country, a highly skilled and trained group.... So it does not take much feminist sensitivity to see that there is something unique about the health industry: here we have a veritable army of female workers, approximately three million, many of them highly trained and/or experienced, dominated by a tiny cadre (numbering about 400,000) of largely male physicians and administrators....

We know that this situation does not prevail in all countries and that it did not always prevail in this one. In the colonial period and the early days of the republic, women served as autonomous healers—general practitioners as well as midwives—and in some states outnumbered male healers. Ann Hutchinson, the dissident religious leader and founder of Rhode Island, was a general practitioner. Harriet Tubman, the Black leader who guided so many slaves to freedom, worked as both a nurse and a doctor.

It could be argued that there is no mystery about the situation of women in health, that it is simply a reflection of the situation of women in our society in general. There is a great deal of truth to this argument: certainly the "family" of health workers resembles nothing so clearly as the family itself, with women playing subordinate and nurturant roles, men playing dominant and instrumental roles. . . . Of course the medical system reflects the sexism prevalent in the society at large (how could it do otherwise?), but it seems also to concentrate and intensify that sexism.

I would like to argue that what we see in health is a kind of *institutional sexism* which reflects not just the sexism which prevails in U.S. society at large but the internal imperatives of the U.S. medical system. . . . As a business, U.S. medicine has evolved in the space of less than 70 years from what we could call a preindustrial phase, characterized by the dominance of the physician as an individual entrepreneur, to what we could call an industrialized phase, characterized by a growing centralization of resources in major medical institutions and complexes of institutions. I will argue that the subordination of women has been critical to the success of medicine, as a business venture, in each of these phases.

Women in the Preindustrial Stage of U.S. Medicine

Let us look first at the preindustrial stage in North American medical history. . . . The United States had had a long history as a relatively underdeveloped colony: there were few university-trained people, and, until very late in the nineteenth century, nothing that could be called a medical profession. While most European countries had had established, university-trained medical professions for centuries, the United States had only a large number of competing "healers" representing various degrees of training and diverse philosophies of healing. . . . The ancestors of today's North American medical profession were just one of the many competing healing sects—a group distinguished by its commitment to a philosophy of healing called "allopathy" and by its demographic composition, almost 100 percent white, male, and middle to upper class. It is difficult from today's vantage point to appreciate the difficulties this group, the self-styled "regular" doctors, faced in the nineteenth century. Not only was there severe competition from other varieties of healers, there was competition within the swollen ranks of the regulars themselves. As a result, the average regular practitioner enjoyed no greater income than an ordinary mechanic of the time.

. . . A great deal, perhaps a majority, of the competition which had to be eliminated was coming from *women:* women lay healers and midwives, women trained in competing medical sects (which, unlike the regulars, had always welcomed females), and, increasingly in the late nineteenth century, women seeking to enter the "regular" medical schools. The point is that the struggle to establish the medical profession as an occupational monopoly and the struggle to oust women from healing roles were, in this country, completely intertwined. . . .

Of course women were not in fact ousted from healing roles. At the same time that the emerging medical profession was erecting barriers to the entrance of women, Blacks, and working-class people and campaigning for the abolition of midwifery, a new health occupation was taking form—trained nursing. In the late nineteenth century doctors were increasingly being trained in hospitals. Hospitals needed to be kept clean and orderly; patients needed to be cleaned and fed. Women, at first upper-class women who were outraged by the filthy conditions in American hospitals, stepped in to do the job, and stayed to train large numbers of less affluent women as permanent nurses. The fledgling nursing profession was made to feel that it was only allowed in on the sufferance of the doctors, and then only at the price of almost slavish obedience. Even so the doctors felt threatened by their female co-workers. The *Journal of the American Medical Association* reported in 1901 that many doctors found the nurse "often conceited and too unconscious of the due subordination she owes to the medical profession, of which she is a sort of useful parasite."

The formation of the medical profession and that of the nursing profession were, in this country, complementary processes. Where there had once been a single generalized "healer" who combined both nurturance and technique, there were now two distinct occupations: one concerned with "caring" and maintenance functions, the other concerned with "curing" and technical functions; one female, the other male. This was a division of labor with immediate economic ramifications: the skills which the physicians appropriated for themselves were those which involved the visible use of technology and science (surgery, the prescribing of medications, etc.) and which could thus be most profitably marketed as commodities. The residue of skills left to the nursing occupation were those with a very low market value, on a par, at the time, with the services of untrained domestic servants. Thus, in a society in which health care was (and remains) a commodity, and where human labor is also a commodity, the price of which determines the social "worth" of an individual, the medical division of labor automatically set women in a situation of vastly inferior status.

Social Forces in the Reproduction of Sex Stratification

The basic pattern of sex stratification was established in this country by about the turn of the century, in what I have called the preindustrial phase of the medical system. Now I would like to take a quick look at some of the social forces which helped to reproduce this pattern until well into the middle of the twentieth century.

First... is the fact that, throughout the twentieth century organized medicine has consciously and effectively sought to limit entry to the medical profession by controlling medical school entrance standards and by lobbying against federal expenditures for medical education. This policy has affected not only women but all potential aspirants to medical careers and has served, until quite recently, to limit medical education to white males of upper-middle-class family background.

Second... is the persistent hegemony of sexist ideology, i.e., the ideology that the social division of labor is determined by innate psychological differences between the sexes. Women are more motherly, therefore they should take care of children and sick people; women are good at repetitive work, therefore they should fill the least skilled assembly line jobs; women are indecisive and emotional, therefore they should not be political leaders, airplane pilots, or surgeons; and so on.

. . . The medical profession itself has played a significant role in promoting and reinforcing sexist ideology. For example, we find in an 1848 textbook on obstetrics: "She [woman] has a head almost too small for intellect but just big enough for love." For example, in 1877, Dr. Edward Clarke of Harvard Medical College published an influential book in which he proved conclusively that higher education would cause a woman's uterus to atrophy. Moving ahead to the present, we find in a 1971 textbook on gynecology and obstetrics, the following statement: "The traits that compose the core of the female personality are feminine narcissism, masochism, and passivity." Or then there was the time only four years ago when Dr. Edgar Berman, a former surgeon and adviser to Senator Hubert Humphrey, declared to the press that women are unfit for positions of responsibility because of their monthly "raging hormonal imbalances.". . .

What these doctors are saying, each in his own way, boils down to one thing: women cannot be doctors. . . . In the mouth of physicians, bigotry, superstition, and prejudice are all transformed into "scientific fact." Thus the physicians have been in the enviable position of being able to publicly "prove" that their dominance in the health workforce is only "natural.". . .

Women in the Industrial Stage of U.S. Medicine

... The industrialization of medicine began in the 1930s and accelerated rapidly after World War II. It is a transformation which has been characterized by: (1) the growing institutionalization of the health-care delivery system, with hospitals and clinics replacing the solo practitioner's office as major centers of health-care resources; and (2) a trend toward the centralization of power over local institutions in the hands of a small number of major medical centers. Thus the health industry has been, in a sense, catching up with the other sectors of U.S. industry: health care is no longer a "cottage industry" dominated by individual practitioners. The important unit of the delivery system, the major medical center with its network of affiliated facilities, has come more and more to resemble a typical capitalist business enterprise. Though it is usually a legally "nonprofit" enterprise, it does seek to generate a financial surplus which can then be invested in further institutional expansion or in extremely high payments to its top functionaries, the administrators and fully trained physicians. ...

Nurses were hastily drawn into institutional employment during the depression when the market for home nursing dried up. Today, three-quarters of the nation's active nurses are employees of hospitals. Even female physicians are more likely than their male counterparts to work in hospital or group settings, in part due to the difficulties women often encounter in setting up their own private practices. For so many of the female job categories—the aides, kitchen workers, specialized therapists and technicians, etc.—there has never been a choice: these jobs exist only in the hospital setting.

So in order to understand the subordinate position of women in health today we must look... at the organization and nature of hospital work. Today, in the industrial phase of medicine, many features of the organization of hospital work are analogous to what one would expect to find in any sector of modern industry.

First, there is an elaborate division of labor. For example, one New York hospital lists 42 pay categories of service and maintenance workers, 35 types of clerical workers, and 38 types of technical and professional personnel. And many of these are still further subdivided into narrow subspecialties. Contrast this to the situation at the turn of the century, when only three categories of workers could be found in hospitals: physicians, trained nurses, and untrained housekeeping aides. What has happened in health is much the same thing that has happened in other industries in the past 50 to 70 years: a progressive replacement of the more costly labor of a multifunctional employee by the less costly labor of a less-skilled employee. For example, many of the original functions of the professional nurse have now been dispersed among a host of more poorly paid employees: ward clerks, practical nurses, diet aides, operating room technicians, nurses aides, and orderlies, etc. Similarly, many functions which were formerly physicians' have been spun off to cheaper labor: X-ray technicians, clinical laboratory technicians, inhalation therapists.

We should note right away that there has been a definite sexual asymmetry to the process by which labor has been subdivided in hospital work. Professional nursing, stripped of many of its original functions, has been left in an ambiguous and uncomfortable position—threatened from below by the functionally overlapping but cheaper practical nurses, but barred from moving up without a drastic redefinition of nursing education. For physicians, however, the situation has been totally different. Physicians have spun off fragments of technology as these became routinized (e.g., taking X-rays), but they have also appropriated for themselves each new high-technology function as it has come along (e.g., cardiac catheterization). . . . Finally, as cheap labor replaces more costly labor in the health industry, that cheap labor is likely to be female for the simple reason that female labor is universally cheaper than male labor in U.S. industry.

Another feature of hospital work which finds its parallel in all other industries is the concentration of planning and intellectual work in a group which represents a decreasing proportion of the total workforce. In 1900, for example, physicians alone accounted for 52 percent of the health workforce; in 1970, physicians and administrators together comprised only 12 percent of the total. Yet there has been no dispersion of their power to the growing army of lower-level workers. Physicians and administrators (with variable amounts of input from trustees) make decisions about overall institutional priorities, about the deployment of revenues and capital, about the types of care which will be offered. The physician himself has, as he has spun off functions, come more and more to play the role of an executive or manager: his orders (for injections, medications, lab tests, etc.) determine the work of scores of other workers who are not expected to grasp the intellectual rationale for the tasks they are asked to perform, but only to perform them reliably and repetitively.

These two features of modern hospital work—the minute division of labor and the concentration of the intellectual control of the work in a diminishing proportion of the workforce—are almost universal features of work processes, at least in countries which have followed Western patterns of industrialization. As Harry Braverman has demonstrated in his seminal study of labor in U.S. society, neither of these features of the work process is a natural or automatic result of advanced technology. Rather, they are the result of the conscious efforts of management to gain control over the work process, given the fundamental class antagonism between workers and employers in capitalist society. In many industries this "rationalization" of the work process has gone much further—to the point where the labor of the individual workers is reduced to a single repeated motion or set of motions, and *all* intellectual control of the work process is vested in a tiny elite of engineers and managers. In fact, by comparison to other industries, the [rationalization of the] work process in health is far from complete: it has been impossible to fully concentrate control of the work process in the hospital's executives (physicians and administrators). And, I will argue, it is for this reason that the subordination of women in the hospital workforce—*as women*—persists and flourishes in the modern health workplace.

Let me give just a few reasons why the rationalization of the work process in health is necessarily incomplete, at least in those areas directly involved with patient care. First, the work is inherently unpredictable: patients do not always have coronaries or babies on time or in the presence of the appropriate category of health worker. This means that whatever division of labor exists on paper in the personnel manager's office is always vulnerable to the exigencies of the actual work: practical nurses very often end up doing what registered nurses do; registered nurses very often end up performing tasks legally reserved for physicians; and so on. Second, the nature of the "material" (human beings) means that lengthy prior study is never a guarantee of on-the-job omniscience. The physician may know all about the ionic composition of the patient's blood, but the aide—who does the actual bedside care in most hospitals—may possess equally vital information about whether the patient has eaten that day, or has become depressed, etc. All knowledge relevant to the work process cannot be concentrated in any one functionary, unless that functionary is willing to do almost *all* of the work. Finally, hospital workers are in general highly motivated and committed to their work—at least compared to workers in the many U.S. industries which make useless or destructive products. Most patient-care workers have their own understandings of what good patient care is, and many will try to achieve their standards even at the risk of being disciplined for "insubordination."

So health work can never be fully rationalized along the lines developed in other industries. So long as the material is human beings and not, say, automobile frames moving along on a conveyor belt, it will be impossible to reduce the work to assembly line procedures, and it will be impossible to fully separate manual from intellectual effort. What this means is that in the health industry there is a real problem of the legitimization of authority.... It is ultimately not only interpersonal authority which is at stake but the power to allocate money, to determine institutional priorities, and to dictate the conditions of work.

And with this we return to the situation of women in the health workforce today, for I contend that the "solution" to this problem of authority has lain in the sex—and race—stratification of the health workforce. Sex and race stratification make the authority structure seem natural, even though it is not justified by the nature of the work and may, in fact, often be counterproductive to good patient care. When a doctor speaks to a female underling, he is not simply one highly trained functionary speaking to another, less highly trained co-worker; he is a *man* speaking to a *woman*. His authority, then, does not need legitimization through superior knowledge, experience, or commitment to service on his part; it is built into the relationship. . . . Sex and race stratification play a legitimizing role throughout the occupational spectrum, as sociologist Carol Brown writes.

> Much of the "natural" behaviors between occupations turn out to be based on the sex of the incumbent rather than the status of the occupation. Male doctors do not treat male subordinates the same way they treat female subordinates . . . Studies of female doctors show that they often try to identify with their occupational authority and are perceived as "arrogant" in trying to get the same assistance from nurses and other women subordinates that the men get automatically. . . . Similar problems arise with a woman chief technician running a partly male department, or a black therapist with white therapy aides. Male orderlies often resent orders given by female nurses. The behavior patterns seen in hospitals between women and men of different occupations are very much sex-status patterns, just as the interpersonal relations between blacks and whites of different occupations are racial relations.

To summarize, I have tried to account for the subordination of women in the U.S. health industry by looking first for its origins in the preindustrial phase of medicine, then at some of the social factors which helped to perpetuate the original sexual division of labor and power, and finally, by looking at the stabilizing role of sex stratification in the contemporary, industrialized health industry. A philosophical observation may be in order here: from a distance, the ancient theme of male supremacy and female subordination, which runs through almost all human cultures in one form or another, seems to be as unremarkable and removed from history as the actual physical difference between the sexes. But as we look closer, as I have tried to do in the particular case of health, we find that male supremacy is not just part of the monotonous biological background against which human history is enacted; it takes different forms and plays different roles in different historical circumstances. In the nineteenth century, the ideology of male supremacy served as an important weapon in the male "regular" physicians' struggle against competing kinds of healers. Today the situation is entirely different: the physicians and administrators, who are essentially co-managers of the health workplace, are sitting atop an ever broader and higher pyramid of so-called ancillary personnel who are almost entirely female. In this situation, the ancient theme of male supremacy serves a new purpose: it helps to buttress the pyramid and make it seem as if this were the only natural way to organize health work.

But things are already changing so fast that I hesitate to put anything in the present tense. Largely due to pressure from the women's liberation movement, medical schools have been admitting more and more women in the last few years. And, in part because of the rising feminist consciousness in this country, women health workers have been showing more and more militancy around their own needs and around patient-care issues. Nurses as well as other health workers are showing an increasing readiness to organize themselves as workers and, when necessary, to strike or take other job actions to win their demands. With the growing numbers of women in medicine and with growing militancy among all women in health, sex differences will cease to be the automatic rationale for occupational stratification, and sex *deference* will cease to be a palliative for class antagonism.

In fact, we may be entering a stage where women health workers find that the greatest barrier to change is not so much sexism as it is the hierarchical divisions among women workers themselves. The principle which has led to these divisions—that of replacing costly labor with cheap labor—automatically engenders deep resentments and anxieties. It can lead to a sterile professionalism which uses the banner of feminism to advance the status of a particular occupational group, with little or no regard for sister workers in other job categories. But, I think, and here I may be overly optimistic, that there is a growing consciousness of this danger among women in health today—a realization that it is not only the distribution of women within the hierarchy which must be changed but the hierarchy itself. A realization that it is not only the role of women in the division of labor which is wrong but the division of labor itself.

. . . Can we hope to make the changes we would like to make in the health sector without making much more profound changes in our society? Can we hope for a health-care system that is both egalitarian and effective within the context of a social system which is based on class, race, and sex inequities? And if not, if more broad and revolutionary changes are required, then we must ask ourselves: Where do we start?

Ronald L. Numbers

The Third Party: Health Insurance in America

Contemporary headlines reporting congressional debates on national health insurance plans seldom suggest the long history behind the concept of assured prepaid medical care. Health insurance legislation has been under considera- tion since 1916, when it was briefly supported by the American Medical Associ- ation (AMA), the official voice of physicians. In the following article, Ronald Numbers, historian of medicine at the University of Wisconsin, outlines how the AMA has since come full circle, through decades of opposition, to a stance of limited support for the concept of national health insurance.

> No third party must be permitted to come between the patient and his physician in any medical matter.
> *American Medical Association, 1934*

American medicine in the 19th century was essentially a two-party sys- tem: patients and physicians. Medical practice was relatively simple, and doctors—out of economic necessity more than to preserve an intimate physician-patient relationship—personally collected their bills. Most practi- tioners billed their patients annually or semi-annually, although those with office practices usually insisted on immediate payment. They were not, how- ever, always free to charge what they pleased. In many communities local medical societies established schedules of minimum fees and instructed mem- bers never to undercut their colleagues. There was little objection to provid- ing free care for the poor—or to overcharging the wealthy—but generally the American medical profession preferred fixed fees to the so-called "sliding scale." When hospitals began to mushroom late in the century, they, too, charged patients directly according to fixed prices.

But even in the 19th century a small, but undetermined, number of Ameri- cans carried some insurance against sickness through an employer, fraternal order, trade union, or commercial insurance company. Most of these early plans, however, were designed primarily to provide income protection, with perhaps a fixed cash benefit for medical expenses; few provided medical care, and those that did, like the plans sponsored by remotely located lumber and mining companies, generally contracted with physicians at the lowest possible prices. This type of "contract" practice restricted the patient's choice of physician, allegedly commercialized the practice of medicine, sometimes resulted in shoddy medical care—and always elicited the opposition of organized medicine. During the latter half of the century the American Medical Association (AMA) repeatedly condemned arrangements that provided unlimited medical service for a fixed yearly sum and urged the profession to maintain "the old relations of perfect freedom between physicians and patients, with separate compensation for each separate service."

Widespread interest in health insurance did not develop in the United States until the 1910s, and then the issue was compulsory, not voluntary, health insurance. . . . Inspired by developments abroad and the spirit of Progressive reform at home, the American Association for Labor Legislation in 1912 created a Committee on Social Insurance to prepare a model bill for introduction in state legislatures. By the fall of 1915 this committee had completed a tentative draft and was laying plans for an extensive legislative campaign. Its bill required the participation of virtually all manual laborers earning $100 a month or less, provided both income protection and complete medical care, and divided the payment of premiums among the state, the employer, and the employee.

The medical profession's initial response to this proposal bordered on enthusiasm. . . . The *Journal of the American Medical Association* hailed the appearance of the model bill as "the inauguration of a great movement which ought to result in an improvement in the health of the industrial population and improve the conditions for medical service among the wage earners.". . .

Physician support at the state level was similarly strong. . . . Reasons for favoring health insurance varied from physician to physician. According to the *Journal of the American Medical Association,* the most convincing argument was "the failure of many persons in this country at present to receive medical care"; but the average practitioner, who earned less than $2,000 a year, was probably more impressed by the prospect of a fixed income and no outstanding bills. Besides, the coming of health insurance appeared inevitable, and most doctors preferred cooperating to fighting. . . .

By early 1917, however, medical opinion was beginning to shift, especially in New York, where the AALL was concentrating its efforts. One after another of the county medical societies voted against compulsory health insurance, until finally the council of the state society rescinded its earlier endorsement. Both friends and foes of the proposed legislation agreed on one point: the medical profession's chief objection was monetary in nature. . . .

The medical profession was, of course, not alone in opposing compulsory health insurance. Commercial insurance companies, which would have been excluded from any participation, were especially critical; and some labor leaders, like Samuel Gompers, preferred higher wages to paternalistic social legislation.

America's entry into World War I in April 1917 not only interrupted the campaign for compulsory health insurance, but touched off an epidemic of anti-German hysteria. . . . As the war progressed, Americans in increasing numbers began referring to compulsory health insurance as an "un-American" device that would lead to the "Prussianization of America."

. . . This repudiation of compulsory health insurance was not, as one writer has suggested, the result of "an abdication of responsibility by the scientific and academic leaders of American medicine." Nor was it primarily the product of a rank-and-file takeover by conservative physicians disgruntled with liberal leaders. The doctors who rejected health insurance in 1920 were by and large the same ones who had welcomed—or at least accepted—it only four years earlier. . . .

Many factors no doubt contributed to such changes of heart. Opportunism undoubtedly motivated some, and the political climate surely affected the attitudes of others. But more important, it seems, was the growing conviction that compulsory health insurance would lower the incomes of physicians rather than raise them, as many practitioners had earlier believed. With each legislative defeat of the model bill, the coming of compulsory health insurance seemed less and less inevitable, and the self-confidence of the profession grew correspondingly. "This Health Insurance agitation has been good for us," concluded one prominent New York physician as the debate drew to a close. "If it goes no farther it will have brought us more firmly together than any other thing which has ever come to us.". . .

In 1925 the New York State Medical Society reported that health insurance "is a dead issue in the United States. . . . It is not conceivable that any serious effort will again be made to subsidize medicine as the hand-maiden of the public." The victorious New York physicians had every reason to be confident, but they failed to reckon with economic disaster. The Great Depression invalidated many assumptions about American society and threatened the financial security of both hospitals and physicians. . . . The net income of physicians during the first year of the Depression dropped 17 percent, with general practitioners suffering the biggest losses. In some regions, particularly the cotton-growing states, collections from patients fell 50 percent, and the situation grew worse as the Depression continued.

In response to this disaster, several hospitals began experimenting with insurance. By 1937, when the American Hospital Association began approving such programs, there were 26 in operation with 608,365 participating members. The motives behind these early endeavors are difficult to determine. In two recent studies of Blue Cross, for example, Odin W. Anderson stresses the altruistic spirit of the pioneers, while Sylvia Law emphasizes their economic interests. There is, as one might expect, some evidence for both interpretations. Voluntary hospital insurance, said Michael M. Davis in 1931, has "the double aim of furnishing a new and broader base of support for hospitals and of helping small income people to meet their big sickness bills." Economic concerns are, however, easier to document than altruism. It is significant that although financially disinterested civic organizations occasionally contributed funds to establish hospital insurance programs, "in most cases the initiative and main drive for the starting of the various plans came from the hospitals of the community—from hospital administrators and trustees." In his 1932 survey of prepayment plans Pierce Williams concluded that hospitals had promoted insurance primarily "to put their finances on a sound basis."

Physician reaction to these early experiments in hospital insurance was mixed. Those affected the most seemed pleased. . . . The AMA, however, was openly antagonistic, characterizing prepayment plans "as being economically unsound, unethical and inimical to the public interests.". . . The AMA's solution to the problem of financing health care was "to save for sickness."

Despite these negative pronouncements, health insurance continued to grow. . . . In 1934, President Franklin D. Roosevelt appointed a Committee on Economic Security to draft legislation for a social security program, which, everyone assumed, would include health insurance. Pressure from organized medicine, however, forced the President to drop health care from the bill he sent to Congress in 1935. Undaunted, progressive members of his administration continued to agitate for compulsory health insurance and in 1938 held a National Health Conference in Washington. This event aroused great popular interest in a government-sponsored health program, resulting the next year in Senator Robert F. Wagner's introduction of a bill to provide medical assistance for the poor, primarily through federal grants to the states.

In view of these developments, the AMA reversed its position on voluntary health insurance, hoping that such action would quiet demands for a compulsory system. In 1937 the House of Delegates approved group hospitalization plans that confined "their benefits strictly to the facilities ordinarily provided by hospitals; viz., hospital room, bed, board, nursing, routine drugs." A short time later the association began taking credit for promoting the growth of hospitalization insurance, which it had so bitterly opposed only a few years before.

At the same time it was giving its blessing to hospitalization insurance, the AMA was working out a physician-controlled plan to provide medical care insurance. In 1934 the House of Delegates took a tentative step in that direction by agreeing on ten principles to govern "the conduct of any social experiments." These included complete physician control of medical services, free choice of physician, the inclusion of all qualified practitioners, and the exclusion of persons living above the "comfort level." The delegates stopped short of endorsing health insurance and made a point of emphasizing the traditional view that medical costs "should be borne by the patient if able to pay at the time the service is rendered."

In February 1935, shortly after the Committee on Economic Security reported to the President, the House of Delegates met in special session—the first since World War I—to reaffirm its opposition to "all forms of compulsory sickness insurance." Recognizing the need to offer an alternative to government-sponsored insurance, the delegates encouraged "local medical organizations to establish plans for the provision of adequate medical service for all of the people . . . by voluntary budgeting to meet the costs of illness." The language was vague, but the intention was clearly to foster the creation of society-controlled medical insurance plans.

In the aftermath of the National Health Conference of 1938 the AMA called a second special session on insurance. This time the House of Delegates approved the development of "cash indemnity insurance plans" for low-income groups, controlled by local medical societies. By offering cash benefits instead of service benefits, physicians hoped to retain their freedom to charge fees higher than the insurance benefits whenever it seemed appropriate. In 1942, to meet competition from commercial insurance companies, the AMA took the final step of approving medical service plans.

. . . [In 1946] when the AMA created Associated Medical Care Plans, the precursor of Blue Shield, there were 43 medical society plans with a combined enrollment of three million members. In most places coverage was limited to low-income families, who would otherwise have been among the least able to pay physicians' fees.

The threat of "socialized medicine" was no doubt the most compelling reason why organized medicine decided to embrace health insurance. As the demand for compulsory health insurance grew, more and more physicians came to see voluntary plans as their "only telling answer to federalization and regimentation." . . .

But fear of compulsory health insurance was not the only reason why the medical profession changed its mind. By the late 1930s many physicians were also discerning potential benefits in health insurance. A 1938 Gallup poll showed that nearly three-fourths of American doctors favored voluntary medical insurance, and over half were confident that it would increase their incomes. Health insurance, predicted one Milwaukee physician, "would do away with the uncollectible accounts.... It would offer to the physician an opportunity of earning a living commensurate with the value of the service that he performs." Furthermore, by paying for expensive services like x-rays and laboratory tests, it would enable doctors to practice a better quality of medicine....

Despite a genuine concern for the welfare of their patients, doctors did not embrace health insurance primarily to assist the public in obtaining better medical care. In fact, throughout the 1930s spokesmen for organized medicine repeatedly denied that health care in America was inadequate and attributed the good health of Americans to "the present system of medical practice," that is, to the traditional two-party system....

Proudly displaying the medical profession's stamp of approval, health insurance entered a period of unprecedented growth. By 1952 over half of all Americans had purchased some health insurance, and prepayment plans were being described as "the medical success story of the past 15 years." Behind this growth was consumer demand, especially from labor unions, which after the war began bargaining for health insurance to meet rapidly rising medical costs that were making the prospect of sickness the "principal worry" of industrial workers. Following a 1948 Supreme Court ruling that health insurance benefits could be included in collective bargaining, "the engine of the voluntary health insurance movement," to use Raymond Munts's metaphor, moved out under a full head of steam. Within a period of three months the steel industry alone had signed 236 contracts for group health insurance, and auto workers were not far behind.

Growth statistics, however, do not tell the whole story. Although most Americans did have some health insurance by mid-century, coverage remained spotty. In 1952 insurance benefits paid only 15 percent of all private expenditures for health care (see Figure 1). Besides, the persons most likely to be insured were employed workers living in urban, industrial areas, while the unemployed, the poor, the rural, the aged, and the chronically ill—those who needed it the most—went uninsured.

With voluntary plans failing to protect so many Americans, the perennial debate over compulsory health insurance flared up again.... To head off passage of such legislation, the AMA in 1946 began backing a substitute bill, sponsored by Senator Robert A. Taft, which authorized federal grants to the states to subsidize private health insurance for the indigent.

The basic problem, as the Association's spokesman Morris Fishbein defined it, was one of "public relations." The medical profession had "to convince the American people that a voluntary sickness insurance system ... is better for

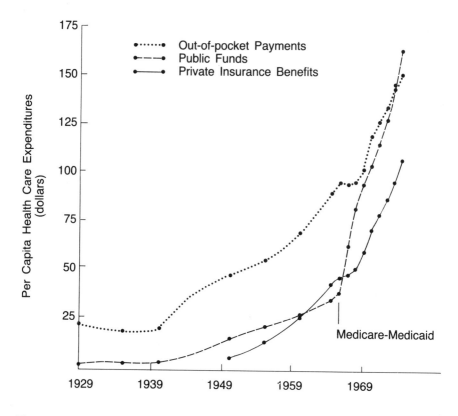

Figure 1: Sources of health-care expenditures in the United States. Source: Nancy L. Worthington, "National health expenditures," 1929–74," *Social Security Bulletin,* February 1975, 38:16.

the American people than a federally controlled compulsory sickness insurance system." Actually, most Americans needed little convincing. . . .

Truman's surprise victory in 1948, at the close of a campaign that featured health insurance as a major issue, convinced the AMA that it was time to declare all-out war. . . . The showdown came in 1950 when organized medicine won a stunning victory in the off-year elections, forcing many candidates to renounce their earlier support of compulsory health insurance and defeating "nearly 90 percent" of those who refused to back down.

Throughout this controversy representatives of organized medicine insisted that the country did not need compulsory health insurance, just as they had insisted in the early 1930s that voluntary insurance was unnecessary. "There is no health emergency in this country," said a complacent AMA president in 1952. . . .

What Americans needed, said the doctors, was more voluntary insurance, which had worked out so well that most physicians by the early 1950s no longer thought coverage should be restricted to low-income groups. The financial and political benefits of health insurance were so great, the medical profession jealously protected it. . . .

The election of a Republican administration in 1952 effectively ended the debate over compulsory health insurance, and organized medicine breathed a sigh of relief. . . . Encouraged by their physicians and by the constantly rising costs of medical care, an increasing number of Americans purchased health insurance, until by the early 1960s nearly three-fourths of all American families had some coverage. Still, this paid for only 27 percent of their medical bills, and many citizens, especially the poor and elderly, had no protection at all.

This problem led Representative Aime Forand in the late 1960s to reopen the debate over compulsory health insurance with a proposal limiting coverage to social security beneficiaries. In 1960 Senator John F. Kennedy introduced a similar measure in the Senate. To organized medicine, even such restricted coverage amounted to "creeping socialism," and the AMA would have none of it. The association's "strongest objection" continued to be that "it is unnecessary and would lower the quality of care rendered," the same argument it had been using since the 1910s. Its only concession was to approve a government plan providing assistance to "the indigent or near indigent," which would benefit physicians as much as the poor. Thus in 1960 Congress, with AMA approval, passed the Kerr-Mills amendment to the Social Security Act, granting federal assistance to the states to meet the health needs of the indigent and the elderly who qualified as "medically indigent."

If the medical profession hoped to forestall the coming of compulsory health insurance by this small compromise, Senator Kennedy's election to the presidency that fall soon convinced them otherwise. Upon occupying the White House, he immediately began laying plans to extend health insurance protection to all persons on social security, whether "medically indigent" or not. The AMA denounced his plans as a "cruel hoax" that would disrupt the doctor-patient relationship, interfere with the free choice of physician, impose centralized control, and—worst of all—undermine the financial incentive to practice medicine. They would not only endanger the quality of medical care, but would discourage the best young people from entering the field. Despite these ominous predictions, Congress in 1965 voted to include health insurance as a social security benefit (Medicare) and to provide for the indigent through grants to the states (Medicaid). Thus, after 50 years of debate, compulsory health insurance finally came to America.

In 1967, just two years after the passage of Medicare, third parties for the first time paid more than half of the nation's medical bills. Many Americans continued to be without health insurance, but seldom by choice. Although critics frequently attacked the insurance business, no one advocated a return to the two-party system. In the opinion of one observer, the acceptance of health insurance was a phenomenon "without parallel in contemporary American life." Prepayment plans benefitted both providers and consumers of medical care, but especially the providers. . . .

Compared with the relatively tangible benefits of health insurance for hospitals and physicians, those to patients are more difficult to calculate. Prepayment plans undeniably gave Americans greater access to medical care than ever before, eased the financial strain of paying medical bills, and brought peace of mind to millions of policyholders. A grateful public showed its appreciation by buying increasingly comprehensive coverage. But it is not certain that they enjoyed better health for it. On the one hand, there are studies showing that "those who were eligible for Medicaid were likely to have better health than similar groups who were not." But other studies indicate that although Medicare apparently encouraged more expensive types of treatment, like surgery rather than radiation for breast cancer, recovery rates remained roughly the same.

Under health insurance from 1941 to 1970, life expectancy at birth in America did increase from 64.8 years to 70.9 years. But again it is hard to determine how much—if any—of this should be credited to improved medical care, much less to the way in which it was financed. By the early 1970s even organized medicine was downplaying the ability of the medical profession to prolong life and preserve health. As Max H. Parrott of the AMA testified in 1971, choice of life-style had become as important as medical care in determining the nation's health: "No matter how drastic a change is made in our medical care system, no matter how massive a program of national health insurance is undertaken, no matter what sort of system evolves, many of the really significant, underlying causes of ill health will remain largely unaffected." In a society in which heart disease, cancer, accidents, and cirrhosis of the liver all ranked among the top ten killers, it was indeed unrealistic to expect health insurance to cure the nation's ills.

5 The Organization of Health Care

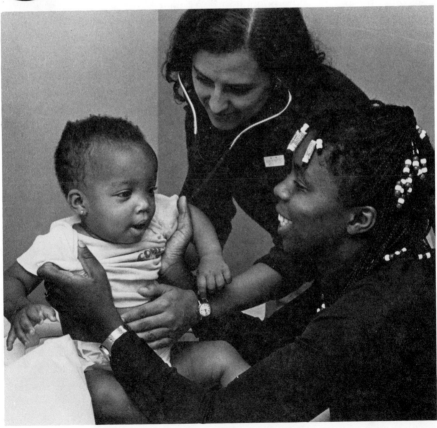

MARK TUSCHMAN

In the preceding chapter we considered the various societal forces in the past that have shaped present-day medicine. This chapter will focus on the vast array of facilities and services that serve the nation today. A fundamental question springs up immediately: How does the U.S. health care system meet the needs of the population? We have evolved a disease-oriented, private enterprise, high-technology, specialized system, which is in the throes of spiraling inflation. While expressing satisfaction about their own personal care, most Americans readily admit to dissatisfaction with the system.

The statistics of its use tell some of the story. Americans average four physician visits a year, and 14 percent of the population is hospitalized each year, amounting to more than 230 million days of hospital care for over 29 million people. These figures suggest the magnitude of the health care industry.

Size itself is a problem. All aspects of the health arena have experienced astronomical growth in the last ten years. The health labor force has more than doubled; at the same time, it has expanded horizontally into hundreds of professions, whose services conform to the emphasis on specialization and high technology. Hospitals are the largest part of the system, employing 75 percent of the work force. The amount of money spent on hospital care increased from $50 per person in 1960 to $300 in 1977. Much of this cost relates to the tremendous growth in technology witnessed in the past decade, including sophisticated electronic heart monitors and CAT head and body scanners, as well as more routine but widely applied laboratory testing facilities.

The issue of costs is inevitably at the core of much of the health policy debate. In 1978, $192.4 billion was spent on health care, representing $863 for every man, woman and child in the country. These figures reflect the exceptionally high inflation of the health dollar as well as other cost factors, which will be further discussed in Chapter 8.

How can the system be influenced to better serve people's needs? The debate has been raging over the decades. One response to widespread dissatisfaction has been a dramatic increase in the government's influence over the allocation of health care resources. Political momentum is growing for some form of universal health care coverage. At the same time, many analysts and policymakers plead for caution. They warn that present dimensions of cost increases, expanding utilization of facilities, and growing complexity of government intervention could create a health care quagmire.

The authors in this chapter provide a variety of perspectives about these issues. In "Overview of Health Services in the United States," Paul R. Torrens, of the School of Public Health at the University of California, Los Angeles, details the gaps that exist in the allocation of health care resources for different segments of society and analyzes the various approaches to solving current problems.

Dr. William H. Glazier, a professor of community health, addresses some of the issues raised in Part I of this series concerning the relationship between medical care and health. In "The Task of Medicine," he points out that as disease patterns have altered in this century, medical care has not effectively adapted to the changes. He stresses the need for a new emphasis on the chronic illnesses that plague us today. Eric J. Cassell's article, "Our Sickness Care System," reveals a similar concern. An internist and professor of public health, he describes the substantial lack of knowledge about health and the need to focus the attention of medicine on the care of the sick. With that accomplished, he notes, we can turn our attention to what health is and how it can be achieved.

"America's Health Care System" provides another dimension to the issues. It looks at how people actually obtain health care—where they go for care, how often, and who pays for it—as well as their attitudes about the treatment they receive. The article appraises the national survey of access to medical care in 1975–76, which used a statistically representative sample of almost eight thousand U.S. citizens, and discusses the survey's implications for national health policy.

The final article in this chapter, "All-Night Vigil at Emergency Hospital" by reporter Allan Parachini, demonstrates how one small segment of our vast health care system served a large city between midnight and dawn one night in April.

Paul R. Torrens

Overview of Health Services in the United States

The frequently criticized fragmentation of health service may be caused in part by the fact that the United States has not a single health care system, but many. In the selection that follows, Paul R. Torrens describes four major systems— private practice, local government, military, and veterans (VA). He notes the differences among systems in the quality of medical care they provide and in the role played by the patient in making individual choices. Torrens is chairman of the Division of Health Services and Hospital Administration, School of Public Health, at the University of California, Los Angeles.

When visitors from abroad come to the United States, particularly those engaged in health services in their own country, they frequently want to know about "the American health care system" and how it works. They are usually puzzled by the answer they get:

> There isn't any *single* 'American health care system.' There are many separate sub-systems serving different populations in different ways. Sometimes they overlap; sometimes they stand entirely separate from one another. Sometimes they are supported with public funds and at other times they depend solely on private funds. Sometimes several of these different sub-systems use the same facilities and personnel; other times they use facilities and personnel which are entirely separate and distinct.

It should not be surprising that there is this multiplicity of health care systems (or sub-systems) in the United States, given the historical development of health services in this country.... Private medical practitioners, voluntary non-profit hospitals, city and state government hospitals, military and veterans hospitals, and health insurance plans of a variety of forms and origins all developed in the United States at the same time, separately and for specific purposes. The resulting picture has been described as having "a rich diversity of opportunities and approaches for meeting the health care needs of a population that has in itself a rich diversity of people and situations." It has

156

also been described as "chaotic, uncoordinated, overlapping, unplanned, and wasteful of precious personal and financial resources." The reality probably lies somewhere in between. . . .

Middle-Class, Middle-Income America
(Private Practice, Fee-for-Service System)

It is appropriate for two reasons to first consider the system of health care utilized by a "typical" middle-class, middle-income individual or family. First, this system is frequently described as *the* American health care system (all others, therefore, immediately becoming somehow secondary to it), and second, this system is frequently said to include the best medical care available in the United States and perhaps anywhere in the world.

The most striking feature of the middle-class, middle-income system of care is the absence of any *formal* system at all. Each individual or family puts together an *informal* set of services and facilities to meet their own needs. . . . Two other characteristics are also immediately noteworthy. First, the service aspects of the system concentrate around and are coordinated by the physicians in private practice. Second, the system is financed by personal, non-governmental funds, whether paid directly out-of-pocket by consumers or through private health insurance plans. . . .

Public health and preventive medicine services for the middle-class, middle-income system are provided from two different sources. Those services which are aimed at the protection of large numbers of people *en masse,* such as water purification, disposal of sewage, and air-pollution control, are provided by local or state governmental agencies. Frequently those agencies are called "public health departments." These agencies usually provide their services to the entire population of a region, with no distinction between rich and poor, simple or sophisticated, interested or disinterested. Indeed, these mass public health services are common to all of the systems of health care to be discussed. Those public health and preventive medicine services which are aimed at individuals, such as well-baby examinations, cervical cancer smears, vaccinations, and family planning, are provided by individual physicians in private practice. If a middle-income family desires a vaccination in preparation for a foreign trip or wants their blood cholesterol level checked, the family physician is consulted and provides the service. If it is time for the new baby to have its first series of vaccinations, the family pediatrician is usually the one who provides them.

Ambulatory patient services, both simple and complex, are also obtained from private physicians. Many families use a physician who specializes in family practice, while others use an array of specialist physicians such as pediatricians, internists, obstetrician/gynecologists and psychiatrists who provide both primary care and specialty services. When special laboratory tests are ordered, x-ray films required, or drugs and medications prescribed, private commercial for-profit laboratories or community pharmacies are used. Many of these services, from individual preventive medicine services to complex specialist treatments, are financed by individuals through out-of-pocket payment since most health insurance plans do not provide complete coverage for these needs. When the middle-income family begins to use institutional services, such as hospital care, the source of payment shifts almost completely from the individual to third-party health insurance plans.

Inpatient hospital services are usually provided to the middle-class, middle-income family by a local community hospital that is usually voluntary and non-profit. The specific hospital to be used is determined by the institution in which the family physician has medical staff privileges. Generally, the smaller, less specialized, more local hospitals will be used for simpler problems, while the larger, more specialized, perhaps more distant hospital will be used for the more complicated problems. Many of these larger hospitals will have active physician-training programs, conduct research, and may have significant "charity" or "teaching" wards.

The middle-class, middle-income family obtains its long-term care from a variety of sources, depending on the service required. Some long-term care is provided in hospitals, and as such, is merely an extension of the complex inpatient care the patient has already been receiving. This practice was more common in the past but utilization review procedures have increased pressures on the hospital to reduce the length of time people are hospitalized. More commonly, long-term care will be obtained at home through the assistance of a visiting nurse or voluntary non-profit community-based nursing service. If institutional long-term care is needed, it will probably be obtained in a nursing home or a skilled nursing facility, usually a small (50–100 patients) facility, operated privately, for profit, by a single proprietor or small group of investors. The middle-class, middle-income family usually pays for its long-term care with its own funds, since most health insurance plans provide relatively limited coverage for long-term care.

When middle-income families require care for emotional problems, they will again use a variety of mostly private services. However, as the illness becomes more serious, families may, for the first time, rely on governmentally-sponsored service. When emotional problems first begin to appear in the middle-class family, the patient will probably turn to the family physician who may provide simple supportive services such as tranquilizers, informal counseling, and perhaps referral for psychological testing. The physician may even arrange for the patient to be hospitalized in a general hospital for a rest, for "nervous exhaustion," or for some other non-psychiatric diagnosis. As the emotional problems become more severe, the family physician may refer the "patient" to a private psychiatrist, or to a community mental health center which most likely will be a voluntary non-profit agency, or under the sponsorship of one (such as a voluntary non-profit hospital). If hospitalization is required, the psychiatrist or the community mental health center is likely to use the psychiatric section of the local voluntary non-profit hospital if it seems that the stay in a hospital will be a short one. If the hospitalization promises to be a long one, the psychiatrist may use a psychiatric hospital, usually a private, non-governmental community facility.

In those cases in which very extended institutional care is required for an emotional problem and where the patient's financial resources are relatively limited, the middle-class family may request hospitalization in the state mental hospital. This usually represents the first use of governmental health programs by the middle income family, and as such it frequently comes as a considerable shock to patient and family alike.

In summary, the middle-class family's system of health care is an informal unstructured collection of individual services, put together by the patient and the private physician to meet the needs of the moment. The individual services themselves have little formalized relationship among themselves, and the only thread of continuity is provided by the family's physician or by the family itself. In general, all the services are provided by non-governmental sources and are paid for by private funds, either directly out-of-pocket or by privately financed health insurance plans.

For all its apparent looseness and lack of structure, the middle-class family's system of health care allows for a considerable amount of decision and control by the patient, and more than that of the other systems to be discussed. The patient is free to choose the physicians, the health insurance plan, and frequently even the hospital. If additional care is required, the patient can seek out and utilize (sometimes over-utilize) that care to the limit of the financial resources available. If the patient does not like the particular care being provided, dissatisfaction can be expressed in a most effective manner: the patient can seek care elsewhere from another provider.

On the other hand, the middle-class family's system of care is a poorly-coordinated, unplanned collection of services which frequently have little formal integration with one another. It can be very wasteful of resources and usually has no central control or monitor to determine whether it is accomplishing what it should. Each individual service may be of very high quality, but there may be little evidence of any "linking" taking place to ensure that each service complements each other to the maximum extent possible.

One special sub-set of the middle-class, middle-income model now involves millions of patients in this country. When people reach age 65, they are automatically eligible for Medicare, the federally sponsored and supervised health insurance plan for the elderly. A patient covered by Medicare benefits can utilize the same system of care as the middle-income family, including private practice physicians and voluntary non-governmental hospitals. The main difference now is that the bills are paid by a federal government health insurance plan, rather than the usual private plan in which the typical middle-class family is enrolled. The physicians are the same and the hospitals are the same; only the health insurance plan is different.

Poor, Inner-City, Minority America (Local Government Health Care)

A second major system of health care in the United States serves the poor, inner-city, and generally minority population. While the specific details may vary from city to city, the general outline is well-known throughout all major cities of the country. If it was important to study the middle-class, middle-income system of care because it represented the *best* health care possible in this country, it is equally important to study the poor, inner-city system of care, since it frequently represents the *worst*.

The most striking feature of the health care system of the poor, inner-city resident is exactly the same one that was so outstanding in the middle-class system: there is no *formal* system at all. Instead, just as in the middle-class system, each individual or family must put together some *informal* set of services, from whatever source possible, to meet the health needs of the moment. There is one significant difference, however: the poor do not have the resources to choose where and in what style they will obtain their health services. Instead, they must take what is offered to them, and try to put together a system from whatever they are told they can have.

There are two other important characteristics of the system. First, the great majority of services are provided by local government agencies such as the city or county hospital and the local health department. Second, the patients have no *real* continuity of service with any single provider, such as a middle-class family might have with a family physician. The poor family is faced with an endless stream of health care professionals who treat one specific episode of an illness and then are replaced by someone else for the next episode. While the middle-class system of health care was able to establish at least some thread of continuity by the continued presence of a family physician, the poor family is not able to maintain any thread of continuity at all.

The poor obtain their mass public health and preventive medicine services, including a pure water supply, sanitary sewage disposal, and protection of milk and food from the same local government health departments and health agencies that serve the middle-class system. In contrast to the middle-class system, however, the poor also get their individual public health and preventive medicine services from the local health department. When a poor family's newborn baby needs its vaccinations, that family goes to the district health center of the health department, not to a private physician. When a low-income woman needs a Papanicolau smear for cervical cancer testing or when a teenager from a low-income family needs a blood test for syphilis, it is most likely that the local government health department will give the test.

To obtain ambulatory patient service, the poor family cannot rely on the constant presence of a family doctor for advice and routine treatment. Instead, they must turn to neighbors, the local pharmacist, the health department's public health nurse, or the emergency room of the city or county hospital. It has often been said that the city or county hospital's emergency room is the family doctor for the poor, and the facts generally support this: when the poor need ambulatory patient care, it is quite likely that the first place they will turn is the city or county hospital emergency room.

The emergency room also serves the poor as the entry point to the rest of the health care system. The poor obtain much of their ambulatory services in the outpatient clinics of the city/county hospitals, and to gain admission to these clinics, the poor frequently must first go through the emergency room and be referred to the appropriate clinic. Once out of the emergency room, they may be cared for in two or three specialty clinics, each of which may handle one particular set of problems, but none of which will take responsibility for coordinating all the care the patient is receiving.

When the poor need inpatient hospital services, whether they be simple or complicated, they again usually turn to the city or county hospital to obtain them. Admission to the inpatient services of these hospitals is usually obtained through the emergency room or the outpatient clinics, thereby forcing the poor family to use these ambulatory patient services if they wish later admission to the inpatient services. The poor may also turn to the emergency room, the outpatient clinics, and the inpatient ward or teaching services of the larger, voluntary non-profit community hospitals. Since these hospitals are frequently teaching hospitals for the training of physicians, they often maintain special free or lower-priced wards. It is to these wards that the poor are usually admitted. Since the care in the teaching hospitals is generally as good or better than might be obtained at the local city or county hospitals, many poor are willing to become teaching cases in the voluntary non-profit hospitals in exchange for better care in better surroundings. By and large, however, the city and county hospitals carry the largest burden of inpatient care for the poor.

If the long-term care situation of middle-income people is generally inadequate, the long-term care of the poor can only be described as terrible. In contrast with the middle-class, much of the long-term care of the poor is provided on the wards of the city and county hospitals, although not by intent or plan. The poor simply remain in hospitals longer because their social and physical conditions are more complicated and because the hospital staffs are reluctant to discharge them until they have some assurance that continuing care will be available after discharge. Since this is very often uncertain, poor patients are likely to be kept longer in the hospital so that they can complete as much of their convalescence as possible prior to discharge.

The greater bulk of the long-term care of the poor is provided in the same type of nursing homes or skilled nursing facilities that are used by the middle-class: small (50–100 patients) facilities, operated for profit by a single proprietor or a small group of owners. One major difference between the two systems is the quality of the facility used, the middle-class generally having access to better equipped and better staffed nursing homes, and the poor having access to less expensive, less well-equipped facilities. Another important difference between the middle-class and the poor is that the middle-class, middle-income patients are more likely to pay for their own care in these institutions, while the poor have their care paid for by welfare or other public, governmental funds.

It is interesting to note that the system of health care for the middle-class utilizes entirely private, non-governmental facilities until long-term care for mental illness is required; at that point, a governmental facility, the state mental hospital, is used. By contrast, the system of health care for the poor is composed almost entirely of public, government-sponsored services until long-term care is required. This is usually provided in private, profit-making facilities, the first such use of private facilities by the poor.

The convergence of the poor and the middle-class systems of care in the small, private profit-making nursing homes is important, since it represents an important feature of our multiple sub-systems of health care. In a number of instances, several systems of health care that are otherwise quite separate and distinct will merge in their common use of personnel, equipment or facilities. The emergency rooms of the city or county and voluntary non-profit teaching hospitals, for example, will serve as the source of emergency medical care for the middle-class family that cannot reach its own family physician. It will also serve as the family physician for the poor family that has none of its own. The private, for-profit nursing home will serve as the source of long-term care for the middle-class family, and may provide the same function for the poor. The radiology department of the voluntary non-profit teaching hospital will provide x-rays for the middle-class patient whose care is supervised by a hospital staff physician in training. This does not mean that there is any real, functional integration of the separate systems of care because of their common use of the same facility or personnel. Rather, the model is more like that of a busy harbor in which a variety of ships will berth side-by-side for a short period of time before going on their separate ways for their separate purposes.

In their use of services for emotional illness, the poor return once again to an almost totally public, local government system. Initial signs of emotional difficulties are haphazardly treated in the emergency rooms and outpatient clinics of the city or county hospital. From here patients may be referred to the crowded inpatient psychiatric wards of these same hospitals, but are just as likely to be referred to community mental health centers operated by local government or voluntary non-profit community agencies. When long-term care in an institution is required, the poor are sent to the psychiatric wards of the city or county hospital, and then from there to the large state government mental hospitals, frequently many miles away.

In the past, health services for the poor were usually free, at least to the patient. Neither the local health department, the city or county hospital, nor the state mental hospital generally charged for their services, regardless of the patient's ability to pay. In the last few years, both local health departments and city and county hospitals have been forced to initiate a system of charges for services which were previously free. They have done this to recapture third-party payments to which the poor patient might be eligible, and patients who are unable to pay are still ordinarily provided the services they need. . . .

Under Medicaid people whose income and resources are below a level established by the individual states can utilize a state government–sponsored health insurance program to purchase health care in the private, middle-class marketplace. . . . Medicaid has succeeded to a degree in moving poor patients from local government hospitals into voluntary non-profit teaching hospitals, but its greatest effect has probably been in moving poor patients into private, profit-making nursing homes and skilled nursing facilities. . . . And, for all its problems, the Medicaid program has allowed certain aspects of the middle-class, middle-income system of health care to be shared with the poor, inner-city minority system of health care, a blending, merging, or sharing of re-sources and services that is characteristic of the American health care system and which makes it so difficult to evaluate any one sub-system separately.

In summary, the system of health care for the poor is as unstructured and informal as that for the middle-class, but the poor have to depend upon what-ever services the local government offers to them. The services are usually provided free of charge, or at low cost, but the patient has relatively little opportunity to express a choice and exercise options. Poor patients often can-not move to another set of services if they dislike the first one offered, since those first offered are usually the *only* services available.

As with the system of health care for the middle-class, the system for the poor is poorly coordinated internally and almost completely unplanned and unmonitored. It is certainly as wasteful of resources as the middle-class system, but because of the external appearances as a low-cost, poorly-financed system, the exact extent of wasted resources is difficult to document. At the same time, the great positive virtue of the health care system for the poor, its openness and accessibility to all people at all times for all conditions (albeit with considerable delays), is difficult to evaluate adequately as well. An optimist would view health services for the poor in this country today as considerably better than they have ever been before. A pessimist would say that they still have a long way to go towards meeting even minimal acceptable standards for care. Both would be right!

Military Medical Care System

A person joining one of the uniformed branches of the American military sacrifices many aspects of civilian life that non-military personnel take for granted. At the same time, however, this person receives a variety of fringe benefits that those outside the military do not enjoy at all. One of the most important of these fringe benefits is a well-organized system of high quality health care provided at no direct cost to the recipient. Certain features of this military medical care system (the general term used to include the separate systems of the United States Army, Navy, and Air Force) deserve comment. First, the system is all-inclusive and omnipresent. The military medical system has the responsibility of protecting the health of all active duty military personnel wherever their military duty may take them, and of providing them with all the services that they may eventually need for any service-connected problem. The military medical system goes wherever active duty military personnel go, and assumes a responsibility for total care that is unique among American health care systems.

The second important characteristic of the military medical care system is that it goes into effect immediately whether the active duty soldier or sailor wants it to or not. No initiative or action is required by the individual to start the system, and indeed, the system frequently provides certain types of health services, such as routine vaccinations or shots, that the soldier or sailor would really wish not to have. The individual has little choice regarding who will provide the treatment or where, but at the same time, the services are always there if needed, without the patient having to search them out. If a physician's services are needed, they are obtained; if a hospitalization is required, it is arranged; if emergency transportation is necessary, it is carried out. There is little that the individual can do to influence how medical care is provided, but at the same time, there is never any worry about its availability.

The third important characteristic of the military health care system is its great emphasis on keeping personnel well, on preventing illness or injury, and on finding health problems early while they are still amenable to treatment. Great stress is placed on preventive measures such as vaccination, regular physical examinations and testing, and educational efforts towards prevention of accidents and contagious diseases. In an approach that is unique among the health care systems of this country, the military medical system provides "health" care and not just "sickness" care. . . .

Veterans Administration Health Care System

Parallel to the system of care for active duty military personnel is another system operated within the continental United States for retired, disabled, and otherwise deserving veterans of previous U.S. military service. Although the Veterans Administration (VA) system is in many respects larger than the system of care for active duty military personnel, it is not nearly as complete, well-integrated, or extensive. At the present time, the Veterans Administration system of care is primarily hospital oriented and not really a "health care system." The VA operates 171 hospitals throughout the country which provide most VA care. In recent years, the VA has increasingly provided outpatient services and now maintains more than 200 outpatient clinics; however, the major thrust of VA health care is still focused on the hospitals. . . .

Perspectives

In recent years, there have been various approaches to the problem of reorganizing these separate sub-systems of care so that they function together in a more integrated and effective fashion. Although these proposals have often been limited to specific aspects, such as financing or quality of care, their overall purpose has generally been to move the various pieces of the American health care system into a better and more efficient relationship with each other.

William H. Glazier

The Task of Medicine

William H. Glazier focuses on the health care needs of the population and suggests that medicine is ill-equipped to confront the health problems of modern society. Comparing the nature of illness today with that in 1900, he argues that the fee-for-service system is incompatible with current needs. A professor of community health at the Albert Einstein College of Medicine in New York, Glazier argues for a community-based system that would address today's needs for health education, maintenance, and management of chronic illness.

The medical system of the United States is able to meet with high efficiency the kind of medical problem that was dominant until about 40 years ago, namely infectious disease. It also deals effectively with episodes of acute illness and with accidents that call for advanced, hospital-based biomedical knowledge and technology. The system is much less effective in delivering the kind of care that is more often needed today: primary (first-contact) care and the kind of care needed at a time when chronic illnesses predominate. They are the degenerative diseases associated with aging and the diseases that can be characterized as man-made because they are associated with such things as smoking and environmental contaminants. For these diseases medicine has few measures and not even much comfort.

My colleagues and I in the department of community health at the Albert Einstein College of Medicine of Yeshiva University have been much concerned with this shortcoming of the medical system. Since the college is in a community (the borough of the Bronx in New York City) with large numbers of people who are poor, elderly, Puerto Rican or black, we see the deficiencies regularly. When these people seek medical help (and part of the weakness of the present medical system is that it deals only with people who present themselves as sick), they are likely to find themselves very sick indeed and in a long-term regime of treatment involving costs that they cannot possibly meet out of their own resources. The problem, which is by no means limited to the Bronx, is to fashion a medical system that deals as well with the chronic diseases as the present system deals with the infectious diseases and the complicated hospital cases and that handles the costs in a way that is acceptable not only to the patient but also to the society at large.

Until as recently as the beginning of the present century the expectation of life was short in the United States, largely because of the toll exacted by the infectious diseases, particularly among children. The first advances against the infectious diseases resulted from a series of developments in which medical technology and the work of physicians with individual patients played a relatively minor role. The more important factors were the improvement in the standard of living and the effectiveness of public health measures. Because of the rise in the standard of living, people had a more balanced diet, received better education (so that they knew more about taking care of themselves and how to avail themselves of medical help) and had more money to spend on medical care if they needed it. The decline of tuberculosis, for example, is believed to be largely attributable to improved diet.

Meanwhile governments at all levels were moving to purify public water supplies, handle sewage in such a way that it would not be a contaminant, improve housing conditions, drain mosquito-breeding swamps and provide education in health care, particularly for mothers and children. Efforts of this kind led to the decline of such infectious diseases as typhus, typhoid, cholera and malaria.

The role of medicine during this period cannot be dismissed as insignificant. The conquest of smallpox, for example, surely resulted from the discovery of an effective vaccine and the provision of vaccination as a medical procedure. Nonetheless, it was as recently as 1915 that Lawrence J. Henderson of the Harvard Medical School could justifiably make his celebrated remark that the average patient had no better than a 50-50 change of benefiting from an encounter with the average physician.

The beginning of what might be described as the "golden age" of clinical medicine in the United States can be put at about 1922, when the discovery of insulin made possible the control of diabetes. Clinical medicine came into its own as a force against infectious disease with the discovery of the sulfa drugs in 1932. It was in that period too that the effects of earlier advances in physiology and bacteriology and the improvement of medical education resulting from the Flexner report of 1910 began to tell.

*   *   *

The great change in the nature of the health problem during this century is illustrated by a comparison of the 10 leading causes of death in 1900 and 1970. In 1900 three of the 10 (tuberculosis, influenza-pneumonia and diphtheria) were directly infectious and three more (gastroenteritis, chronic nephritis and diseases of early infancy) were closely related to infectious processes. By 1970 none of the first 10 causes of death was an infectious disease except for influenza-pneumonia and certain diseases of early infancy, and in both of these groups the mortality rate was far below the level of 1900.

Today the list is headed by heart disease, cancer and cerebrovascular lesions—all chronic diseases. The first two have increased by 268 percent and 240 percent respectively since 1900 in terms of deaths per 100,000 people. Other chronic diseases, such as general arteriosclerosis and diabetes, have emerged as leading causes of death. Of every 100 males born in the United States this year, 83 are likely to die eventually of a chronic disease; in 1901 the rate was 52 in 100. The likelihood of dying of an infectious diseases is now about six in 100, which is about one-sixth of the rate in 1901.

The death rates tell only part of the story, since the chronic diseases also afflict large numbers of the living for long periods of time. According to estimates made in 1968, heart and circulatory disorders afflicted 26.2 million people in the United States, mental and emotional disorders 20 million and arthritis and rheumatic diseases 16 million. The inescapable legacy of improved health in early and middle life is the increased prevalence of these less tractable forms of disease and disability in middle and later life.

The infectious diseases have a fairly abrupt onset and a finite duration. In the medical structure that has evolved to deal with them the person who feels sick visits or calls in a physician, who prescribes and administers a treatment that nowadays usually ends fairly soon in recovery. The chronic diseases, on the other hand, typically have a gradual onset and an indefinite duration. A patient with a disease such as cancer, arteriosclerosis or emphysema may go about for months or years before he realizes that he is afflicted. Indeed, the case of the person who is unaware that anything is wrong until he is struck down by a heart attack has become common.

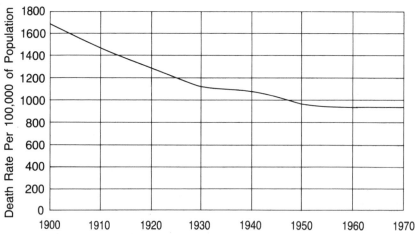

Death rate in the U.S. declined steadily until about 1950 and then leveled off. Infectious diseases, which took a heavy toll among the young, are much reduced as a cause of death, whereas the chronic diseases that are associated with aging have become a major cause.

The medical care system encounters several different types of problems in dealing with the chronically ill. In the first place, it is essentially a passive system, that is, it does not go into operation until a patient takes the initiative by visiting a physician or a clinic. Often by the time a patient with a chronic illness takes this step it is late in the progress of the disease. For many of the chronic diseases much of the treatment is directed to symptoms rather than being curative. The regime of treatment is also likely to be protracted and costly. Another type of problem is that the system is geared to the one-to-one, episodic relationship in which the patient sees a physician, receives treatment and pays a fee. The system is unwieldy and inefficient when, as is often the case with chronic disease, the patient requires care by several physicians with different specialties, by other professional people such as nurses, therapists and social workers and by different institutions. Finally, the system is in a better position to take care of the patient who is so incapacitated that he has to be in a hospital bed than the patient who is ill but more or less able to go about his normal business—and such patients constitute about 85 percent of the total.

In sum, the technology and medical procedures available for coping with the diseases that afflict the population have been expanded and improved, but the structure of the system that deploys the technology and resources has tended to remain fixed in a mold determined by medical and social circumstances that are quite different from those that exist today. The

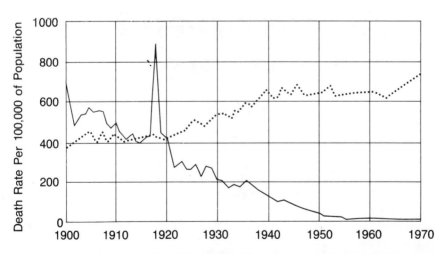

Changing role of infectious diseases (solid line) and chronic diseases (dotted line) as causes of death in the U.S. during the period from 1960 to 1970 is portrayed. Chronic diseases include both degenerative ailments associated with aging and diseases that can be called man-made because they are associated with such behavior as smoking and with such phenomena as environmental contamination.

result is a mismatch between the technology of medicine and the apparatus that delivers care. Many observers see this mismatch as the cause of the crisis in medical practice, medical education and health care in the United States today.

*   *   *

It should be emphasized that the crisis does not arise from any shortage of medical personnel or the other resources employed in providing medical care. On the contrary, the people and the facilities (hospital beds, sophisticated machines, nursing homes and so on) have increased in number over the past decade, both absolutely and per capita, although the distribution of the components of the system is conspicuously uneven. The nation suffers from a misuse (sometimes an overuse) and a maldistribution of medical technology and medical services. Indeed, the root of the crisis is the growing social demand for a more effective and fair distribution of the medical potential created by the scientific and technological advances of the past 50 years. A related problem is the growing lack of primary care, which is what used to be provided by the general practitioners whose number is dwindling steadily as physicians turn increasingly to specialization. General practitioners also used to help patients adjust to the increasing disability of chronic, degenerative disease.

The crisis is articulated mainly in dollar terms, which is understandable in

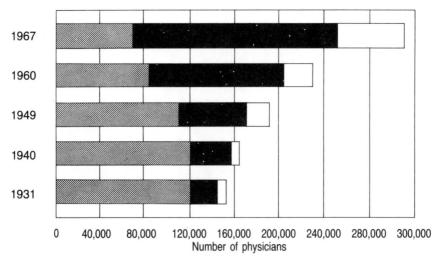

Active physicians in the U.S. have tended increasingly to be in specialty practice (solid) rather than in general practice (shaded). The trend makes it more difficult for people to obtain primary care, which is what was traditionally provided by general practitioners. The white portions of the bars represent hospital physicians who are interns and residents.

view of the enormous flow of public funds into the health care industry during the past few years. For example, both the demand for medical care and the cost of it have been heavily affected by the 1965 amendments to the Social Security Act, which created Medicare and Medicaid. (Medicare is for the aged, Medicaid for the poor; Federal funds are employed to help pay for the medical care of both groups.) Five years after the inauguration of these programs the Federal outlay for personal health care had risen above $14 billion per year from a starting level of about $3 billion.

In fiscal 1971 the amount of money spent in the United States for all types of medical care was $75 billion. At $358 per person, this sum represented 7.4 percent of the gross national product. Five years earlier medical expenditures were $212 per person, or a bit less than 6 percent of the gross national product. One can therefore see why concern over what is being delivered for the money is rising, particularly in the light of evidence that the delivery system is not as efficient or equitable as it might be.

Most of the legislative proposals addressed to the health care crisis seek to moderate or control expenditures by trying to make each dollar provide more medical care. The reasoning behind many of the health bills in Congress seems to be to find ways to make the individual physician more available to the individual patient and to do so, if possible, without spending more. The goal is apparently to provide everyone with the kind of services now available

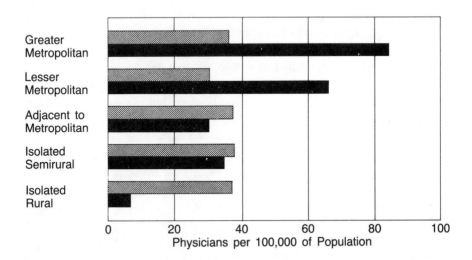

Distribution of physicians is shown according to the type of community and type of practice, with shaded bars representing general practitioners and solid bars representing specialists. The uneven distribution is an obstacle to efficient delivery of medical care.

to the people who can afford to buy the best in medical care, either out of their own resources or because they have ample medical insurance.

*   *   *

Even if the best of existing physician-patient relationships could be provided for everyone, which is financially and practically out of the question, it can be argued that this approach is wrong. It would seem more appropriate to think in terms of setting different priorities for the delivery of health care, considering the problems raised by the growing prominence of the chronic diseases and the fact that some 85 percent of the sick can be cared for at the primary and ambulatory level. The priorities I have in mind would rest on the assumption that the present organization of the medical system—a fee-for-service arrangement for treating discrete episodes of illness—is incompatible with the need for more primary care and with the continuity of care that is necessary for the emerging patterns of disease.

The modern "epidemics" of cancer, heart disease, arthritis, mental illness and so on present medicine with a more complex task of organization and treatment than it has had before. One reason is that the diseases appear to have multiple causes, including behavioral and social factors. Smoking, overeating, overdrinking and lack of exercise are patterns of behavior that seem to contribute to the onset and severity of certain chronic diseases. Social factors, including the tensions resulting from the pace of modern life and the alienation and despair of ghetto life, are reflected in such problems as alcoholism and drug addiction. The complexity of the medical task is also increased by the long-term, sophisticated and expensive nature of the treatment often required.

The answer to the mismatch of technology and delivery is for medicine to orient itself toward a more interventionist approach, by which I mean that the physician and the medical system should be prepared to take the initiative in delivering medical care, rather than leaving the initiative to the patient. The system should reach out to people seeking out those who for genetic reasons or because of their work or way of life may have a predisposition to a disease, carrying on health education among those at risk, pressing among the poor the case for better nutrition for children so as to forestall crippling disabilities in later life and reminding patients who are identifiably ill of the need for specific measures of treatment. In taking this approach medicine would be recognizing the fact that in the chronic diseases its present capability is more for helping than for curing. Since cures are lacking for most chronic disease, the need is for intervention at the point in time for each patient or group of patients when intervention would do the most good in maintaining functional capability under the existing circumstances.

A related need is to recognize that the task of preventive medicine has changed. Preventive medicine was once a wholly public concern: public health officials took the lead in the administration of inoculations, the drainage of swamps, the control of disease-bearing insects and other measures to protect large segments of the population from disease. Now it has also become a private concern. The onset of certain diseases, including some of the chronic ones, can be prevented or postponed by action directed at individuals or groups of individuals who have characteristics of age, sex, occupation or behavior that put them at high risk. Screening of groups and selective testing for specific diseases according to an individual's risk factor will inevitably become a significant part of medical care. The risk of cancer associated with smoking comes to mind in this context; one could also cite other diseases that arise from exposure of susceptible individuals to a particular environmental hazard.

A further need is to redesign medical education so that physicians and other health personnel are trained and challenged to provide primary care and to deal with the chronic diseases. Most medical education still emphasizes the treatment of acute illness and injury (which is not to say that such treatment should be slighted). Few medical people are trained in long-term management of chronic illness and in home care. Medical services must be restructured along similar lines.

A particular problem to be taken into account is the demonstrated reluctance of many people to take the positive step of seeking medical advice, even when, as in the case of national health services such as the one in Britain, the cost will be borne by the society rather than the individual. A study of the British system has estimated that only one person in four with symptoms seeks medical advice. A related problem is that health statistics, being measures of people who go to doctors, fail to show the full extent of social pathology and of undiagnosed diseases.

*   *   *

In my view the medical delivery system would work best if groups of medical personnel were organized to deal with defined population groups, whether in communities or in places of employment. The medical task would involve not only the care of the sick but also the monitoring and health education of the not yet sick. The medical group would have a broad base of knowledge of the population group that it was serving—knowledge including the demographic characteristics of the population, the environmental factors affecting different subgroups, the economic situation of the people and the behavioral patterns in the group. People who presented themselves as sick would of course receive treatment, as they do now. In addition, however, the system would also be in touch with people who were not sick, or not known to be sick, providing them with information on health, suggesting periodic checkups and screening individuals thought to be susceptible to particular illnesses.

One can envision a useful role for modern computer regimes in such a system. The memory of the computer would contain the name of each member of the group, the record of the system's contacts with him and an indication of his particular susceptibilities or needs if he had any. If a specific crisis arose, such as a period of heavy air pollution, the computer could produce the names of the people who ought to be urged to come in for a checkup because they were vulnerable to respiratory afflictions. If certain members of the group had been fitted with a cardiac pacemaker, the computer would contain information indicating when each pacemaker might be expected to run down, taking into account the condition of the patient and the nature of his activity, so that notice could be sent to him whenever it was time for the pacemaker to be checked.

In such a system it would be feasible for each member to pay (or for a public or private agency to pay in his behalf) what might be called a health-maintenance fee, probably on an annual basis, in exchange for which he would receive the continuing comprehensive attention I have described. The significance of such an arrangement is that it shifts the focus of medical care away from treatment of illness, although that is still provided, and toward the maintenance of health. A few arrangements of this kind are being tested, notably the Kaiser-Permanente program, which has operated successfully on the West Coast for many years.

It is implicit in what I have been discussing that the distinction between health and illness, which was clear when the infectious diseases were the main problem, is much less clear now that chronic diseases predominate. In this situation both the medical profession and the society at large confront questions about what levels of health maintenance to seek and about deploying medical resources to achieve them. How far should society and the medical system to go maintain life in the face of incurable disease? If a costly procedure such as dialysis is available to prevent death from kidney failure, to whom and in what way should dialysis be made available? How much of the gross national product should go into health care? What are the acceptable bench marks for analyzing and evaluating the program? Since poverty and poor health are so closely linked, to what extent is it better to seek improved health by attacking poverty rather than by deploying medical resources? Such questions cannot be answered by medicine alone; they require the formulation of social policies and their expression through the political system.

Eric J. Cassell

Our Sickness Care System

While many critics raise alarms about the "health care crisis" and propose a shift in medical emphasis, planning, and funding, Eric J. Cassell commends the excellence of the nation's "sickness care" system. A physician and clinical professor of public health at Cornell University Medical College, he claims that medical care is and should be focused on the care of the ill, the cure of disease. Health care, although vitally important and closely related, involves different concepts and may need to be addressed by personnel and institutions separate from the medical system.

The trouble with the American medical care system probably dates to about 1940. That was when the Hospital for the Ruptured and Crippled changed its name to the Hospital for Special Surgery. Until that time, and without physicians or patients being self-conscious about it, doctors took care of the sick. Medical care was sickness care, not health care.

I suppose the reason the hospital changed its name (and that "sterility clinics" became "fertility clinics" and "birth control" became "family planning," and you can think of others), was trouble raising money. Medicine had a merchandising problem. Clearly, the Hospital for Special Surgery sounds better than Ruptured and Crippled. Which is more appealing, "Mental Health Clinics" or "Mental Illness Clinics"? And where would you rather go when you need a doctor, to a "Health Maintenance Organization" or a "Sick Patient Facility"?

Recently, one of the really fine foundations that funds medical care research announced a program for the "health impaired elderly." Why could they not be called the "old and sick"? That is what they call themselves. Clearly, the word "health" sounds better and, I suppose, sells better than the word "sickness." And bathroom tissue outsells toilet paper, especially if it is facial quality.

The trouble with good merchandising is that it only works if we come to believe in what it is selling. Really good merchandising convinces the seller as well as the customer. And that is what has happened in medical care.

Health and Illness

Medical care—doctors, nurses, paraprofessionals (another bit of merchandising), hospitals, clinics and so on—is about the care of the sick, not about health. Health and illness are probably hardly related, much less the opposite of each other.

Most people know now that the health of a population is not primarily related to its medical care. Having many doctors and hospitals does not necessarily make people healthy. A healthy population is more likely one in which people do not get sick in the first place, rather than get sick and then better.

We have become steadily healthier along with (and probably because of) the improvements in sanitation, diet, housing, education, and general environment that have marked this century. That knowledge has been interpreted as showing that the doctors and hospitals we have are not necessary, much less more of them. A sounder conclusion is that the doctor's job is to take care of sick people, not that we do not need doctors. And taking care of the sick should not be confused with health care—which is different.

By and large, American medicine has done a first-class job of taking care of diseases. We do more—cure more, repair more, return more people to function from more conditions—than ever before in the world's history. And well-earned praise could go on and on. We have been so effective that we, with the help of our merchandisers—the media, health popularizers, fundraisers and so on—have raised expectations right into never-never land. These days, if someone breaks a leg in an auto accident and limps as a result, most people will blame the doctor for the limp.

The point is that American medicine is not a health care system. It is a *sickness* care system and a very good sickness care system. It is expensive. It is overly devoted to its technology, it cares more about diseases than sick persons, it needs a good hard shove to keep it moving, but it is effective.

Even if you do not agree, every time you see the word health, as in health care delivery, or health insurance, try substituting the word "sickness" and then see what that does to the statement in which the word "health" was used. I think you will see that many issues appear in a different light when things having to do with health are separated from those related to the care of the sick. For example, health care cost efficiency may mean just that—or it may mean not spending money for the care of the sick. Especially the poor and sick.

There would be nothing wrong with merchandising the care of the sick by calling it health care (Lord knows, hospitals have enough difficulty raising money), if it did not interfere with the care of the sick and even more with promoting health.

Often, people point to our disappointing infant mortality rates to show that we are not getting enough for our health dollar. Much research has shown that the death of infants is more related to social class, family income, diet or the educational level of the mother than to the availability of doctors. That is true in countries where national health services are present as well as in the United States. Infant mortality, then, is one measure of the *health* of a society, but it is *not* a measure of the adequacy of medical care, which is where the dollar goes.

We hardly even have a health dollar (much less a healthy one). Sickness care adequacy is measured by things such as the mortality from prostate surgery (very low) to the percentage of people unhappy with the care they got (not so low). Costs of these items can be compared from nation to nation. So, too, can measures of unmet needs. By staying on the subject of the care of the sick, we might better focus on our very real medical care problems and decide how to solve them.

Equally important, we might be able to start working on how to have a healthier population, and how each of us, individually, might promote our own health.

At first glance, it seems reasonable that health is on the same continuum as sickness—that being healthy is the opposite of being sick. I do not think that health and sickness are more than passingly related. They seem to be part of the same idea: both occur in persons, both have something to do with the body, knowledge about health and sickness have certain facts in common, and sickness seems an obvious obstacle to being healthy. That is, it would appear that a good step on the road to health would be freedom from disease.

On the other hand, most of us know people who have disease—a stroke, arthritis, heart attacks—who seem remarkably healthy. Sometimes they even say that since the heart attack they have never been healthier! Clearly, state of mind is important, but as innumerable new joggers will testify, the state of the body seems to have something to do with it also.

That health involves body, mind and spirit is an idea that stretches back into antiquity, but considering how modern understanding of those parts of the human condition are divided among so many different specialists, it is small wonder that we know so little about health.

Meanwhile, because of the confusion, we see people whose concern for their health leads to endless consumption of vitamins, frequent visits to doctors (anything doctors know about health they picked up on their own; they certainly received no formal training—who would have taught them?), and to sad scenes such as young runners counting their pulses. Even books about "holistic health" are full of references to alternative medical therapies.

Therapies, legitimate or otherwise, may be good for your sickness but not necessarily for your health. Lester Breslow, dean of the School of Public Health at UCLA, has turned his attention to the problems of studying health quite apart from sickness, and so have a few others. It was his team that demonstrated that people who eat breakfast, sleep seven hours, do not smoke cigarettes, drink in moderation, exercise, are happy in their work, and so on, live longer than people with other habits. In other words, all the things mothers tell you to do but which are seldom done (even by mothers).

Seaweed by the Ton

The obvious answer, health education, has by and large failed to bring about necessary and sustained changes in lifestyle. People will eat raw seaweed by the ton more easily than change the amount of water they habitually drink.

In fact, our knowledge about what health is and how it is achieved or promoted is woefully inadequate. Even trying to define it is difficult. The research methods that have worked so well for disease do not do the job. The two problems, conquering diseases and achieving a healthy population, must be separately addressed. It is probable that different concepts and methods or even different personnel and institutions will be required.

Obtaining sufficient funds for research about health would, in itself, face major obstacles. The sources of money are almost always oriented toward disease. The National Institutes of Health are the National Heart, Lung and Blood Institute, National Cancer Institute, National Institute of Arthritis and Metabolic Diseases, and so on. There is no institute concerned with health. (Except the National Institute of Mental Health and there they have a division for rape prevention but no division for schizophrenia.)

The time has come to recognize that medical care is about the care of the sick and not primarily about health. Realizing that will allow us to continue to pursue the best sickness care system in the world. At the same time, we can turn our attention to understanding what health is and how it can be achieved. When, with the lowest death rate and the most effective medical care in history, the whole nation seems to spend its time fearing the air it breathes and counting its heartbeats, learning what health really is cannot come a moment too soon. Who knows, it may even turn out that a healthy population requires less medical care.

America's Health Care System: A Comprehensive Portrait

A national survey to determine if U.S. citizens get the health care they need, and what they think about that health care, highlights many of the same characteristics and weaknesses of the health care system discussed by other commentators in this chapter. Patients are overcoming many barriers to access and report general satisfaction with care received, the survey finds, but they perceive a crisis in health care and express concern about rising costs. The survey was conducted by the Center for Health Administration Studies at the University of Chicago.

In the world of business, a variety of indicators reflect the ups and downs of economic activity. Selected separate indicators, for example, comprise the Consumer Price Index, Department of Labor employment statistics, Dow Jones stock averages, and others.

Magazines such as *Business Week* and *U.S. News and World Report* each have identified certain indicators which they believe reflect the state of the nation's economy. *Business Week*'s includes net tons of steel, kilowatt hours of electricity, freight car loadings, board feet of lumber, wheat prices in Kansas City, gold prices in London, the prime interest rate, the Federal Reserve money supply, housing starts, and many others.

For businessmen, government officials, economists, bankers, and investors, such indicators are considered essential to decision making. They tell where the economy of the nation is going, and they guide and influence those who have a hand on the tiller.

Adapted from "A New Survey on Access to Medical Care," Special Report Number One/1978, published by the Robert Wood Johnson Foundation.

In the business of health, too, a variety of specialized statistics show how some parts of the system are performing currently:

—the infant mortality rate has decreased in the last five years by 19 percent

—more than 230 million days of care are rendered to 29 million patients admitted to hospitals each year

—health expenditures total 8.6 percent of the gross national product—$140 billion annually

—federal Medicaid payments to states total almost three-quarters of a billion dollars each month

—the ratio of doctors to population has increased from 139 per 100,000 in 1960 to 162 in 1976.

Analysis of these statistics, however, only skirts the fringes of a central question: is health care available to those who need it, and what kind of barriers must be overcome to obtain care? In the jargon of health policy analysts, this crucial issue goes by the phrase access to care.

In "people terms," however, access translates into a multitude of factors which together determine whether or not persons obtain the medical care they need. Is a doctor available? How far away is the doctor's office? How long is the trip? How long does it take to get an appointment? How much time does the doctor spend with the patient? How much does the visit cost? How will the bill be paid? Was the patient satisfied with what the doctor did?...

The national survey of access to medical care was carried out by the Center for Health Administration Studies of the University of Chicago.* The field work was conducted by the University's National Opinion Research Center between September 1975, and February 1976. It is based on a sample of 7,787 persons and is statistically representative of the U.S. population.

The study focuses on many factors believed to affect access for the entire population. Moreover, data for each indicator can be examined for subgroups of the total population—sub-groups defined by a number of important variables, including age; sex; race; income; region of the country; suburban, urban, and rural residence; and education levels. ...

In a number-oriented society, nothing makes a problem come alive so much as the measurement of it. Walter Lippmann, a half century ago, said: "The printing of comparative statistics of infant mortality is often followed by a reduction of the death rate of babies... the statistics make them visible, as visible as if the babies had elected an alderman to air their grievances."

---

*Principals in the study are: Lu Ann Aday, study director; Ronald Andersen, principal investigator; and Gretchen Voorhis Fleming and Grace Chiu, assistant study directors, all of the Center for Health Administration Studies, University of Chicago. The study has been published in *Health Care in the United States: Equitable for Whom?* (Sage Publishing, 1980).

Grievances, indeed, have been aired about America's health system: its cost, and its accessibility to such groups as minorities, rural and inner city residents, and the aged. Attempts have been made to fix deficiencies. Medicare and Medicaid are examples.

The new University of Chicago study promises to provide abundant information enabling an assessment of the impact of these and newer health initiatives. This information will give new currency to the debates which shape changes in the nation's health laws—ranging from recommendations of seeming minor consequence to the sweeping changes implicit in proposals for national health insurance.

Professional organizations, Congress, state legislatures, and other groups will be able to evaluate the relative needs of population groups believed to have particular problems obtaining medical care. Similarly, over time, these data may define the nature of the so-called crisis in American health care. The study's principal strength derives from its attempt to go beyond the raw numbers and to interpret and analyze what they mean. . . .

Traditional Health Indicators in Perspective

Much past analysis of the subject of access has focused on counting doctors (with suggested remedies concentrating on increasing the supply of physicians) and has emphasized mortality and morbidity statistics.

But the first approach is akin to analyzing the energy shortage only by counting corner gas stations. And the latter falls short because traditional mortality and morbidity statistics fail to reflect adequately much that the health system does. A health care system provides useful outcomes other than prevention and cure—reassurance and encouragement, for example. . . .

To illustrate, the clinical capability of pinning broken hips among the injured elderly has not changed the nation's gross mortality statistics, but it has increased the utilization of medical services and it contributes substantially to improving the quality of these patients' lives.

Similarly, take the case of a woman visiting a physician because of a lump in her breast. A diagnosis which reveals the lump is benign does not show up in morbidity statistics, but that diagnosis represents a major benefit to the patient.

It is statistical intangibles such as these—quality of life, samaritanism, and reassurance—that separate mortality and morbidity statistics from the real world.

The Study: Who Gets What Care

The national survey investigates five principal dimensions impinging on access to care: *source* of care, *convenience* of care, actual *utilization* of care, the

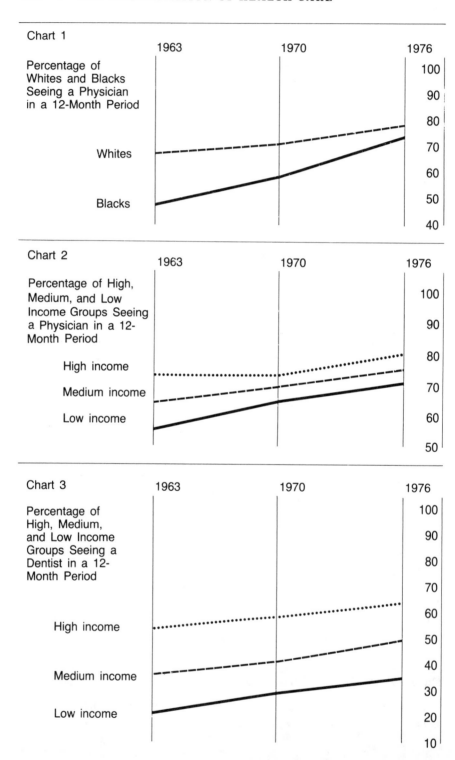

Chart 1

Percentage of Whites and Blacks Seeing a Physician in a 12-Month Period

1963   1970   1976

Whites

Blacks

Chart 2

Percentage of High, Medium, and Low Income Groups Seeing a Physician in a 12-Month Period

1963   1970   1976

High income

Medium income

Low income

Chart 3

Percentage of High, Medium, and Low Income Groups Seeing a Dentist in a 12-Month Period

1963   1970   1976

High income

Medium income

Low income

need for care, and the patient's *satisfaction* with care received. It examines all in considerable detail.

In the 1976 survey year, 76 percent of the population—160,000,000—saw a doctor. The percentage of infants and small children seeing a physician was highest: 87 percent. The percentage declines sharply in the middle and late years of childhood, then climbs slowly through the adult years to a level of 79 percent for those 65 or older.

The report's most significant findings show that the population at large—and every sub-population group studied—has better access to medical services today than in 1970 or 1963.

There are some instances of dramatic change. Chart 1 shows the improvement experienced by blacks since 1963 in one important measure: percentage seeing a physician at least once in the previous year. And Chart 2 shows how the gaps between persons of different income levels have narrowed, though discrepancies continue.

"These trends," says Andersen, "correspond to those which might be expected as a result of the implementation of Medicaid and Medicare in 1966. Medicaid and most health center programs begun since 1963 were designed to serve the low income population of all ages."

The removal of financial barriers appears to have major impact on whether or not various groups have access to care. Whereas physician utilization by low and medium income groups has moved closer to that for the upper income group (Chart 2), the same narrowing of utilization has not occurred for dentist visits (Chart 3). Andersen concludes: ". . . dental services are least apt to be covered by existing financing mechanisms and it is this service for which the greatest inequities in use by family income and race . . . continue to persist."

The study places special emphasis on whether or not persons surveyed indicated they had a regular physician or regular source of care. Previous studies

---

Legend for charts on facing page: **Chart 1.** The percentage of the black population seeing a physician has increased substantially since 1963. While a small gap in physician utilization remains between blacks and whites, it has closed dramatically since 1970. The Chicago researchers report that the largest gains were made in areas of the central city. **Chart 2.** A comparison by income shows how low income groups have increased their use of physician services. Between 1963 and 1970, both low and middle income groups moved toward the high income group. During the next period, all three groups moved upward together in utilization. **Chart 3.** The impact of insurance is revealed in this chart showing the percentage of the population seeing a dentist. For all income levels, the utilization of dentists is lower than for physicians. And the gaps between high, medium, and low income groups in 1976 are not significantly different from 1963. One reason: 88 percent of the population have some form of medical insurance; only 18 percent have dental insurance.

have shown a strong correlation between having a physician and seeking medical service when illness occurs. More than 78 percent of the population claim to have a physician they see regularly; another 9 plus percent report a regular source of care (e.g., a clinic), but without identifying a particular physician.

That leaves almost 12 percent who have neither a physician nor a regular source of care. Andersen speaks frankly of this group: "Though this may appear to represent a small proportion overall, it means that there are actually an estimated 24 million people who can identify no particular place or provider as their regular point of entry to the health care system."

The survey data reveal that low income groups, urban blacks and Spanish heritage persons in the Southwest were less apt than whites to have their own doctor. And for all races, persons below the poverty level were less likely to have a regular source of care than those above.

Other findings include:

—11 percent of the population spent at least one day in the hospital in the survey year

—52 percent had a physical exam

—49 percent saw a dentist

—rural farm dwellers were less likely than city residents to see a physician

—low income Spanish heritage persons were least likely of all ethnic groups to see a physician

—most persons can reach their regular course of care within 30 minutes

—blacks, when in their doctor's office, wait longer to see a physician than whites

—city residents use specialists more frequently than other groups

—rural residents and farmers make greatest use of general/family practitioners

—64 percent of the population can obtain a doctor's appointment within two days; 8 percent have to wait more than 2 weeks.

Moving toward a Measure of Medical Need

Although the survey's findings clarify the picture of access to health care for different population groups, a central and intriguing question remains: are people really getting the medical care they need?

One of Andersen's colleagues, study director Lu Ann Aday, puts it this way: "Is the level of access to the system medically appropriate or not?"

To probe this important area, the Chicago researchers have taken their methodology a step beyond some methods already in widespread use and have pursued a new experimental approach which utilizes what is called the symptoms-response ratio. This approach, they say, "reflects the difference between the number of people with a given mix of symptoms who contact a physician at least once for the symptoms and the number that a panel of medical professionals say should contact a doctor for the symptoms."....

This phase of the study—still in its early stages of development and refinement—is important and has already proved to be controversial. But Andersen strongly believes that the study of access demands a way to measure need and he and his team intend to continue to pursue this approach.

If, in fact, differences do exist between what patients do and some doctors think they should do, it perhaps should not be considered surprising. Medicine is an inexact science and wide variations exist in the beliefs, opinions, and perceptions of doctors, as well as patients.

Are People Satisfied? What Americans Think about the Care They Obtain

Whether or not people are satisfied with their medical care, the Chicago researchers believe, is an important dimension of access and one part of the survey measures satisfaction: how patients feel about their encounters with the system.

Studies on consumer satisfaction in many areas, including health, have been increasing in recent years. Critics of this approach argue that patients are not appropriate judges of their health experiences because they lack sufficient technical knowledge to make an informed judgment.

The study team does not agree with that contention. Gretchen Fleming, assistant study director, notes: "Querying consumers derives from the very notions on which democracy itself is defended—that it is appropriate for the public to be invited and even urged to voice judgments, and that such opinions should be taken seriously. Should consumers' views appear ill-informed to policy makers or those who possess more technical information on the subject, it is their (the policy makers) prerogative in turn to try to convince the consumers otherwise by making further information available to them."

The study probes in some depth whether patients are satisfied or dissatisfied with the care they receive. Time spent waiting to see a doctor and the amount of information given to the patient by the doctor are major areas of dissatisfaction. But no factor rivals cost as a cause of dissatisfaction.

As with all aspects of the study, each factor has been analyzed by income, age, race, region, sex and other variables, and the following generalizations can be made:

—satisfaction with care received increases with age
—persons in the South are least satisfied
—persons with higher income and more education are the most satisfied
—blacks are less satisfied than whites

—persons who see their own doctor regularly are more satisfied than persons who see different doctors in a series of visits

—rural blacks in the South are least satisfied of all groups

—people of Spanish origin in the Southwest are less satisfied than other whites.

The study team has carried its analysis of satisfaction and dissatisfaction an important step further.... For example, dissatisfaction with the amount of time it takes to get to the doctor's office ranges from a low percentage of 4 percent for those who required less than 15 minutes to a high of 37 percent dissatisfied if the trip took over 30 minutes.

"It is very clear that the kinds of events that surround delivery of care strongly affect people's levels of satisfaction," the study team concludes. "Consumers in general are not inclined to be highly critical of their medical care."

The Paradox of Personal Satisfaction and Perceived Crisis

But then comes a paradox. Despite the survey data which show, generally, a high level of satisfaction, as well as increased access to the health system for Americans of all ages and races, the study also shows that 61 percent of the population—125,000,000 people—believe there is a crisis in health care in the United States. And another 26 percent are so uncertain they cannot deny it.

Why this paradox exists is a mystery still to be probed.... It could be a product of the human propensity to seek reassurance and support when in need. When people contemplate their own medical care (i.e., "Were you satisfied with what your doctor did for you?"), the response is from the perspective of a patient—each individual is then a statistic of only one and answers are shaped accordingly.

It is quite another matter to respond to questions about health in the abstract, simply as a part of the aggregate (i.e., "Is there a crisis in health care?").

In spite of these mixed perceptions about what goes on in America's health care system, the national survey of access to medical care provides important new insight into the how and why of a system and is a study of importance likely to be analyzed for years.

Allan Parachini

All-Night Vigil at Emergency Hospital

This journalistic account of one young doctor's night of work in an emergency hospital provides a personal view of the health care system, exploring the experience of patients as well as hospital employees. It also serves as a reminder of the growing importance of accidents and violence as major health care problems in modern society. Allan Parachini is a staff writer for the Los Angeles Times.

I t is somewhere between 11:30 and 11:45 p.m.

Fred Levin goes with the traffic flow on Imperial Highway where the broad boulevard makes its transition from Inglewood through a slice of Los Angeles County and, finally, into Watts.

"This is my quiet period usually," Levin explains as his silver and black compact travels along Imperial, approaching the intersection of South Wilmington Avenue. "I know that I'm going to be working all night and this stretch of the drive is going to be my last chance to have any peace and quiet."

He wears brown corduroy jeans, a green hospital gown top and a white coat. Falling out of the white coat pockets are a stethoscope, an otoscope (a flashlightlike device for looking into ears, nose and mouth) and a dog-eared medical reference book or two.

Clipped unceremoniously to the lapel of the white coat is a plastic name tag that says "Fred Levin, M.D."

Down a few blocks on South Wilmington, Levin turns into an employee parking lot at Martin Luther King General Hospital. At one corner of the parking lot a lighted red and white directional sign says "EMERGENCY."

For the next eight hours, in the middle of this Friday night, the King emergency room will be what Fred Levin simply calls "work." It is a classic understatement.

Levin parks the compact and walks toward the emergency entrance. He is a young man, about 25, in the second year of a three-year residency training program. For several months each year, Levin is assigned to King Emergency.

As the Massachusetts-born Levin talks, there is the sound of New England.

"Trauma" comes out "traumer" as he describes medical school at Boston University.

Five years ago, taking training in emergency medicine would have been looked on with disdain.

But Levin is working to be certified in a new specialty, emergency medicine, that is quickly forcing recognition of the sophisticated nature of critical care. Since 1975, a specialty society for emergency room doctors has been organized and emergency medicine has imposed rules for its own specialty board certification test.

Levin will be eligible to take the exam in a little more than a year. He plans to spend his life in emergency rooms, not by default but meticulously on purpose.

On nights when Levin is lucky, he gets to go home after only 10 or 12 hours. When he's not lucky, the tour stretches to 24 hours. He climbs a few steps to the emergency room ambulance driveway and looks around.

"So far, so good," he says. "I can always tell we're in for it if there are more than two ambulances here when I arrive. If all the ambulances have their lights flashing, then you really know you're going to have a tough night."

This night's first sign bodes well. Only one ambulance is parked under the canopy. Its red lights are turned off.

*   *   *

An emergency room or a hospital, any honest doctor will say, is run by—and is only as good as—its nurses. By the time he has parked the car and walked up the ramp, Levin has unhesitatingly flattered King Emergency's nurses no less than four times during the 30-minute drive from his apartment.

There will be a dozen of them this Friday night, assigned to the "red" and "blue" treatment teams—red for injury and other trauma cases and blue for patients with medical problems like fever, asthma and heart attack.

The nurses include:

Sarah Patterson, a tall, imposing woman who is supervising nurse for King Emergency's midnight-to-8 shift, a job she has held for five years. She says she prefers all-night hours because it insures she is available during the day if her three children need her.

Willie Jones, who first started working at King Emergency before the hospital actually opened in 1972. She clearly has a skill necessary in emergency medicine: the ability to size up a patient quickly in the first few seconds after he arrives. She has eyes that seem to be able to perform a thorough medical analysis in a single glance.

Janice Autry, the lady with the only key to King Emergency's pharmacy. No one except her can distribute the narcotics and other medicines patients will use this Friday night—no exceptions, not even doctors. She is the kind of nurse who always turns out to have just started to do what a physician turns to tell her to do. And, when the doctor realizes this, she always smiles.

11:55 p.m. The midnight-to-8 shift of Levin, two other physicians, Patterson, Jones, Autry and assorted other nurses and attendants make rounds, reviewing with Dr. Karen Dix, who is finishing her 4-to-12 tour, the status of every one of the 20 patients who lie on litters in King Emergency waiting to be treated.

Dix has just started when a woman's voice starts screaming "Wilbur! Wilbur!" The screams fill the entire King Emergency complex—actually a suite of more than a half dozen interconnected treatment rooms, holding areas and office and storage spaces.

Dix continues, but the "Wilbur! Wilbur" cries punctuate everything she says.

The last patient on rounds is the one doing the moaning. She is alone in a little cubicle marked "Burn Care Room." As the medical team stops outside the door, she stops calling for Wilbur and cries out "Doctor! Doctor! Nurse! Nurse!"

"You may recognize this lady," Dix begins. "She is the same lady who was admitted late yesterday."

It seems Burn Care Room Lady is 26 and a habitual user of the drug PCP, which makes her suicidal. A night earlier, she had cracked open her forehead and been rushed to King Emergency where the gash was stitched and her drug symptoms relieved.

She is back again and again has taken PCP. Then, because she believed that, under the drug's influence, she saw God and was instructed to destroy herself, she jumped through a plate glass window on Friday afternoon, opening an enormous gash on one arm.

She had lost quite a bit of blood by the time she got to King Emergency. Her cuts have been stitched, but she will not lie still long enough to be X-rayed and cannot be mixed with other patients because she screams continuously.

Jones tries to calm her. Burn Care Room Lady will have none of it.

12:15 a.m. Occupying Bed 6 is an alert, but concerned young man who frets to Levin about missing work. He is, he explains, Robot Man, a character in a laser light show that performs on stage with musical revues.

Robot Man's problem is that he was accompanying his father to a store "when two guys come up to us and say, 'Give us all the money.'"

Street-wise, Robot Man and his father complied. Robot Man, who had the proceeds from his previous night's performance with him, put $1,000 on the sidewalk. The holdup man, both of whom were armed, picked it up.

"They told us it wasn't enough," Robot Man recalls. Dissatisfied, one of the gunmen leveled a shotgun at Robot Man's father. Robot Man stepped between them and the gunman pulled the trigger, spraying buckshot that hit Robot Man in both legs and one hand.

As Levin gently probes the buckshot wounds, Robot Man smiles, clearly aware he is lucky to be alive. He protests that because he can't walk, he can't work. But the protests are gentle.

Levin sends him to X-ray.

12:30 a.m. The man in Bed 5 has been patient. At about 2:30 in the afternoon he was in an automobile accident, suffering facial injuries. For the last couple of hours, he has been waiting for the results of his X-rays while other, more critically ill and injured patients have been treated at King Emergency.

Figuring to stitch the gashes around Bed 5's left eye, Levin does a routine test of the man's vision and starts to look concerned. The left eye will not focus. Levin takes him to an eye chart. The results are no better.

His demeanor unchanged, Levin asks Bed 5 if he wears glasses. Bed 5 says he does not. Well, then, there may be a problem, Levin explains. Bed 5 listens stoically. Within five minutes, Levin is on the telephone to a consulting ophthalmologist, arranging a special appointment for a complete examination at 7 a.m.

*   *   *

Levin starts to write an order for some lab tests, but Patterson tells him there is a problem. The automated machine that tests blood samples for electrolytes, a key test, has broken down. Now, instead of a two-hour wait for results from the financially pressed county-owned hospital's overburdened laboratory, four hours will be necessary.

Levin shrugs. "You learn not to get upset," he says. "That's the way it is."

12:40 a.m. Bed 5's neighbor, Bed 4, is being attended by Dr. Otis White, another emergency medicine resident who has stayed overtime from the 4-to-12 shift to deal with Bed 4.

It is another hold-up casualty. Bed 4 says he was jumped suddenly by at least two men with knives. He doesn't remember exactly how much they got from him, but they left him on the sidewalk, stabbed in the head, stomach and back, before they fled.

The wounds are horrendous, though Bed 4 will survive and, in fact, is fully conscious and talking coherently. His explanation, to an outsider, is remarkably matter-of-fact. It is as if this kind of thing happens to him all the time.

As White stitches the head wound, a 3-inch gash down to the skull, Levin goes to look at Bed 4's X-rays.

In a small, dark room lined with lighted viewing boxes, Levin positions studies of Bed 4's head, chest, stomach and back. He sees something he hadn't expected. Bed 4 has a large-caliber bullet lodged in his abdomen.

There is also a clear mark on the X-ray of his head that indicates a fractured skull. "It looks like someone really whacked him," another doctor comments. Bed 4 explains. The bullet is from when he was shot a year or two ago. He is more vague about the skull fracture. He says he really doesn't remember how that happened. No, he says, he doesn't think anyone hit him there.

Later, the wounds stitched and all lab tests negative, Bed 4 will calmly dress in a blazer, sport shirt and dark green slacks, like someone about to go out on a date. True, the top half of his head is wrapped in bandages and blood is still oozing from the deep gash.

But as he walks out of King Emergency, he will be singing quietly to himself. He will turn as he passes a young lady walking in the corridor and pat her on the buttocks with his discharge form.

"How old is that guy?" someone will ask. "He looks 35, maybe 40." "No, he's 20," Levin will reply.

Hospital administrator Mel Iizuka will shake his head in disbelief and mutter: "There is a whole lot of life that's gone into those 20 years."

1:30 a.m. Robot Man's X-rays are ready. Levin searches a cabinet for Robot Man's file, but doesn't find it. "What did I say his last name was?" Levin asks, a little distracted.

He turns as Dr. George Wall, an older, pipe-smoking radiologist on duty, strides through the door.

"Have you reviewed the guy with the buckshot yet?" Levin asks. Wall looks perplexed.

"Buckshot? Well, OK, but buckshot where?" he asks, seeking some clue to differentiate this buckshot wound from others he has seen recently.

"Legs and hand," Levin explains. Wall shakes his head and puffs on his pipe. Finally, Levin finds Robot Man's file. Wall scans the X-rays and reaches for a microphone that is connected to a dictation system. The films show small white dots around all of the bones of Robot Man's lower legs.

Wall is dictating a technical report, in which he describes "metallic fragments that resemble buckshot. Period."

No attempt will be made to remove the buckshot, Levin explains. In recent years, doctors have discovered that taking bullets out that are not interfering with regular body functions is more risky than leaving them in.

So Levin and Wall scan the X-rays to make sure none of the buckshot is resting against bone joints or likely to interfere with nerves, blood vessels or arteries. The best treatment, they decide, will be to send Robot Man home, buckshot intact.

"Robot Man is gonna hurt tomorrow," Levin concludes.

*   *   *

Out in the reception area, Henry Killings looks around. Yes, he says with a slight smile, he does get kidded occasionally about his last name, since he is head security guard on the midnight-to-8 at King Emergency.

He talks about his job. There is a balance to be struck, he explains, between the need for a smooth hospital operation and accommodation of the needs of the people who live near King Emergency.

"We're always open and the people here know that," Killings says. "We have people in our neighborhood who actually have no place to go, so they come here. They want to sleep, but if we let them use the waiting room as a hotel, the patients would be crowded out.

"We ask them what they are doing here and if they aren't patients or people who came with patients, we try, politely, to ask them to leave."

Killings scans the waiting room for regulars and sees none. On the uphol-tered benches, however, several families are asleep. Killings calls over a guard and tells him to canvass discreetly the waiting room for squatters.

2:05 a.m. On a litter in a corner of King Emergency, a father and two of his daughters wait patiently. The younger girl, about 8, has a large piece of ad-hesive tape across her chin.

"Dr. Levin, they've been here since 5 p.m.," a nurse says. The delay is unfortunate, but things can happen that way at King Emergency. Levin walks over to the litter.

The little girl sees Levin coming and glances at the white coat and the stethoscope. "Is it going to hurt?" she cries. "No! No!"

The father smiles. The girl, he says, fell off a skateboard and hit her chin on the driveway pavement. "Take your hand away," the father tells the girl. She complies. Levin pulls on surgical gloves and reaches for suturing material. The girl starts to cry again as Levin administers a local anesthetic so he can stitch the cut.

"This is terrible, huh?" Levin says to the girl. "What a bad present for you."

The father and nurse Jones gently hold the crying girl to keep her from thrashing. Levin sneaks in four deft stitches, then pulls off the gloves. As suddenly as it began, the girl's tearful struggle ends as Levin walks away.

2:45 a.m. Levin has finally stitched the cuts of the automobile accident victim in Bed 5. The man's wife has joined him after arriving on an RTD bus, but because their only car was destroyed in the accident, the couple has no way to get home.

The extent of the damage to Bed 5's left eye is still unknown, however, so the couple finds a quiet corner of the waiting room and sits down to pass the time until the eye specialist arrives at 7 a.m.

A few minutes later, Killings and one of his guards—aware that the man is a patient—see the two exhausted people in an embrace, sound asleep.

Killings looks at them for a moment, then turns, having decided not to disturb their sleep, and walks away quietly.

3:10 a.m. Levin does a doubletake as he walks past a litter.

"She fell off her moped," a nurse explains.

"Wait a minute," Levin protests. "She fell off her moped yesterday. I treated her yesterday for falling off her moped. What's going on?"

"Well," says the nurse, "she fell off her moped again."

"Rosie, Rosie," Levin says to the patient. "what did you do this time?" The groggy woman mumbles something. Levin looks at her left knee, which is a mass of blood.

Levin cleans and bandages the wound, concluding it will—just barely—not have to be stitched. The woman starts to get up to leave.

"She says she's fallen off before, but never got hurt before yesterday." Levin says. "She says she's had the moped for two years. I suppose there is a limit to how long it will last."

4:30 a.m. Levin looks worried for the first time. He is looking at the lab test results of a young woman who walked in saying she just didn't feel well.

She stayed for a while, but then got impatient waiting for the lab report and left. The problem is that the test indicates she is probably bleeding internally and has lost so much blood that her life may be in danger.

"She has a hematocrit of 14," Levin says of the woman's test report. The test is a measure of blood volume and condition. Normal for a woman is 42 on a scale of 100. "If she's lost that blood suddenly—and we don't know if she has or hasn't—a hematocrit of 14 may not be consistent with life."

For the next hour, a nurse will keep calling the telephone number the young woman wrote on her admission form. Finally, someone answers; the young woman has arrived home. The situation is rather generally explained and the nurse pleads for the woman to return.

Reluctantly, she agrees.

"We can't stop them," Levin says. "They get up and walk out the back door with a lot worse problems than that."

5:20 a.m. First light.

In the 10-bed holding area at the back of King Emergency, a psychiatric patient feigns a seizure. Dr. Otis Rounds looks at him, and tells him to stop faking. But the noise has started to rouse the rest of the litters.

All of the holding area patients are psychiatric cases. Many of them, including four that have arrived during the night, are also people under the influence of PCP. It is an applied lesson in the patterns of drug abuse.

Except for dealing with several alcoholics, in this entire Friday night, King Emergency has had patients with problems with only one drug, PCP. There has been not a single heroin overdose nor any other narcotic case. Just PCP.

The hospital is caught in the middle.

Though King is building an 80-bed psychiatric unit, there is no place to put mental patients now. And on weekends, nearby Metropolitan State Hospital does not accept new admissions so King Emergency turns into a psychiatric treatment ward.

A man wearing a yellow shirt walks in and hands a clerk a note detailing his history. Killings and two other guards overhear him emphasize that he has spent more than 17 years in various California state prisons.

"I've been classified as a manic depressive," Yellow Shirt says, "with homicidal tendencies. But I never, to my knowledge, killed anyone, except they said I killed someone in 1960 and then they gave me shock treatments for it."

King Emergency has no choice but to give Yellow Shirt a litter to sit on until Metropolitan State Hospital will take him. It may be Monday morning before he leaves.

5:40 a.m. Dr. Otis Rounds is having trouble with one of the psychiatric patients, who turns out to be an alcoholic going into a violent case of the delirium tremens. The man gets dressed and tries to walk out, with an intravenous tube still attached to his arm. Angered, he tears the tube out.

Rounds tries Valium to relieve the DT symptoms, recognizing that withdrawal from alcoholism is a more dangerous medical procedure than withdrawal from heroin. Finally, after three doses of Valium, the man calms. Rounds admits him as an inpatient.

7:25 a.m. Levin is dealing with a perplexing case, a 61-year-old with uncontrollable asthma. The man walked into King Emergency at his wits' end. His medicines stopped working for him after he moved to Los Angeles from

Detroit three weeks ago and he has been unable to get more than 30 minutes sleep without going into an attack.

At morning rounds, Levin explains the situation to Dr. Zemmar Lenoir III, King Emergency's chief resident in internal medicine.

But it is late and Levin's tour is nearly over. Lenoir prepares to take over. "Let's get to the bottom of this," he says, looking at his patient. The man looks relieved. Detailing a nurse to work full-time with the asthmatic, Lenoir pulls curtains around the bed for privacy and prepares for what will surely be a difficult day with the asthmatic.

8:45 a.m. Levin parks his car in the garage under his apartment building.

"I guess I'm used to it," he says, "but I'm not that tired."

Levin has two consecutive days off—an unusual occurrence. He and his wife Linda, a nurse who is also an art student, have planned a weekend of camping. For five days, Levin has been assembling newly purchased sleeping bags, backpacks and a tent.

He unlocks the front door to the apartment and asks:

"Do you, by any chance, have a map of Joshua Tree?"

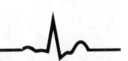

The fact that physicians and medical organizations are more interested in disease than in health might be regarded as an expression of professional bias, but this attitude corresponds in reality to a widespread human trait.

—René Dubos

6 Specialists, Generalists, and New Health Practitioners

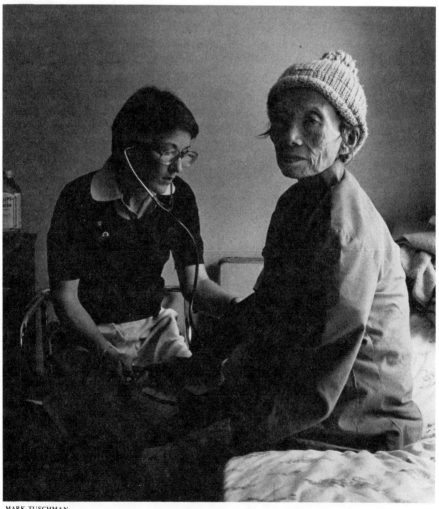

MARK TUSCHMAN

The influence of Abraham Flexner on modern medical practice can hardly be overestimated. He had a vision for the future, which has been realized beyond all expectations. In 1908, with support from private foundations and the blessing of the American Medical Association, Flexner set out to inspect the state of American medical education. Two years later he issued a report to the Carnegie Foundation that included a series of recommendations for sweeping reform. As a result, medicine went through a period of purification. Restrictions were placed on medical education to assure that institutions were organized on scientific principles. The capricious days of teaching medicine for commercial purposes were ended.

While Flexner's whirlwind tour had the laudable effect of eliminating much of the undesirable element from medicine—the charlatans and incompetents—some of its far-reaching effects could hardly have been predicted at the time. Not the least of these was the decline in importance of the family doctor. Medicine entered an era of academic science, and it became centered in the hospital and laboratory. Doctors had for a long time treated individuals—their births, illnesses, and deaths—in the context of home and community. Scientific medicine ushered in an explosion of technology and specialization; the human element was often neglected. Doctors were no longer healers of the sick; they cured disease.

In reality, the old-fashioned family doctors were limited in their understanding of the biological foundations of disease, and their arsenal of treatments lacked the potency of modern science. But with all their limitations, they did not isolate the patient from the experience of disease and disability, and they offered a continuity of care that is unavailable in many quarters today.

The spiraling development of medical technology and academic science led to the subdivision of medical practice into more than sixty-five specialties and subspecialties. As a result, complex life-threatening disorders are better understood; on the other hand, few professionals have been trained to specialize in the treatment of the common, uncomplicated health problems that account for 90 percent of visits to doctors.

The articles in this chapter focus on issues related to specialization, and they discuss the role of new health practitioners (such as the nurse practitioner from the Visiting Nurse Association of San Francisco, shown in the photo at the beginning of this chapter), who provide some of the routine services of the old-time physicians. Their influence is still small, and issues remain unresolved concerning their utilization in doctors' offices, clinics, and hospitals. Their potential contribution is great: they could contribute to resolving physician shortages and maldistribution; they could offer personalized, supportive care that is not available from specialists; they could help to contain costs; they could offer opportunities for greater numbers of ethnic minorities to participate in the health care sector. But it is also possible that they will not be well used; they could be swallowed up in the fragmented, complex, unintegrated system and serve only to reinforce its present inadequacies.

Abraham Flexner was a product of his time, and the first article in this chapter gives us a vivid glimpse of what medicine was like at the turn of the century. "Levi Cooper Lane, M.D." is a portrait of a general surgeon, painted by his student Emmet Rixford, in the days when there were few trained nurses and surgery was often performed in the home or in the doctor's office. The scenes portrayed in this article are in stark contrast to conditions today, as described in Parachini's article in the last chapter and in the remaining articles in this chapter.

In "Health Employment and the Nation's Health," economist Christine E. Bishop reviews the training and employment situation for doctors, nurses, and others in the health workforce. She pinpoints a number of inadequacies and barriers endemic to the system and evaluates some common policy prescriptions. Dr. C. Glenn Pickard, Jr., of the University of North Carolina Medical School, centers on "Midlevel Practitioners: Nurse Practitioners and Physicians' Assistants"—their evolution in the field, their training, what they actually do, and how they can contribute to solutions of many problems that plague the health care system. Nicholas Lemann, in "Let the Nurses Do It," traces a number of fundamental problems we face today back to the Flexnerian fixed code for medical education. A contributing editor of *Washington Monthly,* he explores possibilities for improving medicine and lowering fees by altering educational requirements to fit the realities of what practitioners actually do. Rosemary Stevens, a leading analyst in the field of health systems management, closes this chapter with a discussion of the "Health Manpower" policy issues that are part of the current debate in government circles.

Emmet Rixford

Levi Cooper Lane, M.D.

Many people who are critical of modern medicine for being overspecialized and impersonal lament the loss of the "old-fashioned" doctor, who treated his patients in their homes and showed loving concern for them as individuals. In the following selection, Emmet Rixford, a San Francisco doctor, sympathetically describes the practice of Levi Cooper Lane, a general surgeon, in the late nineteenth century. At the time, hospitals were just beginning to lose their unfavorable reputation as institutions for the destitute, and surgery, like other medical treatment, was often performed in the home or the doctor's office, with medical students sometimes serving as both surgical assistants and postoperative nurses.

Doctor Lane a Hard Worker.—Doctor Lane was an indefatigable worker. A splendid anatomist, he kept his anatomy alive and constantly refreshed by doing a little dissecting each week. In fact he had a private dissecting room on the fifth floor of the college where in preparation for any serious surgical operation he was wont to make dissection of the part in order that he might not be found wanting in the anatomy of the region on which he was to operate. In his relations with his faculty and students, he was always master. His students he knew by name, often exciting wonder that he could remember so accurately the names of so many students. But he had a system about it, a geographical classification, he knew and remembered the town from which the student had come. His teaching was chiefly by lecture, in which he had the ability to make such strong pictures that they were easily remembered. During the college term he would often invite a group of senior students Sunday morning to witness an operation, done in the largest room in his office, the men's waiting room. He had a few bedrooms on the second and third floors which served as hospital.

Sometimes, when the operation was slow and tedious, he would quote from some classic writer or from Shakespeare. He knew Macbeth, and on one occasion was reciting a passage when his attention was suddenly required in the operation. A sepulchral voice from the back of the group of students went on and finished the scene. It happened that one of the students was C. B. Bishop, a comedian in the old California Theater Stock Company.

Doctor Lane was accustomed to take two students from each junior class to serve as house officers in his office in the afternoons, substituting that work for work in the clinic. I had this privilege for two years, as did my associates, Dr. William Fitch Cheney and Dr. Stanley Stillman, and others. There were no trained nurses, or very few, in those days and we students prepared everything for the operation; one gave the anesthetic, another assisted, and one was assigned as nurse to take care of the patient and watch him for the first twenty-four or forty-eight hours. It was a valuable experience. On Sunday afternoon when practice was quiet, Doctor Lane would often call his students into his office and read us a chapter from Hippocrates or Lucian or Tacitus, translating as he went along.

Doctor Lane had a wonderful nose. He said, "These young men have to have a thermometer to make a diagnosis of typhoid fever. They don't know typhoid. If one knows typhoid fever he can make the diagnosis on entering the room." And that nose of his could smell a cigarette further than anyone I ever knew.

On one occasion I asked him for a vacation, saying that some friends had planned a tramp in the Sierra and that I would like to go. His reply was that "if you feel you need a vacation, of course you should have it." Then he looked off, as was his wont, over his glasses, and I waited knowing that something more was coming. He said, "When I was your age I missed but two days in my office in fifteen years."

His Physical Health.—I noticed on a number of occasions that he would leave the operating table in the midst of an operation to be gone for perhaps ten or fifteen minutes, during which time we, his assistants, ligated small blood vessels and otherwise carried on minor parts of the work, when he would return and finish the operation. I often wondered why he left the room. Years afterwards I heard him say that he suffered from indigestion and many times would have to leave the operating table to go out and empty his stomach.

When asked as to his health, he always said it was excellent and slyly remarked to us afterwards that he always gave that answer because otherwise he would have to answer the same question again; and yet he was a great sufferer from sciatica, though few were aware of it. He used to say with wonderful meaning, "It is a great thing to relieve pain."

Doctor Lane's Offices.—Most of his surgery in his active years was done either in private houses or in some of the numerous cheap boarding houses south of Market Street, or in the upper rooms of his office. The front room on the top floor was generally used for more important operations and I can remember sitting up all night many and many a time watching the patient that had been operated upon in the morning. We always knew when morning was coming by hearing the clatter of the vegetable wagons as they came in slow procession down Mission Street from the gardens of South San Francisco.

The office on the ground floor comprised four rooms, a front room, the men's waiting room, the women's waiting room where Doctor Lane had his desk and kept his records, between these, his private office, opening into each of these rooms. There was his examining couch, his instrument cabinet, and a folding bed for the old man who acted as night watchman. Hanging by a thong on the door frame was a pick-handle, to be used for defense in emergency. The fourth room was a sort of laboratory where we young men waited his pleasure.

Doctor Lane's fees were moderate, yet the volume of his office business was such that I remember a certain day in which work was slack enough to cause him to remark that for twenty-five years his office visits had averaged more than $50 a day. Old soldiers always appealed to him. He said that any man who had been in Andersonville Prison could have his services without charge. I shall never forget an old miner or prospector who had had some surgical operation, coming downstairs to pay his bill. Doctor Lane had done some operation upon him and the man was ready to leave. Doctor Lane said, "Have you paid your board bill upstairs?" "Yes." "How much money have you?" With some pride the miner answered, "$75," as if that to him was quite a sum. Doctor Lane said, "Well, I think that $75 will do you more good than it will me."

Doctor Lane's Knowledge of Human Nature.—Doctor Lane was a great student of human nature. He was absolutely intolerant of shiftless, lazy people. On one occasion he performed a small operation on a boy, for which he would ordinarily have charged $5; perhaps it was opening a boil. Doctor Lane was more interested in the father than in the operation. He sensed something in the man that did not ring true. With his penetrating glance which forced an answer of truth, he asked the man what he did for a living. The man stammered and finally acknowledged that he was a beggar. "What!" said Doctor Lane. "You, an able-bodied man, stand on a corner and accept alms from people who have earned their living by work! I will charge you $30 for this operation." The man paid it in nickels and dimes. After Doctor Lane's death I told the story to Mrs. Lane. She laughed and said, "That accounts for it, for one evening Doctor Lane came home from the office chuckling and presented me with a bag of nickels and dimes. Many of them were bad."

When antisepsis finally reached San Francisco, Dr. C. E. Farnum, who was demonstrator of anatomy and who assisted Doctor Lane in much of his work, persuaded Doctor Lane to use Lister's carbolic acid spray in an operation. The machine failed to work properly and sprayed Doctor Lane perhaps more than the germs that were trying to get into the wound. Doctor Lane threw the machine out of the window and continued the operation on his old plan.

He was wont to classify surgeons as good or bad according to how they treated fractured elbow, so certain was he of the superior advantages of the straight position. If the surgeon used it, he was a good surgeon, otherwise not. Doctor Lane got splendid results in his treatment of the fractured elbow in children, which consisted of putting it up in straight position, to be sure, but taking off the dressing each day and forcibly bending the elbow through its full range of flexion. This was very painful to the child, as I know, because I often had to hold the child. In other words, although we now know the straight position is not the best, Doctor Lane got good results by molding the callus by this persistent manipulation and gradually adjusting the fragments into normal position. It was because Dr. Oscar H. Allis of Philadelphia treated fractures of the elbow in the straight position that Doctor Lane invited him to give one of the courses in the Lane Medical Lectures.

Nothing would rouse Dr. Lane's ire like a suit for malpractice. He often said he would cheerfully take the witness stand in defense of his bitterest enemy to fight a malpractice suit, and yet when a patient was brought to him with a bad result from an improperly treated fracture, Dr. Lane sent the patient back to his doctor saying, "Let him finish it." To me he said, "It might do him good to take a little of his own medicine. That doctor was the prosecuting witness in a viciously fought malpractice suit against a fine old doctor in his town who brought him into the world." Dr. Lane felt that for anyone, especially a doctor, to act as prosecuting witness against the man who had brought him into the world, was the very acme of ingratitude.

Doctor Lane's Kindliness of Heart.—Doctor Lane, an austere man, was still the embodiment of kindness to the unfortunate. I once heard him say that he did not wish any man to feel too poor to have his services. On one occasion I happened to be walking with him on the street, and when he saw me step upon a cockroach that happened to be crossing the pavement, he said, "His life was not worth much, but it was precious to him." When caring for a child he had equal regard for the feelings of the mother, and said to us, "Remember that it is her child."

As a surgeon, Doctor Lane was not greatly original and, unfortunately, kept very brief and imperfect records, so that although his practice was enormous he left very little that the student of today can use. He worked out vaginal hysterectomy as an original anatomical study, not knowing that the operation had been done in the early years of the nineteenth century in France and had been forgotten. A mother brought her child to him suffering with microcephalia. The mother said, "Can you not as a surgeon unlock my child's brain? The bone is closing in on it." This suggestion of the mother led Doctor Lane to perform the operation of craniotomy, in which he preceded

Lannelongue by many years. The operation was, of course, futile because the real trouble was maldevelopment of the brain itself.

In his money matters, he had many opportunities for favorable investment. Mackay, of Comstock Lode fame, gave him a tip as to probable movements in the stock market. In refusing the tip, Doctor Lane's reply was that his mine was in his office, but an associate took the tip and realized handsomely.

Doctor Lane's Gift of Cooper College and Lane Hospital.—In building Cooper College and Lane Hospital, Doctor Lane was proud to put up a tablet reading: "This building, erected by Levi Cooper Lane, with moneys earned by himself in his profession, is dedicated to suffering humanity and to the medical profession in the hope that the former may here find refuge and relief and the latter exercise of its humane skill and intelligent sympathy." But his course in building Lane Hospital was fraught with many difficulties and strenuous opposition from property holders in the neighborhood. One property holder send him an anonymous postal card, threatening to blow up him and his institution with dynamite if he persisted.

I had the honor to assist Doctor Lane in his last surgical operation which was for the removal of a cancerous breast. He was so weak that it required much mental effort to complete the operation. At one stage he said, "Give me more light; I can't see in the depth." I handed him his old scissors that he had used for many, many years, saying, "Use these, Doctor Lane; they have been there so often they would scarcely need light." He smiled, and after the operation held up the scissors and said, "Never cut adhesive plaster with those scissors. That's what Doctor Cooper said to me when he gave them to me forty years ago."

After a long and exhausting illness, death finally came on February 18, 1902. The nurse in attendance said he suddenly woke from a drowse, partially sat up and said, "Oh, it is death, it is death," and expired. Doctor Stillman and I were not far away and, when reaching the room and learning of it, Doctor Stillman said, "I wonder what it looks like when seen so close at hand."

Christine E. Bishop

Health Employment
and the Nation's Health

In this overview of positions, duties, training, and earning patterns of health workers, economist Christine E. Bishiop shows how these factors affect the cost, availability, and quality of health care. She discusses the roles of foreign medical graduates, "physician extenders" such as physician assistants and nurse practitioners, allied health workers, and related health sector employees, and assesses the factors that will influence the makeup of the health work force of the future.

Health workers are the ultimate producers of health services. One cannot imagine health care without their experienced observation, diagnostic judgment and caring hands, and their overriding sense of responsibility to their patients. It is no surprise that the salaries of health personnel constitute a large share of the cost of health services. Because of their diversity, it is difficult to generalize about health workers. Some, like physicians and dentists, receive many years of scientific training, and are permitted under law to take full responsibility for diagnosis and treatment of patients. Others, like nursing personnel and technicians of many types, have shorter, more specific training and are hired by hospitals and other providers to care for patients under supervision. Still others, like secretaries, maids, and food service workers, have little training specifically related to health care but perform necessary functions in our health institutions. Trends in the training and employment of health workers and trends in their earnings do much to determine the availability and quality of health care for Americans, and the cost of that care.

Physicians and dentists are at the pinnacle of the health occupational structure. They undertake long educational programs at professional schools at great expense to themselves and with large direct and indirect public subsidy. Many pursue specialty training. Although a number of career paths are open to them, including research, teaching, and salaried employment, most work as independent entrepreneurs in individual or group private practice. They are typically paid by their patients or by their patients' insurance, private or government, on a fee-for-service basis.

There were 379,748 physicians in the United States in 1974, about one for every 550 Americans. Yet people in many parts of the country, especially in isolated rural areas and central cities, have difficulty finding a family physician, both to provide care when they are acutely ill and to provide the kind of comprehensive continuous care which, over a lifetime, may prevent disease. Does this mean that there is a shortage of physicians? It is easy to see how a shortage might arise. Medical schools are very expensive to establish and operate, and for many years the number of places in medical schools did not expand as rapidly as the growing demand for physician services induced by population growth, rising incomes, and increased insurance coverage. In addition, the "pipeline" of medical education is a long one; a college graduate entering medical school can be licensed to practice only after four years of study followed by a year of internship at a hospital; and most new graduates seek specialty training in residency programs of two years or more. Year after year, experts have estimated our national "need" for physicians, usually based on ideal physician-population ratios, and have demonstrated that future shortages are inevitable, given the rate of production of new physicians. In response, state and federal assistance to medical schools has encouraged their rapid expansion: while 7,574 new physicians were graduated in the academic year 1965–1966, by 1975–1976 medical schools graduated 13, 561, a 79 percent increase in the rate of production of new physicians in ten years. But the increase in the number of physicians has not solved the problem of access to medical care for many Americans. Statistics reveal a wide variation in physician-population ratios by location: in 1974, these ranged from 78 per 100,000 in South Dakota to 237 per 100,000 in New York. In 1970, 132 counties in the United States had no physicians, an increase of 34 since 1963. Compounding geographical maldistribution is the long-run decline in the availability of physicians providing primary care, which stood at 94 per 100,000 population in 1931 and has fallen to 55 per 100,000 in 1974. (Primary care practitioners include general practitioners, pediatricians, internists, and physicians in a newly developing specialty, family practice. Residency training, i.e., hospital training beyond internship, is not required for general practice.)

A large inflow of physicians trained abroad has been permitted and even encouraged because of the perceived shortage of physicians. In 1974, 21.8 percent of United States physicians were educated abroad and foreign medical graduates (FMG's) held almost one-third of all internship and residency positions. FMG's in general appear to be less well prepared than American graduates, and questions have been raised about the influence of our dependence on FMG's on the quality of American medical care. In addition, an increasing number of American citizens, rejected by medical schools in the United States, are attending medical school abroad and hoping to return to the United States as transfer students, or for postgraduate training and practice.

The Health Professions Education Assistance Act of 1976 is a further attempt by the federal government to address these problems. It provides support to medical schools only if a substantial proportion of their affiliated residency positions (50 percent by fiscal year 1980) are in primary care specialties; a scholarship program is established to pay tuition, expenses, and a stipend to medical students who agree to practice in designated underserved areas; and the problem of underprepared FMG's wishing to immigrate to the United States is addressed. This legislation is the most far-reaching attempt so far to influence the distribution as well as the supply of health professionals, in recognition of the impact of distribution on the quality and availability of health care for the American people.

Paying the Doctor. The availability and quality of medical care are also affected by the way physicians are paid in our health care system. While a significant proportion of their work is performed in hospitals, most physicians are not paid by these health institutions, but by their patients, on a fee-for-service basis. Physicians earn more if they perform more fee-generating services, and they typically work long hours: non-federal physicians in office practice worked an average of 49.9 hours per week in 1974.

They also earn more if fees rise. For most goods and services, price directly influences the consumer's decision; he or she evaluates carefully whether the item is worth its price, and high prices are likely to discourage purchases. The prices of physician services do not play this role for many consumers, who are covered by private health insurance or by government health programs (Medicare and Medicaid) for in-hospital physician care and, increasingly, for some outpatient care as well. Physicians have apparently been able to raise fees without reducing the demand for their services or affecting the financial situation of individual patients, since third parties (insurance companies and government agencies) pay the bills. . . . Rapidly rising fees feed health cost inflation, and physician fees are clearly a significant component of rising national health expenditures.

Plans and programs to improve the availability and quality of health care in this country and to control its total cost may involve changes in the way physicians are paid. Under a prepaid group practice arrangement, for example, individuals pay the group practice organization a premium or capitation which covers all health care for a year. If physicians, who make most decisions about patient care, choose less costly modes of care when appropriate (for example outpatient care instead of in-hospital treatment for certain conditions) and avoid tests and procedures that have only marginal value for patient health, savings can be returned to the organization for distribution to physicians and/or the membership. Physicians are thus not paid for doing more to patients, but are rewarded for saving costs and maintaining member health (hence the term "health maintenance organizations," or "HMO's," which applies to both prepaid group practice and fee-for-service foundations for medical care). Public policy has encouraged the growth of prepaid group practice, and any comprehensive national health insurance program may be expected to further reinforce any cost-saving aspects of this practice. It has been argued that physicians will not work as long hours for salaries or group rewards as they work for individual fees; this may prove true, but is less of a cause for concern in light of our expanding physician supply. . . .

Other Health Workers

Over 4.2 million people, about one-twentieth of the labor force, were employed providing health services in 1970. Fewer than half a million were physicians, dentists, and other independent professionals. Who are the rest and what do they do? There are actually more workers filling clerical, service and managerial jobs in the health care sector than are providing the specialized professional and technical services we tend to associate with health care. We will consider the training and supply of specialized technical workers, sometimes called "paraprofessionals," or "allied health workers," before returning to the health labor force as a whole, which includes many workers who could find employment in their occupations in other industries.

Allied Health Workers. The training for entry into the allied health field ranges from short post–high school courses and on-the-job training in health institutions to doctorate-level preparation. Because of rigid certification and credential requirements, this training is seldom transferable from one health job to other closely related jobs; in other words, even though trained individuals have learned a great deal about health and illness both formally and through on-the-job experience, they cannot easily build on these basic skills and understanding and transfer them to the next job up the occupational ladder. . . .

This situation, in which training leads to certification at a specific level and is not transferable to other levels, applies to many health occupational groups. Certification and licensing programs have been sought by these groups themselves both to uphold standards of training and, it appears, to limit employment in certain jobs to their own members. Licensure restricts specific health care tasks to individuals with specific training credentials. This means that health workers, more than most workers in our economy, are locked into essentially dead-end jobs with few advancement possibilities. Trained workers are like pegs of a specific shape, with jobs as slots of equal specificity; a mismatch can be costly both for workers and employers and for the public.

Shortages of key personnel can arise if training has not kept ahead of demand; for example, for many years, hospitals found registered nurses in short supply. On the other hand, more individuals may be trained than there are jobs available, leading to unemployment for trained workers and wasting the investment in their training. Policymakers have responded to the credentialing situation with a moratorium on licensure of new allied health occupations and the development of credentials based on proficiency.

Other Health Employees. A full consideration of the health labor force and its impact on the American health system must include the many health sector employees who are not specifically trained in health care: maids, food service workers, secretaries and managers, who are employed in institutions, clinics, and health professionals' offices. The number and wage rates of these workers affect health costs. It should also be recognized that changes in the health system may lead to unemployment for this group, which includes a disproportionate number of people (women, blacks, unskilled service workers) who may be at a disadvantage in finding employment in the general labor market.

Health workers, particularly hospital workers, have been receiving larger raises in pay than workers in the general labor force. This is true for workers not specifically trained for health occupations as well as those in jobs peculiar to the health sector. Wage practices in hospitals differ from those in other sections of the economy; hospitals are able to pass labor cost increases on to the government and private insurance companies, and thus to the public; rate regulations that restrict cost pass-through may change this. Unions are only now becoming a significant influence on the hospital scene, especially since the National Labor Relations Act has been applied to non-profit hospitals only since 1974. These developments affect hospital costs and the supply of workers to hospitals; a recent report to the Council on Wage and Price Stability finds, however, that the unusually rapid increases in hospital wages are responsible for a relatively small portion of hospital inflation.

Health Employment and Health Care Problems

Can we solve our country's health care problems through changes in the training and employment of the health labor force? Let us examine some commonly asserted policy prescriptions for a cure.

It has been suggested that the availability of physicians and dentists be increased. Unfortunately, producing more physicians is unlikely to make medical care more available in shortage areas and in primary care. Policies that alter the location and specialty decisions of physicians may be necessary; required national service for all physicians has been considered. The availability of physician services might be increased by the use of "physician extenders" (PE's), workers who are prepared to do part of a physician's work under his or her supervision, either in the physician's office or in a remote location. For years, physicians have been delegating certain tasks to nurses, aides, and secretaries assisting them in office practice; nurse practitioners give well-baby care and routine prenatal care, and take over other patient care functions from physicians; and recently a new occupation has been created, the "physician assistant," who typically has less training than the baccalaureate nurse and takes on some of the physician's tasks. A relevant question, however, is whether the technical ability of physician extenders to perform efficiently will actually bring about their widespread use, especially in an era of increasing physician supply. Physicians working alone in fee-for-service practice appear unwilling to assume the burdens of management involved in hiring PE's and delegating many tasks to them, even though patient loads can be increased in this way. The widely asserted "need" for specially trained physician extenders has not necessarily been translated into a demand for their services, and people seeking training as nurse practitioners and physician assistants under programs designed to expand the availability of physicians' services may not find jobs waiting at the end of their education.

Interestingly, dentists have been effective in expanding the availability of dental services through the employment of assistants, hygienists and, recently, expanded-function dental auxiliaries. Almost 85 percent of all dentists employed some type of assistant in 1970. Many of these workers are technically competent to perform many dental tasks under a dentist's supervision. However, state licensure laws sharply limit how much a dentist may delegate to his assistants.

It has also been suggested that the quality of patient care can be improved by further training and certification for health workers. Judgments about the quality of health care often appear to be made on the basis of the credentials of the workers providing care rather than on the outcome experienced by the patient. Standards for accreditation and for avoiding malpractice suits in health institutions are often based not on the actual competence of health workers but on their educational credentials. Further emphasis on training and credentialing may improve quality, but it will also increase the rigidity of the health job structure and increase health labor costs.

The development of manpower plans to avoid shortages of health personnel is also urged. Planning for future labor demand is important, especially given the inflexibility of the health job structure. If shortfalls in supply can be avoided, new programs can go forward and wages for certain shortage occupations will not be raised. However, planners too often cite the "needs" for various types of personnel (for example, aides to assist the elderly at home, or physician assistants) when such personnel are actually unlikely to find employment in the current health system. In addition, requirements based on desired ratios of personnel per population may not be translated into future jobs: changing health technology may alter the occupational mix of health employment, cost controls may restrict labor input, and changes in the way we pay for health care may change both the amount and the mix of future health labor demand.

C. Glenn Pickard, Jr.

Midlevel Practitioners: Nurse Practitioners and Physicians' Assistants

The demand in the last two decades for more personal, accessible, and less expensive primary health care has led to the development of "midlevel practitioners." Workers in the new positions of nurse practitioner and physician's asistant seek direct responsibility for patient care and appropriate remuneration for their work. In the following selection, Dr. C. Glenn Pickard, Jr., discusses the contributions that midlevel practitioners can make in personalizing medical care and increasing its effectiveness as well as the problems that need to be resolved in using these health care professionals. Pickard is associate professor of medicine at the University of North Carolina School of Medicine.

In the 1960s an absolute shortage and maldistribution of physicians in the United States initiated a public outcry for more primary care services. These needs were felt most acutely by rural and inner-city areas. The major causes of this shortage and maldistribution were threefold:

1. The shift in medical education and practice from the general practitioner to the specialist.

2. The tendency of specialists to congregate in the larger towns and, in the case of major cities, in the suburbs.

3. Increased expectation on the part of the consumer.

Nurse practitioner and physician assistant programs developed from this mandate for change, for improved service, and for an expansion of physician services. In the decade since their first development, a wide range of names have been applied to various roles included within these two broad categories: Physician's Assistant, Physician's Associate, MEDEX, Child Health Associate, Pediatric Nurse Practitioner, Family Nurse Practitioner, and Nurse Midwife; however, the generic terms *physician's assistant* for the nonnursing roles and *nurse practitioner* for the nursing roles have assumed general if not universal currency. The term *midlevel practitioner* applies to all such roles.

Historical Perspectives

The force for change that led to the development of these programs is probably best understood in historical perspective.

In primary care practice, there are relatively small number of conditions that account for the great majority of patient encounters. These conditions are not particularly complicated, and their management does not require the elaborate and costly training of a physician. Thus the idea of a health professional with fewer medical skills than a physician to whom the physician might delegate the management of the more simple recurring problems was developed and was formally substantiated by studies on the content of general practice. . . .

Medical care services traditionally have been provided by physicians working with a variety of assistants and colleagues with whom they have shared the tasks and functions of medical care. Foremost among these supporters have been nurses, and over the last decade a series of events has made the evolution of the nurse practitioner role a logical one. During this period nurses assumed more and more roles and responsibilities in areas previously considered "medical practice." (Even such a simple act as the taking of a patient's blood pressure was once considered a "medical act.") As nurses became more skilled and physicians were increasingly consumed by more complex tasks, a wide variety of such tasks were de facto delegated to nurses. Nurses accelerated this process by assuming responsibility for many procedures, such as administration of intravenous medications, diagnosis and management of arrhythmias in coronary care units, and service as triage officers in emergency rooms. In areas more closely related to primary care, public health and occupational health nurses expanded their skills and practice in the provision of primary medical care services in both rural and urban communities. Thus, the role of the midlevel practitioner evolved throughout the nursing profession before and coincidental with the demand for more primary care providers.

Other developments presaged the evolution of the physician's assistant. The military service had long used highly trained corpsmen to assist the physician in providing medical care. The escalation of the Vietnam war resulted in the training of large numbers of such men, and in the late 1960s many of these highly trained health care providers returned to civilian life. Furthermore, physicians returning from military duty had been impressed with the skill and utility of well-trained corpsmen. They formed a reservoir of available manpower for provision of primary care. However, retraining was necessary to adapt their military training and experience to the medical problems of the civilian community.

Thus, the role of the midlevel practitioner had its origin in two quite different groups—registered nurses and exmilitary corpsmen.

Evolution of the Midlevel Practitioner Role. Nurse Practitioners: For many years physicians had informally trained office nurses and hospital-based nurses to assume increasing responsibility for medical management. It was the development of formal training and service programs in educational institutions, however, and the reports of these in the medical journals, that provided the major stimulus to the rapid development of additional programs in the 1960s.... In the hills of eastern Kentucky many program developers in the 1960s discovered the long-ignored model of the Frontier Nursing Service, in which nurses had for 40 years been the major providers of primary care in a collegial relationship with physicians.

Drawing on these and other early models, a wide variety of programs were developed in the late 1960s and early 1970s, so that by 1973–1974 a survey showed 83 programs preparing nurse practitioners (NP's).

Although there was a rapid proliferation of a wide variety of programs for the preparation of nurse practitioners, many common features among them began to define the nurse practitioner role. The nurse practitioner learned to use the traditional medical diagnoses and to render medical treatment for the conditions commonly occurring in primary care practice. In addition to these medical practice acts, the nurse practitioner continued to provide nursing care to patients largely in the area of patient education, patient care and counseling, preventive health care, and family planning. Thus, the evolving nurse practitioner role involved a combination of "traditional nursing" and newly acquired medical diagnostic and management skills.

Physicians' Assistants: The development of the physician assistant (PA) role was more complicated, since it involved the introduction of a completely new person into the health care system. The skill and capability of the corpsmen in the military was generally accepted. The challenge was to reorient these skills for primary care in the civilian health care system. Duke University was a front runner in the development of training programs of this type. They developed a two-year curriculum that trained multipurpose physicians' assistants who could assume a wide variety of tasks either in the physician's office or the hospital. Although not specifically oriented to primary care, graduates could assist physicians in many of the routine tasks of primary care practice. The MEDEX program differed from the Duke program by placing less emphasis on didactic teaching and more emphasis on clinical, on-the-job training with a physician.

In both cases the concept was to provide an assistant to the physician who could perform the less complicated tasks and thus enable the physician to use his time better in caring for the needs of the patients with more complications. In these training programs less emphasis has been placed on those aspects of patient care traditionally provided by nurses such as personal care, counseling, and patient education. A large amount of overlap has developed between the two roles, however.

The Midlevel Practitioner's Role

The genesis and evolution of the midlevel practitioner's role having been described, the next logical question is "What are the midlevel practitioners doing in actual practice?" A large number of papers have appeared in the nursing and medical literature describing the role and function of both nurse practitioners and physicians' assistants. A detailed summary of these reports was published by Cohen et al. in 1974 as part of a broad evaluation of midlevel health practitioners. In general most studies of nurse practitioners and physicians' assistants have confirmed that both types of practitioners are capable of managing a wide range of the problems encountered in primary care practice. A generalized description of the types of encounters managed would include the following: well-child care and checkups or physical examinations for patients of all ages; preventive health care including immunizations and special screening and early detection procedures such as Pap smears, tonometry, and spirometry; management of acute minor illnesses such as upper respiratory tract infections, uncomplicated urinary tract infections, viral gastroenteritis, and influenza; management of minor trauma including suturing of superficial lacerations and caring for minor strains and sprains; management of stable chronic illnesses such as essential hypertension, arteriosclerotic cardiovascular disease, and diabetes; care and counseling for a wide range of psychiatric problems such as chronic anxiety, mild depression, and psychosomatic complaints; and management of uncomplicated pregnancy and provision of a full range of family planning services including birth control pills and other means of contraception. . . .

Thus the studies available to date suggest that the midlevel practitioners are performing in the role projected for them in a satisfactory manner that is well accepted by patients. It must be emphasized, however, that the number of practitioners is still small and the studies are few in number and of limited generality. It will be several more years before firm general conclusions can be drawn regarding their role in primary medical care.

Although the nurse practitioner role developed many proponents, such a movement inevitably stirred up opposition from several quarters. Many physicians rejected the entire idea as second-class medicine that should not be permitted to develop. Many nurses also took a dim view of the developments, particularly those aspects of the movement that required that nurse practitioners practice under the supervision of a physician. They argued that nursing had established itself as a separate discipline and that to return to physician-dominated practice would be regressive and unacceptable. A statement in 1970 by the American Medical Association calling for the training of 100,000 nurse practitioners brought a prompt rejoinder from the American Nurses Association in which it was clearly stated that medicine had no business deciding what nurses should do.

In the development of the PA's role as in the case of the nurse practitioner there were opponents as well as enthusiasts. Physicians feared the training of "second-class doctors" who might balk at physician supervision and seek to establish independent practice. Nurses generally resented the intrusion of yet another worker in a field already crowded by a host of other professionals. They particularly resented and rejected the notion that the PA's were assuming a position superior to that of nurses and therefore were capable of giving orders to nurses.

Both evolving roles faced a series of common problems that had to be resolved to permit continued growth.

Medicolegal Questions

A series of interrelated legal issues have been raised by the evolution of mid-level practitioners. The issues have centered around the development of each group separately.

The majority of problems regarding the status of PA's were confronted in the late 1960s in conjunction with the evolution of the pioneering Duke University PA program. A conference attended by experts from around the nation was held at Duke in 1968, and the proceedings of this meeting provide an invaluable source of information regarding questions of legality. These questions included the following: What should be the status of the PA in society and who should sanction the status? For what functions should they be licensed, certified, or recognized, and by whom? What control should the appropriate regulatory agent have over the PA, and how should this control be exercised?

In response to these questions it was concluded that regulatory and licensing authority should be vested in individual state governments following the precedent of the other health professions. . . .

Malpractice. Malpractice is one of the first issues to arise in almost any discussion of midlevel practitioners, whether with health professionals or with consumer groups. In case a patient treated by a PA or NP feels that grounds for a malpractice suit exist, who is guilty and subject to suit, the PA, the NP, or the responsible physician? It is generally agreed that any or all could be sued, because all health professionals are legally responsible for their own personal actions. Therefore, most PA's and NP's have been advised to acquire malpractice insurance of their own. . . . This controversial issue involves all health professionals and . . . is presently the subject of a critical debate, the outcome of which is not clear.

Financial Aspects

The great majority of midlevel practitioners are paid a straight salary by the employing physician, group of physicians, clinic, or community health center organization. This salary is usually set after negotiation between the midlevel practitioner and the responsible practice group. Little consideration has been given to the income-producing ability of the practitioner. Unfortunately there is a paucity of data available on this subject, and the actual limits of salaries are not well documented. It is essential that future salary levels be correlated with levels of income generated, productivity, quality of care, and other factors.

At the present time, across the nation, physicians' assistants are often paid more for comparable services than are nurse practitioners, with little regard for training and prior experience. This seeming discrepancy is based on several factors:

1. Nurse practitioners' salaries usually conform to prevailing nursing salaries in the area, with nurse practitioners receiving salaries at a level comparable to that of a hospital head nurse, a nursing supervisor, or a senior nurse in a public health department.

2. Most nurse practitioners are female, and despite recent developments in the area of equal rights for women, in many areas women continue to be paid less than men in comparable jobs.

3. Physicians' assistants were able to convince their employers of their potential worth and were able to negotiate higher salaries without the constraints of fitting into a previously existing salary range.

4. In some cases PA's have been willing to work longer and more irregular hours than nurse practitioners, thus justifying higher salaries.

5. Nurse practitioners are more inclined to include functions such as patient education, counseling, and home visiting in their practice. These time-consuming activities reduce the number of patients seen and in the short run reduce the income-producing ability of the nurse practitioners. It is also sometimes difficult to pass the cost of such services on to the patient in a fee-for-service system. These combined factors result in lower salaries to nurse practitioners.

Nationwide the trend, based on anecdotal data, seems to be that physicians' assistants' salaries are leveling off or declining slightly, while nurse practitioner salaries are increasing. . . .

Training

The proliferation of training programs for physicians' assistants and nurse practitioners during the period of rapid growth and development beginning about 1965 has resulted in a vast array of educational experiences. As might be expected during this early period of experimentation, there were few norms or standards, and program developers were encouraged to try new approaches to health professional education. During this period programs ranged from a few weeks to a few months of informal on-the-job training to two or three years of training at the master's degree level. At this juncture, after approximately a decade of experimentation, several general patterns of educational experience for both physicians' assistants and nurse practitioners have evolved that enable one to describe several general types of programs that encompass the majority of current programs. In the discussion that follows, an attempt will be made to outline these general programs without discussing the infinite variations that continue to exist.

Physician's assistant programs in general fall into two broad categories: (1) the two-year program granting academic credit and requiring or highly recommending prior collegiate experience and (2) the one-year program, usually a noncredit course with heavy emphasis on prior experience and on-the-job practical experience. . . .

Nurse practitioner programs fall into two general categories: (1) two-year programs, usually at the level of a Master of Science in Nursing, and (2) one-year programs, usually nondegree and therefore open to registered nurses with diplomas or associate degrees as well as to nurses with baccalaureate and master's degrees.

The two-year master's program often combines those courses usually found in nursing master's degree programs, such as advanced theories of clinical practice and graduate courses in life, physical, and behavioral sciences, along with physical diagnosis and medical management. Seldom are nurses required to have physician sponsorship, and the graduates are broadly prepared for a variety of roles. . . .

*   *   *

In response to a demand for improvements in the availability, accessibility, and cost of medical care, the midlevel health practitioner has arrived on the health care scene. Physicians' assistants and nurse practitioners have moved to the fore in attempts to provide answers to this vexing problem. Despite a host of problems involving financial, legal, clinical, and other questions, the models seem well established and evidence of a real contribution to the solution of health care delivery problems is accumulating.

Nicholas Lemann

Let the Nurses Do It

Doctors and other health workers differ greatly in their levels of education, status, and salary; yet these contrasts are not necessarily reflected in the level of patient care or proficiency each exhibits. Observation of medical teamwork dramatically illustrates that many non-physicians can and do provide basic medical care. Citing the influence of Abraham Flexner in the early part of this century on the development of the present system, Niholas Lemann, an editor of The Washington Monthly, *raises the controversial question of how we can make competence, rather than education and professional status, the basis for determining who should treat a patient, and for what fee.*

A few months ago I spent a couple of days watching open-heart surgery being performed. The operating room was full of people: a supervising nurse, a scrub nurse, a few residents who just watched, and three surgeons doing the actual cutting and sewing.

Besides all of them, there were two others. At the head of the operating table, dressed in green surgical scrubs, stood an anaesthesiologist, who kept an eye on the patient's heartbeat, blood pressure, brain waves, potassium level, and other vital signs, and sometimes, at the suggestion of the lead surgeon, injected one drug or another into his bloodstream. Over to the side, also dressed in green surgical scrubs, sat a perfusionist, whose job it was to operate the heart-lung machine, which pumps and oxygenates a patient's blood during open-heart surgery so as to allow the heart to lie still for a time. Like the anaesthesiologist, the perfusionist kept an eye on various vital signs and occasionally, at the surgeon's request, made an adjustment or two.

The perfusionist looked young and wore a beard, so I assumed he was a resident and was impressed that someone in only his seventh or eighth year of post-college training would be given such an important job to do. Once after an operation I approached him outside the operating room and said, "Do they always let residents run the heart-lung machine?"

He looked surprised. "I'm not a resident," he said.

"Oh, so you've finished your training?"

"No, I'm not a doctor. I'm a medical technician. I only went to school for two years."

"How much money do you make?"

"Fifteen thousand dollars."

"How much does the anaesthesiologist make?"

"About $150,000."

Anyone who spends much time around a hospital will see non-doctors and doctors working together so closely that the difference between their functions is sometimes invisible to the naked eye. What you can't see is that while the work is often similar, the money they make isn't even in the same ballpark: everybody involved in the medical world who isn't a doctor earns somewhere between a fifth and a tenth of what doctors earn. Having been to medical school seems to affect one's income a lot more than it affects one's ability to treat patients effectively.

It's difficult for most people to accept the idea that many matters of health care are fairly simple and can be done well by people without much training, but it's true. In less delicate kinds of surgery than open-heart, one sometimes sees a nurse-anaesthetist, rather than an anaesthesiologist, at the head of the table. If radiologists and pathologists didn't wear long white coats it would be difficult to tell them apart from x-ray and lab technicians just by looking at what they do. Ordinary registered nurses can be seen giving shots, inserting intravenous lines, and setting splints—and in some remote rural clinics, they do all of that without a doctor even being present. The lordly surgeon has no non-doctor equivalent who is allowed to cut and sew—but in 1977, when it was discovered that William MacKay, a salesman of prosthetic devices, had performed an artificial hip replacement at Smithtown General Hospital on Long Island, the hospital's defense was that MacKay did this kind of thing all the time. There are some medical acts, like sewing up wounds, that simply don't correspond to educational attainment—whether or not you can sew up someone is a matter of how good your hands are, not how smart you are. Some people who aren't doctors in fact do doctors' work all the time now; those people (indeed, anyone) ought to be legally *allowed* to perform medical tasks according to their ability to master them, not their educational credentials.

Non-doctors can do many of the doctors' tasks just as well, but the law reserves responsibility for the work for the doctors. That means it's very difficult to explore which medical matters can be handled perfectly well by people without an M.D.—that is, where the line should fall between sewing up a cut and doing open-heart surgery. It means non-doctors are often prohibited from doing things that everybody knows they're competent to do. It means that non-doctors can't perform medical services independently, directly charging patients their own bargain rates instead of doctors' sumptuous ones. And that's one reason your medical bills are so high.

What doctors know that non-doctors don't seldom has a direct bearing on what they actually do all day in their practices. Most American doctors have taken two years of chemistry, one of physics, one of biology, and one of math in college; two years of further classroom training in the basic sciences in medical school; two more years of medical school spent rotating among the medical and surgical specialties to get a taste of each one; one horrible, grueling, sleepless year as an intern; two slightly more pleasant years as a resident; and possibly more advanced specialty training after that. The reason for all this training is, first, that doctors provide a more important service than anyone else—and in matters of life and death it's best to err on the side of over-preparing people. Second, in the same way that knowing Latin and Greek was once thought to subtly enrich the performance of adult occupations completely unrelated to those languages, it's thought today that the year the obstetrician spent taking organic chemistry, or his three months on a neurology rotation, will give him a breadth of knowledge and understanding that make him do a better job. Most doctors will readily admit that what they actually do all day doesn't require seven years of training to learn. But they usually say there are four or five moments in the course of a month when having been through all that gives them an appreciation of some delicate shade of meaning that the technician at their side wouldn't be able to pick up.

So in an ideal world, all that training is probably a good idea, just as it would probably be a good idea to require all government employees to read *Remembrance of Things Past*. Certainly there are some areas of medicine, like brain surgery, where the idea of someone going into practice after a couple of years of training is pretty terrifying. But for much of the rest, it's a question, as the economists say, of marginal utility: are the subtle benefits of requiring so much training of those who practice medicine worth the costs?

One of the costs is medical education, which is not only enormously expensive but also is almost completely financed by federal, state, and local governments, and by private philanthropy. And all that is only a fraction of the cost of medical education, since having the degree gives a doctor the license to charge so much for his services. There's also the problem of distribution: the longer a doctor trains, the more likely he is to become a specialist in a big city, and that has left us short on primary care in rural areas—exactly the kind of work that paramedics can do well, and inexpensively. Finally, there's a problem of opportunity: medicine as it is now structured is open almost exclusively to those who have decided on it as a career by age 18 or 19, and who are mature enough at that point to be able to do well in advanced science courses. Every doctor can tell heartwarming stories of the 32-year-old housewife who went back to school, took her pre-med courses, and became a doctor, but by and large medicine is more closed to the late bloomer than any other field.

By the same token, those who do become doctors do so only at a high price in lost breadth of non-medical experience and human contact.

The Flexner Influence

In a society where the reasons for just about everything seem impossibly complex, the reason doctors have to train so long is relatively simple. The structure of medical education and licensing in America today are to an amazing extent the product of the assiduous efforts of one man, Abraham Flexner, who died in 1959 at the age of 92. Understanding what Flexner did helps explain why medicine became so dependent on a long training period and therefore so expensive. And because Flexner was very much a product of his times, it also helps explain why the professions were created in the first place and how they became so powerful and so remunerative. . . .

Flexner . . . settled in New York and went to work for the brand-new Carnegie Foundation. His first assignment there was to travel around the United States and Canada and write a report on the state of medical education. . . .

His prescription was that 115 of the 155 schools should simply shut down, and that the remaining 40 be assiduously reorganized on scientific principles, with strict admission requirements, full-time faculties, up-to-date labs, and plenty of affiliated hospital beds. He realized full well that this would mean fewer doctors, and that was fine with him; under his scheme the care would be better, and the profession would be able to offer greater financial inducements in order to attract people of quality. . . .

Flexner's report, published in 1910 as Bulletin Number Four of the Carnegie Foundation, was an immediate success—partly because its findings were so shocking and its suggestions so sensible, and partly because it was music to the ears of the fast-growing AMA, which saw in Flexner's program better health care, more respect from the public and, of course, more money. . . .

In Love with Technology

Until the end of World War II, the world that Flexner made functioned pretty much as it was supposed to: schools produced doctors of high quality who were primarily into general practice and spread themselves fairly evenly around the country, charging generous but hardly ruinous fees.

Then, in the late forties, things began to change very fast. Rich, victorious, optimistic, in love with technology, and determined to provide a better life for its citizens, the government began to pour money into the structure of professions and institutions that had been born in the first decade of the century and that seemed to be working so perfectly. . . . Medicine received more of the government's money and attention than any other area. Biomedical research was funded by the new National Institutes of Health. Hospitals were built under the Hill-Burton Act. The passing years brought OEO grants, health manpower grants, Medicare and Medicaid, nursing homes, clinics, funding for medical schools, grants and loans for medical students, and the enormous growth of private health insurance. In 1930 the nation spent $3.6 billion on health, 13 per cent of which came from the government; 40 years later our health bill was $69.2 billion, with 37 per cent coming from the government.

By the end of the war the physicians-per-thousand-population rate was less than half of what it was when Flexner wrote his report, and even today it is substantially less; so naturally all this new money vastly increased the earnings of doctors. From 1960 to 1977 the consumer price index for doctors' fees nearly tripled. Each citizen spent, on the average, $17.52 on doctors' bills in 1950, $30.57 in 1960, and $145.84 in 1977. Between 1960 and 1976, the average income of doctors more than doubled. More and more doctors coming into practice were choosing specialties over general practice and the cities over small towns and rural areas, partly because specialties are more advanced and prestigious and partly because they're better paid. In 1965, 22 per cent of American doctors were in general practice; in 1975, 12 per cent. Today there are about 350,000 doctors in the country, averaging about $100,000 a year before expenses and $60,000 after, which makes them by far the highest-paid occupational group in the country.

Those numbers are the reason why it's now worth wondering whether Flexner's wonderful system is still the answer. Today there are about a million licensed registered nurses in the country, making an average of about $12,000 a year. If their pay stays even in the same ballpark, obviously the more of what is now reserved for doctors that can be turned over to them, the less health care will cost. Organized medicine always resolutely opposes that kind of measure, and not only out of financial self-interest—most doctors also share Flexner's horror of charlatans and butchers being allowed to practice, and just as you probably can't imagine that somebody who hasn't been to college could do your job, they can't imagine that somebody who hasn't been to medical school could do theirs.... But with prices where they are it's well worth figuring out a way to ensure competence via less training, or less of the kind of training that is an automatic passport to $60,000 a year. The functional difference between doctors and non-M.D. health personnel just isn't anywhere as great as the economic difference.

For example, obstetricians are doctors who deliver babies, and nurse-midwives are nurses who deliver babies. The obstetricians train seven years, the nurse-midwives considerably less, and as a result the obstetricians think the nurse-midwives don't know what they're doing. But at one California hospital, when two nurse-midwives came in, the infant mortality dropped from 23.9 to 10.3 per thousand. When the doctors succeeded in kicking out the nurse-midwives, the rate went up to 32.1 per thousand. Similarly, lab technicians (with no M.D.) and pathologists (with an M.D.) often do the same work. So do x-ray technicians and radiologists. Psychiatrists and psychoanalysts go through four years of medical school and three of internship and residency, and then use almost none of what they learned there in their daily work. Optometrists (without an M.D.) have shown that they can do much of what ophthalmologists (with an M.D.) were for years successful in reserving for themselves. Nurse-anaesthetists can do much of the work of anaesthesiologists. Rural and inner-city clinics have had happy experiences using nurses to run the show completely, including prescribing some drugs.

More generally, the internship, which is so horribly unpleasant that it usually convinces doctors that no amount they're later paid could be too much, need not be so pointedly torturous. There is some point to doctors spending a year seeing a lot of patients, and even some point to doctors having to stay up all night two or three times. But *every* night for a year? This is a case where the older doctors ought to be given more, not less, work: they should have to share the burden of late-night hospital duty so that everyone would do it occasionally rather than a few doing it constantly.

Of course, there will always be difficult and specialized cases that the non-doctors really aren't equipped to handle—the high-risk mother's delivery, the elderly patient's anaesthesia, the delicate eye surgery, the psychiatric emergency. It's essential that non-doctors in medicine know how to spot a difficult case and send it on to someone who knows how to treat it, just as general practitioners send on their difficult cases to specialists. But to do the bread and butter, we just don't have to pay what we're paying now. Most doctors admit that they learned how to do their jobs mostly by standing around and watching other people do it. People who haven't gone to medical school can learn in the same way. . . .

The flaw in Flexner's perfect vision is that the fit is loose; it's possible to do the job without having had the schooling, and to have had the schooling and not be able to do the job. Seventy years ago, when the professions were new, that was a minor point. Now that they control most of our services and a good portion of our money, it isn't so minor any more.

Rosemary Stevens

Health Manpower

The maldistribution of the health work force is a major barrier to the delivery of needed health care. Inequitable access and quality of care are caused partially by the shortage of physicians in rural and inner-city areas and by the increase in specialization and consequent shortage of primary care practitioners. Lemann and Pickard suggested the development of midlevel practitioners as one solution to maldistribution; health systems specialist Rosemary Stevens analyzes nationally coordinated regional planning, incentives, regulation, and funding as another approach to the problem. Her article includes a discussion of American values and the extent to which government should interfere with the traditions of private enterprise and professional control by medical organizations.

The Federal Government has become a major contributor to health manpower: directly in grants to health manpower education and indirectly through subsidizing professional incomes in massive Federal reimbursement schemes for medical care, notably Medicare and Medicaid. Since some geographical areas and populations have far more health care available to them than do others, one might expect a strong governmental interest in the regional and interregional distributions of health manpower that may have resulted from its investments—even the ultimate regulation of the numbers of personnel in all major health occupations and geographical areas. In fact, government has shown a reluctant interest in this phenomenon. Yet politicians can no longer accept that as inevitable. There is a tussle between the rhetoric of equity, implying as it does, a reasonably even spread of health professionals across the population, and the diffused power structure of the health care system.

Health services are, of course, complex organizations. The U.S. health care system is a congeries of thousands of independent interest groups and competing bureaucracies, each pressing its own policies. Decisions on the supply, entry standards, curricula, and competence of professional workers are usually delegated by government to—or just assumed by—the professions. The leading professional associations thus have a major impact on policies in the manpower field. A second important set of interests has arisen in the steady expansion of hospital facilities, with their large employee groups and training programs, and in the interchange of interests between hospitals and health care planning groups. Government is a third force to be reckoned with as public investment in health care has risen to the present 40 percent of all expenditures. The question this paper deals with is, How far do, and should, hospitals, health planning agencies, and government intrude on the traditional arrangements where manpower distribution lies solely in the discretion of the profession.

Regionalization of health manpower, in the sense both of distributing appropriate manpower with reasonable equity and efficiency across the face of the United States and of insuring adequate care at the local level, has become a topic enmeshed in the broader power plays of health care development. Congressional committees see professional monopolies as villains constricting the free operation of the market system. Hospitals and other organizations compete with each other for prominence in the local health care scene and for control of regional health care planning agencies. Professional associations and professional schools often see hospitals as presumptuous and government as a monster encroaching on hard-won prerogatives. It is against this richly woven background that the "regional" questions must be dissected, for one sector's "regionalism" may be anathema to the next; and the motivations behind each may be quite different.

Regionalization of health *manpower* is of central importance to any discussion of regionalization of health *services*. Yet there is no structure or authority for the development of coordinated health services at the regional level. Thus government manpower policies to date have been largely indirect. Meanwhile, the partial efforts that have been made and those now being considered have imposed peculiar stresses on the health professions, notably on the organization and independence of the schools of health sciences and of the various associations of the medical profession.

Ducking the Regionalization Issue:
Buildings Do Not a System Make

Health care facilities have cast a spell over the way we tend to think about modern health services. The very phrase, "the health care industry" inspires images of vast hospitals and disciplined teamwork between work crews and equipment. Death is translated as a pinpoint of light faltering across an EKG machine. Cure becomes the happy coincidence of drugs, therapy, research, and effective machinery. For those for whom less dramatic metaphors are applicable, there are other institutions: nursing homes for the elderly and chronically sick, community mental health centers, State psychiatric hospitals, neighborhood health centers, health maintenance organizations. Health services have become a world of buildings. It is only a step from here to the notion, implicit in all health planning legislation to this date, that the regulation of buildings will lead to regulation of the entire health service industry.

That notion would have considerable appeal if the buildings—the institutional framework of medical care—were also the employment centers for the 4.4 million persons who actually work in the health care system. In that case, one could encourage a health care system through clusters of institutions in each region or area. Physicians, nurses, therapists, technicians, attendants, secretaries, and other members of the army of 200 or more health service occupations, would either be employed by an organization or would have full-time contracts for specified services.

The employer would decide how many personnel were required in each category to serve a particular population, and would hire, fire, and remunerate accordingly. The allocation of funding to a regional health consortium, channeled through its institutions, would thus have a direct impact on the distribution of health manpower in that area, and in relation to other areas. For example, a regional health agency might decide to employ more nurse practitioners as a partial substitute for physicians in primary care. Since, under this scheme, the organization would have an effective monopoly of the job market in medical care, this decision would expand the demand for nurse practitioners in the area and reduce the demand for primary physicians. In areas in which the demand for primary physicians was met, there would be no job openings; physicians would have to practice somewhere else. In aggregate, there would thus be a shifting of personnel within and across regions according to the supply of available jobs.

How neat and tidy all this is. However, it bears little relation to the way in which health manpower is actually distributed. Hospitals do, it is true, employ about 2.9 million of the 4.4 million persons engaged in the health care industry, and the numbers have been rising year by year. Indeed, the 7,000 hospitals in the United States reported a net gain of almost 1 million employees between 1965 and 1974, a major reason for the escalating costs of hospital care. But to depend on health care facilities to provide a rational distribution of personnel for health services is a distorted view of the power situation of the industry.

While hospitals are the major employers of health employees, they are by no means the only employer. Health workers are employed in the country's 20,000 nursing homes, in health maintenance organizations, in home health agencies, in the Veterans Administration, in Indian Health Services, and in many other services, programs, and institutions. Many health workers are self-employed: pharmacists, dentists, optometrists, physicians. The combined result is not an industrial employment situation that could be rationalized into national, regional, and local units through the structure of employment *per se.* It is rather a hodgepodge of professionals, technicians, clerical workers, and others, clustered in different settings. . . .

The dichotomy between the rhetoric of "planning" and the realities of private enterprise in key health professions, notably in medicine, provides an essential element underlying any discussion of regionalization of health manpower. . . .

Physicians in particular are largely immune to the changing politics of hospital planners. While the number of physicians employed by hospitals has been going up, such physicians are still a minority. There were 360,000 physicians in non-Federal practice in the United States in 1975. Only 21 percent were in hospital-based practice, the great majority in residency training positions. . . . Most key health professionals are not employees; their work and location of their practice cannot be directly controlled through the manipulation of potential places of employment, unless, of course, American society were willing to accept an element of direction far beyond anything so far seen in the health care industry. Control of the distribution of health manpower through the job market, *i.e.* through employment by health care institutions, remains a possibility, but one which would require substantial changes in the health care system. Such a shift would assure the virtual disappearance of the private practitioner.

Axiom: Political Boundaries and Regions Are Frequently Antithetical

A second factor that is sometimes forgotten by the more enthusiastic proponents of regionalization is that health professions and occupations are not regionally organized. There is no general recognition of medical service areas on a prescribed geographical basis. Perhaps the State comes closest to providing a geographically defined territory for health manpower, overseeing and coordinating programs in higher education within the State and licensing 30 or so health care occupations, the number varying from State to State. Yet States are far from ideal planning units. In some respects, especially in terms of bringing medical care to the people, they may be too large, while in other respects, as in the training of professionals, they may be too small. Certainly most States are too large geographically to define the supply and distribution of health manpower with precision. . . .

Geopolitically, of course, city boundaries make no more sense and frequently makes less sense than State boundaries as areas for health manpower planning. Economic catchment areas and the domain of City Hall rarely coincide. Yet there is probably no "perfect" planning area. . . . There are wide differences in health manpower from region to region, according to available measurement, and . . . the differences are not necessarily internally consistent across all professions. Within broad categories—the richer States and areas having a more generous health manpower supply, the poorer the least generous—each place reveals its own idiosyncracies.

Such patterns are hardly surprising, reflecting as they do an assorted combination of influences. Environmental factors combine to play some part in the patterns of manpower distribution. These include climate, the general income of an area, expected professional income, professional connections, previous experience in the area (for example, as a student in a local professional school, or in postgraduate training), the availability of facilities, medical expectations of a population, coverage of particular services under a State Medicaid program, job openings in fields such as nursing, and other factors. There is no single overarching element. Since there has up to now been no regional agency responsible for medical care in a defined service area, assessments have not been made of what overall distribution of manpower is appropriate to a specific population or place. . . .

Tallying up numbers, evaluating workloads, providing forecasts and plans, predicting shortages in one field and excesses in the next, are tasks the new health systems agencies (HSAs) may perform admirably. These are, however, empty exercises unless coupled with a will to improve the actual array of health manpower or with authority to implement agreed-on changes. There is no single employer of health care workers at the local level but, rather, a myriad of occupational situations; therefore, authority cannot be exerted through the direct actions of a powerful employer. The scope of action is therefore limited. Efforts can be made via the HSAs to supply health workers to places where there are clearly deficiencies. This relatively noncontroversial approach exists in the Federal National Health Service Corps, which supplies personnel (usually physicians) to "medically underserved" areas. Efforts to upgrade shortage areas are also built into planning and Health Maintenance Organization (HMO) legislation as a priority, and into educational programs through manpower legislation. But dealing with identified shortages is one thing; tackling the much broader question of regional distribution of health care personnel is another, requiring as it does fundamental approaches to the power structure of the industry. It is here that battle is joined between the health care institutions, the health professionals and—increasingly—Federal agencies that are heavily subsidizing manpower production.

The situation is one of unclear goals and diffused responsibilities. The fact that members of the affluent middle class have available to them relatively much more service than do the poor, and that suburbanites have more than inner-city residents or the rural population, is generally regarded as "maldistribution." Federal programs in the last decade, if anything, appear to have exacerbated the situation. Yet, the goals of the social programs and the general use of tax funds suggest that the direction rather should be toward equalizing health care opportunities.

But it is one thing to say that "equity" should be the goal, another to devise practical solutions. Physically removing personnel from one area or population to another is clearly undesirable, even if feasible. Maldistribution will not be ameliorated by *re*distribution of those already in the system. As far as practical priorities go, the major task at the Federal level is to devise mechanisms where at least the new graduates of Federally sponsored educational programs will be encouraged to work in needy areas—and discouraged from entering the richer sectors.

The Parameters of the Problem—and Possible Solutions

How are new graduates to be persuaded to work in inner cities and rural areas, and—perhaps of more impact—persuaded not to work in the richer parts of attractive cities? Even such limited goals pose problems of Federal initiative.

Outright direction of health manpower, no matter how life has changed, is still alien to the traditions of American medical care. But there are other possibilities that may well become part of the U.S. health care system. At one end of a range of future options, proxy "employers" could be developed to cover virtually all the health occupations. The number of practitioners could be limited in each State, city, or health service area by, for example, controlling licenses, hospital staff privileges, or permits to receive funds from Medicare or even from private health insurance. . . .

Puny and Partial "Solutions"

. . . The Federal approach to the regionalization of health manpower through regional health services has thus been both spotty and coy. Regional planning agencies (HSAs) promise to be exhortative rather than directive. Regional health care systems (HMOs) may be of limited application. Regional qualitative review agencies (PSROs) may or may not serve as a focus of interest for physicians. Regional educational centers (AHECs) may produce additional numbers of personnel required in their service areas but will not redistribute health manpower overall. Nor will the promise of manpower to underserved areas through the National Health Service Corps have an effect on the health manpower available to the general population.

While these approaches are partial attacks on different elements of regionalization, congressional concern over the distribution of health manpower is growing. Federal aid to increase the supply of health professionals and to develop experimental, "innovative" programs such as the sponsorship of physician assistants has led to increased services for some population groups.

But it has also led to increased costs without concomitant general improvements in the equity or efficiency of medical care. Yet any goals to develop more equitable access to health manpower and to encourage their efficiency have obvious regional implications. Equity assumes some effort to use funding to even the supply of manpower between richer and poorer areas within and among health service regions. Efficiency assumes a trim manpower supply with appropriate referral and coordination among its members. . . .

Conclusion

. . . There can be no comprehensive attempt to plan health manpower on a regional basis (that is, with a reasonably equitable distribution of personnel among regions and a reasonably effective distribution within each region) unless such manpower is part of a regionally organized service system. The classic national-regional-district model of planning is possible when: (1) governmental structures are authoritarian, for example, in health services of the U.S. armed services or Veterans Administration; (2) health services are developed in virgin conditions, in areas or to populations that have not had adequate health care before (and where professional organizations are weak), for example, the provision of services to medically underserved areas through the National Health Service Corps; (3) physicians and other personnel work as employees or quasi-employees (for example, under exclusive contract), as in health maintenance organizations. These are not the predominant patterns of organization of physicians and other key managers of medical care in the United States—at least not yet.

That does not mean that decisions about health manpower cannot be taken and do not need to be taken on a regional basis. Maldistribution of health services and maldistribution of health manpower are virtually synonymous. As congressional concern about maldistribution has grown, the regional allocation of health manpower has become a matter of primary interest, notably in debates about the rising costs of medical care and about the impact of Federal grants to health professions education. The distribution of health manpower in various parts of the country, between urban and rural areas and within the sectors of major cities, has been debated *ad nauseam* in health manpower hearings. Lacking the means to influence the major health professions to accept regional manpower planning voluntarily, and lacking the desire to confront and override the major health professions, Congress has chosen to exert its influence indirectly. The result has been a series of "chippings" at the edges of the system.

The combined impact of the various forms of indirect regulation over professional activities—at least as they exist at present—promises to have little effect on the distribution of health professions among or within specific regions. But while the location and function of independent practitioners remains a jealously guarded professional prerogative, other traditional privileges of professional monopolies are being eroded. As a result of indirect efforts to redistribute physicians, medical schools are now firmly tied to government direction on the grounds that they are "national resources." In the current climate of antiprofessionalism, the work of individual practitioners promises to be much more heavily scrutinized than in a direct health service system. Licensing will probably be made more stringent, surgeons watched for "unnecessary surgery," physicians for hospital admissions, all for potential malpractice liability. Yet, while the effect of indirect regulation taken as a whole may be to control aspects of practice other than the location and population served, the primary problems seen by Congress will continue to be the maldistribution of personnel and the need to ameliorate that maldistribution in the interest of equity. There is a basic conflict between action and rhetoric.

In present circumstances, no single regionalization policy for health manpower is likely to be effective as a means of providing interregional balances or regional service networks. The development of educational centers in underserved areas may have some impact on regional service systems, and some on manpower distribution. Detailed Federal regulation of medical schools, however, carries the danger of rigid entry patterns and curricula without concurrent service advantages: entrenched systems are rarely changed by tinkering with entrance and education. Programs involving loans to students that can be paid back by service in needy areas have yet to prove their worth. Providing services to needy areas through the National Health Service Corps can be effective but, as yet, is of limited application. Taken together, the programs may lead to marginal improvements in distribution but no more than that.

Major redistribution of manpower on a regional basis will have to await fundamental changes in the health care system or in insurance reimbursement mechanisms. There may never be equity and/or efficiency in the health care system. However, three potential forms of regional control are long-term possibilities: these may be termed employment, quasi-employment, and restrictive regulation. A marked shift of independent practitioners to employee positions would create a job market in which the controlling force would be health care employers, including hospitals and HMOs. Distribution would be managed through job opportunities and job restrictions.

Passage of a national health insurance scheme with specified funds channeled through regional reimbursement agencies could create a different form of market. Distribution would be controlled through the flow of funding to private practitioners. Instead of a monopoly of jobs, there would be a monopoly of professional incomes.

Restrictive regulation is a third possibility, particularly in the absence of either of the other possibilities. State licensing boards or regional planning agencies could simply prescribe how many practitioners, of what kind, would be permitted to practice in given areas. Such mechanisms would be similar to certificate-of-need requirements for the development of facilities. National health insurance which requires each individual to register with a primary physician is another potentially interesting restriction which could have major effects on the distribution of care.

Each of these three approaches is administratively straightforward. HSAs provide a potential structure for implementation. While the HSA may not be the appropriate "region" for all manpower considerations, and while data sources clearly need developing, the delay in reaching regional manpower goals is not one of governance or ignorance, but of political ambivalence.

Medical students are more aware of questions of distribution than were their predecessors a decade ago; indeed, the Student American Medical Association has been calling for a draft of all medical graduates into underserved areas. The American Medical Association is working with HEW to provide physicians on a voluntary basis to relieve National Health Service Corps personnel for meetings and vacations, and is developing national guidelines as a basis for regional standards of hospital care for PSROs. The PSROs themselves provide new regional groupings. Specialty groups are concerned about the number and distribution of residency positions in their specialties; a concern stimulated in part by congressional investigation. States are moving to reform their licensing boards before the Federal Government does it for them. Regional concerns are implicit in all such activities.

Yet, while there is a general commitment to the ideals of regionalism by all concerned, government, institutions, health professions, there is reluctance to approach the ideals or the ideas directly—at least yet. Indirect regulation promises to have some, though little, effect on regional and interregional distributions. The process of regulation is, however, important in developing discussions and consensus as to whether more direct measures may be necessary. Meanwhile, apparently unintended effects of indirect regulation may affect the long-term situation. It is possible, for example, that regulation of independent medical practice may become so oppressive that physicians and others will prefer employment in groups, if only to facilitate records review or to provide group malpractice insurance coverage. Any such move would have obvious regional connotations.

Such thoughts are, at present, only speculative. The professional monopolies are under stress, but that does not mean the development of regional health care systems. While independent practitioners may well have most to gain by supporting a comprehensive and uniform national health insurance program in which they would emerge with increased power through professional organizations, the emotional and political signposts are still in the other direction. The debates over regionalization of health manpower promise to continue for a long time to come. At this point, for the long-term future, we, like Jimmy the Greek, can only offer odds on or against certain modes of regionalism, or perhaps, in a more scholarly tradition provide—as I have tried to do here—outlines of the implications of current developments.

7 The Right to Health Care

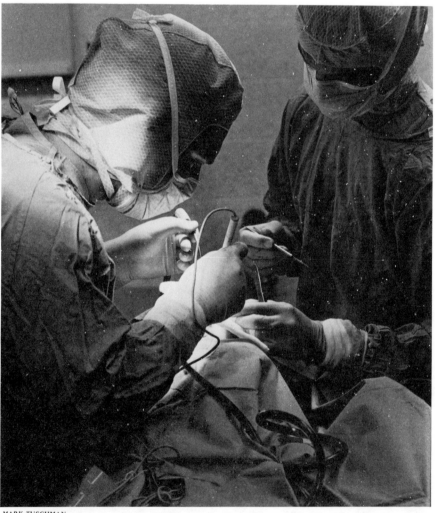

MARK TUSCHMAN

O ur review of medical history demonstrates enormous discrepancies between medical accomplishments at the turn of the century and the technological wonders of modern diagnostic and treatment procedures. The introduction of such technologies as organ transplants, pacemakers, coronary bypass surgery, kidney dialysis, insulin therapy, and intensive care nurseries has saved countless lives. The costs of these procedures, however, are astronomical. Kidney dialysis, alone, can cost over $40,000 a year for each patient. The cost of saving the life of a premature infant that weighs under 2.2 pounds can run over $40,000 for a few months in an intensive care nursery. These somber financial realities create ethical dilemmas concerning who receives care and who is left out or receives inadequate treatment. The high cost of some procedures also can mean that some people are forced to bear devastating financial burdens, while others face no financial responsibility at all.

The federal government helped ease health care inequities in 1965 when it began paying for the care of the aged and indigent through Medicare and Medicaid. There are many restrictions, however, on who is eligible for these funds, on what procedures will be covered, and on how much will be paid for each procedure. Benefits also vary tremendously among the fifty states.

Because medical care can affect not only the quality of life but life and death itself, there is reason to question whether it should be a commodity to be bought and sold on the open market. But when we begin to talk in terms of a "right to health care," we face some complex dilemmas. Should *all* procedures be made available to everyone who *needs* or *wants* them? Or, should everyone be guaranteed a certain minimal level of care? If so, how would this level be determined? Can we guarantee the same rights to people in Alabama and California? In remote rural areas and urban population centers? If health is conceived as a right, will we impinge on the prerogatives of doctors to treat whom they choose?

The modern technologies that have so expanded the abilities of medicine to intervene in all aspects of life—procreation, birth, behavior, and death—have raised philosophical questions that go to the very core of our social institutions. Questions of bioethics constitute some of the most sensitive issues in the realm of health care, often precipitating basic confrontations with human values. Abortion. Suicide. The right to die. Euthanasia. Genetic engineering. Experimentation on human subjects. Prenatal diagnostics. All these issues and many others have enormous implications, raising questions about the definition and control of life and death.

In this chapter we address an ethical question that embraces political, social, and economic issues, as well as our cultural values: Is basic health care a right that is guaranteed to all our citizens? Philip R. Lee and Albert Jonsen, of the University of California, San Francisco, School of Medicine, discuss "The Right to Health Care" in terms of our cultural traditions, and they recommend a balanced approach to obtaining equity.

Daniel Callahan, who has been writing about ethical issues in medicine for many years, offers a seasoned summary of the complex ramifications of this question of public philosophy in "Health and Society: Some Ethical Imperatives." He includes a discussion of personal responsibility and the idea that the population at large should not have to bear the financial burden for those who have poor health habits. Another term for this approach is "victim blaming." At its center is the question of how we strike a balance between individual desires and the public good.

In "Public Health as Social Justice," Dan E. Beauchamp, a professor of health administration, defines justice as a fair and equitable distribution of society's burdens and benefits. He then shows how social, political, and ethical processes intersect in public health policy. He defines "the public health ethic," which calls for a broad social movement to wrest control of medicine from the present power structure in order to make the furthering of human life the first priority of public health policy.

The final article in the series, by Brian Abel-Smith of the London School of Economics and Political Science, draws on the experience of Great Britain to evaluate the U.S. attempt to gain equity in health care distribution. His approach is to define "Minimum Adequate Levels of Personal Health Care."

Philip R. Lee and Albert R. Jonsen

The Right to Health Care

The concept of "right to health care" elicits varying responses: economists estimate the vast cost; politicians wonder whom national health insurance will really serve; physicians worry about excessive regulation of their profession; linguists, philosophers, lawyers, and bioethicists debate the meaning and legitimacy of rights and especially of a right to health care. In the following selection, Drs. Philip R. Lee and Albert R. Jonsen of the University of California, San Francisco School of Medicine introduce the subject of health care rights and illustrate several of the complex questions it raises.

We must have a decision by all countries that it is the right of everybody to have access to health care." These words, spoken recently by Dr. H. T. Mahler, Director General of the World Health Organization, echo a passage in the Universal Declaration of Human Rights, adopted in 1948 by the United Nations General Assembly. The Declaration proclaims that "everyone has the right to a standard of living adequate for the health and well-being of himself and of his family, including food, clothing, housing and medical care." Some 20 years later, in 1969, the American Medical Association resolved, "It is the basic right of every citizen to have available to him adequate medical care."

Declarations and resolutions are relatively easy to devise and to ratify. Decisions that implement them are often exceedingly difficult. Dr. Mahler's call for "a decision" casts the broad and laudable declarations into the maelstrom of political debate, economic argument, and professional anxiety. The right to health, or to health care, or to medical care is a concept that inspires such debate, argument, and anxiety.

One aspect of the political debate rages around the establishment of national health insurance, with its specter of "government control of medicine." The economic argument challenges the overall public cost of such insurance, the effects on the costs of care itself, and its cost effectiveness. The professional anxiety focuses on the physician's freedom to fulfill his responsibilities to patients and the possible deterioration of the intimacy of patient-physician relationships. All these issues have been exposed and argued at great length.

The purpose of this [article] is not to rehash these debates, but to state a conceptual framework within which they might be better understood and evaluated. Claiming a "right" too often comes down to proclaiming a slogan and demanding a program to match. Slogans are poor vehicles for understanding. Stating a "right," in our western philosophical and political tradition, has been much more than sloganizing. It has been an attempt to propose a certain understanding about the moral relationships between human beings.

The great revolutionary documents, the Declaration of Independence, the Bill of Rights, the French Declaration of the Rights of Man, and their classical philosophical counterparts, Locke's *Two Treatises* and Mill's *Liberty,* propose universal fundamental rights, such as right to life, liberty, and the pursuit of happiness. These are obviously broad and vague concepts. Yet their value lies in immense efforts, made by generations, to incorporate them into definite, perceptible social institutions and procedures. In themselves, they assert one thing: the fundamental autonomy of all persons and their fundamental equality before the law and the power of the state. They require fair and humane treatment of every human person. In practice, they are spelled out in such rights as due process, free expression, and free association. The last two rights, unlike the former, can be limited and even overridden when they come into conflict with others' rights or with the public good. Thus, Justice Holmes' famous dictum, "no one has the right to cry 'fire' in a crowded theatre," expresses the qualified nature of such rights.

There are, then, two distinguishable meanings of "rights." Fundamental rights reflect a basic understanding about persons dwelling in a humane community. They affirm that it can never be morally proper to deny to any person, in any circumstances, fair and humane treatment. Qualified rights are the practical implications of fundamental rights. They stand unimpeded until and unless one's exercise of them interferes with another's legitimate claims. Civil law, contracts, social standards, and sanctions are devised to work out a balance, to arrange the priorities, and to settle the disputes.

The right to *health* is a fundamental right. It expresses the profound truth that a person's autonomy and freedom rest upon his ability to function physically and psychologically. It asserts that no other person can, with moral justification, deprive him of that ability. The right to *health care* or the right to *medical care,* on the other hand, are qualified rights. They flow from the fundamental right, but are implemented in institutions and practices only when such are possible and reasonable and only when other rights are not thereby impeded.

The fundamental right to health is justified by inspecting the nature of human persons. To the extent that "being healthy" lies within human power, it is clear that being healthy is a precondition for being free and autonomous. The qualified right to *care* is justified only by inspecting actual conditions of society and of medicine.

A qualified right is justified when it becomes evident that the benefits and burdens of a society are unfairly distributed. Unfair distribution means distribution whereby some benefit, while others are deprived. A justified right to care would then be a call to find ways to redress the inequities and to redress them in a way that neither destroys the essence of medical care nor treads on other justified rights. Translating the concept of the right of every citizen to health care into specific policies and programs requires that the costs be determined, the sources of financing be identified, and the means of providing the services be delineated.

Federal support for health care programs has long been justified on the premise that certain groups of individuals (e.g., the aged, the poor, the mentally ill) bore an unusually heavy burden of illness and did not, in fact, have access to the kind and quality of medical care required. A host of programs were established in an attempt to overcome the obstacles to access and to solve what was looked on as social injustice. These began with small grants to state health departments for maternal and child health services in the mid 1930s, included an increasing number of programs for persons with a variety of illnesses (e.g., tuberculosis), and now include massive expenditure of funds for the purchase of medical care for the aged and the poor, authorized by the Social Security Amendments of 1965 (Medicare and Medicaid). Other groups of people who were considered to be in special need (Native Americans, Alaskan natives) or whose contributions merited special status (members of the armed forces, veterans with service-connected disabilities) were provided medical care directly.

The importance of social justice in the evolution of federal health care policies is illustrated by the programs for the development and expansion of family-planning services to the underserved (usually the poor or educationally disadvantaged) and the extension of Medicare benefits to patients with end-stage renal disease. In the case of family planning, millions of poor men and women did not have equal access to available family-planning services. As a result, they were having many more children than they wished, and they were having children more often than they wished. The costs to the unwanted children, to the families, and to society were high. The basic objective of the family-planning program was to foster individual and family health and to provide free choice in the number and spacing of children. Without access to adequate family-planning services, the poor could not exercise that right equally with families and people in better socioeconomic circumstances.

Similarly, many patients with end-stage renal disease did not have the money to pay the high costs of chronic kidney dialysis and transplantation. They bore a burden of illness and cost that was disproportionate to that of other members of society. The Social Security Amendments of 1972 extended Medicare coverage to persons with end-stage renal disease, thus permitting a more equitable access to needed services without financial catastrophe for the patient or the family.

In both of these cases, a balance has been achieved by extending the right to certain types of medical care to people in need. The goal was to do this without undue financial burden to others, without denying others access to medical care, and without limiting unduly the freedom of physicians and other providers to provide the services in a manner most appropriate to the needs of the patients.

The right to health care need not be a slogan for revolution. It need not be a program for a particular economic structure. It should be the expression of a moral concern about inequities that may presently distort the system of health care. Secondly, it should be the impetus to reform the proved inequities by carefully devising social and economic structures that respect to the highest degree possible the justified rights of the public and the health professions. The goal has been defined clearly by Professor Anne Somers: ". . . the object is to design a single system with enough flexibility—regional, financial, ethnic, and other variations—to allow for the persistent differentials, and then seek to close the gap and raise the standards of the least advantaged groups."

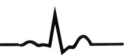

In health there is freedom. Health is the first of all liberties.

—Henri Frédéric Amie (1879)

Daniel Callahan

Health and Society: Some Ethical Imperatives

The right to health is only one of many ethical issues related to biological research and medicine. Philosophical questions about abortion, human experimentation, organ transplantation, euthanasia, and other controversial medical practices involve broad societal values and concepts of rights and obligations. Daniel Callahan, of the Institute of Society, Ethics, and the Life Sciences, explores these relationships in the context of national attitudes toward individual and public good.

Whether induced by internal or by external circumstances, every major social change in a society forces a confrontation with its values. Nowhere is this more evident than in the changes that have been wrought in medicine. In earlier societies, people were necessarily fatalistic about illness; there was little the physician could offer beyond psychological comfort and minor palliation. Modern medicine, by contrast, commands a powerful arsenal of weapons to forestall death, relieve pain, cure malignancies, and rehabilitate the crippled. But this power, impressive as it is, is nevertheless still less than absolute, and thus it poses particularly difficult questions of a kind which previous generations had no need to consider....

In its power, then, to change the conditions of birth and death, to alter ways of life and behavior, to impose new dilemmas about the relationship between individual and social good, medical research and clinical practice force a new confrontation with some of the oldest of human questions. What do we account as "happiness," and what should medicine's role be in bringing it about? What is a "good life," and how much health is necessary for it? What is a "good death," and what are the possibilities and limitations of medicine in contributing to that? How much sacrifice of individual health can society demand in the name of general health? How far must society go in making use of medical means to satisfy individual and sometimes idiosyncratic desires?...

The development of new values as they become necessary to manage modern medicine, the modification of old moral standards, and perhaps the outright jettisoning of still other traditional norms are the ineluctable consequences of advances in medical research, clinical application, and mass delivery of health care. . . .

A logical place to begin an examination of the moral choices at stake is with the concept of "health" itself. From there it will be possible to move to the special problems posed by technology, not only in medicine but in the culture more generally. Finally, a direct examination of the increasingly vexing questions of rights and obligations and of decision-making processes can be confronted.

The Concept of "Health"

Like most other very general concepts—"peace," "truth," "justice," "freedom"—that of "health" poses enormous difficulties of definition. We all know experimentally and intuitively what it means to be sick: we hurt, and, to a greater or lesser extent, we cannot function well. That the pain or misery we feel can lead in many cases to death—either socially, by disability or impairment, or literally—only increases the burden; a reminder that we are mortal. Yet even when we attempt to grasp the notion of "health" by looking at what are normally taken to be its opposites—illness, pain, death—complications immediately arise. People can adapt to illness, learn to put up with their "disease," and to cope with the fact that their body is performing in something less than an optimal way. Moreover, as the sociologists of medicine have taught us, people respond to and interpret illness in very different ways; what is considered sick in one culture or group may be considered health in another. Nevertheless, most people in most places have a rough idea of what they mean by "ill"; a recognizable area of human experience is evoked by the term, even if the borderlines can be exceedingly fuzzy.

To move from a definition of "sickness" to one for "health" is, however, not so easy. The term connotes bodily integrity, the absence of pain and infirmity, the state of a well-functioning and thus unremarkable organism. In a curious way, like "goodness," it can seem bland, if only because the alternative states of human affairs are so marked by drama and suffering. However bland the concept, the reality it invokes is regarded as eminently desirable. When one is in "good health" it is not even noticed: when one is not, it is desperately desired. . . .

How much health do people need? How much and what kind of sickness should be combatted? These are exceedingly difficult questions to answer, in great part, as I noted above, because of the enormous variation among individuals and groups in their tolerance for, and interpretation of, illness. Nonetheless, attempts have been made to find some reasonably objective standards for defining "illness," because without a working definition, there is no way to determine the nation's health needs. These efforts have, on the whole, taken the form of trying to establish a cost in dollars for various illnesses, both in terms of lost wages and in terms of the cost to the economy from illness and disease. Complementary to these calculations are those that employ cost-benefit techniques to determine the net economic gain resulting from investment in research and delivery systems sufficient significantly to reduce the incidence and impact of various diseases. Parallel attempts are made on social grounds: these ordinarily point to the disparities in the incidence of various diseases and disabilities among different groups and classes of people that indicate, not surprisingly, that the downtrodden (whether because of race, age, poverty, or geographic location) bear a disproportionate and thus inequitable burden of poor health.

The advantage of attempts to determine national health needs is that they allow in principle a considerable degree of quantification: reasonably accurate comparisons can be made between alternative health-policy strategies. In practice, however, the objectivity of their figures is frequently more illusory than real. Statistics can only be developed by making a number of arbitrary assumptions, some quantitative, others entailing value judgments. While it may be possible, for instance, to calculate in a rough way the economic cost to society of arthritis, it is by no means as easy to calculate the psychological cost to the afflicted individuals or their families. While unhappiness (even if those afflicted are economically "productive") ought surely to have a place in any full equation, it does not readily lend itself to calculation. In making comparisons between the full costs of different diseases (economic and psychological), is it possible, say, to find any very reasonable way to compare arthritis and hemophilia? Because of the far greater incidence of the former, one might say that the total sum of suffering is greater, but the impact of the latter (not to mention the cost) is probably far greater in terms of individual suffering. . . .

I am not trying to argue here that techniques for determining health needs should be abandoned. They at least reveal some interesting and suggestive figures, speculations, and projections providing those responsible for making policy decisions with something to work on, and something in this case is better than nothing. But they do evade the most difficult problem: that of determining the positive moral weight to be given to the pursuit of health in a society and the negative moral weight to be given to illness and disease. Just what is good "health" anyway, and just what is evil about illness, disease, and death? These are nasty questions to ask, because if put too bluntly they imply a callousness to a major source of human misery and an indifference to the destructive effect of illness. But if they are not asked, it will be impossible to reach some decision regarding the limits to be placed on the quest for health and the priority to be given to societal health needs within those limits.

Two social realities are, at present, bedeviling that necessary task. The first is the almost total breakdown of the ethical distinction between "need" and "desire" in our culture. The second, closely related to the first, is the continuing utopian lure of technology, a lure whose net effect is to thwart any attempt to place limits on medical aspiration. . . .

Rights, Obligations, and Decisions

Two slogans, the "right to health" and the "right to health care," encapsulate the thinking that has recently dominated medicine in this country. The two have arisen in a society that is under great pressure to extend the scope and application of its individual rights, particularly welfare rights, and in the face of rising costs in medical care combined with the fact that an absence of care can now more often make the difference between life and death. A plausible case can be made for asserting that until a half-century or so ago the nation laid the greatest emphasis on the obligations of the individual toward society, while now the emphasis is increasingly upon the obligations of society toward the individual. It is a shift that most find attractive, and nowhere is it more strikingly apparent than in the debate over the methods of medical-care payment. Few public voices would dare support a laissez-faire approach to the cost of medical treatment any longer. Health, it is at least ostensibly agreed, cannot be treated as one more commodity to be sold only to those who have the money to pay the bill.

The slogans about "rights" provide the ideological and political ground on which to lay the foundation for some other solution to the distribution of medical care. But the language of "rights" is notoriously slippery, not only because opinions differ regarding their nature and basis but also because rights that are claimed are not all compatible or consistent with one another. What does it mean to have a "right to health"? It might mean that everyone has a right not to be sick. But that is to enter a claim against the weaknesses of the flesh and against all of those natural processes that lead to disease and bodily decay. That kind of claim could only be entered against God Himself, or nature, or the evolutionary process. Clearly, the claim can be entered; just as clearly, it will not be honored.

The right might mean that society has an obligation to guarantee the health of its members. But even the most superb present and foreseeable medicine cannot guarantee that a person will always be healthy. Then, one might say that, if no society can guarantee the health of its members, the right implies at least an obligation to make the attempt. Even that more modest formulation raises problems: Just why, for instance, is any one person responsible for the health of another, particularly if the one bears no responsibility whatever for the lack of health of the other? More generally, on what basis can it be said that citizens have a mutual obligation for one another's health? Perhaps it can reasonably enough be said that citizens have an obligation not to jeopardize the health of others, but it is an enormous step from there to claiming that the good health of all is the responsibility of all. No plausible argument can be made that would justify that step. The concept of a "right to health" neither makes sense in itself nor provides the basis for any kind of rational social policy.

The "right to health care" is, if properly qualified, a more promising idea. A society can, out of concern for the general welfare, decide to invest in the improvement of its level of health. Our society and many others have already made that decision. Whether a society has an *obligation* to do so—especially vis-à-vis other ways in which it might invest its resources—is a question I will not wrestle with here. I am only asserting that it *may* quite legitimately make that decision. Once it has done so, the question arises as to who has a claim on the resources thus put aside, and under what circumstances. If the "right to health care" is construed to mean, as it commonly is, a right to "equal access" to the general health care which the society has decided to make available, then it is at least in theory possible to conceive of an equitable arrangement for guaranteeing that access. The presumption behind "equal access" theory is that, whatever the total amount of general resources devoted to health, all should have a chance to avail themselves of some fair portion of it. Occasionally, however, the "right to health care" seems to be construed in a way which differentiates it very little from a more general "right to health." It is seen as a claim to whatever resources are needed, even those as yet undeveloped, to guarantee as much health as possible. This more extreme version consequently entails many of the same theoretical and practical problems as a "right to health" does.

The "right to health care," even in its more modest form, is not without its problems as it competes with other welfare rights. It is possible in the cases of education, nourishment, housing, and income to establish minimal levels of need and (assuming the availability of money) to meet each of them (e.g., the mandatory twelve years of education in this country). This cannot be so readily done in the case of health, primarily because of the great variety of illnesses which can afflict people and the great discrepancies in the expenses attendant upon treating each of them. One person may need penicillin for a few days to save his life, another may need open-heart surgery; still another may need an expensive drug for his entire life (as is the case with the hemophiliac).

A strict theory of equity would require that each person get what he needs to save his life. But that means that some will get much more than others, which is in a sense inequitable. Further complications arise when decisions must be made about the magnitude and type of health-care services and facilities to be made available. Using the utilitarian rule of thumb, the "greatest good for the greatest number," it could be argued that the emphasis should be placed on meeting the health needs of the largest number of people. Yet that kind of decision could result in great injustice to those unfortunate enough to be afflicted with statistically rare diseases or with conditions which require unusually expensive or long-term treatment. Still another complication arises when decisions must be made about limits. Should everyone have equal access to health care regardless of age or physical condition? Should an eighty-year-old person have the same free access to open-heart surgery as a child? Should a person who has consumed a great deal of expensive health care over the years have as much right to future treatment as the person who has hitherto required little or none?

What about those whose illnesses can be traced to their poor living and health habits? Evidence is accumulating that many major diseases—lung cancer and heart disease, for instance—often are the direct result of (to use an old term) "abuses" of the body. Why in the world, one might ask, should the public bear any responsibility to provide health care for those who bring their illnesses upon themselves? The question is worth dwelling upon a moment primarily because it can reveal a naïveté about the causal context of disease, and about human nature as well. Take the case of the heavy smoker. In one sense, of course, he could simply stop smoking; if he continues, despite all the known evidence regarding its harmful effects, he has no one to blame but himself. But is that really true? After all, he has been bombarded since youth by high-powered advertising in favor of cigarettes, he has been exposed to their ready availability, and he may have taken up smoking—thus establishing an addiction—well before he was fully aware of what he was getting into. Just how "free," then, is his choice to continue smoking?

It is also by no means clear just why some people smoke and others do not: genetic predisposition, unrecognized psychological demands, the absence of some necessary vitamins or minerals? Unless one is willing to entertain a rather primitively moralistic view of human behavior, it is not so easy to explain why people do undertake, or maintain, harmful habits in life. No one has, at any rate, been able to show that smokers are, as a group, generally less responsible, less moral individuals than non-smokers; nor that the obese, who run a higher risk of heart disease, are less virtuous or poorer citizens than those who are sensibly thin.

Even if it were possible to work through some of these problems, there would still be a final difficulty. While it has been shown that certain ways of life lead to a higher incidence of certain diseases, it has also been shown that those same diseases can appear in the absence of all those causes. For that reason, if for no other, it would be impossible to *prove* that someone's disease was the result of his culpable, willful irresponsibility. Many who smoke do not contract lung cancer or any other disease traceable to smoking; and many who do not smoke do in fact contract those same diseases. Given all of these contradictions, or possibly paradoxes, a public policy based on assigning personal responsibility, and denying health care accordingly, could amount to an exceeding unjust arrangement.

Lurking behind these issues is the abiding problem of the relationship between individual good and common good. American medicine has been based upon the value the society places on the individual; the medical researcher is free to pursue whatever interests and challenges him; the medical patient is free to seek whatever kinds of medical care he thinks he needs, including the freedom to determine what he wants to regard as a medical condition; physicians, patients, and researchers are all free to determine their own value systems and their own ethical codes; everyone is free to get whatever he is willing to pay for, just as everyone is free to live the kind of life he wants, whatever the costs to himself or to society of hazardous living habits. Obviously, a number of practical limitations stand in the way of a full exercise of these freedoms....

The most important changes which American medicine is likely to witness in the next few decades will come from a systematic questioning of those premises. The beginnings of that challenge can already be seen....

Dan E. Beauchamp

Public Health as Social Justice

The right to health may be defined as protection from disability or premature death. Dan E. Beauchamp, a professor of health administration at the University of North Carolina, examines basic models or theories of justice that support a public health policy to provide such health protection. Market justice, based on individual responsibility and providing only those benefits that are earned, presents barriers to health protection. Social justice, on the other hand, emphasizes the need for collective action in controlling hazards and sharing the burdens produced by ill health.

Anthony Downs has observed that our most intractable public problems have two significant characteristics. First, they occur to a relative minority of our population (even though that minority may number millions of people). Second, they result in significant part from arrangements that are providing substantial benefits or advantages to a majority or to a powerful minority of citizens. Thus solving or minimizing these problems requires painful losses, the restructuring of society and the acceptance of new burdens by the most powerful and the most numerous on behalf of the least powerful or the least numerous. As Downs notes, this bleak reality has resulted in recent years in cycles of public attention to such problems as poverty, racial discrimination, poor housing, unemployment or the abandonment of the aged; however, this attention and interest rapidly wanes when it becomes clear that solving these problems requires painful costs that the dominant interests in society are unwilling to pay. Our public ethics do not seem to fit our public problems.

It is not sufficiently appreciated that these same bleak realities plague attempts to protect the public's health. Automobile-related injury and death; tobacco, alcohol and other drug damage; the perils of the workplace; environmental pollution; the inequitable and ineffective distribution of medical care services; the hazards of biomedicine—all of these threats inflict death and disability on a minority of our society at any given time. Further, minimizing or even significantly reducing the death and disability from these perils entails that the majority or powerful minorities accept new burdens or relinquish existing privileges that they presently enjoy. Typically, these new burdens or restrictions involve more stringent controls over these and other hazards of the world.

This somber reality suggests that our fundamental attention in public health policy and prevention should not be directed toward a search for new technology, but rather toward breaking existing ethical and political barriers to minimizing death and disability. This is not to say that technology will never again help avoid painful social and political adjustments. Nonetheless, only the technological Pollyannas will ignore the mounting evidence that the critical barriers to protecting the public against death and disability are not the barriers to technological progress—indeed the evidence is that it is often technology itself that is our own worst enemy. The critical barrier to dramatic reductions in death and disability is a social ethic that unfairly protects the most numerous or the most powerful from the burdens of prevention.

This is the issue of justice. In the broadest sense, justice means that each person in society ought to receive his due and that the burdens and benefits of society should be fairly and equitably distributed. But what criteria should be followed in allocating burdens and benefits: merit, equality, or need? What end or goal in life should receive our highest priority: life, liberty or the pursuit of happiness? The answer to these questions can be found in our prevailing theories or models of justice. These models of justice, roughly speaking, form the foundation of our politics and public policy in general, and our health policy (including our prevention policy) specifically. Here I am speaking of politics not as partisan politics but rather the more ancient and venerable meaning of the political as the search for the common good and the just society. . . .

In the case of health, these models of justice form the basis of thinking about and reacting to the problems of disability and premature death in society. Thus, if public health policy requires that the majority or a powerful minority accept their fair share of the burdens of protecting a relative minority threatened with death or disability, we need to ask if our prevailing model of justice contemplates and legitimates such sacrifices.

Market-Justice

The dominant model of justice in the American experience has been market-justice. Under the norms of market-justice people are entitled only to those valued ends such as status, income, happiness, etc., that they have acquired by fair rules of entitlement, e.g., by their own individual efforts, actions or abilities. Market-justice emphasizes individual responsibility, minimal collective action and freedom from collective obligations except to respect other persons' fundamental rights.

While we have as a society compromised pure market-justice in many ways to protect the public's health, we are far from recognizing the principle that death and disability are collective problems and that all persons are entitled to health protection. Society does not recognize a general obligation to protect the individual against disease and injury. While society does prohibit individuals from causing direct harm to others, and has in many instances regulated clear public health hazards, the norm of market-justice is still dominant and the primary duty to avert disese and injury still rests with the individual. The individual is ultimately alone in his or her struggle against death. . . .

Market-justice is perhaps the major cause for our over-investment and over-confidence in curative medical services. It is not obvious that the rise of medical science and the physician, taken alone, should become fundamental obstacles to collective action to prevent death and injury. But the prejudice found in market-justice against collective action perverts these scientific advances into an unrealistic hope for "technological shortcuts" to painful social change. Moreover, the great emphasis placed on individual achievement in market-justice has further diverted attention and interest away from primary prevention and collective action by dramatizing the role of the solitary physician-scientist, picturing him as our primary weapon and first line of defense against the threat of death and injury.

The prestige of medical care encouraged by market-justice prevents large-scale research to determine whether, in fact, our medical care technology actually brings about the result desired—a significant reduction in the damage and losses suffered from disease and injury. The model conceals questions about our pervasive use of drugs, our intense specialization, and our seemingly boundless commitment to biomedical technology. Instead, the market model of justice encourages us to see problems as due primarily to the failure of individual doctors and the quality of their care, rather than to recognize the possibility of failure from the structure of medical care itself. Consequently, we seek to remedy problems by trying to change individual doctors through appeals to their ethical sensibilities, or by reshaping their education, or by creating new financial incentives.

Government Health Policy. The vast expansion of government in health policy over the past decades might seem to signal the demise of the market ethic for health. But it is important to remember that the preponderance of our public policy for health continues to define health care as a consumption good to be allocated primarily by private decisions and markets, and only interferes with this market with public policy to subsidize, supplement or extend the market system when private decisions result in sufficient imperfections or inequities to be of public concern. Medicare and Medicaid are examples. Other examples include subsidizing or stimulating the private sector through public support for research, education of professionals, limited area-wide planning, and the construction of facilities. Even national health insurance is largely a public financing mechanism to subsidize private markets in the hope that curative health services will be more equitably distributed. None of these policies is likely to bring dramatic reductions in rates of death or disability. Our current efforts to reform the so-called health system are little more than the use of public authority to perpetuate essentially private mechanisms for allocating curative health services. . . .

Social Justice

The fundamental critique of market-justice found in the Western liberal tradition is social justice. Under social justice all persons are entitled equally to key ends such as health protection or minimum standards of income. Further, unless collective burdens are accepted, powerful forces of environment, heredity or social structure will preclude a fair distribution of these ends. While many forces influenced the development of public health, the historic dream of public health that preventable death and disability ought to be minimized is a dream of social justice. Yet these egalitarian and social justice implications of the public health vision are either still not widely recognized or are conveniently ignored.

Seeing the public health vision as ultimately rooted in an egalitarian tradition that conflicts directly with the norms of market-justice is often glossed over and obscured by referring to public health as a general strategy to control the "environment." For example, Canada's "New Perspectives on the Health of Canadians" correctly notes that major reductions in death and disability cannot be expected from curative health services. Future progress will have to result from alterations in the "environment" and "lifestyle." But if we substitute the words "market-justice" for environment or lifestyle, "New Perspectives" becomes a very radical document indeed.

. . . The central task of public health, then, is to complete its unfinished revolution: the elaboration of a health ethic adequate to protect and preserve all human life. This new ethic has several key implications which are referred to here as "principles": (1) controlling the hazards of this world, (2) to prevent death and disability, (3) through organized collective action, (4) shared equally by all except where unequal burdens result in increased protection of everyone's health and especially potential victims of death and disability.

These ethical principles are not new to public health. To the contrary, making the ethical foundations of public health visible only serves to highlight the social justice influence at work behind pre-existing principles.

Controlling the Hazards. A key principle of the public health ethic is the focus on the identification and control of the hazards of this world rather than a focus on the behavioral defects of those individuals damaged by these hazards. Against this principle it is often argued that today the causes of death and disability are multiple and frequently behavioral in origin. Further, since it is usually only a minority of the public that fails to protect itself against most known hazards, additional controls over these perilous sources would not seem to be effective or just. We should look instead for the behavioral origins of most public health problems, asking why some people expose themselves to known hazards or perils, or act in an unsafe or careless manner. . . .

Public health, ideally, should not be concerned with explaining the successes and failures of differing individuals (dispositional explanations) in controlling the hazards of this world. Rather these failures should be seen as signs of still weak and ineffective controls or limits over those conditions, commodities, services, products or practices that are either hazardous for the health and safety of members of the public, or that are vital to protect the public's health.

Prevention. Like the other principles of public health, prevention is a logical consequence of the ethical goal of minimizing the numbers of persons suffering death and disability. The only known way to minimize these adverse events is to prevent the occurrence of damaging exchanges or exposures in the first place, or to seek to minimize damage when exposures cannot be controlled. . . .

Thus, the familiar public health options:

1. Creating rules to minimize exposure of the public to hazards (kinetic, chemical, ionizing, biological, etc.) so as to reduce the rate of hazardous exchanges.

2. Creating rules to strengthen the public against damage in the event damaging exchanges occur anyway, where such techniques (fluoridation, seatbelts, immunization) are feasible.

3. Creating rules to organize treatment resources in the community so as to minimize damage that does occur since we can rarely prevent all damage.

Collective Action. Another principle of the public health ethic is that the control of hazards cannot be achieved through voluntary mechanisms but must be undertaken by governmental or non-governmental agencies through planned, organized and collective action that is obligatory or non-voluntary in nature. This is for two reasons.

The first is because market or voluntary action is typically inadequate for providing what are called public goods. Public goods are those public policies (national defense, police and fire protection, or the protection of all persons against preventable death and disability) that are universal in their impacts and effects, affecting everyone equally. . . .

The second reason why self-regarding individuals might refuse to voluntarily pay the costs of such public goods as public health policies is because these policies frequently require burdens that self-interest or self-protection might see as too stringent. . . .

Fair-Sharing of the Burdens. A final principle of the public health ethic is that all persons are equally responsible for sharing the burdens—as well as the benefits—of protection against death and disability, except where unequal burdens result in greater protection for every person and especially potential victims of death and disability. In practice this means that policies to control the hazards of a given substance, service or commodity fall unequally (but still fairly) on those involved in the production, provision or consumption of the service, commodity or substance. The clear implication of this principle is that the automotive industry, the tobacco industry, the coal industry and the medical care industry—to mention only a few key groups—have an unequal responsibility to bear the costs of reducing death and disability since their actions have far greater impact than those of individual citizens. . . .

Right-to-Health. . . . Perhaps the most important step that public health might take to overturn the application of market-justice to the category of health protection would be to centrally challenge the absence of a right to health. Historically, the way in which inequality in American society has been confronted is by asserting the need for additional rights beyond basic political freedoms. (By a right to health, I do not mean anything so limited as the current assertion of a right to payment for medical services.) Public health should immediately lay plans for a national campaign for a new public entitlement—the right to full and equal protection for all persons against preventable disease and disability.

This new public commitment needs more than merely organizational and symbolic expression; ultimately, it needs fundamental statutory and perhaps even constitutional protection. I can think of nothing more helpful to the goal of challenging the application of market-justice to the domain of health than to see public health enter into a protracted and lengthy struggle to secure a Right-to-Health Amendment. . . .

A second step on the path to a fundamental paradigm change is the work of constructing collective definitions of public health problems. Creating and disseminating collective definitions of the problems of death and disability would clearly communicate that the origins of these fates plainly lie beyond merely individual factors (but, as always, some individual factors cannot be totally ignored), and are to be found in structural features of the society such as

A young physician examines a patient at San Francisco's Haight Ashbury Free Medical Clinic—a unique facility that provides vital care to people who cannot afford mainstream medicine.

the rules that govern exposure to the hazards of this world. These new collective descriptions, as they create more accurate explanations of public health problems, would in and of themselves expose the weakness of the norm of individual responsibility and point to the need for collective solutions.

These new definitions of public health problems are especially needed to challenge the ultimately arbitrary distinction between voluntary and involuntary hazards, especially since the former category (recently termed "lifestyle") looms so large in terms of death and disease. Under the current definition of the situation, more stringent controls over involuntary risks are acceptable (if still strenuously resisted by producer groups), while controls over voluntary risks (smoking, alcohol, recreational risks) are viewed as infringements of basic personal rights and freedoms.

These new definitions would reveal the collective and structural aspects of what are termed voluntary risks, challenging attempts to narrowly and persuasively limit public attention to the behavior of the smoker or the drinker, and exposing pervasive myths that "blame the victim." These collective definitions and descriptions would focus attention on the industry behind these activities, asking whether powerful producer groups and supporting cultural and social norms are not primary factors encouraging individuals to accept unreasonable risks to life and limb, and whether these groups or norms constitute aggressive collective structures threatening human life. . . .

In building these collective redefinitions of health problems, however, public health must take care to do more than merely shed light on specific public health problems. The central problems remain the injustice of a market ethic that unfairly protects majorities and powerful interests from their fair share of the burdens of prevention, and of convincing the public that the task of protecting the public's health lies categorically beyond the norms of market-justice. This means that the function of each different redefinition of a specific problem must be to raise the common and recurrent issue of justice by exposing the aggressive and powerful structures implicated in all instances of preventable death and disability, and further to point to the necessity for collective measures to confront and resist these structures. . . .

Conclusion

The central thesis of this article is that public health is ultimately and essentially an ethical enterprise committed to the notion that all persons are entitled to protection against the hazards of this world and to the minimization of death and disability in society. I have tried to make the implications of this ethical vision manifest, especially as the public health ethic challenges and confronts the norms of market-justice. . . .

Brian Abel-Smith

Minimum Adequate Levels of Personal Health Care

Compared to Europe, the United States has been slow to add health care to the public services provided to all citizens. In the following selection, British scholar Brian Abel-Smith justifies the provision of a minimum level of health care as a reasonable national priority. He notes that definition of "minimum health care" may depend on budget limitations, physician expectations, and regional differences.

The historical process by which our societies, through their legislatures, have come to decide that particular services should be provided or made available as a right, has been long and complex. Moreover, motives have often been mixed. But we have nevertheless reached the stage when some needs have become socially recognized—the need for a minimum income in certain defined contingencies; for compulsory education for all children; for the exercise of controls over the use of our environment; for the provision of a wide range of public services from roads to parks, from fire engines to policemen. In Europe, two social needs have been much more widely accepted through legislative action than in the United States—the need for a minimum of personal health care and, less successfully, the need for a minimum standard of housing.

In every field where a service is publicly provided it has been necessary to define a level of provision. This is true of a service in cash, like public assistance, as well as of a service in kind, like education. The ceiling for cash assistance has usually been determined by minimum earnings for full-time work, though exceptions have been made to treat more generously those (such as the disabled or aged) for whom work is not in prospect, or those with large families in order to prevent children from being seriously deprived. . . . In the case of benefits in kind—particularly health care benefits—there are no relatively simple limiting criteria. . . .

Justifications for a Minimum Level of Health Care

If I were asked today to give a justification for a developed society securing the provision of a minimum of health care, I should say that, as in the case of education, there is no one single simple rationale. First, it is clear that the rationale of protecting society from infectious disease is now of much narrower application than in the past. But this rationale does still justify a wide range of public health measures, as well as the provision of various services, such as immunization, as part of primary personal health care.

The lack of consumer knowledge is a second consideration. One cannot know how important it may be to get personal health care until one has contacted a trained health professional. I recognize that one may still not know. But the relative lack of knowledge, compounded often by a discounting of health risks, suggests that access to primary care should be part of any minimum.

Thirdly, it is widely accepted that society has a duty to protect children from the more serious consequences of having a parent or parents who are too ignorant, negligent, or poor to provide their child with a necessary minimum. This argument points to a comprehensive, if not compulsory, assessment and treatment service for children, similar to our minimum education requirement.

The fourth and more general argument is essentially based on economic security. Illness can destroy working capacity and thus seriously reduce ability to pay for health care when it may suddenly become a high expenditure priority. The major change that has occurred over the last century is the growth in the gap between average monthly income and the amount of personal health-care expenditure that a physician may decide is "needed" in the course of a month. What is "needed" in this sense cannot be known in advance. This argument indicates a high priority for the coverage of catastrophic expenses, including long-term expenses, as part of any minimum. This leads to the questions of how much expenditure is regarded as catastrophic and what standard of care should be provided. To define a catastrophe in terms of the same sum of money for all does not seem to be in line with other social arrangements. It could be argued that any monthly expenditure that brings remaining income below a minimum-but-adequate level of living is catastrophic for the individual or the family. Alternatively, it could be argued that any expenditure that lowers substantially the level of income given to replace earnings is catastrophic—in other words, that free health care should be provided to those not at work who have no more than a minimum of savings. . . . One of the reasons for providing services in kind is that what is required varies with individual circumstances that need to be professionally determined and are not known in advance.

A fifth reason is the interest that society has in the restoration of working capacity or of capacity to fulfill social function if ultimately society has decided to provide for those who cannot provide for themselves. A sixth sense is a sense of social solidarity—what none of us thinks rightly should happen to our neighbors—which in turn raises the key question "Who is my neighbor?"

But beneath all this lies the central question: What is a minimum of personal health care? Should we be talking, as I did earlier, of physician-defined needs for health care, or of epidemiologically-defined effective health care, or of the informed consumer's felt needs if it is possible to make such a concept operational in health care, or of some other definition? What the physician decides should be provided varies widely in different cultural, economic, and organizational settings. . . . Moreover, as the physician has little motivation, let alone data, on which to determine the most cost-effective way of achieving a medical outcome, there is considerable room for achieving similar results at lower cost.

Effect of Physician Expectations on the Level of Provision

It is particularly difficult to think through the concept of a minimum in a society where physicians working in acute care have become accustomed to the quite exceptional luxury of expecting to use virtually whatever resources they want to use. This expectation has been passed on in medical education and has become almost enshrined as a professional ethic.

I have said that this is a quite exceptional luxury and would argue this point in four different ways. First, . . . few other countries have a general system of health insurance where the cost largely determines the premium, rather than the premium determining the cost. Secondly, virtually no other occupation, professional or otherwise, has a similar expectation. The teacher, the architect, the lawyer, the accountant each has normally to keep a sharp eye on his paymaster's pocket. And no similar license is given to the road engineers, the bus drivers, the firemen, the factory inspectors, the coastguards, the swimming pool attendants, or the health educators even when they can prove that they can save life at a lower cost than can the physicians. Thirdly, the physician working with the chronic mentally ill or mentally retarded does not have a similar expectation. Fourthly, the expectation is limited to a narrow sphere, even for the physician working with the physically ill. If a physician wants to order diagnostic tests, or use surgery or pharmaceuticals or other treatments, he expects the sky to be the limit. But if he were to decide to prescribe an electric hoist, a stair lift, an electrically powered vehicle, or just a concrete ramp to enable a wheelchaired patient to get in and out of his home, the physician's expectations and the public's suddenly become circumscribed. There is a strange contrast between the amount spent in the remote hope of reducing disability compared with the amount spent to enable the disabled to compensate for their disabilities and attain greater independence and an improved quality of life. It is by no means self-evident that expenditure on one possible route to death prevention should be unlimited while others are tightly budgeted, or even that valiant attempts to postpone death at extraordinary cost are on a quite different plane from that of the prevention of poverty, crime, violence, illiteracy, or slum housing.

How does all this help in thinking through what one means by a minimum? In my values, the services of a primary-health-care team, which includes a personal physician, come first in any specification of a minimum. The functions of this team might be to provide twenty-four-hour continuing care, including a willingness to give house calls by day and by night, to provide the requisite immunization and searching assessments to children, to provide family planning services to women of childbearing age, to provide nursing in the home and regular health checks for the elderly and disabled, to give counsel to the worried and support for the dying and bereaved, and to work with the population served to improve health by encouraging greater self-reliance and changes in behavior. I see this as the essence of personal health Care. And in this context I would give *care* a capital letter. I do not believe that this floor can be established without toughly maintained ceilings on most hospital budgets and on hospital use of medical manpower.

The financial cost of this part of a minimum would not be great when viewed as a proportion of total present health-care spending. And I do not venture an estimate of what it could save in terms of hospital costs, though the saving would potentially be substantial. The major cost would not be in dollars at all but in changes of professional attitudes and expectations, in a fundamental reorientation of education purposes and processes and of public expectations of personal health care and personal responsibility.

This concept of primary care is of course not far from what some Health Maintenance Organizations (if the term is not outdated) seek to provide. But for many Americans it would be more than they are accustomed to receiving, or at least different. It would, of course, be for the personal physician to say when referral to a specialist is necessary and, in most cases, for that specialist to say when admission to a hospital is required.

Defining an Adequate Minimum

I see the key problem as the definition of an adequate minimum for hospital care. One possible solution is for this minimum to be determined, as in the case of education, by the total budget available for the minimum—which would have to be high enough for most people to choose the minimum—leaving those who want something better to pay twice to get it. Thus, I see the establishment of a ceiling in the facilities most people use as one of the essential steps to establishing a floor and ensuring that this floor actually exists in every geographical area. . . .

A limited budget forces those responsible for spending it to determine their priorities. Local politicians, consumers' representatives, local health professionals, and others working in health services may all wish to participate in the dialogue about how the money should be spent. Some priority decisions need to be made regionally to prevent the duplication of expensive equipment and to secure a concentration of rare specialties. Other decisions need to be made more locally. This may well mean that the precise definition of what is included in a minimum varies somewhat between different parts of the country. This avoids the need for centralization and standardization. And to some extent it protects central legislators from having to define priorities in detail by directing criticism to those responsible locally for making decisions about how "their" budget should be spent.

Somehow budget limits work in education. What is different about health that justifies a different solution? Both educational care and health care can have major influences on the life chances of individuals. Somehow, as I have said, limited educational resources are distributed between competing needs in response to the pressures of consumers and the professional judgments of teachers. The result may seem to many of us imperfect but this does not mean that we would all necessarily agree on what the right distribution should be. The problem is to establish an effective dialogue in health care—on how any budget should be spent.

Part

III Problems
in Paradise

There is a fundamental irony about the issues discussed in this book. Scientific achievement is at its zenith, and health care reaches more people than ever. And yet, there is growing public concern about the state of health and medicine. Why should this be so? Scientific advancement has made promises that it could not keep, and public expectations have not been met. American citizens and their policymakers are distressed about a broad range of health care issues, but inevitably certain selected problems are at the core of dissatisfaction and disenchantment. We address in this section three of the most persistent and burdensome problems faced by contemporary medicine—costs, inequities, and drug use.

Cost is undoubtedly the greatest thorn in the side of medicine. Medicine is capable of doing much more than we can afford for it to do. In Chapter 8, we consider the degree and extent of inflation in health care expenditures, and we focus on the solutions being considered for addressing this continuing spiral. It is also important to look at the forces that have propelled costs out of control, not the least of which have been our unrealistic expectations about what medicine could and should do. Clearly, there are many more basic reasons behind inflation than doctors' incomes and the way that medical care is paid for. We must begin with the system of payment itself.

In Chapter 9, we explore groups of people within our country who are not receiving adequate medical attention. This may be the greatest and most senseless tragedy. Medicine and society know how to address the needs of these people; but their inadequate treatment is an ugly legacy of a private enterprise approach to health care.

Chapter 10 considers the complex issues surrounding the use, prescription, regulation, and application of potent modern drugs. Some of them keep us alive and improve the quality of everyday life. Some are abused, misunderstood, and wrongly prescribed. The government is the watchdog. The consumer must weigh the roles of doctor, drug industry, and government—an impossible task unless the consumer is better informed about the risks and benefits of any drug therapy and can accept greater personal responsibility for understanding the issues.

8 Why Does Medical Care Cost So Much?

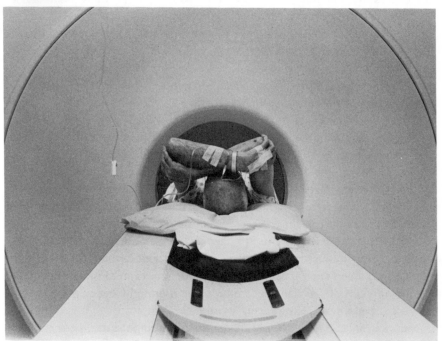

MARK TUSCHMAN

I ssues relating to medical care costs have been raised in each section of this book. They underlie every aspect of the health care system and they influence all policy questions. Any basic policy change relating to health care expenditures inevitably affects us all. There are four fundamental forces behind the tremendous upward spiral of the health dollar. The three most obvious causes are inflation, improved and costly techniques and technologies (such as the CAT scanning machine illustrated on the preceding page), and an increase in the number of people who use the services. The fourth factor is the structure of the system itself—the way we pay doctors and hospitals. Medical care costs have increased by over 429 percent since 1965, a rise far in excess of the general rate of inflation in the economy. It has been estimated that medical costs in the future will double every five years.

What many Americans don't realize is that everybody pays the $200 billion national medical bill. We pay in taxes that finance Medicare, Medicaid, biomedical research, health professions education, and much more; we pay in wages lost to employer contributions to huge medical insurance premiums; we pay in the high costs of goods and services in other sectors of the economy; and we pay when we receive medical services that are not covered by government or private insurance.

One look at the system we use to pay health care providers tells us that it is inefficient. Doctors and hospitals are paid according to the quantity of services they provide. Their incentive is to provide more care. Patients have little incentive to curtail services because they are insulated from costs by government or private health insurance programs that pay for care. In a traditional free market, incentives exist for both consumers and producers to keep prices down. This efficiency is lost in the health care market.

There are many benefits in the system as it exists, not the least of which is that it is serving more and more people, particularly the aged and indigent. Still, greater consideration of costs must be introduced. The solution surely does not lie in stopping technological change or in serving fewer people. But there are a number of proposals that would motivate doctors and hospitals to operate more efficiently. There are also proposals that would require all consumers to pay a percentage of their medical bills, thus introducing an incentive for them to consider the volume of services they use. Another possible approach is the promotion of health maintenance organizations (HMOs), in which consumers pay a fixed premium in exchange for receiving all necessary medical care. There is some evidence that HMOs can achieve cost savings without sacrificing quality.

The articles in this chapter explore the forces behind skyrocketing costs and the various proposals for holding down expenditures. The opening piece from *Time*, "Health Costs: What Limit?" provides a general overview of the cost picture, as well as a review of the data that depict the relative pressures that emanate from particular segments of the health care economy. Philip R. Lee, in "Technology and the Cost of Medical Care—The Physician's Responsibility," explores similar ground with an emphasis on the physician's role in containing costs. Sociologist David Mechanic addresses the sensitive issue of "Rationing Medical Care." He points out that any change in the current rationing system will have far-reaching consequences and will irrevocably alter the relationship between physicians and patients. However, he argues, it may be possible to apportion resources more fairly through the use of explicit rationing techniques.

Time

Health Costs: What Limit?

In this Time *cover story, the spiraling costs of medical care are dramatically documented. Individual costs, national expenditure, and percentage of gross national product devoted to medical care are charted along with an analysis of how doctors, hospitals, technology, employers, insurers, and government intervention all inflate costs.*

As recently as 1965 the nation spent $38.9 billion in medical outlays of all kinds (hospital bills, physicians' fees, lab tests). That amounted to 5.9% of total spending for all goods and services. Since then the bill has increased by 429%. This year [1979] the total is expected to reach $206 billion, or 9.1% of the gross national product. The White House estimates that at the present rate of increase, medical costs will double every five years, a rise far in excess of inflation. Says Dr. Richard Corlin, president of the Los Angeles County Medical Association, with only mild hyperbole: "We are now in a position to spend the entire national budget on medical tests and procedures."

Prices of the most routine facilities and treatments are staggering. Samples: in 1969 Massachusetts General Hospital charged $80 a day for a semiprivate room. Now the bill is $189 a day. Ten years ago, a baby could be delivered at Manhattan's New York Hospital–Cornell Medical Center for $350 in hospital bills, exclusive of the obstetrician's fee. But when 6-lb. Priscilla W. was born there in a fine uncomplicated delivery, she cost her parents $2,800—more than $450 a pound—$1,300 of that for the hospital.

It is true that most medical bills are covered by Government programs or by employer-paid private insurance. But many citizens who long kidded themselves into believing that, as a consequence, medical inflation did not hurt them, now realize that they do pay the bills. They pay in taxes needed in part to finance Medicare and Medicaid. They pay in smaller wage increases than they would get if private employers were not saddled with huge medical insurance premiums. They pay in price hikes that result directly from those premiums. The health insurance costs that Ford Motor Co. pays for its employees add $130 to the price of every car the company makes.

A growing number of policymakers... are convinced that the nation must slow the surge in health costs as part of any effort to control the general inflation that saps the economy and erodes the dollar. But any attempt to do so must be based on a clear understanding of why those costs are so high in the first place, and that understanding is not easy to acquire. The economics of medicine are so unlike those of any other market that even many doctors and hospital administrators find them illogical.... Medical costs do follow a kind of logic, based on two factors that make medicine an economic anomaly:

—Medicine is inherently a seller's market. The customer (patient) has no bargaining power; he initiates only one decision—to see a doctor. The sellers (doctors and hospitals) then take over; they decide what services the patient needs, and do not ask but order him to buy. Unable to diagnose his own illness, the patient has little choice but to obey.

—In American medicine, government and insurance payments have removed all effective limits on demand, and thus price. Though sellers' markets always tend to rapid inflation, they usually are subject to at least one rough check: prices cannot rise so high that the buyers simply become unable to pay. That used to be true of medicine, too, in the now dimly remembered days when patients paid nearly all the bills out of their own pockets. No more: the saddest irony of the medical inflation is that it has been triggered largely by an effort to bring quality medical care within everyone's reach.

Starting with Blue Cross in the 1930s, and continuing through the post–World War II trend for employers to provide medical insurance for their workers, private insurers have picked up a giant chunk of hospital-doctor bills. In 1965 Congress chipped in, providing Medicare payments for those over 65 and Medicaid assistance for the poor. There are still gaps in the coverage: the 20% or so of the bill that the typical Medicare patient must pay can be a severe burden; the long illness that exhausts inadequate insurance benefits is a terror to the middle class. Nonetheless, the system of "third-party payments" has become so comprehensive that patients today pay directly a mere 6% of all hospital bills and 39% of all physicians' fees. The government picks up 55% of hospital bills and 24% of doctor bills; private insurers pick up 37% of each....

Unquestionably, this system has saved innumerable lives and improved the nation's health by encouraging people to seek medical care that they could not otherwise afford (few could without insurance: total payments to doctors and hospitals will work out to more than $3,500 this year for a typical family of four). But the system could hardly have been better designed to fan inflation if that had been its purpose. It has in effect repealed for medicine the last vestiges of the law of supply and demand, a free market equivalent of the law of gravity, and made health care a market of weightlessness: what goes up keeps going up.

Patients now are asked to produce their insurance or Medicare cards before they state their symptoms; once satisfied that they are covered, they rarely even ask what the treatment will cost. Thus demand expands no matter what happens to the national income. Increases in supply do not hold down costs, as they would in a conventional market; quite the opposite. Hospitals build more beds than there are patients available to occupy them: some 25% of the more than 1 million hospital beds in the U.S. are unused on any given day. Then the hospitals must charge more than ever to cover the cost of maintaining those empty beds. . . .

The supply of doctors has increased gradually to 2 per 1,000 population from 1.5 in 1960. But to the chagrin of classical market theorists, no competitive fee cutting has occurred. Indeed, one physician calculates gloomily that every time a new doctor begins practice the nation's medical bills go up another $250,000 per year. Reason: the typical physician generates that much additional business in the tests and hospital admissions.

*   *   *

That might not be the case if the insurers and government bureaucrats who pay the bills kept a sharp eye on costs. But they do not. The Blue Cross movement, which affiliated with the American Hospital Association in 1937, has not rigorously questioned hospital bills until recently. Congress, when legislating Medicare and Medicaid, tacitly agreed to forget about cost controls as part of a bargain to keep the medical profession from opposing the program. Instead, one of the ways the Governmment reimburses hospitals for the care of Medicare-Medicaid patients is on a "cost plus" basis, and it asks few questions about the cost. Blue Shield and commercial insurers generally pay "usual, customary and reasonable" physicians' fees (U.C.R. in medical jargon). That gives doctors an incentive to charge all patients top dollar, so that they can establish those fees as U.C.R. The few fumbling attempts to contain costs have not worked. . . .

*   *   *

Some insurance practices operate directly to drive up costs. Many insurance companies will pay for lab tests only if they are done in a hospital on a supposedly sick patient. The result is to encourage hospitalization of untold thousands of people who could be diagnosed and/or treated at far less cost in a doctor's office. Says one Houston physician: "Say a man in his late 30s to early 40s complains of chest pains. I tell him he needs a thorough physical. In the office my fee would be $45, the tests $250, for a total of $295. But I have to put the patient in the hospital, so his insurance will pay for it. Everything is slow in the hospital, so figure he will be there three days. The cost increases from $295 to $900, but his insurance company will gladly pay for it."

Federal and state governments promote unnecessary hospitalization too. In the Miami area, a February survey found four times as many chronically ill Medicaid patients being treated in hospitals as in nursing homes. Dr. Gerard Mayer, who directed the survey, explains: "Medicaid in Florida makes such low payments to nursing homes that the homes limit the number of beds available to indigent patients. The catch-22 is that the patients wind up waiting in hospitals which are even more expensive" because Medicaid *does* pay nearly 100% of basic hospital costs, whatever they are.

The worst result of the system of third-party payments, however, is a far more insidious one: since the government and private insurers pick up most medical bills, no one in the system has an incentive to hold down those bills. On the contrary: if a doctor or a hospital substitutes an inexpensive treatment for a costly one, he or it merely collects less money from Medicare, Medicaid, a Blue plan or a private insurer.

The lack of necessity to watch costs would be inflationary in any business. (In health care it has been catastrophically inflationary, because powerful underlying forces—economic, psychological and technical—would be working to drive up bills even if a determined effort were made to hold them down. Among these forces:

—Hospitals are inherently expensive places. They must maintain elaborately equipped facilities—emergency rooms, for example—24 hours a day, even though those facilities are used only sporadically. They are labor-intensive: the general ratio is 2.64 employees for every hospital bed. Aggressive unions have forced hospitals to raise the once depressed wages of their nonprofessional people (cooks, cleaners, clerks) so sharply that, for example, wages and benefits now take 70% of the budget of New York Hospital–Cornell Medical Center, *vs.* 35% only 20 years ago. The introduction of expensive machinery raises rather than lowers labor costs. For example, if a hospital buys a CAT (computerized axial tomography) scanner, a kind of super X-ray machine, it must also hire highly trained, highly paid technicians to run it.

—Doctors feel they have a right to charge high fees—the median income is a towering $65,000 a year—to make up for the long training they must undergo and the 80-hour weeks that many say they put in, and to compensate them for bearing the responsibility of making life-and-death decisions. . . .

—Most important, medicine has become an industry employing costly technology as sophisticated as that found in the space program. . . . Doctors generally agree that expensive technology is used much more often than it needs to be, again because no one is watching costs. For instance, hospitals scramble to buy the fanciest equipment available. Secretary of Health, Education and Welfare Joseph Califano charges that hospitals in Southern California contain enough CAT scanners to serve the entire Western United States.

. . . One reason for the emphasis on machinery: the prestige of a hospital is judged by the quality of the doctors on its staff, and the most talented doctors gravitate to the hospitals that boast the most advanced facilities.

Doctors, too, tend to order every test that a patient could conceivably need. In part, that is done to reassure patients or to protect themselves against malpractice suits. . . .

A fierce dispute rages over how much unnecessary surgery is performed on Americans each year. Though the precise figure is impossile to pin down, no one doubts that at least some doctors will operate on patients who could get by without surgery simply because the Government or a private insurer will pay.

If the diagnosis of why medical costs are shooting up is reasonably clear, the course of treatment that could bring those costs under control is anything but clear. It is easy enough to insist that new technology should be subject to rigorous cost-benefit analysis, but if a new machine costs . . . $5 million, and saves one life in ten years, who is to say the price is not justified? Asks Dr. David Thompson of New York Hospital–Cornell: "If you decide to do without some product of the new technology, which one would it be? And are you willing to take the chance that it won't be available when you, the patient, need it?"

More fundamentally still, the system of third-party payments may be the root of much medical inflation, but the old-fashioned alternative is a kind of rationing of medical care by ability to pay that the nation now would rightly find abhorrent. Says Rashi Fein, a noted Harvard medical economist: "Medicine is a social product like education. To ration health in terms of price is not the hallmark of a civilized society. You can differentiate between rich and poor with Cadillacs and yachts, but not with medicine."

Yet unjustified surgery, unnecessary hospitalizations, unneeded tests and an unwillingness even to consider costs do no one any good. The time is past when the nation could accept the resultant inflation as an inevitable side effect of good health; the price is simply becoming too high. . . .

What then can be done? . . . in the U.S., the Carter Administration's immediate proposal is a bill imposing mandatory controls if the medical profession does not clamp down itself. Government interference is, of course, anathema to hospital officials and doctors. . . .

Nevertheless, on balance, the combination of third parties paying most hospital bills and the noncompetitive nature of hospital care seems to have forced costs so completely out of control that, despite the obvious risks, only the Government may be able to clamp on a lid.

National health insurance is a perplexing matter to assess. The issue is also confusing because it takes so many different forms, and the costs, some of them stupendous, are so difficult to pin down. Nearly all sponsors seem to agree, however, on one point: the current mood against increased spending precludes any costly health insurance programs for some time. . . . Public sentiment is building irresistibly for the eventual enactment of some kind of universal health insurance plan. The present programs vary wildly but have one thing in common: the costs keep rising.

Beyond the politicians' remedies, there are more immediate, if less comprehensive steps that the profession and the various insurance plans already in force could take to control costs.

The first essential is to reform insurance practices. Some beginnings have been made: Blue Cross–Blue Shield will no longer automatically pay for a battery of tests administered to every patient who enters a hospital unless each test is specifically ordered by the attending physician. Insurance policies should be rewritten to pay for lab tests and other care administered in a doctor's office rather than a hospital. If Congress will not push the Blue plans and private insurers in this direction, corporations could and should. . . .

The Governmment should revise Medicare and Medicaid reimbursement formulas to pay hospitals a set amount for, say, removal of a gallstone, rather than costs-plus. . . . Califano and some state regulators also are launching a drive to require that a majority of the directors of any Blue Shield plan be laymen. At present, many Blue Shield plans are dominated by doctors, who, to put it delicately, have no great zeal to question fellow physicians' fees. Hospitals could keep a far sharper eye on costs. . . .

*   *   *

On a far larger scale, one of the most promising alternatives to the traditional medical system is group-practice health maintenance organizations, which hire doctors to work on salary rather than charging fees for specific services, and sign up hospitals to take on their patients. A customer joining an H.M.O. pays a set monthly fee. . . . That fee entitles the subscriber and his family to any medical services they may need, from a routine physical exam to open-heart surgery.

Many physicians argue that the only way the U.S is going to bring its medical costs under control is by emphasizing preventive medicine instead of crisis care. They stress exercise, weight control, cutting out drinking and smoking. Says Dr. Hoyt D. Gardner, president-elect of the A.M.A.: "America *medically* suffers more from affluence—and consequent self-indulgence—than from poverty." But not many doctors are genuinely optimistic that much will be done.

No great optimism is justified either when it comes to cutting medical costs overall. Medicine cannot be made cheap, given the costs of its technology, and by its nature it cannot be anything but a seller's market. But U.S. health care bills do not have to shoot up as rapidly as they are doing now. The big question is whether doctors, hospital administrators, insurers and employers can devise ways to bring the public the benefits of technology at an affordable price, without a federal whip being held over them.

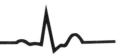

MARK TUSCHMAN

One of the most expensive and also one of the most successful of the new technologies involves neonatal intensive care for newborns.

Philip R. Lee

Technology and the Cost of Medical Care—the Physician's Responsibility

Since physicians control most health services and determine what procedures will be used in medical care, their decisions have a great impact on health costs. In the following article, Dr. Philip Lee, director of the Health Policy Program at the University of California, San Francisco, argues that doctors could make more economical use of technology. Lee notes, however, that Medicare and Medicaid reimbursement methods have encouraged increased expenditure for technology. Fee-for-service or "usual, customary, and reasonable" (UCR) charge methods provide a powerful incentive for excessive use and inappropriate application of technology with resultant increases in the costs of care.

T he rising cost of medical care is one of the central health policy issues of the day. It is likely to remain so as we move into the 1980s. The rising cost of medical care has become an urgent problem for consumers, for third parties (private insurance, government), for physicians, for hospitals, and other providers of medical care.

In 1978, health expenditures totaled $192 billion, or $863 for each person in the United States. While health care costs have increased at an annual rate of over 12 percent in recent years, there is no agreement that such increases are essential to good medical care. The major element in the rising costs of personal health care has been hospital costs—now accounting for 45 percent of the national expenditure for personal health care.

There are three basic elements that account for the rising cost of care:
—inflation in the economy generally, and in the health care sector particularly (50–60 percent);
—increased complexity and/or intensity of care (30–40 percent), and
—increases in the size and aging of the population (10 percent).

It is not an easy matter to estimate the impact of the physician's role on cost, nor to fully measure the amount and direction of technology's impact on cost. It is clear, however, that the statistics often understate the physician's role as the primary decision-maker regarding the utilization of health services. The physician's decisions directly affect the types of services ordered and provided, the quality of medical care, the access of patients to necessary medical services and the cost of these services. Although physician services made up only 21 percent of the total personal health care expenditures in 1978, it has been estimated . . . that physicians exert some direct control over approximately 70 percent of personal health care expenditures.

Medical technology accounts for a significant portion of the cost attributable to both hospital and physician expenditures. The Congressional Office of Technology Assessment has defined medical technology as "the set of techniques, drugs, equipment and procedures used by health care professionals in delivering medical care to individuals and the system within which such care is delivered." Although we must be concerned about the full range of technologies including laboratory, x-ray, medical diagnostic and surgical procedures, as well as the organized application of multiple technologies in intensive care units and operating room suites, I will focus most of my attention on the common laboratory and x-ray procedures.

These are sometimes referred to as the "nickel and dime" technologies, as opposed to the "big ticket" items such as computed tomographic scanning or coronary bypass surgery. I include in technology costs both the costs of the technology and the cost of the utilization of the technology. Although most of the analyses of the impact of medical technology on costs have concentrated on hospital costs, several attempts have been made to assess total system costs and the treatment costs for selected illnesses.

In examining the impact of medical technology on the costs of medical care Victor Fuchs of Stanford University estimated that technology accounted for 0.6 percentage points of the 8.0 percent annual rate of increase of total health care spending between 1947 and 1967. In examining cost increases over a longer period, 1930 to 1975, Selma Mushkin and her associates estimated that technology reduced the annual rate of spending by 0.4 percentage points. In this study Mushkin and her colleagues at Georgetown University's Public Services Laboratory estimated an increase in health expenditures of 3150 percent between 1930 and 1975. Population growth and the changing age composition of the population accounted for 16 percent of the increases and price changes or inflation accounted for 42 percent. The residual increase was made up of the growth in third party payments and the growth in real disposable income, minus the cost-reducing impact of medical technology.

Although economists have questioned some of the assumptions, data and methods in these studies, most clinicians would agree that many of the advances in medical technology have, in the aggregate, been cost-saving. These include: penicillin and other antibiotics for use against infectious diseases;

poliomyelitis, rubella and measles vaccines; antihypertensive drugs; and drugs in a variety of other therapeutic classes. Some of the more recently developed, non-pharmaceutical medical technologies, such as renal dialysis, electronic fetal monitoring and various kinds of intensive care units, have undoubtedly increased the cost of care while often improving the quality of care—in some cases, such as total hip replacement, dramatically so.

It has been the rapid development of "machines" in medicine applied from before birth to the termination of life—that has been the cause of increasing concern. Do the benefits justify the costs? Are the machines safe? Are they effective?

As medical science has advanced and new drugs, equipment, procedures and techniques have proliferated, there has been a dramatic change in the relationship of the federal government and the private sector with respect to medical technology. Although there has been some regulation of prescription drugs since 1906, it was not until 1938 that a manufacturer had to prove that a drug was safe before it could be marketed. In 1962 the Food, Drug and Cosmetic Act was amended also to require proof of efficacy. Although the new requirements have caused some controversy, they are well accepted, and the relationships between the federal government, the drug industry and the medical and pharmacy professions are reasonably clear cut.

Since 1965 far more important changes have taken place in three areas that will have a significant impact on medical technology: health care financing, health planning and medical device regulation. Prior to these developments, and except for the regulatory function of the FDA, the federal government played a limited role in the way that medical technology was developed or applied.

Medicare and Medicaid have had the most profound impact on the use of medical technology, particularly because the reimbursement methods adopted have fostered the use of technology. For example, in 1972 Medicare coverage was extended to persons under age 65, with end-stage renal disease and requiring kidney dialysis or renal transplantation. Federal expenditures for Medicare and Medicaid exceeded $31 billion in fiscal year 1977, while Medicare expenditures for the care of about 40,000 end-stage renal disease patients have now reached approximately one billion dollars annually.

The 1972 Medicare amendments not only extended coverage to patients with end-stage renal disease, they also enacted two regulatory provisions that affected the use of medical technology. Professional Standards Review Organizations were created to review the appropriateness of hospital care provided to Medicare and Medicaid beneficiaries. The law also required that hospitals seeking to make capital expenditures in excess of $100,000 secure approval by the state health planning agency.

Next came the Health Planning and Resource Development Act of 1974, which created the Health Systems Agencies at the local level and state health planning agencies with certificate-of-need authority to limit major capital expenditures by hospitals.

Finally, in 1976, Congress enacted the Medical Device Amendments to regulate the safety and effectiveness of medical devices.

These developments have expanded significantly the role of the federal government in the development and use of technology. In analyzing these developments, Dr. Richard Rettig of the Rand Corporation has recently noted:

> . . . First, the shift toward a greater federal role in medical technology derives from the general failure of the medical marketplace to consider both costs and benefits of medical services in the decision to produce such services. The factors contributing to this situation include extensive third-party reimbursement of medical services which removes the incentive to patients and physicians to economize in the use of medical services, the influence of physicians in affecting patient demand for medical care as well as in controlling its supply, the limited information possessed by health care consumers and a propensity to rely upon physician judgment, the incentive to practice defensive medicine to avoid the threat of medical malpractice liability, and the tendency of hospitals to engage in non-price competition for physicians through the acquisition of expensive medical technology.

It is important to examine carefully Dr. Rettig's assumptions, for if they are correct they will result in even more federal regulation of physicians and medical technology, unless some major changes can be initiated by the medical profession.

What do we know about the impact of medical technology on the cost of care beyond the general data provided in the studies by Fuchs and Mushkin? A major advance in our understanding of the impact of technology on medical care was made by Anne Scitovsky and Nelda McCall in their study of patients treated at the Palo Alto Medical Clinic in the periods 1951 to 1964, and 1964 to 1971. Although the initial study did not deal primarily with the impact of medical technology on cost, it identified changes in treatment as a significant factor affecting costs. The changes in treatment included the use of new techniques or new drugs, the substitution of specialists for nonspecialists, increases or decreases in the use of specific services such as laboratory tests or days of hospital stay, the substitution of inpatient for outpatient treatment, or changes in the mix of services. In their initial study they found that in five of the eight conditions studied "costs rose more (some of them substantially more) than they would have risen if treatments had remained unchanged."

The follow-up study compared the 1964 data with data for 1971. . . . Although real costs declined for five of the eleven conditions studied, the cost-raising aspects of technology exceeded the cost-saving ones. In fact, the real cost increase for treating one condition, myocardial infarction, far outweighed the combined cost savings of the five conditions for which real costs decreased (maternity care, cancer of the breast, closed reduction of forearm fracture with regional or general anesthetic, pneumonia, duodenal ulcer).

Perhaps the most significant finding was not simply the increase in cost, but the dramatic increase in the use of laboratory procedures, x-rays and prescription drugs over the 20-year period from 1951 to 1971. For example, the average number of laboratory tests performed on a patient with a perforated appendix rose from 5.3 in 1951 to 14.5 in 1964 to 31.0 in 1971. For maternity care, the number rose from 4.8 per case in 1951 to 11.5 in 1964 to 13.5 in 1971. . . .

In 1975, Scitovsky carried her studies one step further and examined the national data available on the utilization of outpatient laboratory tests and outpatient x-rays. She estimated that there were an average of two laboratory tests per doctor's office visit, including visits to hospital clinics and emergency rooms. . . . Based on her studies, Scitovsky estimated that from \$4.8 to \$6.7 billion may have been spent for outpatient laboratory tests and x-rays in 1975. This amounted to 25 percent to 35 percent of estimated expenditures for outpatient physician ancillary services and five to six percent of total health care expenditures in 1975.

While Scitovsky has examined the common procedures and their impact on cost, others have examined the more spectacular innovations such as open-heart surgery, renal dialysis and transplants, brain scans and intensive care units. The examination of the impact of these and other technologies on hospital costs has led to estimates that as much as 75 percent of the hospital cost increases in the period from 1955 to 1975 was due to increases in real inputs per patient day. Others have estimated that the greater intensity of the use of services, much of it associated with new technologies, accounts for 30–40 percent of the cost increases.

Recently, Dr. Herbert Abrams, professor and chairman of radiology at Harvard Medical School, has begun to examine the use of radiologic procedures. The cost of these procedures, both inpatient and outpatient, rose from over \$4.7 billion in 1975 to \$6.1 billion in 1977 and probably more than \$7 billion in 1978. In 1977, over 240 million radiologic examinations were performed. These are not insignificant numbers. While particular attention has been paid to new imaging methods, which are expensive and highly visible, most of the costs lie elsewhere.

Prescription drug use also has increased rapidly in the past 30 years. The benefits in some cases have been spectacular. In other cases the seriousness and magnitude of adverse drug reactions, and the improper use or irrational prescribing of drugs, have marred the benefits. The average number of prescriptions dispensed by community pharmacies, discount stores and dispensing physicians rose from 2.4 per person per year in 1950 to 6.9 in 1976, almost a threefold increase in 26 years.... We find that about 2.7 billion prescriptions are currently dispensed—or 12.7 per person per year.

One of the questions that must be asked with respect to the use of any technology—laboratory tests, radiologic procedures, prescription drugs, medical devices, medical diagnostic procedures or surgical procedures—is whether or not the technology is used rationally or appropriately.

I believe that there is substantial evidence that the use of prescription drugs—particularly antibiotics, psychoactive drugs, analgesics and estrogens—is often unjustified or inappropriate. For other classes of drugs, particularly antihypertensives, use may be inappropriately low. There is not only overuse of prescription drugs, such as the use of antibiotics in the treatment of the common cold, but there is also widespread noncompliance on the part of patients with drug regimens that are prescribed appropriately by physicians. In the past, the patient was blamed for this problem and various characteristics of such patients were described. Research in recent years, however, has led to greater understanding of noncompliance and has shown that it is very much related to the physician-patient relationship, physician behavior, and patient knowledge, expectations and motivation.

The use of laboratory tests and radiologic procedures is also intimately tied to physician behavior and is, in my judgment, closely linked to the present policies of third parties (private insurance, government) related to physician reimbursement and to the fee-for-service system of reimbursement.

The problem, however, is not simply one of overutilization or inappropriate utilization of these technologies. Excessive use of radiologic procedures, as Abrams points out, embodies three aspects: excessive radiation per film, excessive films per examination and excessive examinations per patient....

In an analysis of the dynamics of medical technology use, two of my associates at the Health Policy Program, University of California at San Francisco, Dr. Steven Schroeder and Jonathan Showstack, noted that "the fee-for-service reimbursement system contains large incentives favoring technology intensive medical practice."...

There are other factors, however, that may affect physician behavior with respect to the use of medical technologies. Increasing specialization and the identification of specialties with particular procedures is one of the factors identified by Dr. Robert Chase of Stanford Medical School when he was serving as President of the Board of Medical Examiners....

Although all of these factors are important, physician reimbursement is certainly a key factor in the use of medical technologies. There are currently two principal fee-for-service methods of administering third party reimbursement for physician services—a benefit schedule and a fee screen system. A benefit schedule (fee schedule) is essentially a list of specific physician services, with either monetary or unit values attached to it, specifying what third parties will reimburse for a specific service. A fee screen system, often called the usual, customary and reasonable (UCR) charge system, essentially allows physicians to set their own level of reimbursement. To limit the liability of the third party carrier, this system establishes a maximum level of reimbursement based on several criteria, often including the physician's specialty and practice location. The UCR system is used by Medicare and by many private health insurance carriers. It has been estimated that in 1975 approximately 130 million persons out of a total of 170 million persons with private health insurance coverage for physician services had policies that used the UCR system.

Research in recent years has revealed a good deal of information about physician reimbursement:

—The usual, customary and reasonable (UCR) method of fee screens has often been singled out as inherently inflationary, because under this system reimbursement levels are based on provider charge experience;

—Efforts to control costs through governmentally imposed price controls or Medicaid fee schedules have proved largely successful in curtailing unit prices, but not overall expenditures. Physicians increase the number of services provided and shift to more profitable case or service mixes;

—When procedural terminologies (defining what services are billable) are changed from a relatively simple nomenclature to a more comprehensive system, prices charged by physicians tend to rise more rapidly than they would otherwise;

—Methods of reimbursement may affect patients' access to care. If fees are too low, access will be impeded;

—Methods of reimbursement may affect both specialty and geographic distribution of physicians; and

—Finally, there has been a shift in the conventional wisdom from the view that consumer behavior is the main determinant of medical resource use to the view that physician behavior is more important.

In examining some of the current data on the use of medical technologies, I have stressed the role of the physician who is the primary generator of the use of medical technology. I have stressed that the use of medical technology is adding significantly to the cost of medical care, particularly care provided in the hospital. I have noted that it is probably the "nickel and dime" technologies rather than the "big ticket" items that are contributing most significantly to cost increases. Finally, I have postulated that the current fee-for-service system, particularly the usual, customary and reasonable (UCR) method of reimbursement, provides a strong incentive for the physician to use medical technologies in the course of providing care.

I believe that these observations are correct. I believe that they pose a major challenge to the medical profession to reexamine the factors that are driving costs up so rapidly and to consider alternatives to the present cherished UCR system of reimbursement.

David Mechanic

Rationing Medical Care

Attempts to reduce or contain health costs must be viewed in the context of their impact on the quality of medical care. In this careful analysis of the effect of various cost-containment strategies on patient care, sociologist David Mechanic examines both economic and behavioral factors that determine the effectiveness of these strategies. The theory and intention of a plan to contain costs may be subverted by the habits and responses of hospitals, physicians, or patients. Asserting that rationing of medical care has always existed, Mechanic recommends research to determine a balanced mix of cost-containment solutions that will achieve necessary economies while protecting access, quality of care, and trust between physician and consumer.

As medical care costs continue to rise, the containment of those costs has become an issue of high priority throughout the world. . . . Discussions abound on techniques of cost containment but with little comparison of the alternatives and their implications for patient care. In the discussion that follows, I want to review major alternative approaches for rationing the provision of health care through an examination of the assumptions implicit in each of these approaches. Rationing for medical care has always existed through the fee-for-service system. The total amount of medical care provided was a product of what people were willing and able to pay and of the limits on personal economic resources. In recent decades the growth of third-party payment and public subsidy has eroded the controls implicit in fee-for-service arrangements and large co-insurance and deductibles. As a greater proportion of health care expenditures is paid through insurance or public programs, neither the physician nor the patient has incentive to forgo medical care whose value is even remotely possible. One consequence is a highly inefficient and cost-ineffective pattern of service.

Rationing may occur by influencing the behavior of the patient or the physician or the administrative structure of the medical care plan. Fee for service, for example, imposes barriers to access and use among potential patients. In contrast, capitation payment (payment of a fixed amount per patient for a given time interval regardless of the number of services provided), requires the physician to make more explicit decisions as to the allocation of his time and effort among patients.

Fixed prospective budgeting procedures, in turn, demand that administrators make more explicit decisions concerning the provision of manpower and facilities. As the mix of rationing techniques in medical care changes, the relationships among physicians and between patients and physicians also change.

* * *

There are three basic types of rationing, each directing its influence differentially on patients, doctors, or health plan administrators. In any complex medical care program all occur together, but in different combinations.

Fee-for-service rationing refers to economic barriers imposed on the consumer, such as fees or other cost-sharing arrangements. The most frequently used rationing devices are co-insurance and deductibles.

Implicit rationing, the second type, refers to established limitations on the resources available such as in fixed prospective budgets, limitation of available hospital beds, and restrictions on specialists or specialty positions. The National Health Service of England and health maintenance organizations (H.M.O.s) are typical examples of implicit rationing.

The third type, explicit rationing, refers to direct administrative decisions affecting the provision of care, exclusions of coverage within health care plans or in respect to particular subpopulations, limitations on the availability of specific types of visits or procedures, pre-review of the use of certain procedures, utilization review, and required intervals between the provision of certain services.

Rationing through cost sharing is based on the assumption that this reduces the consumption of medical care. Cost barriers have a larger effect, however, on the use of ambulatory care or medications than on more expensive services under control of the physician. However, it is believed that when the patient must pay part of the hospital care costs, he or she is more likely to put pressure on the doctor for earlier release, and that the physician takes the patient's insurance into account in ordering health care procedures and in his other decisions. Whether or not cost sharing actually reduces consumption, it succeeds in shifting part of the cost burden from the plan or the insurance policy to the consumer, and thus reduces the aggregate cost to the plan.

The use of cost sharing as a form of rationing raises some questions. First, to what extent does cost sharing affect the use of different types of services and procedures? Second, in respect to procedures such as hospitalization and surgical intervention, which are under the control of physicians, to what extent do patients actually influence physicians as a result of cost-sharing pressures? Third, to what extent are physicians aware of the co-insurance and deductible provisions of their patients' insurance policies; and if they are, how does it affect their behavior? These are obvious issues, but we have only the most fragmentary data on them. Economists differ in their estimations of the elasticities of medical care consumption; it is clear, however, that cost-sharing provisions affect use of services under the control of the physician. Effects are particularly substantial in the use of ambulatory, psychiatric, and dental services, for example. The extent of the effects differs, depending on the specific cost-sharing arrangements and on the economic status of the persons involved. Cost sharing affects the poor and the affluent differently, and results in inequalities in the distribution of medical care. . . .

Cost sharing as a rationing device is often opposed because of its differential effects on persons with different incomes, because it is believed to create barriers to necessary care, and because administration of such mechanisms is costly. Advocates of such rationing seem to believe that patients are sufficiently knowledgeable to distinguish between serious and trivial symptoms, and that cost sharing encourages them to make that distinction. Certainly this is true in some cases, but studies of illness behavior suggest that patients' decisions to seek care are influenced by factors other than those which physicians deem most important from a medical standpoint. Patients give more attention to symptoms that disrupt ordinary activities and routines than to those that may pose greater potential threat but are more innocuous. The assumption that worried and fearful patients can make accurate judgments of the medical significance of their symptoms is inconsistent with the notion that such judgments are a major function of the physician. In retrospect, many patients' complaints are trivial, but what the patient seeks is reassurance from the physician that this is the case, and relief from uncertainty and anxiety. It is strange to hear, on the one hand, that the ordinary patient can make such judgments, and, on the other, that only a physician with eight or ten years of medical training is competent to deliver first-contact care.

If patients can make wise decisions about when care is necessary, then one would anticipate that cost sharing would result in a different mix of services, because patients who are more seriously ill would be more likely to seek care. The fragmentary data on this issue suggest that cost-sharing provisions exert an over-all rationing effect on medical care usage for both trivial and serious maladies. For example, increases in the prescription charge in the National Health Service affect not only drugs used primarily as placebos but also drugs for serious chronic illness. Even without cost barriers, it is difficult to maintain surveillance and adherence to therapy among persons who have such serious conditions as hypertension but are not symptomatic. Although patients respond primarily to the way symptoms affect them, the role of the physician is to assess the implications of particular symptoms for a person's future health status. The fact that physicians often make an expensive diagnostic appraisal of ordinary symptoms suggests that the clinical significance of such procedures may not be as simple to assess as cost-sharing advocates imply. It seems, therefore, that if more stringent rationing is to be applied, it will be applied more rationally in relation to those who have most expertise and knowledge and who are in a better position to distinguish the serious from the trivial. Implicit rationing shifts expenditure decisions from the patient to the physician.

*   *   *

Implicit rationing assumes that when professionals face resource limitations they are encouraged to make sound clinical judgments on the priority of need and efficacy of intervention. When budgeting is open-ended, as in cost reimbursement, there is less pressure on the professionals to exercise selective judgment. Fixed budgets, it is assumed, require professionals to examine their decisions more carefully.

Implicit rationing is based on various assumptions about the behavior of physicians: that they are sufficiently programmed by their training to make scientifically valid judgments of need and priority of need; that they will be motivated to act ethically and to take whatever measures are best for the patient as opposed to other interests; and that, because of their proximity to the contingencies of care, they are in the best position for good decision-making.

Although these assumptions seem reasonable, various contingencies of medical practice make them less powerful than they may appear. First, there is considerable uncertainty in medical practice as to the amount of care necessary for many problems. Also, the relationship between most processes of care and outcome are at best ambiguous. Thus, the clinician's judgments in such matters are likely to reflect his or her training and style of practice more than any rigorous criteria of effectiveness. This is a weak basis on which to make rationing judgments.

Second, physicians engage in complex and subtle interactions with patients that affect both patient response and physician behavior. Physicians find it difficult to refuse services demanded by more sophisticated, knowledgeable, and educated patients; and such refusal is made even more risky because the standards themselves are so vague and physicians may lack confidence in their own rationing criteria. Physicians, thus, are more likely to ride with the tide, rationing more stringently when there are no protests from patients, but being somewhat more liberal in the use of resources when patients expect and demand this. The problem is that the more sophisticated and aggressive patients receive a disproportionate share of health services, while those who are less educated and more passive may receive fewer services even though they may have greater need.

Further, the assumption that implicit rationing allows physicians to make more professional decisions because it separates their professional judgments from fee considerations is plausible but weak. Physicians are influenced in many ways by their training, by personal needs, and by the desire for prestige and recognition. In the absence of economic incentives they may work at a more comfortable and leisurely pace, devote less time to their patients, give a disproportionate share of their time to more interesting and prestigeful tasks, and generally organize their schedules so as to have a more stimulating and attractive day. There is evidence, for example, that when capitation is the primary mode of payment, physicians devote fewer hours to their patients than do fee-for-service physicians; they refer patients to other types of facilities more readily; and they may be more inflexible and less responsive in dealing with patients. In short, implicit rationing by itself, without carefully worked out incentives affecting remuneration, recognition, and peer acceptance, does not guarantee appropriate allocations of limited resources or equitable behavior in the care of patients.

*   *   *

What has been said of physicians seems even more true of institutions. In recent years various incentive reimbursement programs have been developed to encourage hospitals to use resources more efficiently. The assumption is that the economic incentives would encourage better planning and more rational decision-making. What are not taken into account are the fluidity and decentralization of decisions within hospitals and the hospitals' inability to control their own decision apparatus. . . .

What is said of hospitals is also true of medical staffs of large medical groups. We understand very little about the behavioral factors affecting the decisions of individual physicians; and each physician recognizes the legitimacy of interference in his clinical responsibilities only to a very limited extent. . . .

Developing incentives within capitation systems for both efficient and high-quality care is a formidable challenge. The development of such incentives must take into account not only the uncertainty of practice and the ease with which formal procedures can be thwarted, but also the training and ideology of the physicians, the pattern of peer influences that is presently relatively weak, and the situational contingencies likely to affect performance such as work load, availability of ancillary assistance, and patient mix. The difficulty of achieving any effective direct control over professional decision-making is one argument for an administrative approach to rationing. Explicit rationing is such an approach.

The use of explicit rationing techniques has been based on a number of assumptions. First, it has been assumed that when governments or administrators exercise more centralized control over the allocation of health funds and the establishment of priorities among varying health care options, a more equitable distribution of resources is likely to occur than through either fee-for-service or implicit rationing techniques. Through more centralized control it is theoretically possible to assign funds in relationship to ascertained need of particular population groups, to apportion resources more fairly among different geographic areas, and to establish areas of health care investment with better cost-benefit outcomes.

Second, it is assumed that aggregate data available to administrators, together with the results of careful studies and controlled clinical trials when they exist, serve as a better basis for allocation decisions than the individual judgments of practitioners who may work from clinical impressions and experiences that lack any scientific basis.

Third, explicit rationing in part takes the burden of rationing from the physician and gives it to an outside administrative authority, thus alleviating conflicts of interest inherent in the doctor-patient relationship in which the physician has the major responsibility for denying services to patients and reducing the stresses in that relationship.

As to the first assumption, it is correct, at least in principle, that planning authorities can determine total expenditures, allocation of health care resources among varying population groups, the appropriate mix between physicians and other health care personnel, and the distribution of resources between primary and secondary care levels. Moreover, administrators can exclude payment for procedures that are likely to yield low benefits or that are of high risk relative to their benefits. Or, by requiring pre-review or by specifying the credentials for eligibility for reimbursement, administrators can control the incidence of these processes and specify who is to perform them. The conception of this planning process, however, is excessively rational and fails to take into account the susceptibility of these processes to political influences or public pressures. Even the most cursory examination of health planning reveals sober evidence of the wide gap between rational planning and political outcomes.

There is little evidence to support the belief that explicit rationing per se will result in a fairer allocation of health resources. Indeed, problems of medical-resource redistribution are probably no different than those of income redistribution generally, and are subject to the same kinds of political pressures.

It is likely that redistribution is most possible when resources are expanding, but extraordinarily difficult otherwise.... When funds are made available on an equal basis theoretically—as in the Medicare program in the United States—large inequalities still occur because of the unequal availability of physicians and facilities.

Problems exist as well in respect to the quality of administrative decision-making. In theory, allocation decisions made on an aggregate data base are probably better than individual clinical judgments. But the fact is that in many areas adequate data are not likely to be available in a form that allows firm decisions to be made. . . .

It is not likely that effective guidelines can be written to cover these complicated situations without creating a host of new problems. Standards may be effectively established for some situations, but medical practice in general will continue to require a great deal of professional discretion.

Another problem with explicit rationing is that those who develop regulations and guidelines are often not involved in the complex and variable contingencies of everyday practice. They do not have the sensitivity that comes from working with the problems themselves. In trying to formulate general principles for different settings, the result may be injustices and absurdities. This can be prevented in part by a sensitive process of review and commentary on proposed regulations; but even under the best of circumstances, standard rules fail to cover adequately contingencies that occur in actual delivery of health services.

One advantage of explicit rationing is that it shifts the burden of responsibility for denying certain services from the physician to the administrative staff of the program or to the financing agent. Physicians are insulated from the charge that they are promoting their own interests against those of the patients. Such problems are increasingly likely in those incentive systems that provide bonuses to physicians for cost-effective practices and that require them to share losses when there are cost overruns. In a pure explicit-rationing system, physicians can still advocate doing everything possible for patients; the physicians can serve as the patients' representatives in relation to the plan. To the extent that there are limits on the services available, it is the system that does not provide them rather than the physician who denies them. This insulates the patient-physician relationship from suspicion and hostility which may become more common in systems that require physicians to play a strict rationing role. It has been suggested that to put the physician into the latter position is unethical because it undermines and dilutes his or her primary responsibility to the patient. The argument is that the physician better understands the complexity of the individual patient's case and the patient's clinical needs than does an administrator.

Any system is likely to involve a mix of types of rationing. This is what occurs in almost all non-fee-for-service practice. The issue is to understand better what a good mix is, not only from the point of view of achieving economies, but also from the perspective of improving the doctor-patient relationship and increasing the opportunities for that relationship to be built on trust and mutual respect. This is a big challenge, one that deserves a commensurately large research agenda.

9 Inequities in Health Status and Health Care

One of the most startling facts about the American health care system is that the 34 million people in the poorest families, families with incomes below $6,000 per year, are on the average twice as sick as the rest of us. They spend more than twice as many days ill in bed or otherwise unable to carry on normal daily activities. Overall, the poor have benefited less from modern health care techniques than other groups.

Although annual health care expenditures increased very rapidly between 1964 and 1979, many Americans today suffer the same inequities in access to care that they did fifteen years ago. For many who are poor, the circumstances are alarming.

Despite widespread government-financed medical care coverage for the poor through Medicaid and Medicare, millions of people still receive no benefits. Those who do have coverage still have heavy out-of-pocket costs. Also, they often lack continuity of care and a means for understanding and communicating with the system. Considering the money that has poured into their treatment, it is astounding that so little has been accomplished in improving the health of poor people.

Although it is estimated that the vast majority of poor people enjoy fairly good health, about one-quarter of them suffer from severe chronic illnesses that render them totally or partially disabled. These are the same diseases that afflict other Americans, but for the poor, these conditions are more severe and more widespread. Low income people aged 45 to 64 are about twice as likely to be partially disabled as their contemporaries with higher incomes, and four times more likely to be severely disabled.

Does low income cause chronic illness or is illness bred by poverty? Clearly both conditions—poverty and chronic illness—lead to this vicious cycle. Poverty nourishes illness and premature death. It creates lives that are filled with stress when the maintenance of good health habits is difficult or impossible; it often prevents adequate nutrition; it increases one's exposure to accidents and violence; and once poor people become sick or disabled, it is doubly difficult for them to regain their health. Chronic illness leads to lower income and less adequate living conditions; it increases stress, depression, and deteriorated health.

Why does our health care system fail to generate better health conditions among the poor? Is there something amiss in the balance between spending for medical care and spending for other social programs? Is it impossible to improve the health of the poor? Economist Harold Luft opens this chapter with a discussion of the complex relationship between "Poverty and Health." Clearly, socioeconomic, occupational, and educational factors influence health and thereby the ability to earn money. David Mechanic explores the poor fit between medical institutions and the needs of the poor in "Inequality, Health Status, and the Delivery of Health Services in the United States." He reviews some of the common recommendations for improving the health of poor people—national health insurance, HMOs, preventive medicine—but he clearly sees these as inadequate unless they are accompanied by changes in underlying social conditions. Economist Karen Davis, in "Health Care of Low-Income Families," looks at the statistical evidence on low income and access to care, particularly in relation to current inflation and unemployment. She uncovers some startling evidence concerning inequities in access to care, and she raises some issues concerning the impact of widespread economic stress on the health of Americans.

The final selection in this chapter, "Health and Human Resources," is a description of poverty and its obvious health implications by Raymond Wheeler, a physician who examined hundreds of people in the rural South and Appalachia.

Harold S. Luft

Poverty and Health

Numerous studies have shown a correlation between poverty and health prob-lems. An examination of this relationship raises complex social, economic, and medical issues. Analyzing poverty both as a cause and a result of illness, Harold Luft, of the University of California, San Francisco's Health Policy Program, traces the change of research emphasis over the past two decades from "medical care" to "health problems." Policy recommendations based on biomedical and socioeconomic research focus on strategies for reducing the incidence, severity, and impact of health problems on all citizens, especially on the poor, who are most burdened by inequities in health status and access to care.

M ajor changes are currently taking place in both professional and pub-lic discussions of health problems. In the 1960s the major focus was on medical care and its provision. For many reasons, the emphasis is now beginning to shift to the causes and consequences of health problems. . . .

Health problems are widespread even among the under sixty-five, non-institutionalized population. There is ample evidence of this in the National Health Interview Survey and other sources. Furthermore, these same data show a strong association between poverty and the presence of health problems.

The question is, Does poverty cause poor health, or does poor health cause poverty? My first task is to unravel the lines of causation, at least for major, long-term health problems. The published data of the national health surveys and other, less well known, but more specific surveys, allow an identification of some key determinants of health problems. Low income, low education, and the occupations held by the poor *do* have an important *causal* role. But a "health problem" can be anything from controlled hypertension to totally disabling quadriplegia. Thus, my second task is to identify factors that lead a given level of functional limitation, such as a bad back, to be more or less disabling. As will be seen, people with less education, those initially in low paying jobs, blacks, and women are more likely to be adversely affected by a health problem and to suffer greater reductions in labor force participation and earnings. Those people who often begin with a greater chance of being in poverty tend to experience greater disabilities and become even more impoverished. This leads to my third task—measuring the individual and social effects of disabilities on personal earnings and the extent to which social welfare programs help alleviate the individual burdens. The costs of disability are large and account for a substantial fraction of poverty in America. While various programs help to shift some of these costs to those better able to bear the burden, much more needs to be done. Therefore, my final task . . . is to discuss some of the policy issues that must be addressed. . . .

From Medical Care to Health Problems

Social Policy and Access to Medical Care. The 1960s saw the culmination of several decades of effort on the part of advocates for social reform. The War on Poverty and the Great Society brought social action programs for the poor and, in the health arena, the establishment of Medicare, Medicaid, and Neighborhood Health Center programs. These programs marked the first major successes for the national health insurance advocates who had been maintaining the struggle for such social welfare legislation since the early 1900s. It was hoped that these programs would redistribute resources, remove the financial barriers to medical care, and make it accessible to all. Furthermore, the imminent passage of a national health insurance program promised to remove the last barriers to the perceived "wonders of modern medicine."

The causes for optimism in this period are not hard to discern. The 1950s were a period of rapid innovation and dissemination of antibiotics and new vaccines for polio and other childhood diseases. New surgical techniques were making possible kidney transplants and open heart surgery. Other breakthroughs were occurring at a regular rate. It therefore appeared that the major social responsibility was to make the fruits of medical research available to everyone.

The underlying assumption was often a rather simple model of disease in which a single agent, such as a virus, bacterium, or genetic break, causes a lesion that then develops into what is recognized as disease. The goal of medicine is then relatively simple—find the causal agent, eradicate it in the patient, and repair the damage that the disease has done. Within this framework, people get sick and medical care cures them. Thus, it is particularly unfortunate if there are some people for whom medical care is inaccessible because of financial barriers or supply shortages within certain geographic areas. The new financing schemes of the 1960s, Medicare and Medicaid, were instituted to provide insurance coverage for the two major groups who could not afford private insurance coverage, the elderly and the very poor, respectively. Even if the poor had insurance to pay for medical care, the providers were often not available in the inner cities and rural ares. This led to the development of neighborhood health centers to bring the providers to the people, and medical schools were called upon and given support to train more physicians.

These programs were at least partially effective in meeting their goals. The proportion of the poor and elderly with insurance for medical care increased from about 30 percent in 1962–1963 to about 75 percent in 1970. There was also a redistribution of services toward those traditionally underserved groups. For instance, instead of the poor having the lowest number of physician visits per capita, the utilization rates have become comparable across income groups. Although these were impressive changes over a rather short period of time, not all the goals of equality of access have been met. Medicare and Medicaid reimbursement levels are sometimes so low that some practitioners will not accept such patients. Existing programs have not been effective in attracting medical resources to the inner cities and the rural areas while, at the same time, federal funds for targeted programs such as the neighborhood health centers have dried up. Even the utilization data are misleading. Although per capita physician utilization is now about equal across income groups, those data show substantial differentials in terms of utilization patterns and utilization relative to "need." The poor are much more likely not to see a physician at all within the year, and if they do see one, it is much more likely to be in a clinic or emergency room. If one controls for medical need by the presence of chronic conditions or symptoms, the poor are still less likely than the nonpoor to receive care even if they are eligible for Medicare or Medicaid. Thus, more remains to be done in improving access to the medical care system.

Questioning the Value of Medical Care at the Margin. While there is still concern about access to care, in the 1970s some observers began to question whether more medical care for everyone is really an appropriate goal. The emphasis, it seems, is beginning to shift from *medical care* to *health* and to the prevention of *health problems.* This shift is not anti–medical care. Instead, it recognizes the many true benefits of medicine while questioning whether the marginal (or incremental) gains of increased expenditures in medical care exceed the benefits that could be obtained by spending the extra resources on other means of improving health. . . .

At the same time that people have been questioning the efficacy of medical care at the margin, they have also begun to think more about the quality of life. Lately there has been growing concern about environmental quality and the quality and safety of consumer products. In terms of health, people are beginning to question whether extreme measures should be taken to prolong life, if little can said for the quality of that life. This issue . . . will become more important as the population ages and the proportion of people with chronic health problems increases.

An Overview of the Extent and Impact of Disability. The relationship between health problems and poverty is strong and can be measured in several ways. About 65 percent of poor families consisting of at least a husband and wife include a disabled adult. At least 30 percent of the disabled who are currently poor are poor *because* of their health problems; among white men this figure is close to 75 percent. Disability is responsible for at least 9 to 18 percent of *all* poverty among the nonaged. Similarly, at least 23 to 31 percent of all non-aged poor white men are poor because of their disability. Furthermore, the transfer payment programs do a very inadequate job. Payments total only about 40 percent of the lost earnings and remove from poverty only 40 percent of the disabled who were impoverished by health problems.

The probability of the average person in the eighteen to sixty-four age group becoming disabled within the year is 1.24 percent. Obviously, average incidence rates are misleading, since the probability increases substantially with age. More importantly, it varies with socioeconomic characteristics. The probability of an adult in a low (under $4,000) income family becoming disabled in a given year is about twice that of one in a family with $8,000 or more, after adjusting for age, race, sex, and education. Similarly, the likelihood of disability for someone with nine years or more of school is less than half that of someone with less than nine years, after adjusting for age, sex, race, and income. Furthermore, the twofold difference in disability incidence between black and white men is entirely explained by their differences in income and education.

Although these socioeconomic characteristics appear to be important causes of disability, they are, at least in part, serving to represent the influence of various occupational factors. Such factors play two rather different roles in disability. The first role is the traditional one of occupational hazards or conditions that lead to or exacerbate certain health problems. These are characteristics such as dust, fumes, stress, and the like. The second way that job characteristics influence disability is when specific activities are required, such as lifting or finger dexterity, that interact with a corresponding functional limitation. For instance, a back injury is likely to have more severe implications for a longshoreman than a watchmaker.

Other socioeconomic characteristics also have an influence on the severity of specific functional limitations. Education is particularly important in allowing job flexibility and in enabling people to shift to other jobs with a smaller loss in earnings. Education is also much more significant for those who "normally" have a smaller range of job opportunities—for example, the poor, blacks, and women—than for white men who had well-paying jobs before the onset of their condition. These differences lead to different behavioral responses to health problems. In general, white males are better able to obtain alternative jobs, although at a substantial reduction in weekly earnings, while blacks are more likely to be forced out of the labor force because of health problems.

This review has highlighted a number of points. Perspectives on health and medical care are in the process of undergoing substantial changes. In the 1960s and early 1970s the focus was on assuring equity in access to medical care and on making more care available. Increasing costs and insufficient evidence that more medical care produces benefits worth the cost have led to a shift in focus. There is now a growing concern for the prevention of health problems and care for those with disabilities.... Disabling health problems impose substantial economic costs. They are also more likely to occur among and to severely affect certain already disadvantaged subgroups.

Policy Questions Concerning Health Problems

This background discussion leads to a consideration of policy issues in three broad areas: efforts at reducing the incidence of health problems, activities to reduce the severity of a given health problem, and programs to reduce the impact of disability on the person and his or her family's socioeconomic status. These three areas will be discussed in turn.

Reducing the Incidence of Health Problems. It appears to many that reducing the incidence of health problems is primarily a medical issue. However, by far the major emphasis of medical research is on the treatment of disease, not its prevention. Those studies that are concerned with the causes of disease usually focus on a single factor, not multiple, interactive causes. Thus, one major policy question is how to begin to shift the research interests of the medical community to broaden our understanding of what to do in terms of prevention.

Prevention, itself, involves two rather different foci. Primary prevention focuses on reducing or eliminating the causes of health problems. Secondary prevention focuses on the early detection and treatment of disease. Screening and automated multiphasic testing programs have been suggested for various conditions. Some studies, however, indicate that many such programs are very expensive and may not be worthwhile. The costs go beyond simple financial expenses; in some situations, errors may lead to unnecessary surgery and disfigurement. In others, such as mammography, the test itself is hazardous enough so as to be recommended only for high risk people.

The policy questions related to the socioeconomic and environmental issues in prevention touch upon almost the whole range of human endeavor. One in five disabilities is caused on the job. Thus, the importance of reducing occupational health and safety hazards should be given high priority. Government agencies currently set standards for workplaces and make some effort at enforcement, while Workers' Compensation programs are designed to make the costs of occupationally caused disabilities part of the cost of production. How effective are such programs, what incentives do they provide, and how can they be improved upon? In a broader social sense, who should bear the costs of disability or hazard reduction—the employer, the employee, the consumer, or society at large? Hazard reduction consumes resources that may be used for other purposes—how safe a society do we really want? Similar questions arise with respect to nonoccupational hazards, such as the safety of various consumer products. Probably more important are various types of individual behavior like smoking, drinking, and overeating. To what extent should people be encouraged, allowed, or discouraged from partaking in such individual vices and, if the current situation is nonoptimal, how should it be changed? Still other questions relate to broad social policies that may be supported for many different reasons. For instance, pure income support programs like a guaranteed annual income are likely to reduce the various stresses of poverty, allow people to have better housing and food, and safer products. But, at the same time, cigarette consumption may increase.

Reducing the Severity of Health Problems. A second group of policy questions focuses on what can be done to reduce the severity of health problems. Obviously, the individual's medical status is of major importance, and advances in treatment and physical rehabilitation are vital. But there are many areas in which broader policy activities may have a substantial influence on the extent to which a health problem results in job changes and unemployment. For instance, should vocational rehabilitation programs be expanded along present lines or changed substantially? What is the role of racial and sexual discrimination in the labor market, and would the reduction of such discrimination differentially affect the disabled? Can educational programs be established to provide people job skills and flexibility that can serve as implicit insurance in case they develop a health problem? Can employers be given effective incentives to hire the disabled; should they be required to do so? Do business cycle swings differentially affect the disabled?

Reducing the Impact of Health Problems. The third area of policy concern is alleviating the effects of disability on the individual and his or her family. How large are such effects and what do they involve in terms of income loss, extraordinary medical and other costs, anxiety, stigma, and so forth? Are insurance schemes possible to compensate for the income losses? What are the incentives implicit in such schemes and do they encourage or discourage efforts to rehabilitate the individual? How feasible is it to provide medical care "insurance" for someone with a known health problem? Who should bear the extra costs that may be involved? When designing policies in all of these areas, attention should be paid to the problems of feedback loops. Is it feasible to develop a scheme whereby linkages are created between the causes of health problems and their consequences so that the incentives exist to encourage the reduction of hazards, where possible, and the payment of equitable compensation where hazard reduction is not possible? Such a system might then develop its own dynamic toward improving the health and well-being of the population.

Good health to the poor is the lifeline to all else.

—*Philip R. Lee*

David Mechanic

Inequality, Health Status, and the Delivery of Health Services in the United States

Noting that health priorities reflect societal values, David Mechanic illustrates that inequities in the availability and quality of health care are based on attitudes toward age, chronic diseases, and disability as well as income, ethnicity, and race. The availability of equal access to an adequate level of medical and health care for all, he argues, will therefore depend on a shift in national values and priorities as well as on a basic reconstruction of the health care system.

Innumerable studies have demonstrated that the poor have a greater prevalence of illness, disability, chronicity, and restriction of activity because of health problems than those of higher status, and that they have less accessibility to many types of health services and receive lower quality care.... Social programs to ameliorate the consequences of illness, disability, and poverty have evolved slowly in the United States, and they have been typified by strong moral overtones and a tight hold on the purse strings.... General assistance in this country, and in the tradition of the English poor laws, has always been grudgingly provided with a conviction on the part of many that those on welfare or receiving other social benefits are undeserving and must be policed, supervised, or otherwise discouraged from becoming too dependent on the taxpayer.

In the area of health services, similar attitudes have prevailed. Although there have been many areas of the country, particularly in large cities, where the poor have been able to obtain health services from municipal or university hospitals, such services have often been characterized by fragmentation and impersonality and have frequently affronted patients' human dignity....

In discussing social inequality and health, we cannot neglect the fact that stratification in health care is based not only on income, ethnicity, and race, but also on a variety of other implicit value systems that order the availability of care in terms of the character of the disorder, the age of those affected, the degree of chronicity and disability, and the like. Differential attitudes in the delivery of health services persist in relation to patients with irreversible chronic diseases, geriatric patients, alcoholics, drug addicts and psychotics, and other patients who require intensive rehabilitation services. Many of these categories of need tend to be associated as well with low income and minority status, but they pose more general problems.

Also, medical and other health priorities reflect the ethos of the society. A recent analysis, for example, illustrated that research in sickle-cell anemia, a problem concentrated among black Americans, received only a small fraction of the support and interest given to many other diseases causing less overall morbidity but which affect the more affluent. Since then, the federal government has initiated a more significant program. The previous failure to develop a reasonable program in this area had little to do with the potential research-ability of the field or the promise of new developments. In the past decade, the concentrated efforts and attention devoted to attacking paralytic polio, in contrast to feeble efforts in closing gaps in infant mortality, must be understood within the context that the incidence of polio was higher in the middle classes than in the lower classes. The areas receiving official recognition and attention depend, in large part, on the ability of affected groups to make their needs known and to organize in order to stimulate official response. In this context, the problems that most affect the poor have less public visibility and less impact on political and administrative processes. Clearly, we must give more attention to considering how social priorities are determined and how the needs of those less vocal or sophisticated can be properly weighed against the claims of other groups.

Some Aspects of the Relationship between Social Inequality and Health

Inequalities in health and health care develop in a variety of ways. I can appreciate that when the needs are so pressing, one becomes impatient with subtle distinctions in theory and concept. Such distinctions, however, are helpful and it is necessary to understand them in effectively closing the gaps in accessibility to health care and differential health status. Whatever our aspirations might be, there are no indications that in the near future we will experience a radical transformation in our values, our economic system, or in the distribution of wealth; and thus we must anticipate attacking the problems of health in an arena of scarce resources. The resources that become available must be used effectively in closing the gaps that we know exist and in preventing the further occurrence of differentials in areas where preventive intervention has some possibilities for success.

It is widely appreciated that the relationship between poverty and health status is part of a vicious cycle. Illness and disability are major causes of dependency and low socioeconomic status, and traditionally the lower income of the poor has limited their opportunities to receive services to increase their functional capacities and, indirectly, their income potential. Although in recent years the Medicaid program has improved the medical care situation of many poor persons, it is generally true that rehabilitation of the functional capacity of the ill and disabled is an underdeveloped aspect of our entire health care system, and frequently adequate services are just not available. In addition, persons who are seriously disabled and visibly handicapped are exposed to various forms of discrimination in employment as well as in other life areas, and often cannot use the skills and education they have because of arbitrary exclusion from the work force. Much social legislation for health services in the United States is oriented toward the irreversibly disabled (the deserving unfortunate), and frequently persons who are rehabilitable cannot receive public support for rehabilitation without first becoming indigent. Thus, social legislation often produces incentives against rehabilitation and gainful employment, and our social ethos defines the ill and disabled as lesser citizens.

Although the literature is uncertain concerning the relationships between the occurrence of disease and socioeconomic status—and, of course, this varies from disease to disease—it is clear and unequivocal that when the poor become ill, they suffer consequences more serious than those experienced by more affluent classes. The poor are less likely to receive adequate treatment, are more likely to come into treatment during more advanced stages of their illness, and are more likely to experience persistent morbidity and disability. Moreover, the social position of the poor exposes them to lesser social protection for themselves and their families in that their jobs are generally less secure, they have less income to tide them through a serious illness, they are less protected by sick leave and other social arrangements, their illness is more likely to impinge on the performance of their work, and their living environment is less conducive to recovery and freedom from worry. The consequences of illness for the poor make illness a more frightening and disruptive experience, and probably encourage denial of illness and reluctance to enter treatment during its less evident stages of development.

I raise these issues, in part, because the problems characteristic of the cultural orientations and inclinations of the poor-sick for receiving medical care must be understood within the existential situation they face. When some segments of the poor come into contact with large medical bureaucracies, professionals often define their behavior as ill-adapted, and complain of the difficulties of delivering necessary health services to the poor. The poor, of course, are in no sense monolithic, and it is dangerous and misleading to offer generalizations about them as a special class. Yet a variety of studies have shown that one more frequently finds among the poor tendencies which make them less receptive to preventive care, less likely to conform to medical regimen, less oriented toward taking precautions necessary to maintain their health, less informed about health matters, and the like. To some extent, such responses reflect limited education, cultural and social deprivation, apathy and neglect, and fear. The responses also indicate the experience of the poor with impersonal medical institutions, inconsiderate personnel, and resulting humiliation. But such tendencies also reflect a problem of fit between social institutions developed by middle class Americans with middle class concepts that are not adaptive or sensitive to the special difficulties the poor may have in accommodating to such forms of delivery of health care. In agreeing that there is a great deal more that can be done in structuring preventive and other services so that those in need of them find them more compatible with their orientations and understandings, we must also recognize that there are significant differences in the manner in which populations orient themselves to health and health institutions, and that such differences cannot all be explained by the lack of commitment, interest, and other limitations of health personnel. The poor have special needs and problems that must be taken into account, but in any situation of scarcity of personnel and other resources, health facilities similarly face serious operational difficulties. We know that many medical and social programs oriented toward the poor and disabled frequently end up servicing those with lesser need. Such programs can be structured so that they are more responsive to the hard-core poor and disabled, but it is unlikely that the problem of providing access and service can be remedied if we underestimate the degree to which the client's orientations and reactions may be an important barrier to bringing about some reasonable fit. It is only when we recognize such facts that we begin to develop programs and procedures that overcome them.

Inequality and Mortality

The reduction of mortality, improvement of longevity, and the maintenance of a high level of health status is largely the result of improvements in nutrition, housing, sanitation, and the quality of life. At the present time, the major causes of mortality and morbidity in the population—such problems as heart disease, cancer, stroke, accidents, mental disorders, and the like—are not impressively affected by medicine as it is practiced, and much of the medical care provided is ameliorative and supportive. Such care is important and should not be disparaged, but a realistic attack on the problem of health must recognize the true potentialities and limitations of medical practice. Similarly, major problems of health among the disadvantaged young—such as drug addiction—have not been easily amenable to medical control, and much of the solution to these problems may lie outside the traditional practice of medicine. Moreover, the unhappiness and the despair of the old, abandoned in their later years without function or status, or the alienations of the young depend more on social values and conditions generally than on the activities of health workers. I raise these issues because many of the problems of health related to inequality will not be simply responsive to the expansion of services, but require a more profound recasting of social values, practices, and priorities. This will demand efforts more pervasive than those that can be mustered by the health sector alone.

In this essay, I shall restrict my attention to efforts possible through the health sector as it is traditionally seen with the understanding that health does not operate in a vacuum, but is responsive to the larger forces that shape society and people's lives.

The most persistent and impressive inequality in the health care area is the disparity between white and nonwhite infant mortality in the United States. Such differences are extremely large; the nonwhite rate has been almost double the white rate for some years, and although both whites and non-whites have made progress in recent decades, the gap itself has persisted and has even given evidence of increasing. . . .

The factors affecting infant mortality are intertwined in a complex web, and it is not easy to isolate one or another factor as a major determinant. The opportunity of a new infant to survive is affected by the stature and health of the mother, which is in turn affected by her early nutrition and development, which may be a product of her social background, the economic status of her family, and so on. Similarly, socioeconomic status is associated with the rate of illegitimate births, parity of the mother, age at the time of childbearing, quality of medical care received, and the like.

The best predictor of infant survival is the birth weight of the infant. . . . Low-weight infants are more likely to be born to mothers who are under 15 years of age, nonwhite, of lower socioeconomic status, of less education, and among those who smoke. . . . Low-weight infants who constitute less than 10 per cent of all births are a group at special risk, and it is imperative that this population receive effective prenatal and postnatal care and other types of health services. It is not clear, however, how this group can be most effectively identified.

There are a variety of other factors correlated with the occurrence of infant mortality, but none of these has an effect as large as birth weight. These factors include race, parity, maternal age, socioeconomic status, and illegitimacy. . . . The crucial point, however, is that extreme poverty is often associated with a pattern of living and orientations that involve extremely high risks of infant mortality, and this argues very strongly for particular attention to such high risk areas which insures the development of adequate patterns of prenatal, maternal, and child care.

It is reasonably clear that well-organized public health efforts, associated with improvement in the overall life conditions of the poorest segments of our population, can result in a substantial decrease in the magnitude of infant mortality in the United States. It is extremely difficult to estimate specifically what constitutes a reasonable reduction in infant mortality given the tremendous variations characteristic of the living environments and cultures of the United States. Speaking relatively conservatively, I see no good reason why the national rate cannot in the coming years be reduced to a level of 15 or 16 deaths per 1000 live births. . . .

Mortality among adults also varies significantly by race and socioeconomic status. At almost every age, nonwhites and the poor suffer a higher risk of mortality. . . . Although the trends are approximately similar to the situation described relevant to infant mortality, it is more difficult to provide evidence that these differentials can be markedly influenced by changes in the organization of medical care rather than more basic changes in the life circumstances of the poor.

There are no doubt circumstances where, for example, the lack of availability of medical facilities decreases the longevity of nonwhites and the poor relative to whites and those better off—for example, such as access to good medical care following a heart attack—but much of the differential is a product of more embracing life disadvantages that the poor must face. Just as it is difficult to specify precisely the effects of medical care in general relative to other life forces, so it is difficult to specify how much specific gain can be achieved through better medical services as compared with a decent job, adequate housing, and a neighborhood free of the pathologies of drug addiction, alcoholism, and alienation. . . .

Some Notes on Forms of Health Care Delivery and the Poor

Much of the problem of bringing health care services to the poor involves eliminating economic barriers to care and providing the required manpower and facilities for providing adequate care. There is evidence that suggests that major gaps in care can be closed if such conditions are fulfilled in a reasonable way. The utilization of health services, of course, will also depend on social and cultural orientations toward the types of care provided, the manner in which care is organized, and the responsiveness of health personnel to medical consumers. Access to medical care decreases as costs increase, and costs must be measured not only in money terms, but also in terms of time, inconvenience, distance, embarrassment, or whatever.

Traditionally the poor, particularly in large cities, have depended very heavily on public clinics and outpatient departments for their care.... There is also evidence that differences in the basic pattern of use of services continue to persist.... Those with less knowledge and sophistication in particular, but probably all of us as well, require more than the episodic and fragmented care characteristic of large hospital outpatient clinics. Although the well-educated and sophisticated consumers of medical care complain about the growing impersonality of care and the lack of responsiveness of medical personnel, such persons are often able to exploit existing resources through their aggressiveness, their ability to obtain information, and their demands for respect and courtesy.

Those who are less sophisticated and assertive, because of lack of education or cultural orientation, are frequently confused and intimidated by the vastness and complexity of the large medical bureaucracy, and by the interchangeability of people and roles. The poor family with multiple difficulties, in particular, must deal with a variety of agencies and personnel to obtain needed care involving great time, patience, and initiative. Not only is the location of such care fragmented and confused but, frequently, no serious attempt is made to coordinate services or to deal with the array of health problems in its family context or in any relationship to one another. No matter how good any particular service may appear, when poorly coordinated, the overall pattern of care may be inferior and poorly fitted to the needs or social conditions of the persons involved....

Providing Health Services for the Poor

Recently, there has been an outpouring of analyses on the health care crisis. The typical discussion concludes with the recommendation that the solution to these problems lies in the development of widespread prepaid group practice, preventive care and health maintenance, and the use of a variety of new paramedical personnel as well as more effective use of those already in evidence. I do not wish to belittle these recommendations for there is much in their favor. But we should be aware that the central feature in current discussions of health care has continued to be the growing cost of services. As such costs have risen, they have put pressure on many different interest groups who together make up a powerful force in political affairs. As government through an incremental process has assumed payment for a greater proportion of the costs of medical care for the old and the poor, resulting inflation in the health care area and higher taxes have aroused many middle class consumers and have put considerable financial pressures on state finances as well as on the federal treasury.

Although the health problems of the poor are of concern to governmental and other groups, these interests are only part of the larger set of interests which are coalescing and forming a countervailing force against more traditional interests in the health field. It is not at all clear from current discussions how well the poor will do within the context of the types of reforms generally being advocated, but it is reasonably clear that in the absence of general reforms of our health care system, which bring benefits to many segments of the American population, the benefits provided to the poor will be unequal to the scope of the problems they face. It is already clear from the Medicaid program that coverage for the poor or near-poor will be fragmentary and uneven from area to area if the approach is a categorical one and if it is heavily dependent on tax support from the states and localities.

In the last analysis, we must recognize that the health care problems of the poor are a product of the larger sociopolitical system and of the more general organization of health care services in America. As long as these problems are seen as nothing more than slight maladjustments of what is basically a constructive approach to meeting the health needs of the country, it is unlikely that an adequate solution will be found. The poor are not a sufficiently powerful interest group to effectively compete in the establishment of priorities or in the distribution of available facilities, manpower, and services. Moreover, the problems of health care are only one part of a more complex pattern of social, economic, and environmental difficulties. It appears then that the health care needs of the poor can most constructively be met within a larger and more basic reconstruction of health care institutions in America, which insure access to medical care for all and which establish a minimal level of health service available irrespective of social status or geographic area. It is doubtful that this can be achieved without greater direction over professional behavior. Access to care for all is available elsewhere in the world and under social and economic circumstances that pose greater pressure on national resources. The fact that the United States has still failed to achieve such modest goals is shameful. But even when we do, we will have hardly begun to face the underlying conditions that make the plight of the poor so difficult and their pathologies so prevalent. These problems will require a more frontal attack on our national values, our priorities, and our system of social stratification itself.

Karen Davis

Health Care of Low-Income Families

For the poor, the vicious cycle of unemployment, inflation, and health problems has not been slowed—even by massive Medicaid and Medicare programs. Economist Karen Davis notes that the poor person has limited options in seeking medical care and that the dual stresses of unemployment and inflation increase the likelihood of health problems. Policies to contain medical costs must be coupled with improved public health programs if the chain of poverty and ill health is to be broken.

Americans spent $485 on average for the medical care of each person in fiscal year 1974. At current rates of inflation in health care costs, this sum will increase to $560 in the following year.* This rapid increase in cost is difficult to meet at a time when general price inflation and rising unemployment are placing severe strains on families' financial resources.

All Americans share in the burdens imposed by rising medical care prices. Unfortunately, however, this burden falls more heavily on those who can least afford it—low-income families and the elderly who devote a larger share of their limited incomes to health care services. Unlike higher income families, those at the low end of the income scale have few options for mitigating the impact of inflation. They find it impossible to substitute lower cost services for more expensive kinds of health care since they already seek out the lowest cost forms of health care available. Many low-income families will be forced to postpone medical care, particularly preventive care services, and thus may expect greater health problems in the future. At the same time that access to medical care services is curtailed, rising costs of essential items such as food and heating and the stresses of unemployment may well undermine the health of many.

Government programs are not currently offsetting these adverse pressures. Instead, lower income families and the elderly are finding reduced assistance from outside sources. The real value of public medical care programs which attempt to provide special assistance to the poor—such as the neighborhood health center program—have declined in recent years as budgetary outlays

---

*Ed. note: The estimated figure for 1979 was $920.

have failed to keep pace with the cost of services. Even the Medicaid program, which has experienced rapid increases in expenditures, now provides fewer real services per recipient than it did in the early years of its operation. Despite Medicare, the elderly, too, have been hard hit by inflation and now pay more for medical care than before Medicare's initiation in 1966. . . .

The lag between changes in economic conditions and the reporting of statistical health care data makes it difficult to assess the consequences of these events. However, if policy action awaits the collection and dissemination of data on the current period, many may suffer needless and possibly irreparable damage to their health.

This does not require that health policy action relating to current economic conditions must take place in a vacuum. Much has been learned from past experience that can be applied to predict future changes. Economic theory bearing on the reaction of consumers to changes in prices and real incomes can also provide some insights in the health care area.

Past Trends in Health Care Services and Income

For many years, low-income families received less medical attention than others despite their more severe health problems. During the 1960s, the introduction of several major public health care programs reversed this pattern. For the first time, low-income persons could visit physicians and be hospitalized more frequently than higher income persons. . . . In just a seven-year period from 1964 to 1971, low-income people made up the gap between their use of medical services and that of others, and for some age groups actually began to see physicians more frequently than middle-income persons.

While this progress is encouraging, the goal of equal access to medical care for all persons has yet to be achieved. The overall trends, in fact, conceal some remaining, serious deficiencies.

Most importantly, not all of the poor have been reached by public programs. In 1974, over 6 million persons with incomes below the poverty level, or about 28 percent of the poor, were ineligible for Medicaid.

A study by Davis and Reynolds indicates that the poor not covered by Medicaid have not shared in the improved access to medical care. For example, children whose families had incomes below $5,000 but who did not receive welfare assistance averaged 2.8 visits to a physician in 1969, compared with 4.6 visits for children in families with incomes above $15,000. Failure to have financial assistance in meeting the cost of health care continues to deny many poor people the access to medical care enjoyed by more fortunate members of society.

Comparison of medical care utilization among income classes is also misleading unless some adjustment is made for the greater health problems of low-income people.... Instead of surpassing middle-income persons, low-income persons uniformly use less medical care than all other income persons with similar health conditions. For example, high-income elderly persons see physicians more than 70 percent more often than low-income elderly persons not on welfare, and 63 percent more often even than those elderly persons covered by both Medicaid and Medicare.

There is also considerable evidence that low-income families do not participate in "mainstream" medicine of quality, convenience and style comparable to that received by more fortunate persons. Low-income families—whether on welfare or not—are much more likely to receive care from general practitioners rather than from specialists, in a hospital outpatient department rather than in a physician's office, and after traveling long distances and waiting substantially longer for care.

While much remains to be done to achieve the goal of adequate access to medical care for all persons, much real progress has occurred in the last eight years. This progress, however, is now threatened by the detrimental effects on health care arising from poor economic conditions, declining real incomes, rapid increases in medical care prices, loss of insurance coverage among the unemployed, and cutbacks in support from public health care programs.

Unemployment, Inflation, and Health Problems

Evidence is accumulating that periods of economic stress—caused by rising unemployment or inflation in the prices of essential goods and services—can have serious detrimental effects on health. A study by Brenner has examined the relationship between economic cycles and health statistics over a period covering the past 125 years. Brenner finds that recessions and loss of employment increase death rates from a variety of causes. Some adverse health reactions occur only after a considerable lag. A wave of heart attack deaths follows recessions by three years; kidney-failure deaths take an upturn two years following recessions; and strokes increase two to four years following an economic downturn. Other changes in health are more immediate. Infant mortality rates increase rapidly in recessions, as do admissions to mental hospitals.

Brenner links these changes in health to three sources of stress caused by periods of economic downturn. First is the struggle for the basic necessities of life: food, clothing, shelter and heating, health care, and education for children. Worry and anxiety about the ability to provide these essential items for the family place great stress on family heads. Even if those working do not lose their jobs, fear that they will do so and that their savings will be inadequate affect far more families than just the unemployed.

The second factor cited by Brenner is the loss of ego satisfaction and social standing that accompanies unemployment. If the family is forced to turn to relatives or to welfare for assistance, feelings of self-worth and adequacy may deteriorate rapidly.

Finally, Brenner emphasizes that these factors often induce greater consumption of alcohol and tobacco. This increased consumption often shows up in greater long-term illness, traffic deaths, murders, and suicides.

Less is known about the relationship between inflation and health. Inflation in the prices of essential goods and services has been quite marked in recent years—particularly in prices for food, fuel, and medical care. Some of the effects of this inflation are similar to that of unemployment—the stress of not knowing if the family will be able to make ends meet, to feed hungry children, and to protect the family from cold weather illness.

In other cases, the impact of inflation may have mixed effects. Rising food costs may reduce overconsumption of food by some people and cause food purchasers to evaluate more carefully the nutritional value of the food basket. Many nutritionists may welcome the reduction in sugar consumption resulting from the rapid rise in cost of that commodity.

Other effects of rising food costs and declining real incomes are not so fortuitous. A newspaper account recently documented the case of an elderly woman trying to survive on a monthly Social Security check that left her only sixty-five cents a day for food after paying rent and other essential services. She was found dead, weighing seventy-six pounds; the coroner concluded that the cause of death was malnutrition, or quite simply that she starved to death. For others the consequences of malnutrition may not be so immediate: pregnant mothers have babies who start life with a disadvantage that they may never overcome; children go hungry, miss school, or are unable to learn; and elderly people are weakened and vulnerable to illness. For these, the link between inadequate diets and shortened lives, reduced productivity, and diminished enjoyment of life may be harder to trace, but no less genuine.

Rising fuel prices can also be expected to have mixed effects on health. Reduced automobile travel and slower speeds instituted as fuel conservation measures are already reflected in declining traffic deaths. But for others high fuel costs mean death. Newspapers publicized the case of an elderly Schenectady, New York, couple who died from cold after the utility company turned off their heat. In the St. Louis area, five children died in fires apparently caused by space heaters being used in place of ordinary heating. In Keystone, West Virginia, another five children—and a young Marine who tried to rescue them—died from a fire caused by an overheated kitchen stove being used to keep the house warm. These factors and the increased reliance on kerosene may partially explain the fact that a leading medical diagnosis among Medicaid patients under nineteen in Tennessee is burns. Inadequate heating may also increase the susceptibility to and seriousness of respiratory illness among the elderly and infirm. Increased air pollution resulting from a relaxation of standards may further intensify this problem. . . .

Summary

The current economic condition with twin problems of rapid increases in prices and rising unemployment poses serious difficulties for access to medical care. More and more persons will find themselves in need of assistance in obtaining needed medical care, while at the same time sources of support from governmental programs are being curtailed. Much of the progress which has been made in the last eight years in improving the access of low-income families to adequate medical care may well be reversed unless specific actions are taken to control the cost of medical services to all persons and to maintain the real value of public medical care programs.

Effects of general price inflation, rising unemployment, and inflation in the costs of health care services which have the most important implications for the poor include:

—Loss of employment usually implies loss of private health insurance coverage.

—Persons below the poverty line may well begin to increase in number, but public assistance income eligibility limits are not being automatically adjusted to reflect rising prices and declining real incomes.

—Current economic conditions may undermine the health of the poor by contributing to inadequate nutrition, housing, heating, and increasing stress and anxiety.

—The elderly and low-income families spend a much higher fraction of income on medical care services and, hence, are particularly affected by inflation in health care costs.

—Lower-income families are unable to mitigate the impact of inflation by substituting lower cost goods and services since they already choose the lowest cost services available.

—Limited resources for meeting health care costs will induce many to postpone early and preventive medical care, a situation leading to possible deterioration in health.

—Expenditures per recipient of services have declined in real terms in Medicaid, the maternal and child health programs, and the neighborhood health center programs.

—Medicare has had constant real benefits per beneficiary over the period from 1972 to 1975. Amounts paid directly by the elderly, however, have increased markedly from $300 in 1966 to $450 in 1973 (including Medicare premiums).

—Escalating physician charges may cause physicians to supply fewer services to patients. Furthermore, physicians may reduce services even more for patients covered by public programs or direct-paying patients who are unemployed or encountering financial difficulties.

—Traditional charity care facilities are likely to become increasingly crowded as more patients require assistance in obtaining medical care.

Raymond Wheeler

Health and Human Resources

Placing malnutrition and inadequate health care in the larger framework of wasted human and natural resources, Dr. Raymond Wheeler reports on the research of the Southern Regional Council and the Citizens Board of Inquiry into Hunger in the United States. His eyewitness account of poverty and disease among southern farm and migrant workers and their children dramatically illustrates the tragic results of inequitable distribution of income and health care. A significant "health gap," with poverty and disease at one end and adequate income and health care at the other, is a reality in the United States in 1980.

Wherever we went, in the South, the Southwest, Florida or Appalachia the impact was the same, varying only in degree or in appalling detail. We saw countless families with large numbers of children isolated from the mainstream of American culture and opportunity, possessing none of the protections of life and job and health which other Americans take for granted as rights of citizenship. The conditions of migrant workers were poignantly recorded in a recent NBC documentary. Some of the detail of that program was disputed by landowners and employers, but certain facts are beyond question. If a farm worker is injured in the field or if he becomes ill from exposure to pesticides (we heard of and saw many instances of both situations) he does not receive Workman's Compensation. If he is sick or cannot find work (and there are many days when work is not available) he does not receive unemployment insurance. There is no realistic minimum wage to guarantee him adequate pay for his work. If Social Security payments are deducted from his wages, few records are kept by the crew boss on which he can later base a claim. He has no health or hospital insurance to provide him with minimum medical care and he does not earn enough to purchase it. The farmer is not even prohibited from working young children in the fields if their parents, desperate enough for money to buy food and shelter, choose to take their children out of school or bring along their pre–school age children to pick the vegetables.

We saw housing and living conditions horrible and dehumanizing to the point of our disbelief. In Florida and in Texas, we visited living quarters constructed as long cinder-block or wooden sheds, divided into single rooms by walls which do not reach to the ceilings. Without heat, adequate light or ventilation, and containing no plumbing or refrigeration, each room (no larger than 8 × 14 feet) is the living space of an entire family, appropriately suggesting slave quarters of earlier days. I doubt if the owners of fine racing horses or dogs along the East Florida coast would think of housing their animal property in such miserable circumstances.

In all of the areas we visited, the nearly total lack of even minimally adequate medical care and health services was an early and easily documented observation. Again, that which most Americans now agree to be a right of citizenship, was unavailable to most of the people whom we saw. The standard procedure of requiring cash for services and a cash deposit before hospital admission, places an impossible burden upon those least able to afford the high cost of being sick.

We saw hundreds of people whose only hope of obtaining medical care was to become an emergency which could not be turned away. We heard countless stories of driving 50 or 100 miles to a city general hospital after refusal of care at a local hospital. Mexican-American citizens of the U.S. told us of crossing the border into Mexico for medical treatment which was less expensive and for care which was kinder, more humane than they could obtain in their own communities. We heard of diagnoses and treatment by nurses, endless waiting for simple procedures such as immunization of small children, and degrading treatment by medical personnel.

Most of these people live constantly at the brink of medical disaster, hoping that the symptoms they have or the pain they feel will prove transient or can somehow be survived, for they know that no help is available to them. Only two groups have any hope of relief: those who are somewhat better off financially and those who are most critically ill. Some of the people we saw were not seriously ill, or perhaps not ill at all, but none of them knew, and most had never had the opportunity to find out if they were healthy or whether tomorrow might bring disaster. Our group was not equipped to offer very much in the way of definitive treatment for the vast amount of illness that we saw. Perhaps the most constructive and most helpful acts that we performed involved the opportunities to assure some, who had never seen a physician before, that they were, indeed, well and could continue their struggle to survive without the nagging fear of physical disability or death.

For the majority of the hundreds of people we examined, it was a different, frustrating, and heartbreaking story. We saw people with most of the dreadful disorders that weaken, disable, and torture, particularly, the poor.

High blood pressure, diabetes, urinary tract infections, anemia, tuberculosis, gall bladder and intestinal disorders, eye and skin diseases were frequent findings among the adults.

Almost without exception, intestinal parasites were found in the stool specimens examined. Most of the children had chronic skin infections. Chronically infected, draining ears with resulting partial deafness occurred in an amazing number of the smaller children. We saw rickets, a disorder thought to be nearly abolished in this country. Every form of vitamin deficiency known to us that could be identified by clinical examination was reported.

I doubt that any group of physicians in the past thirty years has seen, in this country, as many malnourished children assembled in one place as we saw in Hidalgo County.

Dietary histories were all the same—beans, rice, tortillas, and little else. The younger children, especially, were undersized, thin, anemic, and apathetic. The muscles of their arms were the size of lead pencils—a sign of gross protein malnutrition. Many had evidence of multiple vitamin deficiencies and almost without exception their skins were rough, dry, inelastic with the characteristic appearance of Vitamin A deficiency. I remember vividly the shock I received when one young boy was brought in who was well nourished and I touched his skin—warm, soft, resilient—unlike any I had seen all day and I called to the student with me to come and put his hand on that child in order that he might refresh his memory of what a healthy skin feels like.

The children we saw that day have no future in our society. Malnutrition since birth has already impaired them, physically, mentally, and emotionally. They do not have the capacity to engage in the sustained physical or mental effort which is necessary to succeed in school, learn a trade, or assume the full responsibilities of citizenship in a complex society such as ours.

10 Modern Medicines: Miracle or Menace?

MARK TUSCHMAN

The growth in American drug sales during the past twenty years demonstrates a remarkable increase in drug use. In 1954, U.S. drug firms reported domestic sales of approximately $1.3 billion; by 1965 sales had risen to $2.8 billion; and in 1977 the figure stood at an estimated $8.7 billion. Increases have been exceptionally high for psychotherapeutic drugs, pain killers, antibiotics, and hormones. It is estimated that over 70 million Americans regularly use prescription or over-the-counter drugs, and pharmacists dispense over 12 billion prescriptions each year. Doctors are prescribing more and more drugs, to patients both inside and outside hospitals, than ever before. Two-thirds of all office visits to a physician result in one or more prescriptions.

How can we explain the increase in drug taking and prescribing? Is it resulting in better health? There is some evidence that many doctors consider that a visit to their office is an indication for a prescription. This is true despite the fact that most potent modern drugs carry with them serious risks, and we are uncovering major hazards in their use. It is estimated, for example, that 15 percent of women aged 45 to 64 take oral estrogens for menopausal symptoms. This may involve over three million women at any one time. The risks of these drugs include hypertension, ovarian cancer, endometrial cancer, blood clots in the veins, and gall bladder disease. Most alarming is the risk of cancer, which increases by as much as eight times when estrogens are used. How much of this is justified? Do the patients realize the risks? Many women take these drugs because of anxiety, depression, and fatigue. Do these symptoms justify the risks of cancer and hypertension?

There is also the more general problem that, because of vaccines and drugs, we have so lowered our exposure to many diseases that we have lost our natural immunities. As a result, we have become particularly vulnerable to virulent germs. Even "miracle drugs" sometimes provide only partial solutions to medical problems, obliterating one disease only to provide a favorable environment for another. Furthermore, new strains of germs, beyond the magic of medicine, seem to develop almost as fast as we find treatment for older forms. As René Dubos has pointed out, there are too many disease-causing microbes in the world for us ever to be able to conquer them all, and disease will always remain a threat.

Drugs, of course, have done much to ease mankind's suffering, but the problems associated with their use have tempered somewhat our enthusiasm for them. Today, the issues of drug prescribing patterns, drug promotion, government regulation, overmedication, and patient information are all laden with controversy. With all the triumphs of drug therapy, there have been millions of needless tragedies born of ignorance, carelessness, and greed. The expanding role of the government, particularly through the Food and Drug Administration (FDA), reflects the growing concern with drug misuse. A number of major policy issues are currently undergoing review concerning curbing irrational prescriptions of certain dangerous substances, informing patients about the drugs they take, expanding the role of pharmacists, placing limitations on inappropriate drug promotion, and educating physicians about drug safety.

Dr. Milton Silverman and Dr. Philip Lee have two excerpts from their book, *Pills, Profits, and Politics,* in this chapter. In the opening article, "The Revolution in Drugs," they present a historical outline of drug use from primitive societies to the twentieth-century drug boom.

Robert L. Kane takes a balanced approach to a most sensitive issue: iatrogenic disorders—casualties of the hospital and doctor's office. In "Iatrogenesis: Just What the Doctor Ordered," he asks us not to sweep such doctor-induced problems under the rug, but he also warns against using them to indict the entire health care system. Kane divides iatrogenesis into four categories—conscious risk, unexpected complications, inept care, and overzealous care—demonstrating that some problems are unavoidable, while others are inexcusable. They result from all manner of failures: failure of drug company, doctor, hospital personnel, and of patients themselves.

Donald Kennedy, now president of Stanford University, is a biologist who served as Commissioner of Food and Drugs under President Carter. In "Creative Tension: FDA and Medicine," he responds to the accusations of those who believe the FDA is overzealous in its watchdog capacity. His remarks serve to reinforce the complexities of the issues, including the shortcomings of medical education and the need for patient education.

In the final selection in this chapter, "Future Strategy: Prescription for Action," Doctors Lee and Silverman offer an appraisal of prescription drug policy issues, as well as suggestions for reform. They underscore the need for enhancing the role of physician, pharmacist, industry, and government, and, like Kennedy, they urge that patients be given a more active role in their own therapy.

Milton Silverman and Philip R. Lee

The Revolution in Drugs

The introduction of sulfa drugs in the late 1930s and of penicillin in the 1940s initiated what might be called "the great drug therapy era." Drs. Milton Silverman and Philip Lee chronicle the miracles and discoveries: conquest of infections, prevention of crippling, symptomatic relief of mental illness, and increasingly sophisticated research and technical application. These developments have spawned a massive, powerful drug industry and the growing interest of consumers in not only the benefits but also the hazards of drug use.

In 1935 a group of German scientists and physicians announced the discovery of a new drug for the treatment of staphylococcal, streptococcal, and other infections. Its generic or public name was sulfanido-chrysoidine. It was patented and put on the market under the brand name Prontosil. This was the first of the so-called wonder drugs. Although Prontosil was an important agent, it was hardly the most important ever to be discovered. Its introduction, however, triggered a chain of events destined to open what medical historians may well call the great drug therapy era.

The nature of this remarkable period may be measured by many yardsticks: the exciting conquest of deadly infections, the relief of crippling, and the symptomatic relief of mental illness; or the skyrocketing increase in the number of prescriptions written by physicians, and in expenditures for drugs; or the mounting investment in drug research, the increasing sophistication and technical skill of drug investigators, and the soaring growth of the drug industry.

But there are other and more disquieting measurements: the avalanche of new prescription products introduced each year, the vast increase in drug promotion, the mounting confusion among prescribers, the impact of drug advertising on medical journal editorial policies, the strong ties between the drug industry and leaders of organized medicine, and the deep involvement of the industry—whether by accident or design—in medical education.

There is the expanding and carefully nurtured tendency of the public—and much of the medical profession as well—to depend on a pill for the solution of every problem of mankind, physical or mental or social. There is the inclination of a patient to request a specific drug, or even to demand it, from his physician. There is the obviously related trend to utilize such drugs as alcohol, marijuana, LSD, and heroin as escape routes from the uncomfortable realities of life.

There has also come the appalling realization that adverse drug reactions—due in large part to well-intentioned but irrational prescribing—are now responsible for a million or more hospital admissions annually in the United States alone, tens of millions of days of prolonged hospitalization, thousands of preventable deaths, and the resultant expenditure of *billions* of dollars each year.

Such developments, both the good and the bad, did not arise suddenly in the midst of the twentieth century. Their roots extend at least back to the beginning of recorded history.

To Discover a Drug

As far back as records go, it would appear that drug discoverers followed one basic rule: whatever the substance, be it animal, vegetable, or mineral, if it can be broken into bite-sized portions, or dissolved in a liquid concoction, or spread as a salve, try it on a patient. In some instances this version of research merely speeded the death of the victim. In others, the patient recovered or at least survived because of the treatment, or in spite of it.

By 1700 literally thousands of drug products had been tested and endorsed as useful at one time or another, but only about two or three dozen were actually effective....

A major change in this kind of drug discovery and drug use was signaled in 1805, when a twenty-three-year-old German pharmacist, Friedrich Sertuerner, reported the extraction of morphine from crude opium. This was the first isolation of a pure, powerful drug from a crude and generally unreliable product. It led during the next century to the isolation of a host of other valuable products: alkaloids like quinine, codeine, atropine, and cocaine, and a wide assortment of naturally occurring vitamins and hormones.

Starting in the mid-nineteenth century, the first important synthetic drugs made their appearance: nitrous oxide (1844), ether (1846), and chloroform (1847) as anesthetics; amyl nitrate (1867) and nitroglycerine (1879) for anginal pain; chloral (1869) for sedation; and antipyrene (1883), acetanilid (1886), and acetophenetidin (1887) for the control of pain and fever. Introduction of the last three marked the entry into the pharmaceutical field of the German chemical industry, which would dominate the world's drug production until 1914.

With the outbreak of World War I, the international drug situation suddenly changed. England, France, and the United States, cut off from their traditional supplies of German drugs and other synthetic chemicals, were obliged to create their own "fine chemical" industries, which first merely duplicated the products originally created by German scientists and then began developing new products on their own. (Until this time American contributions had been limited in number, but they included two of the first general anesthetics—nitrous oxide and ether—along with the discovery of Vitamin A and Vitamin D, and the isolation of epinephrine and thyroxin.)

Then came the Prontosil affair. This brick-red chemical, of undoubted value in the treatment of infections, had been patented in 1932 by the I. G. Farbenindustrie, but was not introduced until 1935. The reasons for this delay in getting such a desperately needed lifesaving drug on the market have never been clearly established. A few months later a group of French scientists at the Pasteur Institute revealed that the complex Prontosil molecule consisted of two chief components: a reddish dye with no significant antibacterial value, and a powerfully active substance known as sulfanilamide. Ironically, it was quickly noted, sulfanilamide had been patented many years before as a dye-intermediate—by the I. G. Farbenindustrie—but this patent had long since expired.

These events had two immediate effects. First, the dramatic account of sulfanilamide was widely publicized in medical journals and in newspapers and magazines all over the world, and the demand for the new drug skyrocketed. Second, drug companies in England, France, Germany, and the United States, quick to see the potential sales in this new field, began to synthesize, test, and rush to the market a vast number of sulfanilamide derivatives which could be patented and promoted.

This approach, which began in the late 1930s with the sulfa-drugs, and which was intensified by the introduction of penicillin in the mid-1940s, heralded the start of the great drug therapy era. It was marked not only by the introduction of new drugs in great profusion and by the launching of large promotional campaigns, but also by the introduction of what are known as "duplicative" or "me-too" products—those which offer the physician and his patient no significant clinical advantages, but which are different enough to win a patent and then be marketed, usually at the identical price of the parent product, or even at a higher price. . . .

Today it is clear that the great drug therapy era had brought the following changes:

1. In place of the relatively few drugs, many of them of natural origin, available to physicians as recently as 1935, there were thousands of products, most of them created synthetically and most of these introduced since World War II. It was estimated, for example, that American physicians have available for prescription about 6,780 single drug entities and 3,330 combination products, giving a total of some 10,000 products in 14,250 different dosage

forms and strengths, all produced by only fifty-three manufacturers. The number marketed by hundreds of other manufacturers, most of them relatively small, was unknown. An even larger number—more than 100,000 products—was available without prescription.

2. The locale of drug discovery had changed remarkably. During the nineteenth century and the early years of the twentieth, most new drugs had been discovered by individual investigators, who carried on their studies in their own pharmacies or clinics and worked in such European countries as Germany, France, and England. Since 1938 most new drugs had been discovered by teams of scientists, who worked in drug industry laboratories and mainly in the United States. Whether this American domination will continue is, however, now a matter of some doubt.

3. Unlike many of the older agents, which were by and large relatively ineffective but also relatively safe, the new drugs were often far more powerful—and far more toxic. . . .

4. The impact of these new drugs on the public health had been extraordinary, although they were often given somewhat more credit than they deserved.

The Impact on Health

The germ-killing sulfa-drugs and the antibiotics helped to slash the death rates from the once-dreaded streptococcal diseases, such as acute rheumatic fever, and puerperal sepsis or childbed feber, and from pneumonia. Similar victories were achieved against scarlet fever, erysipelas, streptococcal septicemia, meningococcal meningitis, staphylococcal infections, and typhoid fever, and puerperal sepsis or childbed fever, and from pneumonia. Similar victories were achieved against scarlet fever, erysipelas, streptococcal septithese infections had been steadily dropping in the United States since about 1910. Nonetheless, these new agents manifested a striking effect in making recovery not only more certain but far smoother and quicker. Patients suffered less pain, tissue damage, and disability, and required less hospitalization—or none at all. As costly as some of these new drugs may have been, the total cost of medical care in the treatment of an illness was substantially lower, and patients were able to return to normal activity in a fraction of the expected time. . . .

In the case of tuberculosis, death rates in the United States had been going down steadily since at least the turn of the century, presumably as the result of improved sanitation, the pasteurization of milk, better nutrition and housing, and the use of lung-collapse and other surgical procedures. With the introduction of streptomycin, para-amino-salicylic acid, and isoniazid, the rates were forced even lower.

The syphilis death rate, which had continued to rise even after the discovery of Paul Ehrlich's "magic bullet," arsphenamine, dropped dramatically after the introduction of penicillin. The drop, however, had actually begun in this country as early as 1935, in part as the result of a nationwide drive by Dr. Thomas Parran, then the surgeon general of the Public Health Service, together with Paul de Kruif and other science writers, to bring the facts of syphilis prevention and syphilis treatment into the open.

In the tropics, death rates from malaria were slashed by the combined application of new quinine derivatives and other antimalarials, DDT sprays, and swamp drainage. The combination of these approaches—better drugs, insect control, and improved hygiene, and also the use of vaccines—served to control such age-old infections as cholera, bubonic plague, dysentery, typhus fever, yellow fever, and a host of parasitic infections that had long flared in both tropical and subtropical areas.

Hypertensive heart disease, once one of the most deadly killers, was brought under control, allowing patients to live more normal lives, soon after the discovery of hexamethonium, hydralazine, and the Rauwolfia alkaloids.

The discovery of insulin, and later that of tolbutamide, have had no appreciable effects on the diabetes death rate per hundred thousand, which has continued to climb (perhaps as a reflection of the growing percentage of the elderly in the population) but these drugs have made it increasingly possible for diabetics to live longer and more comfortably. Figures from the Joslin Clinic show that the duration of life after the onset of diabetes was only 4.9 years during the preinsulin period 1897–1914. Since 1965 it has been 16.7 years. Even more startling are the effects in diabetics below the age of twenty; in the period 1897–1914, the average survival for them was only about 2 years after the disease was first detected, but by 1960 the average survival period had gone up to 24 years.

Similar triumphs in increased longevity or in prolonged control of symptoms have been achieved with new drugs in the treatment of epilepsy, parkinsonism, asthma, thyroid disease, and even certain types of cancer. The new steroid hormones have provided useful weapons against arthritis and, in the form of oral contraceptives, against unwanted pregnancies. New vaccines have come close to wiping out poliomyelitis and offer the promise of eradicating mumps, measles, and rubella.

With the advent of the new tranquilizers and other psycho-pharmacologicals, it has become possible for the first time to reverse the ominously growing number of patients in mental hospitals, and consequently to slash the high costs to society for prolonged institutional care. In recent years the reduction in the number of patients in mental hospitals may also reflect the tendency to treat such individuals on an outpatient basis in their home communities.

There is at least some evidence that new attitudes and approaches in these hospitals may have played an equally important role. But although the tranquilizers and related drugs have significantly controlled mental symptoms, they have thus far failed to cure mental illness, and there is growing apprehension that their frequent use to cushion or camouflage what are simply the normal problems of living may be seriously harming many millions of patients.

Still other drugs, by making possible smoother anesthesia and safer operations, have in turn made possible the development of a wide variety of advances, including open-heart surgery, tissue and organ transplants, more effective cancer surgery, and the surgical treatment of epilepsy.

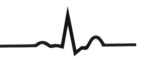

Supposedly we have the highest standard of living in any country in the world. Do we, though? It depends on what one means by high standards. Certainly nowhere does it cost more to live than here in America. The cost is not only in dollars and cents but in sweat and blood, in frustration, ennui, broken homes, smashed ideals, illness and insanity. We have the most wonderful hospitals, the most gorgeous insane asylums, the most fabulous prisons, the best equipped and the highest paid army and navy, the speediest bombers, the largest stockpile of atom bombs, yet never enough of any of these items to satisfy the demand. Our manual workers are the highest paid in the world; our poets the worst. There are more automobiles than one can count. And as for drugstores, where in the world will you find the like?
—Henry Miller

Robert L. Kane

Iatrogenesis: Just What the Doctor Ordered

In medical care as in physics, for every action there is a reaction. For each therapy or drug prescription, there is a risk. The causing of illness by medical treatment is called iatrogenesis. In the following article, Robert Kane describes the iatrogenic illnesses caused by drugs, surgery, technologies, and other therapies. He argues that the physician's primary commitment not to harm the patient demands information, investigation, and action to prevent destructive drug prescription and other iatrogenic treatments.

At a time when we are entranced with prevention, perhaps we might look closer to home for problems to conquer. One area worthy of prevention subvention is iatrogenic disease. It is so important, in fact, that it is worth coining a word everyone seems to use, but one which is conspicuously absent from the dictionary, "iatrogenesis."

The term refers to the production of disease by the manner, diagnosis or treatment of a physician or some other member of the health care team. There are some who are prepared to indict medical care in its entirety as iatrogenic, claiming at best it is addictive and, at worst, dangerous. But let us not rush too quickly to issue a new Surgeon General's warning about potential hazards of visits to the doctor. We must recall that disasters make the news. Good outcomes do not get the same publicity. When we look at the denominator—the rate at which people are exposed to potent medical innovations—we may conclude that things are better than we thought....

Medical care represents a balancing of alternatives not unlike the second law of thermodynamics: For every action we take, there is a risk (reaction). Each therapy carries the danger of producing some untoward effects—a side effect, an excessive dosage. The possibility of benefit must be weighed against the physiologic cost of treatment. In a technologically sophisticated society, the line between doing good and causing harm may become very fine. Each time we identify an illness we intervene in the patient's life, changing his status and sometimes his entire lifestyle. If iatrogenesis is considered the production of morbidity through treatment, then iatrogenesis is ubiquitous; it is a part of every step of medical care. The salient issue is not whether iatrogenesis occurs or how it can be avoided, but rather how it can be identified and minimized.

We need to consider a range of iatrogenic disorders from the mere obvious consequences of drug therapy and surgery to the more subtle problems of diagnosis, labeling and general excess zeal. Iatrogenesis quickly raises issues of ethics and effectiveness that are discussed elsewhere. For purposes of this discussion, we will consider four classes of iatrogenesis.

1. *Conscious risk*—many diagnostic and therapeutic decisions require the therapist to choose a procedure or regimen with a known risk. Each surgical procedure and most drugs fall into this category.

2. *Unexpected complications*—even when care is provided according to the best established techniques, a complication may arise. . . .

3. *Inept care*—errors of judgment, lack of skill, inadequate knowledge or superficial attention can have disastrous consequences. . . .

4. *Overzealous care*—the creation of dependency is a dangerous side effect. Inadequate concern about the psychological aspects of illness can be as crippling as physical ones. So, too, can one produce economic cripples—individuals and whole societies. . . . The choice of an expensive form of treatment (e.g., hospital) when a substantially less costly and equally effective alternative is available represents one way in which medical care can lead to excessive utilization of resources. . . .

Hospitals are dangerous places. An estimated 2 million nosocomial* infections (or 7 such infections per 100 admissions) occur annually, accounting for 150,000 deaths and costing over $1 billion annually. Almost one-third of hospitalized patients experience at least one adverse drug reaction during hospitalization and about 3 percent of hospital admissions to general medical services are due to adverse drug reactions. In a recent study of teaching hospitals, almost half the patients were exposed to one or more potentially dangerous procedures and 14 percent of those undergoing procedures experienced complications.

Drugs

Drugs are ubiquitous poisons. It is estimated that 75 million adult Americans take an average of two drugs regularly (at least once a week and usually daily). Over 15 million people take aspirin regularly; 10 million regularly use anti-hypertensives; over 5 million take oral contraceptives, tranquilizers, or antacids.

The utility of a drug depends upon its correct usage for the proper con-

*"Nosocomial": Pertaining to a hospital or infirmary. —Ed.

ditions in the correct amounts. Even when used correctly, drugs may have untoward effects that we accept as part of the cost of therapy. Despite an active regulatory process which requires a great deal of testing at both the animal and the clinical level, drugs are released only to discover that they cause serious problems when used in broad populations.

Drugs may be misused. The misuse can result from ignorance or it may be a deliberate departure from accepted practice. The use of amphetamines as stimulants and anorectic agents is a flagrant example of the latter. Ignorance is more difficult to identify and control. A recent survey suggests that there is a variation in knowledge about some common drugs and their uses. Some quality of care studies have uncovered inappropriate use of drugs like antibiotics. Other, even more potent drugs, are likely misused as well. Aside from narcotics, no special requirements beyond a medical license are imposed on physicians using even the most sophisticated drugs. The general practitioner can prescribe powerful anti-cancer regimens. One proposal that has appeared from time to time is a limitation on the right to prescribe certain classes of drugs according to specialty training or other evidence of special preparation. The alternatives appear to be a continuation of the *laissez-faire* approach or a retrospective surveillance with subsequent revocation of privileges for persistent offenders—neither of which is particularly attractive.

Perhaps the most common form of drug abuse is the excessive use of many forms of drugs without adequate justification. The most commonly misused prescription drugs are tranquilizers and antibiotics. The former constitute the most frequently used drugs and are liable to be prescribed indiscriminately and continued almost indefinitely. We have, as a result, produced a national epidemic of drug addiction, perhaps far more dangerous than the illicit drug trade we hear so much about.

Surgery

Many of the dilemmas of the prescription pad have their parallel in the scalpel. There is a basic risk of surgery associated with the use of general anesthesia (approximately one death per 1000 anesthetic inductions) and there are specific risks associated with various operations. There are those who claim we are too quick to operate and those who feel we are indiscriminant. Beyond operative mortality, the complications from surgery include both the direct effects of organ disruption and secondary effects on physical and psychological functioning.

The relative benefit of surgical intervention has been subjected to more careful scrutiny of late. Cost-effectiveness analyses provide provocative data to dampen our enthusiasm for many elective surgical procedures. Surgical rates in the United States are substantially higher than those observed elsewhere but it is not always clear how that information should be interpreted. For example, the families of physicians show a higher rate of elective surgical procedures than a comparable group of families of other professionals. Within regions, there is a wide variation in elective surgery rates. No consistent patterns can be demonstrated to relate the variation in surgical rates with either precipitating morbidity, availability of resources or different standards for selecting patients. However, the fact of the variation is seen as presumptive evidence that at least some proportion of the higher rates represent excesses. . . .

In some instances, the controversy may focus on the efficacy of the procedure itself. Currently the place of coronary bypass surgery is caught up in such heated debate. The past decade has witnessed growing enthusiasm for direct surgical intervention on blocked coronary vessels. Lists of case reports enthusiastically testify to the beneficial results of the bypass procedure. But there is growing recognition of the need for more significantly controlled trials of new therapies, even in surgery. . . .

Meanwhile, the patient is left in the middle. The operation is expensive and debilitating. It carries an operative mortality risk of 1–4 percent. At the same time, it is a treatment for a common, painful, disabling, and life-threatening condition. Everyone wants the operation to work; when, then, should a recommendation for the procedure be construed as iatrogenic?

The surgeon's capacity to mutilate implies a great responsibility. Women appear to be particularly vulnerable targets—so much so that some feminists have begun to label hysterectomy an iatrogenic disease secondary to male chauvinism. Whatever the etiology, the performance of hysterectomies does not seem to be highly sensitive to external forces. Relatively simple surveillance can produce substantial changes in performance rates.

The removal of a breast is both physically and psychologically traumatic. Even beyond the implications of breast cancer itself, the disfigurement and possible loss of function in an upper extremity extract high prices from afflicted women. One would want to be very sure that there were clear advantages in survival rates from the more debilitating mastectomy procedures compared to simpler operations (perhaps in combination with other modalities such as radiation or chemotherapy). Once again, the picture is far from clear. Extensive dissection of breast tissue, lymph nodes, and attendant destruction of muscle mass has not been shown to yield consistently better survival rates than more modest surgical therapy.

At a slightly more subtle level, there is also much room for improvement in the way we manage surgical patients. Pre-operational information and support reduce stress and reduce post-operative distress. We thus have available a technology to alleviate unnecessary suffering.

Other Therapies

Our lack of consistency in treatment is not limited to the use of drugs or surgery. Witness the history to date of our management of acute myocardial infarctions. As our capacity for technologic intervention increased, the site of care has shifted increasingly to the hospital and then to specialized units within it. Perhaps nothing epitomizes this technological revolution so well as the coronary care unit. Once again, a host of enthusiastic case reports extoll the value of this therapeutic breakthrough and, once again, there is a dearth of controlled studies to test the concept. By now the CCU has become standard medical practice and denial of its "benefits" to a control population is virtually unthinkable.

Nonetheless, there are reports that suggest some degree of temperance of our enthusiasm. On one hand, we have studies that recount the terrible psychologic burden of patients treated in such a unit. On the other hand, we have a few controlled studies to indicate that, at least for some groups of patients, home care is as effective as CCU care.

Moreover, we run the risk of inflicting disability on disease. Tremendous energies expended on the treatment of coronary heart disease may produce a cardiac cripple. Our treatment of the disease has changed with time and fashion. A quarter of a century ago we began to move the heart attack patient from bed to chair. Now we are seeing increasing urging for early ambulation and early discharge from the hospital, but no signs of consensus. . . .

This question of conservative versus active management of patients can be found in other aspects of medicine as well. Each time the patient is caught in the middle, he risks both physiologic and psychologic trauma. Controversies continue about such issues as the value of strict control of diabetes mellitus or dietary management of peptic ulcer disease. Each urging of stricter limitations on patient behavior implies restricted lifestyle and additional stress. This may be a high price to pay for ambiguous efficacy.

In many respects, our successes breed our dilemmas. As we develop the means to artificially reproduce the function of organ systems, we create a series of moral and social problems. Who has the right to continue or to terminate life functions? When do the costs outweigh the benefits? . . .

Diagnosis

The physician-taxonomist is addicted to diagnosis. The process of labeling implies understanding and suggests at least a prognosis, if not a treatment. This critical care step then offers the patient reassurance that the dreaded entity is, in reality, something more benign or it may mean that the patient's whole future is blighted by the announcement of an affliction. This business of labeling is indeed a weighty responsibility.

Reviews of the degree of inter-observer variability do little to reassure us about the reliability of clinical judgment. Three types of diagnostic problems are particularly troubling: false positives, false negatives, and labeling without benefit. . . . The final question . . . is whether we ought to bother with diagnosis at all. There exists in medicine, as in most pursuits, a certain degree of the Mt. Everest syndrome: When asked why he climbed the mountain, an adventurer replied, "Because it's there." It is useful to pause in our enthusiasm to label and ask ourselves to what end we do it. . . .

Fundamental Issues

We began by listing several classes of iatrogenesis. We close the presentation with a set of related questions:
1. Who should be responsible for the results of treatment?
2. What level of performance is reasonable?
3. How can iatrogenesis be monitored?
4. How can iatrogenesis be minimized?

We raise these questions in full recognition that no simple or permanent answers are feasible. The responsibility for the outcomes of care opens a Pandora's box. Issues of informed consent, patient compliance, institutional and individual licensure come quickly to mind. . . . However, it is important to recall our initial premise: Medicine is not yet, and likely never will be, an exact science. At best it represents a set of known probabilities. For the most part, we must choose between doing nothing and proceeding on the basis of insufficient data. Either choice represents a risk. . . .

At the same time, the practicing physician is constrained by the progress of the field in general. Patients and physicians alike may be anxious to adopt the therapeutic recommendations based on vanguard data. In many situations, it may be more prudent to delay dissemination of a new technique through means such as special licensing until adequate trials can be conducted and evaluated. At present there are few restrictions on physician behavior. State licenses to practice medicine tend toward the permissive endorsement of "medicine and surgery in all its branches." Our only checks lie in hospital staff privileges and malpractice insurance coverage—both quite fallible. . . .

We need some means of reminding the profession of its cardinal tenet, "Primum non nocere."* Regulation is not likely to be effective nor can we rely on exhortation. Pragmatically, our best defense is an informed consumer

---

* "Above all, do no harm." —Ed.

who can at least inquire about the risks and implications of diagnosis and therapy. Such a solution is not likely to satisfy those in search of a foolproof safeguard, but it is probably an accurate reflection of the situation as it is and as it will be.

Finally, we must acknowledge our great need for more information. We have alluded to some of the problems of monitoring untoward reactions. Constant scrutiny and an active data retrieval system are of paramount value in this pursuit. We also need far more information about what are reasonable expectations of outcome for various treatment modalities. It will only be by studying the varying rates of successful intervention across sites that we can identify those with good results and isolate the approaches they employ in order to foster those over other means.

Donald Kennedy

Creative Tension: FDA and Medicine

The U.S. Food and Drug Administration regulates the production and use of new medicines and technologies. A former commissioner of food and drugs, Donald Kennedy assesses the causes for doctors' hostility to regulation. He recommends that education of medical professionals include examination of the drug regulation process, benefit-risk analysis, social research, and personal health behavior. Drug package inserts for patient information, regulation procedures, and drug legislation are additional issues on which Kennedy proposes continued dialogue between medical practitioners and the FDA.

Since joining the Food and Drug Administration, I have been exposed to a remarkable array of correspondence from well credentialed practicing physicians. Some of them are my former students from Stanford, others are former classmates at Harvard, and still others seem not to require any help from prior acquaintance. Many believe that the FDA is failing in its obligation to the medical profession in several ways: by appearing to ignore the wisdom of clinical experience in its decisions about drugs; by denying American physicians a number of new medicines readily available overseas and unduly delaying those developed domestically; and by regulating through edict rather than through education.

Let me begin by observing that a certain amount of tension between medicine and government regulatory activities seems unavoidable, appropriate and possibly even creative. I do not intend, by raising that prospect, to justify continuous hostility. But there are important respects in which the objectives of the two groups differ, and may even be in productive opposition.

We therefore should probably not expect, or even seek, to work in complete harmony, but surely we should do everything we can to avoid frank hostility, or outright misunderstanding. A first step in preventing such negative outcomes is a process that Lincoln called "disenthrallment."

For its part in the disenthralling process, I think the FDA has to liberate itself from the notion, with which it more than occasionally comforts itself and its medical constituency, that it regulates drugs and devices but not doctors.

As much as we might wish otherwise, to regulate technology is to regulate practice. The Agency has never been, and is not now, anxious to exert direct regulatory control over the way in which physicians and other health professionals work. But like other regulatory agencies, FDA has turned an important corner from policing the health-care system against fraud, quackery and bad manufacturing practices, to functioning as a regulator in the transfer of health technology. We have to be evaluated on the basis of how well we perform that function, and in a comprehensive way that counts loss of innovation as a cost.

For its part, American medicine must shed the view that regulation is something so fundamentally distasteful that it is best ignored. Let me hasten to say that negative conclusions about regulation do not bother me, if they are argued on the basis of a clear understanding of the process. But my communications from practitioners reveal, I think, a real deficit in the way in which medical education has dealt with the subject.

Shortcomings of Medical Education

My first point is that medical schools ignore the institutional aspects of health, and that the regulatory process is particularly neglected. For example, I can find only a few medical schools in which the pharmacology course includes an adequate examination of the process for the approval of new drugs. I think doctors ought to know much more than they do about adverse drug reactions, how to report them, and how to draw conclusions from the results, and that they should be much more familiar than they are with the basis for making risk-benefit assessments. The average physician in the United States will receive over $4,000 worth of direct drug advertising this year; it takes the drug industry less than a decade after graduation to surpass the public investment in the medical education of each doctor in the country. That is reason enough to make us want the nation's medical schools to teach something of the social calculus of balancing drug efficacy and risk.

Secondly, I think medical schools—along with the rest of society—should be asking whether, in research and education, they emphasize the important questions instead of merely the answerable ones.

The right outcome measures for our work in health will eventually depend on a set of disciplines related to populations and to population health: epidemiology, nutrition, toxicology and the applied behavioral sciences. Already, we have learned that most indexes of population health, although not materially affected by the density or cost of traditional curative medical practice, are highly sensitive to such variables as income, gender, education, behavior and geographic location. It is not surprising that these relations are poorly understood, since, even in our leading medical schools, the relevant scientific disciplines have been fragmented or poorly represented or both.

Central to the needed reform is a change in the relative emphasis given in medical schools to the disciplines that pertain to populations rather than to individuals. The training of physicians now emphasizes the reductionist sciences so heavily that there is little time for learning about biostatistics; yet the public policy decisions about therapeutic tools in medicine all depend critically upon questions of sampling. . . .

My third point emerges from the new data on population health. It is by now clear to almost everyone that personal health behavior is an absolutely critical determinant of health outcomes. Many physicians agree that the improvement of health behavior—which under the best of circumstances seems difficult to achieve—depends at least upon self-knowledge. That requirement fits well with what I think of as the idealized role of regulation. Regulation, after all, arises as a consequence of the generation of public costs by a private activity; the best regulation is a clear signal that identifies these costs and allows members of the public to avoid them voluntarily. Sometimes, the regulator has to do more, as when the costs are impossibly cryptic or public understanding is inadequate. But in most cases the regulator's task is to provide information—and this role puts FDA in the middle of the health-education business. Perhaps the best example is the matter of patient package inserts.

Package Inserts for Patients

Patient labeling for certain classes of drugs, especially those that are taken chronically in outpatient situations (and most especially those that are elective and are associated with serious side effects), has a largely untapped potential for patient education. We initiated such labeling in 1971 for oral-contraceptive drugs, with a good deal of co-operation from organized medicine. Labeling for IUD's went into effect last November. Estrogen labeling was also established in late 1977 but is under a legal cloud: we were sued by the American College of Obstetrics and Gynecology (ACOG) and by the Pharmaceutical Manufacturer's Association in Delaware, but the judge refused to grant a preliminary injunction staying our regulation. Some doctors, as the ACOG brief makes clear, are worried that long lists of adverse reactions and risks may deter patient compliance, reflecting a legitimate professional concern. This legal maneuvering conveys a clear message: it is getting harder for us to require patient labeling as it becomes clearer to the industry and the medical profession that we are serious about it for a variety of drugs, not just for a few special cases. . . .

To summarize, one does not have to advocate "deschooling medicine" to observe that the process of patient education involves both health professionals and government. The settings in which that education takes place are predominantly conversations between doctors, pharmacists, nurses and patients, and communications between government and citizens primarily through labeling. I believe strongly that the latter vehicle has been inadequately exploited. We want more patients to have more information in plain language about their own therapy; that not only will improve their compliance with a medical regimen but also will improve the state of self-knowledge that helps bring about more health-promoting behavior. I simply cannot see any reason to doubt that the co-operating patient is more to be desired than the merely compliant patient.

The "Drug Lag"

A recurring theme in my correspondence from physicians is the assertion that FDA regulation is denying to American medicine drugs readily available overseas. The "drug-lag" accusation is, in my view, serious. I have given it a good deal of attention in the past six months. It turns out that much of the evidence supporting the claim that, because of the efficacy requirement of United States drug law, this country characteristically lags behind others in the introduction of new drugs suffers from serious deficiencies. These deficiencies are of three kinds: failure to make distinctions between quality and quantity; lack of comprehensiveness; and insufficient analysis of differences in the methods chosen by various nations to regulate drugs.

Looking first at the qualitative-quantitative distinction, I would point out that the FDA is not defensive about its failure to approve some drugs for use in the United States. On the contrary, it is a justifiable source of pride. Although thalidomide is an oft-cited example, its exemplifying power remains undiminished by hard wear—and it is not unique. Furthermore, each of the six leading countries in drug innovation (France, Germany, Italy, the United Kingdom, the United States and Japan) might be said to have a "drug lag." Thus, of the 39 drugs introduced in 1976 in Germany, 32 were not available in the United States, and 37 were not available in Japan. Conversely, of the 15 drugs introduced in the United States 13 were not available in Japan, and 11 were not available in France.

. . . A painstaking analysis of the literature on international rates of drug innovation shows clearly that a multitude of factors, only one of them remotely "regulatory," affect international drug innovation rates. Among the factors are the multinational character of many pharmaceutical companies and differing rates of exchange.

Finally, the way nations have chosen to regulate drugs often reflects a general policy stance rather than a specific approval process. Our own orientation involves documentation, the protection of persons involved in experiments, democratic procedures, openness and accountability. Time penalties are levied by this approach—just as they are by all forms of government by consent. Thus, important trade-offs are involved in streamlining procedures to gain time, and any dispassionate analysis of the "drug-lag" question must balance what is gained against what is lost when the process is attenuated.

I know that many physicians believe, as I do, that the debate over drug lag—no matter how convincing the arguments may be—is essentially arid as compared with our concern about specific drugs that are available elsewhere but not here. I do not want it said of FDA that when doctors asked for drugs, we gave them debating points: the important question is whether there are ways of speeding the new-drug approval process without losing something valuable in so doing. There are two ways, one a temporary but important expedient, and the other a long-range solution. The first involves an effort currently being undertaken by the Agency to give "express" treatment to drugs of unusual potential therapeutic benefit, and to devise other mechanisms for reducing approval backlogs. This effort is so well advanced that it may be nearing the point of diminishing returns. Only so much can be done administratively.

Limitations of Present Legislation

What is needed is careful attention to the features of the law that require us to be overly conservative in the approval process. It is extraordinarily difficult for FDA to know what is actually occurring with a specific drug after it is in the marketplace, because formalized systems of drug-experience reporting are lacking. Even if that difficulty were remedied, an indefensibly protracted hearing process would be needed to remove a questionable drug from the market—during which it could still be sold—unless a rarely invoked summary power were used. The restrictions on removal might be justified if the FDA had full information about a drug before approval was granted, but the scale of testing guarantees that we do not have full information.

A thousand volunteers or so, at most, are involved in the clinical phases of drug approval. Because rare events occur rarely, it is obvious that novel adverse reactions may appear when the number of persons exposed to a drug increases by several orders of magnitude. It is in the marketplace—under real conditions of exposure, possibly involving interactions with foods, with other drugs or with atypical genetic constitutions—that the real element of the risk equation is revealed.

If a physician were required to practice under similar conditions—access to only a fraction of the patient's history, no ability to modify the diagnosis or the treatment protocol and full accountability for the outcome—there would, I suspect, be a similar tendency toward conservatism. So it is with FDA; given the limitations under which the law requires us to operate, we seek to find out as much as we can before we grant approval. This tendency to sacrifice speed for comprehensiveness has been reinforced by the trend of Congressional oversight; FDA has seldom been asked to account for nonapproval of a drug, but has been severely criticized at times for approving drugs that proved to have a less favorable risk-benefit balance than we thought....

A Proposed Reform of New-Drug Laws

In view of these and other deficiencies that have emerged in the 40 years since our basic statute was enacted and the 16 years since it was substantially amended, almost everyone who has looked carefully at the situation... has concluded that sweeping statutory reform is the most essential element for improving the new-drug approval process.

Milton Silverman and Philip R. Lee

Future Strategy: Prescriptions for Action

Concerned by the seriousness of iatrogenic diseases, drug overutilization, irrational prescribing, and the rising cost of medications, Milton Silverman and Philip R. Lee urge the public as well as physicians, the drug industry, and government to take steps to assure that drugs are used to improve our health. They believe that clinical pharmacology should be required for medical students and continuing education for practitioners. Other recommendations include widely accessible and objective drug information, industry controls, new roles for pharmacists in community education and counseling, and drug insurance. They also analyze the role of government in research, regulation, and payments as well as consumer education.

Much of the use of pharmaceutical agents in this country has been rational and brilliantly successful. Lives have been saved, pain has been alleviated, the anguish of severe mental illness has been tempered, crippling has been prevented, recovery has been made quicker, and some age-old plagues have been essentially obliterated.

But it is only too evident that a significant portion of drug use, both prescription and over-the-counter, is unnecessary and irrational. This misuse is largely the result of (1) the lack of skepticism or the outright naïveté of both physicians and patients; (2) the flood of advertising and other drug promotion that has too often been unobjective, incomplete, or misleading; (3) the lack of readily available drug information that is objective; (4) the widespread use of a drug on the usually false premise that "it may not help but it won't hurt"; and (5) the equally widespread belief among the public that there is or must be a pill for every ill.

Unfortunately, irrational drug use has often been condemned principally on economic grounds. To those who focus their attention solely on the financial aspects of the problem, the solutions are self-evident: cut the price of drugs, slash the profits of the drug industry, revolutionize the drug patent system, or turn the pharmaceutical industry into a national public utility. The high prices of some drug products and the incredible inconsistencies of drug pricing in general cannot be readily justified by ordinary economic arguments, and not even by the industry's constant emphasis on the riskiness of its operations. The present drug patent system is not perfect, and the advantages and disadvantages of changing it should be carefully weighed by the health professions, economists, the drug industry, the Congress, and society in general. The profits of the drug industry are large, but there is no substantial agreement on whether they are too large. Moreover, putting a discriminatory ceiling on the profits of an industry might well place a similar ceiling on inventiveness, ingenuity, and creativity that would eventually harm society.

To our minds, any attempt to solve the problem just to save money, either the patient's or the taxpayer's, is of secondary importance. The primary objective is not lower costs but better health. The significant challenge lies in minimizing irrational prescribing and irrational self-medication in order to improve the quality of health care and the patients' health, limit drug dependence of any kind, and prevent needless drug-induced illness and drug-induced death.

In any consideration of the steps that might be taken, it must be emphasized at the outset that the drugs now available, when used appropriately, can be a boon to mankind. Society must see to it that every patient needing drugs for the prevention, control, or treatment of disease can obtain them. Access to these vital products should be assured by insurance programs, government subsidy, or whatever other technique may be practical.

Society urgently needs new drugs that are better than the ones we have today—more effective, safer, less costly, able to prevent or alleviate diseases that are now uncontrollable. But there is no great need for drugs that are only new. Such me-too drugs, offering no substantial clinical or economic benefits, merely litter the pharmaceutical landscape.

The achievement of these primary goals will require action by physicians, pharmacists, industry, and government, and especially by the public—as patients, as purchasers of drugs, as taxpayers, and as voters. The public must take far more vigorous action and accept far more responsibility than it has ever taken or accepted in the past.

The Physician

Medicine is too important to leave exclusively to the doctors, but medical problems both on a day-to-day basis and in terms of long-term policy can scarcely be solved without them. The record has shown that the prescribing attitudes and practices of many physicians are marked by serious deficiencies. . . . As a vital step in controlling irrational prescribing, the need to improve the teaching of pharmacology and especially clinical pharmacology for medical students and medical residents in training has been stressed repeatedly. Equally important are programs of continuing education for physicians already in practice, especially where these can be conducted in community hospitals, teaching hospitals, and university medical centers.

To improve the accessibility of objective, accurate drug information, a number of options are open. The package insert, which is now financed by the industry, should be replaced by an industry-financed, medically edited, and government-approved compendium listing and describing every prescription drug product legally on the market. It should be updated periodically and be supplemented with price information. Special journals dealing specifically with prescribing (*The Medical Letter* is an outstanding example) should be published by private groups of experts, should not be dependent on any drug advertising, and should be distributed at the expense of the government to all physicians in practice. . . .

Physicians face another problem—the detail man. This industry representative, or salesman, is the source of much excellent information for physicians on brand-name drug products. But biased, inaccurate, or overzealous detail men pose problems for which practical solutions remain to be found. To improve the situation, it has been proposed that all detail men be trained and recruited from the ranks of pharmacy graduates, that they be required to undergo continuing education, that they be licensed by a government agency, that they be required to provide each physician with an FDA-approved statement summarizing those claims that are based on fact, and even that local medical societies establish "truth squads" that will follow up a detail man's presentation with whatever corrective material may be necessary. The most effective control, however, will rest on the ability of the individual physician to view all claims with a high degree of skepticism and sophistication. . . .

In many hospitals, there is now a Pharmacy and Therapeutics Committee—which usually includes both pharmacists and physicians—that seeks to guide the prescribing pattern of all physicians on the staff. In some instances, they may offer only informal suggestions, which any physician is free to accept or reject. In others, the hospital committee has clear authority to permit or ban the use of any product.

In many hospitals, the committee decisions are reflected in a formulary, or list of the approved drugs that may be prescribed and that will be stocked in the hospital pharmacy. Often, they ban costly brand-name or me-too products which, in the committee's view, are not clinically needed. Similar formularies have been adopted by some voluntary health insurance systems and by various state and federal health programs. Any substantial extension of the formulary system, especially in Medicare and other federal programs, has been vigorously opposed, however, by the drug industry.... We continue to believe ... that drug formularies can have an important place in improving the quality of medical care.

The next obvious step must be the extension of the formulary system and the involvement of the clinical pharmacist outside of the hospital. These community programs could best be undertaken by group practice clinics and by county medical societies. Such a step, involving reasonable guidelines established by the physicians themselves with the advice of pharmacists and other experts, should be begun on a voluntary basis. But if the guidelines are not set up by health professionals in the community, under growing federal health programs they will almost certainly be set up by the government....

Medicine and its allied professions must take a more careful look at the prescribing competence of particular individuals or groups of prescribers.... There are some physicians whose records of constantly irrational prescribing are so deplorable that a hospital or a local medical society might require that each of their prescriptions be reviewed and countersigned by a drug expert. In the past there have been physicians whose prescribing of narcotics has been so atrocious that they have been prohibited from prescribing such drugs for many years or even for life. It is conceivable that the prescribing patterns of certain physicians have been so irrational, and have resulted in so much injury to their patients, that all their prescribing rights must be banned. And these are responsibilities which must be accepted by the medical profession itself.

Finally, physicians must make a searching examination of the role largely forced upon them by society—a role in which they feel obliged to function as universal healers. They should seek nonchemical methods to assist patients suffering from the social and emotional stresses of life.

The Pharmacist

In the hospital, the pharmacist can function most effectively in the control of irrational drug use by serving as consultant and adviser to nurses, to patients, and most significantly, to physicians. Out of the hospital, in community pharmacies, the pharmacist must also play a more responsible role. Here his advice can also be helpful to prescribing physicians in the community, but often it will be he alone who can serve as consultant to the patient, particularly where over-the-counter drugs (OTCs) are concerned.

He can function as perhaps the most readily available source of information on OTCs in the community. He can refuse to stock and sell remedies he considers ineffective or inappropriate. He can advise all potential purchasers that such products as OTC headache remedies, available at a wide range of prices, have essentially no difference in clinical value. He can also alert the patient to the problems he may encounter because of drug interactions, particularly if he keeps adequate drug records on the patients who consult him.

Many pharmacists—particularly recent graduates—have been trained to serve as clinically oriented professionals and are eager to do so. Under a system that rewards them only by success in merchandising—the more sales, the higher their income—they face economic penalties that make clinical pharmacy a career that may be emotionally satisfying but financially disastrous. There would appear to be one clear-cut solution. The system must be so changed that the professional pharmacist, like his colleagues in other health professions, will receive compensation based on the value of his knowledge, his skill, and his time. For the community-based pharmacist, this calls for a fee-for-service approach, under which the pharmacist would receive the identical professional fee regardless of the price of the product he dispenses. It would be appropriate—but more difficult to achieve—if the pharmacist were to receive compensation whether the patient elects to buy a drug or not to buy. (For the pharmacist associated with a prepaid group practice, of course, the professional compensation is a simple matter and can be readily determined within the organization.)

Since pharmacists are already involved in filling prescriptions under federally financed programs, and since the likelihood is great that this involvement will increase over the coming years, consideration should be given to legislation and regulations that could enable pharmacists to contribute even more effectively to the quality of health care. Thus, as a requirement for participation in federal programs, it might well be made mandatory for pharmacists to maintain drug records on all out-of-hospital patients and to consult these records before dispensing any prescription. They should similarly be required to counsel these ambulatory patients on the nature of each prescription, the reason why it was ordered, the results that are expected, the adverse reactions that might occur, and any special precautions needed for proper use and storage of the drug. In order for the pharmacist to offer the most helpful guidance, it should be required that all prescriptions carry the physician's diagnosis, either spelled out or given in code symbols, if the prescription is to be accepted for reimbursement under any federal program. Under such programs, no prescription should be approved for reimbursement if it carries such vague instructions as "take as directed."

Pharmacy schools should be urged or required to give their students sufficient training in measuring blood pressure, pulse rate, and similar physical signs, so that, with the approval of the physician, the pharmacist can carry on effective surveillance of patients undergoing long-term treatment for such chronic diseases as pernicious anemia, diabetes, and hypertension—permitting refills as indicated, calling for laboratory tests, and urging the patient to seek a physician visit when this is indicated. Consideration should be given to the proposal that practicing pharmacists be required to take periodic postgraduate courses as a prerequisite for license renewal—a suggestion that has already been made for physicians and other health professionals—or that pharmacists voluntarily taking postgraduate refresher courses should qualify for higher professional fees. Some states are already implementing requirements for continuing education in pharmacy.

Industry

A responsible drug industry should undertake on its own the following steps:

—Reexamine its research directions, company by company, to determine if they are in the best interests of both the company and the public

—Minimize efforts to develop and market me-too products

—Improve the quality of evidence submitted to obtain FDA approval of a new drug

—Relinquish its position as chief educator of the medical profession on drug use, and return this role to the health professions, providing no-strings-attached grants for the development of programs in clinical pharmacology and clinical pharmacy, as well as in continuing education

—Eliminate the practice of distributing free drug samples unless these are requested by prescribers (Some companies have already abolished this practice on their own. California has banned it by state law.)

—Reduce the quantity and improve the quality of drug promotion, facing up to the fact that at least some detail men have been far overstepping the boundaries of objectivity

—Moderate the quantity of OTC promotion directed at the public, and be prepared to face the possibility that the public may demand that drug advertising be shown to be as safe and effective as the drug itself

—Consider the evidence that the industry has perhaps unwittingly taken a leading role in inducing physicians to overprescribe antibiotics, psychoactive drugs, and other products, and the charges that it is involved in a campaign of "mystification" aimed at dreaming up new diseases to be controlled by old drugs and to use medical treatment for nonmedical ailments

—Phase out the use of brand names and instead, if the companies have the pride in their own firms which they so fervently claim, let them market drugs labeled only by generic name plus company name.

It seems likely, however, that the industry will make what we believe to be essential changes only when these are required by law, or when the industry discovers that a continuation of some of its practices has become unprofitable.

We may now be on the verge of witnessing the application of such an economic level through the further expansion of government-financed health programs.'

The Federal Government

In each of the three broad categories in which the federal government plays a role—research, regulation, and purchase or reimbursement—existing programs can be strengthened and policy alternatives should be considered. In research and research training, it has been difficult to generate the kind of public and congressional support for pharmacology, pharmaceutical chemistry, and related fields that has long been available for more glamorous assaults on cancer, heart ailments, and such crippling diseases as poliomyelitis and arthritis. There is now a need to strengthen university and independent, nonprofit research institute programs in such areas as pharmacology and toxicology. . . .

Drug Insurance

In the opinion of many longtime observers of the political scene, it is only a matter of time before some version of national health insurance or national health service will be enacted. It is not yet clear whether such a program will involve an insurance approach, with reimbursement provided by the government for most or all health expenditures; a national health service approach, with physicians and other health workers directly employed by the government; or the compulsory payment of premiums to private companies by employer and employee, with government subsidy provided where needed.

Under any of these methods, it seems almost certain that the coverage will include prescription drugs. Depending on how the ground rules are written, such drug insurance will have a major impact—possibly a revolutionary influence—on the prescribing and dispensing of drugs and on the drug industry itself. . . .

And Last But Not Least

Patients themselves cannot escape the charge that they, by their own attitudes and actions, have contributed in a devastating fashion to the incidence of needless drug use, adverse drug reactions, drug-induced injury, and drug-induced death. They have pressured a physician to prescribe, even against his better judgment. They have insisted on getting a prescription mainly on the grounds that their insurance will cover it. They have become prescription shoppers, going from one physician to the next to obtain a multiplicity of medications, and frequently have neglected to mention their use of multiple drugs when giving their medical histories. They have taken a drug prescribed for another member of the family and used it themselves, presumably in the belief that two diseases marked by similar symptoms must call for the identical therapy.

When they have been given a prescription drug with specific directions, the odds have been alarmingly high that they would take far too little or far too much. According to one review, "The percentage of patients making errors in the self-administration of prescribed medications, with few exceptions, has ranged between 25 and 59 percent.... In addition, 4 to 35 percent of the patients were misusing their medications in such a manner as to pose serious threats to health."... Part of these failures to comply with directions may be the result of inadequate instructions. "In our society," it was stated, "better instructions are provided when purchasing a new camera or automobile than when the patient receives a life-saving antibiotic or cardiac drug."...

Patients as well as physicians have the right to know the scientific basis supporting all claims of drug safety, efficacy, quality, and costs. Unless patients have this right, and the wit to act on the knowledge available to them, all the other steps proposed to achieve the goal of rational drug use—improving the education of physicians, modifying the system of pharmacist compensation, controlling drug detail men, and all the rest—will have only limited impact.

Certainly each patient should be able to ask both his physician and his pharmacist about the known values and hazards of any drug he is supposed to take. Each container of an OTC product should be labeled to indicate not only the approved uses of the drug but also its major hazards, and all this information should be presented in simple terms and in suitably large type. Similar information should be included in every advertisement recommending the use of the product. Furthermore, the caution should be present not in such general terms as "The Surgeon General has determined that cigarette smoking is dangerous to your health," or "Any drug you are about to swallow may work against you," but "This drug may cause gastric hemorrhage," "This drug may cause you to fall asleep when you are driving," or "If you are pregnant, this drug may cause you to produce a defective child."...

Some prescription drugs—antibiotics, steroid hormones, sedatives, tranquilizers, digitalis, and the more potent analgesics—should be dispensed only when a brief, simple statement is attached to point out the probable effects, the possible side effects, and the hazards of not taking as directed. The inclusion of such a warning statement with each container of prescribed oral contraceptives has now been required by FDA, and could profitably be applied to other drug classes. No prescription should be dispensed with such easy-to-misunderstand directions as "take as needed" or "take as directed." A patient is entitled to be reminded of precisely why, how, and when a drug is to be used, and when it is likely to deteriorate after storage and should therefore be discarded.

The influence of public disclosure should not be underestimated. . . . In any nationwide effort to provide long-needed drug information to the public, a vital part must be taken by the public media. . . . We would hope that, on their own, the media will develop and implement practical methods of controlling misleading drug advertising before the public demands that all public drug advertising be terminated.

Prescriptions for action, such as those we have considered, require analysis by a variety of individuals, groups, and institutions. As we have noted, the problems will not disappear if the alternatives we have proposed fall on deaf ears, or are blocked by apathy or the opposition of special interests. There is no single focal point for responsibility, but it is clear that six are central: physicians, pharmacists, the drug industry, government, the mass media, and organized groups of consumers. After studying and living with these problems for the past seven years, we believe that the next round will belong to the consumer.

IV The Search for Solutions: Frontiers of Knowledge

The search for knowledge—first at the patient's bedside, then in the laboratory, and now in the community and society at large—has been a principal means of transforming our ideas about health and disease into actual health care and public polices affecting health. Biomedical, behavioral, and social science research encompass many thousands of paths of inquiry seeking new knowledge to benefit mankind. Billions of dollars are invested in research every year by the federal government, foundations, and private industry.

Research is often divided into two camps—basic and applied. Basic research is fundamental inquiry aimed primarily at understanding a phenomenon or subject without regard for immediate application to practical purposes. Applied research is concentrated on an area for explicit practical goals; it is "mission-oriented" research. There is often a conflict between the two. Many scientists believe that basic research is the only pure line of endeavor, that applied research is a bastardization of science, which merely redigests basic research. On the other side of the fence are policymakers, the general public, and other scientists who argue that the time has come for us to cash in on all the time and money invested in biomedical research and apply it to practical problems. Although the costs and benefits cannot be easily computed in dollars and cents, the conquest of many infectious and nutritional diseases in the past fifty years is evidence of the dramatic contributions of research.

One great frontier in modern biology and behavioral science is understanding the perplexing structure and function of the brain and the age-old mind/brain paradox. In the social sciences one of the major challenges is the aging process and how it is affected by socioeconomic factors and society's perceptions of the aged. For example, senile dementia, which has long been thought to be a disease due to physical deterioration of the brain, perhaps related to hardening of the cerebral arteries, is now understood far more clearly. Social networks and social support systems, not physical disease, are the determining factors in this disorder for many individuals.

Biomedical research will continue to focus on the cellular-molecular mechanism and processes of disease. Such research can lead to new understandings which, in turn, will permit us to intervene physically, biologically, and chemically in the treatment of disease.

Behavioral science is increasingly linking the behavior of individuals with a greater understanding of brain function through research in neurobiology, neurophysiology, neurochemistry, and neuropharmacology. The linking of old disciplines to create new fields of research has occurred over and over again.

Social science provides the third foundation of health research. We have repeatedly learned that many health problems cannot be solved by biomedical research alone. They require instead a more comprehensive approach. Social science looks at people in the context of the world, the community, and the family in which they live. It tries to uncover why people are sick or well, the likelihood that they will stay that way, and what can be done to care for the sick and restore their health. It also looks at the way services are organized, financed, and provided, as well as how people use and pay for services. It takes into account lifestyle, as well as social, environmental, economic, and physical characteristics. Today the research field faces new challenges and fiscal and political restraints, and there are distinct expectations about outcomes of research. Social scientists and biomedical researchers compete for limited funds that will affect the health of the nation.

In Chapter 11, we address the issues and controversies currently involved in biomedical research with a particular emphasis on the fields of molecular and cellular biology, genetics, and neurobiology, which are among the most significant and promising areas of biomedical research today. In Chapter 12, we examine the contributions of social science research with particular emphasis on research on aging. The greatest research need in this area lies in the critical application of social science tools to a better understanding of how the political, economic, and social institutions of society affect the aged and the process of aging as well as the occurrence of disease and its impact on the population.

11 Biomedical Research

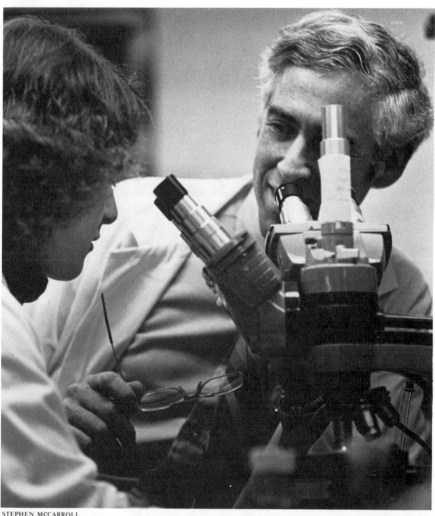

STEPHEN MCCARROLL.

The excitement, the challenge, the mystery, and the "almost ungovernable biologic mechanisms at work in scientific behavior at its best" are vividly and eloquently described by Dr. Lewis Thomas, the preeminent spokesman for medical research, in "Natural Science." Scientific research, in contrast to the popular notion, is not a lonely endeavor. Quite the contrary, it is communal, interdependent, and social. Science is not easy to plan; its outcomes often are unpredictable; yet it has been "the most powerful and productive of things human beings have learned to do together in many centuries."

Professor Renée Fox, a distinguished sociologist, also examines medical research, but for its cultural and societal roots. Medical research is highly valued, not only because it is part of the scientific, logical pursuit of knowledge, but even more because it is the primary means through which disease will be conquered and premature death vanquished. In "The Sociology of Modern Medical Research," she describes the need for organization in order to conduct such research and the special ethical issues posed by the necessity of conducting experiments on human beings. She concludes by noting two developing patterns in medical research: the tendency for modern medicine to become more social in outlook, and the greater interest in moral dilemmas and existential questions that confront physicians.

Planning of medical research and obtaining the best results from the billions of dollars currently spent for it concern medical researchers Henry Wechsler, Joel Gurin, and George Cahill in "Biomedical Research: An Overview." They trace the rapid developments in medical research and the multiplicity of advances in treatment that have resulted. They also address the thorny issue of how we can effectively select areas of promising research, and how to weigh such factors as the difference between nonfatal but almost universal diseases, rare but universally fatal diseases, and diseases that cause much pain, suffering and disability to a great many people. Describing the difference between basic and applied research, they stress the importance of maintaining strong support for basic research.

One of the exciting frontiers of research—molecular biology, particularly the use of what is popularly known as recombinant DNA technology—is the subject of a popular essay by Matt Clark and his colleagues at *Newsweek* magazine. The implications for medicine and many other fields are profound.

"Someday," Clark notes, "bacteria will be turned into living factories. They will churn out vast quantities of vital medical substances." They may also help alleviate the world's food shortage. Developments in the past seven years, since the first successful recombinant DNA experiments were repeated, have dramatically transformed biology and created the foundation for a new scientific revolution. As a result, great strains have erupted within the scientific community, particularly related to enticing commercial opportunities presented to many leading investigators. Other strains reflect concern about the possible consequences of redirecting the course of biological evolution. A noted biologist, Robert Sinsheimer, points out that "it is the success of science that has ended its pleasant isolation from the strident conflict of interests and often passionate clash of values." In "Caution May Be an Essential Scientific Virtue," he describes the potential benefits and inherent risks of the course that has been embarked upon.

Lewis Thomas

Natural Science

In this brief excerpt from the award-winning The Lives of a Cell, *Dr. Lewis Thomas conveys the physical, emotional, and spiritual aspects of scientific investigation. Basic research involves both the individual imagination and an active pooling of ideas from a variety of sources. The scientist is preoccupied with observation and experiment rather than with the ultimate application of discoveries, which are treated in the next few selections.*

The essential wildness of science as a manifestation of human behavior is not generally perceived. As we extract new things of value from it, we also keep discovering parts of the activity that seem in need of better control, more efficiency, less unpredictability. We'd like to pay less for it and get our money's worth on some more orderly, businesslike schedule. The Washington planners are trying to be helpful in this, and there are new programs for the centralized organization of science all over the place, especially in the biomedical field.

It needs thinking about. There is an almost ungovernable, biologic mechanism at work in scientific behavior at its best, and this should not be overlooked.

The difficulties are more conspicuous when the problems are very hard and complicated and the facts not yet in. Solutions cannot be arrived at for problems of this sort until the science has been lifted through a preliminary, turbulent zone of outright astonishment. Therefore, what must be planned for, in the laboratories engaged in the work, is the totally unforeseeable. If it is centrally organized, the system must be designed primarily for the elicitation of disbelief and the celebration of surprise.

Moreover, the whole scientific enterprise must be arranged so that the separate imaginations in different human minds can be pooled, and this is more a kind of game than a systematic business. It is in the abrupt, unaccountable aggregation of random notions, intuitions, known in science as good ideas, that the high points are made.

The most mysterious aspect of difficult science is the way it is done. Not the routine, not just the fitting together of things that no one had guessed at fitting, not the making of connections; these are merely the workaday details, the methods of operating. They are interesting, but not as fascinating as the central mystery, which is that we do it at all, and that we do it under such compulsion.

I don't know of any other human occupation, even including what I have seen of art, in which the people engaged in it are so caught up, so totally preoccupied, so driven beyond their strength and resources.

Scientists at work have the look of creatures following genetic instructions; they seem to be under the influence of a deeply placed human instinct. They are, despite their efforts at dignity, rather like young animals engaged in savage play. When they are near to an answer their hair stands on end, they sweat, they are awash in their own adrenalin. To grab the answer, and grab it first, is for them a more powerful drive than feeding or breeding or protecting themselves against the elements.

It sometimes looks like a lonely activity, but it is as much the opposite of lonely as human behavior can be. There is nothing so social, so communal, so interdependent. An active field of science is like an immense anthill; the individual almost vanishes into the mass of minds tumbling over each other, carrying information from place to place, passing it around at the speed of light.

There are special kinds of information that seem to be chemotactic. As soon as a trace is released, receptors at the back of the neck are caused to tremble, there is a massive convergence of motile minds flying upwind on a gradient of surprise, crowding around the source. It is an infiltration of intellects, an inflammation.

There is nothing to touch the spectacle. In the midst of what seems a collective derangement of minds in total disorder, with bits of information being scattered about, torn to shreds, disintegrated, reconstituted, engulfed, in a kind of activity that seems as random and agitated as that of bees in a disturbed part of the hive, there suddenly emerges, with the purity of a slow phrase of music, a single new piece of truth about nature.

In short, it works. It is the most powerful and productive of the things human beings have learned to do together in many centuries, more effective than farming, or hunting and fishing, or building cathedrals, or making money.

It is instinctive behavior, in my view, and I do not understand how it works. It cannot be prearranged in any precise way; the minds cannot be lined up in tidy rows and given directions from printed sheets. You cannot get it done by instructing each mind to make this or that piece, for central committees to fit with the pieces made by other instructed minds. It does not work this way.

What it needs is for the air to be made right. If you want a bee to make honey, you do not issue protocols on solar navigation or carbohydrate chemistry, you put him together with other bees (and you'd better do this quickly, for solitary bees do not stay alive) and you do what you can to arrange the general environment around the hive. If the air is right, the science will come in its own season, like pure honey.

There is something like aggression in the activity, but it differs from other forms of aggressive behavior in having no sort of destruction as the objective. While it is going on, it looks and feels like aggression: get at it, uncover it, bring it out, grab it, it's mine! It is like a primitive running hunt, but there is nothing at the end of it to be injured. More probably, the end is a sigh. But then, if the air is right and the science is going well, the sigh is immediately interrupted, there is a yawping new question, and the wild, tumbling activity begins once more, out of control all over again.

You would be surprised at the number of years it took me to see clearly what some of the problems were which had to be solved. . . . Looking back, I think it was more difficult to see what the problems were than to solve them.

—Charles Darwin

Renée C. Fox

The Sociology of Modern Medical Research

Defining medical research in its broadest terms, sociologist Renée C. Fox traces the interplay of research priorities and methods with contemporary value systems and assumptions about human nature. Medical research, traditionally performed by detached individualists, is increasingly characterized by collective effort and social outlook. It is also characterized by the growing use of human subjects and evolving interest in the moral implications of possible biomedical developments.

Medicine as an institution turns around the relationship between health and illness, and the physical and psychic capacity of individuals to perform in their social roles. Medicine is concerned with the ultimate conditions of existence and the problems of meaning associated with them. It is linked with birth, life, pain, suffering, anxiety, mortality, and death. Medical research is a way of inquiring into and striving to control the body, mind, psyche, and environment as they bear upon health and illness.

Medical research occupies a strategic place in modern society. Like modern science, of which it is an important part, it is accorded strong and extensive value. It is a symbolic as well as concrete expression of the social structure and cultural tradition. And it epitomizes some archetypically modern forms of competence, achievement, and yearning.

Cognitive Assumptions and Mode of Thought

The mode of thought on which modern medical research is based is an emergent, eclectic product of the biological and behavioral sciences. In its ideal form, it applies logico-rational thought to phenomena that are related to health and illness. Through observation, interviewing, and experimental techniques, information is amassed and refined. Instruments that enhance observation and increase the control of data range in power and complexity from the stethoscope to the electron microscope. The data collected are ordered by conceptual schemes, the highly generalized and systematic sets of ideas that constitute the framework for scientific thought. They provide investigators with insight-provoking ways of formulating questions and seeking answers about an otherwise intricate and confusing empirical reality.

At the same time, conceptual schemes bind the investigator to a particular way of conceiving reality, so that he tends to find what he looks for. Other characteristics of medical scientific thought help curtail this penchant. Great methodological and ethical value is attached to null hypothesis reasoning, the rigorous attempt to systematically disprove or rule out the premises on which a piece of research is founded. The medical researcher is expected to be a specialist in uncertainty who is engaged by the tentativeness and incompleteness of medical knowledge. He advances knowledge by laying bare these uncertainties, as well as by mitigating or dispelling them.

The highest prestige in modern medical research accrues to contributions that constitute a "breakthrough" in knowledge. This is a primary factor in the numerous disputes over priority that have occurred in the history of scientific research. In medical research such breakthroughs have the added cogency of promising relief or cure to suffering patients. Clinical investigators in the dual role of caring for and conducting experiments upon patients with conditions outside of current medical competence nourish this hope in themselves and their patients.

The value system in which modern medical research is rooted is associated with transcendent assumptions about the nature of man and the universe. Nevertheless, the problems and questions with which it deals are sharply distinguished from religious concerns: it addresses itself to the mechanisms of health and illness, life and death, rather than to the meaning of their occurrence. . . . Modern medical research also tries to detach itself from what it regards as the biasing effects that the ideas of specific religious traditions would impose on investigation. . . . Modern medical thought is resolutely antimagical in intent, if not always in fact. . . .

Value Orientations and Some Variants

The cognitive assumptions and mode of thought of modern medical science are interrelated with the value orientations on which it is premised. The value of rationality provides the raison d'être for all forms of modern scientific inquiry, and a strongly felt commitment to progress in rationally understanding health and illness is institutionalized in medical research. The pursuit of logical, orderly, generalized but open-ended knowledge is valued for its own sake, and as an expression of man's higher intellectual and moral faculties. But this pattern of rationality derives even more sustenance from the supposition that it is the primary means through which diseases will be vanquished and adventitious death overcome. . . .

The role that affect is supposed to play in this rationality is shaped by a value conception of detached concern. The medical investigator is supposed to be emotionally involved in the search he conducts, to care about the knowledge it may bring forth and the practical fruits of that knowledge. At the same time, he is to maintain a detachment that blends objectivity with organized doubting. The truth that he seeks is concepts, facts, and techniques that transcend those he would achieve if he were influenced by unexamined and unbridled sentiments.

This value orientation shades into universalism. Judgments of the reliability, validity, and import of the findings of medical investigators, along with eligibility for the status of researcher, are supposed to be dissociated from particularistic considerations. Scientific competence and excellence are considered to be the only appropriate criteria for these judgments, and the scientist's personal qualities or the social attributes of sex, age, race, nationality, class, religion, and political persuasion are believed to be irrelevant.

Finally, modern medical research is poised between individualism and collectivity orientation. The investigator is enjoined to follow the paths of knowledge that scientific inquiry opens up to him, no matter how lonely or heterodox they seem to be. But he is also expected to recognize that the knowledge he utilizes and that he helps to create does not belong to him. It is the property of a community that extends far beyond social groupings of which he is a member, and beyond his own historical time. The medical scientist is expected to be aware of the social consequences of his research, though the concept and scope of these responsibilities are not clearly designated. Rationality, instrumental activism, detached concern, universalism, individualism and collectivism describe the ethos of science as it has developed in modern Western societies. . . .

Scientific Magic

. . . Precisely because he approaches matters related to life and death in a scientific way, the modern medical investigator lives with the problems of uncertainty and the therapeutic limitations of medical science. He also confronts the unanswered why's of illness that fall outside the boundaries of science. These challenges help to trigger and shape the search for more adequate medical knowledge, but they are also a source of considerable strain. One of the coping mechanisms investigators develop is essentially magical, though it may be disguised to some extent in research procedures. Scientific magic tends to be more elaborate in groups of medical researchers with physicianly responsibilities to care for patients who are also their subjects. Scientific uncertainty, the limitation of therapy, and problems of meaning are compounded for these physicians, who make and use more scientific magic than their colleagues whose investigations are confined to the laboratory.

A pattern of scientific magic that characterizes all genres of modern medical researchers consists of investigators making levity-accompanied wagers with each other about what the results of particularly important and/or risky experiments will be. This ironic ritual symbolically comments on the apparent lack of order, predictability, and sense in the phenomena they are exploring. In it they express self-mocking chagrin over their inability to understand, know, predict, and control; and they protest against what seem to be existentially absurd processes or entities associated with illness, and with the efforts to comprehend it. Finally, this game of chance is an affirmative petition for success. The investigators who engage in it pit their own intelligent guesses against the unknown in ways that mimic the more speculative aspects of scientific research They hope that their projections will have a positive relationship to the answers they seek.

Scientific magic seems to grow directly out of the limitations of rationality in modern medical research, and the strains that this imposes on investigators. Although scientific magic parodies the basic value premises of rationality and of instrumental activism, it is a latently institutionalized pattern in modern medical research. It ritualizes the optimism of medical investigators concerning the meaningfulness of their activities. It appears to be a necessary condition enabling investigators to further knowledge and technique according to the cognitive and moral canons of modern science.

Social Structure and Organization

. . . Modern research is characterized by a progressive division of labor, increasing specialization and professionalization. Biochemistry, rather than anatomy, pathology, or bacteriology, is the reigning basic medical science. The lone researcher is a relatively rare phenomenon. Increased knowledge, specialization, and the intricacy and expense of medical technology require that research be conducted by teams of investigators as a cooperative enterprise. The commitment to teamwork, however, is more than a rational recognition of the most practical way to proceed. Collaboration is considered to be morally as well as intellectually superior to an aloof, aristocratic individualism. Established, prestigious, comfortably remunerated status-roles and careers exist. These are primarily in the university, but also in government and industry. They are not the prerogative of amateur gentlemen scholars. Rather, they are open to persons from wide-ranging social class backgrounds, primarily on the basis of their training and accomplishments.

The greater part of modern medical research is carried out within the framework of large, formal organizations that are essentially bureaucratic.

These structures accommodate the changing configurations of medical science, including the rise of new disciplines and subfields, and shifts in the content or scope of basic and applied goals. Furthermore, medical researchers are linked to one another by informal scientific and collegial exchanges, mutually read publications, and membership in loosely organized professional societies. These ties go beyond their formal affiliation with a particular university, government office, or firm. Thus, modern medical research is not coordinated and controlled by one centralized political or economic body. Its florescence is encouraged by the steadfast, enterprising support of government agencies, business firms, universities, and professional associations....

Experimentation with Human Subjects

A final key attribute of modern medical research is the extensive participation of human subjects in its inquiries and experiments. The furtherance of medical knowledge and skill, most particularly therapeutic innovation, involves a sequence of steps that weave back and forth between the laboratory and the clinic.... Human experimentation has increased in magnitude, complexity, and potential peril, and has been accompanied by increasing concern for the ethical and legal character of medical research.... Several codes for human experimentation ... have attempted to define the principles and conditions for research with human subjects, while reaffirming the importance of applying "the results of laboratory experiments ... to human beings to further scientific knowledge and help suffering humanity."...

Certain medical and surgical developments have quickened concern about the increasingly dangerous and subtle abuses that could result from them. The outbreak of infantile limb deformity (phocomelia) in Western Europe in 1961 and 1962 caused by the drug Thalidomide was one such potent occurrence. In the United States, for example, it precipitated passage of the Drug Amendments Act of 1962, which legally empowered the Food and Drug Administration to exercise specific kinds of controls over the clinical testing of new drugs on human subjects.

More recently, organ transplantation has come to be a paradigmatic case of the problems that have classically accompanied clinical medical research and of new phenomena, premonitory of intricate ethical issues, that future investigators and their human subjects will encounter. Concern about the ethics of human experimentation has focused on the difficulty of obtaining truly informed, voluntary consent from the subject, of striking a proper balance between the potential benefits and risks to him, and of protecting his integrity and privacy. Organ transplantation has added new dimensions to these questions. Obtaining consent for a transplant involves complex interactions between the medical team, potential donors and their kin, and the candidate recipient and his relatives. Transplantation has also brought other issues into prominence, including the justification for inflicting a major surgical injury on a live donor in order to help a dying recipient; the symbolic meaning of the human heart and other vital organs; the allocation of scarce organs; the transcendent meaning of the gift-exchange between the donor and the recipient, versus the mutual tyranny it can impose on them; the appropriate definition of death; the distinction between the extension of life and the prolongation of death; and the existential and social implications of the physicianly commitment to do everything medically possible for terminally ill persons.

The fact that in a modern society many persons are willing to act as research subjects—and, in numerous instances, are even eager to do so—needs explanation. Since this form of participation in medical research achieved a greater degree of acceptance in American society than in any other, identifying the factors that have contributed to its support is instructive. The institutionalization of the role of research subject involves a widespread belief in the practical importance and moral excellence of scientific research, and medical research in particular. Contributing to it by taking the role of a research subject is thought to be a humanitarian and potentially heroic act. These individuals demonstrate their readiness to endure the discomforts and hazards of pioneering experiments partly for the self-surpassing goals of collective health and well-being. Thus, the motivation of patients who serve as human subjects often has two facets. It expresses their hope that new insights or treatments may be developed that could directly benefit them; it testifies to their disinterested conviction that, as one patient-subject put it, it will be "for the good of medical science and the humane benefit of others in the future."

"Advanced Modern" or "Post-Modern" Medical Research?

A few comments on some shifts in orientation that medical research is undergoing in American society will provide an epilogue to this sociological overview. These emerging patterns appear to be microdynamic expressions of changes in the society at large, and they raise vital questions about the magnitude and significance of these changes. Do these trends constitute "advanced modern" developments—that is, are they further extensions of the value system and social structure underlying modern scientific research? Or will they prove to be "post-modern" in the sense of being sufficiently discontinuous and incompatible with the social and cultural attributes of modern science to represent a break with them? Although it is too early to formulate definitive answers to these questions, it is important to ask them.

Two developing patterns are especially notable. The first is the tendency for modern medicine to become more social in outlook. Greater emphasis is being placed on the extent to which society is responsible for health and illness. Good health and medical care are coming to be viewed as basic human rights. Social arrangements are increasingly referred to in explaining the persistence of certain illnesses and the emergence of others, as well as to account for injustices in the delivery of medical care. And the belief that illness, along with poverty, pollution, overpopulation, and war, can be brought under control by the organized implementation of public conscience is gaining momentum.

One of the consequences of this new orientation for medical research is an augmenting pressure on investigators to address themselves to "relevant" matters. The definition of what is relevant is veering toward massive efforts to eliminate certain diseases. In this respect, cancer has become symbolic of the most recalcitrant, painful, and lethal medical disorder in modern society to be overcome. But even more pronounced is the demand for solutions to social and economic problems that adversely affect health and its care. This development seems to call into question some of the commitments that have given modern medical inquiry moral and material support. After a decade of steady expansion in funds allocated by the United States government for medical research, the growth rate in federal support has leveled off and is now beginning to decline. In addition, particularly among younger people, a crescendo of doubt is being expressed about the intellectual and ethical values of scientific research and its pertinence to social issues.

The second major alteration through which modern medicine seems to be passing is a shift toward greater interest in the moral enigmas and existential questions that confront physicians. The sources of this new awareness are complex. In part, it grows out of the stage in knowledge and technique that modern medicine has reached. Understanding and control of disease and death have been impressively advanced. The potential human life span has been greatly extended. And yet people still fall ill and die. The juxtaposition of these accomplishments and limitations has reawakened reflection on philosophical and religious questions. Are disease and death inalterably a part of the human condition? If so, why? What does this tell us about the nature of man and the purpose of his existence?

Resuscitative techniques and organ transplantation have contributed to the fact that the cessation of breathing and heartbeat are being superseded by irreversible coma, or the so-called brain-death symdrome, as the criterion of death. The discussion that has surrounded this process has increased physicians' consciousness of the fact that codified notions of death are approximate and arbitrary, and do not solve philosophical or religious questions about what death really is. The debate about heart and lung death versus brain death has also brought physicians to consider in a new way the ambiguities concerning where the prolongation of life ends and the prolongation of death begins.

Participation in organ transplantation in the role of medical professional, donor, or recipient has increased cognizance of widespread, essentially mystic conceptions about the human body, even in a science-oriented society. Furthermore, participation in the network of giving and receiving established by transplantation can be a religious experience. Many report that it has enhanced their self-understanding and self-worth and given them a sense of commitment and oneness with humanity unlike any they have known before.

In addition, physicians and biological scientists in collaboration with lawyers, theologians, philosophers, and social scientists, are trying to foresee the moral and spiritual implications of possible biomedical developments. Notable among the futuristic biomedical phenomena with which they are concerned are the widespread transplantation of all human organs, including the brain; the implantation of various kinds of artificial organs; genetic engineering, including cloning (the asexual reproduction of genetic carbon copies of an adult); and behavior control through neurophysiological or pharmacological manipulation of specific areas of the brain.

The entwined existential and social orientation that seems to be emerging in modern medical research is probably not an ephemeral happening. The best indicator of this is that the young men and women who have entered American medical schools over the past few years are increasingly engaged by this perspective. Their commitment is born out of their protest over what they consider to be the deficiencies of the medicine they have inherited and out of their belief in what it could become. Whether or not we are moving from the modern to a post-modern phase of medical research will be ascertained in the course of their generation.

Henry Wechsler, Joel Gurin,
and George F. Cahill, Jr.

Biomedical Research: An Overview

Advances in biomedical research read like science fiction and give today's researchers the theoretical tools with which to answer questions that could not have been conceived a hundred years ago. Henry Wechsler, Joel Gurin, and George F. Cahill, Jr., joint editors of The Horizons of Health, *highlight recent research accomplishments and recommend improved dissemination of results, careful setting of priorities, and a reasoned balance of basic and applied research. Psychosocial research, they argue, is also necessary to facilitate the translation of biomedical findings into improved medical care.*

No applied science affects our lives as directly and personally as medicine. It is not too difficult to conceive of a world without nuclear power; but where would we be without penicillin? Without the medical advances of the last century, those of us lucky enough to survive would live under the constant threat of diseases that no one understood and for which only ineffective remedies were available.

The distance between the physician of 1877 and today's doctors is as great as the gap between the Wright brothers and Neil Armstrong. Medicine was a rugged profession a hundred years ago, when the physician had to rely on ingenuity, persuasion, luck, and improvisation to overcome the great technical obstacles he faced. An early doctor's bag contained few effective tools. Heart disease could be treated with digitalis, malaria with quinine, and pain with opium; but for most other disorders, the physician could just prescribe a variety of useless potions and salves that were nonetheless used in desperation and blind faith. The stethoscope and the reflex hammer were the major available diagnostic instruments. One can imagine the awe that the physician of a century ago would feel at today's sophisticated tools for visual diagnosis. What would he think of the computerized radioscanning techniques that can locate tiny areas of damaged tissue in inaccessible organs like the pancreas and brain and can display those tissues on a television screen? How would he like to use a fiberoptic tube to look directly at an ulcer in the patient's stomach, search for a site of bleeding, or examine a small lung tumor?

Medical science, like the other sciences, progresses at an ever-accelerating rate; and revolutionary changes in the diagnosis and treatment of disease have taken place within the professional lifetimes of most doctors practicing today.

The analysis of substances in the blood did not even become a major method of diagnosis until around the time of World War II; and even twenty years ago, no one could have imagined the automatic multichannel analyzers now used to study blood samples. These machines measure the levels of minerals, enzymes, and waste products in the blood and indicate which of these fall outside the normal healthy range. Some machines can even be programmed to give different possible diagnoses based on blood sample data, indicate the probability of each diagnosis, and request further information from the physician.

In the past few years, all sorts of devices have been invented to take over the function of faulty parts of the body. Synthetic heart valves, blood vessels, hip and knee joints, and teeth can all be used to replace their natural counterparts when they fail; and scientists are even working on mechanical glands to supply missing hormones just as the body needs them. Electronic pacemakers can keep the heart beating regularly, and people who suffer kidney failure can live their lives, albeit restricted, with the aid of a dialysis machine.

Surgeons can now perform operations long thought to be technically impossible. The heart-lung machine has given us open-heart surgery; laser beams are used to correct abnormalities in the back of the eye; and organ transplants are no longer in the realm of science fiction.

Chemical approaches to treatment have also advanced at an incredible rate. The therapeutic drugs in use today are radically different from those prescribed just a decade ago; and with the important exception of aspirin, insulin, digitalis, some antibiotics and a few other very useful standbys, the physician's pharmacopoeia has changed completely since the 1950s. These advances in drug therapy have been intimately connected to progress in our theoretical understanding of biology at the molecular level.

Molecular biology and biochemistry are probably the youngest and fastest growing of the modern sciences. As recently as 1953 James Watson and Francis Crick first outlined the structure of DNA, which codes the body's genetic information; virtually all of modern biochemistry has stemmed from this revolutionary insight. Researchers now have the theoretical tools to begin answering questions that could not have been raised before. Even the deadly mystery of cancer may soon be solved by modern biochemical research. Cancer cells are characterized primarily by their ability to multiply almost indefinitely, gradually taking over larger and larger areas of the body. This disease process is gradually beginning to be understood as scientists study the very basic biochemical processes that control normal cell division in growth, wound healing, and the replenishment of blood cells.

Since a great deal of knowledge and expertise is required to do research in any disease process on the molecular level, medical researchers have become increasingly specialized; and as a result, communication has become a major problem. Most doctors find it very difficult to keep up with the most recent discoveries and technological innovations in any field of medicine but their own specialty; and many remain ill informed even of advances in their own chosen field. Formal and informal programs have been developed to help physicians continue their medical education.... Medical research has taken on an air of mystification that is nearly impossible for an intelligent person without special training to penetrate. Of course, news of sudden "breakthroughs" does filter down through the popular press; but these bits of information, frequently distorted, can hardly give even the most avid newspaper reader a sense of the interrelationship of different research discoveries or any concept of the way in which research priorities are and should be determined.

. . . Nearly three billion dollars of federal money is now spent on medical research every year; and while this is only 10 percent of the annual federal budget for health, it is still a sizable sum. In addition, medical research often has human as well as financial costs; ethical problems abound in any study of human subjects. The examination of children with an extra Y chromosome for possible behavioral abnormalities has become a central controversy in genetic research. Serious ethical questions were also raised by a much publicized study carried out by the University Group Diabetes Project to determine whether or not certain antidiabetic drugs actually shorten the life span of patients using them. These two groups of studies demonstrate the sensitive issues involved in much medical research and underscore the need for public accountability.

But the most important aim of publicizing research information is not to put limitations on medical research; rather, it is to ensure that medical investigators can work effectively. Health care cannot progress unless ample resources are allocated to the research projects that are likely to lead to the greatest benefits. Ideally, federal funding should be used not only to support existing research programs that are crucial to national health care, but also to attract talented scientists to areas of research that might otherwise be neglected. Individual researchers are not necessarily the best people to judge the relative importance of different kinds of medical research. For many years it was unfashionable to study alcoholism or mental retardation; consequently, we have remained largely ignorant of the factors involved in these conditions. One way to correct such imbalances of research activity is to allocate substantial amounts of public money to important areas that are being inadequately investigated; once the money is available, qualified scientists will certainly be attracted to the field.

A well-informed and careful approach to research funding is not an idealistic goal; it is an absolute necessity. Yet the people who control the distribution of funds—administrators, legislators, and ultimately the general public—have had little sound basis for deciding between competing claims for the little research funding that is available. This unfortunate state of ignorance has not been anyone's fault; it has simply been a natural by-product of growing specialization in medical science. This situation can be corrected by making research information more accessible. . . .

Since resources are limited, the basic problem is to ensure that adequate support goes to those diseases that are deemed the most serious. But it is very difficult to determine exactly how much money is being spent on research into a given disease area or how serious a health problem that disease poses. Funding for basic research may not be counted as money spent to combat a given disease, although such basic research may ultimately lead to the understanding and control of an illness. . . .

Everyone agrees that research into cancer and heart disease must have a high priority because these two types of disorder are the major causes of death in the United States today. But how much money should go to combat dental disease, a universal, if nonfatal, cause of human suffering? Many diseases that are not major causes of death may cause a great deal of pain and substantial loss of productivity for a long period of time, either directly or through their complications. Diabetics can be maintained with insulin injections, and people who have suffered kidney failure can usually be kept alive and productive through dialysis. But diabetics still frequently develop circulatory problems or become blind; and dialysis is an extremely expensive procedure that keeps many patients alive but cannot necessarily keep them healthy. Finally, causes of death that predominate among the young cause a greater loss of "life years" than those that strike older people and from this point of view may be considered particularly important. For example, automobile accidents may be responsible for the loss of more years of life than any other cause, largely because teenagers are prone to car accidents.

Even if the decision is made to allocate a certain amount of money to research on a given disease, it remains to be decided what type of research should be funded. The fundamental distinction that has been made in the past has been between basic and applied research. The goal of basic research is the investigation and evaluation of theoretical principles. Hypotheses are tested again and again until the results of a number of different experiments all agree to support one theoretical concept. The process of basic research is one of continual probing, questioning, and examining; theories that seem sound at one time may be totally revised a few years later. Applied research, in contrast, makes use of theories that are well enough established to be regarded as fact. The task of the applied researcher is not to break new theoretical ground but to integrate what is already known and thus come up with a new technique for preventing, diagnosing, or treating sickness.

Applied research has yielded dramatic new methods of health care. The truly impressive technological innovations that have come about in the last few decades—advances in radiology, orthopedics, and surgical technique— have come about primarily through the engineering skill of applied researchers. Careful application of theoretical knowledge has also made possible the development of hundreds of new drugs for the treatment of specific diseases.

Since the results of applied research are often so dazzling and since they can come into practical use almost at once, a research program aimed at finding a specific treatment for a certain disease may be funded more readily than a program whose goal is a more general theoretical understanding of the biological processes that lead to illness. This is unfortunate, because such basic research has proven to be absolutely necessary to medical progress. Jack Mendelson and Nancy Mello point out quite accurately that the polio vaccine would never have been developed if all available funding had gone to support the applied goal of building iron lungs for polio victims. The concepts used to develop the life-saving vaccine came from years of basic medical research, much of which appeared on the surface to be unrelated to the clinical problem of polio.

Obviously, neither basic nor applied research is better than the other; both are appropriate approaches to different diseases at different times. Rather than blindly championing one method or the other, medical researchers— and the people who support them—must develop a sense of what type of research is needed if they are to use their time and resources as efficiently as possible. In the 1950s, dozens of scientists were intent on finding a chemical cause, and a chemical cure, for schizophrenia; but the vast majority of the theories and remedies proposed at that time turned out to be worthless. Seymour Kety attributes this record of failure to the desire to find applications before anyone had basic theoretical principles to apply. Many investigators were ready to propose chemical theories and cures for mental illness at a time when no one even knew that the transmission of signals between neurons took place through chemical (rather than electrical) processes. Such heroic theorizing in the face of ignorance demonstrates the strong prejudice that exists in favor of any research that offers the hope—however spurious—of providing an immediate cure for a major disease.

Today, the value of basic research in certain cases seems to be better appreciated. It is generally acknowledged, for example, that the problems of cancer and atherosclerosis will almost certainly remain insoluble until we have a better theoretical appreciation of the processes underlying these disorders; and a large proportion of funding for the study of these diseases is directed to scientists engaged in basic research. In other areas, however, investigators are still strongly pressured to find cures and immediate solutions, while the most basic theoretical problems remain unsolved. This has certainly been true in the study of alcoholism and the addictions. Vast amounts of money have been spent to treat these disorders, yet it has been impossible to develop any really effective treatment programs as long as the actual nature of these conditions remains poorly understood. This is not to deny the importance of treatment programs for alcoholics and drug addicts; obviously it is vital to help such suffering people in whatever way possible. But basic research into these disorders is essential if their treatment is ever to become truly curative rather than palliative.

In many ways, it is more difficult to begin to study the fundamental processes underlying a given disease than it is to devise treatments for that disease; until the illness is understood at some theoretical level, one simply does not know what to look for.

Careful epidemiological studies can be invaluable in helping the researcher focus on probable causes of disease. The hardest diseases to study are those that develop years or even decades after the individual has been exposed to the causative agent, but with careful epidemiology, even these disorders can be linked to their causes. Different types of cancer have been shown to be associated with a number of environmental agents, ranging from sunlight to asbestos, by studies of their prevalence in groups of people preferentially exposed to these environmental stimuli at some point in their lives. And recently, a number of serious neurological disorders have been attributed to the presence of slow-acting viruses that remain in the body for decades after the initial period of infection is over. The time lag between cause and effect in these diseases is so great that the actual causes might never be suspected without long-range studies that demonstrate the relationship of the agent to the disease that appears years later.

"Targeted" research programs represent another approach to understanding the origins of disease and devising methods of treatment. These are highly organized programs, usually of applied rather than basic research, that are directed toward specific goals. Some recent targeted programs have been aimed at the improvement of drug treatments for cancer, at the development of better artificial kidneys, and at determining whether or not viruses are involved in human cancer.

It would be fairly easy to plan research if breakthroughs always came as a result of long-range, careful, directed programs. But things do not work so rationally. Many of the most valuable insights into specific diseases have come from totally unexpected sources. The drugs chlorpromazine and iproniazid revolutionized the treatment of schizophrenia and depression, respectively, and studies of the chemical action of these agents have provided much of the basis for our understanding of the chemistry of severe mental illness. But when these drugs were introduced, no one had the slightest idea that they would have important psychological effects; chlorpromazine was first used in the treatment of surgical shock, and iproniazid, as therapy for tuberculosis. Even the most apparently esoteric research may lead to important clinical applications in the treatment of major diseases. The virus that causes hepatitis, for example, was discovered by a geneticist examining blood constituents in a tribe of Australian aborigines. . . .

In view of its central importance, it is certainly strange that basic research has often been seen as a luxury that the public cannot afford. When available funds become scarce, it is usually the basic rather than applied research that suffers the first budget cuts. Probably the primary reason for this is the often considerable time lag before the knowledge gained through basic research actually leads to improvements in health care. The action of heart muscle has been largely understood at the biochemical level, but this understanding has still not made it any easier to treat heart disease. In contrast, new drugs can be used to control disease as soon as they have been approved by the Food and Drug Administration. Drug research, technological innovation, and other applied approaches thus often seem a better investment than basic research in terms of the probable short-term payoff.

Unfortunately, research planners have tended to ignore the fact that a short-term boon can turn into a long-term disaster. In recent years, it has become all too obvious that new agents introduced before their effects are completely understood can lead to health problems worse than those they were originally intended to prevent. Diethylstilbestrol (DES) was given to pregnant women for many years to prevent miscarriages; but the daughters of women who were given DES during pregnancy are now known to run a risk of vaginal cancer. Nitrates have found long use as meat preservatives that prevent the growth of bacteria that cause botulism; now these chemicals, too, have been shown to be cancer-causing agents. Even antibiotics are no longer seen as the miracle cures they once appeared to be. When improperly given, these drugs can dangerously upset the natural balance of the microorganisms that normally live within the body. Worse, certain kinds of antibiotics may literally poison people who are especially sensitive to them. . . .

Advances in medical care do not automatically follow discoveries made in the laboratory. Psychosocial research is clearly necessary if biomedical research findings are to be translated into improved medical care more quickly and effectively. . . . The issues involved in planning medical research are as complex as the actual medical problems that researchers try to solve. As our understanding and control of disease has become increasingly sophisticated, it has become more and more difficult to develop a sense of the interrelationship of research in different fields and to estimate the value of different approaches. This major communication problem must be solved if research is to be planned rationally and carried out efficiently. . . .

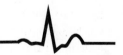

Thousands upon thousands of persons have studied disease. Almost no one has studied health.
—Adelle Davis

**Matt Clark with Sharon Begley
and Mary Hager**

The Miracles of
Spliced Genes

*The ability to create new forms of life by splicing genes, or recombinant DNA,
is a revolutionary development in biomedical research. Research using this new
technology is based on knowledge and adds new scientific information, but its
suggested varied applications raise complex ethical, moral, economic, safety,
and scientific issues. The following article from* Newsweek *explains how genetic
engineering is accomplished and explores some of the ethical and commercial
implications of the research.*

Scientists call it "the construction of biologically functional bacterial plas-
mids *in vitro.*". . . What it means is the creation of new forms of life.

The technology, popularly known as recombinant DNA, is only about
seven years old, but it has already become routine. In laboratories all over the
world, biologists are taking genes from one organism and planting them into
another. So far, the gene splicers have succeeded in inducing bacteria to make
human insulin and several other hormones. And that's only the beginning.
Someday, bacteria will be turned into living factories: they will churn out vast
quantities of vital medical substances, including serums and vaccines, to fight
diseases ranging from hepatitis to cancer and the common cold. "Anything
that is basically a protein will be makable in unlimited quantities in the next
fifteen years," says David Baltimore of the Massachusetts Institute of Technology.

Revolution. The impact of genetic engineering on the world's economy
could almost equal the recent revolution in microelectronics. Single-celled
organisms might yield the proteins that now come from cattle, which would
help alleviate world food shortages. Implanted genes could increase the yield
of alcohol from corn. Genetically engineered bacteria are being designed to
eat their way through oil spills and to extract scarce minerals from the soil.
"There has been a golden age of chemistry and a golden age of physics . . .
now it's biology's turn."

As pure science, recombinant DNA represents the most significant step in genetics since James Watson and Francis Crick discovered the double helix in 1953. It will enable scientists to identify each and every one of the 100,000 genes in the human cell. This knowledge might be used to replace defective genes with healthy ones and overcome such genetic diseases as hemophilia and sickle-cell anemia. Some technologists even suggest that the breakthrough will enable science to fashion "better" human beings. By harvesting genes at will, researchers also hope to find the answers to baffling biological questions. How do cells with the same genes differentiate into skin, muscle and nerve? What makes a normal cell turn malignant? "Recombinant DNA will not only let us understand diseases such as birth defects and cancer, but will also help us understand ourselves.". . .

All scientific revolutions—from Galileo's observations of the planets to the splitting of the atom—evoke the cry of heresy. Recombinant DNA is no exception. . . . Among the first to challenge the new technology were scientists themselves. They feared that bacteria containing noxious genes could burst out of the lab and spread the earth with a man-made plague of untold horror.

While they pondered such scenarios, scientists imposed upon themselves a moratorium on most recombinant studies. Expanded research programs began in 1976 only after the National Institutes of Health issued guidelines imposing strict safeguards in the laboratory. Fortunately, no real-life Andromeda Strain has emerged, and scientists agree that their worst anxieties were unfounded. . . . In January [1980], the NIH relaxed its guidelines to facilitate research.

Locked Drawers. Now the scientists have other concerns. They worry that the pristine realm of pure science may become contaminated by the tantalizing economic promise of the new DNA research. They fear that exclusive patents may become as coveted as Nobel prizes. A California researcher was accused by university colleagues last year of taking chemicals vital to a recombinant project to a commercial firm. Because of such incidents—some real, some rumored—scientists worry that the free exchange of information traditional to science will give way to closed notebooks and locked drawers.

. . . Bargains between the scientist and the entrepreneur have been struck before. But in this deal, the item for sale is nothing less than the fundamental chemical blueprint of life—the gene. The form and function of every living plant and animal are determined by molecules of deoxyribonucleic acid (DNA) formed into the famous double helix. . . . Whenever cells divide, the DNA duplicates itself, passing on its genetic inheritance to the next generation of cells. DNA also guides the cell in the manufacture of proteins essential for life, including hormones like insulin, antibodies to fight disease, hemoglobins to carry oxygen and enzymes that carry out chemical reactions. . . .

Fragment. In recombinant technology, DNA is spliced from one type of

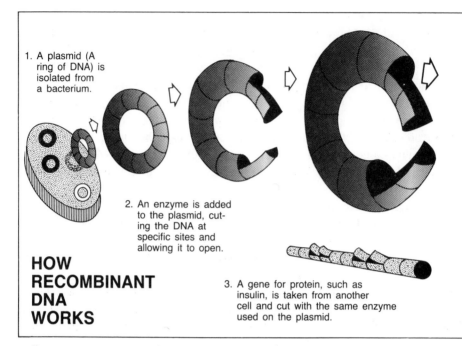

1. A plasmid (A ring of DNA) is isolated from a bacterium.

2. An enzyme is added to the plasmid, cutting the DNA at specific sites and allowing it to open.

HOW RECOMBINANT DNA WORKS

3. A gene for protein, such as insulin, is taken from another cell and cut with the same enzyme used on the plasmid.

cell to another (diagram). Researchers take bacteria, viruses, animal cells or plant cells, break them apart and extract the DNA. They use enzymes to cut the DNA chemically at specific points along its length. They can then pull out a DNA fragment with the particular array of bases they want to study. . . .

Potent Poisons. The possibility of accidentally spreading genes that make bacteria resistant to antibiotics was one of the concerns that triggered the debate over the safety of recombinant research. And under the new NIH guidelines, research on resistance genes remains largely restricted. Also under tight controls are experiments involving the DNA of disease-causing bacteria or viruses, and genes for the synthesis of potent poisons. Such research must be carried out in top-security "P4" labs, in which workers must change clothes and shower before leaving, and handle their bacteria under sealed hoods to ensure containment. No such research is going on now. Under the revised guidelines, nearly 80 percent of recombinant research can be done with the sterile procedures that normally prevail in any hospital lab. These include decontaminating items before disposal and a ban on food at the workbench. . . .

Some researchers believe that the safety issue is being swept under the rug. "For the first time, biologists have a chance to get rich so there is very strong peer pressure to go along.". . . Allegedly, some researchers have lost their jobs for voicing their concerns too publicly. . . .

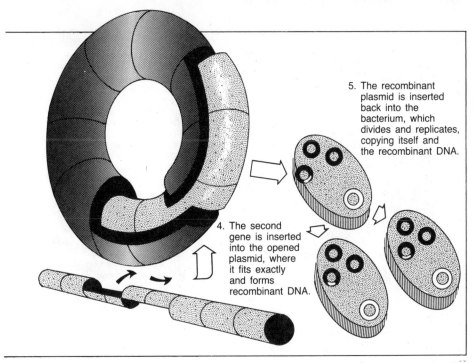

5. The recombinant plasmid is inserted back into the bacterium, which divides and replicates, copying itself and the recombinant DNA.

4. The second gene is inserted into the opened plasmid, where it fits exactly and forms recombinant DNA.

Chains. Among the first recombinant products to be manufactured in enormous quantities will be human insulin. Insulin is a protein consisting of two chains of amino acids. . . . The insulin now used by diabetics comes from cattle or pigs and contains impurities that can cause allergic reactions. Once full-scale production begins, human insulin made by bacteria promises to provide a cheaper and safer alternative. Recombinant techniques have started to produce other important human proteins. . . .

Scientists are also using recombinant methods to unravel basic mysteries about genes. One is how genes are regulated. All cells, except eggs and sperm, contain a complete set of genes, but most of them don't do anything until they are somehow "turned on." At least one type of genetic regulation has now been explained. . . . This work uncovered principles of gene regulation that may let scientists insert genes of higher organisms into bacteria, and also switch them on.

Scientists can now also determine both the exact sequence of bases in a piece of DNA and the precise locations of genes within chromosomes. There are hundreds of thousands of possible combinations of sequencs within genes; because researchers have the ability to produce genes in enormous quantities, they can finally study enough genes to map the bases.

Similarly, biologists can tell how the total of more than 100,000 human genes fit into the 46 chromosomes. To accomplish this, scientists clone a gene

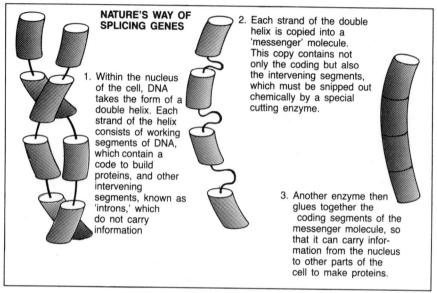

NATURE'S WAY OF SPLICING GENES

1. Within the nucleus of the cell, DNA takes the form of a double helix. Each strand of the helix consists of working segments of DNA, which contain a code to build proteins, and other intervening segments, known as 'introns,' which do not carry information

2. Each strand of the double helix is copied into a 'messenger' molecule. This copy contains not only the coding but also the intervening segments, which must be snipped out chemically by a special cutting enzyme.

3. Another enzyme then glues together the coding segments of the messenger molecule, so that it can carry information from the nucleus to other parts of the cell to make proteins.

and mix it with chromosomes whose DNA spirals have been split down the middle. The DNA bases of the "test" gene automatically find their natural partners in the appropriate split chromosome.... Thus, researchers will learn both which chromosome the gene naturally fits and where on that chromosome the gene normally rests. This "gene mapping" might make possible the cure of inherited diseases like sickle-cell anemia and hemophilia, which result from defects in a single gene. If scientists locate the proper chromosome, they could repair the defective gene or insert a properly functioning new gene into the cell.

Clue. The new DNA research could even help cope with the riddle of cancer. J. Michael Bishop and his colleagues at UCSF have cloned genes of viruses that cause tumors in chickens and isolated those that turn cells malignant. One of the tumor-causing genes instructs the cell to make an enzyme that transfers phosphate molecules to proteins. "Our hypothesis is that this transfer of molecules causes cancerous growth," Bishop says. So far the hypothesis has not led to the development of a therapeutic strategy.

Scientists have also found that the tumor genes that invade the cell are virtually the same as genes that already inhabit it. Bishop suggests this may indicate how cells grow and differentiate: if the invading gene causes cancer by making cells proliferate uncontrollably, its harmless counterpart might normally control growth and differentiation. Thus, the study of cancer, a medical problem, may lead to a better understanding of the science of cell differentiation.

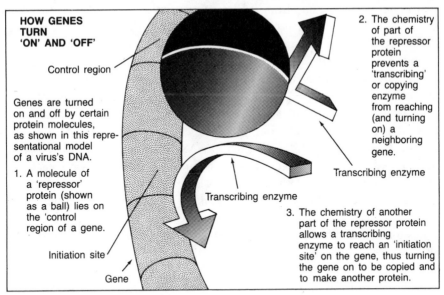

HOW GENES TURN 'ON' AND 'OFF'

Control region

Genes are turned on and off by certain protein molecules, as shown in this representational model of a virus's DNA.

1. A molecule of a 'repressor' protein (shown as a ball) lies on the 'control region of a gene.

Initiation site

Gene

Transcribing enzyme

2. The chemistry of part of the repressor protein prevents a 'transcribing' or copying enzyme from reaching (and turning on) a neighboring gene.

Transcribing enzyme

3. The chemistry of another part of the repressor protein allows a transcribing enzyme to reach an 'initiation site' on the gene, thus turning the gene on to be copied and to make another protein.

Now that gene splicing is so relatively easy, scientists find they can re-examine old genetic dogmas. Until recently, for instance, microbiologists assumed that the genes of bacteria were just like those in higher organisms. But scientists led by Phillip Sharp at MIT and Philip Leder of NIH independently discovered a startling difference. All the bases in bacterial DNA are read by enzymes three by three and translated directly into amino acids. But in viral and mammalian DNA, they found, the elements of DNA that code for amino acids that are used to make protein are separated by sequences that don't seem to get translated into any protein at all.

The discovery of these intervening sequences, or "introns," alters the conventional picture of how human genes work (diagram, p. 378). DNA bases are copied into a molecule of ribonucleic acid (RNA). But before the appropriate information is carried to the region of the cell where amino acids are assembled to make proteins, enzymes must first process the RNA. They must cut the introns out of the RNA and splice the remaining coding segments together. "This discovery is the biggest thing yet to come out of cloning DNA.". . .

If genes are divided into pieces, nature must have a reason. . . . Piecemeal genes may have helped man evolve. Words separated by spaces can be moved around to form meaningful new sentences with less confusion than if words were strung out in an uninterrupted line. Similarly, . . . the messages of DNA can be shuffled more easily into new combinations that make new genes if they are separated by introns. These fresh combinations of DNA might change the character of a cell and give the organism a selective advantage.

Another surprise came from the lab of Alexander Rich at MIT. Rich and his colleagues made crystals of DNA and found that they didn't look anything like Watson and Crick's graceful spiral. The pioneers of the double helix propounded their model from studying vague X-ray scattering patterns. Rich's crystals yielded sharp pictures that showed individual atoms in DNA for the first time. The crystallized DNA formed a zigzag shape that twisted left instead of a smooth curve that twisted right. It is still uncertain why or when it takes that configuration at times.

Ideal Human. Rich thinks that the "Z-DNA," as he calls it, may possibly be involved in cancer. Cancer-causing chemicals could more easily reach the exposed bases. The smooth spiral of DNA can change into the Z form at special sequences of bases, so a small number of such transformations could attract carcinogens and trigger the start of cancer. Rich also believes that genes may change from smooth to Z-DNA to turn themselves off in certain circumstances. "It's still like a new baby," he says. "We don't really know yet what it will grow up to be."

At the extreme of the new genetic research is the question of whether gene splicing could be used to create the ideal human being. Reputable scientists regard that prospect as fantasy. It is one thing to understand the basic blueprint written in the genes; it is quite another to translate the blueprint into an individual. In the formation of any organism, many gene products interact, and the circuitry is staggeringly complex. Besides, the final product of the genes—be it an Einstein or an idiot—is also shaped by environment. "Because of these complexities, . . . attempts to modify human beings through genetic manipulation is a policy of false eugenics. It will do more damage than it will anything else."

There is much that scientists don't know about DNA, and one tangential element of their rapidly advancing research troubles many of them. They fear that the commercial potential of their findings may hamper the flow of information that helps make research succeed. Traditionally, many important scientific ideas have arisen from free and informal contacts among researchers. The Cohen-Boyer collaboration that led to the first recombinant DNA breakthrough began over sandwiches during a lunch break at a biology symposium. "Scientists go off in the evenings and kick ideas around," says MIT's Sharp. "People who are being secretive won't participate and they'll suffer for it."

Ethics. The tantalizing lure of profits from recombinant DNA has already intruded on the sanctity of the academic lab. Scientists were shocked last year when Peter Seeburg, an assistant of John Baxter's at UCSF, left for Genentech and took with him some material to be used in producing growth hormone. Some researchers questioned the ethics of Seeburg's action, but he maintains that he had started the project and was entitled to the material and a share in any patent rights that might come from it.

The role of commercialism in DNA research may be decided soon by the U.S. Supreme Court. Last year, the Court agreed to decide whether new forms of life can be patented. If they can, a scientist and a company would be entitled to sell the resulting product exclusively for seventeen years. Should the Court rule against patents, some scientists fear that their colleagues will resort even further to secrecy. "I hope we will be able to go the patent route and publish freely," says a university biologist who is also associated with a private firm. But others find no benefit in this manner of exclusivity. "There is enough potential in the field that it doesn't need patent protection to stimulate activity," says MIT's Baltimore.

Research Standards. DNA research has attracted so much attention from the public, and from investors, that it has generated still another anxiety—what researchers call "science by press conference." Instead of presenting their work in traditional fashion to a scientific journal, where it can be "refereed" or evaluated by authorities before it is published, some scientists now rush their findings directly to the media. . . . Such premature announcement of results could reduce scientists' credibility and lower the standards of research. But many scientists remain confident that pure science and industry can work together. "Biologists have been unworldly," says Rich. "Chemists have been living in the commercial world for 50 years and still do exciting research."

To good scientists, research is exciting for its own sake. That's why they split atomic nuclei, listen to electronic impulses from the galaxies and fiddle with strands of DNA in the first place. Whether their discoveries simply add arcane footnotes to the scientific literature or launch whole new fields of industrial endeavor remains of secondary concern. The burgeoning gene research promises to do a great deal of both. It will lift the curtain further on the ultimate secrets of life on Earth. And it will also enrich the lives of the planet's restless inhabitants.

Robert L. Sinsheimer

Caution May Be an Essential Scientific Virtue

Experiment is always hazardous and requires careful risk-benefit analysis. Biologist Robert L. Sinsheimer urges extreme caution in the field of molecular research to stay within the limits of risk set by our societal moral sense. Like other biochemical questions discussed in Chapter 7, issues raised by recombinant DNA research have broad environmental, medical, legal, economic, and humanistic implications.

Troubled scientists and confused laymen may wish that the recombinant DNA issue would go away, but it will not. Mankind is about to extend its dominion by redirecting the course of biological evolution. Inevitably, this must change not only the world in which we live, but also the way in which science functions in it.

It is the success of science that has ended its pleasant isolation from the strident conflict of interests and the often passionate clash of values. The great discoveries in molecular and cellular biology—in particular the elucidation of the structure and functions of the nucleic acids—have provided us with a definitive understanding of the nature of life. Earlier in 'this century splendid discoveries in physics and chemistry provided us with a definitive understanding of the nature of matter. From that understanding has come the technology to reshape the inanimate world to human purpose—and many are less than pleased with the consequences. Now the description of life in molecular terms provides the beginnings of a technology to reshape the living world to human purpose—to reconstruct our fellow life forms, each, as are we, the product of three billion years of evolution—into projections of the human will. And many are profoundly troubled by the prospect.

With the advent of synthetic biology we leave the security of that web of evolutionary Nature that, blindly and strangely, bore us and all of our fellow creatures. With each step we will be increasingly on our own. The invention and introduction of new living forms may well be irreversible. How do we prevent grievous missteps, inherently unretraceable? Can we in truth foresee the consequences, near- and long-term, of our interventions?

Genes, composed of DNA, provide the basic molecular blueprints for the design of living organisms. The recombination of genes providing new arrangements of DNA has always been a mechanism for the generation of genetic diversity *within species* (and thus an essential factor in evolution). However, the new technology of "recombinant DNA" provides the capability to recombine genetic material from the *most diverse* species, i.e., to mix genes from animals and plants and microorganisms, and thereby to produce novel organisms not derived by the usual evolutionary processes.

I suggest that it is impossible to predict from present knowledge the properties of such organisms and therefore the consequences of their introduction into our biosphere. Most would probably be innocuous. Some could, by design and selection, become of very great value for human purpose. Others might possibly, inadvertently, become a considerable peril to present human, animal or plant life.

If these novel organisms could be fully contained while they were under study, there would be much less cause for concern. However, the recombinant DNA technology is currently feasible only in microorganisms and in particular in the organism *Escherichia coli,* a microbe indigenous to man, animals, soil and plants. The continued total containment of microorganisms has never been accomplished even under the most stringent conditions. The proposed use in the work of "crippled" bacterial strains with reduced likelihood of survival outside the laboratory is certainly a valuable precaution; however, pragmatically, I suggest that the likelihood of error, of accident, of culture contamination, etc., will inevitably frustrate the goal of total containment.

Because we are concerned here with self-reproducing organisms, this hazard has a novel and irreversible character. Once released, and finding an appropriate ecological niche, these organisms cannot be recalled nor their manufacture ceased. They will be with us potentially forever.

By our wits mankind has become the master of the extant living world. Will short-sighted ingenuity now spawn new competitors to bedevil us?

The apparent significance of the potential hazard of recombinant DNA depends markedly upon the perspective in which the issue is seen.

Viewed narrowly the potential hazard seems slight. Most of the novel microorganisms will likely be innocuous. A few, by careful design and selection, will be of value for human purposes. A few might inadvertently be perilous. The chance of release of these organisms is statistically small, although it can hardly be null. The chance of a series of events necessary to produce a plague seems slim in any one experiment.

Viewed broadly, however—over long years, in numerous environs, with countless experiments—a far larger penumbra of hazard appears.

We are ignorant of the probable consequences, near- and long-term, of crossing the well-developed barriers to genetic recombination between species. We, and all higher organisms, figuratively live immersed in a sea of microorganisms. Our intimate and inevitable interactions with these ubiquitous forms—some beneficial, some pathological—are, however, on the metabolic level, not at the genetic level. The introduction of genetic intercourse between microorganisms and higher organisms may provide opportunities for the subsequent evolution of new forms of pathogens and new modes of transmission of disease. If the diseases concerned have long latent periods (as do cancers or slow virus diseases) they might not become apparent until the causative organisms had become widely disseminated.

Because of these potential major hazards of likely low but, in truth, incalculable probability, I would advocate extreme caution in the development of research in this field. I suggest such research be restricted to a small number of laboratories providing the maximum possible containment, under supervision, to insure that all possible precautions are in fact employed.

I would also advocate the transition as rapidly as feasible of such research from the *Escherichia coli* organism to some other organism adapted by nature to survival in only a very restricted and extreme environment and far less intimately associated with man. It is only the reservoir of knowledge accumulated over the past 25 years concerning *Escherichia coli* that makes it the organism of choice. An extensive program of research could likely provide alternatives within a few years, if the delay is accepted and the effort is made.

We can have no assurance that science will not bring us into a more dangerous world. The search for knowledge has often been hazardous; many explorers have faced great perils. Now the hazards can encompass the planet. For our knowledge now gives us great power and we may not continue to rely upon the resilience of Nature to protect us from our follies.

New circumstances bring new perspectives. As scientists we have had the rare luxury to pursue truth, unconflicted by compassion. Caution has been an unfamiliar virtue, while boldness and curiosity have been hallowed.

As we cut free the strands of our inheritance, a different blend of virtues may be in order and other traditions may be helpful.

We should not underestimate these stakes, now and in time to come. We will need to establish in each time a sense of limits commensurate with our finite vision and shaped by our sense of the moral—limits within which we believe we can explore without fear and with decency and beyond which we ought to tread most gingerly. These limits will change continually as knowledge grows. In their definition and redefinition we should involve all who can help and respect all of those affected.

As scientists who seek to understand Nature we should not unthinkingly and irreversibly perturb it. As human beings we have a responsibility always to be concerned for our fellows and our fellow creatures and the future generations.

12 A Social Science Perspective: Research on Aging

Although they comprise only 10 percent of the population, older Americans bear a disproportionate burden of chronic illness and disability. Americans are living longer than ever, and the elderly, on the average, enjoy better health, but the problems are growing because their numbers are growing rapidly. Despite the increasing size of this minority, their situation in society is deteriorating in many ways. Advancing age requires a difficult transition in life at best. For most people it means sudden, often mandatory retirement, a substantial drop in income, and other social adjustments. This transformation is further hindered by the lack of support provided old people just at a time when they are required to give up their sources of income. We are living longer but feeling worse.

The problems of old age cannot be approached simply from the medical point of view. Experience demonstrates the integration between individuals and their environment—social, physical, and economic. In recent years social science research has uncovered major evidence about health and disease in old age. It has driven home the central character of social, economic, and family circumstances as major factors influencing the health of people over 65. We live in a society where a third of our old people survive at or near the poverty level. Their health is depleted by their living conditions.

The authors in this section comprise some of the major spokespersons for change in national policy concerning the elderly. They are also proponents of social science research to illuminate the causes of deteriorated health in old age. H. Jack Geiger, a physician who has demonstrated a long-term commitment to provide health care to the disadvantaged, presents a sober picture of the socioeconomic factors that influence the health of older Americans. He also describes current social epidemiological research that has critical implications for the health of people over 65. Sociologist Carroll L. Estes addresses policy issues that underlie the life circumstances of many old people in "The Social Construction of Reality." At the core of current policy lie certain assumptions about the aged that Dr. Estes challenges as both erroneous and inaccurate, and she demonstrates that these values and perceptions are behind the failure of many public programs.

Maggie Kuhn is a leader in the fight to amplify the voice of the aged. In her open letter to gerontology specialists, she calls for a new agenda in aging research, focusing on the socioeconomic structures affecting the aged. Too often the aged have been the objects of gerontological research, she observes, and "they are seen as problems rather than victims, persons experiencing problems created by society." She calls for new research methods, particularly to better understand the relationship of the individual to society.

Robert Butler represents the best example of American public service. As director of the National Institute on Aging, he has demonstrated a remarkable dedication to serving the nation's elderly. In "Questions on Health Care for the Aged," he reviews the needs of older people and discusses the government programs designed to respond to the growing gaps in services.

H. Jack Geiger

Health Policy, Social Policy, and the Health of the Aging: Prelude to a Decade of Disaster

Health does not depend on medical care alone; the quality of physical and social environments can also be major determinants of health. In the following article, Dr. H. Jack Geiger of the City College of New York cites research to illustrate the direct connection between inappropriate social policies and increased susceptibility to disease and premature death. The medical problems of aging citizens, often caused by low income, unemployment, and loss of a meaningful role in society, are exacerbated by fragmented, age-segregated medical services that fail to address the underlying problems. Geiger predicts that the health status of the aged will worsen unless public policymakers heed the results of social research and provide opportunities to maintain or develop independence, productivity, and social support systems.

There is a dreadful irony in the words with which Robert N. Butler launched *Why Survive? Being Old in America*—a book intended to change things. "As this book went to press [in 1975]," he wrote, "... the situation of the average older person was becoming increasingly desperate. In the past year food prices had risen 15 per cent, fuel a monstrous 45 per cent, housing 12 per cent, health costs 50 per cent—with no end in sight. Anxiety among all age groups was pervasive. Being old in America has become more difficult than ever. At the highest levels of government, there is talk of cutting social programs, and the Social Security program is being attacked; nor are there any immediate or imaginative programs in the making to mitigate the anomalous combination of inflation and recession."

That was five years ago. Inflation in food, fuel, housing and health care is worse. Recession is worse—indeed, recession has become the explicit goal of federal economic policy. At the highest levels of government, social programs *are* being cut—or cancelled outright. Social Security is under attack. Being old in America has become more difficult than ever.

It is these concerns—the social policies that determine the nature and quality of the social environment, the biological environment, the physical environment, rather than "health policy" narrowly defined in terms of the provision of medical care—that are central to any consideration of the health of elderly populations. For the aged in particular, medical care is important to the quality of life, but the absolute levels of well-being, illness and mortality are determined far more profoundly by what we eat, how we are housed, the extent to which we are sheltered from dangers in the physical and biological environments, and even more by whether or not we have work, are part of a supportive familial or social group, have a place in the general social order. For the elderly, then, social policy *is* health policy.

And social policy now, in my view, portends a decade of disaster for the health of older Americans, regardless of our ultimate actions in the area of medical care. Consider some of the "eight great needs of older adults" as defined by Congress in the 1981 White House Conference on Aging Act (S. 2850):

"1. There is a great need to improve the economic well-being of older individuals." Yet inflation, the single greatest threat to the health of the elderly, has passed 17 per cent annually and is heading for 20. The costs of food, housing and medical care have risen faster than the overall Consumer Price Index—but it is the CPI that determines the level of Social Security benefits. One in four elderly Americans now lives in poverty (the income level, $4931 per year for a family of two, is ludicrously, but officially, defined by the federal government as "near poverty"!). At 18 per cent inflation rates, a $10,000 annual pension will have only $5,000 in purchasing power in five years.

"2. There is a great need for expanding the availability of suitable and reasonably priced housing for older individuals, together with services needed for independent or semi-independent living." The federal government's own estimate is that 120,000 new housing units are needed each year for the population over 65; the federal government now provides assistance for the construction of 18,000 a year, and even that level is threatened by current budget-cutting campaigns. The 10 million older Americans now living in or near poverty presently must spend one-third of their budgets for housing and utilities alone; the likelihood is that this proportion will rise.

"3. There is a great need to promote greater employment opportunities for middle-aged and older individuals who want or need to work." The goal of present governmental anti-inflation strategies, however, is to create an "economic slowdown"—that is, to reduce jobs, increase unemployment, and therefore to increase a competition for jobs in which older citizens will inevitably fare poorly. At the same time, budget-cutting is intended to reduce supportive services to the unemployed and those on low incomes. Finally, unemployment will intensify a growing deadlock between the society as a whole and the elderly. At present, three workers are paying into pension systems for every retiree drawing a pension; in 50 years, by which time the United States will have 50 million persons over 65—a 50 per cent increase— the ratio will be only 2 to 1. Fewer persons working—and contributing—in the next decade will inevitably (and sharply) raise taxes to support Social Security and related benefits, and further the distorted image that the elderly are a national drain rather than a national resource.

It is not mere apocalyptic rhetoric to suggest that lower incomes, unemployment and loss of social validation as workers and contributors, poorer and more expensive housing, costlier food—and therefore less of it—and diminished support services will result in significantly higher morbidity and mortality rates for those over 65. Decades of public health experience validate the exquisite correlation between standard of living and mortality rate, and more recently macro-economic studies in the United States have begun to turn up specific correlations between economic depression and rates of institutionalization, mental hospital admissions, cardiovascular and renal disease, and the like.

But there is more—a body of brilliant work in social epidemiology that is beginning to point to an understanding of the health effects of variations in the social milieu. It has particular relevance (even poignance, as I hope to show) for the elderly; curiously, its special implications for those over 65 remain unexplored.

On the basis of numerous animal and human studies, epidemiologist John Cassell and his colleagues have constructed a general model for exploration of the relationships between changes in the social, biological and physical environments and the incidence of disease. There are, Cassell suggests, three general principles or hypotheses related to increased susceptibility to disease.

The first of the factors associated with increased susceptibility is social disorganization, as measured by any of a wide variety of indicators. Social or familial disorganization has been related to increased rates of tuberculosis, deaths from stroke, prevalence of hypertension, and coronary heart disease.

A second variable is domination and subordination. Not all members of a population, Cassell noted, are equally susceptible to social or familial disorganization. Systematic and regular differences have been observed in animal studies, with the more dominant animals showing the least deleterious health effects and the subordinate ones having the most extreme responses.

A third variable is the presence and effectiveness of protective factors— buffers which cushion the shock to the individual, in physiological or psychological terms, of social disorganization. These include social buffers—chief among which may be the nature and strength of the group supports provided to the individual.... In humans, small-group studies have shown that the degree of autonomic arousal which can be produced by requiring solutions to what in reality are insoluble tasks is more extreme if the group is made up of strangers than when it is made up of friends. Contemporary studies of the epidemiology of tuberculosis in the United States and Britain have shown that the disease occurs more frequently in "marginal" people—that is, people who for a variety of reasons are deprived of meaningful social contacts.

In sum, Cassell argues, the health consequences of social disorganization will not be universal, affecting all people in the same manner. A more adequate formulation would hold that such consequences would be dependent on:

—The importance or salience of the relationships that become disordered under conditions of social disorganization;

—The position of the individuals experiencing such disordered relationships in the status hierarchy;

—The degree to which the population under study has been unprepared by previous experience for this particular situation (i.e., has had insufficient time to adapt), and

—The nature and strength of the available group supports.

What is so striking about this list is its applicability to the probable consequences of present social policy for the elderly in the next five to ten years. If we hypothesize increased social disorganization—meaning unemployment, recession, continuing inflation—then it is a series of *central* relationships (those that center on work, housing and family) that are attacked in people whose webs of relationships have already grown limited and fragile. Further, the elderly are already subordinate in the status hierarchy, a minority suffering bitter oppression despite the fact that they constitute the one minority that we will all, ultimately, join. Finally, the availability and strength of group supports will simultaneously be diminished by the currently proposed reductions in social service programs.

Much of the work on which this model is based was done on migrant populations—in-migrants from other nations, rural-to-urban migrants within the United States, inter-regional migrants. Almost invariably, migrant populations were found to be more vulnerable—less prepared, perhaps, by previous experience, and given insufficient time to adapt. In this respect, I believe, we have made the transition to old age in the United States also a kind of migration—a last, poignant journey to a new social status, to subordination, to disordered relationships, relative social and economic deprivation—with little in the way of adequate preparation and with diminishing social and group support. Current social policy can only intensify this process—and *increase* ill health, disability, and premature death among the elderly.

It is against this background that one must turn, at last, to a consideration of health policy in its narrower sense, the provision and financing of medical care and related resources. It is, obviously, an area of particularly great importance to the elderly; although they comprise roughly 10 per cent of our population, the National Center for Health Statistics estimates that their health care costs account for about 30 per cent of the nation's spending for health services.

In superficial ways, the record looks good. Between 1966 and 1974, health care spending for the elderly more than tripled, from 7.9 billion dollars to 26.7 billion. In 1974, hospital care spending for the elderly totaled 12.6 billion dollars, of which more than 9 billion came from public funds; nursing home care cost 6.3 billion dollars, of which nearly half was publicly funded; and physician's services totaled approximately 4 billion dollars, of which some 2.5 billion was publicly funded. Yet during that same period, out-of-pocket spending for medical care by the elderly increased. What is more important, the pattern of expenditure does not mean that services fit or are appropriate to the needs of the elderly. Since 1969, Medicare's share of the total has been declining—and Medicare from the start has been oriented toward short-term rather than long-term care. Its provisions have been weakest on the ambulatory, preventive and related services required for chronic illness—yet 85 per cent of the elderly have chronic illness.

The spiraling costs have, inevitably, led to pressures for cost containment. But the probability is that—in an exact parallel to general social policy—medical cost-containment, like general budget-balancing, will take place on the backs of the poor and the elderly. Providers will defend high-cost acute-care technologies that have high income yields—thus the great push for selective catastrophic illness coverage, with its inevitable consequent proliferation of coronary care units, CT scanners, and the like. For ambulatory and preventive chronic illness services, coverages are likely to be reduced and provisions for "co-insurance" or "co-payment" (those marvelously deceptive public-relations terms! Has anyone ever been paid a co-salary?) will increase, despite good evidence of the probable effect:

"[According to a 1978 Rand Corporation study,] requiring a $1 copayment for physician visits appears to decrease the demand for ambulatory care by 8% and increase the demand for hospital inpatient services by 17% . . . there was a 3 to 8% increase in overall program costs. Thus, out-of-pocket payments for ambulatory services . . . could be self-defeating as a method of controlling costs."

It is, perhaps, unduly pessimistic to predict a decade of disaster in the health of America's elderly. But it is difficult to foresee any other consequence of social policies that increase susceptibility to disease and health policies that limit medical care responses at early, remediable stages of disease. Since all of us, obviously, will grow old, it is our own fates that we are now determining in our policy choices.

An everchanging, rhythmic biotic adventure of varying individuals, health is a part of the weave of life, coloring it brightly here and there, subtly shading it there, obvious in one place, obscure—almost lost—in another.

—Benjamin A. Kogan

Carroll L. Estes

The Social Construction of Reality: A Framework for Inquiry

Like Geiger, Carroll Estes, director of the National Aging Health Policy Center at the University of California, San Francisco, believes that many of the elderly's problems result from our conceptions of the aged. Estes analyzes the translation of this warped "social construction of reality" into an "aging enterprise"—the network of age-segregated agencies, programs, and businesses created by the Older Americans Act and related legislation. She argues that social, political, economic, and cultural factors are essential to understanding the true situation of the aged and developing realistic perceptions, strategies, and public policies for their (our) future.

> Today there is a cruel and ironic contradiction in the fate of our older citizens. Never before have older people been able to look forward to so many years of vitality. But never before have they been so firmly shouldered out of every significant role in life—in the family, in the world of work, and in the community.*

The major problems faced by the elderly in the United States are, in large measure, ones that are socially constructed as a result of our conceptions of aging and the aged. What is done for and about the elderly, as well as what we know about them, including knowledge gained from research, are products of our conceptions of aging. In an important sense, then, the major problems faced by the elderly are the ones we create for them.

The lot of these elderly persons, the length and quality of their lives, their participation in community affairs, and their personal levels of gratification are primarily determined by social forces. Although individual differences in such matters as inherited economic status, marital status, and racial and ethnic origins have their influence, the key determinants of the standard of living enjoyed or endured by the aged are national social and economic

---

*John W. Gardner, *No Easy Victories* (New York: Harper & Row, 1968), p. 153.

policies, political decisions at all levels of government, the power of various organized interest groups, and the policies of business and industry.

The policies that social institutions produce reflect the dominance of certain values and normative conceptions of social problems and their remedies. These value choices and definitions of existing conditions are not derived from consensual agreement of the members of society, nor do they result from happy compromises among those persons most affected by them. Some individuals and groups bring greater resources of class, status, and power to influence the definitions of social problems than do others. Although the aged themselves, for example, may attempt to influence socially determined priorities and the resultant public policies, they are only one among a growing number of groups that are vitally interested in determining policy choices on their behalf.

The Aging Enterprise

. . . This term describes the congeries of programs, organizations, bureaucracies, interest groups, trade associations, providers, industries, and professionals that serve the aged in one capacity or another. Major components include physicians, hospitals, the Social Security Administration, the Administration on Aging, state and area agencies on aging, congressional committees on aging, as well as the nursing home and insurance industries. The aging enterprise includes, but extends far beyond, the so-called aging network—a term coined to describe the many agencies spawned and funded under the Older Americans Act. In using the term *aging enterprise,* I hope to call particular attention to how the aging are often processed and treated as a commodity in our society and to the fact that the age-segregated policies that fuel the aging enterprise are socially divisive "solutions" that single out, stigmatize, and isolate the aged from the rest of society. . . . For us, the challenge is to make explicit how certain ways of thinking about the aged as a social problem (and the logical extension of these views into social policies) are rooted in the structure of social and power relations and how they reflect and bolster the social location of their adherents and proponents.

Ideology and Paradigm

One prominent ideology in American society defines old age as a problem characterized by special needs that require special policies and programs. This belief supports governmental interventions that separate the aged from the rest of society. This belief has had a powerful and pervasive influence on public policies for the aged. The second ideology fosters the belief that the democratic process is synonymous with interest-group bargaining and that the public interest is adequately represented in such processes. This belief system, in turn, justifies the determination of social policies for the aged largely as a consequence of interest-group accommodation among the agencies and professionals that make up the aging network. These two ideologies—separatism and pluralism—are at the core of American social policy for the aged.

Almost as important as ideology have been the paradigms used to define the problems of the elderly and specific solutions for them within the framework of federal policies, including the Older Americans Act. The impact of a dominant paradigm on perception is "one of reality definition" and provides a recipe that makes the problem routine by explaining it. Paradigms are the coherent frameworks in which disparate facts are ordered and related. As applied to social policies, the principal function of paradigms is to guide policy construction by organizing certain facts into causal theories that then specify appropriate policy interventions. Because they include problem definitions and the ordering of what is considered relevant and valid knowledge, paradigms limit intervention choices by systematically excluding consideration of alternative frameworks (or interventions). Paradigms themselves may take on the character of ideologies as well as reflect ideologies.

As defined in the Older Americans Act, the problem of the aged is seen as primarily one of fragmentation of services. The paradigm implicit in this definition limits the scope of intervention efforts and results in an emphasis on planning, coordination, and pooling of resources to create comprehensive service systems as the major solution. The vagueness and ambiguity implicit in such terms as *planning* and *pooling* has given different interest groups and professionals the opportunity to redefine the solution as falling within their own special domains of responsibility. In this process, the aged are perceived as dependent and in need of the special services prescribed and provided (largely) by these professionals.

Existing institutional and power relationships are maintained by a policy paradigm that imposes problem definitions that in turn legitimate the rationalization (through planning) and reorganization (through coordination) of existing services. The inherent contradiction of such a paradigm is that it cannot solve the problems of the aged because it never addresses them. The vague mandates, constricted programs, and measured appropriations of the Older Americans Act have resulted in services that reach only a small percentage of the elderly. The contrast between the sweeping objectives of the Older Americans Act and the limited authority provided to the Administration on Aging and other agencies created and supported under the act points to the symbolic nature of the act. This symbolism is not inconsequential, however, in that it generates rising expectations and demands, thereby expanding the resource base of organizational service providers, while simultaneously confusing the public and, most importantly, the aged themselves as to the realistic potential for American social policy to alter their social status and improve their condition.

The Social Construction of Reality

For the past thirty years research on the problems of the aged has focused largely on the individual and the adjustment of the individual to circumstances that for the most part were externally determined. Equally important has been the interpretation of research results. Knowledge is socially generated; it emerges from the ordering and interpretation of facts. It may be accepted as factually legitimate, based upon empirical demonstrations of proof or upon the judgments of proclaimed experts and authorities who possess status and power. The less the knowledge base is empirically proven, the greater the influence of social and political factors in the interpretation and acceptance of data as knowledge.

As definitions of reality become widely shared, they are institutionalized as part of the "collective stock of knowledge." Although socially generated, such knowledge and expert opinion take on the character of objective reality, regardless of inherent validity. This "knowledge," in turn, heavily influences both the perception of social problems and ideas on how to deal with them. It is in this sense that the aged have only the social problems that have been "given" them by society. Thus, social researchers and others involved in the design and implementation of intervention programs are not neutral in their influence. "Rather, they are actively engaged in modifying and structuring social reality for the aged."

Theories of Aging. Although empirical research in aging provides a partial basis for policy development, even more important is the potential contribution of gerontological theory to the underlying rationale for those policies. Because social scientists, as well as policy makers and other elites, contribute to social constructions of reality, the production of gerontological knowledge and its role in public policies deserves careful study—particularly in light of the sociological observation that empirical and theoretical advances occur as a consequence of the interaction between (1) technical development and elaboration (research methodologies, empirical findings, and knowledge) and (2) extratechnical sources, such as changes in sentiments, in background assumptions, and in the personal realities of scientists and those around them. This central point, that there are nonobjective social and political bases to development of knowledge and ideas, should be kept in mind as we discuss some prominent theories in aging because the ideas advanced in these theories may shape or justify social policies for the aged.

Since the early 1960s, four major social theories of aging have emerged. In order of their development, they are: (1) disengagement theory, (2) activity theory, (3) developmental theory, and (4) symbolic interactionist theory. Disengagement theory postulates the mutual withdrawal of the aging individual and society. Described as intrinsic to the process of aging and beneficial for both society and the aged individual, disengagement theoretically functions to prepare society for the replacement of its members when they die. At the same time, this process is said to assist the individual in preparing for his or her own death. . . .

In contrast to disengagement theory, activity theory holds that high levels of social activity result in high morale and life satisfaction. . . . This theory views older people as aging successfully if they continue (or replace) their social involvement. . . .

The developmental or life-cycle theory stresses the psychological or personality aspects of the aging process. One of its basic tenets is that persons, young and old, are not alike and have their own personalities and styles of living. . . . Some adherents of the theory argue that with age, individuals gain a greater sense of freedom to do what they want, while caring less about what others think. Therefore, there are many ways of growing old, just as there are many ways of becoming adolescent or middle aged. Policy based on developmental theory could rationalize the continuance of laissez-faire approaches to problem solving. A logical extension of this idea might be that concerted policy interventions are unnecessary or not feasible because of the multiple variations in the aging process of different individuals.

Finally, the symbolic interactionist view of aging . . . argues that it is possible for the interactional context and process (the environment, the persons, and encounters in it) to significantly affect the kind of aging process a person will experience; changes in the interactional variable may produce results that are erroneously attributed to inherent maturational changes. Disengagement, low self-esteem, and dissatisfaction are seen as resulting from the interpretations and meanings generated in encounters between the aged and others. Both the self and society are seen as capable of creating new alternatives. . . . Because symbolic interactionism focuses on both environment and individual, one policy emphasis might be on interventions that seek to modify environmental constraints (for example, the elimination of age discrimination in employment) and another on those directed to the needs of the individual, such as Medicare.

Each of these theories has been criticized on theoretical and methodological grounds, and their empirical support is either weak or incomplete. . . . None of these theoretical approaches has accorded sufficient attention to the social, economic, and political conditions that dramatically affect not only the elderly but those of all ages. The inadequacy of much of the research on old age comes from its focus on what old people do rather than on the social conditions and policies that cause them to act as they do. . . .

The social construction of reality perspective provides several useful insights: The experience of old age is dependent in large part upon how others react to the aged; that is, social context and cultural meanings are important. Meanings are crucial in influencing how growing old is experienced by the aging in any given society; these meanings are shaped through interaction of the aged with the individuals, organizations, and institutions that comprise the social context. Social context, however, incorporates not only situational events and interactional opportunities but also structural constraints that limit the range of possible interaction and the degree of understanding, reinforcing certain lines of action while barring others.

Older persons individually are powerless to alter their social status and condition because their problems and appropriate remedies are socially defined, largely by the dominant members of society. Since the labels and definitions applied to any group in society result from reciprocal relationships in which the relative power, class, and social standing of interactants play a part, the aged cannot unilaterally alter their relationship to the rest of society. . . .

The Political Economy and the Definition of the Problems of the Aged

Political and economic conditions affect how social problems, including the problems of the aged, are defined and treated. Or, to put it more directly, the state of the economy influences social policies. For example, when the economy is expanding, optimism abounds and resources for dealing with social problems are likely to increase. Conversely, in times of economic restraint, less costly, limited, and in fact inadequate social programs tend to be produced, and their predictable failure then provides a rationale for debunking efforts at social change and for limiting additional resource investments for the disadvantaged. Such government policy contractions occur precisely when the disadvantaged are hardest hit by the same deteriorating economic conditions that foster the retrenchment policies. . . .

If inflation and a no-growth economy persist, social problem definitions and social policies will increasingly reflect these conditions. Continuation of the current fiscal crisis, both in America and worldwide, will likely engender a lowering of public expenditures for welfare programs in the face of strong counterpressures to protect individual spending power by maintaining current levels of personal disposable income. Hence, social problems of the aged in the late 1970s and into the 1980s will probably be defined in terms of an orientation with disengagement theory that is geared toward individual pathologies and the functional incapacity of the aged. This would be consistent with the return to policy trends that emphasize individual responsibility and productivity. The 1978 Older Americans Act reauthorization includes, for example, a mandate for the Administration on Aging to develop and demonstrate long-term care services. The growing concern with the elderly who are in frail health also reflects this shift in emphasis—to label aging as primarily a problem of personal functioning is to deny recognition of the aggregate marginal economic and social status of the aged, while drawing attention to individual problems. Such a reorientation provides the necessary market development for an expanded service economy. . . . At the same time, such policies demonstrate political responsiveness to the anticipated demographic explosion of the elderly and their growing political organization. . . .

The conservative role of social science has been a sore point for the Gray Panthers, as illustrated by their public and somewhat bitter criticism of the profession of gerontology: "Gerontology has assumed the deterioration of the aged, and has attempted to describe it in terms which ignore the social and economic factors which in large measure precipitate that deterioration. By reifying the attribute 'old,' gerontology reinforces societal attitudes which view older people as stuck in an inevitable chronological destiny of decay and deterioration. . . . When persons who are old, poor, and stigmatized by society become objects of gerontological research, they are seen as problems to society, rather than as persons experiencing problems created by the society. The natural result of such research is to suggest ways in which older people may adjust to society, rather than how society might be changed to adjust to the needs of older people." The efforts of the Gray Panthers and other aging-based organizations to confront and redirect societal processing and treatment of the aged are critical to the very necessary construction of a new reality about old age. . . . Aging is something that is done to the chronologically old; that is to say, aging "is not a biological transformation . . . it is a political transformation.". . .

Since the labels and definitions applied to any group in society result from reciprocal relationships in which the relative power, class, and social status of interactants play a part, the aged cannot unilaterally alter their relationship to the rest of the society. Nevertheless, the active resistance of the elderly to labels applied to them may contribute to altering the unjust treatment so often accorded them. And as noted by Geiger, current attitudes toward the aged, far from appearing by accident, are "a product of a social structure and a political economy that disposes of people as if there were not enough economically productive work to go around."

Strategies for the Future

What then can we say about the requisite construction of a new reality about old age? It calls for a new perception of old age and a clear understanding of the social, economic, political, and cultural factors that create the very problems now being assiduously discovered by social scientists and policy makers. It calls for a new research agenda as well. Without knowledge about those facets of old age that are socially produced and more knowledge about economic contributions and consequences of aging in the United States, policies for and attitudes toward the aged are likely to continue as symbolic gestures aiding the structural interests that dominate the political scene. It calls for an appreciation which a true "sociology of knowledge" in gerontology might provide in understanding the scholar's and policy maker's contribution to the transformation of objective conditions into public problems and policies. Further, and even more important, it calls for a true "sociology of knowledge" in gerontology that would make it possible to understand how the scholar and policy maker transform objective conditions into public problems and policies. . . .

The long-range goal must be policies that provide for an adequate income, a job, decent housing, and health care; that alter the objective condition of the aged; and that change the social processes by which social policies are made and implemented in such a way that the public interests, rather than private special interests, are served. To accomplish these objectives requires the development of a comprehensive national policy on aging that does not segregate the elderly, stigmatize them or place them in a dependent and depersonalized status. To achieve such a national policy will require basic changes in our values, in our attitudes, in our behavior, and in our actions toward the elderly.

The choices are clear. It is time that America became dedicated to the task of transforming old age itself and, in the process, to dismantling the aging enterprise.

Margaret "Maggie" E. Kuhn

An Open Letter

The National Convenor of the Gray Panthers, a coalition of old and young activists working for social change for the elderly, challenges traditional theories on aging. She recommends a radical redefinition of gerontology (the study of the physiological and disease processes associated with aging) and extensive social science research on age-related issues such as "victim-blaming," age-segregated services, and self-help and advocacy models. The Gray Panthers see an urgent need for social analysis based on new research exploring interactions between societal values and the personal problems of the aged.

The argument in this letter is for a radical gerontology which goes beyond the usual social division of sex, race, and age. I believe its scope should reach beyond "life satisfaction adjustment" to the structural conditioning and constraints of society, and to the forces that improve and enhance the quality of life and make society more humane and just.

It seems important . . . to make implicit at the outset those constraints in the institution of gerontology which mitigate against any radical reordering of social and economic priorities. As Robert Binstock has so frequently observed with reference to aging-based organizations, "the very incentive systems that create and sustain their organizational viability—the interest of their members and the pursuit of their trades and professions—preclude them from testing the extent of their power to achieve fundamental changes for the aging."

Out of experiential knowledge of what it means to grow up and grow old in a postindustrial, "serviced" society we suggested some of the concrete ways in which these constraints appear in the content and direction of gerontological research as well as in teaching of gerontology. We propose them for continued reflection and response. . . .

1. Social gerontology tends to focus on the individual, to the neglect of the socioeconomic structures and forces that segregate, stereotype and victimize old people. Public issues and controversies are often reduced to private problems and complaints and dealt with by a social service shotgun approach that fails to reach those most desperately in need; and actually has a disabling

effect on the near poor by increasing and perpetuating dependency and powerlessness.

Segregated services in senior centers and meal sites under the Older Americans Act and segregated "202" housing programs, though well-intentioned, separate old people from other groups which have been victimized by the malaise of the social order and block possibilities for help in fighting the social system. Such segregated programs and narrowly defined interests virtually guarantee a future backlash by the young.

In a review of the state of the sociology of aging in 1971, Shanas admits that "much of the recent work is concerned with how old persons are integrated into the social system and how family, friends and work serve to effect such integration." A number of investigations of the aging process emphasize "re-orderings of thought and personality independent of social and other environmental events."

Our Gray Panther analysis views the economic system as failing and suffering from a pervasive malaise that mandates fundamental change. Age-segregated services continue to proliferate without recognition of the social isolation and alienation such practices create.

2. Gerontology has sought to identify ways in which old people can adjust to, and become integrated into, existing social systems with the assumption that the system is basically *good* and that its minor flaws can be eliminated by more "gerontological tinkering." When persons who are old, poor, and stigmatized by society become objects of gerontological research they are seen as problems to society, rather than as victims, persons experiencing problems created by the society. The natural result of such research is to seek ways in which old people may adjust to society, rather than how society might be humanized and changed to adjust to the needs of old people. For adjustment, victims obviously need services.

In modern societies services and human relations have become salable products in order to provide profits, jobs for professionals, and capital accumulation for investment. Services also give government bureaus a favorable public image and popular support. The grants which gerontologists receive for research, demonstration projects, the development of new services and service delivery systems often benefit gerontologists and the institutions they serve: not the victims of the system. The researchers applying for grants give little attention to the dissemination of the findings, or their application to policy and practice.

To the extent that gerontologists fail to challenge the system and its social controls, they become agents of social control for older people.

We submit that pioneering studies are needed to:

a. examine the social consequences of "victim blaming" (making the victim of society's injustices "the problem");
b. identify experimental new models of self-help and advocacy;
c. evaluate effectiveness of existing networks of service under the Older Americans Act, etc.;
d. critique the long-term effects of age-segregated services.

We stand by the statement that:

> The government-funded *service delivery* system to older people has been designed in such a way as to foster, on the one hand, a self-perpetuating service delivery network and, on the other hand, a client population that is increasingly dependent on that system for food, recreation, housing, transportation, and similar programs of social welfare. Since the service system exists at the behest of the provider of services rather than the consumer, it is not surprising that it serves primarily the needs of practicing gerontologists and only secondarily those of older people.

3. Gerontology has certain unadmitted preconceptions about old people which reflect the class interests and biases of middle-class educated professionals. These biases are reflected by the gerontological societies as they attempt to meet the needs of several thousand prolific professionals in search of publication, a grant, or professional identity.

Gray Panthers and gerontologists alike have middle-class roots. We need to help each other to move beyond our own class interests to what is, or ought to be, the larger public interest. All of us need to recognize how our goals and attitudes are determined by economic and political structures. This correspondent believes that research as well as advocacy groups would benefit from forthright and vigorous self-criticism, and recognition of the extent to which all of us are conditioned by the prevailing values and priorities of an acquisitive, profit-centered society.

4. There is an urgent need for new research methods, particularly to demonstrate the interaction between the individual and society and to make full use of the experience of old people to form the widest possible data base for radical social analysis. Gray Panthers press for studies and action/research which move beyond developmental psychology to economic political factors and present viable alternatives to the current styles of research.

The new subjects of research should focus on the power elites, the knowledge definers, pharmaceutical houses, the media or the heads of granting agencies. More studies are urgently needed to evaluate the extent to which old people can control and/or provide input in the formulation and implementation of policies and services which purport to "serve the elderly." More research in analyzing and evaluating major age-related social policies in the United States. . . .

As a coalition of youth and age Gray Panthers are not crying for more "goodies" for old people. We are working for basic social change to improve the quality of life for people of all ages. Gray Panthers . . . have been following with great interest the emergence of a radical gerontology which is challenging existing goals, paradigms and methodologies. Participatory radicalism offers a way to work *with* the oppressed rather than *for* the bureaucratic world which *regulates* the oppressed and determines the condition for their survival.

The new life we seek for old people and for all other oppressed and stigmatized minorities will not be secured without basic change in the whole society! The basic social change we envision begins with the thinking of the researchers and scientists who give depth and meaning to social analysis and point to the shape of things to come. We look for some awareness on the part of researchers and advocates of the social consequence of the questions they ask, and a genuine concern for the nature and shape of the future.

We cherish the hope that the continuing dialogue and analysis will make clear what we can do together to address the need for change in Western Society.

Sincerely,

Maggie Kuhn
National Convener
The Gray Panthers

Robert N. Butler

Questions on Health Care for the Aged

As the proportion of old people in the United States increases, the director of the National Institute on Aging (NIA), Robert N. Butler, calls for research toward understanding "our future selves." Research subjects include institutional and home care, nutritional services, housing, transportation, communications, reimbursement, and a variety of issues related to the quality and accessibility of health care. New data provided by research, he argues, will facilitate realistic planning and policies for the comprehensive services needed by the aged.

W hen the National Institute on Aging was created in 1974, Congress required that it develop a comprehensive plan for aging research for use throughout the Department of Health, Education, and Welfare. This was prepared with the assistance of the National Advisory Council on Aging and was titled *Our Future Selves: A Research Plan Toward Understanding Aging,* to remind readers that aging cannot be discussed in entirely objective terms, that everyone who lives will someday be old.

This paper presents selections from the plan which may be useful in establishing national health goals and standards and in guiding the programs of local health planning agencies. The paper is designed to encourage more research on the aging process with the ultimate hope of leading to a more decent and dignified old age for all.

Nations prize longevity and regard it as an outstanding accomplishment when the majority of their citizens live to old age. Average life expectancy, or average age at death, may be regarded as one of the most important indices of social health and overall quality of life within a society. This nation, however, has not been prepared for the "sudden" appearance of large numbers of elderly people.

Our aging society has brought with it a certain proportion of older persons who suffer from poverty, preventable illness, and social isolation. These persons, who can be termed the needy aged, create acute problems in the fields of social and health care. But broader issues stem from the needs of all individuals to adjust to the new rhythms of life that come with increased longevity; to new social phenomena such as multigenerational families, retirement, increased leisure, and changing health status; and to the new opportunities and new problems of adaptation that accompany a long life. And for the society at large, innumerable policy questions arise as the whole social fabric accommodates itself to the changing age distribution.

. . . On the one hand, there are increasing number of the "young-old," persons in their 60's and early 70's who are relatively healthy and vigorous, a large number of whom are retired, who seek for themselves meaningful ways to use their time, either in self-fulfillment or in community participation, and who represent a great resource of talent for society. On the other hand, there is an even more dramatic increase in the proportion of the elderly population which might be termed the "old-old." This comprises persons in their mid 70's, 80's, and 90's, an increasing majority of whom remain vigorous and active but a majority of whom need a wide range of supportive and restorative health and social services.

For historical reasons, the old-old of today represent a disproportionately disadvantaged group. Many were immigrants who came to this country with little formal education; many worked most of their lives at low-skill occupations; many lost their occupational moorings during the Great Depression and did not recoup in the period of prosperity ushered in by World War II, nor did they build up sizable equities under the Social Security program as it developed during the 1940's and 1950's.

In succeeding decades, more and more older people will have been native-born, will have grown up in urban areas, and will have had high school and college educations, will hopefully have been spared from widespread economic catastrophe and will benefit from pension programs, social security, and government service programs of all types. Thus the persons growing old in the future will probably have very different characteristics from those who are presently old.

These different characteristics will in turn lead to vastly differing expectations, and as a consequence there is an urgent need to plan for the future aged as well as for those who are now old.

The need for planning health services is particularly critical.

In general, older people are less healthy and therefore utilize health services more frequently than younger people, at great expense both to themselves and to the health system. Per capita expenditures for health care for those over 65 are six times higher than for children, and almost three times higher than for adults under 65. Two-thirds of their medical and other care expenses of the old are borne by the government, but the residual one-third—amounting to nearly $475 annually per capita—is greater than out-of-pocket expenses for younger groups. In relation to their income, of course, the elderly spend much more for health care on the average than do younger persons.

So far as the health system is concerned, those over 65 require more support and more services than other groups. Constituting only a little more than 10 percent of the population, they occupy a third of all short-stay hospital beds and two-thirds of long-term care facilities. One-half of all government expenditures for personal health care are spent on their behalf.

There are humane as well as economic losses resulting from unnecessary institutionalization of the elderly. Good nursing home care (and some that is not so good) now costs about $50 per day. About a million persons over 65 live in nursing homes. If one-tenth of these patients were able to remain in the community, this country would be saving one billion dollars per year; more important, it would be providing these old people with better lives.

The Aged in Society

In contrast to prevailing myth, most of the "normal" aged—70–75 percent of those over 65 years of age—are intellectually and socially able, productive (given the opportunity), mentally vigorous, interested in their surroundings, eager to participate in the social life of their family, kin, and community. Where there are decrements and apparent declines, the cause is not necessarily the biological process of aging. Rather, the individual may be suffering from other, often controllable impositions only partially related to age—disease, social isolation, poor diet, limited education, economic plight. The inability of some aged persons to cope intellectually and socially is usually due to stresses *associated* with aging rather than *caused* by it. This view, that at least some declines are not inexorably bound to the normal pattern of human development, forces the conclusion that it is possible to prevent or treat many of the intellectual, social, and emotional problems of a significant proportion of the aged population. Moreover, it emphasizes the ability of many of the aged, given the opportunity, to lead independent, self-sustaining, and satisfying lives.

The integration of the older person in society is the norm rather than the exception, as evidenced by the fact that a substantial majority of the aged are intellectually and socially competent. Only a small fraction of the aged are institutionalized. A significant number of the aged who are able to participate socially are excluded, for a variety of reasons ranging from apparent disability or illness to a latent prejudice against any aged person. How the aged respond to stress—illness, deep grief, financial strains—is largely a function of their experience in life. It has little to do with age or aging *per se*. Rather, the capacity to cope depends primarily on education, work patterns, family—all the elements that structure one's life, modulate it, and give it meaning.

The fact that individuality is maintained into very old age requires that effective programs for the elderly provide a wide range of options—in education, in work and leisure, in housing and living arrangements, in social and health services. Pervading these policy considerations is the fact, established by social research, that all modern developed societies have the wherewithal, even with shifting proportions of workers and retirees, to maintain adequate income for the elderly and finance essential services for those who need them. The willingness to do these things is another matter; it is dependent on political judgment, cultural values, national priorities, and principles of equity.

Finally, an issue posing very difficult questions is the ability of modern medical technology to modulate, if not control, the process of dying. Rising concerns generated by humanistic and personal insights have prompted clinical, educational, and other research programs to help seriously impaired or dying individuals and their families. Ethical and scientific issues concerned with the definition of death and the use of technology to prolong life are also emerging in the wake of this new technology.

Health and Human Services and Delivery Systems

Older persons must have access to an effective network of facilities, programs and services to survive short-term crises and meet long-term needs. Without these supports many lose their capacity to live independently or semi-independently in their own homes or communities.

Services for people in the United States are provided by a pluralistic system of government (Federal, State and municipal), private nonprofit (voluntary), and commercial agencies. But many of these agencies have not developed programs that meet the special needs of the aged. For example, the elderly are commonly not provided preventive medical services such as early diagnosis and treatment that can forestall new problems.

Services have frequently been separately developed or legislated with no planned relationship between one system or set of resources and another, with conflicting legislative language, regulations, and funding policies and practices, ambiguous objectives and incongruence between agency or program goals and the needs of older persons.

Given the varied and changing needs of the aged, programs of health and social care must be comprehensive, providing resources ranging from simple information to direct services needed to maintain physical and mental functioning. The design and the evaluation of effective, truly comprehensive programs must be based on systematic, well-planned research and analysis.

Research has been or is being done in several service areas of particular pertinence to the elderly: physical, mental, and dental health; nutrition and food services; physical living environments; employment and other economic supports; the commercial marketplace; transportation; communication; social services; legal and physical protection; education; civic participation; leisure and recreation; and spiritual well-being.

These studies have led to a number of findings that can be usefully applied to improve the quality of health care and service delivery to the aged:

Medical care. Medical knowledge and techniques are available to ameliorate many of the illnesses of late life. But existing health-care systems are organized primarily to deal with acute, episodic illnesses in hospital settings. Institutional health care systems are, by and large, not linked to community-based systems for primary, preventive, rehabilitative or supportive care, although such arrangements are particularly suited to the need for the long-term care of many older citizens. Compounding the lack of adequate facilities for the care of the aged is the fact that medical education does not provide an adequate basis for modern geriatric care. . . .

Comprehensive services. To respond to the growing needs of today's aged and the increasing number of future aged, research in the delivery of comprehensive services is imperative. No community in the United States has a full range of services for the aged, and limited social experiments have not adequately documented the optimum range and mix of health and social care programs. While many of the findings of these experiments have been useful in planning and policy development, what we do know is small compared to what we do not know.

Studies of options for providing continuing of care, including preventive and rehabilitative care and methods for organizing and financing services and their delivery, have yet to be conducted. Two promising models for experimentation are (1) "one-stop" centers, perhaps sited at specially designed housing for the elderly, to which the elderly can come with a minimum of travel and inconvenience and (2) a new type of "health maintenance organization" for older people that provides physician and mental health care, social services, financial assistance, and aides for those who need help with personal and household services.

Studies of these and other models could address such questions as: What are suitable mixes of a range of services? What impact does integration of services have on the older individual? How does integration affect use of services and cost efficiency? What is the role of voluntary groups and agencies? What is the appropriate role of family, ethnic and neighborhood groups in the provision of services? What is the cost and effectiveness of alternative models of service delivery?

Data. Data are needed on what services do exist, their adequacy and gaps, which are and are not used, and who in the population uses them. More exact demographic and epidemiologic information about population trends is also needed to anticipate and prepare for services needed by the future aged, who are ourselves.

Health is a continuing property in the sense that it is present from the ovum until death; it does not disappear during an illness to return on recovery, but the level of health changes throughout life.
                                                        —*J. R. Audy and F. L. Dunn*

Part

V Who Is Calling the Shots?

I mprovements in the health of the American people will require collective action to combat basic social, economic, environmental, and political barriers in modern society. In addition, it will be necessary for individuals to take personal action on their own behalf to safeguard their health and the health of their families. Improvements in our health are also critically dependent on biological, behavioral, and social sciences research—to identify the causes of disease, to find effective ways to prevent and treat disease, and to make the advances available to vast numbers of people. The past, too, has a great deal to teach us. What have we learned in the past few decades that permits some reasonable predictions about the future of health care and the health of Americans in the 1980s?

We pause here to look at current patterns that will affect the health of future generations, as well as to look at signposts that we should heed now, for our own good health. We consider first the politics of health in Chapter 13. Increasingly, decisions made in this sphere dramatically affect our daily lives. However, few of us realize who pulls the strings in the life-and-death circumstances of our society. In Chapter 14 we assess our roles as individuals in caring for ourselves. Can we regain the power over our health that has been abdicated to doctors, hospitals, drugs, and institutions? We close our book, in Chapter 15, with a look at the future of health care in American society, focusing especially on assessing the roles of individuals, the government, and the medical establishment.

13 The Politics of Health

UPI PHOTO

Americans place great trust in their health care providers, in the insurance companies that pay for much of their care, and in the government that regulates, oversees, and, to a great extent, finances the system. In Chapter 13, we will take a look, in one sense, at the "underbelly" of this system: the struggle for power, money, and control of various aspects of health services by a variety of special-interest groups. Underneath the regulations and legislation is a power struggle, the outcome of which ultimately determines the quality of services we receive. It decides who will care for us, when, where, and how; the method by which we will pay for care; where hospitals will be located, their size and facilities. It has great influence on health professions education, and it determines the scope and direction of research.

On the surface, it appears that these decisions emanate from the government. But in reality policymakers take their cues for health care legislation and regulation from a variety of sources. Historically, some special-interest groups, such as physicians, have been able virtually to dictate policy in specific areas. This is beginning to change as more and more interest groups appear on the scene and as consumers take a more active role in attaining public accountability. The four most powerful interest groups are physicians, hospitals, insurance companies, and the drug industry. There are also lobbying groups for dentists, nurses, and many other health professions; for nursing homes and other institutions; for labor and business groups; and for many other participants in the health care arena. While these groups participate in the high quality care we receive, they also are helping to ensure that their own interests are served.

The result of the political process is a fragmented system with diffused energy, often at odds with itself and with the people it is supposed to serve. Rosemary Stevens, of the University of Pennsylvania, in "The Federal Government and the Health Care System," describes the historical factors that have helped to shape the current maze of federal programs that constitute our "nonsystem." She argues that we are heading toward a quagmire of national health insurance that may cause us to lose sight of patient protection and public accountability for all time. Political analyst Douglass Cater, in "Politics of Health: An Overview," expands on Stevens's theme with the notion of a subgovernment of health, which includes policymakers, bureaucrats, and

416

interest groups. Its components often seem to work at cross purposes and to prohibit efforts at a rational health strategy.

Paul Ward's article, "Health Lobbies: Vested Interests and Pressure Politics," takes a detailed look at the special-interest groups that are behind the scenes in policymaking. Vice-chairman of the American Hospital Association's Council on Planning and Management, he views these lobbying activities as an essential dimension of the system, and he has confidence that their guidance will benefit consumers.

Rosemary Stevens

The Federal Government and the Health Care System

More than two hundred federal agencies and departments have uncoordinated and distinctive roles in the provision of the nation's health care. Rosemary Stevens of the University of Pennsylvania illustrates the inflationary effects of the federal role on an already pluralistic, independent health system and argues that we need a more rationalized system of health services. In exploring the boundaries of federal responsibility, Stevens raises questions about public commitment to health care, appropriate participation of government in the development of local services, and the need for a coordinated federal effort in a nationally organized health system.

In other advanced Western countries in the last two or three decades, the development of governmental schemes of health financing has implied an acceptance of national governmental responsibility for the organization of health services. . . .

Rising costs of medical care have begun to provoke middle-class support of proposals for national health insurance. . . . Of itself, however, national health insurance, like Medicare and Medicaid, could serve to increase further both the demand for services, and their costs, in an inflationary spiral, rather than necessarily affect the operation of the health care system. It is in the latter that reform is now chiefly needed. Change is demanded not primarily to take a great leap forward in creating a new health system . . . but by rationalizing, at all governmental and community levels, the unwieldy accretions of programs and services which are already in existence.

The Federal Health Establishment

The pattern of medical care in the United States twenty years from now may not be one of federal domination of health services, in the sense of a monolithic or centralized governmental health service, as in England. Neverthe-

418

less, the key to health services organization is inevitably the present and future actions taken by the federal government. . . .

A direct outcome of a historically weak federal role has been the diffusion of health subsidies over a patchwork of legislation dealing with federal health assistance and service programs. Pockets of federal action are now scattered across 221 different federal agencies and departments. These represent, moreover, a series of distinct approaches as to what the federal role should be. . . . Each program is administered in its own pocket of operations, in the context of its own piece of legislation and its own congressional committees. The disconnections of the federal bureaucracy in health can be readily appreciated by anyone who has attempted to compile a list of all federal involvement in specific health activities or has asked the governmental switchboard for general information. While there are now national centers for health statistics, health services research and development, social statistics, and social security research and information, there is still no central informational service nor ongoing analysis of all federal health programs. . . .

From the viewpoint of the city or neighborhood, the federal health establishment offers a maze of almost incredible entanglement. It is difficult, if not impossible, for local citizen groups or groups of physicians or other health service providers to develop a well-integrated health service scheme for an area or neighborhood which would utilize all appropriate governmental resources now available. Suppose, for example, that a far-seeing group of concerned politicians, physicians, community leaders, and others decides to develop a cluster of interrelated neighborhood health services which would include a health center providing all income groups in the population with a wide variety of specialist services, dental care, community health and home health services, special services for maternity and infant care and for children and youths, school health services and health education, out-of-hospital mental health programs, day hospital facilities for the old and sick, and physical, mental, and vocational rehabilitation services. To do this, they would need help in raising the initial capital and some operating subsidy with respect to services for the poor. Elements of all of these services are eligible for governmental grant or subsidy. Such is the number of agencies and programs involved, however, each with differing requirements in terms of the form and routine of application, the amount of matching funds required, the requirements for participation in the program, the scrutiny of perhaps a score of independent grant-reviewing groups and so on, that any major attempt to link the programs together as one unit is doomed to frustration, at least as yet.

. . . While the government role has been expanding it has been doing so through setting up a series of programs which rarely take account of other programs. Each new program, while extending the range of available services, has added to the system new requirements, qualifications, and barriers, or (like Medicare) has had inflationary characteristics. Programs for resource development and coordination, particularly regional medical programs and comprehensive health planning, have not yet had the funding to influence existing patterns. The mentally sick go to one building, the poor to another, veterans to a third—all set up under the influence of federal funding; yet avoidance of fragmentation has been very low on the priority list of the federal medical establishment. Diffuse responsibility at the federal level has if anything led to ever increased diffusion of services locally.

Boundaries of Federal Responsibility

Organizational diffusion is of course not necessarily undesirable; it may denote a richness of experiment with new forms of service, allow individual patients to have a wide choice of different facilities, and offer the opportunity for constructive competition among various health care schemes, organizations, and agencies. National planning is not necessarily a valid criterion for efficiency. Well-organized neighborhood, citywide, or multicity health systems, whether under public or private auspices, may offer services which are far superior to any nationally organized service system. The experience of independent health insurance plans built around group medical practices, offering a wide range of health services to a defined population, has demonstrated the feasibility in the United States of the development of health services of good quality and reasonable cost through private initiative and effort. . . . For most people in the United States . . . the assumptions on which medical care is provided have not changed since World War I, when there were similar discussions of the need to coordinate the health care system as well as to finance individual medical care. There is still a disorganized system of private practitioners for the comparatively affluent, a disorganized clinic system for the poor, and mixture for those who fall between.

There is no blueprint of how a health service system should be constructed. Given the pluralistic nature of American health care institutions, the continually shifting body of technological knowledge, the existence of regional and local differences in health care resources (and perhaps also in the relative financial and social value put on health services by members of the population), one ideal system may never be attainable, and is probably undesirable. General or multispecialist medical firms, health maintenance organizations, hospital-based group practices, and regional health networks are terms which encompass a wide variety of practical implications. In one place, a hospital may expand its outpatient department into a well-organized health service unit. In another, several hospitals will join together to sponsor a system of community medical care through affiliated centers or multispecialist clinics.

In a third, effective coordination of services may be provided through comprehensive health insurance in private practice, buttressed by well-organized computerized information and records systems and quality control of available services. In a fourth, physicians in partnership will set up new practice networks and programs, employing appropriate staffs and subcontracting for services that they themselves cannot provide. In one area, leadership for change may be generated by state or local health departments, in another by a medical society, boards of hospitals, community action groups, or industrial leadership, or by a combination of one or more of these.

At the same time, however, the specific organizational forms of any health system are in large part dictated, or at least molded, by preexisting organizational structures, professional traditions, and political realities. The appropriate role of the federal government is a crucial issue in current debates, for the government could act in a variety of capacities, ranging from that of administrator of a comprehensive national health insurance scheme to that of a financial collection and standard-setting agency. Decisions have yet to be made whether financing or subsidy should be through general taxation, Social Security taxation, private insurance plans, or a combination of two or more of these; whether the whole population should be covered, or merely those most in financial need; whether a new plan should absorb or complement Medicare; whether other federal programs designed to stimulate health care resources, such as Hill-Burton or grants to medical schools or neighborhood health centers, would remain separate from the health insurance program; what, if any, central controls, policies, standards and public guarantees of service should be set up for the program; and how far a national health insurance scheme, no matter how the money is collected for its financing, should attempt to be more than a bill-paying mechanism and attempt to guide and restructure the health care system. These questions are implicit in all the current proposals for national health insurance.... Under all of the proposals, however, modifications of the system are inevitable, for the hodge-podge of services, programs and facilities which now form American health services cannot readily adjust to the increased demand which would be released through any extended health payment program....

The debates on the proper role and authority of the federal government (more concretely, of the Department of Health, Education, and Welfare or of a new health agency) continue to be dogged by uncertain rhetoric. The phrases "laissez faire" and "regulation" applied to health services tend to appear as if they are alternatives, somewhat along the lines of capitalism versus socialism. Yet the distinction is dangerously simplistic. Laissez faire in many other industries has led not to small-scale, decentralized local industries (of which the parallel in present medical care technology is the health maintenance organization) but to highly regulated chains, mergers, and national corporations. The issue here is not one of regulation per se, but of whether regulation is best exerted by the private or the public sector, for example by the insurance companies or by a government agency. Laissez faire is also often used to imply elements of free-market competition; in turn, competition presupposes well-informed consumers, making an enlightened choice of purchases from competing suppliers. As has been remarked, these conditions do not hold in the health care industry. In particular, consumer information about health insurance entitlements, accessible health services, relative costs and quality, is generally less available in America than in countries that have "socialized" medical systems.

Finally, the federal role itself has been oddly interpreted. There seems to have been a feeling that the proper role of government in health is one not of efficiency but weakness, not of planning but of grantsmanship, not of statesmanship but of irresponsibility. The curious result has been that the federal role in health has been distinguished by minimal consumer protection and public accountability.

Yet it is evident that to promote the supposed advantages of private enterprise—including decentralized control of health services, competition among health systems, adequate public information, and other measures of consumer protection—a strong governmental role is essential. As it is, the clichés surrounding health care provision still stand in the way of free, constructive debate. It is to be hoped that one of the major achievements of the present political prominence of national health insurance will be to air the practical issues.

What are these issues? The first is the degree of commitment by the public, as represented in the Congress, to the provision of adequate health services at various levels of expected cost. This may seem obvious, but the fact that the United States does not yet have national health insurance reflects a degree of indifference on the subject which is obscured in committee presentations.... Even health insurance does not guarantee the availability of appropriate and effective services, and some commitments tend to be only partial and to diminish with time. Medicaid provides a stark example of public interest in "mainstream medical care" for the poor which sank in the quicksands of budgetary difficulties.

A second question which is still unanswered concerns the role of federal funding and/or direction in the development of local service systems, such as health maintenance organizations (or the current proposals for a larger area-wide coordination through grants to stimulate experimental health care delivery systems) which will assume collective responsibility for providing health services to a population or area. Third, there is the related regulation and development of manpower resources. And finally there is the willingness to create strategic organizations responsible for developing federal policies in defined priority areas. In all of these instances there is already substantial federal governmental responsibility through the present operation of the funding system. But there has been, at least as yet, relatively little acceptance of a coordinated federal role in developing a nationally organized health care system.

. . . The signs of increasing congressional and political concern over health care problems reveal at least the beginnings of a movement for the more effective placing of federal tax dollars in the health care industry. Major reform may not be achieved for many years. Indeed, the confusion of federal programs and services may have to grow much worse before any serious overhauls are made. Nevertheless, eventually, the increased demand for health services, their rising costs, the lack of coordination of programs, will make a more directive notion of the federal role imperative.

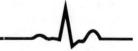

Good health is a basic part of a large dream of opportunity.

—Edward M. Kennedy

Douglass Cater

Politics of Health: An Overview

Describing the U.S. health enterprise as a "subgovernment," Douglass Cater, director of the Aspen Program on Communications and Society, outlines the participation of political groups in the development of health legislation and policy. It is difficult to predict how political forces will shape the nation's subgovernment of health in the future: since there is no model for a national health delivery system, numerous questions remain unanswered.

In the politics of modern America, a new form of federalism has emerged, more relevant to the distribution of power than the old. The old federalism which ordered power according to geographic hegemonies—national, state, and local—no longer adequately describes the governing arrangement. New subgovernmental arrangements have grown up, by which much of the pressing domestic business is ordered.

Health has become such a subgovernment. Any attempt to assess the evolving politics of this major enterprise must include the strengths and weaknesses of this arrangement for the development of policy and the exercise of power. One must take into account the major operatives in the subgovernment of health, who can be divided roughly into five groups: (1) political executives, (2) career bureaucrats, (3) key committeemen in Congress, (4) interest group professionals, and (5) public interest elites. Two criteria determine their eligibility in the subgovernment of health. First, they are continuously interested and involved in this particular area of policy making. Second, they give priority to health policy over competing areas of governmental concern.

This subgovernmental power structure is what the politician must examine when he contemplates further initiatives in the politics of health. It hardly provides a tidy arrangement for governing. Between the political executives and the career bureaucrats, power is uncoordinated. The head of the Veterans Administration or the director of Social Security is scarcely answerable to the Assistant Secretary for Health. In Congress, power over health policy is even more fragmented. The principal stimulators of health demand, the

House Ways and Means and Senate Finance committees, work quite separately from the principal creators of supply, the Senate Labor and House Commerce committees. Interest group professionals present conflicting priorities. One of the major interest groups, the American Medical Association, has pursued a consistently negative course toward any governmental involvement. Public interest elites have been effective in some areas such as medical research, but less effective in others such as health manpower training.

The result, predictably, has been less than orderly development of a national health strategy. Looking back, one may well regret that the approaching crisis in health care was not anticipated long ago and plans made to avoid it. A rational strategy would have first assessed the long-term demands for personnel and facilities. Once these were provided, wider services could have been introduced while the impact on cost and quality of delivery was carefully weighted. An orderly plan would have attempted to achieve a rational balance between hospital and home care, between the supply of doctors and allied health professionals, between preventive and curative health services.

But the politics of health has not worked this way. The Hill-Burton Act, hardened into a formula based on congressional constituencies, helped spawn hospitals around the country with scant regard for the rational distribution of skills and specialties. Manpower training lagged far behind the growing demand. The promise of health services through Medicaid and Medicare was not accompanied by measures to insure control of cost or quality. While there have been federal efforts to spur health planning—the Comprehensive Health Planning Act, the Heart, Cancer, and Stroke Centers, and, more recently, support for Health Maintenance Organizations—the measures have been picayune compared with the forces for disorder.

It is easy to blame the politics of health for the present situation. It is a more difficult task to suggest how a more orderly health strategy might be developed. . . . Which way are we headed? How will political forces shape the nation's subgovernment of health? Several conclusions seem predictable:

—The future politics of health is likely to be no less chaotic than the past. Mighty forces are in conflict. Governmental institutions at all levels lack the capacity to develop broad and long-range plans or to execute them. As a result, the political promises of health care will continue to outrun the performance.

—Still, there will be growing public pressure to improve the governance of health. Medical inflation surely cannot continue at its present rate. Nor can the nation's health enterprise continue indefinitely to claim a rising percentage of our gross national product. If increasing cost is accompanied by declining quality of care, the public call on the politicians will be all the louder. The added cost imposed by medical discovery and innovation will further increase political pressures for a far-reaching national health plan.

—Despite efforts to lessen Washington's direct involvement, through revenue sharing and other measures aimed at decentralization, health policy will continue to be a national concern. The subgovernment of health cannot be confined to state and community jurisdictions. We are no more likely to return to an earlier concept of federalism than we are able to reclaim the old-fashioned Marcus Welby delivery system of health care.

—The model for a national health delivery system in America does not presently exist. Neither the British system, the Kaiser Permanente prepaid plan, nor any of the others provides the perfect prototype. Indeed, there is unlikely to be a single model. Ideally, the politics of health will allow for a variety and competition of models while imposing overall yardsticks of effectiveness.

. . . Where do we go from here? Attention must be paid to various ways to strengthen the subgovernment of health so that it is more responsive and responsible in meeting the nation's health needs. . . .

The question is to decide whether health or economic growth should have priority in determining the type of environment in which we live. —René Dubos

Paul D. Ward

Health Lobbies: Vested Interests and Pressure Politics

The value of special interest groups to public officials, according to Paul D. Ward, is the consensus of opinion and specialized information relayed by lobbyists. Whether protectors of the status quo or promoters of change, health lobbies have an influence on legislators. The health lobby, like the health care system, is fragmented, however, and seldom forms a single coalition, even on a vital issue such as national health insurance. Ward is vice chairman of the American Hospital Association Council on Planning and Management.

In our society lobbies and pressure groups are an essential part of the governmental process. Over the last century their importance has increased, not decreased. They derive their authority from the constitution, that is, the explicit right of citizens, singularly or collectively, to petition their government. As our society becomes more complex, as communications continue to become more rapid and thereby capable of creating a greater mass of concern, as our societal problems become more acute and visible, as the complexities of dependent urban life engulf our pastoral heritage of personal independence, the effect will be to intensify the function of persuasion of government by paid advocates representing certain segments and interests in our society. Complexity of itself demands this. This does not mean, however, that lobbying and pressure group activity should go unregulated or unexposed to the general public; but at the same time their usefulness, in fact their essentiality to government, cannot be denied. . . .

Pressure groups through their lobbyists provide a consensus of opinion from those involved in their groupings; they provide reactions to given courses of action; they provide a major technical input into highly complex matters; and they provide a pathway for the public official into the thinking of at least a portion of that official's constituency. . . . Each pressure group tends to create a consensus of opinion on given issues in certain segments of a government official's constituency that could have, when combined with the consensus of other groups, a profound effect upon the number of years he occupies office. This is not to say that the public official, either in the legislature or the administration, should bow to any consensus. But at least he needs to know when and where the trend is running against his position so that he can advance the arguments of his persuasion more forcefully. Then, if he loses the argument and perhaps, as a result, the next election, at least the public has had the opportunity of hearing and weighing both sides of the question. For better or worse, this is how issues are resolved; it constitutes a large part of the democratic process and is one of the major guiding forces of change in our society.

Categories

There are two broad categories in which we could place lobbies. . . . It may be difficult to argue that any of the lobbies, at least in the health field, belong exclusively in any one category. But we can say that the dominant part of their activities do fall into one category or the other.

The first category we might label as "protectors of the status quo." These lobbyists devote most of their activities to preventing change. When change is supported by them, it is usually to better the conditions of their individual members and not necessarily to enhance the good of the general public. . . .

The second category of lobbyists might be termed "the promoters of change." These groups are usually less well organized, have fewer resources at their disposal, and generally pass in and out of existence with far greater frequency than do those who are "protectors of the status quo."

There have been numerous examples of the promoters of change category in the health field. Most have been groupings of individuals and organizations interested in narrow specific problems related to health care. . . .

APHA

During the period after World War II many looked upon the American Public Health Association (APHA) as the vehicle through which efforts could be focused to bring about improvements in health care. APHA contained the diversity of interests that could perhaps insure its longevity as a political force focused on Washington. But this internal diversity of interest, ranging from pollution to medical care with a full range of political views from conservative to liberal, plus the lack of adequate resources, made highly effective action at the legislative level impossible. Although there have been renewed efforts by APHA to focus on Washington as an instrument of change, its internal structure makes this difficult.

Other groups devoted to single purposes or one-time actions continue to emerge as advocates of change with seemingly little chance of longevity. The

Committee of One Hundred, containing many of the nation's leading advocates of change in our health care delivery system, was formed to support the enactment of national health insurance legislation. Financed largely by organized labor, it admittedly aimed its efforts at one specific type of change and focused, for all practical purposes, on one piece of legislation. Although it might continue as a permanent pressure group if its proposed legislation is enacted, its future source of financial support would undoubtedly have to be broadened and its controlling forces would undoubtedly undergo change. Stability on the promoter of change side is hard to come by. . . .

NIH Programs

The programs of the National Institutes of Health (NIH), in effect, caused the public to become "health conscious." As the research grew in scope and began to bear results, literally reams of press stories covering these results appeared in the news media. The press was eager for articles covering medical discoveries and the vast majority of the articles expressed a hope that some medical problem had been alleviated as a result of research. It was difficult to read a major daily paper for a week without seeing at least one article which provided hope for relief or cure from illness that had not existed before. The majority of the articles or announcements were highly favorable to medical care; they made it appear as if medical care was worth seeking (where there had been some doubt before) and it would be only a short time before all medical problems would be solved. Whenever any subject receives this degree of favorable publicity, the public wants some of whatever it is.

This favorable publicity occurred over a number of years. In fact, it still occurs today except that its effect is modulated by stories of lack of manpower, lack of care, and the high cost of care. Medical care grew into prominence, at least partly on the basis of new hope, and in doing so its basic problems and weaknesses were exposed to an ever-expanding percentage of the public. Health care was declared a "right of all citizens" by Congress and affirmed by Presidents (even though earlier in our history no one had seemed to listen when it had been so declared). The lines were drawn for the making of an issue.

The unprecedented growth of the NIH budget had other side effects in addition to the publicity which stimulated the public's interest in health care. Certainly it had a decided effect on the attitude and structure of medical education. But more important in terms of pressure groups, it created a cadre of medical professionals both in and out of government who had to influence the governmental process in order to survive. In addition it spurred the interest of scores of marginal groups who were interested in one or more of the categorical diseases. Although unorganized as a single focus of pressure on government, these separate groups did tend to generate interest in health care at both the governmental and the public level. At times they tended to cut each other's throats in their eagerness to acquire higher appropriations for their own special interests in the health field, especially during periods of tight controls on the total number of dollars available, but on the whole they did generate new public awareness and concern for health care which contributed substantially to its emergence as a national issue. If these groups were ever able to form a common front by agreeing on a mutually acceptable set of objectives for the health field, their force as a positive pressure group in the politics of health would be unmatched. Whether or not they can find a more effective forum or mechanism than has existed to date through which to accomplish this remains a perplexing questions.

No two lobbies are completely similar in either tactics or procedures. Not only are they generally different from one another in this regard, but any given lobby may change its own tactics from time to time. Each responds to the events that focus on what it considers to be its constituency; it is molded by the personalities of those who emerge as leaders within the constituency and by the counter events in society that react to its positions.

If an organized pressure group takes a certain position through its lobbyist, and this creates a generally unfavorable reaction with the public, then its tactics, procedures, and even positions may well change. One of the difficult lessons to learn in the conduct of our democracy is that often it is as beneficial to focus public reaction on certain lobbying groups through their members in order to urge a change in their position as it is to focus on the public officials. We see this occurring with greater frequency today and undoubtedly this tactic will grow in importance insofar as the formulation of public policy is concerned.

Fragmentation

The lobbies that occupy the health field are relatively recent phenomena when compared with other traditional lobbies. Lobbies concerned with taxes, banking, railroads, liquor, oil and gas, forests, transportation, guns and ammunition, industry, and shipping, to name but a few, are older, more consistent, and perhaps more sophisticated. The health lobbies have received, until recent years, relatively few funds in comparison with the total dollar magnitude of the health industry, and have been low-key in operation. They have been highly fragmented, often fighting with each other, with almost no ability to look beyond their own special and specific interests to the greater interests of the total health field. This fragmentation of the health lobby is due in large part to the way our health care delivery system is organized, and it does make reasonable solutions to some of the problems exceedingly difficult.

In fact, no other major industry in our economy presents so fragmented an approach to the influencing of public policy. For virtually every licensed level of performance, i.e., physicians, nurses, therapists, and so on, there is a separate position and thrust on the issues to be decided. Professionally, medicine is organized on a craft basis, in place of an industrywide basis, and as yet no unifying force has appeared which would cause the individual levels to join together and speak with one voice. Certainly the organized physicians have received the greatest attention since, as a group, they have poured the greatest resources over the longest period of time into the fray, but the per capita costs per physician to maintain this position of dominance may in the long term be self-defeating.

Not only are there several different levels of lobbying input based upon the variety of health manpower classifications and licensure, but there is a major split between manpower and facilities. Organizations representing facilities, and especially hospitals, have a set of goals often at odds with the major manpower groups. To be sure, many examples can be shown where the two forces have converged to support a given position, but there are enough significant issues of increasing importance to seem to indicate a widening of the breach, such as in the way care should be organized, the degree to which services should be facility based, and the methods of paying for care. In fact, one of the fears seldom expressed publicly, but certainly lurking in the background, is that if large health care corporations or health maintenance organizations were created, collectively they might mount a lobbying effort that would dwarf those health lobbies now in existence.

Still another factor provides a major cause for fragmentation of the health lobby. This is the traditional pattern of approaching health problems categorically. Since people usually become ill categorically—i.e., from cancer, respiratory or heart disease, etc.—and not comprehensively, laymen have a tendency to support efforts aimed at diseases with which they can easily identify. This has led to the formation of many organizations built around a single disease. Each one of these organizations, directly or indirectly, constitutes a lobbying force. When they are attempting to influence the government to spend funds for research and services in their special disease areas they tend to compete with each other and may from time to time nullify each other's actions. There have been times when the argument "my disease is more important than yours" has been used by those interested in budget cutting as justification for cutting or not providing new funds to anyone. In the fragmented field of the health lobby it is exceedingly easy to play one group against the other if your goal is to do nothing.

Needless to say, not all lobbies in other fields are unified, but many have found ways to reach agreement on key issues. It might be argued that too much agreement can be as detrimental as no agreement, but at least that would be a novelty in the health field.

The late Senator Everett Dirksen of Illinois, one of the Senate's most eloquent conservatives, used to comment that "nothing can stop an idea whose time has come." He made this comment about the passage of Medicare, a bill that he had opposed with all of his unusual vigor and effectiveness. Medicare had been supported by several lobbies, most of them from outside the health field. Chief among them was the lobby of organized labor. The bill had been strongly opposed by organized medicine, with the notable exception of the National Medical Association, the professional organization of black physicians. The fact is that Medicare, which has to be described as one of the most important, if not the most important, health measures yet passed by Congress, was passed because of forces outside the health-related lobbies. This fact often is not recognized. The lobbying efforts of the Committees for the Aged emphasizing the humane need for care, letter campaigns of various groups demanding that the cost of care of aged parents be lifted from the shoulders of their children who had their own families to protect, church groups, and other civic groups that organized support efforts were all instrumental in their own way in the final favorable vote. But sometimes overlooked are the pressures brought to bear by local government on the federal government for relief from the costs of care that fell on the local property tax when the aged or their children were unable to pay. Costs of care for those over 65 had escalated more rapidly than for any other group and local government was forced to bear a major portion of this cost. The opportunity to shift a portion of these costs from the local property tax base to a social security insurance base was a deciding factor to congressmen who were being increasingly badgered by city and county government lobbyists for such relief. Although the lobbyists for local government maintain a low-profile operation, they have become an increasingly important force on the Washington scene.

Support for National Health Insurance. Does a similar coalition of support exist for the passage of national health insurance? If the Harris poll of last April [1971] is correct, there is certainly overwhelming popular support for some type of national coverage. The poll indicated by a better than two to one margin that the voters favored a "comprehensive health insurance program that would combine federal government, employee and employer contributions into one health insurance system." It is reasonable to assume that if popular support of this magnitude does exist and if remedial action is not taken in the private sector to solve some of the problems behind this public attitude, then pressures will materialize which will cause Congress to act. It is interesting to note that again the major impetus to pass the legislation may well come from groups other than those composed of health professionals.

It is always dangerous to speculate on the type or content of any legislation that may be passed. The question might be asked, however, whether after the passage of a national health insurance program it would be possible to create a combined lobbying effort that would keep the program funded at a desirable level. The example of the highway trust fund and its protectors might serve as a possible indicator of future events in the health field. The highway trust fund is derived principally from gasoline and vehicle-related taxes. Its use by law is virtually limited to building and maintaining the nation's highway and road system. By increasing the related taxes slightly, you theoretically could in time pave the nation. The so-called "transportation lobby," a loose confederation of trucking, automobile, construction, gasoline, and lending institutions, acts to prevent any raids on highway funds for purposes other than highways. Use of the funds for rapid transit or other means of public transportation is strongly opposed to the point that most feel the fund is sacred. Although one can find many drawbacks in this type of development, it follows that the creation of a medical care trust fund under national health insurance may have somewhat the same effect. Since any such fund would be the dominant purchaser of care, and the main supporter of any health care system, there is good reason to believe that most health lobbies would find this an acceptable point around which to rally. Since the rules and regulations adopted for the fund, or even for a system involving use of private insurance carriers, would inevitably be concerned with quantity and quality controls, distribution and pricing, and benefit determinations, there would be an even stronger reason to end some of the anarchy that now exists among the health lobbyists. Add to this the current impetus to create larger corporate-type groups to deliver care which in turn can more easily band together for influencing the political process and it is difficult to believe that the health lobbying field is not going to change substantially during the next decade. These years might be described as the "years of maturing" for the health lobby. . . .

14 The Role of the Individual in Health Care

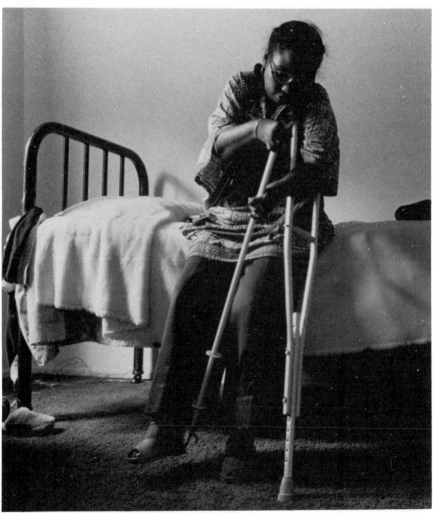

MARK TUSCHMAN

A number of articles in this book have presented an untidy view of the nation's health care system; many of the authors are alarmed at the lack of national health planning, at overspecialization, iatrogenesis, medicalization, spiraling inflation, inequities in access, and other serious problems. In this chapter we address one of the most positive aspects of America's health: the increasing degree to which individuals are assuming responsibility for health and health care. It is true that much of the impetus for individual responsibility has arisen from discontent, disenchantment, and outright rage at the inadequacies of health care services. Nevertheless, the self-care movement is squarely based on the sound notion that we are our own primary source of health care.

Although physicians, policymakers, and the public seldom realize it, individuals and those close to them minister to most health care needs. We are the primary means of preventing disease and disability, and when we are ill, there is a great deal we can do to cure ourselves. This is self-care, a new term that describes an ancient practice.

The renewed emphasis on self-care in the United States takes a number of forms. One of the most encouraging is the move to marshal forces in groups of individuals with common interests or needs. Among the first of these groups was Alcoholics Anonymous, which now has myriad branches serving teenaged alcoholics, children and spouses of alcoholics, and others whose lives are affected by alcoholism. Currently there are five hundred thousand mutual aid groups addressing a multitude of diseases and health issues. Today's diseases in many ways lend themselves to self-help organizations because those who suffer from arthritis (like the young girl in the illustration on the opposite page) or some other chronic diseases such as hypertension and diabetes, are largely responsible for treating themselves on a day-to-day basis. In a group setting they can share successes, setbacks, and emotional experiences, and they often take on added roles such as fund-raising for research, public information, lobbying, and improving public facilities.

Self-care on an individual and group basis touches on many of the issues raised in previous chapters. It has implications for costs, disease prevention, medicalization, access, and quality. Particularly if the public is given adequate education and information, self-care can take pressure off a heavily burdened health care establishment, and many people think that it is bringing issues of health and disease toward a perspective that will enrich human experience, as well as improve health and well-being. However, it should be noted that some critics fear that the new emphasis on self-care might result in individuals neglecting to seek professional help when it is needed, and it might cause us to overlook failures in our medical system.

Frank Riessman, co-director of the National Self-Help Clearinghouse, discusses self-help groups, their dynamics, their triumphs, and their ability to help patients recognize the limitations of modern medicine in "Self-Care and Self-Help: Natural Allies." Charlie Lough and Beckie Stewart analyze some of the more complex aspects of the self-care movement in "Self-Care as a Health Service: Opportunities for Participative Partnerships." The issue of "victim blaming," or the implication that the patient is at fault for illness and failure to get well, is raised in this selection, as is the dependence on medicine that limits human potential. The authors also offer some specific information about self-help kits, mutual aid groups, self-care technologies, and other aids to self-reliance.

Norman Cousins' contribution is important for a number of reasons. Possibly its most compelling feature is that it deftly ventures into the realm of mind-body relationships. Cousins, formerly the editor of *Saturday Review* and now on the Medical School faculty at the University of California, Los Angeles, accomplishes this without stepping on the toes of modern medicine. This is a twilight zone that medical science has relegated to the shadows, and Cousins' own experience with illness and near-death compelled him to illuminate what science has chosen to ignore. His best-selling book, *Anatomy of an Illness (As Perceived by the Patient)*, from which this selection is excerpted, has had an extraordinary impact, bringing to light many dried-up myths about doctors, patients, illness, and well-being.

Frank Riessman

Self-Care and Self-Help: Natural Allies

Self-help groups can increase individual participation in health care and influence the delivery of health services. Frank Riessman, co-director of the National Self-Help Clearinghouse, illustrates the particular success of mutual aid groups in managing chronic illnesses and fostering preventive and educational activities. An integrated human service practice would balance professional help and self-help to increase individual control and participation in the system.

The terms *self-help* and mutual aid refer to the group dimension of self-care. It's my feeling that those who focus their self-care teachings and practices solely on the things people acting alone can do for themselves are ignoring many of the most powerful self-care tools—friends, family, support groups, and community. . . . The principles and practices of mutual aid groups provide a well-developed model for fostering and nurturing social bonds among those practicing self-care.

Gil Evans, in *The Family Circle Guide to Self-Help,* states that there are 500,000 mutual aid groups in the United States, with a membership of fifteen million people. In their book, *The Strength in Us,* Katz and Bender define self-help groups as:

> . . . voluntary small group structures for mutual aid in the accomplishment of a special purpose. They are usually formed by peers who have come together for mutual assistance in satisfying a common need, overcoming a common handicap or life-disrupting problem, and bringing about desired social and/or personal change. The initiators and members of such groups perceive that their needs are not or can not be met by or through existing social institutions.

In addition to being able to provide needed services much more economically than prevailing professional or institutional approaches, there are a number of reasons why the self-help approach is gaining considerable influence. First, there is a strong anti-bureaucratic, populist trend in our society. The small group self-help orientation operates as a countervailing force, reducing alienation and increasing feelings of personal power. Second, self-help approaches are appropriate for a wide range of groups, such as women, youth, elders, and the physically handicapped. Third, self-help activities have proven useful for caring for chronic illnesses (hypertension, diabetes, arthritis, mental illness, cancer, and heart disorders), which afflict fifty percent of our population. Fourth, self-help activities try to improve human services which are inadequate—especially so in their efforts to serve minorities, rural residents, elders, adolescents, and the poor.

Some self-help groups have developed entirely without professional involvement, but many have some interaction with health workers or other professionals.

Let me give a specific example. I have recently been involved in initiating a self-help group for arthritics at Downstate Medical Center in New York. The group members all have scleroderma, a disorder of the connective tissue, and they all have some enormous problems particular to their disease—they have trouble eating, their digestive tract is disturbed, they sometimes throw up in restaurants, their hands are gnarled, and they have a wide range of other problems.

When I was first speaking with the doctors about facilitating this group, they described how terribly off these people were and how bad their situations were. At first I had my doubts as to whether it would be *possible* to form a self-help group.

We started out by sending an invitation, signed by the medical people, to all the scleroderma patients who were being seen at the hospital. There was a tremendous interest. At the first meeting they spent the whole time sharing symptoms and stories and experiences of living with scleroderma.

It was the first opportunity most of them had had to get together with other people like themselves—who really *knew* what they'd been through, who could really listen and understand. It was a terrifically high experience for all of us.

·And after the members got to know each other and the group started to come together, they moved on to helping each other cope with specific problems—dealing with their families, and learning specific exercises and self-care skills. They taught each other to use some of the special devices available to do some of the things that present special problems if you have scleroderma—like tying your shoes, buttoning your shirt, tying your tie, cooking a meal, driving a car. It was clear that someone with scleroderma can learn more from someone with the same disease who has worked through certain problems than from anyone who doesn't know about it from personal experience.

. . . The group is autonomous—it has its own officers and plans its own agenda. Besides doctors, the group has met with a dietician, a podiatrist, and they're looking for a psychologist to present a session on "assertiveness training for arthritics."

When they *do* invite outside consultants, it's the group, not the professional, who calls the shots. The first time the dietician came, she started to give her regular talk on nutrition in general. They stopped her cold. "That's not our problem," they told her. "We're not trying to reduce and we're not worried about eating a balanced diet. Our biggest problem is that doctors tell us we should be eating lots of foods that are high in potassium and some of us can't eat bananas." So they went on to discuss some high-potassium foods.

Group members have also shifted their whole relationships with their physicians. Before the group started, they'd go back and check with their doctor over every little thing—they'd hang on his or her every word. Now they're much more critical—not destructively so, just more realistic about the limits of the doctors' expertise and the need to give the *doctor* feedback and direction.

At one group session a visiting doctor asked exactly what the members got from the group, and one woman answered, "When I look down at Thelma, at the end of the table there, and see the way she smiles and lives with life, I am so *moved* that it gives me strength to deal with my own problems." So the doctor said, "Well you know, that's not always so good. Sometimes you're laughing to keep from crying, and maybe covering up your problems."

And she just shook her head and said, "No, doctor, that's not it at all. It's just that seeing her courage gives *me* courage." This was a lady who would have never dreamed of contradicting her doctor before. The group really let him know they thought he was way off the mark. And he took it very well.

Before the group, I don't think any one of them would have dared disagree. They would have just sat there and listened and discounted their own experience if it was in conflict with his. But now they stand up for what they know. It's been quite impressive to see how the power of the group has grown. So has the way they insist on doing things for each other.

Last winter we offered to arrange transportation to bring them to meetings on cold days. And they told us very firmly, "No, thank you. We can take care of that ourselves." Now to see these people drive is something in itself, because they have some rather severe physical difficulties. But they wanted to do it and they did it.

I think this model—a mutual aid group brought together by a community group or governmental agency—is a very valuable model for the future. I think we'll be seeing a lot of federal funds going into projects like this one. It's a very effective, low-cost way of providing good health care. I think that for such programs to succeed, they must be run by the clients. Professionals may help to initiate such groups, and may serve as consultants and advisors, but it must very clearly be the group members who are in charge.

How Does Self-Help Work?

Mutual-Aid Groups. While "hard" scientific evidence regarding the effectiveness of self-help groups is sparse, there are a number of "soft" indicators that would seem to show that many of these groups do indeed serve their clientele effectively. There are the subjective reports of the members themselves to the effect that they have been helped by the group experience. There is also the fact that the members continue in the group, and while this does not necessarily indicate that they are benefiting, it does imply that they are obtaining some satisfaction. Then, there is the fact that many professional agencies refer people to self-help groups, particularly groups like Alcoholics Anonymous, Gamblers Anonymous, and Synanon which deal with behaviors that have been highly resistant to the usual professional interventions. AA reports that one member in five credits a physician or hospital for directing him or her to AA.

In some cases, there is a kind of face validity. When a self-help group concerned with hypertension enlists people who have previously not been involved in an antihypertensive program, and they remain in the group and follow the regimen, this would seem to have self-evident bearing on the value of the group....

But in the last analysis the power of self-help, mutual-aid groups derives from the fact that they combine a number of very important properties: the helper-therapy principle, the aprofessional dimension, consumer intensivity, the use of indigeneity, and the implicit demand that the individual can do something for him or herself, that people need not be passive, that they have power, particularly in a group—but a group which demands that they do something for each other, a group that while permitting dependence demands autonomy and independence, a group that while giving support demands action and work, a group that is not leader or professional centered, but rather peer centered. In essence, one of the most significant characteristics of mutual-aid groups is that fact that they are *empowering* and thus dealienating. They enable their members to feel and use their own strengths, their own power, to have control over their own lives. This empowering dimension is extremely important for people's health and mental health; it also enhances human service productivity and contributes to effective, integrated service practice.

In addition, many self-help groups combine these features with an ideological, antisystem bias which to some extent limits their bureaucratization and some of the negative consequences of institutionalization....

The Helper-Therapy Principle. Perhaps one of the most powerful mechanisms operative in self-help groups is what has been described as the *helper-*

therapy principle. A derivative of role theory, whereby a person playing a role tends to carry out the expectations, and requirements of that role, the helper-therapy principle states in simplest form that those who help are helped most. . . .

Thus, an alcoholic in AA who is providing help and support to another AA member may be the one who is benefiting most from playing this helping, giving role. However, since all members of the group play this role at one time or another, they are all benefited by this helping process. In a sense, this is true for all helpers whether they be professionals, laypersons, volunteers, or whatever, but it is more sharply true to helpers who have the same problem as the helpee, and this is what is characteristic of mutual-aid groups. While all help-givers may be helped themselves in a nonspecific way by playing the helping role (and this is not an unimportant matter), people who have a particular problem may be helped in much more specific ways by providing help to others who have the same specific problem whether they are alcoholics, drug addicts, smokers, underachievers, heart patients, hypertensives, diabetics, etc. In part this is true because in the process of persuading others they have to persuade or reinforce themselves, not in some general way, but about the various specific problems that they share in common. Becoming committed to a position through advocating it (self-persuasion through persuading others) seems to be an important dimension associated with the helper role.

There are at least three additional reasons why the person playing the helping role achieves special benefits: (1) the helper is less dependent; (2) in struggling with another person's problem which is like her/his own, the helper has a chance to observe his/her problem at a distance; (3) the helper obtains a feeling of social usefulness by playing the helping role.

. . . Helpers functioning in a therapeutic context, whether as professional therapeutic agents or as nonprofessional peer therapists, would seem to benefit from the importance and status associated with this role. They also receive support from the implicit thesis, "I must be well if I can help others." Moreover, their helper roles as such may function as a major distracting source of involvement, thus diverting them from their own problems and a general overconcern with self. Undoubtedly, individual differences account for some people receiving much greater satisfaction than others from giving, helping, leading, persuading, and nurturing.

. . . What is implicit in the operation of mutual-aid groups and all kinds of peer-help situations is that everyone who needs help should have the opportunity to play the helper role. . . .

Consumer Intensivity. Another important aspect of self-help groups is the special involvement of consumers. Victor Fuchs points out that in health, education, and many other service industries, unlike goods production, the consumer frequently plays an important part in affecting the productivity of the service system and the professional provider, if one is involved.

> In the supermarket, laundromat, the consumer actually works, and in the doctor's office the quality of medical history the patient gives might influence significantly the productivity of the doctor. Productivity in banking is affected by whether the clerk of the customer makes out the deposit slip—and whether it is made out correctly or not. Thus the knowledge, experience, honesty, and motivation of the consumer affects service productivity.

Fuchs seems to be suggesting a new classification that might be termed *consumer intensivity:* the more the productivity of the provider depends on consumer behavior, the more consumer intensive we would call the industry or activity. Thus productivity can be enhanced by the fuller use of the consumer, whether as children teaching children, peers counseling peers, doctors teaching patients how to make self-examinations, teachers involving children in their own learning, practically all group therapy, etc. In other words, while consumer intensivity is an essential characteristic of all services, it can be greatly increased by organizing these services so as to involve the consumer more fully; thus, one can say that a service is more consumer intensive to the degree that the consumer provides a greater portion of the service and the professional provides a lesser portion of it.

Consumer involvement not only affects quantity but it has an important and fundamental effect on the quality of all human services, whether education, health care, etc. This is because so much of the essence of the human services depends upon the involvement and motivation of the consumer. . . . An individual's health is dependent upon what he or she does about maintaining it, preventing illness, building positive health. And in overcoming most of the behavior-related disorders of our time, such as smoking, alcoholism, etc., it is obvious that the consumer's self-involvement is decisive. There are countless other illustrations of this in sex therapy, psychotherapy, family planning, and in the so-called coping books—on assertiveness training, transcendental meditation, dieting, relaxation techniques, etc.—where the consumer is obviously the decisive force in helping him or herself, with the professional input restricted to the information presented in the book.

The self-help approach represents the essence of consumer involvement: here the consumers are primary not only in helping themselves, but in helping and serving others like themselves, and in addition the role of the professional service provider is, at most, peripheral.

The Aprofessional Dimension. . . . Self-help mutual-aid groups use much more subjective, peer-initiated, informal, gut-level approaches; disclosures are shared; the participants are judgmental with each other. In essence, the self-help approach reflects a series of dimensions which might be termed *aprofessional*. The professional is much more concerned with a systematic, knowledge-based approach, with the need for distance and perspective, with empathy perhaps, but not identification, with objectivity rather than subjectivity, with practice based on scientific analysis rather than experience or intuition. . . .

The aprofessional dimension featured in self-help groups is not only a powerful counterbalance to some of the intrinsic limitations of the professional knowledge-based, systematic, distanced approach, but it also serves to reduce some of the difficulties which are not intrinsic but extrinsic and related to the way the professional functions in our society. Here I am referring to the elitism, the tendency to mystify, to maintain a monopoly on and high cost for professional service, to be removed particularly from low-income and rural populations, not to be sufficiently accountable and relevant to the consumer, frequently applying outmoded practices because these are the ones in which they, the professionals, were trained. The aprofessional approach is likely to be much more consumer centered, immediately relevant, demystified, not dispensed in a condescending manner, nonelite, more directly accountable to the consumer—at least in terms of direct satisfaction—and far less expensive.

These characteristics make the self-help modality, with its aprofessional dimension, more successful in meeting a broad array of people's needs. Let us turn to the mental health field for an impressive example of the greater applicability of the self-help mode for a wide range of consumer populations. . . . While varying in form from culture to culture there are three universal components which are crucial for a successful psychotherapeutic intervention; these are (1) that the client and therapist share a similar world view, (2) that the client has certain expectations of the therapist's intervention, and (3) the personal characteristics of the therapist. . . . Thus while some people may choose a professional psychotherapist (following the medical model) on the basis of a shared world view, etc., there are many other consumers whose mental health needs might be better satisfied by the intervention of a priest, an astrologer, a yogi, a hypnotist, or a self-help group. Indeed, a consumer-based approach such as the self-help mode with almost as many intervention formats as there are groups affords much greater opportunity to connect with clients' world views, expectations, and systems of belief. Moreover, the self-help aprofessional approach often draws on an activist orientation which values will and faith above understanding. Not only are these dimensions useful in any human service intervention, but they also are more appropriate for many groups in the population which do not share professionals' stress on understanding as the main avenue to change and improvement.

. . . Much of professionals' training and socialization discourages identification, deep concern, full involvement, and caring—qualities which often derive from nearness to the client, feeling like the client in a highly direct, indigenous fashion. In fact, indigeneity, emphasized a great deal in the 1960s along with the development of the paraprofessional movement to mean "coming from or close to the community or clients to be served," is a very important aspect of the aprofessional dimension and certainly a characteristic feature of the self-help mode. While this nearness may result at times in overidentification and an impairment of perspective, it remains a valuable component of human service practice.

An Integrated Human Service Practice. Much human service work can be performed by people with no formal systematic knowledge or training; rather, their ability or skill rests upon their humanness, their feeling for people, their caring, their everyday, down-to-earth experience and common sense, their spontaneity, their availability, their time. This is one of the main reasons why self-help groups can be effective. Because uncontrolled subjectivity and just plain inadequate knowledge can seriously limit the value of the services, there is clearly a need for training, supervision, and professional knowledge for a balanced well-developed human service practice. But the professional input in this balanced programming can be used much more efficiently and judiciously than it is at present. Frequently, tasks are overprofessionalized, causing professional skills to be used when they are not needed and may even be inappropriate. Since human service needs are almost infinite, it is important in a long-range view to recognize that we don't need an infinte amount of professional skill to deal with these needs, but rather that an efficient system should combine the professional with the aprofessional. In this integrated picture of human service practice the self-help mode with its aprofessional, human emphasis can play a vital role, giving people the opportunity to exercise some control over their lives and the services they use.

Charlie Lough and Beckie Stewart

Self-Care as a Health Service: Opportunities for Participative Partnerships

Like Riessman, Charlie Lough and Beckie Stewart see self-care as an essential adjunct to professional care and the greatest hope for improving health care without raising costs. They argue that education for self-care must include promotion of health habits and risk avoidance, therapeutic skills, and information about community resources. Self-help manuals, self-care kits, health counseling, information centers, home technologies, drug package inserts, and mutual aid groups can all assist individuals to improve self-care and form participative partnerships with health professionals.

Self-care encompasses many opportunities for participative partnerships with health care professionals in the prevention, management, and remedy of health problems. These opportunities are being expanded as the "health care system" is extended into the behavioral and social aspects of life. Further development of health education, incentives for health maintenance, and health counseling are needed to support self-care practices as the health care system becomes increasingly complex.

A working definition of self-care has been proposed by Levin as a process whereby a person "can function effectively on his or her own behalf in health promotion and decision making, in disease prevention, detection, and treatment at the level of the primary health resource in the health care system." The person as the *subject* rather than as the *object* of health care decision action is the important concept in this definition....

The relationship between personal self-care and professional health services varies with the complexity and severity of the health problem. The salient question is how much professional intervention is required, not how much self-care is involved....

Lacking the necessary cooperation of the patient, the best laid medical plans are ineffectual, a situation commonly called "noncompliance" by physicians. This critical term implies that the patient is at fault if the therapy is not as effective as it "should be." Actually, a failure of compliance by patients indicates that the appropriate level of shared responsibility between doctor and patient has not been effectively established. In many instances such a situation represents a failure of the professional to assume the proper education or interpretive roles, either individually or as a leader of a team. The role of the patient becomes relatively more important in less serious ailments. Since the least severe illnesses tend to be overwhelmingly common, there are many mild, functional, or self-limited ailments for which the average citizen is fully capable of exercising his own initiative in recognizing the problem and undertaking appropriate therapy. . . .

Unwarranted fears and phobias represent an important impediment to self-reliance. Contrary to common belief, the human body is remarkably sound and resistant to all manner of health hazards. . . . Health care has come to be regarded as a necessity without which citizens might wither and fail. This exaggerated impression does not consider the number of individuals who survive extended periods without access to health care through geographical or voluntary choice. For example, the maldistribution of physicians and facilities leaves large areas lacking adequate health services. Populations in remote and rural areas with adequate nutrition and housing seem to have fewer health problems. . . . Christian Scientists in America are exposed to virtually the same stresses and the same likelihood of minor or severe illnesses as other citizens. They voluntarily avoid the use of health services. Their lives and health do not seem to be jeopardized. . . .

The nature and extent of the individual's responsibility for his or her own health has been clouded and confused in recent years. With the best of intentions, both the health professions and the various levels of government have progressively assumed expanded functions, often tending to usurp the individual's need to make decisions or initiate actions in support of health status.

Deepening Dependence on Professionals

Sophisticated technologies have undermined self-reliance and prompted helplessness in many facets of society. Fifty years ago, the average citizen could be self-reliant in repair of wagons, washing machines, or the simple implements of the time. The inner workings of cars, kitchen appliances, communications instruments, and other necessities of modern life have become "too complicated for the average citizen." The same kind of phenomenon has occurred with relation to health. During our first quarter century, simple remedies prepared at home were clearly competitive with the foul-tasting drugs prescribed by physicians. Few people would have felt it necessary to call upon the services of a physician for the most common kinds of ailments. Today many people have become excessively dependent upon the ministrations of physicians for simple ailments for which self-care is just as effective as professional care for lack of effective therapy.

A large and growing number of people is reacting to the high cost of dependence, particularly among the young. Do-it-yourself approaches to the maintenance of cars, and electrical and kitchen appliances are becoming increasingly popular. A similar reaction in health care has been demonstrated through the growing popularity of self-care practices including diet, exercise, relaxation, stress management, and the large and growing selection of books, manuals, pamphlets, and other sources of information that help people take better care of themselves. Virtually every newspaper and magazine has one or more articles on health matters. Despite the inherent diversity and lack of consistency in the public articles, much of this noncommercial information is basically sound. A number of the social mechanisms for enhancing self-care is already in place. The greatest remaining requirement is to reduce the obstacles and provide positive incentives for citizens to assume more responsibility for health care. Mechanisms by which the typical citizen can safely and effectively manage a large proportion of the common, self-limited ailments represent the most significant approach to improved medical care at a lower cost. . . .

Operational Obstacles

The health care delivery system encompasses characteristics which tend to discourage self-reliance under many different conditions. The utter complexity and diffuseness of the facilities and services provide varying degrees of access or availability. Specialization in medicine fosters hierarchical structures in which the physician occupies the apex and yet is frequently the initial point of contact for the system. The mystic qualities ascribed to medicine coupled with relatively unintelligible terminology and jargon erect barriers to mutual understanding between health care professionals and the public. The fee-for-service tradition reimburses the physician on the basis of the procedures employed (process) and not on the outcome of efforts (product). For this reason, there are strong incentives to be generous or extravagant with services and to discourage initiatives by patients.

Health care professionals too often fail to take patients into their confidence and provide understandable explanations of issues vitally important to a person with a health problem. . . . Extensive research is needed to develop and evaluate practical methods for eliminating or overcoming obstacles to a participative partnership in the encouragement and provision of health care. . . .

Barriers to Understanding

The average American, exposed to enormous amounts of information about health, remains remarkably ill-informed and misinformed regarding the origins and options for management of even the most common illnesses. The root causes of this paradoxical situation stem from many sources: the educational exposure in schools tends to emphasize hygiene, social adjustments, and normal function, almost to the exclusion of study of patterns of signs and symptoms or methods of management for common ailments. The deluge of conflicting information about health matters in mass media and in commercial advertising is sufficient to confuse anyone. The diversity of opinion about the best methods for treating certain common ailments is a reliable indication that none is truly effective. The diversity of prescriptions, over-the-counter drugs, nostrums and folk remedies is equally confounding. A similar degree of senseless confusion surrounds the management of most common ailments, for which definitive treatments are not yet available. Such common complaints are among the leading causes of unrewarding encounters with physicians. Interviews with patients following hospitalization have disclosed that patients are more frequently dissatisfied with the lack of communication than with any other element of the health care delivery system. A principal difficulty lies with the fact that physicians are not noted for their ability to convey the necessary information in understandable form. At the same time, they are reluctant to delegate responsibility for conveying such information to other people. They are justifiably concerned that information may be inconsistent or incorrect when presented by someone who is not entirely familiar with either the details of medicine or with that particular patient. There is a substantial requirement for development of an ever-increasing amount of authoritative health information packaged in useful forms for distribution to citizens. . . .

There are several situations where the promotion of self-care might produce undesirable results. For example, promotion of self-reliance could be used as an excuse to cut budgets for needed attention or services required by specific social segments such as the poor, the elderly, the disabled. Focus on self-care of symptoms may distract attention from causes of illness. There is need to apply the mechanisms of health service evaluation to assess the extent to which self-care might produce unintended side effects. . . .

An important point for policy development in the area of individual responsibility for self-care includes the development of guidelines for promoting individual responsibility for self-care and the use of self-care, while at the same time protecting social rights from being jeopardized. The perceived roles of professionals are not clear concerning the extent to which they could or should foster self-care decision-making and screening. . . . The mechanism for enhancing informed decision-making and the necessary incentives to do so are important research questions.

The concept of a participative partnership between the individual citizen and various health care professionals requires a reexamination of the idea of a "health care delivery system." It is unrealistic to consider some people inside a system delivering some kind of a product to people outside the system. Encouragement of interdependence always and independence often are preferable to utter dependence in health care. Such an approach could contribute to the confidence of the average citizen that health and illness are not beyond comprehension, nor is correct treatment necessarily beyond his/her competence. People encouraged to practice self-care will become more confident of the healing power of their own bodies. . . .

Enhancing Individual Initiatives for Health Recognition and Management of Self-Limited Ailments

. . . Educating people to take care of themselves is a much broader process than simply providing information about home remedies for common illnesses. It is a process whereby individuals become more independent and competent to perform maintenance and therapeutic activities on behalf of their physical, social, and emotional welfare through their own knowledge and experience. They should be able to evaluate their own health status, to seek outside sources as needed, and to provide important elements of primary care. Most importantly, they learn to be self-reliant in caring for their own needs. These self-initiated actions can perhaps best be learned as part of the more general educational objective of reasoned independence.

Education about self-care can take two such forms. The most basic is education for promotion of health maintenance, healthy habits, and risk avoidance. Another dimension is health information encompassing descriptions of diseases and their effects, as well as community resources for information and referral. . . . An excellent starting point would be to establish and publicize authoritative consensus regarding signs, symptoms, and suggested management of common self-limited conditions. . . .

Popular Self-Help Manuals

Books intended to provide basic information on health matters for popular consumption are not new or novel. A variety of valuable books, many paperbound, have appeared in recent years that are specifically intended to improve self-reliance. . . . The best of these manuals or a combination of their best portions could provide ideal textbook material for class presentations at various stages in the educational process.

The books ... employ simple decision trees or algorithms to guide the reader through a series of decisions. They cover most of the common ills that account for 60 to 70% of the reasons for seeking visits with doctors, pediatricians, internists, obstetricians, or gynecologists during a typical year.... Use of decision trees for specific ailments, rather than a collection of such protocols in a manual, also needs testing to determine their efficacy in facilitating recognition and self-management of common, self-limited ailments. Perhaps a given decision tree could be explained on spot television announcements and made available in newspaper ads on a large scale single city epidemiological-type study of its utility for various population segments.

Self-Care Kits

The information and symptomatic treatment for common complaints can also be easily packaged into highly informative kits to be dispensed by pharmacists. The packets could include specific and accurate information covering current knowledge regarding the cause(s), signs, symptoms, and possible indications of complications in understandable language, and supplemented by informative illustrations. ...

The role of the certified pharmacists could be extended to include responsibility to show each kit user how to gain maximum benefit from the material in the packets. They could supplement this information by answering specific questions or dispensing more comprehensive booklets on the subject. In this way, pharmacists could become the natural channel for dispensing information as well as appropriate medications to people at the very time when they are most interested and responsive to information about their own specific problems. ...

Health Counseling and Supportive Self-Care

Health counseling is communication in the form of guidance, information-giving, and reassurance for the purpose of helping people achieve satisfaction from their own decision-making and action-oriented health processes. ... A relatively small proportion of the general public displays complete self-reliance and self-confidence in self-care without consulting a professional. However, the numbers of people who are buying popular self-care manuals, eating natural foods, exercising, and demonstrating concern for their health are quite obviously growing spontaneously. An important obstacle to enhancing self-reliance is the common requirement for reassurance that any particular health concern is not a harbinger of something serious and that a chosen approach to eliminate symptoms is correct and safe. ...

Advice and guidance about health-related problems is by no means confined to doctors, despite the widespread tendency to expect and demand such service.... Health counseling is a major function of all participants in the health care delivery process to varying degrees and in various settings.... Each individual contributes instructions or explanations if the system is working correctly. Despite the enormous diversity of health professionals, there is inadequate provision for a readily visible information channel except through the personal physician.

Health Information Center Concept

The quality and distribution of health care could be greatly enhanced with little additional expense by providing immediate access to a source of reliable information and guidance. For this purpose, health information centers could be established within communities or neighborhoods to provide an exceedingly valuable service....

Consider a central location within a community of 5–10,000 people containing a data bank for which a full-time health counselor is responsible. This data bank would include a detailed listing and description of the available sources of health care over a very wide range of problems. For example, a roster of pharmacies organized by their zip codes could be continually kept up to date, including the names of the pharmacists who would be on call or available at various hours of the day or night. Similarly, the availability of physicians, nurses, and paramedics could be maintained for ready reference, not only in terms of their location, but also of their availability. The location and services available in drop-in clinics in the area should be detailed. The community hospitals in the immediate vicinity or at greater distances should be known, along with the particular kinds of services they are prepared to render. For both legal and practical reasons, this information center would need to have the supervision of a qualified physician to whom problems could be immediately transmitted if the patient did not have a regular physician. The responsible physician could also answer questions or give advice about issues beyond the competence of counselors.

A health information center could serve as a valuable source of reassurance to people who are home-bound and are otherwise dependent upon others in the event of an accident. A valuable referral outlet could be provided for individuals who need to talk to someone about problems which are not necessarily medical....

Medically deprived populations of the country (i.e., central cities) could derive considerable benefit from a central source of information of this sort. It would enable individuals who need guidance into the complex health care system to obtain the kind of help which could both reduce unnecessary demands on the system and at the same time provide rapid response to specific problems with the kind of services which are most relevant.

Aided Self-Reliance

The aids to access described in the preceding paragraphs do not cover diagnosis or therapy. They are intended to facilitate access to the necessary kinds of health care. However, if the person manning the health information center were a trained health professional of one sort or another, with access to a physician, an enormous amount of very useful information could be conveyed on the telephone to help individuals take care of their illnesses. For example, a nurse practitioner or a consulting nurse in such a situation is capable of providing a wealth of information that will tend to resolve a very large proportion of the minor complaints and concerns which beset any family several times a year. This is the operational equivalent of relying upon the clinic nurse of a family physician for such information and has therefore a long tradition. . . .

New Health Professionals. During recent years there has been a rapid emergence of a wide variety of new health professionals. These represent expanded roles for nurses, nurse practitioners, physicians' assistants. They have been trained to relieve physicians of some of the more routine aspects of medical care, in accordance with their particular levels of training, experience, and competence. Persons selected to play the role of the health counselor in a health information center could be selected from this broad selection of health personnel, depending on the particular situation, the nature of the population to be served, and the type and proximity of supervision. In some instances, persons living within the neighborhood could be specifically trained to establish a health information center at home after intensive training in the process. . . .

Technologies in Home Care. Specialized technology of modern health care can effectively support and supplement individual initiatives. Biomedical engineering has produced many home health aides, assistive devices, and handicapped self-help equipment to be used in homes. . . . The management of most chronic diseases (i.e., diabetes, arthritis) necessarily requires a collaborative effort among health professionals, patients, and their families. . . . The skills and knowledge to perform the various required roles and activities can be transferred from professional to patient and family.

Educational services of this kind are numerous and include hospital patient education programs, outpatient programs, clinic-based classes and courses, health maintenance organizations, health education classes, and industrial and occupation health education programs. In all these instances the public receives information to help them more actively participate in self-care activities ranging from decision making to physical care skills. . . .

Mutual Aid Groups. Certain chronic ailments are more amenable to management by nonprofessional peers than by fully trained health professionals.

A notable example is alcoholism, for which Alcoholics Anonymous has compiled a very impressive record of success. There is a bond of sympathy coupled with personal experience which can be supportive and effective in helping deal successfully with persistent problems. For example, patients with colostomies are confronted with unique problems which can be relieved by gaining skills to surmount both the practice and psychological problems of managing excreta. Such mutual aid groups have been expanding in numbers, diversity, and scope as an indication that they serve an important role in the overall health care delivery system. The exchange of information, experience, and support through mutual aid groups could be actively encouraged by the health professions to the benefit of all concerned. . . .

Health is a very large term indeed. It goes beyond the condition of the flesh. It's also a condition of the spirit. Everything we do is reflected in the physical. Over a period of years, the strains and stresses residing in the body often manifest themselves as diseases. The opposite can also be true. And ultimately health doesn't just involve isolated parts of the body. It also involves the whole way we live, the way we think, our social responsibility, our attitude toward the world, our enthusiasm for life.
—*George Leonard*

Norman Cousins

Anatomy of an Illness as Perceived by the Patient

This colorful, personal account of a participative partnership between patient and physician was written to respond to people who expressed interest in rumors that Norman Cousins "laughed" his way out of a serious illness. Whether or not the cure was, in fact, due to the patient's sheer life force and total involvement in treatment decisions, this positive and creative approach to illness suggests the value of the self-care process combined with cooperative health professionals and a strong will to live. Cousins was long-time editor of the Saturday Review *and is now on the Medical School faculty at the University of California, Los Angeles.*

This [account] is about a serious illness that occurred in 1964. I was reluctant to write about it for many years because I was fearful of creating false hopes in others who were similarly afflicted. Moreover, I knew that a single case has small standing in the annals of medical research, having little more than "anecdotal" or "testimonial" value. However, references to the illness surfaced from time to time in the general and medical press. People wrote to ask whether it was true that I "laughed" my way out of a crippling disease that doctors believed to be irreversible. In view of those questions, I thought it useful to provide a fuller account than appeared in those early reports.

In August 1964, I flew home from a trip abroad with a slight fever. The malaise, which took the form of a general feeling of achiness, rapidly deepened. Within a week it became difficult to move my neck, arms, hands, fingers, and legs. My sedimentation rate was over 80. Of all the diagnostic tests, the "sed" rate is one of the most useful to the physician. The way it works is beautifully simple. The speed with which red blood cells settle in a test tube—measured in millimeters per hour—is generally proportionate to the severity of an inflammation or infection. A normal illness, such as grippe, might produce a sedimentation reading of, say, 30 or even 40. When the rate goes well beyond 60 or 70, however, the physician knows that he is dealing with more than a casual health problem. I was hospitalized when the sed rate hit 88. Within a week it was up to 115, generally considered to be a sign of a critical condition.

There were other tests, some of which seemed to me to be more an assertion of the clinical capability of the hospital than of concern for the well-being of the patient. I was astounded when four technicians from four different departments took four separate and substantial blood samples on the same day. That the hospital didn't take the trouble to coordinate the tests, using one blood specimen, seemed to me inexplicable and irresponsible. Taking four large slugs of blood the same day even from a healthy person is hardly to be recommended. When the technicians came the second day to fill their containers with blood for processing in separate laboratories, I turned them away and had a sign posted on my door saying that I would give just one specimen every three days and that I expected the different departments to draw from one vial for their individual needs.

I had a fast-growing conviction that a hospital is no place for a person who is seriously ill. The surprising lack of respect for basic sanitation; the rapidity with which staphylococci and other pathogenic organisms can run through an entire hospital; the extensive and sometimes promiscuous use of X-ray equipment; the seemingly indiscriminate administration of tranquilizers and powerful painkillers, sometimes more for the convenience of hospital staff in managing patients than for therapeutic needs; and the regularity with which hospital routine takes precedence over the rest requirements of the patient (slumber, when it comes for an ill person, is an uncommon blessing and is not to be wantonly interrupted)—all these and other practices seemed to me to be critical shortcomings of the modern hospital.

Perhaps the hospital's most serious failure was in the area of nutrition. It was not just that the meals were poorly balanced; what seemed inexcusable to me was the profusion of processed foods, some of which contained preservatives or harmful dyes. White bread, with its chemical softeners and bleached flour, was offered with every meal. Vegetables were often overcooked and thus deprived of much of their nutritional value. No wonder the 1969 White House Conference on Food, Nutrition, and Health made the melancholy observation that a great failure of medical schools is that they pay so little attention to the science of nutrition.

My doctor did not quarrel with my reservations about hospital procedures. I was fortunate to have as a physician a man who was able to put himself in the position of the patient. Dr. William Hitzig supported me in the measures I took to fend off the random sanguinary assaults of the hospital laboratory attendants. . . .

He reviewed the reports of the various specialists he had called in as consultants. He said there was no agreement on a precise diagnosis. There was, however, a consensus that I was suffering from a serious collagen illness—a disease of the connective tissue. All arthritic and rheumatic diseases are in this category. Collagen is the fibrous substance that binds the cells together. In a sense, then, I was coming unstuck. I had considerable difficulty in moving my limbs and even in turning over in bed. Nodules appeared on my body, gravel-like substances under the skin, indicating the systemic nature of the disease. At the low point of my illness, my jaws were almost locked.

Experts... confirmed the general opinion, adding the more particularized diagnosis of ankylosing spondylitis, which would mean that the connective tissue in the spine was disintegrating.

I asked Dr. Hitzig about my chances for full recovery. He leveled with me, admitting that one of the specialists had told him I had one chance in five hundred. The specialist had also stated that he had not personally witnessed a recovery from this comprehensive condition.

All this gave me a great deal to think about. Up to that time, I had been more or less disposed to let the doctors worry about my condition. But now I felt a compulsion to get into the act. It seemed clear to me that if I was to be that one in five hundred I had better be something more than a passive observer.

I asked Dr. Hitzig about the possible origin of my condition. He said that is could have come from any one of a number of causes. It could have come, for example, from heavy-metal poisoning, or it could have been the aftereffect of a streptococcal infection.

I thought as hard as I could about the sequence of events immediately preceding the illness. I had gone to the Soviet Union in July 1964 as chairman of an American delegation to consider the problems of cultural exchange. The conference had been held in Leningrad, after which we went to Moscow for supplementary meetings. Our hotel was in a residential area. My room was on the second floor. Each night a procession of diesel trucks plied back and forth to a nearby housing project in the process of round-the-clock construction. It was summer, and our windows were wide open. I slept uneasily each night and felt somewhat nauseated on arising. On our last day in Moscow, at the airport, I caught the exhaust spew of a large jet at point-blank range as it swung around on the tarmac.

As I thought back on that Moscow experience, I wondered whether the exposure to the hydrocarbons from the diesel exhaust at the hotel and at the airport had anything to do with the underlying cause of the illness. If so, that might account for the speculations of the doctors concerning heavy-metal poisoning. The trouble with this theory, however, was that my wife, who had been with me on the trip, had no ill effects from the same exposure. How likely was it that only one of us would have reacted adversely?

It seemed to me, as I thought about it, that there were two possible explanations for the different reactions. One had to do with individual allergy. The second was that I could have been in a condition of adrenal exhaustion and less apt to tolerate a toxic experience than someone whose immunologic system was fully functional.

Was adrenal exhaustion a factor in my own illness?

Again, I thought carefully. The meetings in Leningrad and Moscow had not been casual. Paper work had kept me up late nights. I had ceremonial responsibilities. Our last evening in Moscow had been, at least for me, an exercise in almost total frustration. . . .

It was a long flight back to the States the next day. The plane was overcrowded. By the time we arrived in New York, cleared through the packed customs counters, and got rolling back to Connecticut, I could feel an uneasiness deep in my bones. A week later I was hospitalized.

As I thought back on my experience abroad, I knew that I was probably on the right track in my search for a cause of the illness. I found myself increasingly convinced, as I said a moment ago, that the reason I was hit hard by the diesel and jet pollutants, whereas my wife was not, was that I had had a case of adrenal exhaustion, lowering my resistance.

Assuming this hypothesis was true, I had to get my adrenal glands functioning properly again and to restore what Walter B. Cannon, in his famous book, *The Wisdom of the Body,* called homeostasis.

I knew that the full functioning of my endocrine system—in particular the adrenal glands—was essential for combatting severe arthritis or, for that matter, any other illness. A study I had read in the medical press reported that pregnant women frequently have remissions of arthritic or other rheumatic symptoms. The reason is that the endocrine system is fully activated during pregnancy.

How was I to get my adrenal glands and my endocrine system, in general, working well again?

I remembered having read, ten years or so earlier, Hans Selye's classic book, *The Stress of Life.* With great clarity, Selye showed that adrenal exhaustion could be caused by emotional tension, such as frustration or suppressed rage. He detailed the negative effects of the negative emotions on body chemistry.

The inevitable question arose in my mind: what about the positive emotions? If negative emotions produce negative chemical changes in the body, wouldn't the positive emotions produce positive chemical changes? Is it possible that love, hope, faith, laughter, confidence, and the will to live have therapeutic value? . . .

A plan began to form in my mind for systematic pursuit of the salutary emotions, and I knew that I would want to discuss it with my doctor. Two preconditions, however, seemed obvious for the experiment. The first concerned my medication. If that medication were toxic to any degree, it was doubtful whether the plan would work. The second precondition concerned the hospital. I knew I would have to find a place somewhat more conducive to a positive outlook on life.

Let's consider these preconditions separately.

First, the medication. The emphasis had been on pain-killing drugs—aspirin, phenylbutazone (butazolidine), codeine, colchicine, sleeping pills. The aspirin and phenylbutazone were antiinflammatory and thus were therapeutically justifiable. But I wasn't sure they weren't also toxic. It developed that I was hypersensitive to virtually all the medication I was receiving. The hospital had been giving me maximum dosages: twenty-six aspirin tablets and twelve phenylbutazone tablets a day. No wonder I had hives all over my body and felt as though my skin were being chewed up by millions of red ants.

It was unreasonable to expect positive chemical changes to take place so long as my body as being saturated with, and toxified by, pain-killing medications. I had one of my research assistants at the *Saturday Review* look up the pertinent references in the medical journals and found that drugs like phenylbutazone and even aspirin levy a heavy tax on the adrenal glands. I also learned that phenylbutazone is one of the most powerful drugs being manufactured. It can produce bloody stools, the result of its antagonism to fibrinogen. It can cause intolerable itching and sleeplessness. It can depress bone marrow.

Aspirin, of course, enjoys a more auspicious reputation, at least with the general public. The prevailing impression of aspirin is that it is not only the most harmless drug available but also one of the most effective. When I looked into research in the medical journals, however, I found that aspirin is quite powerful in its own right and warrants considerable care in its use. The fact that it can be bought in unlimited quantities without prescription or doctor's guidance seemed indefensible. Even in small amounts, it can cause internal bleeding. Articles in the medical press reported that the chemical composition of aspirin, like that of phenylbutazone, impairs the clotting function of platelets, disc-shaped substances in the blood.

It was a mind-boggling train of thought. Could it be, I asked myself, that aspirin, so universally accepted for so many years, was actually harmful in the treatment of collagen illnesses such as arthritis? . . . Suppose I stopped taking aspirin and phenylbutazone? What about the pain? The bones in my spine and practically every joint in my body felt as though I had been run over by a truck.

I knew that pain could be affected by attitudes. Most people become panicky about almost any pain. On all sides they have been so bombarded by advertisements about pain that they take this or that analgesic at the slightest sign of an ache. We are largely illiterate about pain and so are seldom able to deal with it rationally. Pain is part of the body's magic. It is the way the body transmits a sign to the brain that something is wrong. Leprous patients pray for the sensation of pain. What makes leprosy such a terrible disease is that the victim usually feels no pain when his extremities are being injured. He loses his fingers or toes because he receives no warning signal.

I could stand pain so long as I knew that progress was being made in meeting the basic need. That need, I felt, was to restore the body's capacity to halt the continuing breakdown of connective tissue.

There was also the problem of the severe inflammation. If we dispensed with the aspirin, how would we combat the inflammation? I recalled having read in the medical journals about the usefulness of ascorbic acid in combating a wide number of illnesses—all the way from bronchitis to some types of heart disease. Could it also combat inflammation? Did vitamin C act directly, or did it serve as a starter for the body's endocrine system—in particular, the adrenal glands? Was it possible, I asked myself, that ascorbic acid had a vital role to play in "feeding" the adrenal glands?

I had read in the medical press that vitamin C helps to oxygenate the blood. If inadequate or impaired oxygenation was a factor in collagen breakdown, couldn't this circumstance have been another argument for ascorbic acid? Also, according to some medical reports, people suffering from collagen diseases are deficient in vitamin C. Did this lack mean that the body uses up large amounts of vitamin C in the process of combating collagen breakdown?

I wanted to discuss some of these ruminations with Dr. Hitzig. He listened carefully as I told him of my speculations concerning the cause of the illness, as well as my layman's ideas for a course of action that might give me a chance to reduce the odds against my recovery.

Dr. Hitzig said it was clear to him that there was nothing undersized about my will to live. He said that what was most important was that I continue to believe in everything I had said. He shared my excitement about the possibilities of recovery and liked the idea of a partnership.

Even before we had completed arrangements for moving out of the hospital we began the part of the program calling for the full exercise of the affirmative emotions as a factor in enhancing body chemistry. It was easy enough to hope and love and have faith, but what about laughter? Nothing is less funny than being flat on your back with all the bones in your spine and joints hurting. A systematic program was indicated. A good place to begin, I thought, was with amusing movies. Allen Funt, producer of the spoofing television program "Candid Camera," sent films of some of his CC classics, along with a motion-picture projector. The nurse was instructed in its use. We were even able to get our hands on some old Marx Brothers films. We pulled down the blinds and turned on the machine.

It worked. I made the joyous discovery that ten minutes of genuine belly laughter had an anesthetic effect and would give me at least two hours of pain-free sleep. When the pain-killing effect of the laughter wore off, we would switch on the motion-picture projector again, and, not infrequently, it would lead to another pain-free sleep interval. Sometimes, the nurse read to me out of a trove of humor books. Especially useful were E. B. and Katharine White's *Subtreasury of American Humor* and Max Eastman's *The Enjoyment of Laughter.*

How scientific was it to believe that laughter—as well as the positive emotions in general—was affecting my body chemistry for the better? If laughter did in fact have a salutary effect on the body's chemistry, it seemed at least theoretically likely that it would enhance the system's ability to fight the inflammation. So we took sedimentation rate readings just before as well as several hours after the laughter episodes. Each time, there was a drop of at least five points. The drop by itself was not substantial, but it held and was cumulative. I was greatly elated by the discovery that there is a physiologic basis for the ancient theory that laughter is good medicine.

There was, however, one negative side-effect of the laughter from the standpoint of the hospital. I was disturbing other patients. But that objection didn't last very long, for the arrangements were now complete for me to move my act to a hotel room.

One of the incidental advantages of the hotel room, I was delighted to find, was that it cost only about one-third as much as the hospital. The other benefits were incalculable. I would not be awakened for a bed bath or for meals or for medication or for a change of bed sheets or for tests or for examinations by hospital interns. The sense of serenity was delicious and would, I felt certain, contribute to a general improvement.

What about ascorbic acid and its place in the general program for recovery? In discussing my speculations about vitamin C with Dr. Hitzig, I found him completely open-minded on the subject, although he told me of serious questions that had been raised by scientific studies. He also cautioned me that heavy doses of ascorbic acid carried some risk of renal damage. The main problem right then, however, was not my kidneys; it seemed to me that, on balance, the risk was worth taking. I asked Dr. Hitzig about previous recorded experience with massive doses of vitamin C. He ascertained that at the hospital there had been cases in which patients had received up to 3 grams by intramuscular injection.

As I thought about the injection procedure, some questions came to mind.

Introducing the ascorbic acid directly into the bloodstream might make more effective use of the vitamin, but I wondered about the body's ability to utilize a sudden, massive infusion. I knew that one of the great advantages of vitamin C is that the body takes only the amount necessary for its purposes and excretes the rest. Again, there came to mind Cannon's phrase—the wisdom of the body.

Was there a coefficient of time in the utilization of ascorbic acid? The more I thought about it, the more likely it seemed to me that the body would excrete a large quantity of the vitamin because it couldn't metabolize it fast enough. I wondered whether a better procedure than injection would be to administer the ascorbic acid through slow intravenous drip over a period of three or four hours. In this way we could go far beyond 3 grams. My hope was to start at 10 grams and then increase the dose daily until we reached 25 grams.

Dr. Hitzig's eyes widened when I mentioned 25 grams. This amount was far beyond any recorded dose. He said he had to caution me about the possible effect not just on the kidneys but on the veins in the arms. Moreover, he said he knew of no data to support the assumption that the body could handle 25 grams over a four-hour period, other than by excreting it rapidly through the urine.

As before, however, it seemed to me we were playing for bigger stakes: losing some veins was not of major importance alongside the need to combat whatever was eating at my connective tissue.

To know whether we were on the right track we took a sedimentation test before the first intravenous administration of 10 grams of ascorbic acid. Four hours later, we took another sedimentation test. There was a drop of nine full points.

Seldom had I known such elation. The ascorbic acid was working. So was laughter. The combination was cutting heavily into whatever poison was attacking the connective tissue. The fever was receding, and the pulse was no longer racing.

We stepped up the dosage. On the second day we went to 12.5 grams of ascorbic acid, on the third day, 15 grams, and so on until the end of the week, when we reached 25 grams. Meanwhile, the laughter routine was in full force. I was completely off drugs and sleeping pills. Sleep—blessed, natural sleep without pain—was becoming increasingly prolonged.

At the end of the eighth day I was able to move my thumbs without pain. By this time, the sedimentation rate was somewhere in the 80s and dropping fast. I couldn't be sure, but it seemed to me that the gravel-like nodules on my neck and the backs of my hands were beginning to shrink. There was no doubt in my mind that I was going to make it back all the way. I could function, and the feeling was indescribably beautiful.

I must not make it appear that all my infirmities disappeared overnight. For many months I couldn't get my arms up far enough to reach for a book on a high shelf. My fingers weren't agile enough to do what I wanted them to do on the organ keyboard. My neck had a limited turning radius. My knees were somewhat wobbly, and off and on, I have had to wear a metal brace.

Even so, I was sufficiently recovered to go back to my job at the *Saturday Review* full time again, and this was miracle enough for me.

Is the recovery a total one? Year by year the mobility has improved. I have become pain-free, except for one shoulder and my knees, although I have been able to discard the metal braces. I no longer feel a sharp twinge in my wrists when I hit a tennis ball or golf ball, as I did for such a long time. I can ride a horse flat out and hold a camera with a steady hand. And I have recaptured my ambition to play the Toccata and Fugue in D Minor, though I find the going slower and tougher than I had hoped. My neck has a full turning radius again, despite the statement of specialists as recently as 1971 that the condition was degenerative and that I would have to adjust to a quarter turn.

It was seven years after the onset of the illness before I had scientific confirmation about the dangers of using aspirin in the treatment of collagen diseases: . . . a study showing that aspirin can be antagonistic to the retention of vitamin C in the body. The authors said that patients with rheumatoid arthritis should take vitamin C supplements, since it has often been noted that they have low levels of the vitamin in their blood. It was no surprise, then, that I had been able to absorb such massive amounts of ascorbic acid without kidney or other complications.

What conclusions do I draw from the entire experience?

The first is that the will to live is not a theoretical abstraction, but a physiologic reality with therapeutic characteristics. The second is that I was incredibly fortunate to have as my doctor a man who knew that his biggest job was to encourge to the fullest the patient's will to live and to mobilize all the natural resources of body and mind to combat disease. Dr. Hitzig was willing to set aside the large and often hazardous armamentarium of powerful drugs available to the modern physician when he became convinced that his patient might have something better to offer. He was also wise enough to know that the art of healing is still a frontier profession. And, though I can't be sure of this point, I have a hunch he believed that my own total involvement was a major factor in my recovery.

People have asked what I thought when I was told by the specialists that my disease was progressive and incurable.

The answer is simple. Since I didn't accept the verdict, I wasn't trapped in the cycle of fear, depression, and panic that frequently accompanies a supposedly incurable illness. I must not make it seem, however, that I was un-mindful of the seriousness of the problem or that I was in a festive mood throughout. Being unable to move my body was all the evidence I needed that the specialists were dealing with real concerns. But deep down, I knew I had a good chance and relished the idea of bucking the odds.

Adam Smith, in his book, *Powers of the Mind,* says he discussed my recovery with some of his doctor friends, asking them to explain why the combination of laughter and ascorbic acid worked so well. The answer he got was that neither laughter nor ascorbic acid had anything to do with it and that I probably would have recovered if nothing had been done.

Maybe so, but that was not the opinion of the specialists at the time.

Two or three doctors, reflecting on the Adam Smith account, have commented that I was probably the beneficiary of a mammoth venture in self-administered placebos.

Such a hypothesis bothers me not at all. Respectable names in the history of medicine, like Paracelsus, Holmes, and Osler, have suggested that the history of medication is far more the history of the placebo effect than of intrinsically valuable and relevant drugs. . . .

What we are talking about essentially, I suppose, is the chemistry of the will to live. In Bucharest in 1972, I visited the clinic of Ana Aslan, described to me as one of Romania's leading endocrinologists. She spoke of her belief that there is a direct connection between a robust will to live and the chemical balances in the brain. She is convinced that creativity—one aspect of the will to live—produces the vital brain impulses that stimulate the pituitary gland, triggering effects on the pineal gland and the whole of the endocrine system. Is it possible that placebos have a key role in this process? Shouldn't this entire area be worth serious and sustained attention?

If I had to guess, I would say that the principal contribution made by my doctor to the taming, and possibly the conquest, of my illness was that he encouraged me to believe I was a respected partner with him in the total undertaking. He fully engaged my subjective energies. He may not have been able to define or diagnose the process through which self-confidence (wild hunches securely believed) was somehow picked up by the body's immunologic mechanisms and translated into antimorbid effects, but he was acting, I believe, in the best tradition of medicine in recognizing that he had to reach out in my case beyond the usual verifiable modalities. In so doing, he was faithful to the first dictum in his medical education: above all, do not harm.

Something else I have learned. I have learned never to underestimate the capacity of the human mind and body to regenerate—even when the prospects seem most wretched. The life-force may be the least understood force on earth. William James said that human beings tend to live too far within self-imposed limits. It is possible that these limits will recede when we respect more fully the natural drive of the human mind and body toward perfectibility and regeneration. Protecting and cherishing that natural drive may well represent the finest exercise of human freedom.

States of health or disease are the expressions of the success or failure experienced by the organism in its efforts to respond adaptively to environmental challenge.

—*René Dubos*

15 Health Care and the Future: Individual or Social Responsibility?

MARK TUSCHMAN

In the past one hundred years, there has been a vast improvement in the nation's health; life expectancy has dramatically increased, and infant mortality has sharply declined. These welcome changes were due largely to advances in nutrition through improvements in the abundance and distribution of food supplies; major progress in hygiene and sanitation; and steady increases in the development of immunization against infectious diseases. Most of these measures did not depend on active individual participation. They were the products of evolution in the fields of sanitation and agriculture and a revolution in public health techniques. Gradually the emphasis shifted away from public health toward the application of biomedical technologies in individual medical treatment. Health care became, for many, synonymous with medical care.

In the past decade health professionals have begun to challenge the purely medical approach to health care, and a new constellation of ideas has emerged. As patterns of disease and disability have changed, so has our understanding of disease. We recognize that for many diseases multiple factors are involved—biological, behavioral, social, cultural, and environmental. More and more, it seems, it is what and how much we eat, whether or not we have a job, stresses in daily life and how we deal with them, whether or not we smoke cigarettes, our income, our family and social networks, our degree of physical activity, and safety on the streets and highways, in the cities and in our homes—that determine our level of health.

Modern medical treatment benefits millions of individuals, through life-saving surgical and chemotherapy techniques and through a reduction in the burden of illness and disability. Many people believe that there is a mismatch, however, between current treatment modes and the modern realities of death and disease. Heart disease, cancer, and stroke, as well as accidents, are now the major killers. With the dramatic rise in life expectancy, many of us are living longer, but our chances of developing one or more of the chronic, degenerative diseases have increased. So has the likelihood of living for many years with a disabling illness such as diabetes, arthritis, mental illness, coronary artery and cerebral vascular disease, chronic obstructive lung disease, peptic ulcer, high blood pressure, and cirrhosis of the liver.

Because of this new pattern, health professionals and others are beginning to acknowledge that it is individual and collective action, from self-care to public health, that must be nurtured in order to promote and protect our health. The health status of Americans in the next decade will depend on the quality of actions taken by government, business, and health professionals, as well as by families and individuals acting in their own behalf. It is important to stress that while individual responsibility may well be the key to disease prevention, health promotion, and health care, changes in national health status are unlikely without major improvements in economic, social, and environmental conditions. Sole responsibility no longer lies with doctors and others in the health care system; irrevocably, it is shared by us all.

The late John Knowles, formerly professor of medicine at Harvard and president of the Rockefeller Foundation, discusses "The Responsibility of the Individual" for health and explores the means for enhancing this dimension of health care and health protection. Franz Ingelfinger's article, "Medicine: Meritorious or Meretricious," argues that we expect physicians to do everything—cure our diseases and society's ills as well. In reality, their abilities are limited to a few "truly wondrous" cures. For the rest of our aches and pains, says Ingelfinger, late editor of the *New England Journal of Medicine,* we are no better off than our grandparents.

Lewis Thomas's message in "On the Science and Technology of Medicine" is clear—we must increase our knowledge! He would have us look to biomedical research for the answers to medicine's mysteries, in order to improve the health care system of the future. Robert Claiborne, a writer on issues of science and society, would probably label this approach as an extension of "sickness care." In "A Penny of Prevention: The Cure for America's Health Care System," he urges us to shape the health of future Americans by improving their living conditions—economic, social, and environmental. Not only will people be healthier, they will live in a decent environment that will greatly enrich their lives. He believes that this is a question of values, and the assumptions that are currently in vogue reflect the values of the statement, "them as has, gits."

The final selection in our Reader, "Creating Better Health," closes with a warning. Erik P. Eckholm of Worldwatch Institute cautions that the only way we can insure the health of future generations is to protect the natural environment in which we live. At the rate we are plundering the atmosphere, oceans, soils, and animal and plant life, we are jeopardizing health for the planet's entire population.

John H. Knowles

The Responsibility of the Individual

Noting that the medical profession has reflected our culture's faith in science and technology, the late Dr. John H. Knowles argues that our health problems can best be solved through a combination of individual and social responsibility. He discusses why we have failed to assume such responsibility in the past, and maintains that solutions to health problems demand integration of knowledge from the biological, behavioral, and social sciences.

T he health of human beings is determined by their behavior, their food, and the nature of their environment. The first agricultural revolution occurred 10,000 years ago with the domestication of plants and animals. Nomadic hunter-gatherers settled around their flocks and fields. Nutrition improved, with a resultant fall in mortality and rise in birth rates. The population expanded, but its growth was checked periodically by crop failures and famine, tribal war over scarce resources, infectious disease now easily transmitted by air, water, and food among settled people, and the common practice of infanticide. The population was under 10 million people.

By 1750, the number of people in the world had grown to 750 million, by 1830 to one billion, by 1930 to two billion, by 1960 to three billion, and then to four billion today. This massive growth of population resulted from the fall in mortality rates attendant upon steadily increasing food supplies. Improved nutrition again increased birth rates and resistance to infectious disease. The greater availabilityof food also reduced the practice of infanticide.

The second agricultural revolution had begun in the eighteenth century; it included increased land use, extensive manuring to restore soil fertility, crop rotation, winter feeding, and the widespread cultivation of potatoes and maize. A massive increase in available food was extended still further by the Industrial Revolution of the nineteenth and twentieth centuries through mechanization, extensive irrigation, chemical fertilizers, and pesticides. The "Green Revolution" of the past thirty years further increased food production, and was based on genetic manipulations which produced hardier and more productive varieties of crops, responsive to the more intensive use of water and fertilizer.

More than half the reduction in mortality rates over the past three centuries occurred before 1900 and was due in nearly equal measures to improved nutrition and reduced exposure to air- and water-borne infection. The provision of safe water and milk supplies, the improvement in both personal and food hygiene, and the efficient disposal of sewage all helped to reduce the incidence of infectious disease. Vaccination further reduced mortality rates from smallpox in the nineteenth century and from diphtheria, pertussis, tetanus, poliomyelitis, measles, and tuberculosis in the twentieth century, although the contribution of vaccinations to the overall reduction in mortality rates over the past hundred years is small (perhaps as small as 10 per cent) as contrasted with that due to improved nutrition and reduction in the transmission of infectious disease. An even smaller contribution has been made by the introduction of medical and surgical therapy, namely antibiotics and the excision of tumors, in the twentieth century.

Over the past 100 years, infanticide has declined in the developed countries as changes in reproductive practice, such as the use of contraceptives, have been introduced to contain family size and reduce national growth rates of population, thus sustaining the improvement in health and standards of living. The population of England and Wales trebled between 1700 and 1850 without any significant importation of food. If the birth rate had been maintained, the population by now would be some 140 million instead of the 46 million it actually is. Changes in reproductive behavior maintained a rough balance between food production and population growth and allowed standards of living to rise. A similarly remarkable change in reproductive behavior occurred in Ireland following the potato famines of the eighteen-forties, and birth rates have been sustained voluntarily at a low level to this day in that largely Catholic country.

Improvement in health resulted from changes in personal behavior (hygiene, reproductive practices) and in environmental conditions (food supplies, provision of safe milk and water, and sewage disposal). Cartesian rationalism, Baconian empiricism, and the results of the Industrial Revolution led the medical profession into scientific and technical approaches to disease. The engineering approach to the human machine was strengthened by the germ theory of disease which followed the work of Pasteur and Koch in the late nineteenth century. The idea was simple, unitary, and compelling: one germ—one disease—one therapy. Population factors, personal behavior, and environmental conditions were neglected in such a pure model or paradigm of approach and were picked up by elements less powerful and perceived increasingly as marginal to health, i.e., politicians, state departments, and schools of public health. The medical profession hitched its wagon to the rising stars of science and technology. The results have been spectacular for some individuals in terms of cure, containment of disease, and alleviation of suffering; as spectacular in terms of the horrendous costs compounding now at a rate of 15 per cent annually; and even more spectacular to some because allocation of more and more men and women, money, and machines has affected mortality and morbidity rates only marginally. The problem of diminishing returns, if current trends continue, will loom as large and pregnant to the American people in the future as the mushrooming atomic cloud does today.

I will not berate the medical profession, its practitioners and its professors—they reflect our culture, its values, beliefs, rites, and symbols. Central to the culture is faith in progress through science, technology, and industrial growth; increasingly peripheral to it is the idea, vis-à-vis health, that over 99 per cent of us are born healthy and made sick as a result of personal misbehavior and environmental conditions. The solution to the problems of ill health in modern American society involves individual responsibility, in the first instance, and social responsibility through public legislative and private voluntary efforts, in the second instance. Alas, the medical profession isn't interested, because the intellectual, emotional, and financial rewards of the present system are too great and because there is no incentive and very little demand to change. But the problem of rising costs; the allocation of scarce national resources among competing claims for improving life; diminishing returns on health from the system of acute, curative, high-cost, hospital-based medicine; and increasing evidence that personal behavior, food, and the nature of the environment around us are the prime determinants of health and disease will present us with critical choices and will inevitably force change.

*   *   *

Most individuals do not worry about their health until they lose it. Uncertain attempts at healthy living may be thwarted by the temptations of a culture whose economy depends on high production and high consumption. . . .

Facing the insufferable insult of extinction with the years, and knowing how we might improve our health, we still don't do much about it. The reasons for this peculiar behavior may include: (1) a denial of death and disease coupled with the demand for instant gratification and the orientation of most people in most cultures to living day by day; (2) the feeling that nature, including death and disease, can be conquered through scientific and technologic advance or overcome by personal will; (3) the dispiriting conditions of old people leads to a decision by some that they don't want infirmities and unhappiness and would just as soon die early: (4) chronic depression in some individuals to the extent that they wish consciously or unconsciously for death and have no desire to take care of themselves; and (5) the disinterest of the one person to whom we ascribe the ultimate wisdom about health—the physician. . . .

I believe the idea of a "right" to health should be replaced by the idea of an individual moral obligation to preserve one's own health—a public duty if you will. The individual then has the "right" to expect help with information, accessible services of good quality, and minimal financial barriers. Meanwhile, the people have been led to believe that national health insurance, more doctors, and greater use of high-cost, hospital-based technologies will improve health. Unfortunately none of them will.

More and more the artificer of the possible is "society"—not the individual; he thereby becomes more dependent on things external and less on his own inner resources. The paranoid style of consumer groups demands a fight against something, usually a Big Bureaucracy. In the case of health, it is the hospitals, the doctors, the medical schools, the Medicaid-Medicare combine, the government. Nader's Raiders have yet to allow that the next major advances in the health of the American people will come from the assumption of individual responsibility for one's own health and a necessary change in habits for the majority of Americans. We do spend over $30 billion annually for cigarettes and whiskey. . . .

The barriers to the assumption of individual responsibility for one's own health are lack of knowledge (implicating the inadequacies of formal education, the all-too-powerful force of advertising, and of the informal systems of continuing education), lack of sufficient interest in, and knowledge about, what is preventable and the "cost-to-benefit" ratios of nationwide health programs (thereby implicating all the powerful interests in the health establishment, which couldn't be less interested, and calling for a much larger investment in fundamental and applied research), and a culture which has progressively eroded the idea of individual responsibility while stressing individual rights, the responsibility of society-at-large, and the steady growth of production and consumption ("We have met the enemy and it is us!"). Changing human behavior involves sustaining and repeating an intelligible message, reinforcing it through peer pressure and approval, and establishing clearly perceived rewards which materialize in as short a time as possible. Advertising agencies know this, but it is easier to sell deodorants, pantyhose, and automobiles than it is health. . . .

Attempts to prevent disease and improve and maintain health involve multifaceted strategies and expertise from many disciplines. Fundamental to any and all such attempts is sufficient empirical knowledge, i.e., knowledge gained through observation and trial-and-error experimentation that allows the advocate to convey his information with sufficient conviction to change the behavior of his audience. Although a great deal of information is available, the whole field of preventive medicine and health education needs far more fundamental research and long-term field experimentation. The biological and epidemiological effects of a wide variety of pollutants, the cost-benefit ratios of many available screening services, the influence of financial sanctions on changing health behavior, the use of the mass media and their effect on cognition and behavior, the long-term effects of various therapeutic regimens on the morbidity and mortality of individuals with asymptomatic high blood pressure, the long-term effects of marked reduction of fat in the diet on the incidence of cancer and heart disease, the influence of personal income on the development or cancer and coronary disease (the death rate from both lung cancer and coronary disease is significantly lower for the affluent than for the poor) are all examples of problems that need study. These problems demand for their solution the participation and integration of the disciplines of the biological sciences, the behavioral and social sciences (social, psychology, economics, cultural anthropology, political science), and public health (epidemiology and biostatistics).

It is a sad fact that of a total annual national expenditure on health of $120 billion, only 2 to 2.5 per cent is spent on disease prevention and control measures, and only 0.5 per cent each for health education and for improving the organization and delivery of health services. The national (federal) outlay for environmental-health research is around 0.25 per cent of total health expenditures. . . . Strategies for improving health must include the incorporation of preventive measures into personal health services and into the environment, and individual and mass educational efforts. . . . Carrying out such a strategy involves many variables—convincing the doctor to play his pivotal role (and most medical educators and physicians are singularly uninterested in prevention), altering financing mechanisms to provide incentives to use preventive services (and most health insurance is, in fact, "disease insurance" which does not cover health education and preventive measures), and stimulating public as well as private efforts to exercise restraint on advertising and to exert positive sanctions for dissemination of health information through the mass media.

The health catastrophe related to automobile accidents presents a different type of problem. Here, personal-health services include availability of rapid transportation and first aid, emergency medical services, and definitive acute-care services in regional general hospitals; environmental measures would relate to road and highway construction (including lighting, warning signs, speed limits, safety rails), and the design and construction of automobiles for safety; and educational measures would include driver training, relicensing with eye examination, avoidance of alcohol and other drugs before driving, and reduction of speed. . . .

Conceptually, it is useful to subdivide preventive medicine into three classes: primary prevention and the measures employed to prevent disease, such as vaccination against measles; secondary prevention, that is, the early detection of disease so that active therapeutic intervention can be employed to cure or arrest the progress of the disease—examples are the detection of high blood pressure or the use of mammography to detect cancer of the breast: and tertiary prevention, which comprises those measures that will slow the progress or avoid the complications of established (chronic) disease—an example is the education of the patient with diabetes in the nature of the disease and its treatment: insulin administration, diet control, exercise, urine testing, and care of the feet.... All three forms of prevention require the organization of personal health services, reinforced by environmental measures and mass education. The most good can be obtained, relative to the cost, where large populations can be reached over time, e.g., school, hospital clinic, place of work, or the doctor's office....

*   *   *

... What is the responsibility of the individual in matters pertaining to health? The United States now spends more on health in absolute terms and as a percentage of the gross national product than any other nation in the world.... No one—but no one—can deny the fact that billions of dollars could be saved ... if our present knowledge of health and disease could be utilized in programs of primary, secondary, and tertiary prevention. The greatest portion of our national expenditure goes for the curing of the major causes of premature, and therefore preventable, death and/or disability in the United States, i.e., heart disease, cancer, strokes, accidents, bronchitis and emphysema, cirrhosis of the liver, mental illness and retardation, dental caries, suicide and homicide, venereal disease, and other infections....

*   *   *

The individual must realize that a perpetuation of the present system of high cost, after-the-fact medicine will only result in higher costs and greater frustration. The next major advances in the health of the American people will be determined by what the individual is willing to do for himself and for society-at-large. If he is willing to follow Breslow's seven rules for healthy living, he can extend his life and enhance his own and the nation's productivity. If he is willing to reassert his authority with his children, he can provide for their optimal mental and physical development. If he participates fully in private and public efforts to reduce the hazards of the environment, he can reduce the causes of premature death and disability. If he is unwilling to do these things, he should stop complaining about the steadily rising costs of medical care and the disproportionate share of the GNP that is consumed by health

Table 1. Preventive Medicine Procedures: Middle-Age Adult

Procedure	*Detection-Prevention-Treatment-Implication*
History	Symptoms, environmental exposures, habits, mental status
Height and weight	Obesity, malnutrition, metabolic disease
Blood pressure	Hypertension
Electrocardiogram	Heart disease; baseline for future
Vision (including pressure measurement-tonometry)	Myopia of aging; glaucoma
Spirometry	Breathing disorders; bronchitis, emphysema
Physical examination including dental	Span of physical abnormalities
Breast examination	Cancer (also occurs rarely in males)
Rectal examination	Cancer of rectum and prostate
Sigmoidoscopy	Cancer of rectum and colon
Pelvic examination	Cancer of vagina, cervix, uterus, and ovary
Laboratory Examinations:	
Multiphasic Screening	
Blood cholesterol & triglycerides	Heart disease
Sugar	Diabetes
Uric acid	Gout, heart disease, kidney disease
SGOT	Liver disease
Hemoglobin-hematocrit	Anemia (nutrition, cancer, iron deficiency)
Urea nitrogen	Kidney disease
Creatinine	Kidney disease
Urine examination	Bladder and kidney infection or disease; cancer
VDRL	Syphilis
Tuberculin test	Tuberculosis
Gonococcal culture (usually females)	Gonorrhea
Pap smear (females)	Cancer of cervix of uterus
Stool guiac	Occult blood in stool; bowel cancer
Mammography (females)	Cancer of breast
Chest x-ray	Cancer, emphysema, tuberculosis of lung, heart disease
Tetanus and diphtheria boosters	Infectious disease
Counseling: Health Education	
Nutrition	Heart disease, cancer, liver disease
Smoking	Cancer, heart and lung disease
Alcohol and drugs	Liver disease, accidents
Contraception	Family planning, mongolism
Exercise	Heart disease, vascular disease
Sleep	General health, accidents
Accidents	Alcohol, orthopedic problems
Mental status	Male and female menopause, work, stress
Abortion	Genetic disease; maternal health

care.... He can either remain the problem or become the solution to it; Beneficent Government cannot—indeed, should not—do it for him or to him.

In terms of public policy and the social responsibility of the individual, I believe he should consider the following:

1. Support vastly increased funding to develop the best possible integration of health education into the school system, stressing measures that the individual can take to preserve his own health and knowledge about environmental hazards....

2. Support a far greater national commitment for research in health education and preventive medicine with emphasis on epidemiologic studies, benefit-cost analysis, and the most effective and least offensive ways of changing human behavior.

3. With respect to cigarettes and whiskey, the individual should support greatly increased taxes on the consumption of both, massive public education programs on the hazards of their use, and severe restrictions on advertising. New tax money generated could be used to defray the costs of public education. Consumption should fall and health improve with the above measures. A more extreme additional measure would be to limit amounts available for consumption and to provide subsidies to help producers change to other products.

4. Support the development of genetic-counseling services, family-planning services, and selective abortion.

5. Support the development of age-specific preventive measures, which would include selective screening and counseling services. Preventive services must be tied into a comprehensive system of personal-health services to provide for continuous follow-up. Programs to expand the numbers of qualified individuals in the disciplines of health education and preventive-medicine services and research must be supported.

6. "Disease insurance" should be converted to health insurance. Coverage for preventive medicine and health education would change the behavior of both consumers and producers by introducing economic sanctions. We have barely scratched the surface in our search for those that would be most effective.

7. More attention should be devoted to the family as the basic social unit of the nation. The responsibilities of parents—for using genetic counseling and family planning, for pursuing the proper intellectual, affective, and physical develoment of their children both at home and in school, and for setting the example of individual responsibility and prudence in their own life styles—are paramount. A nation is only as strong as its children and as good as its parents.

8. The shadows of disease and unhealthy habits follow poverty and igno-rance. The greatest costs are incurred, but the greatest benefits can be ob-tained, through preventive medicine and health-education measures aimed specifically at impoverished minority groups in inner-city as well as rural areas. Quite beyond these direct measures, one must understand that total health depends on the eradication of poverty and ignorance, the availability of jobs, adequate transportation, recreation and housing, the level of public safety, and an aesthetically pleasing and physically benevolent environment. Improve health—improve those elements equally which are central to the quality of life. . . .

*   *   *

I began by saying that the health of human beings is determined by their be-havior, their food, and the nature of their environment. Over 99 per cent of us are born healthy and suffer premature death and disability only as a result of personal misbehavior and environmental conditions. The sociocultural effects of urban industrial life are profound in terms of stress, an unnatural sedentary existence, bad habits, and unhealthy environmental influences. The individual has the power—indeed, the moral responsibility—to maintain his own health by the observance of simple, prudent rules of behavior relating to sleep, exercise, diet and weight, alcohol, and smoking. In addition, he should avoid where possible the long-term use of drugs. He should be aware of the dangers of stress and the need for precautionary measures during periods of sudden change, such as bereavement, divorce, or new employment. He should submit to selective medical examination and screening procedures.

These simple rules can be understood and observed by the majority of Americans, namely the white, well-educated, and affluent middle class. But how do individuals in minority groups follow these rules, when their members include disproportionately large numbers of the impoverished and the illiter-ate, among whom fear, ignorance, desperation, and superstition conspire against even the desire to remain healthy? Here we must rely on social poli-cies *first,* in order to improve education, employment, civil rights, and eco-nomic levels, along with efforts to develop accessible health services.

Beyond these measures, the individual is powerless to control disease-provoking environmental contaminants, be they drugs, air and water pollu-tants, or food additives, except as he becomes knowledgeable enough to par-ticipate in public debate and in support of governmental controls. Here, we must depend on the wisdom of experts, the results of research, and the na-tional will to legislate controls for our protection, as damaging as they may be, in the short run, to our national economy.

When all is said and done, let us not forget that he who hates sin, hates humanity. Life is meant to be enjoyed, and each one of us in the end is still able in our own country to steer his vessel to his own port of desire. But the costs of individual irresponsibility in health have now become prohibitive. The choice is individual responsibility or social failure. Responsibility and duty must gain some degree of parity with right and freedom.

MARK TUSCHMAN

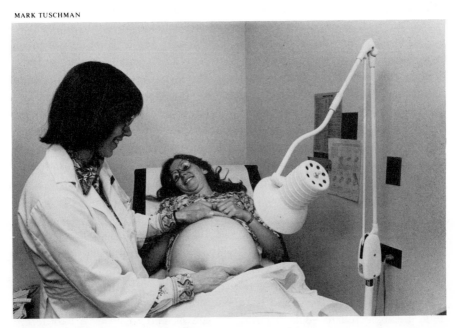

A nurse practitioner at the University of California, San Francisco, Medical Center looks optimistically at the promise of new life.

Franz J. Ingelfinger

Medicine: Meritorious or Meretricious

In spite of remarkable advances in medical therapy and in the development of fantastic diagnostic devices, Americans are increasingly disenchanted with physicians. The paradox can be explained by the high cost of medical care, the overselling of medicine's capabilities, and the expectation that the physician will be both ultrascientific and as empathetic as yesterday's doctor. Dr. Franz Ingelfinger, formerly editor of the New England Journal of Medicine, *questions the ability of doctors to take responsibility for the broad task of improving personal and societal practices disadvantageous to health.*

It is, in my opinion, the unlikeliest of all times for us to be getting ourselves into a depression about medical science," wrote Lewis Thomas. Theodore Cooper, a respected and experienced authority in both medical research and administration, asserts, in appraising today's American medicine, "Never has anything sounded so bad that has actually been so good." But the title of Aaron Wildavsky's essay "Health in the United States" frames the paradox in the choicest of epigrams, "Doing better and feeling worse.". . .

The paradox identified by Thomas, Cooper, and Wildavsky is born of the fact that society, although it itself has abandoned the old-fashioned virtues, still demands to find them in the sons of Hippocrates. Physicians, indeed, are expected to be chimeralike creatures who, on one hand, should be expert in the fabulous knowledge and skills of the scientific century, but on the other, should simultaneously display the humanity, compassion, and devotion attributed to "the good old doc.". . .

The fatherly physician is not only vanishing spontaneously but is hastened in his exit by the boot of the antiauthoritarian activist. American society has opted for the conveniences and efficiencies that are the products of scientific invention, and paramount among this society's goals are financial success and security. Should doctors, who en masse are ordinary if specially educated folk, be expected to seek different objectives and to observe a different ethos?

Like the rest of American society, the doctor has become addicted to, if not the slave of, the device that can be plugged into the electric circuit (at least as long as the necessary sources of energy hold out). The products of technology that he uses in his business—whether x-rays, fiber optics, nuclear imaging, or chemical reactions—are expensive and at times foreboding. . . . If doctors are technologically oriented, hurried, and impersonally distant in their behavior, it is only because they, as a group, mirror the society of which they are an integral part. In contrast, their deviations from the canons of old are particularly exposed to censure, partly because the profession has so insistently professed its dedication to charitable and humanitarian objectives, and partly because in the application of scientific inventions, the doctor has become more and more affluent.

Advances in Medicine: Treatment

. . . The doctor of 1978 has available a vast array of antibiotics to combat infections not preventable by immunization. Tuberculosis, identified by Bunyan as "the Captain of the men of death," and pneumonia, so identified by Osler, are not the killers that they used to be. McKeown is undoubtedly correct in asserting that improved nutrition and sanitation have in a major way contributed to the decline of infectious diseases, but the idea that antimicrobials did not do their part seems a bit farfetched. . . .

Advances in Medicine: Diagnosis

The most fantastic of scientific achievements have, however, taken place in the domain of diagnostics. Indeed, although people still die in our major hospitals, very few die undiagnosed. Samples of bodily tissues and fluids can be obtained with needle-tipped devices designed to penetrate with relative safety into almost any organ or cavity. These samples can then be examined for their structure, immunologic properties, enzymatic activities, and content of organic and inorganic substances. The electron microscope yields pictures of cellular details with good resolution at magnifications exceeding 50,000, and the radioimmunoassay permits detection and measurement of materials present in only picogram amounts.

Chromatographic techniques facilitate the discovery and identification of compounds not previously known to exist in the body. Systems of sequential analysis permit the rapid, efficient, and relatively cheap performance of some 20 common quantitative blood tests. Catheters can be inserted into blood vessels, and, with the injection of contrast materials, allow the definition of large or small portions of the vascular tree. The structure and function of organs can be determined by appropriate radioactive substances. The wonders of radiology appear to be capped by the development of computerized tomography, known as CT or CAT scanning. In this generally noninvasive procedure, x-ray beams are passed through a cross-sectional plane of the body from many different angles; the absorption of these beams is then measures and computerized to yield a density image of the planes studied.... Ultrasonography... may be used to outline a fetus, gallbladder, or pancreas, or to identify the nature and motion of heart valves.... The lining of hollow organs can be viewed and photographed directly by means of flexible fiberoptic tubes....

Disenchantment with Modern Medicine

This imposing array of diagnostic and therapeutic procedures that science has made available to medicine during the 20th century—can certainly be rated as meritorious. Why, then, the discontent, the denunciation of medicine and its practitioners, and even calls—not restricted to Ivan Illich by any means— for demedicalizing ourselves? Why the anguished complaint that, in proportion to the billions spent in the pursuit of health, the prolongation of life, or the enhancement of its quality, is so relatively infinitesimal? Some of the reasons are natural, others social, but a third variety stems from certain meretricious aspects that have tainted medical practice even as knowledge, equipment, and skills have proliferated.

A major natural cause is that life is finite and, in spite of tales of frolicking centenarians in Ecuador and the Caucasus, the span of life is approaching an asymptote. Hence, no matter how many dollars are poured into the effort, the returns in years of life saved will inexorably diminish. The claim, moreover, that, if everyone led an abstemious life and observed all the rules now believed to maintain healthiness "billions of dollars" would be saved, warrants some critical examination. One would expect that taking care of an older, less productive, and increasingly mentally senile population would cost more rather than less; and, even if money were saved by increasing the longevity of those who have already passed the age of 65, that saving would obtain for only a few years. Sooner or later the same deaths and the same expenses would have to be faced. Finally, in spite of the remarkable achievements of certain men and women who live to the age of 80 or even 90, the average quality of life at such advanced ages may well be less rather than greater. Many a man and woman past the age of 75 suffers now only physical deterioration, but increased loneliness and incapacity to do the things that make life worth living. Excessive concern with longevity is, as some have suggested, a disease in itself.

A second natural cause is that the determinants of life are legion, and the defeat of one merely gives opportunity to another. He who is spared a myocardial infarct will have a cerebrovascular disorder (stroke), frequently a far worse fate than a heart attack. She who is saved from cancer A is at risk for cancer B, and, above all, the very therapies that stave off the traditional causes of mortality and morbidity, that is, potent antibiotics, adrenal cortical hormones, and the chemical and radiologic procedures used to treat those with malignant tumors, produce a so-called "compromised" host who may be victimized by microflora that ordinarily are merely commensal. Hence, one is faced by the commonsensical conclusion that saving an elderly person from one illness merely exposes him to another, and also that the morbid effects of certain potent treatments actually increase the susceptibility of the patient to another disorder. Therapeutic success, in a way, thus fertilizes the ground for failure.

Of the social causes that lead to the denunciation of much of medicine, the major one, namely the expectation that the physician should somehow live in an ultratechnologic and impersonal society without acquiring the characteristics of that society, has already been discussed at length. . . . The great abundance of scientific and technologic means available to treat and diagnose illness may be a source of confusion and frustration rather than otherwise. Contributing to this public perplexity are the various schools of thought that make astounding if not outrageous claims concerning the causes, nature, and treatment of the many disorders that still defy medical management. . . . If suddenly the number of available techniques, instruments, and specialists were curtailed, and if health care were to be rationed—as some threaten it may be—much of the criticism of medical care would probably subside rapidly.

Crisis-Care versus Holistic Medicine

Another common complaint, so common as to be a bit trite by this time, is that Hippocrates is crisis-oriented, that he sees his mission as the cure or amelioration of symptoms rather than as the prevention of disease, and that he is committed to the management of sickness rather than the preservation of health. These facts are undeniable; but whether or not they constitute adequate basis for criticism is debatable and depends upon one's point of view. My own feeling is that patients visit doctors in the hope of feeling better, that they want the doctor to exercise a healing function, and that they expect him to render personal health services. For these purposes, he is specifically trained, and for these purposes—if he is a good doctor—he uses his scientific information and exercises his art. . . .

Others would argue that the doctor is a factotum of health, that his general mission is comprehensive health care, and that his approach to the patient should be holistic with emphasis on the patient's total relations with an environment, including his family, his work, and his habits, as well as his natural surroundings. The goals of holistic medicine are, of course, admirable;

nobody would argue that treatment of a disease is preferable to its prevention. Comprehensive prevention, however, entails skills and efforts that are beyond the capabilities of many a good doctor. Preventive health measures are much more influenced by occupations than can shape social attitudes rather than by individual doctors.... Ironically the present emphasis on eliminating "bad" life-styles and opting for the temperate life reflects the success of scientifically based medical practice in controlling acute illness and thus uncovering the importance of degenerative diseases and medicine's relative inability to do anything about them.... The doctor should not be expected to play a major role in changing whatever life-styles may be seriously detrimental. He has enough to do if he takes care of the crisis illnesses that do occur, and if he keeps up to date with the various scientific facts known about their nature and management. Hence, I would not consider the failure of the doctor to practice holistic medicine as substantive evidence of inferior medical practice.

The Overselling of Medicine

Another trouble is that the capabilities of medicine, great as they are, have been oversold. Many parties are to blame. Although individual physicians may be well aware of the limitations of medicine and emphasize them, organized medicine has on the whole encouraged a belief in the doctor's omniscience rather than his ignorance. The news media, whether printed or televised, compete with each other to broadcast the latest "breakthrough" (a word that should be eliminated from the medical lexicon) with findings that are at best preliminary and at worst totally unfounded. But perhaps most culpable are the massive voluntary health groups. In one fearsome advertisement after another, these organizations suggest to the public that, if only a few more dollars were thrown in the research till, the major killer diseases would be contained.... It is organizations such as these, along with medical societies, news media, and politicians that promise too much, that are in large part responsible for the fact that we are feeling worse though actually doing better....

Meretricious Overutilization

The meretricious aspect of the splendid tools and methods with which science has enriched, literally as well as figuratively, medical practice is their overutilization. Not only does the very abundance of medications, equipment, and special techniques create its own demand, but this demand is enhanced by the social, political, and economic factors that prevail in the United States.

The average practitioner is tempted or prodded into carrying out large batteries of tests that are of questionable necessity. Perhaps he wants to provide his patient with the most thorough "work-up" possible, perhaps he feels he has to practice defensive medicine to protect himself from malpractice suits, or perhaps profit motives underlie his actions. Whatever the reason, not all tests are innocuous, and when an unnecessary diagnostic procedure is responsible for pain, incapacity, or even death, the benefits of modern diagnostics become diluted. In analogous fashion, medicines may be prescribed when none are needed, or more potent, and particularly more toxic, products are administered when milder and safer agents would do.

The specialist who has invested in expensive diagnostic equipment is motivated to use that equipment even when the indications are marginal. The hospital that has installed elaborate facilities for some esoteric medical purposes is not anxious to have these facilities remain idle. And the theory that the number of elective operations performed reflect the availability of qualified surgeons rather than the needs of patients has gained so much credibility that more and more insurance systems, particularly those controlled by government, will not pay for certain elective operations unless the need for the procedure is confirmed by a second opinion. At present it is unknown just how many removals of tonsils, gallbladders, wombs, prostates, or hemorrhoids are mandatory, discretionary, or literally unnecessary; that is "instead of contributing to the well-being of a patient, [are] performed because of ignorance, faulty judgment or a desire for personal gain."...

Not only the doctor should be blamed, however, for the meretricious overutilization of the ingenious but usually very expensive medical methods made possible by science. Many a patient demands whatever health services are available, partly because he has ... been oversold as to their value, but principally because, in Wildavsky's words, the patient's simple rule "is to seek care up to the level of his insurance." Thus everyone involved in health services, both providers and consumers in today's popular catchwords, faces no disincentives but is, to the contrary, stimulated to use or seek the "latest" and "best" diagnostic and therapeutic methods that science-based medicine has to offer. The fantastic dollar costs of this medical-social-political-economic exploitation of scientific instruments and skills are stressed ad infinitum...; but equally important, though less often mentioned, are the human costs, the misery and sickness, that are among the disadvantageous consequences when the diagnostic implements and therapeutic modalities of our science-based medicine are overused.

Conclusion

L. J. Henderson, one of Harvard's famous biochemists, is frequently credited with the following aphorism: "Somewhere between 1910 and 1912 in this country, a random patient, with a random disease, consulting a doctor chosen at random had, for the first time in the history of mankind, a better than fifty-fifty chance of profiting from the encounter." Have the patient's chances, as Henderson's words imply, increased appreciably since 1912? The average span of life has of course been prolonged because of the markedly diminished death rates of infants and children, but whether medical care should receive credit for this improvement is much debated. For those who have reached middle and older ages, the possible beneficial effects of patient-physician encounter have not on the average been very impressive. How, in the face of the many medical advances made possible by science, is this relative lack of progress possible? Some of the reasons have already been discussed: the older patient cured of one disease is thereby merely exposed to another; and although the aggressive, interventionist methods used by all kinds of physicians produce some astounding therapeutic victories that were formerly impossible, the same heroic methods produce iatrogenic disease (and death), also formerly impossible. An exact or even approximate balance of accounts is, however, not available.... One would like to think, however, that the beneficial effects of venturesome diagnosis and treatment would outrank the harmful by a ratio of at least five to one.

Another powerful factor must be considered. It is generally believed (another uncertainty expressed by generalization rather than precise measurement) that at least three-quarters of physician-patient encounters are occasioned by complaints that are either self-limited, or for which medicine has no specific remedies. Such patients presumably benefit from seeing a doctor because he listens sympathetically to their words and then consoles and reassures them. This exercise of what might be called the art of medicine has probably not improved since 1912; indeed, social changes and the ascendancy of technology have probably impaired it. Hence, one's evaluation of Henderson's maxim depends to a considerable extent on one's definition of "benefit." If the whole spectrum of medical care is included, ranging from a pat on the back to transplantation of the heart, it is doubtful that the benefit-harm ratio of personalized medical care has changed appreciably over the last 100 years. If, however, attention is focused on certain serious organic diseases—infectious, metabolic, and even malignant—then the contribution of science and technology to modern medicine have been truly wondrous. If the patient of 1978 has the right disease, and consults the right physician with the right scientific knowledge and the right technical skills, there can be no doubt that his chances for improvement by far exceed those of a similar patient two-thirds of a century ago.

Lewis Thomas

On the Science and Technology of Medicine

Although the public perceives a "health crisis," the nation's health has never been better. According to Dr. Lewis Thomas of the Sloan-Kettering Cancer Center, growing awareness of health risks, high expectations of medical treatment, and the unrealistic hope of medical cures for social problems foster crisis thinking. Thomas emphasizes the cost of worry, the positive health and longevity available to most of us, and the realistic possibilities for improving the health care system and solving—in time—the remaining mysteries of disease.

The common theme running through almost all the criticisms leveled at the American health-care system these days is the charge of inadequacy or insufficiency. There are not enough doctors and nurses, and those around lack sufficient interest and compassion; there are not enough clinics, and those around lack sufficient time to see everyone; there are too few medical schools, medical centers, and specialized hospitals, with inequities in their distribution around the country; most of all, there is not enough money, not enough commitment.

And yet, the system has been expanding with explosive force in the last quarter-century. It has been nothing short of a boom.... The question is: What are we improving? What, in fact, have we been trying to accomplish with these vast sums?

An alien historian would think, from a look just at the dollar figures... that some sort of tremendous event must have been occurring since 1950. Either (1) the health of the nation had suddenly disintegrated, requiring the laying on of new resources to meet the crisis, or (2) the technology for handling health problems had undergone a major transformation, necessitating the installation of new effective resources to do things that could not be done before, or (3), another possibility, perhaps we had somehow been caught up in the momentum of a huge, collective, ponderous set of errors. If any of these explanations is the right one, we ought at least to become aware of it, since whatever we are improving will involve, in the near future, an even more immense new bureaucracy, an even larger commitment of public funds, regulations that will intervene in every aspect of the citizen's life, and, inevitably, still more expansion. . . .

The Health of the Nation, 1950–1975

There is, to begin with, no real evidence that health has deteriorated in this country, certainly not to the extent indicated by the new dollars spent each year for health care. On the contrary, we seem to have gotten along reasonably well.

, There is perhaps more heart disease, but this is to be expected in a generally older population living beyond the life expectancy of fifty years ago. Heart disease is, after all, one of the ways of dying, and death certificates do not usually distinguish between heart failure as the result of time having run out and other forms of heart disease, except by noting age. The total numbers have increased somewhat, and perhaps there are also somewhat more cases of coronary occlusion in middle-aged men, but we have not suddenly been plagued, just since 1950, by new heart disease in anything like frightening numbers.

Cancer, stroke, kidney disease, arthritis, schizophrenia, cirrhosis, multiple sclerosis, senility, asthma, pulmonary fibrosis, and a few other major diseases are still with us, but the change in incidence per capita is not sufficient to account for the move from a $10 billion enterprise to a $130 billion one. Aging itself is not a health problem, although a larger number of surviving old people obviously means proportionately more people with the disabling illnesses characteristic of the aged. However, the increased number of such patients since 1950 is not great enough to account for much of the increased investment.

Meanwhile, there has been a general improvement in the public health with respect to certain infectious diseases which were major problems in the twenty-five-year period prior to 1950. . . . On balance, then, no case can be made for a wave of new illnesses afflicting our population in the years since 1950. If anything, we are probably a somewhat healthier people because of the sharp decrease in severe infectious disease.

But this is not the general view of things: the public perception of the public health, in 1975, appears to be quite different. There is now a much more acute awareness of the risk of disease than in earlier periods, associated with a greater apprehension that a minor illness may turn suddenly into a killing disease. There is certainly a higher expectation that all kinds of disease can be treated effectively. Finally, personal maladjustments of all varieties—unhappiness, discontent, fear, anxiety, despair, marital discord, even educational problems—have come to be regarded as medical problems, requiring medical attention, imposing new, heavy demands for care. In addition, there are probably many more people in this country requiring specialized rehabilitation services for disabilities resulting from physical trauma (Korea and Vietnam veterans, automobile- and industrial-accident victims, etc.).

Health-Care Technology, 1950–1975

Has the effective technology for medical care changed in the past twenty-five years to a degree sufficient to explain the increased cost? Is there in fact a new high technology of medicine?

Despite the widespread public impression that this is the case, there is little evidence for it. The most spectacular technological change has occurred in the management of infectious disease, but its essential features had been solidly established and put to use well before 1950. . . . The net result of the anti-infection technology ought to have been a very large decrease in the cost of care.

There have been a few other examples of technology improvement, comparable in decisive effectiveness, since 1950, but the best of these have been for relatively uncommon illnesses. . . . Progress in anesthesia, electrolyte physiology, and cardiopulmonary physiology has greatly advanced the field of surgery, so that reparative and other procedures can now be done which formerly were technically impossible. . . .

We are left with approximately the same roster of common major diseases which confronted the country in 1950, and, although we have accumulated a formidable body information about some of them in the intervening time, the accumulation is not yet sufficient to permit either the prevention or the outright cure of any of them. This is not to suggest that progress has not been made, or has been made much more slowly than should reasonably have been expected. On the contrary, the research activity since 1950 has provided the beginnings of insight into the underlying processes in several of our most important diseases, and there is every reason for optimism regarding the future. But it is the present that is the problem. We are, in a sense, partway along, maybe halfway along. At the same time, medicine is expected to do something for each of these illnesses, to do whatever can be done in the light of today's knowledge. Because of this obligation, we have evolved "halfway" technologies, representing the best available treatment, and the development and proliferation of these are partly responsible for the escalating costs of health care in recent years. Associated with this expansion, the diagnostic laboratories have become much more elaborate and complex in their technologies; there is no question that clinical diagnosis has become much more powerful and precise, but at a very high cost and with considerable waste resulting from overuse.

This way of looking at contemporary medicine runs against the currently general public view that the discipline has by this time come almost its full distance, that we have had a long succession of "breakthroughs" and "major advances," and that now we should go beyond our persistent concern with research on what is called "curative" medicine and give more attention to the social aspects of illness and to preventive medicine.

It does not, in fact, look much like the record of a completed job, or even of a job more than half begun, when you run through the list, one by one, of the diseases in this country which everyone will agree are the most important ones... The ten leading causes of death from disease in the United States in 1974 [were]: cardiovascular disease, cancer, cerebrovascular disease, kidney disease, pulmonary disease, diabetes mellitus, cirrhosis of the liver, perinatal disease, congenital malformations and deficiencies, and peptic ulcer....

The foregoing list accounts for approximately 80 per cent of all deaths in this country. It does not, of course, account for the major part of the work of physicians, nor the greatest element of cost for the health-care system. We are afflicted, obviously, by a great (but it must be said, finite) array of non-fatal illnesses varying in severity and duration, and it is here that the greatest demands for technology are made.... Some of the commonest of these self-limited or non-fatal diseases are: acute respiratory infections, gastrointestinal infections, arthritis, the neuroses, the psychoses, Parkinsonism, and essential hypertension....

The Cost of Worry in the Health-Care System

Nothing has changed so much in the health-care system over the past twenty-five years as the public's perception of its own health. The change amounts to a loss of confidence in the human form. The general belief these days seems to be that the body is fundamentally flawed, subject to disintegration at any moment, always on the verge of mortal disease, always in need of continual monitoring and support by health-care professionals. This is a new phenomenon in our society.

It can be seen most clearly in the content of television programs and, especially, television commercials, where the preponderance of material deals with the need for shoring up one's personal health. The same drift is evident in the contents of the most popular magazines and in the health columns of daily newspapers. There is a public preoccupation with disease that is assuming the dimension of a national obsession.

To some extent, the propaganda which feeds the obsession is a result of the well intentioned efforts by particular disease agencies to obtain public money for the support of research and care in their special fields. Every mail brings word of the imminent perils posed by multiple sclerosis, kidney disease, cancer, heart disease, cystic fibrosis, asthma, muscular dystrophy, and the rest.

There is, regrettably, no discernible counter-propaganda. No agencies exist for the celebration of the plain fact that most people are, in real life, abundantly healthy. No one takes public note of the truth of the matter, which is that most people in this country have a clear, unimpeded run at a longer lifetime than could have been foreseen by any earlier generation. Even the proponents of good hygiene, who argue publicly in favor of regular exercise, thinness, and abstinence from cigarettes and alcohol, base their arguments on the presumed intrinsic fallibility of human health. Left alone, unadvised by professionals, the tendency of the human body is perceived as prone to steady failure.

Underlying this pessimistic view of health is a profound dissatisfaction with the fact of death. Dying is regarded as the ultimate failure, something that could always be avoided or averted if only the health-care system functioned more efficiently. Death has been made to seem unnatural, an outrage; when people die—at whatever age—we speak of them as having been "struck down," "felled." It is as though in a better world we would all go on forever.

It is not surprising that all this propaganda has imposed heavy, unsupportable demands on the health-care system. If people are educated to believe that they may at any moment be afflicted with one of another mortal disease and that this fate can be forestalled by access to medicine, especially "preventive" medicine, it is no wonder that clinics and doctors' offices are filled with waiting clients.

In the year 1974, 1,933,000 people died in the United States, a death rate of 9.1 per 1,000, or just under 1 per cent of the whole population, substantially lower than the birth rate for the same year. The life expectation for the whole population rose to 72 years, the highest expectancy ever attained in this country. With figures like these, it is hard to see health as a crisis, or the health-care system, apart from its huge size and high cost, as a matter needing emergency action. We really are a quite healthy society, and we should be spending more time and energy in acknowledging this, and perhaps trying to understand more clearly why it is so. We are in some danger of becoming a nation of healthy hypochondriacs.

For all its obvious defects and shortcomings, the actual technology of health care is not likely to be changed drastically in the direction of saving money— not in the short haul. Nor is it likely that changes for the better, in the sense of greater effectiveness and efficiency, can be brought about by any means other than more scientific research. The latter course, although sure, is undeniably slow and unpredictable. While it is a certainty, in my view, that rheumatoid arthritis, atherosclerosis, cancer, and senile dementia will eventually be de-mystified and can then become preventable disorders, there is no way of fore-casting when this will happen; it could be a few years away for one or the other, or decades.

Meanwhile, we will be compelled to live with the system as we have it, changing only the parts that are in fact changeable. It is not likely that money problems can induce anyone—the professionals or the public at large, or even the third-party payers—to give up halfway technologies that work only partially when this would mean leaving no therapeutic effort at all in place. For as long as there is a prospect of saving the lives of 50 per cent, or even only 33 per cent, of patients with cancer by today's methods for destroying cancer cells, these methods must obviously be held onto and made available to as many patients as possible. If coronary bypass surgery remains the only technical measure for relieving untractable angina in a relatively small pro-portion of cases, it will be continued, and very likely extended to larger num-bers of cases, until something better turns up. People with incapacitating mental illness cannot simply be left to wander the streets, and we will con-tinue to need expanding clinics and specialized hospital facilities, even though caring for the mentally ill does not mean anything like curing them. We are, in a sense, stuck with today's technology, and we will stay stuck until we have more scientific knowledge to work with.

But what we might do, if we could muster the energy and judgment for it, is to identify the areas of health care in which the spending of money represents outright waste, and then eliminate these. There are discrete examples all over the place, but what they are depends on who is responsible for citing them, and there will be bitter arguments over each one before they can be edited out of the system, one by one.

The biggest source of waste results from the general public conviction that contemporary medicine is able to accomplish a great deal more than is in fact possible. This attitude is in part the outcome of overstated claims on the part of medicine itself in recent decades, plus medicine's passive acquiescence while even more exaggerated claims were made by the media. The notion of preventive medicine as a whole new discipline in medical care is an example of this. There is an arguably solid base for the prevention of certain diseases, but it has not changed all that much since the nineteen-fifties. A few valuable measures have been added, most notably the avoidance of cigarette smoking for the prevention of lung cancer; if we had figured out a way of acting on this single bit of information, we might have achieved a spectacular triumph in the prevention of deaths from cancer, but regrettably we didn't. The same de-spairing thing can be said for the preventability of death from alcohol.

But there is not much more than this in the field of preventive medicine.

The truth is that medicine has not become very skilled at disease prevention—not, as is sometimes claimed, because it doesn't want to or isn't interested, but because the needed information is still lacking.

Most conspicuous and costly of all are the benefits presumed to derive from "seeing the doctor." The regular complete checkup, once a year or more often, has become a cultural habit, and it is only recently that some investigators have suggested, cautiously, that it probably doesn't do much good. There are very few diseases in which early detection can lead to a significant alteration of the outcome: glaucoma, cervical cancer, and possibly breast cancer are the usually cited examples, but in any event these do not require the full, expensive array of the complete periodic checkup, EKG and all. Nevertheless, the habit has become fixed in our society, and it is a significant item in the total bill for health care.

"Seeing the doctor" also includes an overwhelming demand for reassurance. Transient upper-respiratory infections and episodes of gastroenteritis account for most of the calls on a doctor because of illness, and an even greater number of calls are made by people who have nothing at all the matter with them. It is often claimed that these are mostly unhappy individuals, suffering from psychoneuroses, in need of compassionate listening on the part of the physician, but a large number of patients who find themselves in doctors' offices or hospital clinics will acknowledge themselves to be in entirely good health; they are there because of a previous appointment in connection with an earlier illness, for a "checkup," or for a laboratory test, or simply for reassurance that they are not coming down with something serious—cancer, or heart disease, or whatever. Or they may have come to the doctor for advice about living: what should their diet be?, should they take a vacation?, what about a tranquilizer for everyone's inevitable moments of agitation and despair? I know a professor of pediatrics who has received visits from intelligent, well-educated parents who only want to know if their child should start Sunday school.

The system is being overused, swamped by expectant overdemands for services that are frequently trivial or unproductive. The public is not sufficiently informed of the facts about things that medicine can and cannot accomplish. Medicine is surely not in possession of special wisdom about how to live a life.

It needs to be said more often that human beings are fundamentally tough, resilient animals, marvelously made, most of the time capable of getting along quite well on their own. The health-care system should be designed for use when it is really needed and when it has something of genuine value to offer. If designed, or redesigned, in this way, the system would function far more effectively, and would probably cost very much less.

Conclusion

If our society wishes to be rid of the diseases, fatal and non-fatal, that plague us the most, there is really little prospect of doing so by mounting a still larger health-care system at still greater cost for delivering essentially today's kind of technology on a larger scale. We will not do so by carrying out broader programs of surveillance and screening. The truth is that we do not yet know enough. But there is also another truth of great importance we are learning fast. The harvest of new information from the biological revolution of the past quarter-century is just now coming in, and we can probably begin now to figure out the mechanisms of major diseases which were blank mysteries a few years back as accurately and profitably as was done for the infectious diseases earlier in this century. This can be said with considerable confidence, and without risk of overpromising or raising false hopes, provided we do not set time schedules or offer dates of delivery. Sooner or later it will go this way, since clearly it can go this way. It is simply a question at this stage of events of how much we wish to invest, for the health-care system of the future, in science.

The body reflects the attitude of the mind. Improve the function of the body and you must improve the state of the mind.
—*Moshe Feldenkrais*

Robert Claiborne

A Penny of Prevention: The Cure for America's Health Care System

Many critics of our health care system today decry its emphasis on treatment rather than on prevention. But proposals to provide health care rather than sickness care raise controversial questions about payment systems, environmental contamination, unhealthy life-styles, poverty, and the direction of biomedical research. Robert Claiborne, a long-time writer on science subjects, suggests that ending poverty may be the best "health care" investment the nation could make. Economic priorities determine not only who shall live and die, but the degree of health available to the living.

Thanks to pressure from organized doctors and hospitals, Congress has adjourned without imposing even nominal controls on our ever-escalating national health-care bill. This, in turn, could well lessen the likelihood of any meaningful national health insurance system's being voted next session, since the more health costs increase—as they will continue to do—the more national health insurance might be expected to cost the taxpayer.

It doesn't have to work that way. A system of national health insurance containing rational, built-in incentives for cost efficiency can *cut* our anual payments to doctors and hospitals by a minimum of $25 billion—probably nearer $30 billion—within a relatively short time. Even greater savings can be achieved over the long run, provided that doctors, hospital administrators, medical educators, and the general public can achieve a deeper understanding of what health care really is and how we can get better care—and better health—for less money.

The key to that understanding lies in a remark a Blue Cross official made not long ago. "What we have in this country," he declared, "isn't a health-care system; it's a sickness-care system." This is a fundamental truth. What we think of as "health care"—the thing that is currently costing us some $170 billion a year—is overwhelmingly concerned with treating us when we get sick—hopefully, making us better; less hopefully, making sure we get no worse, and, when hope is gone, holding off the inevitable as long as possible.

The bias of American "health care" toward treatment rather than prevention begins (where else?) with the insurance plans, public and private, that pay most of its cost: more than 90 percent of hospital bills, some 70 percent of doctors' bills. Medicare, for example, pays 80 percent of *treatment* costs (within certain limits) for people over 65; yet it is explicitly forbidden to pay a nickel for *preventive* measures. Neither Blue Cross–Blue Shield nor most commercial insurance plans pay for vaccination against such diseases as measles, whooping cough, and polio—though they will usually pay at least part of the much greater cost of treating these diseases. If you get sick, your insurance carrier will usually pick up at least part of the tab; if you try to avoid getting sick, you're on your own.

Oddly enough, this bias persists in the face of a truth known to many doctors and all historians of medicine: the great achievements in the health field in the past century or so have been mainly preventive, not curative. The main reason we enjoy, on the average, longer and healthier lives than our ancestors is not that doctors possess more effective ways of treating our sicknesses— though in many cases they do—but rather that *we get sick less often.*

. . . "Health care" obviously means something much bigger and more complex than our "sickness care" system, overblown though that is. The billions we spend each year on building and maintaining water and sewage systems are in fact monies spent for health care; without them, our bill for sickness care, not to mention our national death rate, would be far greater.

Recent evidence on this point comes from a health center organized some years ago in the Mississippi backcountry. Its clientele was almost entirely black and dirt-poor—thanks largely to the elimination of jobs on cotton plantations through mechanization. Sewage disposal and water supplies were of 18th-century vintage, as was the incidence of such diseases as infectious diarrhea in infants.

The center's personnel, led by Dr. H. Jack Geiger, quickly discovered that preventive medicine was by far the best way of stretching the center's scarce dollars. Treating a single case of infantile diarrhea, says Geiger, could cost some $300; building a sanitary privy—which could prevent half a dozen such cases—cost $75. The center also used some of its funds to help its clients set up an agricultural cooperative, raising food crops on unused land and thereby improving the people's nutrition. As one might expect, the level of health improved.

*   *   *

If adequate nutrition is an important part of health care, as all the evidence indicates, then several other public programs must be seen as part of our health-care system. Food stamps and free lunches for poor schoolchildren (assuming the lunches are both palatable and nutritious, which isn't always the case) reduce the incidence of disease, and thereby reduce our national sickness-care bill. And make no mistake about it—it's *our* bill, not somebody else's. . . .

The search for health care rather than sickness care also raises the question of whether environmental contaminants are related to disease. For some, the answer is clear, indeed notorious: coal dust can produce "black lung," cotton dust can produce "brown lung" (both crippling); asbestos dust can produce a variety of lung diseases, including cancer. Vinyl chloride—the raw material of vinyl plastics—can produce liver and bladder cancer; insecticides such as Kepone can produce nervous disorders or worse.

If to these unquestionably noxious environmental contaminants we add possibly noxious ones, the list stretches out almost to the crack of doom: pesticides, herbicides, food additives and colorings, microwaves broadcast by tens of thousands of sources, air pollutants, diets high in fat. There is an enormous amount we don't know about the effects of these individually, but we can be almost certain of several things about them as a group. First, most or all of them can cause disease in large enough quantities; second, most of them are probably harmless in small enough quantities; third, for few of them do we have any but the vaguest information on how much is "small enough."

There is one thing about environmental contaminants that we can be *dead* sure of. When a given substance is clearly implicated in disease, those who manufacture or sell products containing or emitting that substance will scream the house down. They will deny the scientific worth of the incriminating evidence, denounce anti-pollution legislation as "government interference" and its proponents as soft-headed liberals, "anti-growth" counterculturalists, and environmental freaks. This prediction may seem harsh, but it fits the facts: specifically, the record of the coal industry on black lung, the auto industry on pollution controls, the asbestos industry on asbestosis, and the textile industry, which is currently fighting legislation to control brown lung.

Health care in the environment and the workplace raises companies' costs, and *may* lower their profits—though on the record they generally have recouped their costs or better by raising prices. Sickness care engendered by contaminants raises everybody else's costs. The Department of Health, Education and Welfare estimates that we are currently footing the bill for 330,000 cases of occupational disease a year, 100,000 of which end in death; what the bill is for environmental disease outside the workplace is anybody's guess. As one indication, a recent study estimates that cleaning up air pollution caused by public utilities has saved us $6.6 billion over and above the cost of the clean-up.

Environmental contamination can be controlled by law, but the law can do little about personal environmental factors no less important to our health: what we eat and drink, and how much; the cigarette smoke we do or don't inhale; how fast we drive; and so on. Yet many of the basic facts about this form of health care are clear enough: if we eat a varied and moderate diet, consume little alcohol, smoke few or no cigarettes (preferably of ultra-low-tar brands), exercise regularly and as vigorously as our ages permit, drive at reasonable speeds and fasten our seat belts, our chances of living to a ripe and healthy old age improve markedly.

The connection between lifestyle and health is clear, though many details remain to be filled in; unfortunately, this very clarity has made it a favorite stalking-horse among people opposed to any restructuring of our present grossly inefficient sickness-care system. The fault, they say, is not in the system but in ourselves: if we lived more sensibly, our doctor and hospital bills would be lower. This is undoubtedly true, but it conceals two prime falsehoods. The first is that the costs of sickness care can be lowered *only* by changing our lifestyles. . . . The second is the hidden implication that how we live is entirely the result of rational, voluntary choices. It isn't.

. . . Personal decisions about lifestyles are not made in a vacuum: they are often influenced by institutional decisions. And these, unlike personal decisions, almost always are rational—at least from the standpoint of institutional self-interest. Cigarette smoking, as almost everybody knows, is "dangerous to your health"—yet the cigarette industry is still subsidized by the government in several ways. For example, cigarette manufacturers spend tens of millions a year to induce people to smoke—every penny of it deductible from taxable corporate income, and therefore partly tax-subsidized. . . .

A more direct way of generating healthier lifestyles is through the time-tested method of improving people's living conditions. Persuasive evidence on this point comes from comparing death rates among nonwhites, who are mostly poor, and whites, who are mostly not. For example, the death rate as of 1970 among nonwhite males between 35 and 44—generally considered the prime of life—was more than 2½ times that of whites in the same age bracket. The nonwhites' risk of death from cancer was 60 percent greater; from heart disease, 80 percent greater. Cirrhosis took three times as many blacks as whites; influenza and pneumonia, five times as many; homicide twelve times as many. Can there be any serious doubt that improving living conditions in black and Hispanic ghettos—*not* by handouts but by providing jobs at reasonable pay—would help end this depressing health contrast?

There are those who say we can't afford to end poverty. My own suspicion is that we can't afford not to. Poverty is costing us billions every year in sickness care, billions more in crime—and tens of billions in the "handouts" we give the poor in lieu of the jobs most of them want. A true balance sheet of the dollar costs of poverty versus the dollar costs of ending it might well show that even in purely economic terms, humanity is the best policy.

The problem of health care versus sickness care goes beyond biases in our payment systems, contamination in our environment, and unhealthy life-styles, voluntary or otherwise: it also raises basic questions about the direction of current biomedical research.

It is startling but true that the great health-care measures of the past century or so . . . were to only a minor degree products of the laboratory. Better living conditions, the most important of them, "just happened." The other measures were mainly generated by studies in epidemiology—the study of who gets sick where—plus common sense. . . .

Given the current emphasis on the laboratory approach to disease, it is worth stressing that epidemiological studies, in and of themselves—without help from the laboratory—can provide immediate, practical answers to preventing disease. For example, biochemistry still can't tell us how cigarette smoke causes lung cancer—yet epidemiology has already proved that cancer and smoking are connected, and that not smoking markedly reduces the risk. No less firmly established is the epidemiological connection between poverty and disease—for example, the violence and alcoholism that cut short the lives of so many black and Hispanic Americans. These conditions were epidemic in the 19th-century Irish slums of New York's "Hell's Kitchen," the 18th-century London slums of Hogarth's famous engraving "Gin Lane," and—if the poetry of François Villon is any guide—in the 15th-century slums of Paris. Poverty begets alcoholism, homicide, and other causes of premature death. . . .

It would be easy to conclude from these facts that modern laboratory research is of little relevance to health—and quite wrong. Studies in bacteriology and in the fundamental chemical processes by which living organisms function have contributed significantly both to treating and to preventing disease. But the very successes of laboratory studies have focused the attention of researchers on certain kinds of questions—and largely crowded out other, no less important questions. Biomedical research has produced an enormous mass of facts on the nature of sickness—that is, what happens in people's bodies when things go wrong—and much invaluable information on how the sickness can be cured or contained. But only within the past ten years or so have some researchers begun asking the even more fundamental question: Why?

Nobody knows, for example, why people get influenza. The flu virus is obviously part of the answer, but only part: during a flu epidemic virtually everyone is exposed to the virus, yet only a minority actually gets sick. If the virus makes A sick, why not B and C as well? Even a generation ago, medical science would have replied that B and C had "stronger constitutions" or "greater natural resistance" than A—which were, of course, merely fancy ways of saying what we knew already: A got sick and the other two didn't.

The tendency of researchers to be content with partial answers, or none, to the question "Why?" began with the pioneer bacteriologists. Their answers, though partial, were for their time brilliant: people get sick, not because of "filth," "bad air" (*mal'aria* in Italian) or some malign "influence" (*influenza* in Italian), but from infection with noxious microbes. The conclusions were clear: keep microbes away from people, by providing pure water and food, or by killing or screening out the animals that spread the microbes (as with malaria). If that doesn't work, develop a vaccine that will stimulate the body's own defenses against the microbe. And if *that* doesn't work, then—eventually—give the patient a drug that will kill the microbe.

Simply from the practical standpoint, these were good answers—good enough, in fact, to have (with a major assist from improved living standards) largely eliminated infectious disease as a serious public health problem in prosperous countries. Unfortunately, however, the methods that produced these answers proved ill-suited for tackling *today's* major public health problems: cancer, cardiovascular disease (stroke, atherosclerosis, "heart trouble"), diabetes, rheumatoid arthritis, mental disease. For these conditions, which kill or incapacitate millions of people every year, the brilliant but simple-minded approach of bacteriology simply doesn't work. None of these diseases has any single identifiable predominant cause that, like a microbe, can be kept away from potential victims or, if that fails, isolated in a test tube and used to develop a vaccine or assay an antibiotic.

Insofar as we understand the causes of these "dread diseases"—which, given the billions we have poured into biomedical research, isn't very far— they seem to be largely "multifactorial," that is, produced by the joint action of many factors, some hereditary, some environmental. A person possessing a particular inherited constitution—which nobody can define in any very useful way—develops a given disease if, and only if, he or she is exposed to a number of environmental influences, often over a protracted period. Few of these environmental factors can be identified very precisely, but they undoubtedly include microbes, toxic substances, dietary constituents, and different kinds of psychic stress.

The multifactorial model of disease provides some very clear pointers to the kinds of questions that more researchers should be asking. To begin with, we badly need to know exactly what "inherited constitution" means in relation to specific diseases. Just what inherited biochemical peculiarities make a person susceptible to diabetes, to schizophrenia, to atherosclerosis? Answers to these questions would not enable us to change human heredity; indeed, even if we could change it, the dangers would be far too great. Rather, if we can identify the presence of specific chemical "risk factors" in particular individuals, we can perhaps take steps to correct them through drugs or, alternatively, to shield such individuals from the environmental factors that turn risk into disease. This can already be done with a few rare inherited defects such as phenylketonuria, whose effects (notably, severe retardation) can be reduced or eliminated by removing certain substances from the affected infant's diet.

Where several genetic factors are involved—as seems to be the case with such conditions as diabetes, atherosclerosis and schizophrenia—the risk factors will obviously be harder to identify, but there seems no reason why they can't be found, if enough scientists look for them.

When it comes to the environmental factors implicated in multifactorial disease, some of the answers are already known—but a lot more remain to be discovered. We still have no idea, for example, why of two identical twins, possessing the same inherited constitution, one becomes schizophrenic and the other does not—as occurs in more than half such cases. Here epidemiological studies can provide an invaluable tool: discovering who gets sick, and how their environment differs from that of those who don't get sick. Because of the complexities of the environment, the answers certainly won't be simple, but, again, most of the needed information can probably be found if we take the trouble to look.

The achievements of laboratory science during the past century need no defense from me. But if we are seriously interested in substituting health care for sickness care, we must abolish the assumption—still all too common among both scientists and those who give out research grants—that it is the only kind of science worth doing. At its best, laboratory study can provide answers that are precise, elegant, and practically useful as well. But the far less precise answers of epidemiology, though unsatisfying to some scientific minds, can be no less useful.

One final, basic point needs to be made about both health care and sickness care: however, we wish to deliver them, and in whatever proportions, we must make choices. No system for meeting people's health needs, indeed no economic system, can do everything for everybody; there isn't that much money in the world. And by choosing to spend the available money in one way rather than another, we are choosing—whether we care to recognize it or not—who shall be sick and who shall not; on the bottom line, who shall live and who shall die.

As just one example, consider the much-discussed "coronary bypass," a surgical operation that can prolong the lives of some victims of coronary artery disease (how many is in dispute). About 75,000 of these procedures are being done every year in this country, each at a cost of $10,000 and up—meaning that their beneficiaries are overwhelmingly people in the middle-to-upper brackets. If we were to take the insurance premiums for sickness care now going into coronary surgery and spend it on (say) improving the nutrition of infants and children in urban slums and depressed rural areas, we could probably save at least as many lives as are now being saved by the surgery. Our present ways of distributing and paying for sickness care and health care ensure that it is the coronary patients who will live and the children of poverty who will die. . . .

The question of health care versus sickness care ultimately boils down to the basic issue that confronts every society, past, present, or future: How do we allocate our resources? *What do we want?* Do we want sickness care for everyone who needs it, or only for certain people? Do we want expanded health care, which can certainly save lives and probably save money, over the long run if not the short? Do we want headlong economic growth, more superhighways, a "defense" establishment big enough to devastate the entire globe several times over? Do we want to abolish poverty and clean up the environment? Given our national wealth and native ingenuity, we can have any of these things we choose—but we cannot, now or ever, have all of them.

We have the power to make these decisions, if we choose to grasp it. And if we fail to grasp it, we are *still* making a decision—to maintain the status quo. Whether we accept the responsibility of decision or dodge it, we will still make the choice of who shall live and who shall die, who shall suffer sickness and who enjoy health. The verdict is ours to give: What will it be?

Health, as a vast societal enterprise, is too important to be solely the concern of the providers of services.

—*William L. Kissick*

Erik P. Eckholm

Creating Better Health

Imagining a society in which human health is a positive goal, Erik Eckholm of Worldwatch Institute surveys the essential prerequisites for good health. He considers health problems in underdeveloped countries as well as in the West, and raises philosophical questions about the rights of individuals to choose their own life-styles. Eckholm argues that determining national priorities requires benefit-risk calculations based on how important health is and what it is worth to the population, because the real obstacles to health today are political. Concern for human health must be matched by concern for the total well-being of human life and the environment, he concludes.

No society has deactivated both traditional and modern environmental health threats. Today's more developed societies have markedly cut the toll of traditional disease killers, but they have also created lifestyles and technologies that entail new health risks. Meanwhile, more than a third of humanity must contend daily with age-old scourges. Some unfortunates must cope with both ancient and modern threats.

How would a society that made human health a top priority look? To begin with, in such a society the circumstances of conception and gestation would maximize the chances of each child being born robust and well equipped to survive the perilous early months, and of subsequently leading a long, healthy life. Through judicious family planning, women would avoid giving birth before or after their safest childbearing years, and none would bear large numbers of children. Since prospective mothers would consume well-balanced diets throughout their own lives and adequate dietary supplements during pregnancy, the number of premature or underweight births would be minimized. Pregnant women would not smoke, would not take potentially hazardous drugs, and would not be exposed to toxic chemicals or radiation on the job or at home.

Good sanitation would be a watchword; children's contacts with infectious agents and parasites would be limited, since everyone would live in clean residences with adequate pure water and sanitary sewage faciities close at hand. Nutritional basics would be universally understood; children would be raised on diets that encouraged neither undernutrition nor overnutrition and, from an early age, physical activity would be integral to daily life. Adults would eschew excess calories and fats in their diets, avoid heavy drinking, and get plenty of regular exercise. The number of potentially hazardous environmental agents in circulation would be slashed; only those chemicals that had been rigorously tested for long-term health effects would be added to foods and other products. Smoking would be considered antisocial, and the cigarette smoker would gradually become an extinct species. Workers' health would be strongly protected; if in some cases safeguards and vigilance in the workplace could not guarantee workers reasonable peace of mind about their health, consumers would simply do without particularly dangerous materials and products. Factories would spend what is necessary to eliminate hazardous pollutants. Only low-polluting vehicles would be allowed on roads; and, in urban centers, the widespread use of bicycles and public transportation would offset driving restrictions.

The life-giving properties of such a regime can be inferred, if not predicted precisely. Deaths among infants would be rare, disease deaths among children and young adults rarer still. Infectious diseases would certainly continue to afflict, occasionally fatally, people of all ages but in general would be neither frequent nor life-threatening. Polio, measles, diphtheria, and other diseases would be emasculated by the strategic use of vaccines.

Heart attacks and other cardiovascular conditions would probably take lives among the aged, but they would lose power over the many middle-aged men whose lives they threaten today. Some cancer cases would occur, but the general incidence of cancer would undoubtedly plummet from the levels now prevailing in developed countries. The health of many in middle and old age would improve even as the average length of life was extended. Far fewer people would be debilitated in their forties, fifties, and sixties by circulatory and other ailments than are today.

Beyond the amounts spent to prevent disease, medical expenditures would be concentrated on nonpreventable threats and on the special health (and social) problems of old age. Less money would be wasted trying to save people from ailments that could have been avoided in the first place. Whatever the amount it spent on health care, such a society would get more life for its money than is the rule anywhere today.

What obstacles now keep individuals from enjoying the best possible health? Certainly they are not technological. Achieving the ideal health conditions just described requires no new breakthroughs in medical research—though any that do occur might improve health still more. Nor do insurmountable genetic obstacles bar the way. To be sure, some diseases are inherited and thus not preventable. But only rarely is an individual's health defined by heredity.... Heredity influences individual susceptibilities to the diseases that take most lives today, but environmental factors usually determine whether that potential is realized.

The true obstacles to better health, then, are political failures—failures of nations to organize affairs to minimize environmental health threats, and failures of individuals to avoid self-destructive lifestyles. Significant improvements in health require massive attacks on today's major sources of disease: unjust social systems, skewed investment priorities, carelessly used technologies, and reckless personal behavior patterns.

In rich and poor societies, changes in both government policies and personal habits are essential to better health. Depending on their current health conditions, however, different societies must establish different priorities. In poorer countries, the biggest health gains will follow social reforms that reduce undernutrition and construction programs that provide people with clean water and sewage facilities. In more affluent countries, major health gains will necessarily involve habit-breaking. If cigarette smoking, overnutrition, and sedentary living remain widespread, neither the strictest controls of pollution and toxic chemicals nor the most elaborate medical facilities can improve the health picture much. If, through wise planning, developing countries can possible avoid duplicating all the hazards now associated with industrialism and affluence even as they strive to eliminate traditional health hazards, they will give their people opportunities that money alone cannot buy.

*   *   *

A comparison of mortality rates around the world reveals what should be humankind's top health-care priority: cutting the number of infants and children lost to undernutrition and infectious disease. . . .

Diseases rooted in the ecology of poverty can only be conquered by eradicating their social and physical origins. Major improvements in the health of the world's poorest half will not be achieved with hospitals, doctors, and drugs, but with wells, latrines, land reforms, small-farm credit programs, family planning, and community education. Health strategies, of which medical care should constitute one component, must take account of the broad cultural and economic factors that influence nutritional and sanitary conditions.

The two absolute prerequisites of decent health are an adequate supply of food and convenient access to abundant quantities of reasonably pure water. When these two basic needs are met, infant and childhood mortality inevitably plummets. . . . Development that increases the food production, employment prospects, and incomes of the rural and urban poor will scale down undernutrition; development that promotes economic inequality may worsen it.

According to some estimates, the worldwide burden of infectious diseases would shrink by as much as 80 percent if everyone had access to safe water and made good use of it for proper sanitation. Although providing those who lack them with adequate sanitary facilities is the cheapest and fastest way to improve human health, about one-third of humanity has yet to reap the benefits of the sanitary revolution that swept through Europe and North America in the late nineteenth century. . . .

Family planning services are a third important contributor to good health. At the individual level, uncontrolled fertility directly threatens the well-being of mothers and infants. At the community level, it can undermine even the strongest efforts to wipe out environmental disease-promoters. . . . Family planning will not solve basic development and equity problems, but it is an essential component of social progress. Widely and wisely used, contraception can better the welfare of the present generation as it betters the prospects of future generations, who will have to cope with the environment we bequeath them. Family planning is most apt to be practiced in a climate of economic progress, especially when the survival odds of infants and children are fast improving. But a large share of the more than 300 million couples who do not use contraception lack even the choice, for they cannot obtain reliable contraceptives.

The Chinese system of "barefoot doctors"—men and women with minimal formal medical training who provide rudimentary health services and encourage cleanliness and family planning in their own communities—has recently received much acclaim. These health promoters usually do in fact wear shoes or sandals, but their involvement with their fellow citizens is, as their nickname suggests, unostentatious. Aspects of the Chinese medical-care experience deserve to be emulated in rich as well as in poor countries. At the same time, of course, the underlying sources of China's health progress should be held in mind. Effective "medical" auxiliaries work two jobs. Besides providing vaccines, antibiotics, and safe abortions, they do environmental work and teach their clients how to prevent disease. And, perhaps most important, such health agents have the greatest impact where the broader social prerequisites of good health are met.

In addition to barefoot doctors, poor countries need "barefoot water engineers" who can cheaply provide moderately pure water supplies instead of the more sophisticated and expensive water systems that professional engineers prefer to build. They also need "barefoot agricultural-extension agents" who will advise the struggling small-scale farmers as well as the big landowners who customarily receive most available services and credit. Perhaps the greatest need of all is for "barefoot economists" and "barefoot politicians" who will work for economic reforms that give the dispossessed a chance to better their lot and who will value life above abstract growth indicators.

In rich countries, as in poor ones, further significant gains in health will depend less upon medical science than upon broader social changes. The spiraling cost of medical care in the West is a complex social issue in its own right; but today's massive disease-control expenditures bear surprisingly little relation to overall health trends, except insofar as part of these funds could be better spent on disease prevention. While costly procedures such as organ transplants, the use of artificial kidneys, and heroic efforts to save cancer victims boost medical bills and save some individual lives, they affect the basic health picture only marginally. Funds poured into curative systems in developed countries have reached the point of rapidly diminishing returns.

The limits to the benefits of a costly disease-treatment system are suggested by the American experience. During 1975, American health expenditures *grew* by more than a billion dollars a month, adding up to an annual total of $115 billion. One twelfth of the U.S. national product is now devoured by the medical-care system. Yet American life expectancy is years below and infant mortality is well above the rates prevailing in several European countries where per capita medical expenditures average much less. Although billions of dollars have been spent over the decades on medical research and curative techniques, a white American male of seventy can expect to live only *one year* longer—to age eighty—than could his counterpart at the beginning of the century.

To be sure, health conditions in today's more developed countries shine by any historical standard. Although potential lifespans for those surviving childhood have not been extended much, more people are living long lives than ever before. Yet, each year millions of people in developed countries die or grow infirm unnecessarily early. In the early 1970s, nearly four of every ten deaths in the United States involved victims under the age of sixty-five. . . .

The historical statistics of health progress offer little comfort to the parents of a child smitten by leukemia, the woman widowed at age forty by her husband's heart attack, or the youngster whose mother is carried off by cancer. In developed countries today, preventing deaths and debilities among the young and among the middle-aged should override all other health goals. The same measures that bring down the death and disease toll among middle-aged people will also prolong old age and salve its physical sting, since the seeds of many of the chronic diseases that torment and kill the aged are sown early in life.

To the extent that an ounce of prevention is worth a pound of cure, children and young adults should receive much more attention than their low death rates would suggest. An individual's health in middle and old age is largely determined by personal habits formed and environmental influences first felt in youth. The heart attacks that fell the unsuspecting are usually the culmination of decades of dietary excesses, physical inactivity, and cigarette smoking. So too the smoking and eating habits and the occupational and other exposures to carcinogens that engender fatal cancers are cumulative in their effects.

Personal lifestyles constitute one of the strategic frontiers of preventive medicine in developed countries today. "It can be said unequivocally that a significant reduction in sedentary living and overnutrition, alcoholism, hypertension, and excessive cigarette smoking would save more lives in the age range forty to sixty-four than the best current medical practice," three prominent U.S. medical researchers recently wrote.

By studying the lives of seven thousand men and women in California, Drs. Nedra B. Belloc and Lester Breslow have assembled eye-opening evidence of the health importance of personal habits. They correlated both physical well-being and lifespans to adherence to seven basic practices:

1. sleeping seven to eight hours each night;
2. eating three meals a day at regular times with little snacking;
3. eating breakfast every day;
4. maintaining desirable body weight;
5. avoiding excessive alcohol consumption:
6. getting regular exercise;
7. not smoking

Belloc and Breslow write that "the physical health status of those reported following all seven good health practices was consistently about the same as those thirty years younger who followed few or none of these practices." They found, moreover, that whereas men at age forty-five who follow three or fewer of these practices can expect to live to sixty-seven, those following six or seven of the practices can expect to live to seventy-eight. Similarly, they found that forty-five-year-old women who follow six or seven of the health practices push their average age of death to eighty-one, while women who abide by three or fewer of the practices can expect to die at seventy-four.

Relating behavior, health, and public policy poses profound philosophical questions. Almost everyone would grant an individual the prerogative of choosing a lifestyle that implicitly subordinates personal health to other values. Most would also assign to the individual some responsibility for personal actions. At the same time, psychologists have proven how strongly the social environment can influence personal behavior; and the line between personal prerogative and personal responsibility to fellow citizens is not easily drawn.

How relevant is the notion of individual responsibility when teenagers become addicted to nicotine after seeing their parents, teachers, and possibly even their doctors smoking? How can the children of the Age of Advertising be expected to blind themselves to images of cigarettes as agents of liberation and sexual attractiveness? Can overnutrition be attributed solely to lack of willpower when infants are overfed from birth, when schools teach nothing about the suspected dangers of high-fat diets, and when national leaders speak in favor of subsidies to those who produce butter and eggs?

Not only do most societies fail to educate themselves about the prerequisites of better health; all too often government agricultural policies, tax policies, and other programs support unhealthy lifestyles. It is no affront to individual dignity to suggest that social and economic policies that encourage self-destructive habits should be altered or that advertising on behalf of potentially dangerous products be curbed. Nor need governments hesitate to underwrite programs and economic incentives that promote life-saving personal habits. The molding of a social milieu that promotes enlightened self-interest is not a public infringement on personal rights, but rather a public responsibility to the individual.

If societies have a collective responsibility to build a health-promoting climate, do individuals have, in turn, a social responsibility to try to protect their own health? One's answer to this question depends largely on one's basic assumptions about the purposes of social organization. To the extent that personal behavior infringes on the well-being of others, however, the question of personal responsibility to the community may be reduced in part to a comparatively simple question of fairness. And, as Dr. John H. Knowles has written, "one man's freedom in health is another man's shackle in taxes and insurance premiums." As health-care burdens around the world are increasingly borne by collective groups, whether by those who join health insurance programs or by those who pay for public doctors and hospitals, the finances of medical equity deserve new attention. One way or another, people who act to protect their own health subsidize those who don't. Those who live dangerously—not to mention those who encourage and profit from people's unhealthy habits—account for disproportionate shares of society's health costs, and they must be made to foot a just share of the medical bills.

Eliminating some health threats, of course, lies far beyond the power of the individual acting alone. Only collective behavioral changes and effective public policies can hold down air and water pollution or free workplaces and homes of dangerous substances. A lone individual forsaking his automobile cannot eradicate photochemical smog; radical changes in car design and alterations in a whole city's commuting habits perhaps can. Similarly, a factory worker who handles carcinogenic materials lacks both the scientific knowledge to identify his danger and the political power needed to force corporations to invest in protective technologies.

As both logic and economics suggest, the best way to deal with the health threats posed by modern industrial processes is to prevent them. Pollution can be reduced, deadly substances can be identified and avoided, and the uses of harmful chemicals can be carefully restricted. So long as these tacks fail or remain untried, however, ways must be devised to distribute more equitably the costs of dangerous production patterns. At a minimum, all who initiate or profit by hazardous activities must be forced to compensate generously those who suffer as a result of such activities.

Production that imperils workers or the community is often allowed to continue because its social "benefit" is judged to outweigh the ensuing risks. Seldom, however, do those who enjoy the major benefits face the greatest risks. To date, moreover, no satisfactory means has been devised for ascribing values to either the benefits or the risks involved in a particular production process. How do we determine the social value, as opposed to the market value, of a product, particularly of one that neither survival nor comfort requires? And, apart from the obvious difficulty of appraising suffering and unnecessary death, how are the costs of health risks to be figured when, as is often the case, the magnitude of a given health hazard cannot be determined precisely? Shorn of economic and scientific terminology, benefit-risk calculations are political judgments that reflect assumptions about what things matter and how much these things are worth.

*   *   *

Though environmental-health priorities differ from one country to the next, the study of health conditions and trends everywhere turns up one basic truth: national economic growth and better health are not synonymous. . . . Whatever a country's income level, technological and economic changes that undermine health without providing commensurate social benefits can occur. If "development" is to mean an improvement in well-being, as most would agree it should, then laissez-faire development isn't always development at all. . . . Only a determined polity can give priority to direct indicators of social well-being, such as health and nutritional status, over misleading indicators of progress. . . .

*   *   *

All life forms are shaped by natural evolution and depend upon the earth's basic biological, geological, and chemical cycels for sustenance. *Homo sapiens,* however, is the first species able and willing to alter nature's life-support systems significantly, the first to become a dominant evolutionary force in its own right. Through extraction, production, and combustion, we are disrupting the flows of elements through the soils, biota, and atmosphere; we are changing the biological and geological face of the earth; we are influencing the climate; and we are driving plant and animal species out of existence at an accelerating rate. Humans now create entirely new elements and compounds; following recent breakthroughs in genetic engineering, they also have the capacity to create new infectious agents.

Many environmental alterations have helped to create comfortable and life-prolonging habitats. But humans have neither mastered nor come to a full understanding of the forces of nature, and many inventions and interventions are tried out without adequate concern for their possible consequences. Some have provoked terrible backlashes. As René Dubos observes, man "introduces new forces at such a rapid rate, and on such a wide scale, that the effects are upon him before he has a chance to evaluate their consequences."

The surest way to avoid vicious environmental repercussions is to slow down the pace at which the ecosystem is being altered, and to keep human interventions within the boundaries of human understanding. But whether or not such a prudent course is adopted, humanity's impact on the environment—and hence ultimately on human well-being—has reached the point at which the close surveillance of the earth's life-support systems is essential. Oceans, soils, the air, plants, and animals must be watched for signs of life-threatening changes—for the presence of unexpected pollutants and for unexpected effects from familiar substances or activities. Human populations must be scrutinized for telltale changes in the incidence of cancer or other environmentally induced diseases. Close tabs must also be kept on the number of birth defects, which signal threats to our genetic heritage.

Concern for human health leads inescapably to concern about humans' treatment of the natural environment—living and nonliving. But it also leads to concern about humans' treatment of one another; for the forces that promote poverty remain the greatest threats to human health.

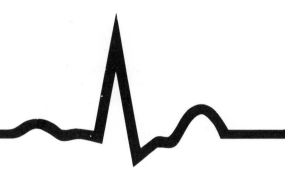

Notes about the Authors

Brian Abel-Smith, Ph.D., is professor of social administration, London School of Economics and Political Science, and author of *Value for Money in Health Services.*

Dan E. Beauchamp, Ph.D., is assistant professor, Department of Health Administration, School of Public Health, University of North Carolina, Chapel Hill, and author of *Contemporary Issues in Bioethics.*

Sharon Begley is an assistant editor of *Newsweek.*

Joyce E. Berlin is administrative assistant, Department of Epidemiology, Harvard School of Public Health.

Rose Elizabeth Bird, J.D., is Chief Justice of the California Supreme Court, the first woman ever to serve in this capacity, and President of the Board of Directors of Hastings College of the Law in San Francisco.

Christine E. Bishop, Ph.D., is assistant professor of economics, Boston University.

Howard Brody, M.D., Ph.D., is a resident in family practice, University of Virginia, and author of *Ethical Dimensions in Medicine.*

Robert N. Butler, M.D., is director, National Institute on Aging, National Institutes of Health, and author of *Why Survive? Being Old in America* and *Sex after Sixty.*

George F. Cahill, Jr., M.D., is professor of medicine, Harvard Medical School; director of research, Joslin Diabetes Foundation; and joint editor of *The Horizons of Health.*

Daniel Callahan, Ph.D., is director, Institute of Society, Ethics and the Life Sciences, The Hastings Center; former executive editor of *Commonweal;* and author of *The Tyranny of Survival* and *Abortion: Law, Choice, and Morality.*

Eric J. Cassell, M.D., is clinical professor of public health, Cornell University Medical College, and a Diplomate of Internal Medicine in private practice in New York.

Douglass Cater, M.P.A., is director, Aspen Program on Communications and Society; visiting professor, Stanford University; author of *Power in Washington* and *The Fourth Branch of Government;* and joint editor of *Politics of Health.*

John S. Chapman, M.D., is professor of medicine, Department of Internal Medicine, University of Texas, Dallas.

Robert Claiborne has been writing on many aspects of science and society for more than twenty years. He is an editor of *Hospital Practice* and author of *Climate, Man, and History* and *Physical Geography: An Introduction.*

Matt Clark is a senior writer for *Newsweek.*

Norman Cousins, Litt.D., is former editor of *Saturday Review;* adjunct professor, Department of Psychiatry, University of California, Los Angeles, School of Medicine; and author of *Dr. Schweitzer of Lambarene* and *Anatomy of an Illness.*

Karen Davis, Ph.D., is lecturer in economics, Harvard University; research associate, Brookings Institution; and author, with Cathy Schoen, of *Health and the War on Poverty.*

René Dubos is professor emeritus of environmental biochemistry at the Rockefeller University. His publications include *Mirage of Health* and *So Human an Animal,* which won a Pulitzer Prize in 1969. His discovery of a bacterial enzyme that destroyed the pneumococcus capsule laid the groundwork for the development of antibiotics.

Erik P. Eckholm works with the Worldwatch Institute, a non-profit organization in Washington, D.C., concerned with global problems, and is author of *The Picture of Health: Environmental Sources of Disease.*

Barbara Ehrenreich, Ph.D., is an editor of *Health Right* and author, with Deirdre English, of *Witches, Midwives, and Nurses* and *For Her Own Good: 150 Years of the Experts' Advice to Women.*

Carroll L. Estes, Ph.D., is professor of sociology and director of the National Aging Health Policy Center, Department of Social and Behavioral Sciences, University of California, San Francisco, and author of *The Aging Enterprise.*

Renée C. Fox, Ph.D., is professor in the Departments of Sociology, Psychiatry, and Medicine, University of Pennsylvania, and author of *The Courage to Fail.*

H. Jack Geiger, M.D., is Arthur C. Logan professor of community medicine, City College of New York. He formerly taught at Tufts University and was the originator of the Neighborhood Health Center program for the Office of Economic Opportunity.

William H. Glazier is associate professor of community health and acting chair of the Department of Community Health, Albert Einstein College of Medicine of Yeshiva University, New York City.

Robert B. Greifinger, M.D., is chief resident in social medicine at Montefiore Hospital and Medical Center and at the Albert Einstein College of Medicine, Bronx, New York.

Joel Gurin is a science writer and joint editor of *The Horizons of Health.*

Mary Hager writes for *Newsweek.*

Robert S. Haggerty, M.D., is professor and chair, Department of Health Services, Harvard School of Public Health, and author of *The Health Care System* and *Community Child Health.*

Ivan Illich, Dr.Fac.Phil., was founder of the Center for Intercultural Documentation, Cuernavaca, Mexico, and is author of *Medical Nemesis* and *Disabling Professions.*

Franz J. Ingelfinger, M.D., was clinical professor of medicine, Boston University School of Medicine, and editor of the *New England Journal of Medicine.*

Albert R. Jonsen, Ph.D., is professor of ethics in medicine, Departments of Medicine and Pediatrics, University of California, San Francisco, and author of *Ethics of Newborn Intensive Care.*

Robert L. Kane, M.D., is associate professor, Department of Family and Community Medicine, University of Utah; author, with Josephine M. Kasteler and Robert M. Gray, of *The Health Gap: Medical Services and the Poor* and *The Behavioral Sciences and Preventive Medicine,* and, with Rosalie Kane, of *Long-Term Care in Six Countries;* and editor of the *Journal of Community Health.*

Donald Kennedy, Ph.D., is president of Stanford University and former Commissioner of Food and Drugs, U.S. Food and Drug Administration.

Arthur Kleinman, M.D., is head of the Division of Social and Cross-Cultural Psychiatry, Department of Psychiatry and Behavioral Sciences, and adjunct professor of anthropology, University of Washington School of Medicine, Seattle. He is editor of *Culture, Medicine, and Society.*

John H. Knowles, M.D., was president of the Rockefeller Foundation; professor of medicine at Harvard Medical School; general director of Massachusetts General Hospital in Boston; and editor of *Hospitals, Doctors, and Public Interest.*

Margaret E. (Maggie) Kuhn is National Convenor of the Gray Panthers.

Philip R. Lee, M.D., is professor of social medicine and director of the Health Policy Program, School of Medicine, University of California, San Francisco; former HEW assistant secretary for health and scientific affairs; and coauthor of *Pills, Profits, and Politics; The Politics of Health;* and *Primary Care in a Specialized World.*

Nicholas Lemann is an editor of *Texas Monthly* and a contributing editor of *The Washington Monthly.*

Charlie Lough, Ph.D., is at the Center for Bioengineering, University of Washington, and is a contributor to *National Priorities for Health: Past, Present, and Projected,* edited by Robert F. Rushmer.

Harold S. Luft, Ph.D., is associate professor, Health Policy Program, School of Medicine, University of California, San Francisco, and author of *Health Maintenance Organizations; Theory, Rhetoric, and Evidence* and *Poverty and Health: Economic Causes and Consequences.*

Brian MacMahon, M.D., Ph.D., is Henry Pickering Walcott professor and head of the Department of Epidemiology of the Harvard School of Public Health, and author of *Preventive Medicine* and *Epidemiology: Principles and Methods.*

Walsh McDermott, M.D., is emeritus professor of public health and medicine, Cornell University Medical College, and a special advisor to the president of the Robert Wood Johnson Foundation in Princeton, New Jersey.

Thomas McKeown, M.D., is professor emeritus, Department of Social Medicine, University of Birmingham, Birmingham, England, and author of *The Role of Medicine: Dream, Mirage, or Nemesis?*

David Mechanic, Ph.D., is John Bascom professor of sociology and director, Center for Medical Sociology and Health Services Research, University of Wisconsin, Madison. He is author of *Poiitics, Medicine, and Social Science; The Growth of Bureaucratic Medicine;* and *A Right to Health.*

Ronald L. Numbers, Ph.D., chairs the Department of the History of Medicine, University of Wisconsin, Madison. He is the author of *Almost Persuaded: American Physicians and Compulsory Health Insurance, 1912–1920* and joint editor, with Judith Walzer Leavitt, of *Sickness and Health in America.*

Allan Parachini is a staff writer for the *Los Angeles Times.*

C. Glenn Pickard, Jr., M.D., is associate professor of medicine, University of North Carolina School of Medicine, and associate attending, North Carolina Memorial Hospital, Chapel Hill, North Carolina.

Frank Riessman, Ph.D., is codirector, National Self-Help Clearinghouse, New York City, and coauthor of *Help: A Working Guide to Self-Help Groups.*

Emmet Rixford, M.D., was a private physician in San Francisco, California.

Victor W. Sidel, M.D., chairs the Department of Social Medicine at Montefiore Hospital and Medical Center and the Albert Einstein College of Medicine, Bronx, New York, and is author of *The Fallen Sky: Medical Consequences of Thermonuclear War* and *Serve the People: Observations on Medicine in China.*

Milton S. Silverman, Ph.D., is lecturer, Health Policy Program, School of Medicine, and researcher and lecturer, School of Pharmacy, University of California, San Francisco. He is coauthor of *Pills, Profits, and Politics.*

Robert L. Sinsheimer, Ph.D., is a biophysicist and Chancellor, University of California, Santa Cruz. He has been internationally recognized for his work in artificially creating strands of DNA.

David S. Sobel, M.D., M.P.H., is a research fellow at the Health Policy Program, University of California, San Francisco; acting chief of preventive medicine, Kaiser-Permanente Medical Group, Santa Teresa, California; author of *To Your Health;* and editor of *Ways of Health.*

Rosemary A. Stevens, Ph.D., is professor of history and sociology of science, University of Pennsylvania; author of *American Medicine and the Public Interest;* and coauthor of *Welfare Medicine in America* and *The Alien Doctors.*

Beckie Stewart is a registered nurse in Seattle, Washington.

Lewis Thomas, M.D., is president and chief executive officer, Memorial Sloan-Kettering Cancer Center; professor of pathology and medicine at Cornell University Medical College; and author of *The Lives of a Cell: Notes of a Biology Watcher,* a National Book Award winner.

Paul R. Torrens, M.D., is professor and chair, Division of Health Services and Hospital Administration, School of Public Health, University of California, Los Angeles, and coeditor of *Introduction to Health Services.*

Paul D. Ward is executive director, California Committee on Regional Medical Programs, and vice-chair, American Hospital Association Council on Planning and Management.

Henry Wechsler, Ph.D., is director of research, The Medical Foundation, Inc., Boston; lecturer in social psychology, Harvard School of Public Health; lecturer in research, Simmons School of Social Work; and joint editor of *The Horizons of Health*.

Raymond Wheeler, M.D., is president of The Southern Regional Council and a member of the Citizens Board of Inquiry into Hunger in the United States.

Irving Kenneth Zola, Ph.D., teaches in the Department of Sociology, Brandeis University, Waltham, Massachusetts, and is coauthor of *Disabling Professions*.

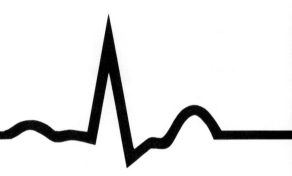

Suggestions for Further Reading

Part I: The Role of Medicine: An Overview

Chapter 1
Medicine and Health

Carlson, Rick J. *The End of Medicine* (New York: Wiley, 1975). Arguing that medicine has little to do with health, the lawyer-author discusses the nature of health, the factors that contribute to it, and the limitations of established medicine in promoting it. Outlines a new paradigm for health care.

Cassell, Eric J. "Illness and Disease: Treating Patients for Both Is the Healer's Art," *Hastings Center Report* 6 (April 1976), 27–36. Making a distinction between disease (which affects the body) and illness (which affects the person), the author stresses the need to treat both the patient and the illness, not just cure the disease.

Cousins, Norman. *Anatomy of an Illness as Perceived by the Patient* (New York: Norton, 1979). This insightful, first-hand account of the author's own experience with illness reveals the intricacy of the mind-body relationship of the patient and illuminates a road to health that surpasses the understanding of ordinary medicine.

Dixon, Bernard. *Beyond the Magic Bullet* (New York: Harper & Row, 1978). Examines the theory of specific etiology—the view that certain diseases are caused by specific pathogenic agents—and traces its history up to the present. Dixon describes the many areas in which the application of this theory is successful as well as those in which it fails, such as cancer, cardiovascular disease, and some forms of mental illness. He considers its political implications for both Western and Third World countries, and concludes that because specific etiology focuses on individual malfunctions and is more concerned with disease treatment than with overall community health maintenance, its value is limited in countries where disease is widespread.

Dubos, René. *Mirage of Health* (New York: Harper & Row, 1979). Traces the history of human disease from prehistoric times to the present and considers health in the context of changing biological and social environments. Examines the origins of Western "magic bullet" medicine.

Eckholm, Erik P. *Picture of Health: Environmental Sources of Disease* (New York: Norton, 1977). Discusses the environmental causes and prevention of disease from a global perspective. Among the topics considered are the hazards of undernutrition as well as those of the "affluent diet," the social causes of cancer, the history of tobacco use, and the problems associated with air and water pollution.

Laframboise, H. L. "Health Policy: Breaking the Problem Down into More Manageable Segments," *Canadian Medical Association Journal 180* (February 3, 1973), 388–393. A good discussion of recent proposals to reform the health care system. Identifies four major divisions in the health field—lifestyle, environment, health care organizations, and basic human biology and clinical adaptations—and argues that persuasive measures can be taken through political action, although government control of the environment would involve certain tradeoffs.

McKeown, Thomas. "A Historical Appraisal of the Medical Task," in Gordon McLachlan and Thomas McKeown, eds., *Medical History and Medical Care* (London: Oxford University Press, 1971), 27–50. Examines how historical improvements in health care have been related to environmental and behavior changes. Pointing out the limitations of the "engineering approach" typically used in Western medicine, McKeown argues that care rather than cure should be the primary focus of medicine.

Silverman, Milton, and Philip R. Lee. *Pills, Profits, and Politics* (Berkeley: University of California Press, 1974). Examines the production and marketing of drugs and the impact of drug overprescription on people's health. Discusses how the prescription drug industry, physicians, and individual patients contribute to the overuse of drugs, and recommends courses of action for the Federal Drug Administration.

Totman, Richard. *Social Causes of Illness* (New York: Pantheon, 1979). A new interpretation of psychosomatic illness that stresses the importance of successful goal attainment in productive, healthful living.

Chapter 2
Health Status and Its Determinants

Center for Disease Control. *Recommendations for a National Strategy for Disease Prevention* (Atlanta: U.S. Department of Health, Education, and Welfare, Public Health Service, Center for Disease Control, 1978). Aimed at advising the Director of the Center for Disease Control on how to reduce unnecessary morbidity and mortality in the United States, this document begins with a brief assessment of existing health problems, then outlines strategies for controlling 12 high-priority problems including alcohol abuse, cancer, cardiovascular disease, dental disease, and motor vehicle accidents.

Danaher, Brian G., and Edward Lichtenstein. *Become an Ex-Smoker* (Englewood Cliffs, N.J.: Prentice-Hall, 1978). Written for the person who wants to become a permanent ex-smoker, this book outlines a step-by-step program to help people overcome the smoking habit and eliminate the lingering urge to smoke.

Farquhar, John W. *The American Way of Life Need Not Be Hazardous to Your Health* (New York: Norton, 1978). This book expresses the knowledge and personal conviction of a physician that what we do in our daily lives largely determines our health. It includes practical advice on such topics as exercise, weight control, alternative eating patterns, how to cope with stress, and how to stop smoking.

Louis Harris and Associates. *Health Maintenance* (Los Angeles: Pacific Mutual Life Insurance Company, 1978). This report, based on a nationwide survey of representative members of the American public as well as business and labor leaders, presents people's opinions about how we can reduce the incidence of disease and promote health. It covers the role of the physician and the employer as well as that of the individual in promoting exercise, good nutrition, and mental health. It also includes suggestions about how to deal with problems related to hypertension, smoking, and drinking.

Nightingale, Elena O., et al. *Perspectives on Health Promotion and Disease Prevention in the United States* (Washington, D.C.: Institute of Medicine, National Academy of Sciences, 1978). An overview of current health promotion and disease prevention programs in the United States intended to guide future program development in the health field. It presents the socioeconomic, environmental, and behavioral factors that should be considered in developing more effective programs, along with examples of successful and unsuccessful applications.

Public Health Service, U.S. Department of Health, Education, and Welfare. *Health, United States, 1979* (Washington, D.C.: U.S. Government Printing Office, 1980. DHEW Publication No. (PHS) 80-1232). This fourth annual report on the health status of the nation is organized into two parts. Part A focuses on the health characteristics of minority groups, nutrition, nonphysician providers of health care, and the assessment of medical technology. Part B discusses health status and determinants, utilization of health resources, health care resources, and health care expenditures.

Surgeon General of the Public Health Service. *Healthy People* (Washington, D.C.: U.S. Government Printing Office, 1979. DHEW Publication No. 79-55071). This recent report prepared by the Surgeon General may come to have as much influence as the 1964 report on Smoking and Health. It summarizes the major risks to health, then presents specific goals for infants, children, adolescents, adults, and older people; finally, it pinpoints actions for health, including preventive health services, environmental health protection, and health promotion.

U.S. Department of Health, Education, and Welfare. "Health and Determinants," in *Health, United States: 1978* (Hyattsville, Md.: Public Health Service, 1978. DHEW Publication No. (PHS) 78-1232). Considers the effects of population growth and distribution on health care needs and funding.

U.S. Department of Health, Education, and Welfare and U.S. Department of Agriculture. *Nutrition and Your Health* (Washington, D.C.: U.S. Government Printing Office, 1980). This recent official document, jointly prepared by two governmental agencies, provides dietary guidelines for Americans. Stressing variety and moderation, it offers easy-to-read, practical advice on how to select a healthful diet. While reasonably complete in itself, the brochure also suggests sources of additional information.

Winkelstein, Warren. "Epidemiological Considerations Underlying the Allocation of Health and Disease Care Resources," *International Journal of Epidemiology* 1, no. 1 (Spring 1972), 69–74. Making clear the distinction between disease care and health care, the author argues that the latter, which includes preventive medicine, environmental control, and human ecology, is the primary determinant of a population's health status and that resources should be allocated accordingly.

Chapter 3
The Medicalization of American Society

Belloc, Nedra, and Lester Breslow. "Relationship of Physical Health Status and Health Practices," *Preventive Medicine* 1 (1972), 409–421. Discusses the relationship of physical health status to lifestyle and daily behavior. Variables include physical activity, amount of sleep, smoking, drinking, and regularity of meals. "Good" practices were found to be associated with better health, and the effects of such practices were cumulative.

Boston Women's Health Collective. *Ourselves and Our Children* (New York: Random House, 1978). A guidebook for parents and for those considering the possibility of parenthood. Topics include factors to be considered in deciding whether to have children, pregnancy, adoption, stepparenting, shared parenthood, various forms of family structure, and professional and lay resources to aid parents.

Caplan, Gerald. *Principles of Preventive Psychiatry* (New York: Basic Books, 1964). Outlining a theory and set of principles to guide the community mental health worker, this book focuses on ways to prevent and control mental illness on a community-wide basis.

Carlson, Rick J. *The End of Medicine* (New York: Wiley, 1975). See annotation on page 517 (Chapter 1).

Cumming, Elaine. "Primary Prevention: More Cost than Benefit," in Harry Gottesfeld, ed., *The Critical Issues of Community Mental Health* (New York: Behavioral Publications, 1972), 161–174. Taking a stand against "popular ideas" about primary prevention in mental health, Cumming maintains that social and moral problems do not necessarily cause mental illness and that popular primary prevention strategies have not yet been tested. These strategies displace needed mental health manpower from the treatment of the mentally ill. Cumming asserts that "the moral and social problems that afflict our society should be attacked because they are insupportable, not because they cause mental illness. . . ."

Dean, Alfred; Alan Kraft; and Bert Pepper, eds. *The Social Setting of Mental Health* (New York: Basic Books, 1976). Writers in this cross-disciplinary anthology stress the community, social, and cultural factors that affect mental health rather than focusing exclusively on the individual. The editors have arranged the articles in such as way that the reader is offered two or more conflicting views on the issues. Topics include the treatment setting, primary prevention, deviance and social control, the medical model, schizophrenia, the family, and intrapsychic versus environmental determinism.

Duff, Raymond S., and August B. Hollingshead. *Sickness and Society* (New York: Harper & Row, 1968). In the context of a university and community hospital, this book focuses on the relationship between the care of medical and surgical patients and the hospital environment. It deals with questions about the role of the hospital social system and the psychosocial environment in delivering care. The researchers followed the patients' "careers" as patients from the time they initially sought help through their hospitalization and convalescence or death.

Fuchs, Victor R. *Who Shall Live? Health, Economics, and Social Choice* (New York: Basic Books, 1974). See annotation on page 523 (Chapter 5).

Illich, Ivan. *Medical Nemesis* (New York: Pantheon Books, 1976). Argues that we have been misled to believe that medicine cures a greater percentage of illness than it actually does. Illich demonstrates how improvements in modern health have been the result of a variety of factors, of which the art of medicine is only one. The book describes how medicine often results in iatrogenesis, not only clinically but also on social and cultural levels. Illich's cure for this iatrogenesis: re-establishing individual autonomy.

Kennedy, Edward M. *In Critical Condition* (New York: Simon and Schuster, 1972). Kennedy discusses health care—particularly the economic aspects—as it applies to individual citizens who suffer illness and hospitalization, giving many illustrative examples of people whose lives have been permanently disrupted by exorbitant medical costs. He also discusses fragmentation of care; the particular hardships of the elderly, disabled, and poor; the health care industry as big business; and the shortcomings of private health insurance. The final chapter outlines his Health Security Program.

Knowles, John, ed. *Doing Better and Feeling Worse: Health in the United States* (New York: Norton, 1977). Appraises the shortcomings and successes of the U.S. "health system"; examines health-care centers, hospitals, medical schools, medical research, governmental agencies, and insurance companies with the aim of redefining existing health care problems. The authors, eminent leaders in the health field, share an awareness of the importance of cultural factors in health care.

Lee, Philip R., and Albert R. Jonsen. "The Right to Health Care," *American Review of Respiratory Disease* 109 (1974), 591–593. The authors distinguish between fundamental and qualified rights, the right to health being an example of the former and the right to health care an example of the latter. The qualified right to health care is justified within the context of inequitable social conditions. Family planning services and the extension of Medicare to cover costs of end-stage renal disease are used as illustrative examples.

Malleson, Andrew. *The Medical Runaround* (New York: Hart, 1973). A strident consciousness-raising book on medicalization.

Norman, John C., ed. *Medicine in the Ghetto* (New York: Appleton-Century-Crofts, 1969). A collection of papers delivered at a 1969 conference on ghetto health care. The papers and discussions are multidisciplinary. Topics include separatism in medical care, the role of the ghetto physician, economic issues, neighborhood health centers, the role of governmental leadership, and community control.

Part II: The Health Care System

Chapter 4
The Shaping of Our Medical System

Abel-Smith, Brian. "Major Patterns of Financing and Organization of Medical Care in Countries Other Than the United States," in *Social Policy for Health Care: Papers Reprinted from the Bulletin of the New York Academy of Medicine* (New York: New York Academy of Medicine, 1969), 13–33. A useful historical overview of the different philosophies underlying the development of medical care in Western Europe, the U.S.S.R., and the United States.

Knowles, John. "The Struggle to Stay Healthy," *Time,* August 9, 1976. Written in honor of America's 200th birthday, this article provides an excellent historical overview of the development of our medical care system, and concludes with an assessment of today's health.

Leavitt, Judith W., and Ronald L. Numbers, eds. *Sickness and Health in America* (Madison: University of Wisconsin Press, 1978). A collection of readings in the history of medicine and public health.

Rosen, George. *Preventive Medicine in the United States, 1900–1975* (New York: Prodist, 1976). A survey of developments in preventive medicine during the first three quarters of this century.

Rosenberg, Charles E. "Inward Vision and Outward Glance: The Shaping of the American Hospital, 1880–1914," *Bulletin of Historical Medicine* 53 (1979), 346–391. A historical account of the origin and development of the American hospital in the late 1800s and early 1900s.

Rosenberg, Charles. "The Practice of Medicine in New York a Century Ago," *Bulletin of Historical Medicine* 41 (1967), 223–253. This account of medicine and its institutions in the 1860s provides a good basis for discussion about what "medicine" means at different times and in different places.

Shryock, Richard H. *Medicine in America: Historical Essays* (Baltimore: Johns Hopkins Press, 1966). A collection of essays on the history of American medicine.

Silver, George A. "Some History," in George Silver, *A Spy in the House of Medicine* (Germantown, Md.: Aspen, 1976). A good survey of the history of medical practice in the United States.

Stevens, Robert, and Rosemary Stevens. *Welfare Medicine in America: A Case Study of Medicaid* (New York: Free Press, 1974). An analysis of the Medicaid program in the United States.

Stevens, Rosemary. "Trends in Medical Specialization in the United States," *Inquiry* 8 (March 1971), 9–19. A discussion of the impact of medical specialization on the structure and practice of twentieth-century medicine.

Stevens, Rosemary. *American Medicine and the Public Interest* (New Haven: Yale University Press, 1974). A historical review of the impact of specialization on the American medical profession and on the institutional and social structures of medicine in the twentieth century.

Vogel, Morris, and Charles Rosenberg, eds. *The Therapeutic Revolution* (Philadelphia: University of Pennsylvania Press, 1979). A collection of essays on the social history of American medicine.

Chapter 5
The Organization of Health Care

Crichton, Michael. *Five Patients: The Hospital Explained* (New York: Knopf, 1970). Through telling the story of five patients hospitalized at the Massachusetts General Hospital in 1969, the author describes some of the changes now occurring in American medicine. The five cases illustrate the hospital's relative lack of ability to continue to care for patients once they leave the hospital; the increasing cost of health care stemming largely from the number of medical procedures that are ordered by physicians; the advances that have made more sophisticated surgery possible; the impact of technology on medical diagnosis and therapy; and the nature of the relationship between patients and doctors.

Dowling, W. L., and P. A. Armstrong. "The Hospital," in S. J. Williams and P. R. Torrens, eds., *Introduction to Health Services* (New York: Wiley, 1980), 125–168. This chapter from a larger text traces the historical development of hospitals in the United States. It describes the forces currently affecting hospital developments, evaluates the characteristics of the hospital system, and goes on to describe the different types of hospitals including community hospitals, for-profit hospitals, governmental hospitals, and specialty hospitals. Current trends and issues in the hospital industry—including hospital cost inflation, the problems faced by small rural hospitals, unionization of hospital employees, and regulation of hospitals—are also examined.

Fuchs, W. R. *Who Shall Live? Health, Economics, and Social Choice* (New York: Basic Books, 1974). This provocative book focuses on a number of themes. The first calls into question the contribution of medical care to the health of the population. It suggests that genetics, environmental factors, and personal behaviors may have a much greater impact on our health than the medical care system. A second theme covers the important role which the physician, as the "captain" of the health care team, plays in regard to health care costs. The third theme calls into question the policy of trying to meet the problem of access to care by turning out more physician specialists and subspecialists. The fourth emphasizes that more medical care is simply going to cost more and must be paid for by everyone through one means or another. The overall central theme of the book is the necessity for choice at both individual and social levels. The author makes several recommendations for providing effective care while controlling costs.

Ginsberg, E. "Health Services, Power Centers, and Decision-making Mechanisms," in John Knowles, ed., *Doing Better and Feeling Worse: Health Care in the United States* (New York: Norton, 1977), 203–214. The author discusses the likely impact of national health insurance on present centers of power and influence in delivering health care. He concludes by calling for moderation in the setting of health care goals and for more realistic expectations of those in positions of power and influence.

Milio, Nancy. *The Care of Health in Communities* (New York: Macmillan, 1975). This is a basic text focusing on discrepancies in health care by geographic region, ethnic group, and income. Comparisons are made between the United States and other countries. Milio stresses the need to examine the interrelationships among the various parts of the health care system itself and between the system and consumers. Particular attention is given to population-based studies which draw on organized input from "consumers-as-citizens." In the process of developing the above points, the author presents a variety of useful data on the health status of the population, use of health services, number and types of health manpower, number and types of health care organizations, and amount and type of health care expenditures.

Phillips, D. F. "The Public Policy Issues Facing Hospitals in the 1980's," in *Hospitals in the 1980's: Nine Views* (Chicago: American Hospital Association, 1977), 215–234. This article summarizes the major points of a national symposium on the American Hospital in the 1980s. The following major policy questions were identified: (1) How should society establish means for determining limits on the quantity of resources to be expanded on health care services? (2) How should society establish a guaranteed minumum set of health care services available for all citizens? (3) How should society establish methods for evaluating the development and use of new medical technologies? (4) How should society achieve better decision-making capability by individuals who are not providers of health care services on matters concerning the appropriate allocation, distribution, and use of these services? (5) How should society exert substantial pressures for the reorganization and restructuring of the health care, education, financing, and delivery system to make it more efficient, effective, or economical? Various approaches to these issues are summarized, including the need for a more coordinated system of regulations, more rigorous evaluation of new medical technology' increased need to provide for greater consumer input into health care decision-making, and the need to better integrate specialty care with primary care services.

Rosenthal, Gerald. "Controlling the Cost of Health Care," in M. Zubkoff, I. Raskin, and R. Hanft, eds., *Hospital Cost Containment* (New York: Prodist, 1978). This article suggests that the current concern over controlling health care costs is relatively recent and is the result of past successes in providing better-trained health manpower, incorporating the latest advances in medical technology and increasing people's access to care. It is no longer feasible to pursue health care goals at any price. Important tradeoff decisions must be made between allocating money to different kinds of health programs versus allocating more money for jobs, housing, education, defense, or transportation. The author discusses current methods of attempting to contain health care costs and indicates that none of these is likely to effectively contain costs in and of itself. Further, a National Health Insurance (NHI) program will likely increase health care cost inflation. Not enough is currently known about how to construct a coordinated package or regulatory strategies to effectively contain costs.

Saward, E. W. "Institutional Organization, Incentive, and Change," in Knowles, ed., op. cit., 193–202. This article describes how institutional providers of health services, in particular hospitals, have traditionally had their policies determined by their professional staffs. The author describes some of the other factors that are beginning to influence the health care system and goes on to indicate how national health insurance will affect the delivery system in the future, particularly the method of paying major providers of services, such as hospitals and physicians. It appears that our value system will dictate that both pluralism and competition will remain significant forces in health care delivery during the balance of this century.

Shortell, S. M. "Factors Associated with the Utilization of Health Services," in Williams and Torrens, eds., op. cit., 48–90. This chapter, part of a larger text, presents basic data on the utilization of health services in the United States. Differences by age, sex, ethnicity, education, family income, and place of residence are presented. Some of the demographic, social, psychological, economic, organizational, and system factors influencing health services utilization are examined. Special issues related to the utilization of services by the elderly and by children are discussed. The expansion of primary care services, self-care services, mental health services, and services to people in rural areas are also examined.

Torrens, P. R., and C. E. Lewis, "Health Care Personnel," in Williams and Torrens, eds., op. cit., 256–286. This chapter describes the numbers, types, and functions of various health personnel, including physicians, dentists, nurses, optometrists, pharmacists, and podiatrists. Issues involving the distribution of health personnel, the role of women in the health care system, and the influx of foreign medical graduates are also examined. In addition, the development of new kinds of health manpower are described along with the conflicts that exist between these practitioners and established health providers. Issues of health manpower productivity and who should control health professionals are also examined.

U.S. Department of Health, Education, and Welfare. *Health: United States, 1978* (Hyattsville, Md.: Office of the Assistant Secretary for Health, National Center for Health Statistics, National Center for Health Services Research, December 1978). This is an annual statistical compendium of health care utilization, costs and expenditures, manpower, facilities, and health status indicators. It shows that increases have not been accompanied by increases in basic use of health services but rather by changes in the size, complexity, and cost of the services provided.

Williams, S. J. "Ambulatory and Community Health Services," in Williams and Torrens, eds., op. cit., 93–124. Contends that most of the contact people have with the health services system occurs in practitioners' offices and hospital clinics. This chapter from a larger book describes the various kinds of ambulatory care organizations, including private office-based solo and group practice, hospital clinics, hospital emergency rooms, ambulatory surgery centers, community-wide emergency medical systems, neighborhood health centers, community mental health centers, free clinics, home health services, school health services, prison health services, and family planning services. The history and organization of group medical practice is examined as well as current prepaid group practices and health maintenance organizations (HMOs). Finally, the author concludes with a list of criteria for assessing ambulatory care systems.

Chapter 6
Specialists, Generalists, and New Health Practitioners

Ebert, Robert H. "The Medical School," *Scientific American* 229, no. 3 (September 1973), 139–148. This article describes how changes in medical education in the 1920s, particularly increasing specialization, hastened the deterioration of the general practitioner's status. It demonstrates how an evolving system of graduate medical education fostered an uneven replacement of physicians in various specialties and resulted in a shortage of general practitioners. Ebert predicts that training opportunities for primary care physicians will gain predominance over programs for specialists.

Jonas, Steven. "Some Thoughts on Primary Care: Problems of Implementation," *International Journal of Health Services* 3, no. 2 (Spring 1973), 177–187. This paper presents the various definitions of primary care and examines the health care crisis in general and the primary care crisis in particular. The importance of team practice in primary care is described, as is the necessity of designating the social physician as team leader. Jonas suggests that certain changes must be made in medical education if we are to find workable solutions to the primary care crisis.

Lee, Philip R.; Lauren LeRoy; Janice Stalcup; and John Beck. *Primary Care in a Specialized World* (Cambridge, Mass.: Ballinger, 1976). Outlines the historical development of U.S. policy pertaining to health manpower and primary health care. Covers issues relating to foreign medical graduates, U.S. physician distribution, the growth of specialization, and the role of physician assistants, and offers recommendations for improving access to primary care services.

Lukomnik, Joanne. "Family Practice." *Health PAC Bulletin* 80 (January/February 1978), 1–2, 25–31. Depicts the old-fashioned general practitioner as an endangered species and explains its disappearance. A renewed interest in generalist-type physicians is attributed to the mismatch between patient need and physician training, the discrepancy between expectation of care and the capacity to pay for services, the inequity between population concentration and doctor distribution, and issues raised by the women's movement. Pressures for a new brand of general practitioner resulted in the creation of a new specialty known as "family practice," approved by the AMA in 1969. After a critical review of family practice training programs and practice styles, the author raises an interesting question: Does family practice promise to humanize medicine or simply to create a new, isolated specialty of "humanistic medicine"?

Petersdorf, Robert G. "The Doctor's Dilemma," *New England Journal of Medicine* 29, no. 12 (September 12, 1978), 628–634. Identifies the major dilemma in medicine today as how to deploy the burgeoning physician manpower needs in a way that is acceptable to society, the medical profession, and patients. Argues that the problem is not one of a shortage of doctors but of maldistribution by specialty and geography.

Sadler, Alfred M., Jr.; Blair L. Sadler; and Ann A. Bliss. *The Physician's Assistant: Today and Tomorrow* (Cambridge, Mass.: Ballinger, 1975). Chapter I of this book describes the "promise" offered by the concept of physician assistantship in improving and distributing health care. The various types of new health practitioners are described in Chapter II. Chapter V discusses the organization of the health team and the problems of leadership and coordination. Though somewhat outdated, this book is still valuable for the evolutionary developments and ideological perspectives it presents.

Stevens, Rosemary. "Trends in Medical Specialization in the United States," *Inquiry* 8, no. 1 (March 1971), 9–19. Traces the development of medical specialization from 1860—when only seven specialties were recognized—to the present. Addresses the issue of how the specialists are distributed and raises questions about what the future might hold, particularly with respect to closing the gap between an educational structure based on an increasingly sophisticated medical technology, applicable to some serious medical problems, and satisfying ordinary health care needs, which are largely unaffected by scientific progress in medicine.

Chapter 7
The Right to Health Care

Childress, James F. "Who Shall Live When Not All Can Live?" *Soundings* 43, no. 4 (Winter 1970), 339–362. Childress discusses the difficult moral problems that arise when there are insufficient medical resources and choices must be made as to which patients shall receive life-saving care. He points out the enormous difficulty in making such choices, particularly when it means that some human beings must be denied care.

Curran, William J. "The Right to Health in National and International Law," *New England Journal of Medicine* 284 (June 3, 1971), 1258. A brief but comprehensive survey of the notion of a "right" to health care in national and international law.

Fox, R. C., and J. P. Swazey. *The Courage to Fail* (Chicago: University of Chicago Press, 1974). This book focuses on the professional, clinical, social, and ethical considerations involved in organ transplantation and renal dialysis. The book examines the uncertainty which many physicians face both in practicing medicine and in the pursuit of new knowledge through research. Issues involving the "quality" of lives that can be saved relative to the costs involved are discussed. Criteria for selecting patients for transplantation or dialysis are also discussed, along with the issue of the patient's "right to die." Rules governing donor's behavior and protection of donor's rights are examined. The experience of the Seattle Northwest Kidney Center is used to illustrate a number of the dilemmas involved.

Gerber, Alex. "Let's Forget about Equality of Care," *Prism* 3, no. 9 (October 1975), 20–27. This article attacks the notion of equality in health care, as well as a "right" to health care. Gerber argues that the very pursuit of equality may be harmful to the quality of patient care.

Pilpel, Harriet F. "Minors' Right to Medical Care," *Albany Law Review* 36 (1972), 462–487. This article reviews the legal impediments confronting minors who wish to seek medical attention for birth control, venereal disease, pregnancy, or psychological problems without the knowledge of their parents.

Shuman, S. I. "The Right to Be Unhealthy," *Wayne Law Review* 22 (1975), 61–86. The author argues, against considerable societal pressure in the other direction, that people have a right to be unhealthy. That right, he says, is part of personal freedom.

Sparer, Edward V. "The Legal Right to Health Care," *The Hastings Center Report* 6, no. 5 (October 1976), 39–47. Professor Sparer analyzes both existing law and recent constitutional rulings on the question of a "right to health care." He finds little direct constitutional support for the idea, but a variety of indirect forms of support.

Veatch, Robert M. "What Is a 'Just' Health Care Delivery?" in Robert M. Veatch and Roy Branson, eds., *Ethics and Health Policy* (Cambridge, Mass.: Ballinger,

1976), 127–153. This article surveys various philosophical theories of justice and applies them to the question of health care delivery. The author also discusses the types of goods that health care delivery systems provide, and points out that they can make a significant difference in the way we think about health care and justice.

Part III: Problems in Paradise

Chapter 8
Why Does Medical Care Cost So Much?

Feldstein, Paul. *Health Care Economics* (New York: Wiley, 1979). The most recent and probably the most comprehensive survey of the field of health economics. The book's author is one of the leaders in the field.

Fuchs, Victor R. *Who Shall Live? Health, Economics, and Social Choice* (New York: Basic Books, 1975). See annotation on page 523 (Chapter 5).

Hughes, Edward F. X., et al. *Hospital Cost Containment Program: A Policy Analysis* (Cambridge, Mass.: Ballinger, 1978). After an analysis of the 1977 versions of Carter's and Talmadge's proposed Hospital Cost Containment legislation, the authors outline their own plan, which includes options for local-area discretion. Provides background on the problem of hospital cost containment and a good discussion of other approaches to the issue.

Knowles, John H., ed. *Doing Better and Feeling Worse: Health in the United States* (New York: Norton, 1977). See annotation on page 521 (Chapter 3).

Rosenthal, Gerald. "Controlling the Cost of Health Care," in Michael Zubkoff, I. Raskin, and R. Hanft, eds., *Hospital Cost Containment* (New York: Prodist, 1978). See annotation on page 524 (Chapter 5).

Russell, Louise B. *Technology in Hospitals* (Washington, D.C.: Brookings, 1979). A survey of the growth patterns of seven major technological innovations in medical care and their subsequent impact on health care costs. Russell concludes that in the long run restraining costs may only be possible by denying health care to some individuals.

Zubkoff, Michael, ed. *Health: A Victim or Cause of Inflation?* (New York: Milbank, 1976). A collection of readable essays examining the cause of rising health costs and offering suggestions as to how to contain them. Provides a good perspective on historical trends in hospital and physician costs and the role of public programs and regulatory efforts in contributing to those trends.

Chapter 9
Inequities in Health Status and Health Care

Bergner, Lawrence, and Alonzo S. Yerby. "Low Income and Barriers to the Use of Health Service," *New England Journal of Medicine* 278 (March 7, 1968), 541–546. A good discussion of the problems of supplying adequate health care to members of low-income groups.

Davis, Karen, and Cathy Schoen, *Health and the War on Poverty: A 10-Year Appraisal* (Washington, D.C.: The Brookings Institution, 1978). A highly readable, data-packed evaluation of a decade of effort, showing some real gains and some continuing major inequities for the poor, rural areas, and the South.

Ford, Amasa B. *Urban Health in America* (New York: Oxford University Press, 1976). A tough-minded look at the real health problems of our inner cities. Ford also outlines some proposals for change.

Geiger, H. Jack. "A Health Center in Mississippi: A Case Study in Social Medicine," in Lawrence Corey, Steven E. Saltman, and Michael F. Epstein, eds., *Medicine in a Changing Society,* 1st edition (St. Louis: C. V. Mosby, 1972). A description of a comprehensive rural health project that made dramatic changes in the lives of a deprived community. It demonstrates that we know some of the solutions, if only we have the will to implement them on a wider scale.

James, George. "Poverty as an Obstacle to Public Health Progress in Our Cities," *American Journal of Public Health* 55 (November 1965), 1757–1771. Two classic descriptions, from the mid-1960s, of the appalling links between poverty, poor health, and inadequate health care, and a look at the resulting human and social costs. These articles were written before the advent of Medicare and Medicaid.

Lewis, Charles E.; Rashi Fein; and David Mechanic. "The Problem of Access to Medical Care" and "Some Options for the Short Run," in *A Right to Health: The Problem of Access to Primary Medical Care* (New York: Wiley, 1976), 3–13; 281–286. A concise analysis of the urgent national problem of access to primary medical care in economically and socially deprived communities. Also offers some possible solutions.

Meyers, Beverlee. "Health Care for the Poor," in Arthur Levin, ed., *Health Services: The Local Perspective* (Montpelier, Vt.: Capital City Press, 1977), 68–78. A good discussion of the problems involved in attempting to provide adequate health care services for the economically deprived. The major emphasis in this article is on the Medicaid program.

Richmond, Julius P. "The Needs of Children," in John Knowles, ed., *Doing Better and Feeling Worse: Health in the United States* (New York: Norton 1977). A discussion of the health care needs of today's children.

U.S. Congressional Budget Office, *Health Differentials between White and Nonwhite Americans* (Washington, D.C.: U.S. Government Printing Office, 1977). Two important studies from the late 1970s showing that only limited progress has been made in improving the quality of life of nonwhites and that the basic problems still exist. Members of poor, minority groups and other deprived populations are enjoying slightly better health, but they are just as far behind in almost every other area.

Chapter 10
Modern Medicines: Miracle or Menace?

Harris, Richard, *The Real Voice* (New York: Macmillan, 1964). An intimate historical account of the passage of the 1962 Kefauver-Harris amendments to the Food, Drug and Cosmetic Act. It provides a good view of drug regulatory politics, and explains the motivation behind the requirements that effectiveness be demonstrated and investigational drugs monitored.

Kennedy, Donald. "Why Our Drug Laws Need to Be Changed," *The Sciences* (May-June 1978), 11–15. A brief summary of the need for (and the nature of) the 1978 administration proposals for further changes in the Food, Drug and Cosmetic Act.

Lowrance, William W. *Of Acceptable Risk* (Los Altos, Calif.: William Kaufmann, 1976). A general analysis of the relationship between science and safety. This is the best treatment to date of the public policy questions surrounding the protection of people against product-associated risk.

Melmon, Kenneth L. "Preventable Drug Reactions—Causes and Cures," *New England Journal of Medicine* 284, no. 24 (June 17, 1971), 1361–1368. Drug reactions constitute a major health problem in the United States. Melmon examines the causes of drug reactions and the effects of such reactions on disease, and describes some of the difficulties involved in recognizing and identifying drug reactions.

Merrill, Richard A. "The Regulatory Environment for Pharmaceuticals in the United States," in J. Z. Bowers and G. P. Velo, eds., *Drug Assessment: Criteria and Methods* (North Holland: Elsevier, 1979). An account of current problems in United States drug regulation.

Silverman, Milton, and Philip R. Lee. *Pills, Profits, and Politics* (Berkeley: University of California Press, 1974). See annotation on page 518 (Chapter 1).

Part IV: The Search for Solutions: Frontiers of Knowledge

Chapter 11
Biomedical Research

Comroe, Julius H. *Retrospectroscope* (Menlo Park, Calif.: Von Gehr Publishers, 1977). In this collection of essays, a physician-scientist-historian traces scientific insights from their beginnings to their final application in medical practice.

Deutsch, Ronald. *The Realities of Nutrition* (Palo Alto, Calif.: Bull Publishing Co., 1976). A no-nonsense presentation of facts about nutrition, written for the general audience. Strikes a good balance between the science of nutrition and cultural dietary habits.

Engle, George L. "The Need for a New Medical Model: A Challenge for Biomedicine." *Science* 196, no. 4268 (April 8, 1977), 129–136. A somewhat technical discussion of the shortcomings of the traditional biomedical model, which ignores the social, psychological, and behavioral dimensions of illness. Engle argues in favor of adopting a new, biopsychosocial model of disease.

Fudenbert, H. Hugh, and Vijaya L. Melnick, eds. *Biomedical Scientists and Public Responsibility* (New York: Plenum Press, 1978). A collection of essays by leading experts about the impact of basic scientific investigation on the delivery of health care and the development of public policy in medical affairs.

Judson, Horace Freeland. *The Eighth Day of Creation* (New York: Simon and Schuster, 1979). The best presentation to date of our present knowledge of molecular biology and its development. Offers the reader an exciting view of nucleic acids, proteins, and genes as seen through the eyes of the people who made the important discoveries in the field.

Lehrer, Steven. *Explorers of the Body* (New York: Doubleday, 1979). An excellent and highly readable account of the history of medical progress, written from a broad perspective.

Academy Forum. *Research with Recombinant DNA* (Washington, D.C.: National Academy of Sciences, 1977). In a remarkably readable symposium, some of the world's leading authorities on recombinant DNA present the pros and cons of genetic engineering.

Seldin, Donald W. "The Medical Model: Biomedical Science as the Basis of Medicine," in *Beyond Tomorrow: Trends and Prospects in Medical Science* (New York: Rockefeller University Press, 1977). Surveys the various criticisms directed at the medical care system, defines the role of the physician in modern medicine, and voices an optimistic note for the future of biomedical science.

Snyder, Solomon. *Madness in the Brain* (New York: McGraw Hill, 1975). The remarkable progress made in our understanding of the chemical and physiological events of the brain is clearly described by a leading psychologist. Includes an excellent discussion of drugs and the mind for nonexperts.

Chapter 12
A Social Science Perspective: Research on Aging

Binstock, Robert H., and Ethel Shanas. *Handbook of Aging and the Social Sciences* (New York: Van Nostrand Reinhold Co., 1976). A compendium of information about the social aspects of aging as well as current research issues, this book is a major reference source for researchers, practitioners, and students in the field of gerontology. The 25-chapter volume is organized into five sections: the social aspects of aging, aging and social structure, aging and social systems, aging and interpersonal behavior, and aging and social intervention. The fifth section contains the only chapter specifically on health, "Aging, Health, and the Organization of Health Resources," by Ethel Shanas and George Maddox.

Butler, Robert. *Why Survive?* (New York: Harper & Row, 1975). This book realistically portrays the experience of older people in the United States today. It examines public policy and programs ranging from retirement, work, and income to death and dying in American medical institutions.

Estes, Carroll. *The Aging Enterprise* (San Francisco: Jossey-Bass, 1979). In this new book, Estes takes a close and critical look at what she calls the aging enterprise—the collection of programs, organizations, special interest groups, trade associations, service providers, and other professionals serving the aged. She demonstrates where the policies and programs designed to help the elderly have gone wrong and what must be done to correct them. She investigates the link between the political, economic, and social action of recent years and the plight of the aged today.

Lowenthal, Marjorie Fiske, and Betsy Robinson. "Social Networks and Isolation," in R. H. Binstock and E. Shanas, eds., *Handbook of Aging and the Social Sciences* (New York: Van Nostrand Reinhold, 1976), 432–456. A good, readable discussion of some of the social aspects of aging.

The National Journal, *The Economics of Aging* (Washington, D.C.: Government Research Corporation, 1978). Part of the National Journal's Policy Forum papers series prepared by government officials, academicians, physicians, and researchers includes a series of articles dealing with the issue of aging in America. It focuses on various aspects of the aging population—its characteristics, its role in national politics, and its impact on the budget—and examines the future of national policy affecting the aged.

Ostfeld, A. M., and D. C. Gibson, eds. *Epidemiology of Aging* (Washington, D.C.: U.S. Government Printing Office, 1972. No. 1746-00027). This publication presents selected research papers delivered at a 1972 conference on aging as well as responses of epidemiologists representing eight fields of interest.

Riley, Matilda W., and A. Foner, eds., *Aging and Society, Vol. 1: An Inventory of Research Findings* (New York: Russell Sage Foundation, 1968). Summarizes the results of social science research on middle-aged and older people. This inventory of findings is arranged according to major substantive focus (for example, mortality and morbidity, behavioral changes, the family). These are then treated from four perspectives: the societal context, the organism, the personality of the individual, and the social roles linking the individual to society. This volume also deals with the state of health of older people, their anatomical and physiological condition, and age-related behavioral changes in perception, motor skill, intelligence, memory, and learning.

Riley, M. W.; J. W. Riley; and Marilyn Johnson, eds., *Aging and Society, Vol. 2: Aging and the Professions* (New York: Russell Sage Foundation, 1969). Includes three chapters on health: "Aging and the Field of Medicine" by Louise Lasagna; "Aging and the Field of Nursing" by Doris R. Schwartz; and "Aging and the Field of Public Health" by Mervyn Susser. The Susser chapter focuses on total populations and communities in examining the distribution and causes of disorder, impairment, and disease in an effort to determine how intervention may bring about or help maintain better health. It affirms the need to recognize and specify the impact of the social environment on the state of health of individuals and populations, and on the very definitions and measurements employed.

Tobin, Sheldon, and Morton A. Lieberman. *Last Home for the Aged* (San Francisco: Jossey-Bass, 1979). An examination of the process by which older people become institutionalized based on studies of the psychological status of the aged before and after institutionalization. The authors show that the greatest psychological damage occurs prior to entering the institution; that passivity sensitizes the elderly to the extreme effects of environmental discontinuity; and that the effects of institutional life—less hope and a perception of lowered capacity for self care—are apparently irreducible. Recommendations address the planning of services to limit premature institutionalization and to improve institutional care.

Vladeck, Bruce. *Unloving Care* (New York: Basic Books, 1980). This book provides a thoroughly critical and informative analysis of the nursing home industry in America. It discusses such issues as quality of care, reimbursement, fraud and theft, working conditions, innovations across states, and solutions for change.

Weiss, Carol H. "Research for Policy's Sake: The Enlightenment Function of Social Research," in Howard E. Freeman, ed., *Policy Studies Review Annual*, vol. 2 (Beverly Hills, Calif.: Sage, 1978). This somewhat theoretical article discusses how social research is used indirectly by policymakers. It concludes by presenting a model for research as social criticism.

Part V: Who Is Calling the Shots?

Chapter 13
The Politics of Health

Brown, E. Richard. "Introduction" and "Epilogue," in *Rockefeller Medicine Men: Medicine and Capitalism in America* (Berkeley: University of California Press, 1979). Traces the current crisis in health care to its roots in modern medicine and corporate capitalism. The author argues that medical care has a relatively small effect on the nation's health.

Cater, Douglass, and Philip R. Lee, eds. *Politics of Health* (New York: Medcom Press, 1972). This book contains a number of articles on different aspects of the politics of health written by individuals who have participated in that process. The subjects discussed include the roles and contributions made by the major participants in the subgovernment of health, including political executives, career bureaucrats, members of key committees in Congress, interest group professionals, and public-interest elites. Numerous examples are provided of how the legislative process has been influenced by each of these groups.

Downs, Anthony. *An Economic Theory of Democracy* (New York: Harper & Row, 1957). This book has become a classic on government behavior. The author uses an economic framework to describe what form of political behavior is rational for government, political parties, and voters in a democracy. While there is no discussion of health issues, the reader can use the ideas presented here to understand more clearly those readings dealing with the politics of health.

Feldstein, Paul J. *Health Associations and the Demand for Legislation: The Politics of Health* (Cambridge, Mass.: Ballinger, 1977). The author presents an economic model of the type of legislation desired by health interest groups. Then the political positions of six health associations—the American Medical Association, American Hospital Association, American Nurses Association, American Dental Association, Blue Cross, and the Association of American Medical Colleges—are analyzed to determine how consistent their political positions on health legislation are with the economic model presented.

Kessel, Reuben. "Price Discrimination in Medicine," *The Journal of Law and Economics* (October 1, 1958). A historical examination of how organized medicine achieved monopoly power. Also discussed are the techniques used in medical societies to prevent price competition and enhance the physicians' ability to charge patients different prices according to their ability to pay.

Marmor, Theodore R. *The Politics of Medicare* (Chicago: Aldine Publishing Co., 1973). This monograph is a case study of the enactment of Medicare. The author attempts to answer three questions: Why did Medicare arise as a political issue at the time and in the form it did? What were the responses to Medicare when it was proposed, and why? What are the reasons for the enactment of Medicare, which represented a sharp break from previous federal health legislation?

Navarro, Vicente. "Social Class, Political Power, and the State: Their Implications in Medicine," in *Medicine under Capitalism* (New York: Prodist, 1976). A somewhat abstract and difficult discussion comparing theories of pluralist power with theories of power elites. The author argues that the capitalist system, not the medical profession, is the main determinant of the nature of medicine in the United States.

Redman, Eric. *The Dance of Legislation* (New York: Simon and Schuster, 1973). A highly readable, personal account of the legislative process. The author, working at the time as a staff assistant to Senator Magnuson, describes the frustrations, bureaucratic in-fighting, and jurisdictional prerogatives of congressional committees involved in drafting and passing the National Health Service Corps Act of 1970. The roles and interests of the federal bureaucracy and the executive and legislative branches of government are traced as a particular piece of legislation becomes a reality.

Chapter 14
The Role of the Individual in Health Care

Berger, Peter, and Richard Neuhaus. *To Empower People: The Role of Mediating Structures in Public Policy* (Washington, D.C.: American Enterprise Institute for Public Policy Research, 1977). A policy framework for considering the full range of nonprofessional health care resources, including individuals, families, and mutual aid is put forward in this book. The authors argue for an approach to national policy which accommodates and facilitates the vital contribution of nonprofessional resources (in housing, education, welfare, and criminal justice as well as health). The book offers a conceptual framework which can help illuminate and sharpen the political implications of self-care and self-help.

Boston Women's Health Book Collective. *Our Bodies, Ourselves: A Book By and For Women* (New York: Simon and Schuster, 1976). Many women collaborated in writing this book, drawing on both relevant scholarly literature and their own experiences. Subjects include reproduction, sexuality, health promotion, rape, self-defense, venereal disease, birth control, abortion, parenthood, pregnancy, childbirth, postpartum care, menopause, and a section on women and the professional health care system. Each topic is demystified, brought down to earth in plain language and without condescension. The social and political context of health is made clear throughout. Health empowerment of women is based on knowledge of their bodies, their person, and the wider social factors which impinge on them. This book is a substantial "course" in women's health as well as a useful daily reference for personal health needs.

Gartner, A., and F. Riessman. *Self-Help in the Human Services* (San Francisco: Jossey-Bass, 1977). This book provides a clear view of the current role and function of the self-help (mutual aid) group and its widening use in health care. Of special value is the emphasis on self-help in mental health, how self-help groups work, and on the potentials and limitations of self-help groups. The authors identify the basis for an integration of the lay health resource with professional resources as a cooperative and complementary (as opposed to competitive) relationship. The references provide a useful bibliography of value to both students of self-help and participants in self-help groups.

Health Facts, published by the Center for Medical Consumers and Health Care Information. Each issue of this 8- to 10-page bimonthly newsletter focuses on a major health problem (cancer, hypertension), health activity (exercise, dental health), or health issue (health care choices). The purpose is to raise the level of informed and effective consumerism through a clear and thoroughly researched presentation of health facts, a balanced analysis of conflicting viewpoints, and a sensible set of recommendations on "what you can do." Bibliographic references, suggested service resources (when appropriate), and additional readings usually are included.

Howell, Mary C. *Healing at Home: A Guide to Health Care for Children* (Boston: Beacon Press, 1978). This book represents the second generation of child-care texts for use at home. The author, a pediatrician and child psychologist, takes the view that the parent, particularly the mother, is the primary health care provider for children. With this in mind, Howell provides information and skills that enhance the parent resource. She clears the air on the crucial health role of parents; provides a perspective and techniques for assessing and monitoring a child's health status; indicates procedures for an examination of a child; offers suggestions for remedies (available for use at home) for minor illnesses; makes recommendations for positive health; and indicates the role of parents in improving the professional health care system. A theme throughout is honoring what the lay parent brings to child health care from his or her own knowledge of the child.

Katz, Alfred H., and Eugene I. Bender. *The Strength In Us: Self-Help Groups in the Modern World* (New York: Franklin-Watts, 1976). This is a classic work on the origins and variations of the self-help (mutual aid) group in the Western world. A delineation of self-help groups by function and style is provided and illustrated with case material. The theory and practice of self-help are joined, making it possible to develop both a descriptive and an analytic understanding. The latter is of special value, particularly those sections that deal with the inner dynamics of the group and the implications of mutual support. The authors, together with other contributors, also discuss the relationship of mutual aid groups with professionals, and the future of self-help as an alternative service strategy.

Levin, Lowell S.; Alfred H. Katz; and Erik Holst. *Self-Care: Lay Initiatives in Health,* 2nd ed. (New York: Prodist, 1979). Based on an international symposium on the role of the individual in primary health care, this book presents a contemporary perspective on self-care as a social phenomenon and as a potential resource for purposeful development. Reasons for the new impetus in self-care are explored from the standpoint of changes in both the public and professional sectors. Ethical, political, economic, and health implications of self-care are discussed and followed by specific recommendations for research. Attention is focused on an international approach to self-care development as a key resource in primary health care. The authors conclude with a look at present and emerging controversies surrounding self-care and prospects for their resolution. There is a 55-page annotated bibliography covering 18 aspects of self-care.

Medical Self-Care: Access to Medical Tools (P.O. Box 717, Inverness, California 94937). Published quarterly, this journal is a multipurpose resource in the development of self-care. Its feature articles focus on specific self-care activities (nutrition, exercise, keeping medical records) and new concepts in self-care (social support systems as self-care). A review of new self-care books and manuals is a standard feature, as is information on self-care and self-help resources and events available to readers nationwide. *Medical Self-Care* represents an amalgam of interests in holistic health, medical self-care, and mutual aid. It is a useful communication tool in "networking" people with a common core interest in self-empowerment in health.

Werner, David. *Where There Is No Doctor* (Palo Alto, Calif.: The Hesperian Foundation, 1977). The intent of this book is to provide the basic knowledge and skills necessary for lay people (particularly rural poor) to provide primary medical care to self, family, and village. In addition to coverage of common ailments (their symptoms and treatment), the book provides a carefully indexed list of medicines, what they are used for, dosage, side effects, and special cautions. There are also instructions to village storekeepers with regard to stocking and dispensing medications; information on supplying a home medicine kit; instruction on how to examine and care for a sick person; practical advice on nutrition and prevention; and advice on serious illnesses that need special medical attention.

Williamson, John D., and Kate Danaher. *Self-Care in Health* (New York: Prodist, 1978). A British general practitioner and a sociologist collaborated on this book that elucidates the role of self-care in primary health care and the implications of that role for national health policies. Although much of the policy reference is to Britain, the basic analysis of self-care as a health service resource can be legitimately applied in considering analogous U.S. health policies. Of special interest is a discussion of the overarching issues of self-care and its impact on the existing professional system and on professionalism itself.

Chapter 15
Health Care and the Future: Individual or Social Responsibility?

Berkman, L. F., and S. L. Syme. "Social Networks, Host Resistance, and Mortality: A Nine Year Follow-Up Study of Alameda County Residents," *American Journal of Epidemiology* 109, no. 2 (1979), 186–204. An important analysis of the association between social networks and mortality. Demonstrates that isolated people who lack social and community ties are more likely to die than those who have extensive ties.

Conroe, Julius H., Jr. "The Witch Doctor, the Which Doctor, and the Wish Doctor," *American Review of Respiratory Disease* 120, no. 5 (November 1979), 1189–1195. A good discussion of the different approaches to the practice of medicine, from the magic of the witch doctor to the science of the specialist, and the problems associated with each.

Dubos, René. *Man Adapting* (New Haven: Yale University Press, 1965). An extraordinary outline of the story of human adaptation. Includes a detailed discussion of the evolution of disease, health, and health care throughout the world, an overview of our social and biological relationship with the environment, and an eloquent treatment of the theme of the interrelationship of all aspects of human life.

Lee, Philip R., and Patricia E. Franks. "Health and Disease in the Community," in John Fry, ed., *Primary Care* (London: William Heinemann Medical Books Ltd., 1980). A detailed discussion of world patterns of health and disease, the major determinants of health, and strategies for improving health status in the world community.

Medawar, P. B. "In Defense of Doctors," *The New York Review of Books* 27, no. 8 (May 15, 1980), 6–11. A review of Dr. McKeown's book (see next entry) representing a point of view that would place greater emphasis on the role of medical intervention in increasing life expectancy. Takes McKeown to task for "simplistic" social medicine view.

McKeown, Thomas. *The Role of Medicine* (Oxford, Eng.; Basil Blackwell Publisher, 1979). Offers an important interpretation of the history of health and the role of social, environmental, and behavioral factors as well as medical science in determining health and well-being. Emphasizes the role of social, environmental, and behavioral factors in the decline of mortality and morbidity in the twentieth century.

Rogers, David E. *American Medicine: Challenge for the 1980s* (Cambridge, Mass.: Ballinger, 1978). Useful summary of the history of medicine and medical care in the United States. Includes an assessment of medicine's accomplishments and failures and delineates an agenda for the present decade.

Sobel, David S. "Introduction," in *Ways of Health: Holistic Approaches to Ancient and Contemporary Medicine* (New York: Harcourt Brace Jovanovich, 1979), 3–11. A concise summary of the approach to medicine and health care that is sometimes termed holistic—a view that combines environmental and social aspects of life with the traditional scientific approach. Includes a discussion of the conceptual differences between traditional and scientific medicine.

Thomas, Lewis. *The Lives of a Cell* (New York: Viking Press, 1974). A frank discussion by a leading scientist of the issues surrounding life, death, and disease in the twentieth century. In just a few years, this book has become a classic in the field of biological science.

Wildavsky, Aaron. "Can Health Be Planned?" The 1976 Michael M. Davis Lecture, Center for Health Administration Studies, Graduate School of Business, University of Chicago. A message from a political scientist on individual and social responsibility for health—medical care does not equal health. The basic theme is that individuals cannot depend on the government or doctors for good health; maintaining good health is an individual responsibility.